Family Guide to Mental Illness and the Law

Family Guide to Mental Illness
and the Law

A Practical Handbook

LINDA TASHBOOK

OXFORD
UNIVERSITY PRESS

OXFORD
UNIVERSITY PRESS

Oxford University Press is a department of the University of Oxford. It furthers the University's objective of excellence in research, scholarship, and education by publishing worldwide. Oxford is a registered trade mark of Oxford University Press in the UK and certain other countries.

Published in the United States of America by Oxford University Press
198 Madison Avenue, New York, NY 10016, United States of America.

© Oxford University Press 2019

CIP data is on file at the Library of Congress
ISBN 978-0-19-062222-0

Dedicated to Tammy Blumenfeld, she's the one with the ratty old address book, and to Judy Tashbook Safern, who made sure that I knew why this book was necessary.

CONTENTS

Preface ix
Acknowledgments xiii
HOW TO Boxes xv

PART 1 Health Law

1. Health Information Privacy 3

2. Disability Benefits: SSDI and SSI 15

3. Guardianship 38

4. Psychiatric Advance Directives 48

5. Involuntary Commitment 57

6. Professional Misconduct 68

PART 2 Criminal Law

7. When the Police Are Called to Help 85

8. Negative Police Encounters, Arrest, and Jail 98

9. Minor Crimes 113

10. Mental Health Court 122

11. Criminal Court Trials and Mental Illness 131

12. Mental Illness in Jails and Prisons 147

13. Criminal Records and Reputations 161

PART 3 Employment Law

14. Employee Reputations and Opportunities 179

15. Employment Discrimination 197

16. Taking Leave and Being Compensated 214

17. Responses to Employment Termination 235

PART 4 Consumer Law

18. Owing Money 255

19. Families and Finance 283

20. Trusts 304

21. Supportive Money Management 327

22. Housing Law 352

PART 5 Death and the Law

23. Missing Persons 389

24. Wrongful Death 398

25. Suicide Law 408

26. The Wills of People with Mental Illness 421

Index 441

This is a book about common legal issues that arise in the lives of adults with mental illness and how the people who are close to them can help. We all have close connections to people who are mentally ill. We do not always want to become involved in their troubles, but we cannot help noticing how unfair and how often troubles seem to find them. Their own communications and actions might bring on some of these situations or make them worse, but that does not mean that these people deserve to suffer. It only means that they can use some help.

Help, what is that? Help might be explaining to your loved one his or her rights and options. This book is full of those explanations. Help might be a brainstorming session in which you both kick around ideas about whether to respond to something and how to express that response. Sometimes help is simply a matter of calling or writing on behalf of your family member. The book gives you facts and legal concepts to use in your brainstorming and communications.

Of course, there are times when help is more involved. You might fill out a form or take responsibility for something that your loved one is not currently able to manage. You could find yourself working on a series of arrangements to solve a problem. This book explains how to provide these different kinds of help in connection with legal matters.

Please do not feel pressured. This book is only a compilation of facts and ideas, not a set of marching orders. It is merely meant to inform you. It will help you decide whether or not to get involved. And if you are ready to take action, the book will tell you which office or government agency to deal with and what process to follow.

Many of the legal topics covered here could arise in the life of any adult, not just one who lives with a mental illness. For example, anybody might run into trouble or need to assert a right with the police, a merchant, an employer, or a landlord. Someone experiencing mental health symptoms, however, may have particular challenges in tolerating or managing some components of handling these legal matters, especially the rigid formalities that are often required by law.

Because legal topics differ according to the state you live in and change over time, the common fundamentals are provided here, along with instructions for finding your state law, should you need that specific information.

Once someone is diagnosed with a mental illness, he or she becomes endowed with certain legal rights and burdened with distinct legal pressures. The new legal rights will come with the status of being disabled. The legal burdens might occasionally require the individual to prove that she or he is able to manage things despite having a mental illness. To make sense of these rights and burdens, this book is organized into five broad parts representing areas of law that apply to adult life: health law, criminal law, employment law, consumer law, and the legal issues associated with death.

PART 1: HEALTH LAW

The book begins with the topic of health law because the process of getting mental health care is the first realm of life that mental illness officially touches. People with mental illness are sometimes called *patients* or *clients* in this section. Most of the adult health law topics discussed are about independence. For example, health information privacy enables people to be independent from their diagnoses and treatments. Social Security disability programs (SSDI and SSI) are associated with a lack of financial independence. Guardianship is available for people who cannot make independent decisions about their daily needs. Psychiatric advance directives express the independent plans that someone makes during a well period in anticipation of future episodes of severe mental illness. The most dramatic mix of mental health care and the law is involuntary commitment—when the legal system permits the medical system to temporarily override a person's independence. Finally, the health law section addresses malpractice, which is how the law of professional misconduct empowers people to take independent control after being victimized by a treatment provider.

PART 2: CRIMINAL LAW

There are various ways that criminal law uniquely affects people with mental illness. In this part of the book, people involved with criminal law are sometimes be referred to as *victim, accuser, defendant*, or *inmate*. When people with mental illness are victims of crime or police misconduct, they can have accommodations and support to help them testify and cope. People who are at risk of being punished for exhibiting symptoms of mental illness can benefit from crisis intervention teams that get them away from the criminal system and into treatment. When people with mental illness do get in trouble with the police, they have rights and opportunities associated with getting arrested and going through mental health assessments in jail, with being convicted of a minor crime, and with having a criminal case in mental health court rather than in the criminal court. In traditional criminal court, there are unique criminal trial defenses available to people with mental illness. If they are convicted, people have rights and remedies connected with their need for mental health treatment. This section also introduces the concept of expungement, which enables criminal records to be erased, and it demonstrates how family members can be liable for associating with, or failing to prevent, crimes.

PART 3: EMPLOYMENT LAW

Employment law has several ways for people with mental illness to find and keep good jobs that match their talents and availability, but sometimes the symptoms that interfere with work tasks may also prevent employees from being able to act on their legal rights. Adding to this challenge is the fact that employment law claims usually have to start at the workplace, rather than in a neutral court or regulatory agency. In this part of the book, people with mental illness are sometimes referred to as *workers* or *employees*. The section begins with an explanation of employee background checks. It then shows how to recognize and report employment discrimination and explains the potential legal consequences of improper conduct at work. Next, it addresses the legal issues that arise when someone has to stop working, at least temporarily, because of mental health symptoms. Employees can sometimes collect workers' compensation for mental suffering that is caused by events at work. They can sue their employers for emotional distress if mistreatment at work is extreme and outrageous. Workers and their caregiving family members can take time off to get regulated with medicine or other treatment under the Family and Medical Leave Act. Finally, if someone on disability, through SSI or SSDI, is ready to return to work, the Social Security Administration has ways of supporting that transition.

PART 4: CONSUMER LAW

Consumer law helps people (typically referred to as *consumers* in this part of the book) whose psychiatric symptoms interfere with their ability to manage money, make financial decisions, and interact in customer transactions. This section covers how the law balances consumers' rights not to be taken advantage of with creditors' rights to get paid for the goods and services that they provide. It also breaks down the personal bankruptcy process and shows how certain mental symptoms can affect a consumer's bankruptcy petition and participation in bankruptcy proceedings. It explains the various legal arrangements that enable families to assist with banking and provide financial assistance without compromising disability benefits. This part also explains financial relationships (powers of attorney, supported decision-making, and conservatorship) through which families can enter into monetary commitments and do business on behalf of a loved one with mental illness. The section ends with housing law issues that particularly affect people with mental illness.

PART 5: DEATH AND THE LAW

Death involves the legal system when it happens under mysterious circumstances, when it is either caused by another person or is self-inflicted, and when the time comes to carry out somebody's last wishes. In this section of the book, people who have died may be referred to as *decedents* or *testators*. The section begins with the possibility that someone has died—the law of missing persons. It then explores the components of a wrongful death claim. The section continues with a discussion of the legal ramifications of suicide. Finally, it shows how wills and estate administration can be affected when the person who died had mental illness.

Tools for the Family

Throughout this book, there are multiple "how to" boxes directed to family members who want to help their loved one with mental illness. These boxes provide guidance on handling practical legal situations. You will notice that many of the issues have Tax Facts sections, which are meant to give you a "heads up," rather than to fully explain tax implications related to the topics. The Tax Facts will point you to IRS publications that have details and exceptions. Every legal issue in the book ends with a resource list of authoritative information that you can refer to as needed. These resource lists point you to primary law sources as well as examples and explanations from authoritative organizations, publications, experts, and government agencies.

As you go forward in this book and in your life, I hope that you will use the information here to help when someone you care about is suffering injustices. You do not have to be a lawyer to effectively help someone with legal troubles and you do not have to stand by and watch helplessly while your loved one gets ignored and mistreated.

ACKNOWLEDGMENTS

I was inspired to write this book by observing good friends in my NAMI group: Anne Handler, Jean Cheppa, Mim Schwartz, Judy Amend, and Lynda Sorch—incredible caregivers in their families. I was constantly encouraged to keep working on it by recalling the experiences of clients in my law practice, patrons in my library, and other people who have found me over the years and asked, "Is this legal? What can I do?" I was aided in writing it by peer reviewers, subject experts, and good editors. Most of the peer reviewers were anonymous to me, but there were two local attorneys, Jacquelyn Connell and Kenny Steinberg, as well as several generous and careful colleagues at Pitt Law—Jerry Dickinson, Larry Frolik, Alice Stewart, and David Torrey—who, in addition to the anonymous peer reviewers, graciously scrutinized and improved individual topics. I interviewed many subject experts for precise tidbits of information. Four helpful experts to whom I'm grateful for lengthy or multiple interviews are Amy Matz, Al Schirmer, J. Michael McCormick, and Ivan Marcus. Several of my students assisted with research tasks along the way. I especially want to thank the first one to be involved with this book, Theresa Donovan, who shared a personal story with me, was encouraging and enthusiastic as I started the work, and has gone on to practice in the field of mental health law. And, oh boy, did I get lucky with editors! Thank you, Sarah Harrington at Oxford, for taking a chance on me and guiding me with great patience and wisdom. And thank you, Kate Scheinman, my developmental editor at The Total Book, for sharing sensible ideas and solid skills and for the months-long wonderful conversation that we maintained in the margins along every page. After more years of writing and editing than I expected, I was energized to finish the book by my many friends who kept asking if it was done yet. I'm sorry for being annoyed by that question in the early days, but I thank you all for reminding me so often that readers were waiting.

HOW TO Communicate With Your Relative's Outpatient Mental
    Health Service Provider 4
HOW TO File a HIPAA Complaint 12
HOW TO Reduce Costs When Applying for Disability 20
HOW TO Help With Disability Evidence 26
HOW TO Help With Disability Hearing Preparation 30
HOW TO Help Your Family Member After a Disability Claim Denial 33
HOW TO Find Guardianship Training and Support Programs 43
HOW TO Inspire Effective Preference Statements 51
HOW TO Be a Good Agent During Temporary Incapacity 54
HOW TO Participate in a Commitment Hearing 60
HOW TO Complain About Hospital Care 62
HOW TO Complain, Generally 70
HOW TO File a Professional Ethics Complaint 72
HOW TO Start a Relationship With a Personal Injury Lawyer 75
HOW TO Help Prove an Intentional Tort Case 79
HOW TO Call the Crisis Intervention Team in an Emergency 92
HOW TO Get To Know Your Local CIT Officers 94
HOW TO Start a CIT Program in Your City 95
HOW TO File a Local Police Misconduct Complaint 99
HOW TO File a Complaint With the DOJ 100
HOW TO Find a Lawyer for a Police Misconduct Case 103
HOW TO Help if Your Relative Waives Her Right To Remain Silent 106
HOW TO Support an Inmate's Mental Health 109
HOW TO Support Compliance With Court Orders 117
HOW TO Support Mental Health Courts 128
HOW TO Find a Criminal Defense Lawyer 132
HOW TO Be Useful in Trial Competence Inquiries 135
HOW TO Be Useful in a "Not Guilty by Reason of Insanity" Case 140
HOW TO Participate in Criminal Court Sentencing 143
HOW TO Help a Prisoner Exercise Legal Rights 155
HOW TO Expunge a Criminal Record 164
HOW TO Interact With Police Investigators 172
HOW TO Talk About Employment Law 180
HOW TO Help Save a Job if an Employee Performs Poorly 188

HOW TO Request Job Accommodations 202
HOW TO File an Employment Discrimination Claim 205
HOW TO Assist With Employment Mediation 206
HOW TO Arrange for Leave From Work Under the FMLA 215
HOW TO Complete a Workers' Compensation Injury Report Form 226
HOW TO Reconcile an Emotionally Distressed Employee's Legal Options 242
HOW TO Report That an SSI Beneficiary Is Employed 246
HOW TO Report That an SSDI Beneficiary Is Employed 247
HOW TO Fix Undue Influence and Bad Contracts 258
HOW TO Help Your Relative With Credit Counseling 263
HOW TO Assist With a Bankruptcy 269
HOW TO Avoid Trouble When Dealing With Your Relative's Banking 286
HOW TO Respond To Your Relative's Questions About an Account 289
HOW TO Cope if You Feel Conflicted About Giving Gifts 294
HOW TO Manage an SSI Overpayment 311
HOW TO Decide Whether To Buy a Tangible Gift or To Contribute To a Special
       Needs Trust 316
HOW TO Be a Good Agent 332
HOW TO Prevent and Handle Bad Conservatorship 347
HOW TO Request Housing Accommodations or Modifications 361
HOW TO Help Someone Get HUD-Funded Housing 363
HOW TO Testify at an Eviction Hearing 369
HOW TO Report a Discriminatory Housing Provider 373
HOW TO Decide What To Put in a Family Caregiver Agreement 379
HOW TO Search for a Missing Person 392
HOW TO Begin a Wrongful Death Lawsuit 399
HOW TO Collect Life Insurance After a Suicide 413
HOW TO Improve Suicide Law 416
HOW TO Help Your Relative Plan His or Her Will 425
HOW TO Contest a Will 433
HOW TO Be an Executor or Estate Administrator 435

Family Guide to Mental Illness and the Law

PART 1

Health Law

Health Information Privacy

Your cousin Isaac has been in mental health treatment since freshman year of college. Now, it is senior year and you are both getting ready to graduate. You have always had each other's backs, so when you see that he is becoming symptomatic, you want to do something about it. You don't know if his medicine isn't working or if he needs to get different professional help. You don't even know if his therapist is aware of the changes you are seeing. What can you do in this situation?

MEDICAL PRIVACY—WHY DO WE HAVE IT?

Medical privacy is likely to be one of the first legal issues that you face after an adult in your family has been diagnosed with a mental illness. It will probably arise when you are trying to be helpful! Perhaps you explain to a mental health worker your perfectly legitimate reason for needing to know something about your relative, only to have that person deny you the information, no doubt declaring something about HIPAA (the Health Insurance Portability and Accountability Act) or a professional code of ethics.

For example, if you know that your son, Michael, is supposed to take medicine, you can help him get the prescription filled and remind him when it is time to take that medicine. If he is supposed to go for therapy or practice certain skills or try particular activities, you can help make those things happen. If he is disturbed by something within your control, you may be able to reduce or eliminate the disturbance. But to do any of this, you have to know some of what the doctor or therapist told your son. If neither Michael nor his mental health professional tells you this stuff, you will not know how to help. No wonder families feel frustrated by medical privacy laws!

Here is the way legal thinkers look at this kind of impasse: We flip the situation over. We realize that, if we are trying to get information, it means that we know part of the story and are trying to fill in the rest. We then look at what we would risk if we reveal what we know in order to get those blanks filled in or to get help.

Think about this in connection with, for example, your daughter's mental health treatment: Ideally, you know how she has been doing since going into treatment. If she seems to be doing fine, you may not have any questions. However, if you see that she is going downhill or falling into bad patterns that you have seen before, you will want to know why. Since you are not her treatment provider (and since you may not even know what to do with an answer to the question "why" even if you get it), consider whether you risk any negative consequences by communicating your observations of your loved one's behavior to the professional who is her treatment provider. You may come across as being interfering and have your questions rejected, but you certainly would not be taking a legal risk. There are no laws saying that families cannot convey their observations to mental health professionals, but the reverse is not true. There are federal laws, such as HIPAA, state laws, and professional ethics rules that prevent professionals and institutions from revealing information to you without the proper release forms.

HOW TO Communicate With Your Relative's Outpatient Mental Health Service Provider

Always know that you should invade the sacred relationship between your relative and his therapist, psychiatrist, or caseworker only when you have a really good reason. If you do have an important reason to get in touch, be prepared to convey that reason in one sentence. Here are some clear examples:

Haley has not eaten anything all week.

Alan was in my house ransacking drawers and demanding money when I got home yesterday.

Cara has been posting extremely long, distorted versions of her memories on Facebook for three days.

Ben experienced a major stressor yesterday; the police pulled him over for having a broken tail light.

Do you notice the language pattern in these examples? They all state a problem and convey how long the problem has been going on or, if it was a one-time event, when it happened. It is important to try to show why this problem is significant. In the Facebook example, it is important to say that the writing is being published online. Writing down lengthy memories for private use may be out of character, but it's harmless. Posting that kind of content online can put relationships, reputations, and personal safety at risk. The only kind of problem that you should bring to the professional's attention is a problem that your loved one is experiencing, not your problem.

If you get a chance to say a second sentence, tell the mental health practitioner how you know that this problem is important and whether you know about past similar situations. Here are some examples of how you can do that:

Five years ago, when she went through a non-eating phase, she passed out on a bus and got hurt.

When he starts digging through drawers and closets, it means his mood is becoming hostile again.

The last time she looked back over her life, she sank into a long and serious depression.

Now he is angry at everyone and everything, just because he got pulled over. He doesn't even want to go to his weekly appointment with you.

This pattern for succinctly notifying the professional about your relative's current problem is based on the way lawyers construct their opening statements in court. Just as lawyers have to quickly summarize their side of the case to a jury, healthy relatives have to be efficient in convincing mental health professionals that their information merits attention. Using this structure, you will not come across as insecure or snooping or anything other than informative.

The professional may ask you questions. Of course, you should answer those as fully and truthfully as you can. If you do not know an answer, just say so. When the professional says "Thank you," that is your cue that she considers the conversation to be over. At that point, your good-bye statement can include an offer of help:

> *Thank you for your time. If you want to see Alan for an extra appointment this week, I can get him over there.*
>
> *I appreciate your taking this call. I don't know what else I should do, so please tell me if you think of anything.*

Do not expect to get information from the professional simply because you have given her information. This is not an exchange; it is merely a method for you to convey important facts about your relative. If you do not have useful information to convey, you probably do not have a legitimate basis for talking about your relative with his mental health provider. In fact, it is possible that either your relative or the mental health provider has identified you as a problem. Your intentions may be good, but your impact may be troublesome. Maybe your son is trying to get out from under your control. There could be all kinds of reasons that it is best for your loved one if you are not involved with his mental health treatment—even though he may need you to provide him with housing or financial support. If the professional declines to answer your questions about your family member, understand that she is merely being protective (not rude) and that she has a legal reason for not divulging confidences to you.

HIPAA AND FAMILY ACCESS TO MEDICAL INFORMATION

HIPAA is huge, detailed, and intimidating. It is the dominant legal authority for keeping medical information private. It is a complex federal statute enacted by Congress that is explained and organized by Health and Human Services regulations. HIPAA details every task involved with storing or transferring patient information. And yet, along with all of the rules about medical centers, computer systems, and security protocols, HIPAA does recognize family involvement with patient care. In fact, it presents three circumstances in which mental health professionals can divulge patient information to family members, "close personal friends," or other caregivers:

1. When the patient has signed a consent form specifically granting permission for a particular person to know his mental health information.

2. When the patient and the family member are together with the mental
   health professional and the patient could object but does not object as the
   professional starts to talk about his condition or his treatment.
3. When the mental health professional believes with his or her best
   professional judgment that it would be in the patient's best interest for
   the family member to know something about the patient's condition,
   treatment, or billing.

In all of these circumstances, mental health professionals are supposed to reveal only the limited amount of information that is necessary right then. Maybe
it is hospital discharge instructions. Maybe it is the drug name and dosage
instructions for a new prescription or the fact that certain foods interfere with
the medication. Maybe it is a referral to an additional service provider. What the
mental health provider reveals has to be practical information that you need in
order to be helpful—this information is not being shared so that you can gossip
about it.

As shown in the scenarios in the HOW TO box, if you effectively convey your
observations to the professional, she may use the "professional judgment" part of
the regulation to involve you as a partner in treatment. If you tell her, for example,
that your brother has been agitated, she may say something like, *Jack is supposed
to supplement his regular medicine with [name of other medicine] when he feels agitated. Do you know whether he ever filled this second prescription? If he did not, are
you available to fill it for him and give it to him?*

Psychotherapy Notes

Here is something very important to know about HIPAA: You cannot find out
what your relative says about you in therapy sessions. Psychotherapy notes get
extra protection under a separate HIPAA rule. These notes contain the most
private of all private information—the thoughts and feelings that the patient
has revealed and the therapist's impressions and questions about what the patient has said. Exposure of this information could be extremely embarrassing
and harmful to the patient. Although therapy notes are not even likely to contain the kind of practical and necessary information that could be revealed to
families and caregivers under the basic HIPAA privacy exceptions, this extra
provision makes it perfectly clear that the therapist's notes from sessions with a
client cannot be divulged to anybody without the patient's specific separate authorization. The only exception to this is another layer of law: If a different legal
provision does require the therapist to report something from therapy notes,
then HIPAA allows the therapist to convey that single piece of information. The
best known example of this is that child abuse laws require therapists to notify
the police about clients who divulge in therapy that they have violently, emotionally, or sexually abused children.

PROFESSIONAL ETHICS, STATE LAW, AND FAMILY ACCESS TO INFORMATION

Rules of professional ethics are another important legal way of protecting patient privacy. Mental health service providers who are licensed by the American Medical Association, the American Psychiatric Association, the American Psychological Association, the American Nurses Association, the American Counseling Association, and the National Association of Social Workers are obligated to maintain client confidentiality. All of these professional associations declare in their ethics rules that respecting confidentiality is critical to therapeutic relationships. A professional who violates these rules by revealing client information can lose his or her license to practice.

You may think that these rules are not exactly laws because they are written by professional licensing organizations instead of by governments, but there is a legal connection: State governments adopt professional organizations' ethics rules into their administrative codes. Therefore, it can be illegal for someone to practice without a license and the ethics rules can be enforced in court.

Unlike HIPAA, the ethics codes do not invite professionals to use their judgment and decide that it is sometimes acceptable to divulge a loved one's information to family members. This is probably why so many mental health professionals refuse to say anything to families. If they lump their refusal into a phrase that includes the word HIPAA, do not presume that they fail to understand HIPAA. It is more likely that when they consider HIPAA's permission to use professional judgment, they fall back on the more restrictive professional ethics codes as their professional judgment.

The professional ethics rules allow private information to be divulged only in the following four circumstances, which are also spelled out in state mental health codes and in HIPAA regulations:

1. When the client presents an imminent danger
2. When a court requires the confidential information
3. When the client consents
4. When an insurance company needs the information in order to pay for treatment.

Imminent Danger

Imminent danger means that someone presents a legitimate current threat to him- or herself and/or to others. A mental health professional who knows her client Jake's ordinary range of moods and triggers and knows his record of past hostility can likely make a pretty good prediction about whether danger is imminent. The professional knows how Jake sounds when he is just letting off steam and how he sounds when he is not able to let go of something. She can figure out whether he is making plans about how, when, and where he will create the danger and whether he has a particular victim or population of victims in mind. She will either know or find out whether Jake has previously hurt people or animals—demonstrating the capacity to cause harm.

If the professional believes that Jake is an imminent danger to somebody, she has a legal duty either to warn or to protect the prospective victim, depending on her state's legal standard. In some states, mental health professionals have only one of these legal duties. The duties can come from statutes (laws) or from cases (past court decisions that identify particular actions as duties). In most states, they are established by statutes and interpreted by cases. The *duty to warn* generally means that the professional should alert law enforcement and the intended victim that Jake presents a danger. The *duty to protect* can also mean that the professional should warn law enforcement and the prospective victim, although sometimes it means that instead of giving warnings, the professional can prevent immediate danger by hospitalizing Jake without warning the police or the prospective victim.

When a professional presents a warning about imminent danger, it is likely to contain just the barest facts: the identification of the dangerous person and the proposed victim or victims and the content of the threat. In other words, Jake's diagnosis, the rest of his therapeutic conversations with his mental health professional, and her impressions of him remain confidential. The professional's impression of Jake's dangerousness is one of the standard legal bases for the duty to warn or to protect, but the professional is not expected to reveal more impressions than that. Therapists cannot report legal violations that do not involve threats and, without a court order, they cannot open treatment records to police investigators.

Because the professional will probably not divulge much information in her warning about Jake, the alert may trigger phone calls from the police and the prospective victim to members of Jake's family. If the professional cannot talk about Jake's mood, behaviors, access to weapons, and so on, maybe his family will. Families do have to cooperate with police investigations or risk being charged with interfering with the investigation. However, nothing in the law obligates families to speak with the person who is being threatened. On the other hand, there is also nothing in the law that prevents them from speaking with that person and providing details to help him or her get prepared and protected.

Court Order

A court could require parts of someone's private mental health treatment information when:

- Deciding whether to appoint a conservator to manage finances for someone with a severe mental illness
- Considering the impact of a personal injury (such as a car wreck) on someone who has a mental illness
- Determining criminal intent
- Making a child custody decision
- Enabling a mental health professional to defend herself in a malpractice lawsuit brought by a patient.

Notice that, in some of these examples, the person with mental illness may want the professional to divulge confidential information, whereas in other examples that person would not want the information to be used.

For example, if a court needs your daughter Maria's mental health treatment information, a lawyer would request that her mental health professional serve as a witness. The lawyer may contact the professional in a phone call, by mail, or with a subpoena. A subpoena is a formal court order to serve as a witness, and a well-informed mental health professional will not agree to serve as a witness without receiving a subpoena. Once the subpoena has been issued, the professional can file a "motion to quash," asking the judge to determine whether the requested testimony or records about Maria are truly necessary for the case. The judge may rule that all, part, or none of the confidential information can serve as evidence.

By forcing this judicial examination, the mental health professional has done her best to protect confidential information. Even if the individual wants the professional to provide evidence in the case, going through the subpoena and motion process ensures that the professional will have to reveal only a narrowly defined set of information. Knowing this, families should not resist the delay and possible expense that the subpoena process may create.

Once the time comes for the professional to testify, she can still assert therapist–client privilege or doctor–patient privilege in response to particular questions from the judge or lawyers. This privilege arises from court evidence rules—yet another source of client privacy protection. There are thousands of court cases that analyze privilege rules because the unique facts of each case can raise questions about privacy. When the mental health professional declines to answer, the lawyers will quickly tell the judge why they think the judge should or should not allow the information to remain privileged.

Often, the judge will require the questioning lawyer to rephrase the question so that the witness can divulge less information. Sometimes, however, the judge will order the professional to answer the question as it was already asked, and in that case, the witness does have to answer the question. If she withholds facts that are critical to the case, the court might find her to be in contempt. Contempt is a crime that can result in fines or jail time for the mental health professional. So, despite all professional efforts to protect client confidences, people who treat clients with mental illness can be made to divulge some private mental health facts in court.

In the end, it is up to the lawyer representing the person with mental illness to try to keep the testimony and written evidence of the person's mental health out of the public record. Families and individuals with mental illness would be wise to stress from the beginning that they expect their lawyer to use all possible measures to prevent disclosure of private mental health information. Perhaps the mental health professional can testify at an off hour, when the public is less likely to be in the courtroom; maybe the evidence can be viewed more privately in the judge's chambers; or maybe the evidence can be sealed after it is presented in court. Health records are routinely excluded from the public records in cases, but testimony and correspondence referring to mental health are not necessarily excluded. Documents filed in court cases are more readily available now than ever before. It is perfectly reasonable for family members to push for their relative's private mental health information to be kept out of those easily accessed files.

Client Consent

When someone gives consent for information to be released from his treatment records, he has to sign a form stating who can have his information, what kind of information can be shared, and when the information can be shared. His instructions on the consent form can override parts of the privacy protection laws, but, overall, the laws continue to apply to his records. Health facilities will have their own HIPAA Waiver Form or Patient Consent Form for this purpose. No matter what it says on the preprinted form, the person getting the treatment is in control of this consent, as long as he or she is a competent adult, and the person can write in any conditions or explanations—as long as they are feasible for the professional. Most people will limit the access to a particular time period and/or a particular purpose, such as helping to deal with a set of transactions.

When someone has a good trusting relationship with a relative, this consent will bring the mental health professional into that relationship—authorizing her to notify the family member of adjustments in treatment or medications and to suggest new ways for the relative to help. Families should remember that the professional does not have to convey information just because a consent form exists. They should not expect the professional to provide them with regular updates on their family member's condition, for example. The consent is almost always intended for use on a need-to-know basis. Most importantly, the person in treatment can cancel the consent at any time.

Another way a person can provide consent for someone else to access his or her mental health information is the durable power of attorney for health care and related decisions. This is a type of consent that applies only when the person experiences very severe episodes of mental illness and is not able to make rational decisions for her- or himself. Depending on where you live, the document may also be called a mental health power of attorney or a durable power of attorney.

Creating a power of attorney agreement involves completing a legal form or hiring a lawyer to compose terms that are acceptable to both the person in treatment and the person entrusted with decision-making power. A durable power of attorney agreement can be written only during a time when someone is able to reliably communicate his wishes, and then it becomes active only when necessary. The agreement will tell exactly how the family and the medical establishment will know that the person has reached a point of needing someone else to make decisions. It will also tell when the person can resume control over his own decisions. (For additional information, see Chapter 4, which covers psychiatric advance directives. Also see Chapter 21, which discusses another kind of power of attorney—the financial power of attorney.)

When Insurance Companies Need Health Information

Health care payers, including insurance companies, HMOs, company health plans, and government medical assistance programs like Medicare and Medicaid, are legally entitled to have a limited amount of patient or client information in order to confirm that billing claims are valid. The billing offices in medical and mental health treatment facilities identify their patients to these payers and supply treatment codes attesting to each patient's particular diagnosis and treatment. This arrangement has been around since long before HIPAA, and at this point, the HIPAA regulations specifically permit treatment offices to communicate private patient information to payers.

In fact, the HIPAA regulations identify payers among its categories of "covered entities" that legitimately need patient medical information in order to conduct their business. Payers are in the business of paying for their members' legitimate treatments. So it is understandable that to conduct their business they have to confirm that each billing claim applies to someone who actually is in the plan, and they have to confirm that the particular treatment is among the services that they pay for.

ADDITIONAL STATE LAWS ABOUT PATIENT PRIVACY AND FAMILY ACCESS

As mentioned, states tend to have some patient privacy provisions in their mental health codes in addition to including the ethics rules in their administrative codes. Most of the state laws relating to client confidentiality tell when information can be divulged and how patient consent has to be handled. Sometimes, state provisions are stricter than HIPAA, and sometimes they are equivalent to HIPAA; they cannot provide less privacy protection than HIPAA provides.

Here are some examples of strict state rules in laws about client consent:

- In Ohio, a client's consent has to be reviewed by the provider's chief clinical officer for medical records to confirm that releasing the information would be in the client's best interests.
- Montana has a unique provision that, even when a client has granted permission for the professional to share confidential client information with a particular family member, the professional does not have to include any confidential information that came from another family member.
- In New Mexico, the authorization form in which the client grants permission to share his health information must include "a description of the manner in which the disclosed information is intended to be used."
- Indiana, Kansas, Maine, Oklahoma, Tennessee, and Wisconsin also require that the consent document spell out the purpose for releasing private information.

Some states do have built-in family short-cuts:

- In New Mexico, client authorization is not required when the professional simply needs to tell the caregiver if there are things to do on behalf of the client.
- Ohio separately allows family caregivers to have information about medications, the diagnosis, and the prognosis without getting written client consent.

- In Minnesota, there is a family involvement law that specifically permits mental health providers to inform families about fundamental client needs that they can fulfill.

IF MEDICAL PRIVACY IS VIOLATED

If a mental health professional violates patient confidentiality, there are many ways to take action. You can take any or all of these actions on behalf of your family member with mental illness, and you can take them at the same time or at different times. For example, the professional's office probably has an internal disciplinary system that will hear your claim. If you want to go bigger, file an online HIPAA complaint that will trigger an investigation of the office where the professional works, file a complaint with the professional's licensure board, or file a lawsuit. (See Chapter 6, which discusses professional misconduct, for more information about licensure investigations and lawsuits.)

You will probably get the quickest and most useful results from simply dealing with the mental health provider's place of work; they can arrange for your relative to work with a different professional within the same office or system and they can take other quick actions to fix whatever went wrong without significantly disrupting your relative's care. If you learn that the problem occurred because of the way the office functions and not just the action of one professional, consider filing a HIPAA complaint.

HOW TO File a HIPAA Complaint

It is very easy to file a HIPAA complaint. Simply complete the online form provided by the Department of Health and Human Services (HHS). (See the Resources section, below, for a link to the form.) If you prefer not to use the electronic form, you can write your own letter to HHS.

The complaint instructions specifically say that anyone can file a complaint on behalf of a patient whose privacy was violated. In fact, the first section of the complaint form asks for information about the person completing it, and the second section asks who the patient is. This proves that HHS expects to get lots of complaints that were not written by the patient victims.

The complaint has to identify by name both the patient and the mental health professional. However, the person filing the complaint can require HHS to keep the patient's identity secret. Of course, if the professional does not know which patient the privacy complaint is about, she will not be able to fully explain what happened. If the patient is identified, the office or individual complained about is not allowed to retaliate against the patient for complaining—whether the patient himself complained or a friend or family member complained on his behalf.

The complaint will only be accepted if it is filed within 180 days of when the privacy violation occurred or when the patient would reasonably have learned that his medical information got out. Once HHS receives the complaint, its Office of Civil Rights will investigate it, looking for systemic problems at the facility where the privacy breach is alleged to have happened. If the investigation uncovers inadequate privacy protections, the HHS Office of Civil Rights will work with the facility to implement new policies, routines, staffing, and other ways of improving the way they handle private information. It may even require the facility to pay a fine to HHS, but it will not specifically intervene in any individual's health services. Even though HHS depends on individuals to notify it about HIPAA violations, it does not have authority to require facilities to apologize to patients or to match them with new counselors. Those outcomes may come about after HHS works with the facility, but it is not a sure thing that the person who filed the complaint will get any direct benefit from it.

RESOURCES FOR PRIVACY

1. Minnesota's Family Involvement Law is at Minnesota Statutes, § 144.294(3) Chapter 147. National Alliance on Mental Illness (NAMI) Minnesota offers a clear and detailed brochure titled "Understanding Data Privacy" at namihelps.org.
2. Some of the state privacy laws that grant more protection than HIPAA provides are: Ohio Code Ann. § 5122.31; Mont. Code Ann. § 53-21-166; and N.M. Stat. Ann. § 43-1-19(c)(2).
3. The Code of Ethics of the National Association of Social Workers is at socialworkers.org. The Ethical Principles of Psychologists and Code of Conduct are at apa.org.

   Psychiatrists, like all medical doctors, comply with the American Medical Association's Code of Ethics and they also comply with the American Psychiatric Association's Principles of Medical Ethics with Annotations Especially Applicable to Psychiatry (available at psychiatry.org).

   Ethics information for assorted types of counselors is available from the American Counseling Association at counseling.org.

   The Professional Standards for the American Nurses Association are at nursingworld.org.
4. For a very thorough examination of client privacy issues, read Mary Alice Fischer, *The Ethics of Conditional Confidentiality: A Practice Model for Mental Health Professionals*. The author is an expert on ethics for mental health professionals. Find additional information at her Center for Ethical Practice at centerforethicalpractice.org. Other good books with information about client privacy are John Parry, *Criminal Mental Health and Disability Law, Evidence and Testimony: A Comprehensive Reference Manual for Lawyers, Judges and Criminal Justice Professionals* (2009), and John Parry, *Civil Mental Disability Law, Evidence and Testimony* (2010).
5. Health Information and the Law, a project of the George Washington University's Hirsh Health Law and Policy Program and the Robert Wood Johnson Foundation, charts state laws about patient consent to mental health records disclosure and state laws about court-ordered disclosures at healthinfolaw.org.

6. The National Conference of State Legislators has a legislative brief and a chart of all fifty states' laws about mental health professionals' duty to warn and duty to protect regarding dangerous clients. In some states, the duty is presented through court cases and in other states it comes from statutes or regulations. States phrase and apply the duties in different ways. Search for the terms *duty to warn* and *duty to protect* at ncsl.org.

7. *Health Information Privacy: HIPAA Privacy Rule and Sharing Information Related to Mental Health*, published by the HHS Office of Civil Rights, is available online at hhs.gov. This guidance document gives clear, authoritative facts about when mental health professionals can give certain patient information to families and caregivers.

8. Most of the HIPAA regulations are in 45 C.F.R. § 164.102-534. To find them, go to ecfr.gov and navigate to Title 45.

    The HIPAA regulation about special protection for psychotherapy notes is at 45 C.F.R. § 164.508.

    The HIPAA regulations about sharing health information are at 45 C.F.R. § 164.510 and § 512.

    The regulation telling when state privacy laws trump HIPAA is at 45 C.F.R. § 160.202.

    The regulations about compliance with HHS and how HHS investigates complaints are at 45 C.F.R. § 160.300-316.

9. HIPAA definitions are at 42 U.S.C. § 1320d, available online at uscode. house.gov.

10. All of the information about HIPAA privacy complaints, including a link to the online complaint procedure and a printable complaint form for those who prefer not to file online, can be found in the HIPAA complaints page at hhs.gov.

11. One of the mysteries about health information privacy is how and when patient information gets into the background database for gun sales—the National Instant Criminal Background Check System, NICS for short. HIPAA and the federal Gun Control Act are reconciled in a regulation at 45 C.F.R. Part 164.512(k)(7). This regulation permits certain health care providers to provide NICS with a client's identity and certain demographic facts but not "diagnostic or clinical information."

2

Disability Benefits

SSDI and SSI

You have always had a close relationship with your father's youngest brother, your Uncle George, who has a mental illness. He had to stop working about a year ago because his symptoms had worsened to the point where he could no longer tolerate the work environment and could not pay attention to tasks for long enough to finish them. You worry about your uncle, and you want to help him create some economic stability by encouraging him to apply for Social Security benefits. What benefits are there, and how can you assist in the application process?

THE SOCIAL SECURITY ADMINISTRATION'S DISABILITY PROGRAMS

The Social Security Administration (SSA) provides disability benefits to adults with mental illness who are not able to "maintain substantial gainful employment." This can mean that someone has never been able to hold down a job or that someone was once able to work but has now developed such pervasive mental symptoms that she is no longer able to work enough to support herself. Chapter 17, which discusses employment, has more information about the *substantial gainful employment* concept. For now, know that it is the key phrase for determining who gets disability benefits and who does not.

The process of applying for disability is called a claim and the person applying, such as your family member, is called a claimant. In fact, the word *claimant* is a clue that the person applying has to do all the work of requesting and proving the need for the benefits. The burden is not on the SSA to call people into the disability program and collect evidence for them; rather, it is up to the claimant to supply all the necessary information.

So how is the claimant—who is disabled by mental illness—supposed to be able to fill out forms and gather proof to make the claim? The same lack of energy and focus, and other symptoms that prevent her from being able to work at a job, make it extremely difficult for her to apply for disability benefits. Somebody needs to help her, and that somebody may very well be you! Be prepared: it is a long and time-consuming process, especially because mental health claims require more proof than physical health claims.

The Social Security regulations that define disabling mental conditions include not only medical symptoms, but also *functional limitations*. This makes sense to anyone who has ever spent significant time with somebody who is experiencing severe mental illness; there is certainly more to mental health than a medical diagnosis. Having to provide this extra proof *does* help claimants who are mentally ill to explain how their mental health interferes with their ability to work, but it also slows down the disability application process.

The SSA has two different systems for paying disability benefits. The first is called Social Security Disability Insurance (SSDI), and the funding for SSDI is money that employees have paid into the Social Security system. The second is called Supplemental Security Income (SSI), which is funded by the government for people who have either not paid into the system or whose income was so low that the percentage they did pay into the system was too low to generate a full SSDI payment. Some people get combined funding from both of these systems.

WHAT ARE DISABILITY BENEFITS?

When someone is successful in claiming disability benefits, she is no longer a claimant. The SSA now refers to her as a beneficiary. Three types of benefits apply once a person has been declared disabled by the SSA:

- Cash benefits, paid every month for as long as the disability lasts
- Government-funded medical insurance
- Eligibility for other government programs and some private services.

Cash Benefits

The amount and start date of the cash benefits depend on whether the person is going to collect SSI or SSDI.

The amount of benefits for SSI recipients is set by the SSA every year and is published on the "payment amounts" section of its website. Although the federal rate is the same for all SSI recipients, most state governments supplement the federal payments with additional money, so the monthly checks differ according to where someone lives. The amount of benefits for SSDI recipients is determined according to how much they have already paid into the system. Disability applicants who have paid into the system can sign-in to "My Social Security" on the SSA's website to find out how much SSDI they are eligible for. See the Resources section at the end of this chapter for reminders about accessing this information.

The SSA calls the beginning of eligibility the "onset date," which is the date that the disability began. However, for SSI claimants, the onset date is the date of the disability application—not the date that the disabling condition began. So the SSA pays SSI recipients "back due" benefits (also known as "back pay") dating to when they filed the application for disability benefits. If, for example, Fred applied for disability benefits a full year before finally seeing a judge and winning in his hearing, he is entitled to twelve months of back due benefits. However, if he owes a repayment to the state public assistance program, the SSA will first pay back that state agency and any other government offices that extended cash assistance due to Fred's poverty. If Fred is in bankruptcy, some of his back due benefits may be turned over to the bankruptcy court and split among creditors. (See Chapter 18 for more information about bankruptcy.) In addition, if he did not have a free representative to help him with his disability hearing, the SSA will also pay the representative's fee out of Fred's back due benefits. Whatever remains of the back due amount, after those payments, will be paid to Fred along with his first monthly payment. Fred would receive that initial monthly payment in the first full month after the SSA has issued a ruling that he is disabled.

SSDI also begins making payments in the first full month after the claimant gets a positive disability ruling, but for SSDI claimants, the onset date is usually earlier than when they filed the disability application. The back due amount for SSDI will typically count back to when the claimant had to stop working. However, some SSDI recipients only become eligible for disability benefits when a medical event happens *after* they stop working. In other words, sometimes people stop working when they experience some, but not enough, symptoms to collect SSDI benefits. If the condition worsens and they later have enough symptoms to meet the SSDI regulations, their disability onset date will be that later date, not the date when they stopped working. In those cases, the back due benefits will count as far back as that medical event. Oddly, after going to the trouble of figuring out exactly when the SSDI disability started, the SSA routinely subtracts five months out of the SSDI back due benefits. So they really pay back due benefits beginning five months after the disability started. Even with this five-month reduction, the SSDI recipient can get a very big lump sum check for back pay.

SSDI Example

Suppose Latoya left a job because she was suffering terrible mental symptoms, languished for several months, eventually went into a mental hospital for a time, then got intensive outpatient treatment, and finally reached the point when she felt able to apply for disability. The records from her job, mental health treatment, and other involvements prior to the application likely prove that she was entitled to the benefits during the time leading up to her application, even though she had not yet applied. Her SSDI onset date would become when her mental condition made it impossible for her to work anymore. Latoya will therefore get a lump sum payment for the disability benefits that she was entitled to collect from the sixth month after the onset date until the present.

Government-Funded Medical Insurance

Government-funded medical insurance also differs depending on whether the claimant gets SSI, SSDI, or a combination of the two. *Medicaid* goes with SSI and, like the cash benefits, coverage begins in the first full month after the claimant has been declared disabled. *Medicare* goes with SSDI and it begins two years after the disability cash benefits have started. Claimants do not have to complete a separate application to start Medicaid or Medicare benefits; the SSA will notify those programs about the claimant's disability status and the Medicaid or Medicare office will mail the insurance card and an instruction packet when eligibility begins.

Medicaid is administered through state agencies, even though it is a federal program. Every state's Medicaid program has to cover certain mandatory medical services for all recipients. These include hospital treatments, doctors' appointments, lab tests, periodic screenings, and some other common services. States can choose whether to cover other medical services, such as dental care, optometry, physical therapy, occupational therapy, and chiropractic care.

Medicare is federally coordinated. Part A and B benefits are provided to SSDI beneficiaries and basically cover medical services associated with hospitalization—whether for a mental problem or for a physical problem or both. Part A generally pays for inpatient costs at hospitals and nursing homes and for home health care. Be aware that Medicare caps coverage for psychiatric inpatient days, and Part A coinsurance requirements go way up after a certain number of days without supplemental insurance. Part B benefits cover medical services associated with going to a doctor's office. These include therapy with a psychiatrist, psychologist, or clinical social worker (as long as the therapist "accepts assignment" via Medicare), a yearly mental wellness visit, depression screening, family counseling, and lab tests. Medicare Part B can also cover most of the costs of structured outpatient mental health services that are provided by a hospital or community mental health center as an alternative to staying in a mental hospital—even occupational therapy and patient education. Disability Medicare beneficiaries can opt to register with a Medicare Advantage Plan or a Medicare Prescription Drug Plan to help offset the costs of prescriptions. If the costs of medication are still unreachable, disability beneficiaries can apply for Social Security's Extra Help program.

Eligibility for Other Programs

The third benefit of having disability status, eligibility for other programs, varies according to what is available in any given community. Housing programs funded by the Department of Housing and Urban Development(HUD) tend to have at least some reserved slots for disability recipients. Some local private (nongovernment) housing options, including various types of group homes, will use SSI or SSDI disability status as proof of eligibility for admission and as a source of rent. Many communities have peer-support programs, vocational training, recreational activities, and meal services for people on disability. Programs that are in place for the elderly routinely allow younger disability recipients to participate along with the senior citizens.

The opportunities for housing, meals, and socialization will not reach out to new disability recipients, but as a family member, you can search for them. County human services offices typically have information about housing. The United Way maintains lists of activities, including classes, social events, and other programs run by nonprofit organizations. Even an ordinary Internet search on the term *disability services* along with a city name can help you find local resources.

THE SOCIAL SECURITY ADMINISTRATION'S FOUR QUESTIONS

The process of applying for disability benefits takes a long time and involves multiple layers of questions.

- The first question is, "Does this claimant have a serious medical condition?" This question is answered in the claimant's initial application and interview with the Social Security office.
- The next question is, "Does this medical condition prevent the applicant from doing the kind of work she used to do?" This question is answered when the applicant finally gets a chance to show how mental illness invades her daily life. That opportunity arrives late in the process, when the applicant submits evidence in preparation for a disability hearing.
- After that question has been answered, the disability process asks, "Can this applicant work full time in a different kind of job than she used to have?" This question is answered by a vocational expert witness at the disability hearing.
- If all of these answers have not convinced the SSA that the applicant is disabled, the SSA asks one last question, "Does this applicant have a combination of symptoms or impairments that together keep her from being able to work?" This question is answered by the medical records, hearing documents, and hearing testimony.

APPLYING FOR DISABILITY BENEFITS

Let's go back now to the start of the disability application process, which begins with a straightforward form, Application for Disability Insurance Benefits. On that form, the person applying for benefits has to identify her health care providers, diagnoses, and basic facts about her education, family members, and employment history. The form does not ask anything about how the claimant feels or acts, even though for claimants with mental illness, that kind of information best demonstrates how disabling the symptoms really are. The claimant (or the family member helping the claimant) is responsible for hunting down names, addresses, phone numbers, prescription details, and dates of service before completing the form. The SSA provides a worksheet for recording all of this information so that you or your family member will not be surprised by the application and will be able to complete it efficiently.

The application form can be completed online, either by the claimant alone or by the claimant with the help of a family member, case worker, or other assistant. Alternatively, the application can be completed over the phone or in person with the assistance of an SSA interviewer who will be sure that the form is completed properly. Anyone completing the online application should know that the SSA provides instructions, called "Helping Someone Apply Online." The instructions say that as long as the disabled person can knowingly sign his or her name on the form, a helper can fill in all of the other information.

The instructions further tell helpers to answer the questions as if the person with the disability were writing the answers. If the person with the disability is too symptomatic to definitely understand that by signing her name she is applying for disability benefits, the helper has to indicate that fact. The SSA will then mail something for the claimant to sign later on. If the applicant is younger than 22 years old and is dependent on a relative, or if the applicant is older than that and a relative has been appointed as guardian or conservator, the family member can apply for disability on behalf of an unwell relative without having the unwell relative sign the form.

It may annoy a claimant whose disability is mental to see that the application asks about irrelevant physical health issues. Some claimants will be inclined not to give that information, but those facts can strengthen the disability claim. When the SSA considers whether there is any job in the national economy that the claimant can do, the case reviewer will look at the total combination of physical and mental symptoms that limit the claimant. A bum knee, asthma, or another physical problem that interferes with ability to do things can really help a claim. If the mental condition alone is not severe enough, physical symptoms on top of the mental health problem may qualify a claimant for disability.

HOW TO Reduce Costs When Applying for Disability

Another significant reason for putting everything into the initial disability application is that the SSA will pay to get the applicant's initially cited health care records. Claimants and their helpers do not even have the opportunity to supply records at this point, because the SSA system has to obtain them. At every other stage of the application process, the claimant has to pay for copies of records, and if the claimant is not earning money, a friend or relative helping the claimant can get stuck paying for records at later stages in the process. Avoid that risk, as much as possible, by listing every available source of evidence up front.

The application has a hefty section asking for facts and contact information that lead to employers and medical providers. After that is a section called "Remarks," which has lots of blank lines where you can write whatever you want. Use the remarks section to list the social worker, the probation officer, the vocational counselor, the landlord, and every other business or service provider who knows the claimant and has witnessed his mental illness. For every one of the information providers, list a name, address, and summary telling what kind of information the SSA can get from him or her.

You may get resistance from the SSA intake worker who helps with the application or from a reviewer who reads the application after you submit it. These people may say something like, *I can only send for records from medical providers.* If anyone at the SSA does seem unwilling to send for items other than medical and employment records, remind him or her that SSA Form 827, Authorization to Disclose Information to the Social Security Administration, which the claimant (or authorized relative) signs as part of the disability application package, specifically says that the disability applicant gives permission for the SSA to see records from other sources. The form includes the following list, exactly as it is written here, of information sources. The authorization would not have this list and require claimants to approve the release of information from these sources if claims could only be based on medical records.

- All medical sources (hospitals, clinics, labs, physicians, psychologists, etc.) including mental health, correctional, addiction treatment, and VA health care facilities
- All educational sources (schools, teachers, records administrators, counselors, etc.)
- Social workers/rehabilitation counselors
- Consulting examiners used by the SSA
- Employers
- Others who may know about my condition (family, neighbors, friends, public officials).

The effort to get the SSA to acquire additional types of records may or may not work, but it is a valid and financially responsible stance to take. The SSA will base its initial decision entirely on the records that it receives directly from health providers, past employers, and the other resources that it occasionally taps for a particular application.

Whether or not the SSA collects all of the relevant records at its expense in the beginning of the case, either you or your family member will later have to obtain and pay for updated records—unless a miracle happens and your relative is awarded benefits as a result of the initial application. Before paying for copies of records, at any point in the disability process, ask every caseworker or indigent service office whether they can obtain free copies of records for the Social Security disability claim. Very often, when caseworkers and needs-based services have a working relationship with the disability applicant, they will have a system for obtaining free records to support these clients' disability claims.

CONSULTATIVE EXAMINATIONS

A Social Security reviewer reading the disability application may require the claimant to see a consultative psychiatrist or psychologist. The SSA will select the mental health professional and will pay for the appointment. When possible, the SSA will arrange for the consultation to be conducted by a provider who already knows the claimant.

The consultation is not meant to go against the claimant's records or to upset her. It is only meant to supplement the application. Claimants who do not get routine mental health care and claimants whose psychiatry or psychology records lack sufficient content tend to have much stronger disability applications when they get these consultative examinations.

Unfortunately, even the consultative examiner is asked to supply only a limited array of information. His or her report to the disability file will describe the applicant's general appearance, thought process and content, mood, cognition, and judgment. These are helpful facts for the file, but they are all temporary characteristics that may be different during the examination than in a job environment.

Even if these features are fairly consistent, they do not depict all of the reasons that someone with mental health symptoms cannot work.

The claimant should give as many examples as possible in response to questions in the consultative examination. This can be difficult to do when someone is experiencing certain symptoms of mental illness, but personal examples are great demonstrations of how mental health symptoms limit the way someone functions. Suppose the claimant is your friend Markie. If the consultative psychologist asks how often something happens, Markie can begin the answer by telling about the most recent few incidents and then note how far apart they were. Markie may say something like, "I know I had a crying jag two days ago because it totally wore me out and kept me from having the energy to even get dressed the next day. And the same thing happened the previous Thursday and made me miss my chance to use the laundry room in my apartment building. It also happened three times last month. Now that I think about it, I realize that I have super tiring crying jags two to three times every month." Hearing this, the consultative examiner will not only know how often the crying jags happen, he will also know that the crying jags disrupt Markie's ability to function for a day or so afterward. In advance of the appointment with the consultative psychologist or psychiatrist, you may want to remind Markie about problems that her symptoms have caused. In this same conversation, you can tell her to look for opportunities to describe examples to the consultative examiner.

THE DISABILITY APPLICATION RESULT

Since the application process provides claimants with little opportunity to show how they function as a result of their mental illness, and the mental health disability regulations *require* proof of functional limitations, the result of a perfectly completed application is almost always rejection. The rejection is a stark bureaucratic letter that comes in the mail.

Nobody claiming a mental disability should feel discouraged by this initial rejection. It does not mean that your loved one is not qualified for disability benefits; it merely means that the SSA needs more information. The basic application process (completing the application, possibly having a consultative examination, and perhaps answering questions from an examiner who reviews the application) is intended to get the core material on file for all applicants and to quickly qualify any applicants whose medical and employment records tell the full story of why they can no longer maintain substantial gainful employment.

So as a helping relative, your primary responsibility is to make sure that, throughout the application process, your loved one meets every SSA deadline and answers every SSA question. You may also need to help gather details for the application and assure your family member that the initial disability rejection letter is really an invitation to continue explaining why she is entitled to disability benefits. After this, you might prepare her for the next discouraging step in the process, a phase known as reconsideration, which is an opportunity to supply additional medical records. The reconsideration phase is efficient for people going through a battery of tests and procedures in connection with a progressive physical problem, but it rarely changes the course of an application that is based on mental disability.

Hiring a Representative

In the second rejection letter, the one that comes after the reconsideration phase, the SSA will explain how to appeal the case at a hearing in front of an administrative law judge (ALJ). The ALJ hearing is the disability application stage when, at last, applicants with mental illness get to present evidence of their functional abilities. To notify the SSA that she wants an ALJ hearing, the claimant will complete the Request for Hearing by Administrative Law Judge. Question 4 on that form says, "I disagree with the determination because. . . ." The determination is the rejection that came in the mail. One of the reasons for disagreeing with the determination is that the SSA has not yet seen evidence of the functional limitations associated with the mental disability. The claimant, or the person helping the claimant with the SSA paperwork, can answer Question 4 by simply writing, "I have a mental health disability and need to show evidence of my functional limitations."

This is the stage when claimants should have a representative—either a disability lawyer or a Social Security claims representative. A Social Security claims representative is typically a caseworker who has completed the SSA's training program to become certified at representing people with disability claims. It is okay to submit the request for a hearing without first having a representative if that is the only way to submit the form on time, but you really should obtain representation before there is a time crunch.

The representative will know how to dig for the unique variety of proof that truly shows how your family member's mental illness interferes with her ability to keep a job. The representative will also know how to interact with the hearing office and how to use the SSA's online Office of Disability Adjudication and Review (ODAR) system to submit evidence electronically. Depending on how busy the hearing office is, the hearing may be scheduled in just a few months or it may not take place until nearly a year after the hearing has been requested.

Claimants living below the poverty line are eligible for free disability representation from social workers, legal aid offices, law school legal clinics, and nonprofit organizations that provide disability hearing representation. To find free representation, begin by contacting the local legal aid office. If legal aid cannot take the case, the intake assistant will know about other sources of free representation. All disability claimants, whether they are applying for SSI disability or for SSDI, can choose to hire a private lawyer. Private lawyers are the law firms that advertise about handling disability cases. If a private lawyer is too expensive, claimants can hire one who will accept the SSA's direct fee payment from the back pay. Recall that back pay is a lump sum of monthly disability payments that are owed to the claimant for the months between becoming disabled and finally getting an SSA determination of disability.

The Appointment of Representative form that the claimant signs upon hiring a lawyer or other representative includes check boxes where the representative indicates whether she waives the fee, will collect the direct payment, or will be paid out of pocket by the claimant or someone paying on the claimant's behalf. If the claimant is working with an office that provides free representation, the representative has to check the box saying that he waives the fee. If the representative agrees to the direct payment that will come from back pay, he should check the direct payment box.

Not all lawyers will accept the direct payment; the claimant or her family should ask about this when they call to schedule their first meeting with the lawyer, before they decide whether to hire him or her. It is appropriate to say, "Will you accept the direct payment from back pay benefits? If not, we will not be able to hire you for this case." Also confirm that the lawyer or representative will not expect you or the claimant to pay out of pocket for investigative costs, such as phone calls, photocopies, travel, or any other expenses that the firm has to pay in order to collect evidence for the case.

The representative has to check the box and sign the form *before* the claimant signs it. A free representative is one who does not get paid at all. If you or the claimant have been told that the representative will take the case for free, but the representative has checked the direct payment box, then you and the claimant do not have to sign the form. Maybe the representative is actually trying to fool you or maybe the representative and claimant have not been able to communicate clearly with each other. In either case, the relationship is off to a bad start, and the claimant may want to look for someone else to represent her.

When a representative checks the direct payment box, and the claimant has agreed to pay the representative this way, he will not get paid unless the claimant is found to be disabled. So if the claimant is found to be disabled, the SSA will send the representative the direct payment check when it sends the remainder of the back due benefits amount to the claimant. Many representatives, including many lawyers, are willing to be paid this way.

When a representative and claimant make a private out-of-pocket payment arrangement, the SSA has to approve it. The SSA does not want people to be cheated out of their benefits by greedy representatives. The SSA will generally approve a fee that is the lesser amount of 25% of the back due benefits or of an acceptable fee announced in the Federal Register. As of this writing, the maximum acceptable fee is $6,000.

Evidence of Functional Limitations

Once a representative is hired, he or she will want to speak with everyone who interacts regularly with the family member who has a mental illness. For example, your cousin Janie's lawyer Antonia would want to ask roommates, family members, and group home staff how Janie manages household chores and basic living routines. Antonia would need to hear stories about how Janie interacts with people. The lawyer has to know about any odd or hostile public behavior, such as when Janie had eruptions in stores or made communications that were inappropriate to the social setting, or if she acted under a phony identity or didn't cooperate with instructions from bus drivers, police, or anyone else in authority.

Maybe the claimant, your son Jeff, is on a team or in a group. If so, make sure to let the representative know so that she can interview the other members. If Jeff goes someplace to hang out on a regular basis, such as a public library or coffee shop, the representative can quietly check with staff there to find out what Jeff does and how he acts. The representative also needs to know about any criminal records documenting Jeff's misbehavior and will likely enter those records as evidence in the disability claim. It is really important to be honest with the representative! The more information she has, the better she can help your relative get disability benefits.

As much as possible, the representative will gather written statements from the people who have true stories to tell about the disability claimant. She may ask one or two of them to serve as witnesses at the upcoming hearing. Professionals, such as group home leaders, staff from homeless shelters, and intensive case managers, make especially good witnesses because they are trained in human behavior and they can describe it with accuracy and authority. They are good at answering judges' questions.

The representative will also try to get disciplinary records and attendance data from the claimant's past jobs. Proof that an employee tended to be late for work or was testy with customers and co-workers can definitely strengthen a disability claim, as can reports about disruptive behavior. Because employers worry about getting sued for defamation or wrongful discharge or for causing emotional distress if they convey anything bad about former employees, they typically will confirm only the job title and dates of employment. To alleviate those worries, the disability representative will promise to use the records only for a disability application and not for any legal action against the employer. She can solidify this assurance by urging the employer to send the information directly to the SSA hearing office. She will then access it from the client's file electronically.

While the representative looks for clues about the existence of witnesses and other functional evidence, the claimant may try to "fake" new evidence by pretending to have a breakdown or other problem. Fake tantrums, however, and fake periods of languishing or other attempts to imitate their own unwell behaviors actually make claimants look like they are not disabled. Although these attempts at producing evidence may be motivated by subconscious desires to improve the case, they tend to demonstrate job skills. The same claimant who says he is too mentally ill to sustain employment has now demonstrated he can identify a problem, devise a plan for resolving the problem, ensure that the resolution will be witnessed or recorded so that the representative can use it as evidence, scope out a location where the event will happen, and probably identify at least one other person to participate in the ruse.

When someone can formulate these thoughts and accomplish these tasks for his disability claim, he has the ability to apply the same skills at a job! When a representative sees a claimant trying to manipulate the evidence in a case, she starts to worry that she is wasting her time and that she is at risk of getting in trouble for representing a phony claim. Experienced representatives avoid telling their clients what kind of evidence they need and warn them about the dangers of trying to manipulate the case.

A Closed Period of Disability Benefits

A disability claimant who begins feeling better and more productive during the disability application process may not be disabled any more by the time she gets a hearing. If her symptoms kept her from working for at least a year and the symptoms were well documented for that period, she may still be able to get disability benefits from the beginning of the back-due period until the point when she became well enough to work again. This is called a closed period of disability.

The problem with seeking coverage for a closed period is that the disability is considered to be over at the end of the closed period. If your family member has an episodic mental illness that might flare up again in the future, he needs his disability case to remain open. So, if it is possible, when the symptoms get better before the disability hearing, claimants with mental disabilities should first establish their disability status and then use the SSA's work incentives program to return to work during well periods as an alternative to requesting disability benefits for a closed period. (See Chapter 17 for a discussion about returning to work after a period of disability.) A good tactical representative will carefully watch the judge during the hearing. If the judge gives any indication of believing that that the claimant currently is not disabled, the wise representative will insist that the claimant was disabled and has a condition that may disable her again. To hedge her bets, the representative will urge the judge to at least consider that the claimant had a closed period of disability.

To make this double-layered plea, the representative will probably say something like:

> *Since my client seems to be temporarily feeling better, she will likely attempt a return to work soon. She is certainly no malingerer. As the evidence demonstrates, her episodic mental illness can disable her for very long stretches of time, in between which she can experience periods of employability. However, if you are not convinced that her particular mental illness is an episodic disability that is worthy of work incentives, please at least consider her to have been disabled for a closed period.*

Chapter 17 has detailed practical information about the SSA's work incentives program, including instructions for participating in it.

HOW TO Help With Disability Evidence

If you don't already know your family member's representative, introduce yourself with a short note or email. This way, the representative can read the message at a convenient time and will not feel interrupted by your outreach, as she would if you called or showed up at her office without an appointment. In your introductory note, tell how you are related to her client, let her know how and when she can get back in touch with you, and summarize the information that you can give her for the case:

> *Ann's dentist has refused to treat her anymore because she behaved badly toward the receptionist several times when she went for check-ups. I can tell you how to contact the receptionist there if you want to get first-hand anecdotes about those episodes.*
>
> *I know all of Ann's friends and can provide names and addresses for them and for other people in Ann's life who observe the way she functions and can tell you how she acts.*

I just want to be sure you know that Ann participates in the local mental health clubhouse for daytime activities, once a week, and that she was dismissed from a volunteer position at the food bank. I am certain that the clubhouse leader and the food bank manager will gladly provide you with affidavits about Ann's poor functionality. I have interacted with both of these people a lot and can make introductions, if you want me to.

You could provide the representative with stories that demonstrate how your relative's mental symptoms manifest. This will show why she cannot find or keep employment. If you are not comfortable writing a paragraph or so to tell each story, at least send a note offering to tell these stories over the phone. The representative or an assistant will be very grateful to hear about these real-life experiences. They will collect clues from the stories and they may include the stories in the written case memorandum that they submit for the hearing. Be sure to direct the lawyer to other family members who can provide additional examples.

Some families avoid telling representatives anything positive about the claimant's good points—her skills, knowledge, affinities, and talents. That is a bad strategy; the representative needs a complete picture of your loved one. Some of the information may even demonstrate functional limitations, such as an inability to stick with a single task, a tendency to only focus on minute things, or a need for utter solitude in order to accomplish tasks. Do not try to second guess your relative's disability representative. She will know whether and how to use any of the information you give her.

If you can give your family member rides to appointments with the representative or to the hearing, tell that to the representative. If you can do any legwork, maybe to encourage witnesses to write the testimony that they've promised to send, let her know that, too. Some witnesses freeze when an official representative asks for a document. Those same witnesses may be more relaxed and able to write if you comfort them and point out that they just need to write a plain note telling true stories about the claimant.

Make sure that the representative knows about any back-up support you can give. She may need you to be sure that the claimant shows up to see a consultative psychologist. She may ask you to encourage your relative to cooperate more fully in the case preparation. She could just want you to fill in missing facts, such as dates and names that your relative does not know. To be truly helpful in the hearing preparation, be as flexible and cooperative as possible.

THE HEARING

Disability Accommodations

The hearing office can accommodate disabilities, but it will know that a claimant needs particular reasonable accommodations only if she or her representative asks for them. Maybe your son cannot tolerate being recorded unless he personally inspects the recording equipment. Knowing this, the hearing office may be able to give him time for the inspection right before the hearing. Perhaps your sister takes medicine that makes her very tired in the morning and she needs to ask for her hearing to be scheduled in the afternoon, rather than in the early time slot initially assigned by the hearing office. The hearing office will make a record of the request for accommodation and will note how the request was fulfilled, but the request will not be considered as proof in the claim for disability. If a claimant does not believe that the SSA provided her with reasonable accommodation, she may file SSA Form 437, Program Discrimination Complaint Form, and submit it to the SSA's Complaint Adjudication Office as explained in the form's instructions.

Video Hearings

Sometimes, the SSA opts to conduct a disability hearing as a video conference. This may be due to a particular location's shortage of hearing judges, the lack of a vocational expert, or other circumstances at the hearing office. Since the participants do not have to all come together in the same room for a video hearing, it can often be scheduled sooner than an in-person hearing. Video hearings are conducted within a private network and are technologically secure. The audio content of the hearing is recorded for the claimant's SSA record, but the video content is not.

Disability claimants are permitted to object to having their hearing by video as long as they object within 30 days of receiving the SSA's notice that a video hearing is planned. The opposite is not necessarily possible: The SSA does not promise that a claimant can choose to have a video hearing rather than an in-person hearing. When a claimant objects to having a video hearing, it is perfectly reasonable to explain how his ability to present his disability may be compromised by having the video hearing rather than an in-person hearing. When a claimant has a representative, the representative should submit the objection on behalf of the claimant. The hearing office will then attempt to arrange an in-person hearing for the claimant.

Arriving for the Hearing

On the day of the hearing, your relative will finally get to tell SSA why she cannot work. When she arrives at the building for her hearing, assuming that she either has an in-person hearing or is participating in a video hearing at a federal government building, she will have to go through security screening. Guards will take away or at least examine any potentially dangerous items that she is carrying. She should not bring mace or any kind of pocket knife, for example. She should expect to remove sunglasses, a mask, or anything else that disguises her features, even if her mental condition compels her to be covered. She and you should be prepared to present photo identification. Because ALJ hearings tend to be held in buildings where multiple federal agencies operate, the security presence does not end at the front door. There will be cameras and security officers throughout the building.

None of the security personnel will know anything about your family member. They may ask what she is doing there. They are simply confirming that she has business in the building. She or you should simply say, "We have a disability hearing in room 123." Nobody working in the building will be out to thwart your relative, and nobody will know her private information. Even the guards and clerical staff in the hearing office will not know about your relative's particular disability claim file. Some of the clerical staff may have handled her file at some point, but only the ALJ and possibly one person on the ALJ's staff will have read it. There is no reason for your family member to worry that anyone other than the hearing participants know about her mental illness.

ALJ hearings typically take about 30 minutes. They do not always start at exactly the scheduled time. Each participant in a hearing has to personally check in at the hearing office after going through the security checkpoint. Friends and relatives who go along for moral support do not have to check in. The check-in is just a system for notifying the judge's clerk when everyone has arrived for the hearing.

The representative will gather your family member's team at a table or, when possible, in a separate room to get ready. Most of the time, the team is just the representative and the claimant. Sometimes, as soon as the representative, the claimant, and any witnesses have checked in, the clerk will immediately appear and say that the judge is ready for them. This does not mean that they have to suddenly go to the hearing. If it is not yet the scheduled time for the hearing to start, the representative can tell the clerk to wait. Of course, it also happens that claimants and representatives have to wait when previous cases extend beyond their expected time.

The period between check-in and the start of the hearing is extremely important for a mental health disability claim. This is when the representative finds out what kind of shape her client is in and tries to get her ready to face the judge. Finally reaching the long-awaited hearing day is enough to upset many claimants. Adding to that, the stress of getting to the building and dealing with all of its federal government scariness can bring out all kinds of anxieties and behaviors. This can be good; representatives want the judge to see their claimants' symptoms. However, the representative has to be sure that her claimant can answer questions and follow the content of the hearing. She may need to calm the claimant down or to focus her on the case.

Some claimants so enjoy having the support of a representative and the attention of a hearing that they arrive relaxed and almost euphoric. This can be damaging to their case. The judge has been led to believe that a deeply troubled person is coming to show how her mental condition prevents her from working, and yet he sees before him a calm and happy claimant who does not seem disabled by mental health symptoms. On the other hand, since judges and representatives frequently see this phenomenon in claimants who are mentally ill, it is not necessarily considered a contradiction to the documents in the case file. In fact, a happy claimant may be particularly good at describing her troubles.

Still, the representative might use part of the preparation time to focus the claimant on the case. She can do this by getting the claimant to recall examples to use in the hearing: *Tell me again what was so bad about that last job.* Or, *What went wrong when you tried that temp agency?* After the hearing, the representative and claimant will have a debriefing, at which time the representative will aim to undo any upset that she caused in the preparation meeting and that came from the hearing itself.

HOW TO Help With Disability Hearing Preparation

As a relative of the claimant, you might play a part in the hearing preparation. Use your best instincts and knowledge of the claimant to guide the representative's strategy. Even if you are at the hearing only because you have to transport your relative back and forth, shake hands with the representative and tune in to the preparation meeting. In fact, during the handshake, you can begin to convey how your relative is doing:

> *Amir did not sleep at all last night.*
>
> *Lisa is so stressed that she yelled at me all the way here in the car.*
>
> *Pam seems happy about all of the attention she's going to get today, but she has not been able to concentrate on anything all week.*

If the representative uses the wrong approach with your family member or cannot get through to him, ask if you can help. You may believe that you are an annoyance, or you may worry that the representative will not like you, but you cannot let this chance at getting benefits fall apart. You know how to read and to cope with your relative's reactions to stress. You may have to demonstrate that knowledge right now, very quickly. If you truly are a nuisance, then say your piece and get out of the way.

> *Dan is not answering your questions because he cannot form words when he is upset.*
>
> *Casey has spent the last 48 hours writing notes for this hearing without taking any time to sleep.*
>
> *I just want to be sure you understand that, despite what she said, Emmy is not mad at you; she is mad at everything.*

If you see that your relative is enjoying the attention too much, use your familiarity to settle him down:

> *Sam, you should not be giggling right now; this is serious business.*
>
> *Corey, I know you like attention, but this is ridiculous; stop acting like you are the lawyer here.*

A good representative will know how to use your information and may even quote it in the hearing. The lawyer also needs the full attention and trust of the client and may need you to stay out of the hearing preparation. If he or she instructs you to be quiet or leave the room, you should do so.

Your job here is to show loyalty to your loved one. She needs these disability benefits. She has been waiting a long time for this day to come. She cannot afford to be misunderstood right now.

During the Hearing

The judge's clerk will come to collect the claimant, the representative, and the claimant's witnesses from the waiting room. They will go to a private hearing room. Social Security hearings are not in courtrooms and they are not open to the public. If the claimant wants to include you or another supportive person present as an observer, the representative must clear it with the judge. This only takes a moment and most ALJ's do allow supportive visitors.

The hearing room does not look like a courtroom. Everyone will sit at tables. The judge's clerk will record everything that is said during the hearing. The recording can only be used for appeals or investigations following the hearing. It will not be made available to the public or to employers, caregivers, or anyone else.

In addition to the judge, the judge's clerk, the claimant, the representative, and any witnesses or an observer that the claimant may bring, there will almost always be a vocational expert in the hearing. This is someone with expertise in finding jobs for people. The SSA hires and pays the vocational expert, but the expert is neutral and has no personal interest in whether the claimant wins the case or not.

The judge will open the hearing by asking the claimant and any witnesses to swear that they will tell the truth. Having read through this claimant's file, the judge may want to begin the hearing with a few of his own questions, which will simply ask for clarification. He may note that Amir's file includes a letter from the volunteer coordinator at the animal shelter and then ask Amir to tell about his typical shift at the shelter. Recalling that Pam's work history included a lawn care job, he might ask Pam to tell what she thinks about the possibility of doing lawn care at this point in her life. The claimant should know that every question presents an opportunity to tell about disruptive mental health symptoms.

When the judge has finished asking his questions, he will invite the representative to question her client. Of course, the representative knows the answers to her questions and has the ability to simply make a statement on behalf of the claimant, but she is not permitted to do that. This is a hearing and the claimant has to be heard. If Amir or Pam forgets to say something important in answering the judge, the representative will ask reminder questions to get those statements on the record. After that, most of the representative's questions will be about independence, ability to complete tasks, social skills, and other aspects of the claimant's functioning. She might ask Amir to talk about his typical day. Once he has told about his routine, she might ask him to tell more about one of the daily activities, guiding him with questions that will demonstrate his inability to concentrate or maintain interest. Next, she might remind Amir about a work environment where he had difficulty participating in team activities. She will ask him to tell her what went wrong in those activities. She will do this in a gentle way. Her goal is not to upset Amir; it is merely to have him demonstrate the functional limitations that he experiences.

When the representative has finished her questioning, the vocational expert will testify. The judge will ask him whether there are any jobs in the national economy that someone with this claimant's symptoms, diagnoses, age, and work experience can do. Notice that the jobs do not have to be available where the claimant lives.

The vocational expert does not have to identify exact job openings. He just has to show that even if the claimant can no longer do the work that he used to do, his impairments will not prevent him from doing other jobs.

When the judge asks the vocational expert to name some jobs, he will tell the expert to believe everything that the claimant presented in the case. This does not mean that the judge believes the claimant; he has not made up his mind yet. If the vocational expert does come up with some jobs that the claimant should be able to do, the representative will cross-examine him to try to get him to admit that the claimant really is not able to do those jobs. No matter whether the expert identifies some job possibilities, the claimant can be found disabled. The judge will send the decision by mail a week or two after the hearing.

LOSING THE DISABILITY CLAIM

If the ALJ concludes that the claimant is not disabled, the claimant can appeal the decision as well as file a new application for disability benefits. The appeal and the new application can both be filed at the same time. The appeal will be a continuation of the old case and the new application will be a completely fresh start: another chance to fill out a blank copy of the online disability application form.

The appeals process, which is handled by the SSA Appeals Council, may go very slowly. It is possible that the new application will get a decision before the appeal is finished. If the claimant is considered disabled based on the new application, she will start getting benefits and the Appeals Council will continue dealing with the old claim. If the claimant is not considered disabled based on the new application, she can apply for an ALJ hearing, but that hearing will not happen until the Appeals Council has finished its work with the old case.

The Appeals Council exists to review mistakes that ALJs make at hearings. The only reason for filing an appeal, instead of filing a new disability claim, is to demonstrate that the ALJ made a mistake. Of course, the claimant and the claimant's representative will believe that the judge made the wrong decision, but judges can reach an unfavorable conclusion even after properly overseeing procedures and thoughtfully reviewing all of the evidence. Actual ALJ mistakes may be misstatements of the claimant's diagnosis, failure to consider all of the evidence, improperly utilizing the Code of Federal Regulations, or blatant prejudice against the claimant.

Ordinarily, lawyers and representatives file appeals; claimants do not file appeals by themselves. Since the representative's income and reputation are affected if he loses an ALJ case, he will earnestly look for a legitimate reason to appeal it. He will need to identify the judge's mistake or multiple mistakes in the appeal document that he files. If, after reading the decision very critically, the representative cannot find a serious mistake that is worthy of appeal, he will cut his losses and tell the claimant that the case is over. This is the end of the claimant's relationship with the representative. If the claimant wants the same representative to help with anything else, she will have to make a new contract with him.

HOW TO Help Your Family Member After a Disability Claim Denial

The most practical way to handle a disability claim denial is to change focus and to look for other ways to get money. If your relative cannot pay for housing and other basic needs and is not already collecting public assistance, she may need to apply for it in order to avoid becoming homeless. The state's public assistance office will match your family member with any aid for which she is eligible. She may get food aid, state disability money, housing aid, or other assistance depending on her particular circumstances and the resources that are available in her state.

If she has already received the full amount of state assistance for which she was eligible, she will be in very desperate need at this point. One way to look for potential resources is to go online and search for the term *homelessness prevention* to help your loved one identify additional nonprofit and government agencies that operate at the county and local level. Such organizations can help with housing assistance, cash assistance, job placement, medical compliance, and other needs. Also, look for disability service agencies; some of them will define disability based on the mental health diagnosis alone, whether or not the client is disabled according to the SSA. These disability agencies sometimes have intensive case managers available to coordinate the whole bundle of services that an individual client needs.

Numerous church-associated organizations also offer resources and services for the poor. The Salvation Army helps with hunger and housing, has a special unit for veterans, and helps to locate missing persons. Union Gospel Rescue Missions address a range of poverty issues, especially homelessness. Many religious denominations operate full-service social work agencies that deal with vocational needs, mental health support, family counseling, and service coordination. These agencies almost always assist the full community, not solely members of their faith.

Every service organization knows about the other local providers, but they do not necessarily offer information about those providers unless somebody requests it. So you may have to assist your relative by networking among agencies. For example, your son might go to the food bank for groceries, but he cannot or will not ask the staff whether they know of an agency that can help him with housing. Therefore, you might call the food bank in advance and inquire, "When Jason comes in for his groceries today, will you please talk to him about some places that can help him find a cheap apartment?"

When a relative seeks referrals on behalf of someone with mental illness, he may be asked, "Why don't you help your relative?" Maybe the answer is, "We are all tapped out," or "She wants nothing to do with us," or "We are helping with other issues, but we need support for this one." The agency is not judging the family when it asks why they are not helping; it is simply trying to get a full picture of the client's circumstances. There is no need to fear the question. As long as the person with mental illness is an adult and not a legal dependent, you have no legal obligation to provide for him. Families can convey that they are inviting the agency onto the team of people who are helping a person with mental illness to live the best possible life.

Other Things To Try If the Disability Claim Is Denied

Another option for your family member to earn money without having to work full-time in an insensitive environment may be to get a job in a mental health service agency. Of course, this could be a terrible work setting for some people with mental illness, but others may be comfortable working in this type of environment. They may like that the employers fully understand how to supervise and manage staff members who have mental illness. People who have lost their disability claims and possess professional skills, such as computer network management, web development, fundraising, or program planning, may feel able to work part-time or full-time in their professional capacity for one of these flexible and understanding employers.

Various types of mental health organizations hire people who have experienced mental illness to serve as peer specialists. For example, peer specialists might staff a phone line, they might plan get-togethers, they might make referrals to community resources, or they might serve as coaches. There are certification programs for peer specialists, so this is specialized work, and sometimes it is just the right fit for people who experience mental illness and are in transition. Some employers of peer specialists provide their own in-house training. People who have been denied disability benefits on the basis that they are not symptomatic enough may well have the energy and desire to do this kind of job.

While applying for disability, your family member should work with her state's vocational rehabilitation office in case she ends up being denied disability benefits. However, if she has not done that, or if she tried vocational rehab in the past but is not currently involved with it, now (after being denied benefits) is the time to get involved. There are two reasons for going to vocational rehab after being denied disability benefits: (1) the person is likely to discover a job path that combines her natural talents and interests with wherever she currently is in life, and (2) should things go very badly when she tries the assessments, training, and jobs presented by the vocational rehab office, the bad experience can serve as helpful evidence in a future disability application.

In fact, all of the involvements identified in this section can result in evidence for a new disability application. Efforts to obtain government services, interactions with case workers at homeless offices or disability agencies, and dealings with prospective and actual employers at places that hire people with severe mental health diagnoses may all show that the person truly is not able to accomplish tasks or otherwise function in job settings.

FILING A NEW DISABILITY APPLICATION

Filing a new disability application is exactly like filing the original disability application, but without the shiny glimmer of hope that made the earlier application process somewhat tolerable. The second time around, the application form is taunting and repetitive. The waiting periods are sheer torture. Unfortunately, the outcome is hardly ever different. The only way to succeed in a disability claim after failing in the last one is to have a new and worse diagnosis or a more severe level of symptoms. It helps to have bad work experiences reflected in the medical records, but the attempts to work cannot be the only new proof submitted with a second disability claim.

The SSA will already have all of the records from the old application, but they need recent records to go with the new application. The onset date for a new disability claim cannot be any earlier than the date of the unfavorable decision. Ordinarily, it is the date of the new application. The whole story has to be told again, but this time the story can only be about how the claimant has been since being declared not disabled the last time.

THE REPRESENTATIVE PAYEE

If a claimant is found to be disabled, but is not able to concentrate or to organize sufficiently to maintain a budget and pay bills on time, the SSA will appoint a representative payee to manage the claimant's disability money. The representative who handles the hearing and the representative payee are usually not the same person, even though they both have the word *representative* in their titles.

The hearing representative will usually indicate, in the hearing memorandum, whether the claimant wants or needs a representative payee. During the hearing, the judge might ask the claimant to tell about her money management. If the judge decides to appoint a representative payee, he will invite the claimant and the representative to suggest a friend or family member for the position.

Representative payee work is relatively easy, and this could be a very positive and supportive way for you to help your loved one. For example, if you are appointed to be your son Brian's representative payee, you would be allocating his monthly disability payments toward his basic living expenses. Most of this work can be done through online transfers. The SSA would directly deposit the money into a bank account that you would be managing for Brian, and then you can set up automatic bill payments to pay certain monthly bills out of the disability money. Brian may have other accounts that he or a power of attorney can control. As representative payee, you do not get to make all of Brian's financial decisions or even necessarily know about his financial activity unless it is related to his continued eligibility for disability benefits or the way you spend the disability benefits on his behalf. Once a year, the representative payee has to file a report with the SSA to demonstrate that the disability payments are being managed responsibly.

Since the representative payee answers to both the SSA and to the person collecting disability benefits, she does occasionally have awkward obligations to deliver bad news from one to the other. If, for example, your son dies, moves into a care facility, or has a change in financial circumstances, you would be responsible for immediately notifying the SSA of that information; you cannot wait until the annual report to convey the news to the SSA. Or if the SSA sends a letter to Brian saying that there will be a change in his benefits, possibly because of some information you provided, you may have to review and explain the change several times before your son internalizes it.

Tax Facts

- SSI disability benefits are not taxed by the IRS. SSDI disability benefits can be taxed. If one half of the SSDI disability benefits plus other income earned that year adds up to more than the annual "base amount" established by the IRS, then the money earned above that base amount will be taxed. This income is treated like all other income: IRS exemptions and deductions will reduce how much tax is owed on it.
- See the *IRS Benefits Planner* at ssa.gov for the most current details about income tax and Social Security benefits.
- The way to avoid paying income taxes on a lump sum of back-due benefits is to show that some of the money is income from past years, not from the current year. In fact, the IRS will send form SSA-1099 to the new beneficiary of disability benefits. This form will list the amount of back pay for each of the past years and the current year. Full instructions for handling the lump sum on tax returns are in IRS Publication 915. Note that there are four worksheets associated with these lump sums.
- In the unlikely event that a taxpayer receiving disability benefits from the SSA has enough income and expenses not only to pay taxes but also to itemize deductions, it is worthwhile to know that the fee paid to the attorney who handled the disability case is a deductible expense. This is also covered in IRS Publication 915.

RESOURCES FOR DISABILITY BENEFITS: SSDI AND SSI

1. The disability chapter from the *Social Security Handbook* is free online at socialsecurity.gov. It contains clear statements from the disability regulations and samples of disability decisions.
2. Disability beneficiaries can use the terms *payment amounts* or *my Social Security account* in the search box on the SSA website (ssa.gov) to find out how much money they are supposed to receive from either SSI or SSDI or both.
3. Read *What You Should Know Before You Apply for Social Security Disability Benefits* (available on ssa.gov) for another view of this process.
4. Your state's disability rights network can answer almost any questions regarding Social Security, Medicaid, Medicare, and other disability support resources in your state. See ndrn.org.
5. The most authoritative source for Medicaid information is your state's health and human services office at healthfinder.gov.
6. Medicare publishes a booklet titled *Medicare and Your Mental Health Benefits* (available at medicare.gov) in which you can find the latest facts about mental health treatments and services that are covered by Medicare.
7. To identify your legal aid office when looking for free representation in a disability hearing, use the Find Legal Aid directory that is maintained by the Legal Services Corporation (see lsc.gov). Alternatively, locate

your nearest bar association in the ABA's directory of state and local bar associations (available at americanbar.org) and then ask the nearest association if there are free local disability lawyers. To find a disability lawyer for a claimant who is not eligible for free legal aid services, look for leads from the Disability Rights Network at ndrn.org, search by city and subject in the Martindale Hubbell Directory at martindale.com, look for lawyers' ads in your community, or use the Justin lawyer finder at justia.com/lawyers.

8. The Extra Help program that helps disabled Medicare beneficiaries pay for prescriptions has a website with instructions, explanations, and forms at ssa.gov.

9. The SSA's guidelines for medical professionals who conduct consultative examinations are online in the "green book." The formal title is *Consultative Examinations: A Guide for Professionals*. See ssa.gov.

10. The listing of impairments, where the SSA identifies the conditions and symptoms that claimants must have in order to be found disabled, is in the Code of Federal Regulations at 20 C.F.R. Part 404 Subpart P Appendix A. It is online at ecfr.gov.

11. The National Organization for Social Security Claims Representatives (NOSSCR) provides clear, helpful facts about applying for disability benefits at nosscr.org.

12. The internal manual that SSA employees use when processing disability applications is the *Program Operations Manual System* and is known as POMS. It is free online at secure.ssa.gov, but it contains much technical language. The manual that ALJs use for disability hearings is called HALLEX. Enter HALLEX in the SSA's search box to access this manual. Lawyers and other representatives will consult both POMS and HALLEX when deciding whether to appeal a case after an unfavorable hearing decision.

13. A disability claimant who requests, but does not receive, reasonable accommodation for her disability at any point in the disability application process can file a Program Discrimination Complaint Form, which is available online with instructions at https://www.ssa.gov/forms/ssa-437.pdf.

14. The Equal Employment Opportunity Commission's Job Accommodation Network (JAN) has links to all of the states' vocational rehabilitation agencies at askjan.org.

15. The SSA provides training, guidance, and explanations for representative payees at https://www.ssa.gov/payee/.

3
—

Guardianship

Your sister Nyla has lived independently for her whole adult life, but now she is not shopping or eating or even bathing with any regularity. You have been going over to her place every evening for several weeks to make sure she takes her medicine, and you therefore see that she is not able to manage herself or her household right now. You want to do more for Nyla and you want to get involved with her mental health treatment, but she has not given you permission to interfere with her home life and her treatment. At this point, only a court can give you that permission; you need to seek guardianship.

THE NEED FOR A GUARDIAN

"Guardianship of the person" is legal authority to make health and lifestyle decisions on behalf of somebody who is incapacitated. Although the technical term is *guardianship of the person*, this chapter uses the term *guardianship* for ease of understanding. Other forms of legal authority, such as power of attorney for health care (also called health care proxy) and conservatorship, are available when people need assistance making health-related decisions or help with financial management. (Medical powers of attorney are covered in Chapter 4 and conservatorship is covered in Chapter 21.)

Guardianship is granted when loved ones and caseworkers convince a judge that somebody can no longer take care of himself and cannot make or communicate decisions about his well-being. Two important things happen in the same successful guardianship court case: A person with severe mental illness is declared to be incapacitated, and another person is appointed to be his guardian and take care of him. The guardian can be an individual or an institution. If the guardian is an individual, the person does not have to be a family member, although a guardian frequently is. Incapacity and guardianship can be temporary or permanent and can be modified by the court.

How do you know if your unwell family member needs a guardian? Well, the evidence will have been mounting for a very long period, probably over a year. For example, with your adult daughter, Rosa, there have been frequent times when you or others have had to manage routine tasks and arrangements that would otherwise have gone undone: washing laundry; stocking soap, toothpaste, and toilet paper; getting treatment for dental and vision problems; calling an exterminator to deal with an infestation; informing the landlord of an ongoing leak or appliance failure; preparing meals, etc. Also, Rosa has required multiple hospital visits in recent years, some of which could have been avoided if Rosa had better personal routines in place.

Furthermore, there have been conversations with others who have raised concerns about Rosa. Maybe a neighbor called you to report scenes or a care provider checked in with the family. Perhaps her supervisor at work or the police called and said to come and pick Rosa up. Her spouse, siblings, co-workers, and friends may be asking each other what is going on with Rosa because some of these relationships have fallen apart.

Your family and other caregivers may have tried less drastic steps along the way—arranging for services to be provided or else taking care of things yourselves. A relative or caregiver may have had temporary or ad litem guardianship for emergency circumstances. An intensive case manager may have been working with your daughter for an extended period. Perhaps a caseworker has declared, "Rosa needs a guardian."

THE GUARDIANSHIP PROCESS

The process of seeking guardianship is just like the process of seeking conservatorship (also known as "guardianship of the estate"), which is described in Chapter 21. The guardianship process begins with a form called a court petition requesting that an individual be declared legally incapacitated. The court, usually probate court or family court, will provide a standard petition form asking for basic facts and examples. The person who is being discussed in the petition has to receive a copy of that petition; nothing about the process can be done behind the person's back, which can make the process very stressful and uncomfortable. If the completed petition form has sufficient information, the court will undertake an investigation. If the petition does not have enough compelling information, it will be denied by the court. The petitioner may later be able to gather additional facts and present a stronger petition that will merit an investigation.

The guardianship investigation will normally include an independent psychological examination of the person who is alleged to be incapacitated. The court might also order psychiatric and social work examinations. Then the court will review documents proving that caregivers and service providers have already tried less restrictive ways of helping the person to manage independently. In some states, the court will conduct a background check of the person who has been nominated to serve as the guardian. This background check will look for criminal records demonstrating a history of abusiveness. When the investigation is complete, the court will schedule a guardianship hearing.

In both guardianship and conservatorship hearings, people come forward to tell unflattering true stories about how their loved one with mental illness can no longer handle things. It is bad enough in the conservatorship hearing, when the stories are about not managing money well. In a guardianship hearing, the stories can be heartbreaking. Relatives, friends, and caregivers—people who are liked and trusted by the one they are accusing of incapacity—report on poor hygiene, bad housekeeping, inadequate eating habits, problematic personal relationships, and other embarrassing and disgusting areas of personal mismanagement. Many people experience some of these negative issues in their lives. People in need of guardianship, however, experience these issues so much that their health and functionality are compromised and most of the people who know them have stories to tell.

The Defendant's Lawyer

The person who is alleged to be incapacitated will almost always be represented by a defense lawyer at the hearing. Every state's guardianship law either entitles or requires people who may require a guardian to have a lawyer. The court will appoint a lawyer or engage a public defender unless the individual chooses to hire her own lawyer. Appropriate lawyers for guardianship hearings are those who specialize in elder law or disability law. The lawyer's job is to represent the client's desire to retain control over his own life, as much as possible, and to defeat the claims that he is incompetent. The lawyer will bring witnesses and other proof to demonstrate the client's competence and will cross-examine the witnesses who say that he needs a guardian. She will also want to confirm that the witnesses are not exaggerating their descriptions and that nobody is seeking guardianship out of greed or a desire for power.

The lawyer will need to become familiar with the client (for example, your daughter Rosa) prior to the hearing, so you or a friend or another family member should provide rides or other help to make sure that Rosa can spend time with her lawyer. If Rosa is unable to express herself, her helper should at least get her together with the lawyer so that they can observe each other and Rosa can hear what the lawyer has to say. The lawyer should tell Rosa what the hearing room will look like and how the judge will act. Watching and listening for reactions from Rosa, the lawyer will also talk about the questions and statements people will present at the hearing.

At the hearing, in addition to challenging claims about Rosa's incapacity, her defense lawyer will offer evidence to show how and when Rosa does demonstrate good self-management. If Rosa can make and communicate her own decisions about self-care—at least under certain circumstances or regarding some aspects of her life—her lawyer will fight to preserve those areas of independence for her. The goal is to minimize Rosa's loss of control. Therefore, even if Rosa truly wants somebody else to deal with everything, her lawyer will try to save every possible opportunity for her to make choices for herself once a guardian is in place. If guardianship is granted, the incapacitated person (in this case, Rosa) becomes known as the *ward* of the guardian.

After the details of Rosa's incapacity are established in the guardianship hearing, the other lawyer in the case—the one representing the prospective guardian, perhaps you—may have the opportunity to include some issues that are specific to the particular situation in the document granting guardianship. State law might require separate hearings or other processes in order to tailor the guardianship terms or it might not permit certain issues to be built into the guardianship at all. Some issues to include in a guardianship arrangement regarding a person with mental illness are:

- Planning for the possibility that the ward will not want to receive psychotropic medications: The courts in some states can specify that the guardian is authorized to follow best medical advice over patient objections when the patient is psychotic. So, if you became your daughter's guardian and she becomes psychotic and doesn't want to take her medication, you can try to force the issue.

- Planning for the possibility that the ward will refuse to go for voluntary hospital treatment: Depending on the ward's state of residence, the court can declare that the guardian has authority to volunteer the ward for admission to the mental hospital when hospitalization is medically appropriate but the ward is not dangerous and in need of involuntary commitment. In other words, if Rosa has missed several days of sleep and is bouncing from one activity to the next and almost constantly chattering, you can tell that she needs help settling down and you can have her evaluated for admission to the hospital.

- Planning to implement systems and services: Not every family has separate people serving as guardian and conservator, but if they do, the two will need to work together on certain arrangements. For example, the court can specifically declare that the guardian will arrange transportation, manage the schedule, and handle other issues that require collaboration with the conservator. Under this arrangement, the guardian can bring Rosa to consult with a nutritionist and then make new meal plans, but the conservator will have to confirm that the consultation is affordable or is covered by Rosa's insurance, file the insurance forms, release funds to pay a co-payment or full bill, and possibly increase the grocery budget. (Chapter 21 covers supported decision-making, which is another approach to handling personal management.)

THE GUARDIAN

Competent Versus Incompetent Guardianship

If someone is successfully granted guardianship, the court will require the guardian to file regular reports on the ward's well-being. Typically, the reports are made on standard forms provided by the court and are submitted once a year. The report forms ask about the ward's condition, actions that the guardian has taken on behalf of the ward, and any major changes in the ward's circumstances, such as new housing or a new therapist.

Meanwhile, the various service providers who interact with the guardian about the ward's treatment and billing will be paying close attention to how the guardian behaves with the ward and how well the guardian is managing the ward's compliance with treatment. If these professionals see any problems with the guardian, they will attempt to deal with the guardian directly, but they may also report the problems to the court. Similarly, family members will have their eyes on the guardian, watching for good and honest care. They, too, can report problems to the court that established the guardianship. The court can call for a hearing at any point that it wants to hear from these witnesses and the guardian. The input from the people who interact with the ward can act as a shield to protect a vulnerable ward from an unscrupulous guardian.

Guardians who keep thorough and well-organized records will be in the best position to file adequate reports to the court and to defend themselves against any claims of insufficiency or dishonesty. Guardians should make a file for each major issue to be managed under the guardianship, such as housing, physical health care, mental health care, socialization, education, and/or employment. Within each of the files, the guardian should make folders for copies of people's contact information, specific incidents, general billing, communications, and any related insights that the ward conveys.

These insights from the ward (for example, Rosa) may be stray comments or the content of deliberate conversations, drawings, or any other form of expression. Over time, patterns will appear in the insights so that the guardian and ward will both come to realize preferences, dislikes, and comfort issues that otherwise may not have been obvious. In addition to these reasons for maintaining files, guardians will have a much easier time managing their guardianship responsibilities when they have all of the information organized in a handy system.

Guardians' Decision-Making Power

The modern concept of guardianship requires that wards have the most freedom possible. This concept comes from the Standards of Practice of the National Guardianship Association (NGA). The standards incorporate the recommendations established at the Third National Guardianship Summit and are endorsed by the American Bar Association. In other words, everybody is behind the standards. Lawyers representing people who are allegedly incapacitated have the standards in mind as they argue to limit the extent of an individual's guardianship. Furthermore, guardians, once appointed, are wise to follow the standards to be sure that they provide the best service.

Basically, the guidelines require guardians to become well informed before making any decisions for their wards. Guardians have to investigate and understand the available choices and the possible outcomes. When they do not understand or know how to do something, they are expected to ask for help, rather than worrying that they may look bad for having to ask. They also have to understand and comply with the ward's perspective.

Guardians are supposed to approach every decision in the ward's best interests and as conscientiously as they would want somebody making decisions on their behalf. At the same time, they cannot be selfish. If, for example, as Rosa's guardian, you are deciding which dentist she should see, the important factors in selecting the dentist should be the dentist's professional skills, knowledge of patients with special needs, and acceptability to Rosa. Issues that are more important to you, such as your convenience, should be secondary to Rosa's needs and preferences.

The guardian who makes decisions about the person and the conservator who makes decisions about finances can be the same person or different people. If one person handles both personal matters and financial matters, she is formally called "plenary guardian," although she is often referred to simply as "guardian." If they are two different people, they will need to communicate with each other, but the guardian should not have to seek the conservator's approval for every spending decision. Their shared and separate responsibilities should be delineated by the court, and early in their relationship they should establish a mutually acceptable system for dealing with each other. It may be necessary for them to meet with the ward's caseworker or a professional/institutional guardian at the beginning of their relationship, to plan their system for working together. In this meeting, or series of meetings, they might plan a general budget, arrange a communication system, set priorities, and confirm their boundaries.

HOW TO Find Guardianship Training and Support Programs

There are many good informational tools available to new guardians. The court will provide at least some basic forms and instructions and typically a handbook. Some court systems offer entire courses for new guardians. Local hospitals frequently have community educational programs about health decision-making and other medical transactions. Enter the term *classes* or the word *events* in a nearby hospital's search box to find out what kinds of programs are on the schedule.

Contact a large, well-known, local senior services provider to ask what sort of guardianship training they provide or know about. They may refer you to a service that works with Alzheimer's patients or people with intellectual disabilities. It does not matter whether the ward is a senior citizen or dealing with a different condition; the guardianship training will be the same for any guardian.

The NGA offers webinars and self-study materials for guardians to learn about individual topics of interest. Among their courses are: Introduction to Guardianship, Public Benefits, VA Benefits, Surrogate Decision-Making, Choosing a Home for Somebody Else, Due or Undue Influence: How Do You Draw the Line?, and A Protocol for Medical Decision-Making. The Center for Guardianship Certification offers a credentialing process for guardians that involves a standardized exam. In preparing for the exam, applicants have to master a set of core competencies that reflect the knowledge and skills necessary to satisfy typical state guardianship laws and the NGA Standards.

MODIFICATION OR TERMINATION OF GUARDIANSHIP

There are happy reasons and also sad reasons for modifying or terminating a guardianship. Among the happy reasons is the ward's improved well-being. The sad reasons include the guardian's bad behavior. For whatever reason that a guardianship has to change, the official way to notify the court is through a petition to modify or terminate guardianship. In some jurisdictions, the petition process will be called restoration of capacity.

The petition is typically a standard form supplied by the court that has been supervising the guardianship. It can be submitted by the guardian, the ward, or any interested party. Although the guardian and interested parties may choose whether to have a lawyer assist them in a modification/restoration hearing, wards are customarily represented by legal counsel. It is reasonable for the ward to expect the court to pay for the same lawyer, or at least the same law office, that represented her in the hearing that established the guardianship. However, state laws do not specifically promise that this will happen. Either a ward or someone watching out for her interests may need to contact the judge's clerk and ask that the court provide the ward with a lawyer, and, if the ward desires it, the same lawyer who helped in the past.

The happy reasons for modification/restoration are easy to document in the petition: a guardian can declare that the ward is now able to handle some of the things that the guardian has been dealing with (for example, the guardian has helped the ward to organize her own hygiene and medication routines). Over time, the ward may be able to take back increasing amounts of control, and the guardianship will be further modified. A ward who could not manage independent living at one point in life may eventually attain a level of wellness and a set of skills that later make her capable of functioning entirely without a guardian. Honest and successful guardians are proud to see their wards regaining independence.

Other guardians prefer not to acknowledge their ward's independence. There are plenty of stories about self-serving guardians who refuse to relinquish control when their wards no longer need them. Often, these are guardians who get paid out of their wards' assets and do not want to give up that income. However, sometimes they are just people who thrive on having control over others. Sometimes a particular guardian is just not a good match for the ward but fights against the ward's independence because of his own ego; he does not want to become unnecessary.

There are also times when a guardianship needs to be modified not because the ward has improved, but because a different guardian is needed. If the guardian is abusing the ward or stealing her money, call the police and Adult Protective Services first and then deal with guardianship court. When a guardian is not committing crimes but is selfish, controlling, or basically not helping his particular ward, you might talk to the guardian or you might opt to notify the guardianship court about it, depending on the circumstances. Consider a scenario in which you manage your daughter's money and someone else serves as her guardian. You have not received any pharmacy charges for your daughter in the past month, although you usually get one per week. You first contact the pharmacy to ask if there is a billing error. The pharmacy tells you that nobody has come to get the prescriptions. At this point, your best move would be to ask the guardian what's going on with the prescriptions. If the guardian does not have a medically valid reason for not getting your daughter's medicine, then you'll want to notify the guardianship court.

Anybody with first-hand knowledge can report the guardian. The proper way for interested parties to notify the court about guardianship problems is to file a petition to modify guardianship, but some witnesses may just want to report what they have seen. The court will not usually have a form or even a required format for this kind of communication, but the judge will take the information seriously if it is composed in a serious manner.

This testimony needs to be in writing and properly addressed to the judge overseeing the guardianship. It has to include the first and last names of the guardian, the ward, and the witness submitting the testimony, and it should tell how the court can reply to the witness by phone, mail, or email. The testimony should have a detailed report of who, what, when, where, and how. The person submitting the letter or report should convey how he got the information, whether he saw it or heard it. He should identify other witnesses by their full names and their relationships to the ward—best friend, pharmacist, landlord, sister, etc. He should tell how the ward is affected and whether the ward's mental health appears to be compromised by the guardian's acts or omissions. Perhaps the witness has not seen or heard anything because the guardian has alienated this person as well as the ward's other friends and relatives. This is also definitely worth reporting to the court. The court will not necessarily act on this kind of report as soon as it comes in; the clerk may file it until it is time for the next routine review of the guardian. On the other hand, someone from the court may make inquiries right away. The response will depend on several factors, including the court's rules and staffing, in addition to the content of the report.

When the court receives a petition for modification/restoration, the court clerk will first notify the ward, the guardian, and the interested party that the document has been received and will be investigated. Unless there is a known safety risk, all of their names will appear in the same notification, so they will all know that the others have been informed about the pending investigation. After notifying the interested parties, the court will seek additional proof of the claims presented in the petition.

The court's investigation into modifying or terminating the guardianship will be very much like the investigation that went with the original guardianship petition. The judge will want impressions from the ward's therapist, caseworker, medical providers, and others who are in close and supervisory relationships with the ward. If there is any opposition in the case, the judge will seek input from witnesses representing the parties' different perspectives. Finally, the court will conduct a hearing and make a decision about whether to reduce or increase the guardian's responsibilities, replace the guardian with somebody else, or declare the ward to be no longer incapacitated and in need of guardianship.

Tax Facts

- The guardian is usually responsible for filing tax returns on behalf of the ward unless the ward has a separate conservator who would handle the tax return along with other financial matters. In the first year, the guardian can deduct, on the ward's income tax return, the costs of getting the guardianship arranged in court. See Internal Revenue Service (IRS) Publication 502.
- Guardians need to file IRS Form 56, Notice Concerning Fiduciary Relationship, along with the standard income tax form (1040, 1040A, 1040EZ) that they file on behalf of the ward.
- If the person acting as guardian is in business to be a guardian, then he or she can deduct the costs of being guardian as business expenses. An example of a deductible business expense would be a computer and software that the guardian purchases and uses just for the guardianship work. See IRS Publication 535.
- If one spouse is the guardian for the other and they file a joint tax return, the guardian spouse can sign both names but write "signed by (Guardian's Full Name), guardian," after the name of the person who is unable to sign. See IRS Publication 17.

RESOURCES FOR GUARDIANSHIP

1. The NGA has a printable seven-page glossary of guardianship terms available for free online. Every new or prospective guardian should have a copy of this on file. To find an experienced guardian, either for networking or possibly to serve as your relative's guardian, search in their membership database at guardianship.org.

2. The NGA has had Standards of Practice for Guardians since 2000. In 2011, when the National Guardianship Network (NGN; made up of the country's ten leading elder care policy organizations) met for its Third National Guardianship Summit, it used the NGA's old standards as the basis for establishing new standards, which are now incorporated into the current version of the NGA Standards. See the full proceedings of the National Guardianship Summit at epubs.utah.edu and the current NGA Standards of Practice for Guardians at guardianship.org.

3. The NGA's *Model Code of Ethics for Guardians* is online at guardianship.org.

4. The American Bar Association's portal to state guardianship laws and annual legislative updates is online at americanbar.org.

5. The National Resource Center for Supported Decision-Making publishes a clear and descriptive guide to state guardianship laws at supporteddecisionmaking.org.

6. Online training for guardians is provided by The Center for Guardianship Certification (CGC). This organization offers practice exams and applications for the states that require certification. Even when state law does not require certification, guardians can learn a great deal from studying for and passing the CGC's general certification exam. See details at guardianshipcert.org.

7. The Special Needs Alliance (SNA) is a nonprofit legal organization with expertise in disability law and government benefits. According to its identity statement, "individuals with disabilities, their families and their advisors rely on the SNA to connect them with nearby attorneys who focus their practices in the disability law arena." See SNA's *Find an Attorney* page for this purpose. Two of their newsletter articles about guardianship and mental illness are: "The other special need: Planning for those with severe mental illness," *The Voice*, 5(3), Feb. 2011, and Martha C. Brown, "Guardianship and mental illness," online only at specialneedsalliance.org.

8. The NGN maintains a resource guide, *Decision Making without Guardianship,* for families who want to see the pros and cons of handling particular transactions with and without guardianship authority. The guide is free online at naela.org.

9. Working Interdisciplinary Networks of Guardianship Stakeholders (WINGS) are "consensus and problem-solving groups" that exist in some states. Each of the networks acts as a partnership between families and various local institutions that provide important information and services to guardians and wards. Read all about WINGS at the NGN website. Families involved with guardianship may want to help establish one of these networks in their community. The free guidebook for creating a WINGS group is also on the NGN website at naela.org.

10. The National College of Probate Judges serves as the central information source for guardianship courts. See its current information about guardianship at ncpj.org.

11. The Center for Elders and the Courts publishes professional reports about emerging legal issues and quality of service in guardianship. Its materials are written for courts, but anybody can read them. Its *Guardianship Basics* is a very thorough explanation of guardianship court practices. Find all of this at eldersandcourts.org.

12. The National Association for Court Management publishes the *Adult Guardianship Guide,* which advises courts about appointing, training, and monitoring guardians, at nacmnet.org.

13. The Uniform Adult Guardianship and Protective Procedures Act (UAGPPA) uses the word *conservator* for a guardian who manages finances and *guardian* for a guardian who manages personal and medical matters. This law has been enacted by all but seven states so far, and it sets the rules by which states will recognize and deal with guardianship relationships that cross state borders. Examples of cross-border issues include: when the guardian and ward live in two separate states, when some of the ward's assets are in another state, or when one or both of them moves out of state after the guardianship has been created. Since a uniform law is a model for states to adopt or modify, not every state's version is completely identical to the UAGPPA. Read the UAGPPA and related information at uniformlaws.org.

14. Adult Protective Services (APS) agencies are government offices that investigate reports of physical, emotional, and financial abuse and participate in prosecuting the abusers. Find your local APS agency and more information from the National Adult Protective Services Association at napsa-now.org.

4

Psychiatric Advance Directives

Jed has been hospitalized for major depression in the past and undoubtedly will be hospitalized for it again. He knows this as well as anyone. There are two things that he dreads about the hospital: being stuck with needles (he needs the hospital to take special steps before giving him IV medicine, for example) and the way everyone presumes that he is violent (which he is not) simply because his hands go into tight fists when he experiences acute depression. He knows that his sister understands him and will speak for him even when he is too depressed to think anything positive about her. The next time he lands in the hospital, he wants them to know about the needles and his involuntary nonviolent fists, and that they should call this sister. If Jed fills out a psychiatric advance directive when he is well, and then becomes incapacitated by a severe episode of mental illness, the hospital will consult that psychiatric advance directive to know what Jed desired prior to becoming incapacitated.

THE REASONS FOR PSYCHIATRIC ADVANCE DIRECTIVES

One of the worst things about episodic mental illness—that is, periods of severe symptoms that disrupt someone's usual life—is the way it terrorizes people. It peeks out from among memories at stray moments, threatening ruin and then retreating until the day that it begins creeping all the way out for a long period of torment. During the longer bad times, there can be crisis periods when people are so unwell that they cannot process or communicate information. These are known as *periods of temporary incapacity.* Psychiatric advance directives are legal tools that people with mental illness create during their well times to tell their family and health providers how they want to be treated if they ever become ill and experience temporary incapacity.

Psychiatric advance directives contain two messages:

1. An explanatory list of treatment preferences
2. A designation of somebody to make medical decisions that are not addressed in that list. This person is formally called the patient's *agent.*

These messages can appear in a single document or in separate documents. If they are in separate documents, the list might be titled Psychiatric Advance Directive—Treatment Preferences, and the designation might be titled Psychiatric Advance

Directive—Durable Power of Attorney for Mental Health Decision-making. If the messages are in a single document, it will probably be titled Psychiatric Advance Directive (PAD).

PADs are a subset of medical planning documents. Other medical planning documents include durable powers of attorney for health care (also called health care proxies) and living wills. In a durable power of attorney for health care, you name someone to make general medical choices in the event that you cannot make or communicate decisions. A living will conveys your end-of-life instructions, including your choices about life support.

WHEN A PAD BECOMES APPLICABLE

Unlike the need for guardianship, which becomes evident through various incidents over time and must be proven in court, the need to follow a PAD arises quickly, and the decision about when to use it is usually made by a doctor, not a court. State laws on advance directives will typically establish guidelines about how to determine when your family member's temporary incapacity starts and stops, whether and how advance directive documents have to be witnessed or notarized, and whether a mental health agent can also be an agent for physical health decisions. For example, the advance directive law may say that a doctor treating your grandmother for schizophrenia can conclude that she is temporarily incapacitated, or it may say that a judge has to make that determination, based on input from a psychiatrist. Some state laws call for multiple medical opinions on a person's capacity. Other state laws entitle people to give their own directions about how everyone can tell that it is time to implement parts of the PAD. Your grandmother may write, for example, that she wants you to make her psychiatric decisions whenever it becomes obvious that she is heavily influenced by a particular delusion that she has experienced in the past. When a person signs a PAD, she should know the circumstances under which her written treatment preferences and the decisions of her agent (the person who will make decisions during the period that she is ill) will be followed. For this reason, a properly drafted durable PAD document will quote the state law criteria.

WRITING TREATMENT PREFERENCES

To make a meaningful advance directive that anticipates what may happen in the mental hospital, your grandmother will probably have to conjure up recollections from past treatments. This can be harrowing and should not be done under pressure. Family members helping with PAD planning should not hurry the process, nag their relative for facts, or involve outsiders whom the relative has not invited. Rather, family members who truly want to be helpful should allow their loved one to put down the desires and limits that are important to her.

There are standard PAD forms, which are available from treatment facilities, state governments, and mental health advocacy organizations; these forms have questions to inspire good planning. They typically contain either blank lines or else "do/don't" checklists where a patient can identify her preferences for facilities, medications, forms of restraint, and modalities of treatment. The forms then provide a line after each preference where patients may write a reason for each preference. Families can build on those broad questions by using the inquiry techniques that a lawyer would use in court. The purpose behind the inquiry techniques is to get people to tell stories about past events and to express their desire for justice; that is exactly what should happen in planning a good advance directive. Here are some examples of how the method can work.

When a PAD form says something like, "I do not agree to receive the following medications," you could ask your grandmother:

- *Have you ever had bad side effects from medicine? What was it like?*
- *Do you remember getting a bad combination of medicines? What happened because of that combination?*
- *Did you ever get too much or too little of any medicine? How did you find out that the dosage was wrong for you?*

Your loved one can include these story details to explain her preferences on the form. For example:

- *When I got 4 mg of that medicine I developed the shakes, but 1 mg seemed to help and did not give me the shakes.*
- *This medicine gave me hallucinations the last time I took it.*

Notice that the pattern of the questions asks people to declare that they have had a bad experience and to describe what happened as a result of that bad experience. These are painful things to think about. Also, out of context, they could set off mental health symptoms, but drafting a PAD is proactive planning that involves using past experiences while not dwelling on them. It may help to tell your grandmother, "This should prevent that bad experience from happening again." "I will make sure they look at this form and know not to give you that medicine." "You are steering things this time. You have rights and you have choices. I will do my best to keep your instructions in front of them."

Not every part of the advance directive form has to rely on experiences, but some of the treatment options on the form can still cause anxieties because of information that the person with mental illness has read or heard. For example, one of the questions could specifically ask your family member to opt in or out of electroconvulsive shock treatment. Another may be about methods of restraint or seclusion. Even someone who has never experienced those treatments can predict how they could affect her and can give instructions in advance of a crisis. Furthermore, because new methods and devices become available all the time, the more descriptive someone's preferences are, the more helpful they will be when the hospital needs to know whether or how to use the new options with your relative.

HOW TO Inspire Effective Preference Statements

Ask leading questions. Leading questions state facts and cause responders to use the facts in forming their answers. This is how lawyers cross-examine witnesses who do not want to talk about unpleasant things. Although lawyers may seem uncaring when they do it, family members can do it in a supportive way. For example:

- *Do you want the hospital to know that a totally dark room will stress you out?*
- *Remember that TV interview about how ECT affects memory? Do you want to write down what you think about that topic on this form?*
- *You know how much you hate it when people touch you without asking first. Do you want to let them know that here, so it's less likely to happen?*

Remember to include physical health issues in the leading questions about being placed in restraints. Physical discomfort is very stressful.

- *If they leave you flat on your back for a long time, is that going to set off your esophagitis?*
- *If your arms are kept in one position for too long, will that bother the bursitis in your shoulder?*

Some people think that information already contained in a medical record does not have to be repeated in an advance directive. That is wrong. It is not enough to have had conversations with providers or even to have notes in the medical chart from past treatments. Patients and families should expect that, in a crisis, the hospital team will not slow down to read carefully through years' worth of records to find out about stray problems with medicines or comments about not wanting particular treatments. All of your family member's guidance should be clear and handy in the PAD.

Legal forms generally exist to structure communications between parties. When the form is generated by the government (like a tax return) or establishes a deal between people (like a sales agreement) the questions on the form have to be completed a certain way in order for the form to be legally valid. But PAD forms are valid even if parts of them are blank or if they include information that is not specifically called for on the form.

Maybe the form only asks about medicines to avoid and does not ask about medications that your grandmother takes for other conditions, such as her high blood pressure. Maybe the form asks for the name of a preferred hospital, but not the preferred conditions in the hospital. Perhaps your grandmother wants to avoid the teaching hospital, for example, so that she does not have to deal with medical students. Don't feel limited by the exact questions on an advance directive form; the form exists to collect your relative's preferences even if those preferences go beyond the form's exact categories or questions.

WHEN HOSPITALS DO NOT FOLLOW TREATMENT PREFERENCES

Advance directives have been around for decades. The legal system and medical establishments take them seriously and uphold them as much as they can. There are times, however, when hospitals are permitted to work around individual terms in an advance directive. When a patient is no longer incapacitated and learns about the hospital's noncompliance with her treatment preferences, she may want to take legal action. Unfortunately, she is not likely to have a valid legal claim unless the hospital blatantly violated the state's advance directives law or her condition was made worse because they did not follow the advance directive.

Even a breach of contract claim is not likely to stick. An advance directive may seem like a contract for services, but that is not what it is. In a contract, both parties agree to do certain things. In a medical service contract, for example, a medical facility agrees to provide care to the patient and the patient agrees to pay for the care. That is, however, not how an advance directive functions. An advance directive is a one-sided communication from the patient, not an exchange of promises.

The patient's right to draft treatment preferences and the hospital's obligation to follow them are in the same legal codes that also require hospitals to provide certain standards of care for all of their patients. So an individual's treatment preferences have to be considered within the context of the hospital's other legal obligations. Treatment preferences also have to be considered in relation to insurance coverage and other legitimate economic conditions in hospitals. The advance directive laws certainly do not authorize patient treatment preferences to override professional medical expertise or emergency conditions.

Despite the probable lack of a legal remedy, there are actions that a patient and her family members can take after suffering an injustice relating to her treatment preferences: She can modify her advance directive in case it is ever needed again, and she can speak up—presenting her story as an example of how things can go wrong. To modify or replace the document, she can keep the good parts of the old PAD and write new instructions to replace the old content that either couldn't be followed or did not turn out the way she hoped it would. If she opts to speak up, she and her family members can write to the state mental health authority or to the hospital administration, perhaps making recommendations or else simply asking that things change. She may even want to tell her story at peer-support meetings, the local clubhouses, NAMI (National Alliance on Mental Illness) meetings, or social service agencies. Talking to these groups, she can caution other patients about the factors that caused her PAD to be misused or ignored. Ideally, people who hear her story will write better PADs for themselves once they know what happened to her. A lot of people can learn good lessons from one person's bad experience.

DURABLE POWER OF ATTORNEY FOR MENTAL HEALTH DECISIONS

A durable power of attorney (POA) for mental health decisions is the part of a psychiatric advance directive that empowers someone, such as a family member, to make mental health decisions on behalf of a person who is temporarily incapacitated.

People with mental health concerns draft a durable POA so that they can choose who will speak for them if ever they cannot speak for themselves. Unlike guardianship, in which a court assigns someone to help, the decision to draft a durable POA and the selection of the person to hold the POA are made by the individual herself. Some people interview and train their decision maker as if they were hiring him for a job. Others simply designate their decision maker and trust him to use good judgment if he is ever needed.

Say that your grandmother would like you to have POA for her mental health decisions. You would have to sign a POA document, agreeing to accept the responsibility. Once empowered, you might be called an *agent*, a *substitute decision maker*, or *the person with durable power of attorney*. If your grandmother has drafted an advance directive with treatment preferences, you will act as a supplement to the preferences, meaning that you will only be called upon to answer questions that are not covered in the treatment preferences. You may also remind the hospital about the treatment preferences if you see that they are not being followed.

As the agent, you will be empowered to start, stop, or continue treatments and medications. You will have access to your grandmother's medical record. You will have authority to select practitioners to treat her. You may never be called upon to make any decisions if your grandmother's written treatment preferences are clear and apply to all of the situations calling for decisions during her incapacity. If you do have to make a decision, it will likely be a very narrow decision. State law will set forth the perspective that you should apply when making decisions on behalf of a patient.

Fundamentally, as the agent, you are required to make your grandmother's mental health treatment decisions with the same care and thoughtfulness that she would use for her own treatment decisions. Knowing this, a person selecting an agent for mental health decisions should select someone who is very thoughtful and careful. More specifically, state law may require agents to make all of the decisions either in the patient's "best interests" or else as they believe the patient would decide, which is referred to as *substituted judgment*. The example given here demonstrates the differences between the best interests and the substituted judgment perspectives:

Suppose Tim is an incapacitated patient who arrived at his current episode of severe mental illness despite taking his long-time medicine exactly as prescribed with perfect regularity for several years; he simply reached a point where the medicine was no longer right for him. Over the years, Tim has told friends and family members, including his brother Mark, who is his agent, that he does not trust and will not take any medications until they have been on the market for at least 5 years without causing worse problems than they are supposed to cure.

The hospital psychiatrist, after studying Tim's record, recommends a new drug that was created for patients with exactly the condition that Tim has. The drug has delivered excellent results to patients just like Tim in clinical trials. In a state that mandates the best interests perspective, Mark would be justified in accepting the new medicine for Tim because science says that it will probably help him. In a state that mandates the substituted judgment perspective, Mark would be justified in declining the new medicine because it has not yet been on the market for 5 years and Mark knows that Tim would decline it if he were able to communicate his own decision.

This example is extreme and is designed only to highlight the differences between state law perspectives. Patients can expect that their priorities, concerns, and other interests will always guide their agents' decisions. There would be no reason for patients to select their own agents if the agents could just make arbitrary decisions or would always yield to the doctor. The whole point of granting durable POA is that people get to direct their health decisions through somebody whom they trust and whom they may have trained to represent them.

HOW TO Be a Good Agent During Temporary Incapacity

In assisting your grandmother, even if you do not need to make decisions during her incapacity, you can still be involved with her treatment. Think of yourself as an advocate, someone in a position to stick up for the patient and to make sure that she gets the best treatment available. If this sounds out of character for you, know that many people find that it is easier to advocate for somebody else than for themselves. You do not have to be pushy or demanding to be a good advocate; you just have to be well-informed and clear in your communications.

To the extent that the hospital permits it, you should personally observe your grandmother. If you have questions about her medication, her room, her diet, her treatment team, or anything else, ask. You can either ask the nurse directly about the issue or you can ask the nurse how to contact the person you should speak to about the issue.

Read the brochures and signs that are available in the hospital. They will tell you about the hospital's policies and treatment philosophies. They may even identify some family education programs that you can attend or some vocabulary that you will want to use.

Take notes when you communicate with hospital staff. Write down the name of the person you are speaking with and the explanations and facts that you are given. Also take note of the date and time that you get the information. Facts and opinions will change as time passes; that is normal. If you have notes, you will be clear about when and why things are changing. Either your grandmother is responding to medicine, the staff are revising the course of treatment, or something else is happening. If you do not have an explanation for the change, you at least have a basis for asking about it when you are told something that differs from the information you previously wrote down.

You should have a copy of your grandmother's treatment preferences so that you can monitor the hospital's compliance with them. If you see any treatment that goes against her preferences, use a three-step process to interact with the nurse:

1. Note what the advance directive says. Example: *Zelda's advance directive says that she does not want medications with substance X in them because they interfere with her digestive system.*

2. Politely point out the contradiction. Example: *I see that the doctor has just prescribed X-deluxe for her.*
3. Inquire about correcting the situation. Examples: *Would it be possible for me to talk with the doctor about revising that medication order? Can you tell me how to contact the doctor? Is there a similar medication that does not contain X but that is used to treat this symptom?*

You do not have to be at the hospital constantly inspecting every single action. You just need to check on your relative so that you know how she is, who is involved with her, and what is going on in her treatment. The hospital staff will call you if they need you. As you develop a relationship with the hospital treatment providers, they will involve you in a therapeutic alliance; you will be a part of the team working to get your grandmother out of crisis and into a suitable transition back home.

RESOURCES FOR PADS

1. The National Resource Center on Psychiatric Advance Directives has excellent introductory information, including helpful videos, articles, and a glossary. Their state-by-state tab gets you to individual FAQ pages summarizing each state's practices and linking to the state's laws, forms, and related sources. See nrc-pad.org.
2. Mental Health America (MHA) provides guidance and advocacy regarding PADs. Look for MHA's glossary and its FAQ page about PADs at mentalhealthamerica.net.
3. The Bazelon Center for Mental Health Law provides a fill-in PAD template form, a fact sheet, policy comments, and legal advocacy resources at bazelon.org.
4. *The Advanced Self Advocacy Plan* (ASAP) produced by the University of Pennsylvania Collaborative on Community Integration is a 29-page questionnaire that will help patients and families to think about all of the topics and perspectives necessary to prepare for a future mental health crisis. See tucollaborative.org.
5. The World Health Organization has compiled authoritative materials about a mental health patient's rights. Various parts of the materials may help patients and families think of ideas to cover in their advance directives. See who.int.
6. The International Society for Ethical Psychology and Psychiatry is an interdisciplinary nonprofit organization that produces thoughtful materials on ethics in mental health practice. Its statements on "Key Issues" are very clear and can help people to phrase their interests as they compose advance directives. The materials are available at psychintegrity.org.

7. *The Mental Health Declaration of Human Rights* sets forth principles for patients' control of their mental health decision-making. The organization behind the declaration, the Citizen's Commission on Human Rights, is opposed to the use of psychiatric medications and other practices in mainstream psychiatry. See cchr.org.

8. The National Institute of Mental Health (NIMH) maintains a descriptive roster of medications commonly prescribed for particular mental health conditions. NIMH's descriptions are simpler and much more straightforward than the details on package labels. See nimh.nih. gov.

9. The National Library of Medicine publishes an alphabetical guide to all medications. Families and patients seeking information about a particular drug or herbal supplement's chemical composition, known side effects, things to know before taking, and other facts can find that information at nlm.nih.gov.

10. The American Psychiatric Nurses Association publishes authoritative resources about restraint and seclusion of psychiatric patients. Their documents include a history of the practices, a position statement, standards of practice, and continuing education material. See apna. org.

11. Regulations about restraining hospital patients are at 42 C.F.R. § 482.13. See ecfr.gov.

12. The *Journal of the American Academy of Psychiatry and the Law* publishes many of its articles free online. They are scholarly articles that use advanced professional vocabulary and discuss complicated scientific principles, but families and patients who search for the term *advance directives* on the journal's site will find comfort and expertise. See jaapl. org.

13. A very practical book about patients' ability to make decisions regarding their health care and the circumstances when professionals should assess, judge, or consider overriding a patient's decisions, is Thomas Grisso's *Assessing Competence to Consent to Treatment: A Guide for Physicians and Other Health Professionals* (1998).

14. The National Mental Health Consumers' Self-Help Clearinghouse has webinars, training materials, and other resources about PADs online at mhselfhelp.org.

15. The National Association of State Mental Health Program Directors maintains a portal to government mental health authorities in the individual states and territories. Patients who have had bad experiences with PADs may want to describe their experience to the state authority. See the portal at nasmhpd.org.

5

Involuntary Commitment

Your daughter's neighbor called this afternoon. Your daughter, Melissa, was acting out in the apartment hallway and someone called 911. An ambulance just took Melissa to the nearest hospital. You race to the hospital and are allowed to see your daughter in the emergency department for a few minutes before being sent to the waiting area. After 2 hours, someone comes to tell you that they have committed Melissa to the psychiatric ward. You think that they've made a mistake, and you want to know what's going to happen next and whether you will have any opportunity to be involved with her commitment.

THE CONCEPT OF INVOLUNTARY COMMITMENT

Involuntary commitment is what happens when somebody who is experiencing psychiatric symptoms is admitted to a hospital without consenting to the admission. Once hospitalized, the person will often be required to undergo mental health treatment against his will. The treatment can happen in the hospital, which is involuntary inpatient commitment (IIC), or in the community, which is involuntary outpatient commitment (IOC). Although it seems like a medical decision because it is about health care, involuntary commitment is really a legal action. Statutes and courts have to authorize involuntary commitment because it interferes with a person's fundamental liberties.

Every state has a mental health code that explains the criteria for involuntary commitment. One common basis for involuntary inpatient commitment is dangerousness; a patient who is an imminent danger to others or himself, possibly from poor self-care, can be committed to a mental hospital until the danger passes. The legal standards for outpatient commitment are more diverse among the states, and they generally also require some degree of dangerousness, usually that the person seems "likely" or has a "reasonable probability" or is "predictably" or is "reasonably expected" to soon be dangerous. Also in the state outpatient commitment standards are requirements like:

- The patient lacks insight or capacity to make informed medical decisions for himself.
- The patient is unable to provide for his own basic food, clothing, and shelter needs, or to live safely without assistance.
- The patient needs treatment to prevent further deterioration.
- Outpatient support exists in the community.

In some states, the law specifically requires that patients be given "the least restrictive alternative," meaning the form of mandatory mental health treatment that best avoids compromising their fundamental freedoms any more than is necessary.

FUNDAMENTAL FREEDOMS

It took until the last third of the 20th century for courts in the United States to thoughtfully weigh mental patients' constitutional rights against society's interests in peace and safety. The courts concluded that, in mental health settings, as in physical health settings, people have a right to privacy that entitles them to opt out of medical intrusions. The courts realized that as long as people have a First Amendment right to access and use information as they desire, they also have the right to be informed about medical risks and to develop their own impressions and decisions based on that information. The legal concept of *battery*, which forbids "non-consensual physical contact" also came to mean that medical patients have the right to be informed about the risks they face with treatment and the right to accept or not accept the treatment. Some courts found that the First Amendment entitled people to be able to communicate about their mental health and their treatment, even if they had to stop taking psychiatric medications in order to think and communicate clearly. The courts declared that public interests had to be narrowly designed to stand up against individuals' due process right to control their own mental health.

The current state laws on involuntary commitment were devised to recognize these fundamental rights. In your state, perhaps someone cannot be physically restrained or forced to take psychiatric medications unless these measures are truly necessary to stop him from immediately hurting himself or others. Maybe he cannot be confined in a mental health facility against his will unless he presents an imminent danger. If he has been taken to a treatment facility in an emergency, he is entitled to participate in the decision about whether to stay there and whether to continue treatment after the emergency has ended. Nowadays, if you are looking for legal support to enforce an involuntarily committed patient's fundamental rights, you should be able to find what you need in your state's mental health code and in your state's court cases.

COMMITMENT PROCESSES

Involuntary commitment (also known as civil commitment), like all other legal actions, is framed by procedural rules. Some of the rules come from the mental health code (such as rules about deadlines in the commitment process) and some are general court rules that are not unique to mental health commitments (such as evidence rules that are used in courts throughout the judicial system, including civil commitment hearings). The procedural rules tell how the commitment is supposed to be carried out. Typically, the rules require an examination by a mental health professional, an assessment of the person's dangerousness, court approval of the decision to commit, and then a hearing soon after the commitment has started. Notice that the court appearances having to do with involuntary commitment are hearings, not trials. Trials are for determining whether somebody is guilty of wrong doing. Hearings are for determining program eligibility and making plans. Some hearings about involuntary commitment do not even take place in a court building; instead, they are held in a hearing room at the hospital or other mental health treatment facility.

When someone is involuntarily committed on an emergency basis, he is typically transported to the mental hospital by police, a mental health crisis service, an ambulance, or other emergency personnel. (See Chapter 7 for detailed information on police crisis intervention teams, which are trained to recognize and respond to people who are exhibiting symptoms of mental illness. Officers on these teams diffuse crises and arrange transportation to the hospital.) Depending on the location and circumstances, a person may be transported to a general medical hospital rather than to a mental hospital. The doctor who examines him in the emergency department at any kind of hospital completes a legal form declaring that the person needs to be involuntarily committed. The hospital then submits the form to court and either holds the person for treatment or, if the hospital does not have space or psychiatric services, transports him to a mental health treatment facility.

Typically, the patient's initial hearing happens after he has been in the hospital for 48 or 72 hours—depending on the length of time that the state law allows for an "examination" period. Within that time, a psychiatrist and others will talk with the person and assess his mental state. They may have given him medicine and taken note of how the medicine affected him. They will also observe how he interacts with staff. Those professional impressions will serve as evidence at the hearing, the main purpose of which is to decide whether the person needs to remain in the hospital.

In a situation where a person has voluntarily entered the hospital, but then wants to leave while still ill enough to be confined, he can be involuntarily committed by the staff. This means that staff will prevent the person from leaving, will fill out an involuntary commitment form attesting to his mental state, and, within the legal time limit, will present medical evidence at the same kind of involuntary commitment hearing that an emergency patient would go through.

The parties to a commitment hearing are the person being detained in the hospital (the patient) and the state. The patient is represented by a court-appointed lawyer and the state is represented by a state attorney who is responsible for civil commitments and the hearing officer, who has a duty to rule on the case at the end of the hearing. The hospital and individual mental health providers are merely witnesses; they are not parties to the hearing, although they are very important witnesses. State laws about commitment hearings tend to identify only mental health providers as required witnesses. In fact, the laws say that the commitment decision is to be based primarily on medical opinions. Whether or not the law specifically says it, family members and others who are close to the patient may also serve as witnesses if they have relevant information to share.

Those seeking to be witnesses may need to dig for information about the commitment hearing, even to get basic facts like when and where it will be held. The hospital will not divulge the time or location of the hearing because that would compromise patient privacy. The hospital may provide the hearing office's phone number. Alternatively, prospective witnesses can search online for the term *civil commitment hearing office* along with the county name. Usually, the civil commitment hearing office is a part of the court that oversees protective services.

HOW TO Participate in a Commitment Hearing

Anyone wanting to testify at a commitment hearing should notify the civil commitment hearing office that he or she wants to be put on the witness list. Potential witnesses could include an employer, a neighbor, or family members. The hearing office will file the prospective witness's contact information and reason for wanting to testify so that the lawyers can decide whether they want to interview and possibly involve this person as a witness.

Let's assume that your sister Lynn has been committed and you want to serve as a witness at her commitment hearing. The hearing office will probably require a conversation between you and either the hearing officer or Lynn's defense lawyer before placing you on the witness list. You should welcome that conversation and consider it an opportunity to begin making plans about the message you hope to convey. Once you are on the witness list, you can expect to receive all communications about the upcoming hearing: reminders about the schedule, identities of the other witnesses, handy facts about the conduct of the hearing, and possibly notes on Lynn's future reassessment hearings.

Here are some examples of how you could be a useful witness in Lynn's initial commitment hearing:

- If you know that Lynn will not be able to speak up for herself at the hearing, your testimony may be the only evidence about what upset her prior to her hospitalization. It can also show some facets of her personality that will help her get the most appropriate treatment.
- Similarly, your testimony can demonstrate Lynn's range of normal moods and behaviors. This would give the hearing a basis for comparison with the medical testimony. With this information, the court can best determine, for example, whether Lynn is actually dangerous or whether she is all talk and just sounds dangerous. Remember that if the hearing is about dangerousness and Lynn is not dangerous, she does not need to be hospitalized against her will.
- If you were victimized by Lynn, you can certainly be a valuable witness at the commitment hearing, especially if Lynn is good at tricking people into thinking that she is well when she is not. You would testify about harm that you or your property suffered during the events leading up to Lynn's hospitalization. You can also ask the hearing officer to order Lynn to participate in family therapy or order the hospital to notify you when Lynn is released. If you truly feel threatened by Lynn and you learn that she is released soon after the hearing, you can go to criminal court and request a protection from abuse order. This is a type of restraining order that will entitle the police to arrest Lynn just for getting physically near you after she is out of the hospital.

The hearing officer and lawyers can question you in the hearing. The questions are meant to explore issues, not to accuse you of doing something wrong, but they can be intimidating. They may ask how much you truly know about Lynn's daily life or what you did or did not do as Lynn's symptoms escalated.

The lawyer representing Lynn will push back against possible exaggerations and false claims and will fight for the least restrictive alternative. The medical witnesses will be more experienced at hearings than the family witness, but Lynn's lawyer will be tough on the medical witnesses, too. Although hearings are often less formal than trials, the lawyer will use the evidence rules to protect her client, especially the hearsay rule. Hearsay is testimony that includes someone else's statements. The hearsay rule prohibits this kind of testimony. Family members often want to present quotes in commitment hearings. For example, you may be tempted to testify that "Lynn just kept saying 'I wish I'd never been born' over and over again." You should know that Lynn's lawyer will object on the grounds that you are trying to present hearsay if you try to quote Lynn this way.

One method that you can use to report Lynn's statements is to contain them within scene descriptions. Here are some examples:

I was terrified that she would hurt herself because she had my car keys and was crying and said she was going to drive into a wall.

I just wanted to get away, but she grabbed my arm really hard and said she would break it. I still have bruises where she squeezed me too tight.

Notice that these statements relate personal experiences, not merely quotations. Lynn will be at the hearing and will have the chance to accuse you of lying. Her lawyer will back her up, contesting your ability to recall exact details and testing your ability to repeat the exact phrase at different times.

As the court determines whether to impose inpatient commitment or outpatient commitment, looking for the legally required least restrictive alternative, it will need to know if a family member is available to provide various forms of support. Recalling that involuntary commitment is used when patients cannot handle their basic personal care and safety, you, as a witness at the hearing, should prepare to either accept or decline responsibility for feeding, bathing, medicating, sheltering, transporting, or otherwise consistently assisting Lynn. You do not have to feel pressured to take on these tasks simply because you have appeared at the hearing. Lynn's hospital treatment team will ask her for names of possible support persons and ideas about who else might assist her outside of the hospital.

If the hearing officer does conclude that Lynn needs to remain involuntarily committed, the officer will issue a court order establishing Lynn's commitment terms. The terms will specify where the commitment will take place (whether inpatient or outpatient), what limits Lynn will have to live under during the commitment, what obligations the hospital has regarding the commitment, whether there are any criminal law issues connected with the commitment, and when the commitment is to be reassessed.

In most states, the court order will say that the commitment can last for "not more than" a certain amount of time; in fact, many patients are hospitalized for much less time than the court order says. Their symptoms improve quickly or they change their own status from involuntary to voluntary. If they become

voluntary patients, they do not have to undergo any more court scrutiny in connection with their commitment. The length of commitment time in the court
order actually comes from the state's commitment statute. It is meant to ensure
that people do not get abandoned in a facility, forgotten by the system. When
someone does remain committed for the full amount of court-ordered time, he
will have a second hearing at the end of that time to determine whether he still
needs commitment and whether it should be in the same form or a modified
version.

QUALITY AND CONTENT OF MENTAL HOSPITAL SERVICES

There was a time when people accused of being "mentally deficient" either in
intellect or sanity could be trapped in a facility for years, getting bad treatment
or no treatment at all. Families can now feel secure that psychiatric hospitals,
like all hospitals, are held to performance standards that are established by
accrediting bodies as well as by law. Every element of psychiatric hospital
management is subject to standards of quality, including medical treatment,
cleanliness, nutrition, facility maintenance, pharmaceutical accuracy, nursing
care, and security.

Although a state's mental health code will contain statutes about psychiatric
hospital management, the state health department, and possibly other regulatory
agencies, will make and enforce precise regulations for how the statutes are carried
out. The regulatory agencies will monitor hospital compliance by requiring hospital
managers to file periodic reports and the facilities to submit to inspections. If a
hospital performs below regulatory standards in any area, the regulating body will
require and oversee improvements. If the hospital does not improve, it may be fined
or forced to close the noncompliant unit.

HOW TO Complain About Hospital Care

Families can report most hospital problems directly to the hospital's administration. The institution will likely have comment cards around the building
as well as a contact form on their website. File a complaint, either through a
nurse or the convenient comment tools, when there is something wrong with
a patient's room (for example, if the sink is not working or the bed is broken) and when professional mistakes do not get corrected (for example, if the
pharmacy keeps forgetting to send up the asthma medicine, or the cleaning
service has not dealt with a mess that was made days before, or the dietary
department keeps sending gluten-filled meals to a patient with celiac disease)
and when patient needs are not being addressed (for example, a nearby patient makes noise all night and keeps your relative awake, or your loved one
is not given phone access during the after-school hours when her children are
available to talk).

Someone from hospital administration will get in touch to say that she received the complaint. Put that reply in a file folder so that the administrator's
name and title and the date of the response are available for future use. If the

administrator writes again to let you know about corrective action, also put that communication in the file. This may be the end of the problem, but if it is not, you have the option of complaining to the state health department. Every state health department has an online complaint form.

While you are on the health department's website for the complaint form, look through the regulations to be sure that at least one of them relates to the problem you are reporting. To file a legitimate health department complaint, you will have to include your own name, the patient's name, and the identities of staff and administrators who have not resolved the issue. As with all complaints, describe who, what, when, where, and how. Explain why the problem is important. Finally, define the resolution that would satisfy you. (For example, you could say, "Please see to it that this sink gets fixed immediately," or "I hope that you will take all necessary measures to ensure that my brother gets gluten-free meals," or even "I trust that you will use your full regulatory enforcement power to improve the hygiene in this facility.") Your chosen resolution may not be possible or may not come about for other reasons, but at least you will have conveyed what you consider to be the best way to fix the problem.

EXPUNGING AN INVOLUNTARY COMMITMENT RECORD

Expunging something is the legal process for having it deleted. In some states, when people are involuntarily committed for no legitimate reason, the commitment record can be expunged. How can anybody be unjustly confined to a mental hospital without a legitimate reason? Maybe a vindictive spouse made a false claim or somebody in public mischaracterized something that he saw or heard. The police or a crisis team then transported the accused person to an emergency department (ED) where, surely after a long wait, an unknown medical team did a quick examination and asked a bland battery of uncaring and unhelpful questions.

In other kinds of ED visits, patients are asked questions like how long they have been in pain, when the bleeding started, and what happened to cause their suffering. But in a mental health workup, the patient's well-being seems secondary to the assessment of whether he is immediately dangerous. ED staff will give the person the full examination that the circumstances call for, they will treat his wounds, and they will ask about his full array of prescribed medicines, for example. But their dominant concern is whether the person is dangerous. And the accused person, who may have arrived at the hospital in police custody, who may have been expressing valid emotion, who may have made another person mad, or, who—for any number of reasons—may have been forced into a police car, dragged to a hospital, and detained, is expected to be calm and pleasant? Anybody could come across badly under these circumstances.

For example, the ED doctor, rushing from one person to the next, gets her first "clue" about your brother, Sammy, from the fact that he did not bring himself to the hospital. When she realizes Sammy was forced to come, she suspects something must be wrong. The goal in the ED is to get patients stabilized. The doctor will run toxicology tests and check for neurological symptoms. She will try to find out about psychiatric history and current pressures, but it's possible that your brother may not be cooperative. A lack of cooperativeness is another clue. Furthermore, a team of several ED staffers may collect Sammy's information in separate spurts. Meanwhile, Sammy does not know if any of these people know what the others are doing or if any of them believe what he is telling them. He may respond with anger or sarcasm: more clues. At some point in this incredibly stressful ordeal, one of the professionals may comment on your brother's physical behavior; perhaps he can't sit still or his fists are clenched. Sammy, feeling accused or threatened in the midst of this aggravating nightmare, might respond by crying, yelling, or rolling-up in a ball. Another clue. At some point, the number of clues justifies filling out a commitment form.

Sammy is admitted to the mental hospital or committed as an outpatient for more thorough evaluation and to get treatment. Maybe he truly does need some mental health care. Nevertheless, if the commitment was unjust because he truly was not dangerous and did not satisfy his state's other legal criteria for involuntary commitment, this should not stand in the way of his future opportunities. Sammy should not have to answer Yes in the future when asked if he has been involuntarily committed to a mental institution. This is why there are laws and procedures for expunging unjust involuntary commitments. Sammy's medical record will still exist, but his commitment form, which is a legal document, will be removed from the court records, and his status of having been involuntarily committed will cease to exist.

To begin the expungement, a lawyer has to petition the judge who handles civil commitments in the city or county where your brother was processed. The lawyer will also request a copy of his commitment form from the court. Sometimes, the court does not have the commitment form. When that happens, the lawyer immediately informs the judge that the commitment was obviously illegal because the proper form was not filed.

If Sammy's form is on file, however, his lawyer will exploit every possible flaw in it. She will question the thoroughness of the ED examination. She may even get testimony from the person who made the 911 call that started this series of events. Her goal is to demonstrate that there was insufficient evidence to commit your brother in the first place. As long as the lawyer can prove that the commitment was made with incomplete or inaccurate information, it has a chance of being expunged.

Criminal record expungements have become much more common in recent years, particularly when they serve the social good. For example, we often see minor charges, such as vagrancy and loitering, being expunged from the records of homeless people so that they can more easily find jobs and homes. If your state does not yet expunge mental health commitment records, although it expunges or suppresses criminal records, consider lobbying for a new law. Although some states put their commitment expungement statutes with their gun registry laws, you can fight for your state's statute to be a due process claim in the civil rights code or to be a modification of your state's civil commitment law.

RESOURCES FOR INVOLUNTARY COMMITMENT

1. To find a state's mental health code, look for a citation from the charts that the Bazelon Center for Mental Health Law and the Treatment Advocacy Center both provide. Alternatively, in a search engine, enter the name of the state and the word *statutes*. That will take you to the statutory code. One you are in the code's website, use either the code's search box or the code's index to look for the word *mental* or the term *civil commitment*. Be sure to carefully browse the table of contents at the beginning of the state's mental health code to get a full sense of its coverage.
2. Protection and advocacy (P&A) agencies are available in every state to monitor and advocate for the rights of people with disabilities. They are experts on disability policy and interact regularly with agencies and facilities that serve people who live with disabilities. Find your state's P&A agency through the directory maintained by the Disability Rights Network. See ndrm.org.
3. The Bazelon Center for Mental Health Law advocates for patients' civil liberties in the commitment context. The liberties are the rights that all medical patients have: the right to decide whether to accept treatment, the right to privacy, the right to decide where to live, and other rights regarding personal autonomy. The Bazelon Center publishes lots of authoritative and clear resources for families to read and they encourage families to be well informed, to lobby legislators, and to use the court system to fight for mental patients' autonomy. See bazelon.org.
4. The Treatment Advocacy Center also works hard to inform and to involve families regarding laws that affect people with mental illness. In addition, the organization seeks to "eliminate barriers to treatment." They are concerned about patients suffering through prolonged periods of severe symptoms and other negative consequences of not getting sufficient mental health treatment. They believe that patients who lack insight about their mental health are unable to make rational decisions about their own care. See treatmentadvocacycenter.org.
5. Mental Health America is opposed to IOC and calls for an increased variety and availability of community resources that patients can access on a voluntary basis. See mentalhealthamerica.net.
6. Therapeutic Justice in the Mainstream seeks to have therapeutic principles guide developments in mental health law. This movement arose in response to the lack of community resources available to help patients fulfill and sustain their outpatient commitments; commitment was functioning like a punishment rather than a treatment. The academics behind the movement offer consultations to courts so that judges will direct patients to appropriate combinations of services for adequate amounts of time to help them get through their current mental health crises. See mainstreamtj.wordpress.com.
7. A good book with recommendations about improving involuntary commitment from the perspectives of both mental patients' rights and society's interests is Bruce J. Winick's *Civil Commitment: A Therapeutic Jurisprudence Model* (2005).

8. Another valuable book related to the topic of involuntary commitment is John Weston Parry's *Mental Disability, Violence, Future Dangerousness: Myths Behind the Presumption of Guilt* (2013). The book demonstrates and denounces American society's rampant prejudice against people with mental illness. It calls for sanist prejudices against people with mental illness to be abolished and for special protections to be created.

9. When a family member feels endangered by a relative who is mentally ill and not confined to an institution, the endangered family member should follow self-protection advice from the National Commission on Domestic Violence. This guidance includes household preparations, communication techniques, obtaining a protection from abuse order from the criminal court, and planning for various outcomes. See ncadv. org.

10. The National Council on Disability is an independent federal agency responsible for advising the president, Congress, and federal departments about the effects of government actions on people with disabilities. Regarding involuntary mental health commitment, they have commented on policies and proposed laws, submitted *amicus* briefs in court cases, and conducted research studies. See ncd.gov.

11. The Centers for Medicare and Medicaid Services summarizes federal regulatory requirements for psychiatric hospitals and links to the related regulations at cms.gov.

12. The U.S. Department of Health and Human Services has a portal to all health regulations. The regulations apply to inpatient and outpatient psychiatric services, including systems for coordinating psychiatric care with other medical care. See hhs.gov.

13. The National Association for Psychiatric Hospital Systems sets forth quality standards and provides accreditation. It has a very strong advocacy program that lobbies for government attention and resources for improving behavioral health. Its guidance on building design, patient and staff safety measures, and quality of inpatient services is used by psychiatric hospitals all over the country. See its website at naphs.org.

14. The American Hospital Association (AHA) is the national organization representing the hospital industry in policy advocacy. It administers professional competency exams and bestows professional certification to assure that hospital managers possess fundamental knowledge. Its Hospitals in Pursuit of Excellence (HPOE) arm provides resources and examples to guide hospitals toward continual improvement. This information and the AHA's behavioral health resources are available at aha.org.

15. The Joint Commission accredits all kinds of hospitals. Its certification is widely recognized as a mark of hospital quality. Its accreditation standards are incorporated into many state regulations and can serve as a list of expectations for families and patients in evaluating their own hospital. See jointcommission.org.

16. Not every state has a specific mechanism for expunging court records of involuntary commitments. Three examples of states

that do have procedures for this are Pennsylvania, New Jersey, and Minnesota. See njexpungements.com for instructions to follow in New Jersey. See mncourts.gov for a fill-in form to get an involuntary commitment expunged in Minnesota. The guidance available for use in Pennsylvania was written by Attorney J. Michael McCormick, who is an expert in gun law. His explanations and arguments can be adapted to any jurisdiction—even those that have not yet considered expunging civil commitment records. See his website, pagunlaws.com, as well as his chapters about restoring firearm rights in the latest editions of *The Law of Guns in Pennsylvania* (Pennsylvania Bar Institute).

6

Professional Misconduct

Your brother, Randy, was abandoned by his psychologist, Dr. Dell. Randy was seeing Dr. Dell as part of the employee assistance program at his job because he was burned out. Dr. Dell went on a long vacation after seeing Randy for four weeks and did not arrange for Randy to meet with a substitute in his absence. He did not follow-up with Randy when he returned from the vacation, even though Randy had sent him two messages asking for help during his absence. Dr. Dell had written in his notes that he was going to refer Randy to a psychiatrist for antidepressants, but he never made that referral. Meanwhile, Randy became increasingly depressed and stopped going to work. He lost his job and then his home. You believe that things would not have gotten so bad if Dr. Dell had done his job right. You think that Randy should sue Dr. Dell on the grounds that his whole world fell apart because of Dr. Dell's professional negligence.

WHAT IS MALPRACTICE IN MENTAL HEALTH PROFESSIONS?

It is way too easy to mistreat somebody with a mental illness, especially when that person trusts you and you know exactly how to push her buttons. You can seduce that person. You can cheat her. You can make her feel terrible. You can betray her confidence. (Of course you would never do these awful things. The word *you* is not specific here. It just means that anybody might intentionally mistreat someone else.)

On the other hand, mistreatment does not have to be intentional. You could forget about something that you needed to handle. You could misplace things. You could be unreliable. There can be lots of ways that you might not do what you are supposed to do. (Again, this is not you specifically: it is anyone who is negligent.)

Even mental health professionals and their institutions—the experts who are supposed to help and protect people with mental illness—have been known to mistreat them. It has happened enough times that there are multiple legal doctrines against it. While the general term for mistreating clients is *professional misconduct*, the legal system identifies several specific offenses:

- Regulations set forth requirements for professional licensure. When a professional fails to fulfill the requirements, she can lose her license. The regulations also establish duties that can be raised in negligence cases.
- State civil court precedents establish the concept of malpractice. Malpractice is a form of negligence. Over time, throughout the country,

malpractice has come to be defined as a "failure to use the reasonable skill and care that a professional in the same field would ordinarily use under similar circumstances." In other words, professionals have a duty to use that level of skill and care; if they fail to do so, they have breached their duty. And, if the failure caused harm to the client, the professional has been negligent. A breach of duty that causes harm is negligence.

- Past cases and statutes identify additional duties that professionals might breach. Victims commonly stack multiple negligence charges in a single case, for example, malpractice, infliction of emotional distress, wrongful death, and general negligence.
- Statutes and civil court cases also identify particular intentional acts (known as *intentional torts*) that can be punished as professional misconduct.
- Criminal codes identify types of professional misconduct that can be crimes in addition to being malpractice. Examples include being under the influence of drugs while treating a client, prescribing medicine incorrectly or unnecessarily, sexually abusing a client, and causing the client's death.
- Regulations, statutes, past cases, and professional standards identify duties for institutions just as they do for individual professionals, but institutions are not able to have human culpability for intent. For this reason, when an institution fails a client, the legal doctrine is usually some form of negligence: failure to maintain an adequate facility, failure to properly supervise employees, failure to protect patients, or wrongful death.

The legal doctrines are the strongest expressions of professional misconduct, and they come with the harshest penalties. For example, if a hospital fails to honor federal regulations about patients' rights, perhaps by having insufficient staffing or abusing and harassing patients, and the patients file a complaint with the Centers for Medicare and Medicaid Services (CMS), the hospital can lose its Medicare and Medicaid funding or even be forced to close. There are also milder ways to define and deal with professional misconduct, particularly in regard to individual practitioners, as opposed to institutions. Clients and their families can respond to professional misconduct in the way that best matches the client's needs and endurance, depending on what the misconduct was.

For example, if your mother's psychiatrist committed an intentional tort or negligence and your victimized mother can tolerate the long-term stress of a court case and truly wants her doctor to be publicly punished, the best action for her to take may be a malpractice lawsuit. Or if the professional has at least violated professional standards and your mom wants her doctor to be punished, but she also wants the mess to end quickly and quietly, she may be more satisfied by filing a complaint with the state licensure board. The important thing to know about licensure boards, however, is that they concern themselves only with disciplining professionals and not with helping victims. For some victims, this is perfect; the less they have to be involved, the better.

Whether or not the professional committed a formal legal violation, a client like your mother, who has been injured or disappointed, can complain to the institution that employs the professional. Unlike the licensure board, the institution will be concerned with helping your mom and will attempt to continue providing her with services, in the care of a different professional, while it also deals with the first professional. No matter which action your mother selects, she will have to begin with a complaint. A lot of people do not want to seem like they are complaining, but *complaint* is the official word for a claim against a professional!

If your mother expects that nobody will believe her or if she is afraid that she will be punished for complaining, she may be especially reluctant to report her mental health provider. As a lone client, she is vulnerable because her trust has been betrayed. She cannot be sure that anyone will do anything about the mistreatment or even that anyone else understands how important the betrayal is. She does not know if she may be mocked for trying to take action. She may not be able to focus on the complaint formalities. In fact, she may be in such a tailspin from the mistreatment that she is furious, or morose, or utterly withdrawn. This is the ideal time for a family member, such as you, to step up and either file the complaint for your mom or to find someone else to help with it—as long as your mother wants the help and approves of the helper.

HOW TO Complain, Generally

Any lawyer will tell you that we file a complaint as a first step to resolving a dispute, not to pick a fight or pointlessly exert power over somebody. With that in mind, we write the complaint to show how we want the situation to be resolved. We describe what went wrong, we show the impact of the problem, and we suggest a remedy that will resolve the problem. This is the general way a complaint gets started.

Think of the complaint as a customer service complaint: For example, your mother went to the service provider for a particular purpose, but she did not get what she was supposed to get and, as a result, she is no better off than she was before. In fact, she may be worse than she was before, or she may not able to take action that she needs to take. For example, she may not be able to motivate herself to see another psychiatrist if her first experience was bad. As your mother's support person, you now call upon the service provider (e.g., her mental health provider) to fix the situation by doing what was supposed to be done in the first place. Or maybe there is nothing that the provider can do to fix things and you just want to prevent the same problem from happening again—to your mom or to someone else. In that case, explain in the complaint that you want the professional to be educated, reassigned, or punished. Also explain what you want for your mom: a new professional, a new treatment plan, an opportunity to speak with an administrator, a referral to an additional service, or whatever you can think of as a possible way to fix the situation. That way, the institution (in your mother's case, the mental health facility) receiving the complaint knows what you are after and can respond in a more satisfying way than it could if your complaint were less clear.

Some institutions have their own formalities for filing complaints—a form or a process of some sort. The formalities are not meant to make things hard for you; they are meant to standardize things so that the office that manages complaints is sure to follow certain steps. Even though the institutional complaint system may feel inconvenient and inefficient, it does result in a paper trail for both the family and the institution to use as a basis for communicating about whatever went wrong in the first place.

Understand that the institution wants to satisfy you. Whether it is an employer/institution or a licensure board, it wants to have satisfied clients and respect for its services. It certainly wants to avoid being sued for mishandling your complaint. If an institution can avoid that claim of general negligence or infliction of emotional distress, it will. So give it a genuine opportunity to make things right. Complete the forms, participate in the communications, and remain open to their efforts while still being firm in your assertions.

CONFRONTING A PROFESSIONAL OR HIS INSTITUTION

The most direct way of filing a complaint is also the most frightening, although it can be the most efficient way to fix the problem. By going straight to the source of the problem, whether it is the individual or the institution, the person filing the complaint (called the complainant) is demonstrating a desire to continue all that has been positive in the treatment and move beyond the bad thing that happened. It is generally a good idea to use this method as a first step.

Helpful phrases to use in direct complaints include:

I don't know whether you know . . .

Here is why this is a problem . . .

Before this happened . . . but now . . .

Would it be possible . . .?

How can we . . .

Use the direct complaint method when the problem is ordinary and manageable and no serious harm has occurred. Most of all, use this method when it seems likely that the professional or the institution can solve the problem. Perhaps your cousin Omar's therapist changed the schedule, or forgot to do something, or made hurtful remarks to Omar. These behaviors probably are not illegal and do not violate licensure, unless they were done in an extreme way. Either the therapist or the institution where he works, or both working together, can arrange a solution directly with your cousin.

Unless the office has already informed you of a specific system for filing complaints, you can expect that any form of direct communication will work. You or your cousin can phone or write to the therapist or schedule an appointment to discuss the problem. Of course, once you do that, he may ask you to go through some formalities, but if you present your complaint in a message aimed at problem solving, he will feel less threatened and may be less formal with you. He will surely want to help; he is not in business to upset his clients.

If you present a complaint directly to a professional on behalf of Omar but without Omar's participation, the professional will not give you any information about Omar or his treatment unless Omar has provided the professional with consent for that. (See Chapter 1 for discussion of patient privacy.) After hearing the complaint from you, the professional is likely to report the conversation at your cousin's next session. The therapist may say something like, "Your family member tells me that you were upset because I cancelled our last four sessions." This is an invitation for Omar to express his negative feelings so that the session can go forward with open and honest communications. The therapist should know how to handle the conversation, including any embarrassment or denials that Omar might convey. Together, the two of them can plan improvements. If the therapist cannot salvage the relationship, at least the problem will have been aired and Omar will have been somewhat empowered. Then he, alone or with a family member, can make new arrangements.

COMPLAINTS ABOUT PROFESSIONAL ETHICS

Each state government includes state professional boards (such as the state board of psychology), that administer licenses and enforce professional ethics rules on behalf of national professional associations, such as the American Psychological Association. The people who serve on each board are members of the board's profession; psychologists serve on the state board of psychology, for example. One part of a state professional board's rule-enforcement function is to maintain its professional rules within the state administrative code. Another part is to respond to complaints about professionals who violate the rules. To be in trouble with the state board is a serious disgrace for a professional. When a psychiatrist, psychologist, or social worker is scrutinized by her peers—the same people who know her name from conferences and articles—her reputation is at stake. When the state board concludes that the professional has violated her professional ethics, they can suspend or revoke her license to prevent her from practicing.

HOW TO File a Professional Ethics Complaint

To file a professional ethics complaint, find the website for the professional licensure board that regulates the person who mistreated your loved one. The boards operate at the state level, so include the state name, the profession, and the word *complaint* in your online search. Here are some examples of searches to use:

- social worker complaint Florida
- psychologist ethics complaint Wisconsin
- mental health Oregon complaint

These searches will lead you to complaint forms and instructions. Family members and others can file claims on behalf of mistreated clients, although at some point the board will likely need to get clarifications and confirmations directly from the client. Take the time to look around the board's website before you file the complaint. Take a look through the ethics rules so that you can specifically identify any that you think were violated. See if the board has guidelines or fact sheets on topics related to the professional's actions. Maybe they even have a page with summaries of disciplinary actions that they have taken. This background reading will give you phrases and comparisons to use in the complaint.

If the complaint you submit is incomplete or does not raise issues related to competence, ethics, or licensure, the board's intake person may consider it to be invalid and dismiss it without further action. If the complaint does make it past the intake phase, it might go through a panel review, in which a small committee determines whether it is worthy of a full investigation. You want your complaint to open an investigation, so take the time to relate the situation to the ethics code or to some other list of standards that the licensure board enforces. All of their codes and standards will be on their website.

Make sure the complaint has descriptive examples explaining who, what, when, where, and how. Quote what your relative has said about the incident(s). If a complaint form does not have enough space for all of your details, attach pages or at least note that you have additional information to provide—a dated list of events, additional examples, copies of emails from the professional, compromising photos, diary entries that your relative wrote, or other proof. The complaint is only an initial communication, so it does not have to be comprehensive; it just has to be convincing. Detailed observations and examples showing that the professional contradicted the licensure board's standards will make for a very strong complaint.

To ensure the most thorough investigation, the licensure board will often ask whether you have already tried to resolve the problem. They may even require you to seek a resolution with the professional's institution before they begin their own investigation. The board will almost always need the client to sign a consent form in case they come into contact with confidential information that she shared with the professional. If the licensure board concludes that the professional did violate a legal ethics obligation, they can charge a fine, require the professional to participate in education programs, put limits on the professional's license, or suspend or revoke the person's license to practice.

Licensure boards conscientiously keep their investigations confidential. They conduct the investigations only for their own purposes—to maintain quality and integrity within their professions. They do not tell clients or clients' representatives about the conduct of their investigations or share with these people any information that they gather when looking into a complaint. They do not even provide their investigative records to lawyers for use as evidence.

They will, however, keep the complainant informed about their progress, but only with general remarks, such as:

We are investigating your claim.

We are following up to let you know that we take these matters very seriously.

We have finished our investigation and are satisfied that Dr. X did not violate his licensure requirements.

We are writing to notify you that Dr. X's license to practice psychology will be suspended for a period of six months.

Licensure boards almost always make their disciplinary decisions public. Like the communications with claimants, the disciplinary decisions tend not to include details; they typically say little more than something like "License inactive for six months," or "License suspended," or "License inactive pending satisfaction of agreed-upon terms." Still, the information is in place so that clients and families can verify a practitioner's status.

LAWSUITS

Lawsuits are serious and public. They are extremely stressful for both the plaintiff (client) who brings the claim and the defendant (mental health professional or institution) who responds to the claim. They involve lots of time and details. In the end, a plaintiff who has an out-of-court settlement or a favorable jury verdict will get only money. Because lawsuits are so full of hassles and aggravation and are so emotionally unsatisfying to plaintiffs, it only makes sense to bring one when a professional has truly caused serious emotional, physical, or financial harm.

Beginning a Professional Misconduct Lawsuit

If a badly treated adult client, such as your stepfather Max, is still alive, family members usually cannot file malpractice or other personal injury suits on his behalf.[1] Most of the time, Max himself would have to bring the lawsuit—although he may be almost fully recovered by the time he is able to cope with the stressful communications and the investment of time that are necessary for this kind of action. Each state's statutory code has a statute of limitations telling how much time can pass before an injured party loses the chance to bring a negligence claim. It is typically two or three years, so if Max wants to bring a claim against his mental health practitioner, for example, he must begin the process before the statute of limitations is up.

Issues in mental health malpractice cases can involve sexual abuse of clients, cheating clients out of money, abandoning clients, failing to deal properly with a client's risk of suicide, prescribing the wrong type or dose of medication, implanting false memories, or putting clients on such an inappropriate course of treatment that their relationships or functionality have become significantly damaged. A 2009 article in the journal *Psychiatry* stated that psychiatrists can put themselves at risk of being sued for malpractice by "Not responding at all (even appropriately within professional standards) to family members who call with concerns about a patient

---

1 A guardian can bring a lawsuit on behalf of someone who is incapacitated. Also, an organization, such as a disability rights group or a civil rights advocacy office, can bring a class action lawsuit on behalf of a group of people who all suffered because of a single professional's bad treatment or an institution's breaches of duty, including failure to adequately supervise an incompetent or out-of-control professional.

with suicidal behaviors." (See Chapter 24 for discussion of lawsuits against mental health professionals whose actions lead to a client's suicide or other untimely death.)

Personal injury lawyers—the specialists who handle malpractice and other negligence cases on behalf of plaintiffs—are known for offering free consultations and for handling cases on a contingency fee basis. The free consultations allow clients and families to shop around for the lawyer they most want to work with. The contingency fee arrangement ensures that clients will not have to pay out of pocket for the attorney's fee. Often, it also means that the client does not have to pay up front the costs of gathering evidence and filing documents in court. Instead, the lawyer gets to keep a high percentage, usually between 30% and 40%, of the settlement or court award when the case is concluded.

The free consultations and contingency fees also give lawyers opportunities to avoid taking bad cases. Bad cases are those involving unreliable clients, false claims, minor incidents, minimal evidence, and factors that will basically be hard to prove. Lawyers who know that they will be paid only if they win or settle the case will accept only cases that look winnable.

HOW TO Start a Relationship With a Personal Injury Lawyer

When your loved one is shopping for a personal injury lawyer, he should plan to meet with at least three before deciding which one to hire. In talking to three lawyers, he will get a valid sense of whether his case is strong, because not every bad act is necessarily malpractice or negligence. Questions to consider when interviewing a potential personal injury lawyer include:

- Do their contingency fee agreements require you to pay any costs out of pocket?
- What similar cases have they represented?
- What kinds of tasks do they usually ask clients and families to do as they proceed with the case?

Let's go back to the example of your stepfather, Max. Once he and his lawyer, Sarah, have agreed to work together, she will need to collect details from Max. This will require multiple meetings and will involve numerous repeated questions and much prodding. Sarah will want to know why Max went to that mental health professional, when he first got clues that something was wrong, and what he did about the clues. Sarah will test Max's memory and accuracy by reviewing the story in different ways. She will gather records and testimonies to back up his claims about suffering harm from the wrongdoing.

At some point early in the attorney–client relationship, offer to help your relative do some of the work that he has to do for the case. This work can be typing a list of contact information for possible witnesses, keeping a calendar of symptom flare-ups, or similar clerical functions. Tell your loved one that he can pass along your contact information to the lawyer if he wants to, so that the lawyer can give you instructions. A lawyer and a client have a confidential relationship (similar to a doctor and a patient), and the only way that you (as a family member) can communicate with the lawyer about the case is with the client's permission. If your relative does pass along your contact information to his lawyer, the lawyer will then ask whether he is willing to sign a confidentiality release—so that the lawyer can speak directly with you. If your family member is not willing to do that, you can still be useful; you just have to deal directly with your loved one rather than with his lawyer.

ELEMENTS OF A NEGLIGENCE CLAIM

No matter what kind of negligence case your family member may bring, there are four common elements that plaintiffs (clients) always have to prove in order to be successful:

1. The defendant (mental health provider) owed a duty to the plaintiff.
2. The defendant breached that duty.
3. The plaintiff suffered harm.
4. The plaintiff's harm was caused by the defendant's breach of duty.

Families can help to prove these elements.

Duty

Duty can have many sources: institutional rules, licensure requirements, standards published by a professional organization, laws, and sometimes even common expectations. Specific examples of duty in mental health treatment settings include:

- The duty to properly diagnose the client
- The duty to properly treat the client
- The duty to appropriately refer the client to other practitioners
- The duty to maintain the client's trust
- The duty to ensure client safety at the treatment facility.

Court cases frequently declare that in malpractice claims, duty exists only between a treatment provider and the client he is treating. Other employees at the facility may have duties and be negligent, but they cannot be charged with malpractice unless they directly treat the client.

As a supportive family member, your role in proving duty would be minimal, if anything at all. At most, it may be helping to prove the relationship that your relative had with the professional. This need occasionally arises when the client had only casual interaction with someone who happened to be a professional, when the client somehow obtained professional services without divulging his true identity or history, when either the client or the professional misunderstood something about their relationship and the professional should have been aware of the misunderstanding, and in other rare or informal situations when it is not clear that a professional–client relationship actually existed.

Breach

Proving that the professional breached a duty is more likely to involve you. A breach can happen through action or inaction.

- If a professional in one specialty, say the field of counseling for mood disorders begins counseling a client in a different specialty for which he is not trained, say marital relations, the counselor may be breaching a duty of competence by working outside of his specialty. That would be an action-based breach.
- Misdiagnosing a client and putting her on a harmful course of treatment is another example of an action-based breach.

These are just two of many possible ways that a professional can commit an action-based breach. Examples of breaches arising from inaction include:

- Failure to respond to a client's urgent out-of-session communications
- Not dealing with an issue that the client has raised in therapy
- Disregarding blatant clues about a client
- Otherwise not dealing with something that a reasonably competent professional would deal with.

As the relative of a client in one of the above situations, your role in proving the existence of a breach would likely be to gather documentation, such as phone messages or emails that the professional's office has sent, insurance statements showing patterns and periods of disruption in the treatment schedule, copies of any forms that your family member had to sign for the professional, and any writings or drawings that he has composed about the treatment. The lawyer will send for copies of records in the professional's possession. The sources that you collect can raise important inquiries and prove facts that do not come across in the professional's records.

Harm

After breach, harm is the next element to prove. Relatives can serve as critical witnesses in proving harm. Anybody who is close to someone living with mental illness can tell when that person is feeling worse. In fact, they are likely to see signs of harm that others may not notice, such as sleep disruptions, various forms of self-deprivation, skin disorders, digestive trouble, changes in alertness and reaction time, and loss of sex drive. Medical records and employment records will document more obvious harm, such as hospital visits necessitated by faulty psychiatric prescriptions and disciplinary action or job loss brought about by the mental health professional's actions (violations of confidentiality or baseless reports of dangerousness, for example). But eyewitness testimony from companions demonstrates the real depth of a client's suffering.

As a relative who wants to support a harmed family member, you could, early in the case, write the lawyer a letter conveying your honest observations. If you do this, you can give the letter to your relative to deliver in person. The letter does not have to be kept secret from your relative. If you don't think that it will upset him, let him read it, and tell him that you want to help him win his case. In the letter, describe the harm your relative has endured, offer to serve as a witness, and provide your full name, relationship to the client, and contact information. If you know that others are available to testify about the harm your loved one has suffered, urge them to also contact the lawyer in the same way.

Cause

The hardest element to prove in a negligence case is cause. Close relations should speak up when they see cause and effect. If your daughter Nora behaved one way before her psychotherapist did something and another way afterward, somebody has to say so. If Nora was fine as long as the professional provided consistent treatment and was not fine when the professional changed or dropped the treatment without a legitimate reason, tell the lawyer about that transition.

This information can go in the same letter in which you document breach and describe harm. Since proof of cause is especially helpful to lawyers, call attention to it by either making "before and after" lists or identifying events in order by date. Even when you do not know exact dates, you can summarize the passage of time in general terms, such as, "after one week," or "within a month," or "between September and November, she became worse every week as she continued with this treatment." Your chronology will alert the lawyer about questions to ask and evidence to find.

OTHER LEGAL CLAIMS

Malpractice and other types of negligence are the most obvious legal claims to bring against mental health professionals and their institutions, but injured clients can also take legal action against professionals who commit intentional torts and crimes. (*Tort* is the convenient word for personal injury.) Intentional torts do not have to arise from duty; they are just harmful actions done with intent. Conversion is one intentional tort that happens in professional relationships. It is the act of converting a person's assets to your own, such as convincing a client to give you a valuable piece of jewelry that was upsetting to her because of the memories it carried. Intentional infliction of emotional distress—purposely upsetting someone (such as when you purposely make noises that will trigger another person's posttraumatic stress)—is another tort. Emotional distress can be a negligence claim, but when a lawyer cannot connect it to a particular duty, she characterizes it as intentional.

Defamation—the act of damaging somebody's reputation—is another intentional tort. So is false imprisonment—keeping somebody in a place against his will. This extremely cruel intentional tort includes physically detaining someone through emotional oppression or by actual locked doors. Another intentional tort that professionals commit against clients is fraud. This tort is more likely to be committed by a nonprofessional claiming to be a professional than by an actual licensed professional; it is the act of causing harm by intentionally misrepresenting important facts to the client. Examples of ways that mental health providers can commit fraud include giving a client a phony diagnosis, falsely claiming to be an expert, and deceiving a client into taking a dangerous risk.

HOW TO Help Prove an Intentional Tort Case

Intentional torts are handled by the same personal injury lawyers who handle negligence. Clients and families do not have to define the specific injuries or even categorize them as negligent or intentional; lawyers know how to do that. Clients and families simply need to convey true and detailed stories, describe genuine injuries, and demonstrate how things changed after the professional's misconduct. With this information, the lawyer can assess how the situation compares to past cases. In other words, the family's role in proving an intentional tort case is to testify about harm and possibly cause, but not duty or breach because they are not elements of intentional torts. (See Chapter 17 for discussion of emotional distress and evidence and procedures in civil court cases.)

CRIMES

The court cases described up to this point have been civil cases. Civil cases are brought by individuals or groups against other individuals or groups for the purpose of being paid money as compensation for suffering harm. When a crime is committed, the criminal case is brought by the government (local, state, or federal) against individuals, and the punishment can include community service, probation, or confinement, as well as fines paid to the government and possibly financial restitution paid to the victim.

Some intentional torts have criminal equivalents. For example, conversion in civil court can additionally be charged as theft in criminal court. Sexual assault in civil court is also sexual assault in criminal court. Negligent prescription management in civil court can be drug dealing in criminal court. The personal injury lawyer representing a victim in a claim of negligence or intentional tort can help him decide whether to report professional misconduct to the police. Once the police receive a crime report, they can investigate it and turn it over to the prosecutor, who will decide whether to bring a criminal court case against the mental health professional.

Criminal justice is no different for mental health professionals than it is for anyone else. (Chapter 7 includes guidance for helping a person with mental illness cope with being a crime victim.)

Tax Facts

- Payments resulting from out-of-court settlements or court judgments for physical suffering do not count as taxable income. Payments for emotional

distress or mental anguish do count as income unless the suffering originated from physical harm.
- If you or your loved one previously filed a tax return deducting medical expenses because you paid out of pocket for medical treatment in connection with a personal injury, then you are supposed to declare as income on your current tax return the part of your settlement or judgment that pays you back for the medical expenses. Internal Revenue Service (IRS) Publication 4345.
- In both out-of court-settlements and jury awards, the following items typically count as taxable income: punitive damages, attorney fees, and lost wages. IRS Publication 4345.

RESOURCES FOR PROFESSIONAL MISCONDUCT

1. The Association for State and Provincial Psychology Boards provides links to psychologist licensure boards and license verification sites in all U.S. states and territories and Canadian provinces. See asppb.net.
2. The National Register of Health Services Psychologists has excellent lists of professional associations and organizations that establish practice standards for psychologists at nationalregister.org.
3. The Association of Social Work Boards links to social work regulatory boards and online license verification sites in the United States and Canada. It also publishes the very informative *Guidebook for Social Work Disciplinary Actions*. See aswb.org for these resources.
4. The American Psychiatric Association has a very helpful Policy Finder in which you can type any term or phrase and find related standards that psychiatrists have to follow. See psych.org.
5. Psychiatrists are licensed and disciplined by their state medical boards. The American Medical Association links to the boards at ama-assn.org.
6. The book by David L. Shapiro and Steven R. Smith, *Malpractice in Psychology: A Practical Resource for Clinicians* (2011), although written for professionals, is a clear and straightforward resource on psychologists' legal obligations.
7. The handbook by Anne Marie (Nancy) Wheeler, J.D., and Burt Bertram, Ed.D., *The Counselor and the Law: A Guide to Legal and Ethical Practice* (2015), tells mental health counselors how to avoid and how to deal with an array of legal claims.
8. Andrew B. Israel, a law professor, wrote *Using the Law: Practical Decision-Making in Mental Health* (2011). This resource explains how and when mental health professionals should consider legal ramifications throughout their interactions with clients.
9. An article published in the August 2009 issue of the journal *Psychiatry* (pp. 38–39) —"What Puts a Psychiatrist at Risk for a Malpractice Lawsuit?" —stated that psychiatrists can be liable for not responding to family input about a client's suicidality. It is available online at ncbi.nlm.nih.gov.

10. *A Practitioner's Guide to Hospital Liability* (2011), published by the American Bar Association (and written by James T. O'Reilly, Jolene Sobotka, and Phillip Hagan), shows lawyers how to critically analyze assorted hospital problems and how to determine whether they are worthy of a lawsuit.

11. To file a complaint with the Joint Commission, which establishes standards for hospital quality, or a grievance with the Centers for Medicare and Medicaid Services (CMS), which requires hospitals to follow regulations about patients' rights that are in 42 C.F.R. 482.13, see jointcommission.org ("report a complaint") and cms.gov ("Appeals and Grievances").

PART 2

Criminal Law

7

When the Police Are Called to Help

Your daughter Pat, who has an anxiety disorder, is a driver for the local peer-support agency that provides assorted social programs for people with mental illness. She called to tell you a story as soon as she got home from work today. One of her weekly passengers, Karen, whom she described as "the most gentle and frightened person in the world," had been mugged a few days earlier. Witnesses had called the police immediately. When the police came and saw Karen's extreme distress about the mugging, they called a CIT (crisis intervention team) officer to help at the scene. Since the CIT officer was trained to interact with people who have mental illness, she was able to help Karen feel calmer and participate in the police report. You and Pat were both surprised by this CIT involvement because you had only heard about CIT officers participating in involuntary commitments.

ENCOUNTERING THE POLICE

There is no reason to presume that your relative with a mental illness will become involved with the criminal justice system, and, if he does, it will not necessarily be because he committed a crime. He may be the victim of a crime, or he may be questioned by police simply because somebody misunderstood him. No matter what prompts a police encounter, the outcome will depend greatly on the police officer's ability to recognize and respond to mental illness. Anyone is likely to feel intimidated and stressed about talking with the police. Someone who has a mental illness may feel the intimidation and stress more acutely and may react in a way that alarms an officer who does not understand mental illness. In the best encounters with police, at least one of the officers present has learned about mental illness through training for a CIT. In the worst encounters with police, an officer mistreats your relative or unnecessarily charges him with a crime.

VICTIMS OF CRIME

Criminal law relates to behaviors that are identified as crimes and how the criminal justice system is supposed to investigate and prosecute the crimes. Toward the end of nearly every state's criminal code and the federal criminal statutes, after all of the crimes are defined, the police practices are delineated, and the prosecution system is set forth, the law covers one more issue: victims' rights. As statistics gathered over many years prove, many people with mental illness are victims of crime. Fortunately, crime victims (whether they have a mental illness or not) do have rights. Unfortunately, asserting those rights can be extremely difficult for people with certain symptoms of mental illness.

Victims' rights are designed to empower people, to give them a voice and a chance to at least get compensated, if not somewhat healed. However, the only way to exercise these rights is to tell and retell everything about the crime. This means answering questions, and victims have to defend their version of the story and the actions that they took when they were being victimized. It also means encountering the victimizer and that person's support team; the victim may have to identify the perpetrator in a line-up or photo array and face that person in court.

Realize that victims of crime, such as your brother Chad, who was assaulted, not only are victims, but also are accusers. As accusers, they subject themselves to scrutiny—which means that the police investigators and the attacker's legal defense team will investigate the accuser while they are investigating the crime. To confirm that his accusation is true, Chad will almost certainly have to disclose private information. Victims of violence may have to submit to medical exams. Victims of identity theft will have to divulge financial records. Most victims have to explain why they were at the place where the crime happened. These are just a few examples of the personal information that victims have to reveal, depending on what happened to them.

The prosecuting lawyer, who brings the case against the attacker, can protect Chad from some of this scrutiny. She can file motions to quash the defense lawyer's subpoenas. She can bring mental health expert witnesses to deflect attention away from Chad's personal treatment and toward professionally recognized characteristics. She can counter every request for information with a demand that the defense lawyer prove that the information would be relevant to the case and that court rules permit the use of the evidence. She can also object that the requests are too broad. These actions protect Chad's privacy as much as possible and may keep him from feeling harassed by the defense team. The actions can also wear down the defense lawyer and make him reluctant to request so much information.

In addition, the Americans with Disabilities Act has provisions that can make the victim's participation in the investigation more tolerable. As offices of the justice system, police departments and courts have to accommodate persons with mental disabilities. One of the accommodations available for victims with mental illness is to be questioned by forensic interviewers, rather than by lawyers, at least in the early information-gathering phase of the case, before it goes to trial.

Forensic interviewers are trained in behavioral science and advanced communication skills. They are described by the U.S. Department of Justice (DOJ) Office for Victims of Crime as competent at conducting nonleading, victim-sensitive, and neutral interviews. Some prosecutors' offices and associations maintain referral lists of forensic interviewers whom they can call upon. If a prosecutor does not have such a resource, victims and families can ask their own therapist to identify forensic interviewers working in the region.

Forensic interview sessions are supposed to gather the information that would otherwise be collected in a meeting with a lawyer. To prepare, the forensic interviewer may request some observations from your family members or from Chad's therapist. The interviewer will talk with the lawyer and obtain the list of questions that the lawyer needs Chad to answer. The interviewer's initial meeting with your brother may involve nothing more than getting acquainted, so that the interviewer can learn how to best communicate with Chad. Over time, the interviewer and Chad will talk about the crime. In the company of a forensic interviewer, your brother can sit, stand, pace, yell, smoke, or do just about anything he needs to in order to provide the requested information. Through this patient and nonconfining process, Chad will explain what happened during the crime, demonstrate some of how the crime has affected him, and show whether he can participate in a trial.

Other helpful accommodations for criminal investigations and trial preparations tend to be about the environment for victim interactions, that is, where the victim is comfortable. Questioning can be done at the victim's home, in a private room at the victim's church, or in another nonthreatening, confidential space, rather than at a law firm or court building. Meetings can be limited in time and topic so that they do not last long and cover only one subject per session. Agreed-upon code words can be used in place of names and vocabulary that cause distress. A court reporter and recording equipment, which are sometimes used when police or lawyers interview people, can be inconspicuous, although the victim will be informed that the event is being transcribed or recorded.

Victims' Rights

Working along with the prosecutor and victim will be a victim rights advocate whose entire job is to enforce the statutes about victims' rights. The victim rights advocate may be employed by the police department, the prosecutor's office, the criminal court, or a local agency that serves particular categories of victims, such as victims of domestic violence. Members of the criminal justice system (police, prosecutors, and court staff) are usually quick to offer victim advocacy. A victim who is not offered this service should know to ask for it.

The victim advocate is the person who interacts with victims and their families regarding the mental health impact of participating in the case. It is possible that an individual victim rights advocate has learned about mental health only in the 30-minute session on victims with mental health issues that is part of the current DOJ Victim Assistance Training (VAT) program, and perhaps in the related VAT sessions, "Trauma-Informed Care" and "People with Disabilities." The VAT sessions do not provide a lot of preparation for working with victims who have mental illnesses. However, some victim advocate jobs do require a degree in counseling, which probably included mental health coursework. (Other victim advocate positions accept applicants with a major in criminal justice, sociology, business, or public administration.) Therefore, while a particular victim advocate will not necessarily know much about mental illness, let alone a specific victim's condition, the advocate will have the authority and resources to engage mental health experts for consultations and services. Victims and their families should feel comfortable advising the advocate about local mental health providers who already have relationships with the victim.

The legal rights that victim advocates enforce are all connected with investigating and prosecuting the crime. In other words, they are rights of victims who help to catch criminals. The rights are not available to victims who do not report the crimes committed against them. Mental health organizations, such as the Depression and Bipolar Support Alliance and the Schizophrenia and Related Disorders Alliance, may provide victim support services, but that is not the same as victim advocacy.

RESTITUTION

One of the especially important victims' rights set forth in criminal codes is the right to restitution. Restitution pays for losses that the victim suffered as a result of the crime. The losses can include property damage (a purse torn by a mugger, furniture burned by an arsonist) as well as counseling fees, lost wages, reimbursement for theft, and medical expenses. Restitution can come from the perpetrator and from the state's victim compensation fund. Victims have to present copies of bills and receipts in order to receive restitution from either source. The victim compensation fund can provide funding based on a police report, so that money is available fairly quickly. Victims or families can apply directly to the fund if the victim advocate is too busy or too slow to do it. Restitution from the perpetrator is available only after a conviction, and then it will trickle through the court's payment system in minimal amounts as the perpetrator either earns money for his prison labor or, if he is not incarcerated, makes payments out of wages from a job in the community.

NOTIFICATION

Victims also have the right to be notified about the perpetrator. The court clerk's office, which uploads case information as it happens, can usually set the system to notify a victim about all or some events in the case, depending on the victim's preference. Alternatively, the victim advocate can manage notifications for the victim. Once a criminal is convicted, the correctional system's updates can also be forwarded to the victim. This way, the victim will know about opportunities to influence the parole board, for example.

Some victims do not want notifications. They would rather not have news about the hurtful person continuing to invade their lives. Other victims want all possible opportunities to speak out against the perpetrator. Some feel at least a degree of control as long as they know what is happening between the person who harmed them and the criminal justice system. Victims can change their minds as often as they need to about whether to get updates by asking the office that sends the notifications to make a quick and easy adjustment in the notification system. Victims have the option of being notified only when the perpetrator's jail or prison release date is set. Family, therapists, and victim advocates can all help the victim to implement a personal security plan before the perpetrator is released.

BEARING WITNESS

Victims have the right to be heard. Even so, many victims do not want to be heard. Maybe they were willing to report the crime in the first place, but they feel revictimized every time they have to tell the story again. Perhaps they are terrified of speaking in court. The right to be heard may feel like a burden. Other victims want to shout their stories from the rooftops; they cannot wait for the judge and jury to hear what they have to say. These victims are disappointed when a perpetrator confesses or enters into a plea bargain. They feel cheated out of having their day in court.

When victims want to be heard but are not needed in court, most systems allow them to be heard at least by the prosecutor. This can take the form of either a conversation or a formal statement—like a speech. State laws and prosecutors' offices differ in their handling of these situations. The victim advocate can set it up according to the court's standards and the victim's needs.

Whether a victim communicates privately with the prosecutor or is called to testify in court, he or his family or victim advocate can usually arrange for special needs simply by explaining things to the prosecutor's office. The explanation may be general, such as:

For therapeutic purposes, it is necessary for this particular victim to submit a written description of his victimization and receive from your office written personalized validation of what happened—not a form letter.

The explanation may need to be more precise, such as:

This victim has tremendous anxiety, but she is required to participate in this prosecution. Can we arrange for her to testify via closed-circuit television so that she will not be in the same room with the defendant?

Closed-circuit television is very commonly used. Less common adjustments—such as bringing a therapy animal to court or wearing a disguise—have been used in past cases. Arranging for uncommon adjustments will probably require input from a therapist or case worker. In very rare circumstances, the victim or someone on his team may have to remind the court or defense lawyer that the victim is merely seeking disability accommodation. In other words, if the defendant's lawyer claims that the jury will be swayed against her client if the victim is permitted to have a particular adjustment, the prosecutor will need to respond by justifying the adjustment.

Victim's Impact Statement

One important way that victims can exercise their right to be heard is with a victim's impact statement. The statement is officially part of the sentencing phase of a trial. It is presented after the defendant has been found guilty and before the judge has decided upon the sentence. In some confession and plea cases, judges welcome victim impact statements before they approve plea agreements or assign punishment.

A meaningful victim impact statement shows the judge how much damage the crime did to the victim. To present the message, whether in writing or in person, victims with mental illness often have to tell how their sense of well-being has been disrupted. This is hard to admit—the feeling of being rattled, shaken, and knocked off balance. Some people, like your relative with mental illness, Helen, worry that it makes them look like something was wrong with them to begin with. Victims should know that judges can impose harsher sentences when they know how the victim suffered and when they understand that everything was basically fine until the crime happened. If Helen had to move to a different home, lost a significant other, spent time in the hospital, missed work, or stopped going someplace or doing something that she used to enjoy, that upheaval can affect the defendant's punishment. Nobody has to be ashamed of feeling trauma.

Experts advise victims to talk only about themselves and their circumstances, not the perpetrator, in victim impact statements. It is too late to talk about the perpetrator; he has been found guilty. Victims should remember that they are talking to the judge. If the statement is done in person, others in the courtroom will be watching and listening, but only the judge has the power to do anything with the statement. Finally, the victim's impact statement has to have a clear ending. To achieve this, it should follow an outline or a story arc. Some victims have a list of thoughts to tell the judge. When they get to the last one, the statement is over. Some victims prefer to tell how they have suffered in date order. Immediately after the crime, they experienced certain things, then it morphed to other miseries, and now this is how things are. Any order is fine, as long as the statement does not become an endless ramble that confuses the judge. This final communication to the court is the only one that the victim gets to make without being questioned afterward. It is the last thing that the judge will hear before deciding the perpetrator's fate.

THE CRISIS INTERVENTION TEAM (CIT)—POLICE TRAINED TO DEAL WITH PEOPLE WHO HAVE MENTAL ILLNESS

A CIT is a team of police officers who have relationships with local mental health agencies and who are trained to do police work with people experiencing bad episodes of mental illness and other crises. The officers are trained to de-escalate crises. Their work with people who are demonstrating psychiatric symptoms is sometimes described as preventing "criminalization of mental illness" because they know when and how to get people into the mental health system, rather than the criminal justice system.

The standard program objectives for a CIT are very nicely articulated by the Missouri CIT Council[1]:

> To train law enforcement officers to distinguish threatening behavior based on a mental illness rather than criminal intent, and to respond accordingly.
>
> To reduce injuries to law enforcement officers and individuals with mental illness that may result from crisis interventions, through training of skills in tactical communications and crisis de-escalation techniques.
>
> To reduce time required for transfer of custody from law enforcement to hospital personnel, so law enforcement may more quickly return to services.
>
> To reduce recidivism of individuals who are high utilizers of law enforcement and mental health resources, by implementing assertive outreach and engagement activities for individuals subject to CIT interventions, so that even those

---

1 Permission to reprint "Program Objectives" from its CIT program flyer was granted by the Missouri Crisis Intervention Team Council.

who have poor insight, deny their psychiatric condition, are noncompliant to treatment and difficult to serve, may be successfully linked to treatment services.

What Will a CIT Officer Do?

A CIT officer arrives at the scene of a police encounter ready to figure out how to de-escalate a crisis that may be in progress and to determine which local mental health resources may need to be involved. If the scene is at a private home, the officer will also assess the condition of the premises, looking for indications of psychiatric symptoms in addition to clues about whether a crime has happened. If the scene is not where the person with mental illness lives, other officers will secure the premises, while the CIT officer focuses on interacting with the person.

No matter where the scene is, the officer will use on-scene input to decide how to open communications with this particular troubled person. Having observed and met with numerous persons with mental illnesses and their families during training and past work experience, the officer will watch the person's behavior. Observing body language, the officer will assess whether the person is lethargic, afraid of touching things, shaky, and so on. Some physical clues will be signs that the person does not have control over himself. Other body language will suggest fear or temper. Listening to the person with mental illness, the officer will tune in for flighty manic speech, conversations with imagined characters or people who are not present, hallucinatory gibberish, confusion, or emotions that do not fit the situation.

If the CIT officer arrives to find someone who is in imminent danger, whether it is the person with mental illness or a potential victim of that person, CIT expertise will be used to get the person to a mental hospital emergency department with the least amount of resistance and dramatics. When the officer finds someone who is in obvious emotional turmoil but is not wielding a weapon or making threats, the officer may call the mobile mental health crisis team, rather than taking that person away in a police car. The mobile mental health crisis team is a gentle crew of mental health specialists, possibly a psychiatric nurse, a therapist, and a social worker—people who work every day in mental health crises. They are equipped to stabilize the person. If the locale does not have a mental health crisis team, the officer may summon an ambulance to transport the person to the hospital for stabilization.

When the CIT officer comes upon a scene that is neither critical nor dangerous, she may just make referrals, telling the family which local agencies to call and specifically what to ask of them. This could happen, for example, when a family says, "Our mother, who has hoarding tendencies, has been rearranging things in her room for two days without eating or sleeping," or "Cousin Mathew believes that the Public Utilities Commission is monitoring his brain through every computer in our house, so he's building a 'safe room' in the basement to keep out the signals, but it is basically an air-tight box where he'll suffocate." Sometimes, a uniformed police officer is the only person who can get the troubled person's attention in times like these. If the family already knows about the agencies that the officer recommends and they cannot get their loved one to go, the CIT officer may be able to facilitate cooperation and transportation.

The presence of a CIT officer does not mean that the incident will result in only mental health treatment or a series of social work services. The officer will file criminal charges if a crime has been committed, but the charges will likely be secondary to the mental health intervention. CIT operating manuals advise officers to file either an arrest warrant or a citation (ticket) for the police department to execute once the person with mental illness has been stabilized by the mental health system.

In other words, if a patient is supposed to be arrested, the police add a written notice to the person's admission file that tells the medical facility to discharge the person into police custody, rather than to home. In fact, when they are initially called to the scene, police routinely check for any past police encounters or outstanding warrants for the person they have been called about. If any outstanding warrants are found, they, too, can be executed by the police as soon as the mental health provider notifies them that the person in question has been stabilized.

HOW TO Call the Crisis Intervention Team in an Emergency

Call 911 to report a mental health–related emergency. Then, as long as your local police department has a CIT officer and you use a well-known mental health term (such as mentally ill, manic, schizophrenic, or suicidal), the dispatcher will probably notify the police to send the specially trained CIT officer to the scene.

Here are some tips to ensure that the dispatcher does send the CIT:

It is not enough to say that your family member is acting violent or threatening. Tell the dispatcher that, for example, your father has a diagnosed mental illness, explain what the illness is, and help prepare the officer for the scene by giving the 911 operator all of the details about your dad's current behavior:

- Does he have a weapon?
- Is he athletic or trained in martial arts? Give facts about his size.
- At this moment, is your father delusional, depressed, hallucinating, manic, spastic, or agitated?
- Repeat any threats that he is making.

To help make the police encounter as safe as possible for everyone present, you or someone else should go outside to flag down the police and tell them where the building entrances are and where the event is happening inside the building. Although you told everything to the dispatcher, give a quick descriptive update to the on-scene police as soon as you can. For example,

My 30-year-old son, Steve, who has bipolar disorder, threw me down the stairs. I don't know if he took his medicine. He is shaking all over and won't talk to any of us.

My 25-year-old sister, Kay, is delusional. She is pulling everything off the shelves and throwing it on the floor. I ran next door. Nobody else is in the house with her.

> *My husband, Ed, is depressed. He locked himself in the upstairs bathroom and is threatening to drink the drain cleaner.*

Once the officer begins to work the scene, stay out of the way! Do not talk unless the officer asks you a question or calls on you to say something. The CIT officers know how to interact with people living with specific mental disturbances; they do not need you to translate for them. All police officers are trained to stabilize situations, so even if there is not a CIT officer present, you should not interfere.

If the incident is not at your house or you are not even present, you can still give some mental health background information to the 911 dispatcher, who will pass it along to police and will know to get a CIT officer on the scene. How will you know about the incident if you are not there? Maybe someone called you from the scene and said, "Lou is here and he's out of control; someone just called 911." Maybe you got a text message or email from your relative saying "I love you" and indicating that he or she is planning suicide.

Can You Call a CIT Only During an Emergency?

You may know that your relative is in the throes of a bad episode that is causing you worry, although you may not know whether there is any imminent danger. In this case, it is still appropriate to call police, but do not call it in as an emergency. When you call 911, tell the dispatcher that you are not calling with an emergency, and that you need police to conduct a welfare check (sometimes called a "check on welfare" or "wellness check") for your family member who has a mental illness. Provide the mental health diagnosis and the address where the police can find your loved one. Explain what has caused you to be concerned and ask the dispatcher to request a CIT officer for the welfare check. The dispatcher will send a CIT officer or another officer to assess whether your relative needs to be transported to a mental health facility. If clues suggest that it is necessary, the police can break down the door to get inside and look for an attempted suicide, a person lost in delusion, or another type of emergency.

Non-Emergency CIT Example
In 2014, there was a killing spree in California that was one man's enactment of his manifesto. His parents lived in a different city, but when his worried therapist called the man's mother saying her son seemed extra troubled, the mother looked to see if she had any new messages from her son, and she found that her son had sent her a disturbing email spelling out his manifesto. She quickly got on the phone with 911, telling the dispatcher what to expect according to the descriptions written in the manifesto, and then she drove to where her son lived. She and her son's father arrived separately and too late. Their son had already killed himself and six other people. Although she was unable to prevent the tragedy, she had done everything she possibly could.

The news stories about that event all noted that sheriff's deputies had visited the man at his home a few weeks earlier. Some of the stories included the fact that a 911 call from the mother had also prompted the earlier visit. Since the son appeared calm and rational to the deputies, they did not have grounds for searching his apartment. They certainly could not arrest him or commit him for mental health care. So it happens, sometimes, that calling 911 and alerting law enforcement about the mental health aspect of a situation does not save the day. Yet, you have to try. The information that you present may save your relative and others from getting injured.

HOW TO Get To Know Your Local CIT Officers

You always have the right to walk into a police station and at least talk to the person at the front desk. If your relative with mental illness has occasional bouts of hostility, or may be seen wandering the streets, or otherwise is likely to attract police attention, it is a very good idea for you to introduce yourself at your neighborhood station and let them know that you are connected with the person and that he has a mental illness.

When you go to the police station for this purpose, ask if there are any CIT officers available to talk with you right then. If no CIT officer is available at that time, talk with whoever is there and ask when would be a good time for you to come back and meet some CIT officers. Some police departments offer to send a CIT officer to your house, to get acquainted under peaceful circumstances. You can ask about that possibility when you are at your neighborhood police station.

To help the police remember your family after your visit to the station or after their visit to your house, you could provide a fact sheet with a picture of your relative, a list of some of the symptoms that could attract police attention, and your contact information—along with an indication of your relationship to the person.

If you are not comfortable calling police attention to your relative, at least get yourself familiar with the CIT team in a less personal group setting. If you have any sort of mental health family support group, arrange for some CIT officers to come and talk to that group. If you do not have a support group, arrange a CIT visit to any group that you are in. If you do not belong to any groups, ask the police department or your public library to coordinate a public presentation by the CIT officers. Sitting in the audience at a public CIT presentation, you will be amazed to discover how many people are worried about relatives with mental illness. You will not need to say anything about your family member, and you can learn how the CIT operates. That way, you will know which faces to look for if police ever do get called to an emergency involving your loved one.

When a City Does Not Have a Crisis Intervention Team

Generally, when police departments have specially trained teams of officers, the teams are directly related to the majority of crimes that the department handles. For example, if a city has a lot of drug activity, the police department probably has a drug task force. If vandalism, homicides, or car thefts are rampant in a city, the police will have teams with expertise in those issues. To have a special team with expertise on one segment of the population, such as people who have mental illness, is a much different thing: it requires a unique skill set in addition to expert knowledge. Furthermore, the assortment of calls that the team handles is likely to be much more diverse than the other teams' calls.

To families who routinely interact with a member who exhibits mental health symptoms, it makes perfect sense that police should be able to recognize and respond to the symptoms. Without this knowledge, police may treat every incident as a crime and every person as a suspect. They might arrive at the scene intending to quickly give orders and to get everything under control, only to discover that calling out orders will not resolve a mental health crisis. They may know how to interact with their own family member who has mental illness, but not with your family member. Fearing a bad result for their loved one, families may not even call the police. They might attempt to resolve the situation on their own, although they themselves could be part of the problem and even though they do not have the authority and neutrality that police have.

Suppose your daughter Penny is unable to calm down and just broke a window. You keep telling her to calm down, but that is only making her worse. You want to hug her, but she won't let you get close. You try offering a snack and her favorite blanket. None of this is helping her. You are all out of ideas and you are only upsetting Penny. You are afraid that if you call 911 for help, the police will handcuff Penny and charge her with a crime for breaking the window. You don't want that to happen; you just want Penny to be calm. If your city has a CIT team and you have heard the officers speak about their CIT work, or you know people who have had good results from the CIT team, you probably would not have let the bad scene with Penny go on for so long. You would have called 911 and asked for CIT support as soon as you knew that Penny was not going to deal with you.

HOW TO Start a CIT Program in Your City

If you want your police department to have CIT officers trained and ready to help in mental health emergencies, then go ahead and generate a demand! You and other families can speak at city council meetings, write letters to the head of your police department, submit a contact form on the mayor's website, send letters to the newspaper editor, and get on local podcasts and TV or radio talk shows. In these communications you will have two goals: to educate the public and the local government about the value of CIT services and to call for local officers to be trained and designated for CIT duty.

There are lots of resources available to help you advocate for a CIT in your community. The detailed materials from Memphis and NAMI, listed in Resources at the end of the chapter, will give you plenty of ideas and precise instructions for raising community support, partnering with agencies, and implementing the police training. One of the most effective ways for you to gather support for a CIT is to tell your own stories about what has gone wrong when police have dealt with your relative, but if you do this in an angry or accusatory way, it will be difficult to establish a positive partnership with the police. You want to do your storytelling to prove the need for CIT service, not to criticize the police or threaten them with civil rights lawsuits. Remember that police departments exist to help people; they will appreciate your effort to inform them about mental illness.

RESOURCES FOR VICTIMS OF CRIME

1. The National Crime Victim Law Institute provides definitions, frequently asked questions, an introduction to the criminal justice system, and a toolkit for enforcing victims' rights. Its Victim Law Library has very detailed explanations of victims' rights as well as copies of "new and noteworthy court opinions." Families and lawyers will appreciate its publication *Practical Tips and Legal Strategies for Easing Victims' Concerns about Testifying.* See ncvli.org.
2. The Treatment Advocacy Center's Backgrounder titled *Victimization: One of the Consequences of Failing to Treat Individuals with Severe Mental Illnesses* summarizes data on the prevalence of crimes against people with mental illness. Read it at treatmentadvocacycenter. org.
3. A large research study about victimization was reported by Sarah L. Desmarais in "Community Violence Perpetration and Victimization Among Adults with Mental Illnesses," published in the *American Journal of Public Health* in December 2014.
4. To learn about the Victim Assistance Training that crime victim advocates get, use the resources from the DOJ's Office for Victims of Crime—Training and Technical Assistance Center at ovcttac.gov.
5. The National Association of Crime Victim Compensation Boards explains victim compensation rights and links to the state victim compensation offices at nacvcb.org.
6. The National Organization for Victim Assistance (at trynova.org) links to state victim advocacy offices and features a full reprint of "The Psychological Trauma of Crime," which is the first chapter of Marlene A. Young's book *Victim Assistance: Frontiers and Fundamentals* (1993).
7. The National District Attorneys Association publishes *National Prosecution Standards* for free online. The standards include sections about conveying information to victims, providing victim assistance, making victims comfortable, protecting victims, and knowing about programs that compensate victims. Find this resource at ndaa.org.
8. Victims and all members of the public can monitor individual inmates by checking the free online inmate locator for their state's correctional system or by registering with VINE—the victims notification network. See usa.gov/corrections and vinelink.com.
9. For guidance about composing a meaningful victim impact statement and more information about victim advocates, see the Washington's Victims Support Services website at victimsupportservices.org.
10. Californians for Safety and Justice publishes a free online manual, *Victims of Crime Act and the Need for Advocacy: A Toolkit for Advocates*

and Victims Services Providers to Ensure Victims of Crime Act (VOCA) Funds Reach Underserved Crime Victims. Families who are not satisfied with victim advocacy services in their communities can use this toolkit to lobby for improvements. See safeandjust.org.

RESOURCES FOR CIT

1. The National Center for State Courts has a good summary of the Mentally Ill Offender Treatment and Crime Reduction Act. This federal law provides funding for states to provide police services like CIT programs. See ncsc.org or look for the full act at uscode.house.gov.
2. The Missouri CIT Council's program objectives for CITs are published in the council's CIT program flyer. See missouricit.org/resources. The "Program Objectives" from the flyer are reprinted in this chapter.
3. To find out if your community has a CIT program, click through the map at cit.memphis.edu.
4. The federal Bureau of Justice Assistance (BJA) operates the Justice and Mental Health Collaboration Program under which local CIT programs exist. The BJA website, bja.gov, gives a detailed compilation of technical support for police departments.
5. The May 25, 2014, *New York Times* article by Adam Nagourney about the California parents who attempted to intercept their son's crime spree, "Parents' Nightmare: Futile Race to Stop Killings," is available at nytimes. com.
6. NAMI (National Alliance on Mental Illness) has a very practical toolkit for advocates who want to start a CIT. The toolkit and other valuable resources are available at the section of NAMI's website about CITs on nami.org.
7. The University of Memphis makes available strong, clear guidance about developing agency partnerships and implementing CIT training, and it makes available samples of CIT policy manuals from police and sheriffs' departments at cit.memphis.edu.
8. The National Association of State Mental Health Program Directors has the old but good *Criminal Justice Primer for State Mental Health Program Directors* available at nasmhpd.org.

8

Negative Police Encounters, Arrest, and Jail

When Nat lost his temper in the store, everything spiraled out of control. Someone called the police, the police were rude and rough and didn't listen to anything, and then they arrested him just for being angry. Now he is in jail and has called you. You plan to go and see him tomorrow, but first you want to know what is supposed to happen when someone is arrested and jailed and may have been victimized by police.

POLICE MISCONDUCT

When someone is experiencing a bad spell of mental illness, he may not be able to hear what people are saying, including commands from police officers. There may be completely different messages in the troubled person's ears and eyes—strong words and images—that make it truly impossible for him to stop writhing or screaming or doing whatever attracted police attention.

It is in these out-of-control moments (when police cannot communicate with a suspect and cannot get the suspect to stop doing something) that unnecessary violence is likely to happen—either by, or against, the person with mental illness. The police are empowered to protect the public and themselves from violence by suspects and they are licensed to use force against suspects who appear threatening. This is often how it happens that innocent people with mental illness get hurt by police.

Hurting a suspect under these circumstances is not necessarily police misconduct, which involves depriving people of their legal rights without a good law enforcement reason. Police are legally entitled to use their discretion in dealing with people because the decisions about controlling a scene or a person who is irrational are not easy and obvious. However, when the officers have the ability and opportunity to control the scene without hurting the suspect and they fail to do so, or when they hurt a suspect more than they need to, it is probably misconduct. Failing to protect people from harm is also a form of police misconduct, so officers cannot just stand around and watch while somebody cuts himself, or bangs his head on a brick wall, or creates a danger to other people.

Use of excessive force is not the only type of police misconduct, and the police sometimes deal with people with mental illness who are not suspects. Police have been known to single out a person, to play on paranoia, to taunt, to gang up, to take a person's belongings, and to use other forms of torment. These bad interactions can happen at any point in police work. For example:

- During an ordinary park patrol, an officer may use the wrong words to tell a person that he should not be sitting or lying where he is. If that person takes the officer's remark badly, the conversation can escalate into a power play.
- During an investigation, an officer collecting eyewitness information may frighten a witness into thinking that she is a suspect.
- While arresting and booking someone, the police might use mockery or shame in numerous harmful ways.
- Worst of all, an individual officer or the law enforcement system may re-victimize a crime victim who lives with mental illness.

HOW TO File a Local Police Misconduct Complaint

It seems awkward and counterintuitive, but you usually have to file a police mis-conduct complaint with the police department, although some cities have a way for you to file it with a central municipal complaint office. Police departments typically have a section called "internal affairs," "internal review," or "internal investigations." At the city level, the complaint office could have a phrase in its name like "municipal review," "municipal investigations," or "city performance," or one of the "internal" titles.

Contact the complaint office as soon as you can, while details are still fresh. Ask whether they require you to complete a particular form or whether you can write your complaint in a letter. Find out exactly what information the office requires you to include in your complaint. It is generally wise to go beyond their requirements and to give every fact that you and the victim know. It is important to be precise about time and location so that the investigators can track down surveillance video that may have been captured by nearby businesses or by the city government's own cameras. Expect that you will need to explain who, what, when, where, why, and how. There are two items to cover in the "how" category of the complaint: Tell how the officer behaved and tell how your relative, because of his mental illness, responded to, and was affected by, the encounter.

Internal review systems take complaints seriously, and they do conduct gen-uine investigations. When they discover wrongdoing, they can retrain or re-assign the offending officer in an effort to prevent future occurrences. Citizen complaints can also result in various kinds of punishments that affect an officer's salary and opportunities for promotion.

Connect With Advocacy Agencies

There is no good reason to stand alone against injustice. Reach out to local chapters of NAMI (National Alliance on Mental Illness), the ACLU (American Civil Liberties Union), the American Psychological Association, and any organizations that you find while searching for the term *disability advocates* and

your city name in a search engine. Tell the organizations what happened with
the police, and ask if they are currently engaged in police misconduct advocacy.
See if they will write letters to the municipal government calling for the matter
to be handled swiftly and thoroughly. Perhaps they have media contacts who
will take up the story. They may already have a file of similar stories and a plan
to file a class-action lawsuit. Advocacy groups provide good advice and support;
count on them to help your family through this difficult situation.

When Local Control of Police Misconduct Is Inadequate

If the local police disciplinary system has not resolved a police misconduct problem,
members of the public can notify the U.S. Department of Justice (DOJ). The DOJ has
authority to investigate public complaints and then to guide reforms in local police
departments if the departments or their municipal governments are not adequately
managing bad police behavior. If necessary, the DOJ can prosecute members of a
police department in criminal court or sue them in federal civil court.

Several federal laws inform DOJ actions. A federal criminal statute about "deprivation of rights under color of law" enables the DOJ to prosecute police for abusing
their official power in ways that victimize members of the public. A federal civil
law called "the police misconduct provision" empowers the DOJ to deal with "a
pattern or practice of conduct by law enforcement officers . . . that deprives persons of rights . . . protected by the Constitution or laws of the United States." This
is the law that applies when the police department or city government has failed to
manage an ongoing series of bad police practices, when they have not taken citizen
complaints seriously, or when their system of correcting problems is not working.
The Americans with Disabilities Act and Section 504 of the Rehabilitation Act of
1973 authorize the DOJ to respond to police behavior that was specifically associated with somebody's mental illness: for example, officers took advantage of anxiety or paranoia, they goaded someone into bad behavior so that they could get
rough with him or arrest him, or they refused to provide assistance that he needed.

HOW TO File a Complaint With the DOJ

There are three separate DOJ complaint channels for reporting police abuses
against people with mental illness. You can file a complaint with any or all of
them. Be sure to tailor each complaint to the distinct type of issue that each
office handles. If you file your complaint through only one of the channels and
your claim also seems applicable to one or both of the other channels, the office
that receives it will usually share it with the others so that they can also investigate what happened. Nevertheless, since you do not have control over the inter-
departmental sharing decisions, you may want to take the extra trouble to file
separate complaints.

Notify Your Nearest FBI Office
The FBI is the criminal investigation division of the DOJ. It is responsible for
finding out whether anyone in law enforcement has committed a crime. Using

excessive force, arresting people for no reason, falsifying evidence, taking or destroying a person's possessions for no reason, and failing to protect people can all count as crimes, in addition to being civil wrongdoing. You can report an individual officer or multiple people in your FBI complaint, and your complaint can be about only one incident and one victim. You can type or handwrite your complaint.

The FBI cannot do a long investigation of every single complaint, so try to grab the investigator's attention by including every piece of information that shows why your situation is especially important: a timeline of exactly what happened, names and other available identification information about everyone involved in the incident(s), all facts about when and where the incident(s) happened, and contact information for witnesses and nearby offices or businesses—with explanations of why you are giving the FBI that information and your reasons for believing that the event was such a bad example of law enforcement that it should count as a crime. Do not rush through the complaint; write it very carefully and be sure to say that you are available to help with the investigation.

Notify the Civil Rights Division

The Civil Rights Division is the DOJ office that deals with complaints about "patterns and practices" of police misconduct that are associated with constitutional issues, such as freedom from improper search and seizure, violations of due process, equal protection, and free speech, as well as laws in the U.S. Code. Civil rights complaints are most effective when they come from groups of people and describe multiple incidents. A single incident or even multiple incidents against a single person will not establish a "pattern or practice" of misconduct.

Notify the Americans with Disabilities Act Compliance Division

The Americans with Disabilities Act (ADA) Compliance Division is the agency to contact when police behavior is particularly targeted against someone because he has a mental illness. It may be the same behavior that you already reported to the FBI or to the CRD, but in this complaint, show proof that it was done to make your relative's symptoms worse, or to mock or belittle him, or to otherwise affect him particularly because of his mental illness. Maybe the police used excessive force against your brother because he behaved in an unusual way. Maybe the police threw your daughter into an even worse state by taking away a nondangerous item that was clearly comforting or important to her. Maybe the police teased your relative about something irrational that he could not help saying. There are lots of ways to discriminate in law enforcement.

What Happens When You File a Complaint With the DOJ?

The DOJ's goal with civil police misconduct is to fix malfunctioning systems and behaviors in law enforcement agencies. With criminal police misconduct, the goal is to punish police who abuse their power.

Criminal Complaints

Once the FBI has investigated a criminal complaint about police, it will be able to tell whether individual officers, administrators, or other members of the law enforcement community have violated any criminal laws. If the FBI thinks that there is proof of crimes, they will charge the person or people with committing the crimes and forward the file to the U.S. Attorney (the federal prosecutor) in the jurisdiction where the misconduct occurred. The U.S. Attorney is responsible for prosecuting the case in federal criminal court.

Civil Complaints

When the Civil Rights Division (CRD) of the DOJ investigates a complaint under the police misconduct provisions, it will begin by reviewing all of the separate encounters in the complaint(s) about a particular law enforcement agency. Then, it will study the law enforcement agency's internal records, which typically include incident reports, training materials, policy manuals, performance evaluations, and documents from the internal affairs office.

During and after the document review, the CRD investigators will interview officers, trainers, supervisors, and other relevant law enforcement personnel who can speak knowledgeably about agency operations and the particular complaints that prompted the investigation. Throughout the investigation, the CRD is looking for facts about how much force was used in each event, how the person with mental illness was acting, what kinds of weapons were in the area, the reasons for calling police to the scene, and other information that will weigh the legitimacy of the police actions against the impact of the actions on the person.

After the CRD finishes investigating a complaint under the police misconduct provisions, it will write a findings letter to the law enforcement agency. The findings letter will explain exactly how the investigation was conducted and what the CRD discovered and decided as a result of the investigation. The findings letter may also recommend new practices and policies for the police department to implement. The DOJ and the law enforcement agency will enter into an agreement that sets forth the methods and timeline by which the agency will employ the new practices and policies. The agreement is called a consent decree, and it is filed in federal court so that the DOJ can quickly go forward with a full lawsuit if the law enforcement agency does not uphold its obligations.

ADA Complaints

The Disability Rights Section has vast expertise in understanding disabilities and the ways that police conduct interactions with people who have disabilities, including mental illness. Its investigations involve the same methods that the CRD uses, but it considers all of the documents and interviews with a knowledgeable perspective on psychiatric conditions. While the Disability Rights Section does recommend reforms to law enforcement agencies, it also has a very active record of suing police departments for discrimination.

HOW TO Find a Lawyer for a Police Misconduct Case

If your relative is injured or otherwise mishandled by police, you or he may be tempted to file a civil court lawsuit over the incident. The process of bringing a lawsuit is, however, extremely slow and stressful. The first reason that police misconduct lawsuits are difficult is that police are given discretion in doing their work. Since the police have to rely on their own quick judgment in responding to emergencies and dealing with all of the different kinds of people who make up the general public, the legal system exempts them from being sued unless there is something blatantly wrong with the judgment they made. The exemption is called *qualified immunity*, an odd term that means that police are immune from being sued unless a typical reasonable police officer would have known that it was wrong to take the disputed action that the officer or law enforcement team took under the circumstances.

The second reason that police misconduct cases are hard is that the court can throw out the lawsuit if the arguments do not show the following facts about the law enforcement behavior:

- It violated a federal law (such as the Americans with Disabilities Act, the Civil Rights of Institutionalized Persons Act, or a corruption statute).
- It violated the Constitution.
- The officer or other law enforcement worker knew that he or she was violating a law.
- The officer or other law enforcement worker acted in his or her official capacity while breaking the law.

When searching for a lawyer to handle a police misconduct case, start with advocacy groups. Will the ACLU or a nonprofit disability law organization take your case? If they will, your burdens will be greatly reduced. The organization will take a stand in your name; it will be their lawsuit as well as yours, and they will be a strong buffer between your family and the police department. If the advocacy groups are not available to take your case, they should at least be able to refer you to civil rights lawyers. Civil rights lawyers are experts at combining statutes and constitutional rights in the claim and they have the best sense of whether state or federal court should handle your particular police misconduct case.

Other organizations that can refer you to civil rights lawyers include the Center for Constitutional Rights, the National Lawyers Guild, the NAACP, Lambda Legal, and the National Council of La Raza. You could also search for the term *civil rights lawyer* on your local newspaper's website. Conducting a search for a lawyer by way of organizations or the newspaper will lead you to information about the lawyers as well as their names.

ARREST AND JAIL

There is an entire field of legal study, called *criminal procedure,* about the ways that police handle crime scenes and suspects. Much of criminal procedure relates to the Fourth and Fifth Amendments to the U.S. Constitution. Although these two amendments apply to the federal government, the Fourteenth Amendment makes them also applicable to state governments. In addition to the constitutional principles, local and state laws and rules establish criminal procedure.

SEARCH AND SEIZURE: THE FOURTH AMENDMENT

The Fourth Amendment sets the basic rules for how police can search people and property and when they can take evidence from a suspect's private property. This legal authority requires police to prove to a judge that there is probable cause to believe that evidence of a crime exists in a place so that the judge will issue a warrant entitling the police to search that place. The amendment also requires that the search be reasonable. Court cases have interpreted the Fourth Amendment to allow police searches without a warrant when the person being searched gives the police permission to search. This is formally called consenting to a search.

However, when the person who consents to a search does not have the mental capacity to realize what she is agreeing to or what could happen when the police conduct a search, it may be possible, later, to convince the criminal court to exclude all of the evidence that was gathered from the search.

Past cases and rules of criminal procedure in each state tell more specifically how to determine when consent was valid. Each state's courts, over time, have created their own list of criteria for believing that someone truly consented to the search. The arguments between the prosecutor and the defense lawyer in attempts to throw out evidence from non-consent searches are very technical and specific. There is certainly not an automatic legal presumption that a person with mental illness is incapable of consenting to a police search.

Police officers who see that someone is obviously delusional, manic, suffering from extreme compulsion, or otherwise out of control will not risk having their evidence excluded. They will go to court and try to get a warrant to search. If the police have a warrant, they do not need permission from a suspect in order to search her home, car, or other possessions. However, since symptoms of deep mental disturbance are not always obvious to those who do not know the person, the police may believe that they did get legitimate consent when, in fact, the person appearing to give consent did not know what she was doing.

If Your Relative With Mental Illness Unknowingly Consents to a Police Search

Perhaps your cousin Hank, who lives with bipolar disorder, is suspected of being involved in a crime. Someone who knows Hank may have seen what happened when the police came to his door. If it was not you, maybe it was a group home manager or a roommate. Ask questions of the witnesses: Did the police look around here? Did they take anything with them? Did they ask Hank for permission before they did that? Would you be willing to tell our lawyer what you saw?

You, and others who are very familiar with your cousin, know if he tends to put on a front of complacency or arrogance when he is really feeling fear. You and they can tell if Hank is talking without thinking. You and they know if he is acting from a different personality or a subtle psychotic state. You all have a lot of information that can be very valuable to a defense lawyer wanting to prevent damaging evidence from being presented in court. So you, because you are a helper to your cousin (and because you may be paying for his lawyer), need to let the lawyer know if there is reason to believe that a police search was done without genuine consent.

To be sure that you are clear and thorough in your message and to avoid paying for an hour of the lawyer's time in which you talk and the lawyer takes notes, send her a letter explaining why you think that a search or seizure may have been conducted improperly. Include details about how Hank was acting and communicating. Identify yourself or others as witnesses, and ask if the lawyer thinks that your relative's Fourth Amendment rights were violated.

SELF-INCRIMINATION: THE FIFTH AMENDMENT

The Fifth Amendment protects people from being forced to serve as witnesses against themselves. One of the most famous cases related to this amendment is *Miranda v. Arizona,* which resulted in the warning that police have to recite before they interrogate a suspect:

> *You have the right to remain silent. If you do not remain silent, anything you say can and will be used against you in a court of law. You have a right to an attorney. If you cannot afford an attorney, one will be provided for you.*

Most people are familiar with this warning and know that they do not have to say anything to the police, but people with mental illness are not always able to stop themselves from communicating. A person with depression might talk because he does not care about anything that has happened or that might happen. A person with schizophrenia may not understand that she is talking to people who have the power to lock her up. Individuals with some types of obsessions may feel compelled to explain very precisely why their irrational actions really do make sense. Various mental conditions may cause someone to be too shocked or terrified to relate to anyone, to realize the impression she is making, or to understand what is going on.

Because the *Miranda* warning only has to be given at the point where police are ready to interrogate a suspect, nobody has a legal right to the warning up until that point. Someone who is out of control can confess to a crime before the police have even said anything. When someone at a crime scene does spontaneously claim responsibility for the crime, police are quick to give the *Miranda* warning. People are welcome to confess at any time, but still the police can question them only after warning them that they have the right not to say anything.

The police ask questions after someone confesses because they have to be convinced that the confession truly is connected to the current crime and because they need to know as much as possible about how the crime happened. If the police think that the person who confessed is irrational or is recognizably mentally ill, they might ask some questions to figure out how well oriented the person is, or they might just transport the person to jail or a mental hospital and ask their questions later.

Whenever the police issue a *Miranda* warning, whether at the crime scene, in the police car, or at the police station, the suspect can either remain silent or waive the right to remain silent. Many court cases have examined the concept of waiving the right to remain silent. They have generally concluded that three characteristics make a waiver legitimate. It has to have been made knowingly, intelligently, and voluntarily. *Knowingly* basically means that the suspect understands that she can choose not to say anything. *Intelligently* is usually understood to mean that the suspect realizes the consequences of answering questions from the police: The police may get proof, or at least clues, showing that she is guilty, and then she will have to go through a trial and punishment, if she is found guilty in the trial.

Voluntarily means that the suspect was not forced to give up her right to remain silent. In the case of someone experiencing an episode of psychosis or cognitive breakdown, voluntariness should be considered in light of the suspect's perception of reality, but courts mainly look at the officers' words and actions, rather than the suspect's perceptions. The only way to get the court to look at how voluntary the waiver really was is to emphasize the "totality of the circumstances." This means that the defense lawyer will show that, although the officers' communications might seem noncoercive in some situations, the court has to think about how the particular defendant saw the police. Perhaps the person has a history of deferring to people in authority. Maybe the person has a severe fear of the government and its employees. Possibly the person was overcome by a fantasy of charming the officers. The defense lawyer would have to present proof to support such a claim.

HOW TO Help if Your Relative Waives Her Right To Remain Silent

You will probably be an important source of proof that your relative's waiver was not knowing, intelligent, and voluntary. For example, if you hear that your daughter Brittany, who has panic disorder, has confessed to something and you believe that she was not in condition to knowingly, intelligently, and voluntarily give up the right to remain silent, get in touch with her lawyer, if possible in writing. You need to present your reasons for doubting the validity of the waiver and to suggest other written sources and people (such as Brittany's therapist, teacher, and boss) who are likely to corroborate your belief. The lawyer can petition the court to examine your daughter's waiver. In your letter, specifically request that the lawyer do so.

Your information will not be the only input used to decide whether Brittany waived her right to remain silent. If the court does get a defense petition questioning the waiver, it will most likely get a forensic psychologist or psychiatrist to assess your daughter's perception of her *Miranda* conversation with the police. Your persuasive letter to the lawyer can specifically ask that the lawyer demand to have a forensic mental health professional involved. In the standard forensic assessment for this purpose, the psychologist or psychiatrist will ask a set list of explanatory questions, such as: Tell me, in your own words, what "anything you say can and will be used against you" means. After the assessment, the forensic psychologist or psychiatrist will submit an expert report to the judge.

HOW DO JAILS DEAL WITH MENTAL ILLNESS?

Depending on a suspect's condition and the available community resources, police have the option of sending a person who is showing symptoms of mental illness to a crisis center or hospital, rather than sending her straight to jail. When police do this, and they believe that the suspect has committed a crime, her admission record will show that she can be discharged from the facility only into police custody. Upon discharge, the police take the suspect to jail for booking.

Once an arrested person reaches jail, any mental health care that she normally receives will almost certainly be disrupted. Numerous professional organizations have called for improved mental health care in jails, demonstrating the damage caused by the care disruptions and proving that the criminal justice system and the inmates are all better off when mentally ill inmates get proper care. A series of federal court cases have established that failure to properly treat inmates' mental problems can be a form of cruel and unusual punishment, in violation of the Eighth Amendment to the Constitution.

Screening

Screening is a quick and limited way to check, as soon as an arrestee arrives at the jail, whether she has an immediate need for mental health intervention. Screening primarily consists of "yes or no" questions. Not every jail conducts intake mental health screenings; they are most common in heavily populated areas with high-traffic jails.

According to the National Commission on Correctional Health Care's *2014 Standards for Health Services in Jails*, all incoming arrestees need to be screened for signs of certain mental problems during the booking phase when they are fingerprinted and photographed. In this admission screening, "Screeners should make adequate efforts to explore the potential for suicide. This includes both reviewing with an inmate any history of suicidal behavior and visually observing the inmate's behavior (delusions, hallucinations, communication difficulties, speech and posture, impaired level of consciousness, disorganization, memory defects, depression or evidence of self-mutilation)." The Commission calls for the screenings to happen within the first few hours of an inmate's arrival at the jail.

The Commission also asserts that the intake worker must ask new inmates what prescriptions they take and arrange for them to continue getting the medications— whether for mental or other illnesses. Since the jail pharmacy is not likely to be fully stocked with every psychotropic medication, there is a huge possibility that an inmate will not be able to get exactly the medication that she took prior to jail. Of course, there is also a possibility that the inmate will not properly identify her medication names and dosages. Families are permitted to contact the jail and to provide correct prescription information, but they may not bring medications to the jail.

Screenings are not meant to be professional mental health evaluations. In most jails, they are conducted by corrections professionals, not mental health professionals. Nevertheless, the standard sets of inmate mental health screening questions were composed by mental health professionals.

Assessment

Assessment is more extensive than a screening and is done when a screening suggests that an inmate may require mental health treatment, when the arrest report suggests a mental health problem, or when the inmate behaves like she has a mental illness. The American Bar Association, the American Psychiatric Association, the Council of State Governments, and the National Commission on Correctional Health Care all say that the assessments should be conducted within 14 days of admission to the jail. Unfortunately, this much time can allow inmates to be bailed out before being assessed but after suffering mental harm.

Assessments are conducted by people who are trained to identify mental health symptoms and to listen for hints about the scope of an inmate's mental disturbance. These trained individuals can be corrections officers, nurses, social workers, or other professionals. No matter what professional background brings them to the assessment duties, they have to be trained in the jail's assessment system before doing the work.

Assessment questions are more open-ended than screening questions in order to collect information about an inmate's mood, motivation, awareness, perceptions, and other signs of mental illness. A common assessment question is, "How important is it for you to get mental health care while you are here awaiting trial?" Since the assessment happens after the inmate has been in jail for some time, it will also reveal information about how confinement is affecting the inmate's mental health.

Inmate mental health assessments inform the jail's mental health department about the types of intervention to use with an inmate and any special needs that the inmate has. Jails will accommodate the special needs with housing, activity, and diet arrangements when they can. When the special needs are about noise levels, or fear factors, or other environmental issues that the jail cannot necessarily control constantly, at least the jail will know how to temporarily calm an inmate by adapting the environment.

Evaluation

Evaluation is a professional mental health workup conducted by a psychologist or a psychiatrist. It results in an actual treatment plan for the inmate as well as the jail's cooperation with the plan:

- Medicine will be dispensed on schedule.
- The inmate will be taken to therapy on schedule.
- The therapist and doctor will keep official medical records about ongoing treatment.

Inmate Participation in Mental Health Care

Despite having the levels of inquiry about inmate mental health and despite being very controlling environments, jails cannot force inmates to reveal that they have been prescribed psychotropic drugs. Nor can they force inmates to take their medicine or to participate in therapy or wellness programs. This is a major distinction between involuntary commitment to a mental hospital and confinement in jail. If an inmate's interference with her own mental health care causes significant problems, the jail can transfer the inmate to a mental hospital for involuntary commitment and treatment. Once the person is stabilized, then guards or police will bring the inmate back to jail.

HOW TO Support an Inmate's Mental Health

If you have a family member with mental illness who is in jail, say your brother Preston who lives with obsessive-compulsive disorder, before concluding that the jail's mental health services are inadequate, carefully search the jail's website for every clue about staff or services that may be associated with mental health. Reach out to the jail's mental health provider so that you can make sure they know about your family member's mental health history and treatment. You can also give them contact information for your family member's usual psychiatrist or other mental health treatment provider. On the visitor information page, see if there is anything about who can visit. Maybe you can arrange for a positive person, such as a friend from the clubhouse, to go during visiting hours and help Preston adjust to jail life. It may even be possible for Preston to have phone calls with his usual therapist.

See if the jail's website has a section about activities or programs. If it does, that is where you can expect to find out about wellness activities and support groups. Urge your relative to participate in the programs, and encourage the jail to invite him to join in. Also look on the website for the words *community* or *local* so that you can see if the jail has partnerships with any mental health providers in the area. Next, go to the community providers' websites and see what kinds of jail services they discuss and whether they identify any staff members whom you can contact about your family member.

If the jail does not have mental health resources and services to help Preston, or if he will not take advantage of the offerings at the jail, you can ask his defense lawyer to try to get him moved to a mental health treatment facility while waiting for trial. This step is referred to as a "petition for diversion." The petition is usually presented to the judge at arraignment—when an inmate is formally charged—but it can happen at another time. When possible, the defense lawyer will get the prosecutor to agree to mental health diversion before presenting the idea in front of the judge.

Diversion is not usually available to inmates who have committed serious crimes and it will be revoked if the patient does not complete the course of treatment. If that happens, the patient has to go back to jail. Sometimes, when the patient successfully completes the mental health treatment that is required in his particular diversion arrangement, the criminal charges are dropped.

If your brother has to remain in jail or is returned to jail and the jail does not have adequate mental health assessments and treatments, consider writing to the state legislature, the state corrections agency, and directly to the jail to advocate for better services. Base your advocacy on an existing set of standards: You could demand that the jail become accredited by the National Commission on Correctional Health Care or that it comply with the standards established by the Mental Health Consensus Project, published by the Justice Center at the Council of State Governments. Or you could identify model processes in other jail systems and call for those to be used in your jail. Considering how much news has been published about mental illness in correctional facilities, it is hard to justify jails that do not have sufficient knowledge or resources to properly serve their inmates' mental health needs. A few letters from families may bring problems to light and influence improvements.

RESOURCES FOR POLICE MISCONDUCT

1. Look in the United States Code (uscode.house.gov) for the statutes about misconduct:
   Deprivation of Rights under Color of Law 18 U.S.C. § 242
   Police Misconduct Provision 42 U.S.C. § 14141
   Americans with Disabilities Act 42 U.S.C. § 12131-12132.
   The DOJ's descriptions of the laws are on the page titled "Addressing Police Misconduct" at justice.gov.
2. Submit a general police misconduct complaint to: Coordination and Review Section, Civil Rights Division, U.S. Department of Justice, P.O. Box 66560, Washington, DC 20035-6560.
3. File a criminal complaint about the police with your nearest FBI field office. Field offices are listed at fbi.gov.
4. Send your discrimination complaint to: Disability Rights Section, Civil Rights Division, U.S. Department of Justice, P.O. Box 66738, Washington, DC 20035-6738.
5. Find examples of current legal actions involving the DOJ's ADA Compliance Division at ada.gov.
6. The DOJ publishes its cases and investigative reports, which are called findings letters, online at justice.gov. A 2012 findings letter about one city's pattern of excessive force against people with mental illness is available at http://www.justice.gov/crt/about/spl/documents/ppb_findings_9-12-12.pdf. A 2014 findings letter about a city where the police tended to use too much force against people with mental illness is available at http://www.justice.gov/crt/about/spl/documents/apd_ findings_4-10-14.pdf.
7. The ACLU website has a discussion on reforming police practices that will help you learn more details about the process. See aclu.org.
8. The National Disability Rights Network will link you to advocacy groups in your state that might collect and compile stories of police misconduct against people with mental illness. The disability rights office would then file a group complaint to the DOJ. You want to connect with a group that is geographically close to you, since police work is local. See ndrn.org.

9. When searching for a lawyer, look in the Martindale Hubbell Legal Directory at martindale.com using *civil rights* as the specialty term and limiting the search to your city or state. You could also contact civil rights organizations, such as the ACLU (aclu.org), Lambda Legal (lambdalegal.org), NAACP (naacp.org), Center for Constitutional Rights (ccrjustice.org), the National Lawyers Guild (nlg.org), or National Council of La Raza (nclr.org). All of these organizations have referral lists to help people find private civil rights lawyers.

RESOURCES FOR ARREST AND JAIL

1. The Annotated U.S. Constitution at justia.com has the exact text of the Constitution plus summaries of the leading cases interpreting each part of it. Find state constitutions, which have very similar criminal procedure rights to those in the federal Constitution, at law.cornell.edu.
2. Link to a state's rules of criminal procedure via the Cornell Legal Information Institute at law.cornell.edu.
3. An excellent book about consent in numerous legal contexts involving people with mental illness is Thomas Grisso's *Evaluating Competencies* (2nd ed., 2003). The author is a forensic psychologist who developed several of the forensic assessment instruments that courts rely on when deciding whether someone has legitimately waived his or her rights.
4. A very informative source about mental illness in jails, including the research behind inmate mental health assessments, is *The Criminalization of Mental Illness,* by Risdon N. Slate, Jacqueline K. Buffington-Vollum, and W. Wesley Johnson (Durham, NC: Carolina Academic Press, 2nd ed., 2013).
5. An example of a quick screening tool is the Brief Jail Mental Health Screen, available from The Gains Center at samhsa.gov/gains-center. The Gains Center for Behavioral Health and Justice works to increase mental health services in the justice system.
6. The National Commission on Correctional Health Care's standards for receiving screening (health screenings during the jail admission process) and basic mental health services are summarized at ncchc.org. The full standards are available in a book published by NCCHC: *Standards for Mental Health Services in Correctional Facilities.*
7. The Council of State Governments' Justice Center Consensus Report has a sensible list of recommended criteria for the full span of jail mental health services, from booking through discharge. It is available at csgjusticecenter.org. Although the criteria are optional, the Justice Center publishes them for free online and offers training to corrections and law enforcement professionals, often in cooperation with government agencies, nonprofit entities, and professional organizations. The standards have to be satisfied in order for a jail to be accredited by the Commission, but jails are not required to have this accreditation in order to operate. In other words, they do not have to comply with the standards.

8. The National Institute of Corrections has produced good, authoritative studies and guidelines about inmate mental health services. Find them at nicic.gov/mentalillness.
9. The American Bar Association's Standards on Treatment of Prisoners are available at americanbar.org.
10. Several organizations jointly produced a great *Advocacy Handbook* to guide individuals and organizations working to improve criminal justice interactions for defendants and inmates who have mental health issues. The Council of State Governments' Justice Center makes it available for free online at csgjusticecenter.org.
11. A recent initiative called "Stepping Up: A National Initiative to Reduce the Number of Inmates with Mental Illnesses in Jails" hopes to inspire more diversion to treatment programs. Read their materials at csgjusticecenter.org.

9

Minor Crimes

A probation officer called about your sister Ivy today. She said that Ivy identified you as someone who can help with her probation. You were totally blindsided by this call and bought yourself some time by scheduling an appointment to talk with the probation officer on Friday. Now you need to get some basic knowledge about probation.

WHAT ARE MINOR CRIMES?

Minor crimes are categorized as being minor because nobody has been badly hurt or lost a lot of money in connection with them. These crimes are either infractions (also known as ticket offenses and summary offenses), which come with a fine, or they are misdemeanors, which may come with harsher punishments, such as community service, participation in training or counseling, probation, or a short jail term.

Minor crimes are sometimes the only reason that many people with mental illness are ever involved in the criminal justice system. For example:

- Somebody complains about Susan out in public, and she ends up being charged with loitering.
- Walking across a street, Bruce is cited for jaywalking or interfering with traffic.
- Your mom creates a scene somewhere and gets cited for disturbing the peace.
- D'Ante gets caught driving without a license or insurance card.

Getting in trouble with the police has a lot to do with who else is around and what else is going on.

Police see all kinds of illegal behavior and do not necessarily "bust" anybody for it, especially neighborhood police, who are familiar with the locals. Sometimes, they can respond to minor incidents just by dispersing people or by talking through something. Maybe they'll give a warning. However, when they get dispatched to a scene because people are complaining or the behavior happens in risky circumstances, they may need to arrest somebody as part of getting control of the situation. Even when they do arrest someone for a minor incident and charge her with a minor crime, it may only result in minor punishment if it comes to any punishment at all.

Defenses are available for most of these minor crimes:

- Susan was not loitering; she was window shopping.
- Bruce always keeps his left foot on the outer edge of crosswalk lines even though the rest of his body is outside of the crosswalk; he is very exact and consistent about that. We submit that since he had that one foot touching the crosswalk, he was not technically jaywalking.
- Your mother did not disturb the peace; she was merely asking a question.

When there is no defense, a defendant like D'Ante might at least get his charges reduced by showing contrition and corrective action.

- When I grabbed my backpack that morning, I forgot that my wallet was not in it. Now I check for my wallet every time I get ready to leave the house. I learned from this experience and I respectfully request that you reduce the charge of driving without my license and insurance card.

Anyone can go to court and fight a ticket if she wants to contest its legitimacy. Misdemeanors, however, are more serious than infractions, and there is no choice but to go to court over a misdemeanor. This can be a scary experience for anyone, but the positive side is that going to court means that a prosecutor has to prove that the person the police charged really did commit the crime. If the particular misdemeanor is identified in the state code as one that can be punished with jail time and if the defendant has low enough income and savings, the court will appoint a public defender to help fight the charge. Otherwise the defendant or her family can hire a defense lawyer.

The initial court appearance in these cases is typically a very quick meeting in front of the judge. If the case is about an infraction, such as driving with a broken tail light or obstructing the sidewalk, the prosecutor will run through a few questions with the police officer who was at the scene and possibly one or two witnesses at most. Then the defendant, or her lawyer if she has one, can question the claims made by the officer and any witnesses. These questions may test a witness's accuracy, memory, and distractions. Specific questions for the police officer can cover those same issues as well as who he talked to at the scene and how he studied the scene. If the case is about a more serious charge, such as shoplifting, this first court appearance will probably not include testimony about the crime. It will basically be an opportunity for the judge to clarify that the defendant, for example your aunt Kate, understands the charges and the possible punishments that may result. She will have the opportunity to plead guilty or not guilty. If your aunt pleads not guilty, she will have a trial at a later date unless she and her lawyer arrange a resolution with the prosecutor before the trial date.

Assuming that the offense is minor enough to be resolved in the initial court appearance, for example when your sister Wendy who was cited for failing to keep her dog on a leash (which enabled her dog to attack another animal), the defendant should arrive ready to communicate quickly after sitting around waiting for a long time. The defense lawyer, whether hired by your sister or her family or appointed by the court, will probably talk with Wendy for just a few moments before seeing the judge. While other cases are being heard at the bench, defense lawyers are likely to walk through the seating area calling out names of the clients they are supposed to represent. As each client raises her hand, the defense lawyer takes her aside, reviews the file with her, and asks for her version of what happened. Sometimes, there are so few public defenders available that the client meets the lawyer only when they arrive at the judge's bench. Still, they will have at least some chance to confer before the case begins.

To prepare for this hurried meeting with her lawyer, a defendant like Wendy should be able to tell her story in a sentence or two. She needs to efficiently say what she was actually doing, describe anything important about the environment, and note whether the police officer was present during the event. Here are some examples:

- *I was running to catch a bus and didn't see that lady in my way, and, then, when I accidentally bumped her, some guy tackled me and held me on the ground until the police came.*
- *I wasn't on anything illegal, but my meds make me very tired, especially when I'm in the sun; I just stretched out on a bench to rest and then that police officer woke me up and wrote me a ticket.*

This same pattern of quickly summarizing the situation is also how the defendant can begin her testimony if she is representing herself without a lawyer. She is most likely to represent herself against an infraction. In both infraction cases and misdemeanor cases, however, the goals in defense are to at least get the charge reduced, if not dropped entirely. To succeed at either of these goals, the defendant and her lawyer (if any) need to show flaws in the prosecutor's assertions.

If the defendant does end up convicted of something in court or through a plea agreement, she and her lawyer can request the lightest possible punishment. The severity of the punishment can depend on how the crime happened, the defendant's record of getting into trouble, and the judge's discretion. If a job or education is at risk, the defendant can say something like, *Please don't make me lose my job over this* or *I take responsibility for what I did, and I hope that you will consider a community-based punishment so that I can keep going to school.* Even if the case does not go well for the defendant, she can at least take some comfort from recalling that a minor crime will come with a minor punishment.

Sadly, the insignificant nature of minor crimes can be completely ruined by a defendant who does not comply with her assigned punishment. For example, if Wendy does not pay her ticket, she can eventually be charged with the additional crime of nonpayment. If she is supposed to be at a hearing, but does not show up for court, she may be arrested and charged with "failure to appear" in addition to her original crime. If Wendy went to court and was assigned to do something that she did not do, she may be charged with multiple additional offenses and could be sent to jail.

Punishments for Minor Crimes

Aside from fines, the three most commonly imposed punishments for minor crimes are community service, training and treatment, and probation. In serious cases, such as those in which someone has a previous arrest record or is charged with multiple minor crimes in combination, she can be put on house arrest while also serving one of the community-based punishments. During her months of house arrest, she has to wear a radiofrequency ankle bracelet that notifies police if she is not within range of her base monitor or at an approved location at the designated time—the location of her community service or the meeting with her probation officer, for example.

COMMUNITY SERVICE
When a judge orders community service, the defendant generally has the opportunity to select from an assortment of community-service placements according to location, task, and relevance to the crime. In some jurisdictions, the criminal court arranges community-service placements only with government offices, such as the parks department and the public library. Other jurisdictions may have community-service arrangements with nonprofit organizations. There is usually an office associated with the criminal court that maintains a roster of the options and manages the placements.

People with community-service orders connect with that office and, along with a staff member, review the available programs. The staff member then contacts the agency where the person wants to do her community service to confirm that the place can currently use the extra person and to set up the schedule. If the person's chosen placement is not available, she will have to accept a different one. As long as the person does the volunteer work for the designated number of hours and gets the paperwork signed by the volunteer supervisor, she will satisfy her debt to society. If the community-service match works out well, the person may opt to continue volunteering. Even if she does not continue as a volunteer, the experience can add to her professional network and possibly result in a job reference that she would not otherwise have. The reference can describe her as a volunteer; it does not need to say that she volunteered at the order of a court.

TRAINING AND TREATMENT
When a court orders a defendant to participate in addiction counseling, behavioral training, mental health treatment, or other educational or treatment programs, it is often an opportunity for the defendant to avoid going to jail. As with community service, she will typically get to choose where she has her placement. Of course, the place that she chooses will have to be approved by the court, and it will have to give her the kind of treatment that the court ordered.

As much as possible, her training or treatment schedule can be arranged around her job and other commitments. Still, she needs to be seriously committed to these court-ordered experiences. She has to go to all of the sessions and participate properly or else the program presenter will not give her credit for attending. If she fulfills the training or treatment obligation, her criminal trouble will largely be behind her. She may still have some fees to pay and other court-ordered tasks to fulfill, but ideally by then she will have new skills and habits or be in a good therapeutic relationship and regulated on her medicine.

PROBATION

Probation is court-ordered supervision. It is frequently combined with community service or outpatient treatment, although it can stand alone. Basic probation is just participation in routine meetings with a probation officer to keep the officer informed about things. For example, people on probation may have to report to their probation officer about getting services from community agencies, refraining from certain activities, or seeking or maintaining employment. The subjects included in each probationer's terms of probation (in other words, the stipulations or conditions) are established according to her crime, where she is in life, and sometimes in relation to her victim. If, for example, Janie's crime involved senior citizens, her probation may include observing and reading about senior citizens.

Note that meetings with probation officers can take place at locations other than the probation office. Sometimes, meetings are at probationers' homes so that the probation officer can confirm any home-based compliance and keep an eye on the probationer's lifestyle.

HOW TO Support Compliance With Court Orders

For a Ticket

A ticket is the most common type of court order. If, for example, your daughter Francesca, who has been diagnosed with clinical depression, gets a ticket for something that she actually did, she has to pay it. Even if she wants to fight the ticket, she may need to pay it up front in order to be assigned a court date. In jurisdictions with that kind of system, the accused person gets a refund check if she succeeds in court. The court cashier can usually work out an installment plan for paying a ticket, but if you can pay it outright for your daughter and she is not a frequent troublemaker, why not do it? If she is not going to fight the ticket, then paying it will be the end of her legal problem. Even if she does take the time and energy to fight it, at least Francesca will know that she has your support. You can make a private arrangement to have her pay you back in small amounts, if that makes sense in your circumstances.

If, however, you are not in a position to pay your daughter's ticket or you think that she will not pay you back, perhaps you can assist with other things. For example, help Francesca save money by going with her to inexpensive stores and consulting on her purchases. Go over her routine expenses and help her decide which ones to cancel so that she will have money for paying her court debt. She may be insulted by this scrutiny, but if it will end her legal problem, it is worth it. Give her a secure place to stash her savings if she does not otherwise have one. When she is tempted to do anything extravagant, remind her that she owes the money. She may think that she deserves an evening out or a special treat, but she needs to pay her debt or risk getting an additional criminal charge.

For a Requirement to Appear in Court

A requirement to appear in court is another simple court order. The defendant, your husband's sister Alexa, has to show up and participate. If your sister-in-law is at risk of missing that court appearance unless she has some backing, give her the backing. She may need someone to wake her up, give her a ride, and sit next to her while she waits for her case to be called. You may not be the person she wants with her, but you can help her to get the person she does want. Maybe you can quietly call her preferred friend or family member to tell them that she would love to hear from them and that she has something important to discuss.

Maybe she just needs some coaching about how to tell her boss that she has to miss work for court that day. You can suggest that she say something like, "I have been called to testify in a court case on this day at this time. They don't know exactly when the case will start, so I'm supposed to be available there for the whole morning. How can we arrange my schedule around this appointment?" If the boss asks what the case is about, she can say "I was told not to talk about it." The court clerk can provide her with a note to later bring back to work, certifying that she was there and participated in a case.

For Community Service

The judge's ruling in a case is the ultimate court order. Sometimes the judge orders that the case is dismissed, while other times the judge orders punishment for the defendant. If the court orders community service for your relative, you may need to help him.

Let's use the example of your brother, John, who was found guilty of littering and disorderly conduct. If the judge orders community service and John is too upset to tune into the choice of a community-service assignment, go through the list of possible placements with him. If he is interested in a specific nonprofit that is not on the placement list, ask the coordinator about the possibility of arranging for your brother to work for that organization. It may be that the only way to get John on board with community service is to arrange a placement with someone he already knows and trusts. If the community-service coordinator resists alternative service ideas and if your family member satisfies the ADA criteria of having an impairment and of being treated for that impairment, or if he is regarded as having an impairment, you can try pitching the alternative placement as a request for accommodation.

On the other hand, your role in arranging John's community service may be to help him get adjusted to the system, rather than trying to make the system adjust to him. You may need to help your brother focus on the available placement options, take him to look at a few places, and just be a sounding board while he gets used to his upcoming obligation. Once the placement is set up, be available with any support that your brother may need. This may just be a weekly phone conversation to hear how the community service work is going. It may be maintaining a file of weekly attendance slips to submit to court. It may be equipping him with supplies, such as a sun hat or work gloves. Above all else, help your loved one to feel good about the service he is providing.

For Participation in Classes or Treatment

If the court ordered John to participate in classes or treatment, he may not realize what a relatively easy punishment it is. He may not feel motivated to learn or to recover just yet. He may not care that his punishment will be much worse if he does not cooperate. If your family member is resistant or unlikely to comply for any reason, you have to make it clear that his participation is not optional. To do this, put it on his schedule and build structure around his appointments. The structure can include a meal before or after each appointment, a routine for getting to and from the appointments, or selecting and preparing clothes to wear for each appointment. Think about all of the steps that you go through when preparing yourself to go to important meetings and put those in place with your brother. You do not have to convey any kind of attitude; you just need to establish a system with him. With this kind of support, he will get accustomed to attending the appointments.

For Probation
If the court orders John to participate in probation, know that probation officers are grateful to have supportive people assisting in the process. They rely on families to supply facts and various forms of assistance. Probation officers commonly begin their relationships with probationers by having them identify people who are helpful to them in particular ways, such as making them laugh, motivating them, listening, or helping with decisions. The probation officer will then try to engage with these supportive people during the intake and assessment phase of the probation to determine how they can participate in the probation plan.

If you get a call or email from your relative's probation officer, you should be honored; it means that your brother has identified you as trusted and supportive. Initially, the probation officer may just ask you for information. He may want to know if there are any triggers that will upset John or if you predict that John will have problems with any of the probation conditions. He may ask generally if you want to be on the probation team or he may have a specific task in mind for you. Take the opportunity to let the officer know about any unusual challenges that your brother is currently facing. The loss of a job or a change in therapist, for example, may have led to the criminal charges and may still be upsetting him.

Brainstorm with the probation officer. Look through the list of probation conditions and think about all of the people in your family who have skills, knowledge, or other reasons for being able to help your brother comply with any of the terms. Here is are some examples:

Maybe the probation office is downtown and your cousin Dorothy works downtown. John may be more likely to keep his weekly downtown appointments with his probation officer if Dorothy schedules something positive with John, like a coffee break or a ride home.

If John has to have periodic drug testing and you expect that he will be anxious about misuse of his test results or even the process of providing urine samples, think of someone who can put his mind at ease. This may be his doctor or a neighbor who works in a medical or legal capacity and happens to know behind-the-scenes facts about drug testing. Ask the probation officer whether you or he can arrange for a conversation with this person, a tour of the testing lab, or some other demonstration that can help to alleviate John's concerns.

Probation officers go to the trouble of reaching out for family support because it genuinely matters to them that their clients succeed in probation. They tend to come into this profession with college degrees in social work or criminology—helping professions. The whole point of their jobs is to keep people out of jail and away from its consequences; they do not want their clients to fail. So they make these plans with the family, hoping to remove obstacles that might keep a client from fulfilling the judge's full probation order. If the judge wants the person to take child-rearing classes, the probation officer will find a training program, feasible transportation, and a facility or family member to watch the child while the probationer takes the class. If the judge wants the person to pay restitution to a victim, the probation officer will organize a payment plan with the client and, if there is a family member associated with the client's money management, will get the family member to fit this new expense into the probationer's budget. As long as family members are willing and able to help, probation officers will get them on board.

Helping Your Relative Have a Successful Outcome

The final word about helping a loved one through a minor crime and punishment is: Your involvement can prevent this bad-enough experience from turning into a worse one. You and others who are close to this relative are uniquely positioned to predict and to spot her inclinations toward noncompliance. She may not realize that she is arranging her schedule, is changing her mind, is getting distracted, or otherwise is at risk of not being where she is supposed to be or doing what she is supposed to do. If the rest of you can find ways to keep her on track, she will get through the criminal experience quickly and with a minimal amount of disruption in her life.

RESOURCES FOR MINOR CRIMES

1. The federal Substance Abuse and Mental Health Services Administration (SAMHSA) maintains a national list of addiction treatment programs that are approved for court-ordered services. Look for it at findtreatment. samhsa.gov.
2. The American Probation and Parole Association has an assortment of free publications and reports on its website (at appa-net.org). Examples include a guide titled *Involving Families in Case Planning* and a handbook titled *Implementing the Family Support Approach for Community Supervision.*
3. *Guidelines for the Successful Transition of People with Behavioral Health Disorders from Jail and Prison,* by Alex M. Blandford, M.P.H., C.H.E.S., and Fred Osher, M.D. (Council of State Governments Justice Center, 2013 csgjusticecenter.org), advises corrections authorities about probation for offenders with mental illness. Although it emphasizes the post-incarceration transition to probation, it contains justifications and guidance that defendants and families can use in pleas for probation as an alternative to incarceration.
4. *Minor Crimes, Massive Waste: The Terrible Toll of America's Misdemeanor Courts,* by Robert C. Boruchowitz, Malia N. Brink, and Maureen Dimino (National Association of Criminal Defense Lawyers, 2009), is a report

about the enormous quantity of misdemeanor cases that burden defense lawyers' workloads and prevent them from having sufficient time to build stronger defenses. The report is available at nacdl.org.

5. The American Bar Association's Standing Committee on Legal Aid and Indigent Defendants (SCLAID) provides examples of good practices in public defender services and publishes standards on public defense and excessive workloads. These resources, as well as conference materials and news items associated with indigence and minor crimes, are available at americanbar.org.

6. The National Center for State Courts has compiled quite a bit of interesting information about the utility and impact of criminal fines. It is published on a website called *Fines, Costs, and Fees Resource Guide* (at ncsc.org).

7. A report titled *Smart on Crime: Reforming America's Criminal Justice System* (U.S. Department of Justice, 2013) declares that one of the Department's priorities is to "pursue alternatives to incarceration for low-level nonviolent crimes." The report is online at justice.gov.

8. Families Against Mandatory Minimums (FAMM) is a nonprofit advocacy organization that encourages courts and legislators to impose criminal punishments that are more likely than prison to have positive outcomes for offenders. Their publication titled *Alternatives to Incarceration in a Nutshell* and other sensible materials are available at famm.org.

10

Mental Health Court

Your nephew Earl cannot tolerate having people talk about him; this is a prominent symptom of his mental illness. It would just be inhumane to put him in a courtroom full of lawyers, witnesses, and jurors all discussing him and the day he messed up. You can look at the court system's website and find out if mental health court is available where he lives. If it is, make sure that he and his immediate family know that this type of court is private and supportive, emphasizing treatment rather than punishment.

WHAT IS MENTAL HEALTH COURT?

Mental health courts are criminal courts that exist exclusively to deal with accusations against people who have mental health problems. Their purpose is to provide jail alternatives. The rules and processes in mental health court are designed to help defendants get out of the criminal justice system and avoid committing future crimes. Mental health courts are trial courts that have rules specifying the combinations of crimes and psychiatric conditions that they can handle. These courts generally do not handle sexual assault cases or murders and they do not have juries participating in case decisions.

Mental health courts are partners with mental health service providers, substance abuse service providers, social work agencies, vocational resources, and other entities outside the justice system. Some of the partners provide guidance to the mental health courts and some provide direct treatment and other services to defendants. All of the partners participate in planning and providing criminal case management that deals more carefully with defendants' mental health issues than standard criminal courts do.

Mental health courts provide defendants with a larger team than the judges, lawyers, and clerks found in most criminal courts. The staff teams in mental health courts include caseworkers (who manage defendants' individual calendars) and treatment staff (who help defendants maintain the best possible medication and therapy routines and develop skills and knowledge that can keep them out of future trouble). The teams are also supposed to make sure that the court's arrangements for each defendant remain flexible and adapt to the defendant's evolution through the system.

How Does a Case Get Into Mental Health Court Instead of the Standard Local Criminal Court?

When a defendant is delivered to the police department by a Crisis Intervention Team (CIT) officer or by officers who collect her from a mental health facility, the intake officer will direct the case file to the mental health public defender (if there is one) or will flag the file for a mental health court referral. Similarly, a defendant identified as mentally ill during the jail intake and subsequent mental health evaluation in jail will be flagged for mental health court consideration.

If the police have not identified a jail inmate with mental illness as a potential candidate for mental health court, either the defense lawyer[1] or the prosecutor can make the referral. Occasionally, a defendant with mental illness makes it past the police and the lawyers without being referred to mental health court until the general criminal court judge sees the case file or meets the defendant in a preliminary hearing and then decides to send the case over to the mental health court.

At any point after the defendant has been charged with a crime, family members, friends, caseworkers, and therapists can refer the case to mental health court. This is best done in cooperation with the defense lawyer. Getting hold of the lawyer for this purpose is rarely a problem when the defense lawyer is a private attorney getting paid by the hour, but it can be challenging when the lawyer is an overworked public defender. On the other hand, the public defender's office may have experience with, and convenient routines for, dealing with mental health court that a particular private lawyer may not have. It is not necessary to involve the defense lawyer with the referral; it just makes it easier. The court may have a referral form on its website. If it doesn't, it will likely provide contact information there so that relatives or friends can call and get instructions for referring a case to the mental health court. The referral will have to include details about past mental health problems, drug and alcohol use, medications, and contact information for a local caseworker or therapist who has dealt with the defendant for other issues prior to arrest.

Intake Process

After referral, the intake process begins. The intake process is the court's routine for preparing a case file so that the case can get on the calendar to be heard by a judge. Intake for mental health court requires a lot of documentation—more than the arrest report and possible "rap sheet" (criminal history report) that are sufficient to get a case on the standard criminal court calendar. The extra intake documents typically include:

- Information from the defendant's mental health record. This will most likely be a letter or completed form from a treating therapist or psychiatrist, not a copy of a full mental health record, although the mental health court does eventually obtain some of the defendant's

---

1 Note that the defense lawyer does not have to be a public defender; private lawyers can also refer clients to mental health court.

mental health records. One important component of the mental health information required at this point in case review is the defendant's history of cooperating with treatment.

- Information from addiction treatment centers (if any). At intake, this will summarize the type of program that a defendant participated in (such as twelve-step, long-term residential, or straight detox), verify addictions, and indicate whether the defendant was compliant with the program. Later in the process, the court will see current addiction treatment records.
- Any available jail-based mental health assessments and evaluations, plus information from the prosecutor and defense lawyer about whether they think that the defendant should instead go through the "unfit to stand trial" process—which is appropriate for a defendant who is too mentally ill to willfully and knowingly participate in mental health court.
- And, possibly, comments and observations by either the defense lawyer or the prosecutor suggesting that the defendant is faking mental illness as a way of trying to get an easy punishment. The suspicion of faking is not likely to exist when one of the lawyers referred the case to mental health court; it tends to happen when a friend or relative made the referral and neither the jail nor the lawyers have seen recognizable symptoms of mental illness in the defendant.

Mental health courts declare their limits up front, so that only the most appropriate cases get referred to them. They aim to process the intake packets as quickly as possible so that defendants do not languish in stress, waiting to find out if they are eligible for mental health court and worrying because they will have to go through the standard criminal court system if they are not eligible.

During the intake process, a mental health professional, the defense lawyer, and possibly other professionals (such as, for example, a special education teacher) will consult with the defendant about the risks and reasons for proceeding in mental health court, as opposed to standard criminal court. They will make sure that the defendant has the mental capacity to genuinely agree to mental health court. They will clearly explain to the defendant what kinds of tasks she will likely have to do as a participant in mental health court. And they will confirm that the defendant understands the consequences of both succeeding and failing in mental health court.

One important aspect of the intake process is about medical records privacy. The Health Insurance Portability and Accountability Act of 1996 (HIPAA) ensures medical records are kept private, although it does have provisions allowing correctional and law enforcement agencies to access medical records. Similarly, the regulations titled Confidentiality of Substance Abuse Patient Records permit correctional and law enforcement agencies to see treatment records. These legal exceptions to privacy allow only limited access by certain personnel in the correctional or law enforcement setting, so mental health courts require defendants to sign a release form entitling the full support team to share all of the same information from medical records. This way, for example, a therapist on the treatment team can speak freely with social workers or court staff, and the mental health records created by the jail can be shared with any non-court employees on the treatment team.

The mental health information shared by the team is usually summarized content that is needed for planning and decision-making. For example:

This client has been depressed for the last two weeks, so I have altered his medications. You might see that he is unusually tired or agitated as the new medication builds to a therapeutic level in his system. Get in touch with me if you see anything unusual—before you hold something against him.

Neither the mental health treatment records nor most of the other records from mental health court are released on the public docket or otherwise made available to anyone other than those working on the case. The public docket may list the criminal charges, and it will indicate whether the defendant was found guilty or not guilty of any of the charges and whether any of the charges were dropped. All of the various professionals working on the case risk losing their professional licenses and suffering other punishments if they divulge confidential client information.

Once a defendant is accepted into mental health court, the case proceeds more like a series of meetings than like the adversarial case that it would be in standard criminal court. Nobody comes to testify against the defendant, there are no cross examinations, evidence is not exhibited and fought over, there is no jury full of strangers making judgments about the incident that landed the defendant in court, and, best of all, courtroom events in mental health court are private—unlike criminal courts, which are open to the public. Since the mental health court process is not about defending oneself and the accused person's status changes during the process, defendants in mental health court are sometimes referred to as "participants."

MAKING A TREATMENT PLAN

The main goal for a participant in mental health court is to arrive at an agreement to participate in treatment for a mental disorder and any concurrent drug or alcohol addictions. This agreement is often called a *treatment plan*, and it is literally a contract between the defendant and the court. The most daunting part of the treatment plan is a guilty plea. The defendant has to admit to being guilty of the crime and has to be willing to take a treatment-based punishment instead of having a trial at which she could be found not guilty.

Why would anyone give up the great American promise of a fair trial with a jury of peers at which the prosecuting attorney has to prove guilt beyond a reasonable doubt? Defendants have numerous reasons: they know how brutal and risky trials are; they want to avoid being locked up with criminals; they want to be able to keep their jobs, housing, and routines; they need and want support; and sometimes they truly are guilty.

In fact, not every defendant who qualifies for mental health court wants that option. For example:

- Some defendants have symptoms of grandiosity or irrationality that prevent them from appreciating the opportunity to have the case heard in mental health court.

- There are defendants who have been let down by bureaucratic systems and are justifiably distrustful of mental health court's very personal and intimidating agreement.
- Some defendants are truly innocent and will have no chance at justice if they plead guilty.

Whatever their reasons for avoiding mental health court, nobody can force defendants to give up their constitutional right to have a jury trial in criminal court.

In addition to the automatic guilty plea, the defendant, perhaps your niece, Aisha, has to agree to be under intensive scrutiny by a whole team of people. The team is designed to help Aisha succeed at the particular combination of treatment and training that the intake process has established for her. Your niece will have to agree to meet with, or report to, members of the team or the whole group at scheduled times. She may have to agree to avoid certain places or behaviors. She may have to agree to volunteer in the community. She may have to agree to complete behavioral training or communication classes or other forms of education to avoid getting in the same kind of trouble again. Someone guilty of being an accomplice, for example, may be required to take lessons in assertiveness and other social skills so that she can say "no" the next time anyone tries to coerce her into a crime scheme.

Finally, Aisha has to agree to be punished in the event that she fails to uphold the terms of the treatment plan. The ultimate punishment is prison and nearly every defendant has to agree to that possibility, unless their crime is not the type to be punished by prison in the first place. Before mental health court sentences someone to incarceration, it will usually implement lighter forms of punishment, called *sanctions,* in an effort to help the defendant be more successful in the treatment plan. The sanctions tend to be more frequent scrutiny, such as more visits with a therapist, more drug tests, or more meetings with the judge, but they might also be short stints in jail or other compromises on freedom.

CASE MANAGEMENT

With the treatment plan in place, a defendant has to work his way through the agreed-on series of programs and tasks. This is a lot of work and it takes a lot of time. The defendant has to do his part; relatives cannot do the tasks that the defendant is assigned to do. For example, if a behavioral therapist requires the defendant to make a list of alternate ways of responding to something that happened, then only the defendant—and not his wife—should think of items to list, and only he should write them down. If a defendant is supposed to describe his ideal peer-support partner, household members may need to stay out of the way for a couple of evenings to give the defendant space and time to think about priorities. The defendant will regularly have to make and fulfill plans and then report on them.

The activities that mental health court defendants have to complete and the reports that they have to present demonstrate how they are taking responsibility. Some of their most critical reports are their routine meetings with the judge. These typically take just a few minutes but convey a lot of information about how the defendant is improving. The judge will watch, over time, for pride and optimism to emerge. These effects of treatment become evident when the defendant's reports tell what he hopes to do next and demonstrate that he now approaches people and problems differently than he did prior to engaging in the treatment plan.

Of course, the judge will not ask obvious leading questions like "Do you still think it was necessary to punch your boss when he told you you'd have to stay late?" Anybody going through mental health court because of an assault charge knows the right answer to that kind of question. The judge will ask more open-ended questions and then watch the defendant's body language for clues about sincerity and thoughtfulness. For example, "What's different about your job plans, now that you're in this treatment program?" "How do you think you're doing in your treatment program?" Some of the judge's questions will be yes or no questions, the answers to which may already be in the file: "Are you going to all of your AA meetings?" Initially, the defendant's answer will most likely just be one word, but eventually, when the treatment plan is really working, she will spontaneously begin to elaborate: "Yes sir. I even go early and set up the chairs. And last week I said something that made a guy really think about his life; he told me so."

If, for example, as a defendant, your youngest sister Laura reaches certain landmarks in her treatment, the judge can—but does not have to—turn the punishment system into a reward system. For example, the judge could allow Laura to come less frequently to the judicial meetings, reduce the amount of months or weeks that she has to participate in the mental health court program (if the treatment team has recommended such a reduction), lower the severity of her charges, or even drop some of the charges. The last two actions may sound surprising. Laura pled guilty to the crime(s), so why use the word *charges*? (Charges refer to the crimes that got her into trouble.) As long as your sister's case is still open, and it is open while she works through her treatment plan, the events that landed Laura in court still count as charges and the judge can still adjust the outcome of the case.

HOW ARE CRIME VICTIMS' INTERESTS REPRESENTED IN MENTAL HEALTH COURTS?

So far, we have discussed people charged with having committed a crime (defendants), but, remember, many crimes also have victims who have suffered because of the crime. Victims, like defendants, get to avoid the spectacle of open criminal court when the case is in mental health court. Victims do not have to relive trauma from the criminal event during mental health court procedures, and they do not have to endure onlookers and possible press coverage. They can still collect financial restitution if the crime caused expenses, and they can see societal benefits from the perpetrator's reformation. They may even realize that their own role in this more humane and healing treatment of the defendant is honorable: rather than merely being cast as victims, they are participants in fixing something.

Recognizing that victims can at least partially heal from their victimization by seeing the perpetrator punished and by having a chance to speak against the perpetrator, experts recommend several ways to allow victims to interact with the mental health court:

- At the intake stage, prosecutors reviewing criminal court files for possible transfer to mental health court can give victims the opportunity to provide impressions of the defendant's mental health or victim impact statements about the crime's effect on themselves and their families. These testimonies from the victims, which can be written or spoken, would then be considered in the decision about whether a case belongs in mental health court as well as in the creation of the treatment plans for the defendant.
- Mental health courts can implement the domestic violence court practice of holding "judicial review hearings," where victims come to watch or testify as witnesses. In these specially convened hearings, the judge hears reports only about the defendant's compliance with requirements involving the victim. For example, is the defendant making the agreed-upon financial installments? Did the defendant send the required apology letter? Is the defendant abiding by the "no contact" order?
- If a victim needs to interact directly *with* the defendant, rather than speak *about* the defendant, in order to work through his or her own recovery, the mental health court can implement participation in community-based mediation with the victim as part of the defendant's treatment plan.
- When victims want to participate orally in any of the previously listed communications, but do not want to be in the presence of the defendant, mental health court can arrange a teleconference or Internet video conversation.

HOW TO Support Mental Health Courts

The number of mental health courts around the country is constantly increasing, but your community may not have one yet. You may want to encourage your court system to start one. If families do not create a demand, the local justice system may not be able to justify the expenses and intensive labor necessary to operate a mental health court. You can get the movement underway by writing letters to the editor of your local bar association's publication and to the editor of your local newspaper.

You may want to rally a group of families to send letters to your local criminal court. To find like-minded families who could join you in the letter-writing campaign, search the online archives of newspapers for terms like *mentally ill defendant, bipolar* AND *court, schizophrenic* AND *police*. The goal in searching news articles with these terms is to identify families whose relative has made news for being involved with a crime and having a mental illness.

You can also find like-minded families through your NAMI chapter and by supplying flyers to any therapy practices that offer family support groups for well relatives. The flyers could either invite people to a meeting about mental health court or just give facts about mental health courts and instructions for sending letters to the head judge in your local court system. If you cannot find instructions for writing to the court system, call your county law library or the reference desk at your public library.

If your community already has a mental health court, keep your eyes and ears open for anything that you can do to make it better. Maybe you can spearhead a fundraiser to supply some sort of equipment that the court needs. Maybe you can lobby the court system to give the mental health court a paint job, or a more private location, or a password-accessible online scheduling tool, and so on.

Or, you may just want to be involved in your own family member's case in mental health court. Family members normally have no place there, but, as with so many services, you can reach out to your loved one's defense lawyer or case manager and offer to serve as an information source or to provide rides or reminders that will ensure that your relative gets to her appointments. And, finally, when you know about any of your relative's mental health court obligations, you can say encouraging words and, at least in the beginning, be sure that she has the time, space, and supplies to fulfill those obligations.

RESOURCES FOR MENTAL HEALTH COURT

1. There is a portal to mental health courts all over the country at samhsa. gov/gains-center.
2. The HIPAA rules about privacy are in Title 20 of the Code of Federal Regulations, Parts 160 and 164. The regulations on Confidentiality of Substance Abuse Patient Records are in Title 42 of the Code of Federal Regulations, Part 2. They are available online for free via ecfr.gov or in a handy guide compiled by the National Governors Association specifically for law enforcement and corrections agencies. The title is: *HIPAA, Corrections, Law Enforcement, and the Courts* (nga.org).
3. The expert report on victims' rights and mental health court is *A Guide to the Role of Crime Victims in Mental Health Courts,* and it is free online at csgjusticecenter.org.
4. There is a very good manual about mental health court operations that includes full case-handling process descriptions from several different mental health courts. The manual is called *Criminal Justice Interventions for Offenders with Mental Illness,* and it is available at www.urban.org.
5. The Council of State Governments offers an excellent free online curriculum on setting up a mental health court (at learning. csgjusticecenter.org).
6. The Bureau of Justice Assistance has a free online manual titled *Mental Health Courts: A Primer for Policy Makers and Practitioners* (available at www.bja.gov).
7. Mental Health America has a strong advocacy statement on behalf of mental health courts at mentalhealthamerica.net.
8. The Treatment Advocacy Center (treatmentadvocacycenter.org) conducted and published results of a nationwide research study on mental health courts in *Mental Health Diversion Practices: A Survey of the States.* This organization works "to promote mental health laws and policies which, if fully implemented by state mental health systems, would

minimize—if never fully eliminate—the tragedy of people with severe mental illness falling into the clutches of the criminal justice system." Its website includes opinion pieces and legal briefs as well as other valuable examples of criminal justice advocacy materials.

9. The Bazelon Center for Mental Health Law has published several strong, favorable reports about mental health courts at bazelon.org.

11

Criminal Court Trials
and Mental Illness

You have heard the phrases on the news "incompetent to stand trial," "not guilty by reason of insanity," "insanity defense." Now that your family member is the one facing trial, you find yourself questioning whether these legal concepts generally help or hurt defendants who have mental illness.

HOW DEFENDANTS WITH MENTAL ILLNESS ARE TREATED UNIQUELY IN CRIMINAL COURT

As discussed in the previous chapter, not all defendants with mental illness have the opportunity to participate in mental health court. In fact, many such defendants end up being tried in standard criminal courts, which have various ways of treating defendants who have mental illness differently from all other defendants. At the beginning of a case, when the prosecutor first presents charges against a defendant who has mental illness, or at some point after that, but before the case goes to trial, the defendant may be judged not competent to stand trial. Or, if the criminal trial does go forward, the verdict can reflect the defendant's mental illness either by finding him *not guilty by reason of insanity* or, in some states, *guilty but mentally ill*. These verdicts can result whether or not there was ever a question about competence to stand trial. Even in jurisdictions that do not offer the option of a guilty but mentally ill verdict, courts can impose a less harsh sentence in consideration of a defendant's mental illness.

When any of these judgments apply to a defendant who has been collecting disability benefits from the Social Security Administration (SSA), whether Supplemental Security Income (SSI) or Social Security Disability Insurance (SSDI), and the defendant is placed in a mental health treatment facility instead of a correctional facility, the disability benefits will stop, just as if he were in a correctional facility. It is SSA policy that anyone "confined in an institution at public expense in connection with a criminal case" is not eligible for disability benefits. Medicare Part A benefits will continue, but Medicaid benefits will not. Family members who collect auxiliary benefits from SSA in connection with a relative's disability will continue to get their auxiliary benefits while the person with the disability is confined. (See Chapter 2 for fuller coverage of SSA benefits.)

To be sure that your confined family member does not get paid undeserved benefits that he will have to pay back, contact your local SSA office as soon as his confinement begins. If a disability payment arrives after he is confined, return it to the SSA immediately. Enclose a copy of the court order, if you have it, or at least a note explaining the court-ordered confinement. When your family member is ready to be released from confinement, his caseworker at the facility will likely initiate his return to benefits. This should be one of the first things you ask about when he comes home. If a caseworker did not handle it, then your relative can contact SSA himself with proof of his release and a request that they resume his disability payments.

HOW TO Find a Criminal Defense Lawyer

Before reading about the criminal law issues that are unique to defendants with mental illness, you may wonder how to get a criminal defense lawyer who will be competent and respectful of your family member. Here are some ideas.

- Look through your local newspaper's online archive for reports about past defendants with mental illness and contact the lawyers in those cases. You will have to hunt around using the news provider's search box, so remember to search for similar and related terms, such as *lawyer* and *attorney, mental* and *psychiatric*, or *judge* and *court*. Also, just to be thorough, use the names of specific mental diagnoses in your search.
- Visit the websites of local mental health organizations and find the lists of present and past members of the boards of directors. In those lists, you will find numerous people with Esq. after their names. Esq. is the abbreviation for "Esquire," which is the professional title for lawyers. Lawyers who volunteer their time to serve on the boards of mental health organizations are likely to understand clients who have mental illness.
- Using the search box in the Martindale-Hubbell Law Directory (http://www.martindale.com/), enter your city name, the word *criminal*, and terms like *psychological* and *mental health*.
- Go to your local bar association's website and navigate your way to its list of various divisions or sections. If there is a section on health law or psychiatry and law or mental health, see if you can click through to a website for that group—just so you can browse around for names and other information about local experts in mental health law. Also, looking again at the bar association's main page, find the link to publications and try to peruse any magazines or newsletters that the organization produces. See who wrote articles in the publications and who is talked about in the articles. If they have a search box, enter *mental* and *psychology* and *psychiatry* and similar terms to see if they lead you to any mention of local experts in mental health law. The American Bar Association has a portal to state and local bar associations at americanbar.org.
- If you have a mental health court in your area, peruse its website and its annual report for the names of lawyers who practice in the court. If none of the lawyers will take private clients, which means that they are all public

defenders and prosecutors, at least ask them for referrals to good lawyers who will understand and represent a client with mental illness. The National Center for State Courts maintains a list of links to mental health courts at http://www.ncsc.org/.
- Remember that your relative may be eligible for public defender services; you may not need to hire a private lawyer.

WHAT DOES "NOT COMPETENT TO STAND TRIAL" MEAN, AND HOW DO YOU PROVE IT?

A defendant is judged *not competent to stand trial* when she cannot understand the court proceedings and cannot participate in her own defense. Participating in her defense includes:

- Being able to talk coherently about what led to getting arrested
- Being able to answer the lawyers' questions
- Understanding what the lawyers and judge are saying
- Having the mental wherewithal to follow instructions.

These are general criteria; some courts will not require all of them in order to find someone not competent to stand trial. Notice that being not competent to stand trial is only about the defendant's current mental state, not about the mental state that she was in when the crime happened.

Only the defense lawyer, the prosecutor, or the judge can open an inquiry into a defendant's competence. For example, let's look at the situation of your nephew, Victor. If his lawyer doubts that Victor is competent, she must file a petition asking the judge to investigate Victor's competence to stand trial. The petition will explain why the lawyer suspects a lack of competence. If the judge is the one with the suspicion, of course, no petition is necessary. Whether the judge approves a lawyer's petition or has her own doubts about the defendant's fitness, she will then arrange to have a forensic psychologist or psychiatrist examine Victor.

State law sets the number of days within which the determination of competence has to be made, typically 30 to 60 days. There is no limit to the number of interactions that the psychologist or psychiatrist can have with the defendant in that time. The defendant may remain in jail, may be confined in a mental hospital, or may be out on bail and getting outpatient mental health treatment during the competence examination period.

The forensic psychologist or psychiatrist will not be someone who already knows the defendant, although it may be someone who works in a community mental health setting rather than at the jail. The court will pay for this examination or series of examinations. Most of the time, the mental health professional has to figure out whether the defendant, in this case Victor, is competent to stand trial and, if the defendant is not yet competent, whether he can be made competent to stand trial.

The forensic psychologist or psychiatrist will meet privately with Victor. This examiner—most likely using one of a few common questionnaires—will ask Victor about trials generally and his case in particular. One such questionnaire invites the defendant to read or hear simple stories and finish sentences about them and the defendant's own case. These partial sentences would be statements like "When Pat was accused of the crime . . ." and "If the jury finds me guilty . . . ."

Another questionnaire requires defendants to describe and predict things about the trial: "Who can ask you questions when you're on the stand?" "Does your lawyer have good plans or are there some things that should be done differently?" Far beyond correct answers to these questions, the psychologist will be assessing the defendant's distractibility, accuracy, confusion, tendency toward fantasy, and other aspects of functioning.

Understand that competence to stand trial is not the same as competence in other legal contexts. Someone who has a guardian may be competent to stand trial but not competent to manage her own affairs. Someone who is competent to have custody of his children may not be competent to stand trial. Again, competence to stand trial is entirely about the person's ability to participate in the defense.

The psychologist or psychiatrist reports back to the judge in writing, and both lawyers will get to review that written report. The lawyers and judge may have agreed in advance to accept the psychologist's or psychiatrist's opinion as the final decision on competence to stand trial. But the judge can always gather more information after reading the report by calling the psychologist or psychiatrist to testify in a hearing about the defendant's competence. The judge will normally use her own knowledge and experience, the lawyers' impressions, and the forensic psychology or psychiatry report to make the final ruling on whether the defendant is competent.

What Is the Significance of Being Not Competent To Stand Trial?

A defendant who is found incompetent to stand trial is ordered, by the court, to get psychiatric and psychological treatment that will make her able to understand court proceedings and to participate in the defense. The judge will require routine reports from the mental health providers to be sure that the defendant is participating in care and to keep track of her readiness for trial preparation. The time that a defendant spends getting healthy enough to stand trial will often, but not necessarily, count as "time served" if the trial results in a conviction.

Unless the case has received much media attention, the eventual jury will not know when a defendant has gone through a period of not being competent to stand trial. Nothing about the competence evaluation or the subsequent treatment can be used as evidence in the case. Competence for trial is irrelevant to whatever happened at the crime scene and whether this defendant committed that crime.

In cases of defendants who are so extremely mentally ill that they may end up having inpatient mental treatment for as long as they potentially could have spent in jail, the prosecutor's office can drop the charges in criminal court and instead go to civil court with a petition to have the defendant involuntarily committed. This would only happen when the mental health reports to the court consistently conclude that a defendant is not improving enough to competently answer the competence for trial questions. Since the civil court may not issue the commitment, the prosecutor does not have to drop the criminal charges before the civil court rules on the commitment petition.

If the civil court does order inpatient commitment, the defendant (who is now a patient) has to stay in the mental health facility until the court orders her release. In other words, court-ordered inpatient treatment ends only when the court is convinced that it should end, and not when a patient opts to leave the facility.

HOW TO Be Useful in Trial Competence Inquiries

There is little for families to do at this point in a prosecution. However, if your relative, say, your sister Jenna, has been charged with a crime and you have a solid and honest alibi for her, you will want to notify her defense lawyer about that alibi. If you were with Jenna in a place other than the crime scene at the time of the crime, or if you know someone else who was, then it is possible that Jenna has either mistakenly confessed to the crime or failed to convey this critically important information. In other words, she may not be participating effectively in the defense if she got charged with a crime that happened when she was somewhere else! Tell all of this to her defense lawyer in writing, and specifically say whether you suspect that your sister is incompetent to stand trial. As always, if a spoken conversation is the only way to get the lawyer's attention, then have that conversation and then send a follow-up note to be sure that your full message gets across.

You do not need to give a full mental health history in the communications with the lawyer, but you can help your sister's defense by saying that she is treated for a mental health problem and by explaining how she acts and communicates during traumatic times. You will know if there have been past circumstances when she has been willing to say anything at all just to get out of a conversation. You know how little it takes to confuse Jenna or to throw her into a false belief. You know whether sometimes she just craves attention of any kind. You know how easily she talks from her imagination instead of her memory. But the defense lawyer, especially one who is barely spending time with your sister, probably does not know any of this and, without your input, may not realize that Jenna could be incompetent to stand trial.

Another essential time to interject your opinion of your sister's competence for trial is when you learn that she is waiving the right to have a lawyer. Your suspicions will probably be higher if she also waived the right to avoid a warrantless search or the right to remain silent. Although not every court will necessarily order a competence evaluation just because a family member claims that a defendant's mental illness caused her to opt out of having a lawyer, you can at least remind the judge about the U.S. Supreme Court case of *Indiana v. Edwards*.

In that case, the defendant Edwards argued that he should not have been required to have lawyers represent him in his two criminal trials. He asserted that, having been found competent to stand trial (after a period of not being competent to stand trial), he was capable of presenting his own defense. The Supreme Court ruled against Edwards, concluding that being competent to cooperate in defense is not the same as being competent to handle the whole defense alone without a lawyer. Courts all over the country, however, are still inconsistent about using the *Edwards* precedent. In some cases, the judges are simply not convinced that a defendant's mental illness is a legitimate reason for denying him the option of handling his own defense. In other cases, the judges think that defendants with mental illness do need to have lawyers to protect them, whether or not they want professional legal help, just in case the mental illness hampers the defendants' judgment, focus, or perceptions. Still, the case is an important example to present when you want your loved one to be represented by a professional criminal defense lawyer.

Finally, in addition to putting the word out if you think that your relative's mental condition is causing her to implicate herself in the crime or waive her constitutional rights, you can offer to serve as a witness in the competency hearings or as a source of background information. Notify the defense lawyer and the judge's clerk if you are available to serve in one of these roles.

NOT GUILTY BY REASON OF INSANITY: THE INSANITY DEFENSE

When a defendant is competent to stand trial, her mental illness may be raised as part of her defense in a claim that she is not guilty because she was "insane" when she committed the crime. A good defense lawyer will raise every possible claim to give the jury reasonable doubt about whether the accused defendant committed the crime. In fact, it is common for criminal defense lawyers to present multiple different defenses in a single case, including some that contradict each other. Among the various claims that the defendant did not commit the crime at all, the lawyer will also raise any affirmative defenses that could make the defendant at least look less guilty. An affirmative defense is one that says, "Yes, but . . . ."

The plea of *not guilty by reason of insanity* is an affirmative defense because its message is: even if this defendant did commit this crime, he only did it because his mental illness made him "unable to appreciate the nature and quality of the wrongfulness of his acts."

This quote is from Title 18 U.S. Code §17 and applies to federal crimes. State cases and codes similarly allow this defense when mental health symptoms compromised a defendant's ability to understand either what she did or what was wrong about it. It is very hard to prove this point, so verdicts of *not guilty by reason of insanity* are not common; some states do not even permit this defense.

There are lots of ways that mental illness can cause someone to commit a crime. A few examples include:

- A post-traumatic stress trigger overtook Carla's mind so fully and quickly that she violently attacked somebody.
- A compulsion led Morris to steal or vandalize.
- A narcissistic personality disorder inspired Lakeisha to evade taxes or commit insurance fraud.
- An extremely irrational delusion drove Chris to stalk or kidnap someone.

The key to the not guilty by reason of insanity defense is proving that, had it not been for the mental problem, this crime would not have happened. Many crimes have two components to prove: That the defendant committed the criminal act and that the defendant intended to commit the criminal act. Often, the not guilty by reason of insanity defense applies when the lawyer shows that the mental problem replaced the defendant's intent. For example:

> *The defendant did not intend to damage county property; his delusions convinced him at that moment that he had to remove the upholstery from the bus seat because it displayed a demonic message.*

When the insanity defense is not about intent, it can be about presence of mind. This may be the explanation when someone has a dissociative disorder and truly was not herself during the crime. Here are two examples:

> *All she could see right then was the memory of her father pulling off his shoe so he could beat her with it.*
>
> *Her melancholy was such a thick and inescapable fog that it surrounded her, blocking every sight and sound and rolling into her nose and mouth when she breathed. She covered her toddler's face with a pillow to keep the fog from getting inside of him, too.*

The Goal of Claiming "Not Guilty by Reason of Insanity"

Not every criminal case is a "who done it?" mystery. When there is clear evidence that the defendant committed the crime, and the lawyer does not expect to get an ordinary not guilty verdict, the wise trial strategy is to fight for the lightest possible punishment. The defense lawyer will raise the insanity defense as a way of getting the defendant into a treatment facility or at least into some form of treatment-oriented punishment in the corrections system. Both of these options are likely to be less harsh than being incarcerated in the general prison population.

Sometimes, decisions of not guilty by reason of insanity are arranged by the prosecutor, defense lawyer, and judge as an alternative to holding a trial. The lawyers make the arrangements and present them to the judge when they are both convinced by the pretrial evidence that the defendant did not know what he was doing and did not realize what was wrong with it when he did it. They cannot usually make this arrangement without the defendant's approval. Most of the time, the defendant has to agree to go without a trial and to participate in mental health evaluations and treatment. Some courts have appointed representatives to accept the terms of the arrangement on behalf of defendants who were deemed to be too mentally ill to participate in it.

When there is a trial and a defense lawyer raises the defense of not guilty by reason of insanity, the idea is to convince the judge and jury that the defendant is already suffering by having to live with mental illness, that the defendant is a sick person—not a bad person—and that the crime would not have happened if it she did not have a mental illness, so she should not have to also suffer from the harshest criminal punishment.

Proving That the Defendant Was Insane When Committing the Crime

The defense lawyer can call witnesses who saw the defendant immediately before, during, and soon after the crime. The witnesses will testify about the behavior they saw and any statements they heard from the defendant. The lawyer or the prosecutor will also present relevant written and video evidence by and about the defendant. For example, the prosecutor could introduce as evidence a threatening letter or social media post written by the defendant to show that she intended to commit the crime. The defense lawyer will then try to convince the court that the writing, video, or social media post is not proof of intent, but proof that the defendant did not know right from wrong or understand that she was doing something illegal.

Both lawyers will have expert witnesses testify about the writings. This part of the trial is called "the battle of the experts." The expert for the prosecution and the expert for the defense will have similar professional training and experience. They will be psychologists or psychiatrists who have seen these kinds of writings before and have treated many patients with diagnoses and histories like the defendant's. They will review the police report, the defendant's mental health record, and other documents associated with the crime. They will review surveillance video and look for physical signs of the defendant's mental condition.

Each expert will meet separately with the defendant to find out about her mental state at the time of the offense. Although there are some standard assessments for experts to use in these examinations, they are not exactly fixed lists of questions. Instead, the standards recommend certain categories of information for the examiner to investigate.

Meeting with the defendant at different times, these experts may get different answers to similar questions or develop such dissimilar relationships with the defendant that their conversations really diverge. For example:

- One expert talking with an accused rapist may learn only about his fixation on a particular victim or category of victims. Another expert, speaking with the same accused rapist, may additionally find out about relevant traumatic experiences in his upbringing.
- Two different experts examining a computer hacker may both identify her power fixation, but only one expert may discover that the defendant also self-mutilates.

Inevitably, the expert witnesses will come to court with some overlapping impressions as well as some contrasting information.

Challenges to Proving "Not Guilty by Reason of Insanity"

Luck, money, and time are behind every successful defense of this type. Luck is critical because, without it, there are no nosy neighbors available to describe the noises they heard, there is no physical evidence representing the frenzy that went on, and nobody saw the defendant before or after the crime. Money is necessary to hire expert witnesses—psychiatrists and psychologists who know all about the defendant's disorder, trauma, medicine, his combination of impairments, and his reaction. Time makes it possible for the lawyer to think about strategies, to read applicable past cases, to meet plenty of times with the defendant and those who know the defendant, and to interview everyone who can give technical explanations.

Another challenge is the ebb and flow of mental symptoms. For example,

- A defendant who committed a crime only because the right combination of triggers and conditions came together that one day may not look "insane" in court.
- A defendant whose mental disorder is normally controlled or whose symptoms simmer pretty consistently may seem, to the judge, just like every other infrequent criminal defendant who is in court for just one stray crime.
- A defendant who was taken from the crime scene straight to a mental health center may have had sufficient time and treatment to feel completely different in meetings with lawyers and expert witnesses than he felt before and during the crime.
- Some defendants whose mental health has improved between the crime and the court preparations may even turn on themselves and compromise their own defense.

What Is the Legal Significance of Being Not Guilty by Reason of Insanity?

Being found "not guilty by reason of insanity" is not the standard form of a "not guilty" verdict. In a criminal case that does not involve this defense, when the judge or jury has found a defendant to be not guilty, the verdict means that the defendant did not commit the crime and is free to leave the courthouse and to control her own life. But when a defendant is found to be not guilty by reason of insanity, it means that (1) the judge or jury concluded that the defendant's mental illness was responsible for the crime, (2) the defendant did commit the crime, and (3) the defendant probably should not be released into the community.

Unless the criminal case was in federal court, state statutes direct what happens when a defendant is found to be not guilty by reason of insanity. If the case was in federal court, then the U.S. Code sets forth the procedure for institutionalizing the defendant after the trial. In federal cases, the defendant will be taken from the courtroom and transported to a "suitable" mental health facility.

Within 40 days of starting the commitment, the former defendant (who is now a detainee) has to have a hearing to determine her dangerousness. At that hearing, the court will determine whether releasing the detainee will "create a substantial risk of bodily injury to another person or serious damage to property of another." If the court does think that those risks exist, the detainee will be put under the control of the U.S. Attorney General.

The Attorney General's office will then transfer control of the detainee out of the federal government and over to the most appropriate agency in the state where the trial was held or where the detainee lives. In other words, the state will take over the costs of this person's inpatient treatment. The state agency will then place the detainee in an inpatient psychiatric facility, which may be the same one that the federal government has been paying for, and will give the director of that facility responsibility for notifying the federal court when the person is no longer a risk to people or property. At that point, the court can either hold a hearing or order the detainee to be discharged without a hearing.

If the original criminal trial was in state court and the defendant was found to be not guilty by reason of insanity, then, as noted above, a state statute will direct what happens next with the person. Some states simply require a post-trial psychiatric evaluation followed by different outcomes depending on the results of that evaluation. In some states, as soon as the verdict is announced, the prosecutor has to file a petition to have the judge order an involuntary commitment. In other states, involuntary commitment is automatic. Furthermore, in some states, the former defendant's next placement depends on whether the crime involved bodily harm. Rarely does the former defendant get to go straight home. Much of the time, the commitment lasts only as long as it takes to make the detainee no longer dangerous.

If the state does send a former defendant to a psychiatric facility upon a verdict of not guilty by reason of insanity, it may be the policy in that state to limit the maximum institutional commitment to the amount of time that this person would have spent in jail, had she been found guilty. Even when this is the policy, a psychiatric facility will not release a dangerous person into the community simply because she has spent a particular amount of time in the facility; the state's ordinary standards for involuntary commitments will justify keeping a dangerous person institutionalized.

HOW TO Be Useful in a "Not Guilty by Reason of Insanity" Case

Lawyers weigh risky stuff in deciding whether to raise a "not guilty by reason of insanity" defense. If the defense works, your relative may not have to go to prison. If it does not work, it may make the jury dislike your family member. Whether or not the defense works, your relative's case may get media attention just because of the insanity claim. And, of course, the claim adds a lot of extra scrutiny and hassle for your loved one to endure: more hearings, more forensic mental health exams, and more delays while the court and the mental health facility try to schedule communications with each other.

You will not help matters by guessing whether the insanity defense is the right strategy to use. Instead, devote your time and energy to promoting your family member's due process rights.

When the lawyers and court personnel are too busy with the details of dozens of cases, you need to be the one who makes sure that your family member gets the speedy trial that is promised in the Sixth Amendment. Ask the defense lawyer if you can have an outline showing how these cases evolve. Consider making a calendar where you can note deadlines, events, and the names and phone numbers of people who are supposed to handle each item. Make friends with the defense lawyer. Do not become a nuisance; just be a caring and useful resource. That way, you can keep in touch to ensure that your loved one's processes are not delayed or overlooked.

Whenever you call the lawyer's office for information (for example, *Has that mental evaluation been scheduled yet?*), offer to do something in return, such as: *Is there anything that I can do to help you facilitate the meeting?* Compliment the person who assists you: *You are so efficient. I am always amazed by how much you know. You are so good at your job.* And remember to thank the person: *I really appreciate all that you are doing to help my husband. I am grateful for all that you do.*

Understand that the lawyer may have tactical reasons for pacing the case more quickly or more slowly than you would expect. Also keep in mind that the lawyer has a lot of information that you do not have regarding the legal system and your relative. There will likely be times when you feel left out or ignored, although the lawyer has to exclude you for professional reasons, such as protecting both client confidentiality and the case strategy.

The lawyer's office will not necessarily have answers to all of your questions; if you don't know where else to get the answers, it is okay to ask someone at the lawyer's office to tell you who will have the information and how you can contact that person. Maybe you are trying to find out when the next hearing is scheduled, or when the forensic report is due to be submitted to the judge, or how to find something on the court's website. The court clerk will be able to answer these court-related questions. He may even be able to show you how to access the case schedule online.

Of course, when you know that someone other than the court clerk has control over information, contact that person. If you can find information independently, without having to call the clerk or law firm, then do so. As you search for information in connection with your family member's court case and as you think about how you will use the information, remember that your purpose is merely to make sure that your family member gets processed as carefully and efficiently as possible; that is due process.

GUILTY BUT MENTALLY ILL

Some states have a guilty but mentally ill (GBMI) statute that offers a middle option between (1) finding someone not guilty by reason of insanity and (2) finding her guilty and punishing her as if she had the mental state to be guilty of the crime. Suppose your friend Sean is on trial for state business tax fraud. Sean understands intellectually that it is wrong to cheat on taxes, but his mental illness causes him to be so extremely distrustful of the government that he refuses to pay taxes. In other words, his mental illness prevents him from realizing that failing to be truthful on a tax return is wrong. Remember that someone can only be found not guilty by reason of insanity if mental illness prevented him from understanding what he did and what was wrong with what he did. Sean's mental illness affected his criminal act, but since he did know what he was doing, he cannot succeed in claiming that he was not guilty by reason of insanity. If he lives in a state that has a GBMI statute and he has been found to be guilty but mentally ill, he is entitled to have mental health treatment included in his punishment.

This entitlement tends to require that the prison provide the inmate with on-going mental health care and possibly, or sometimes just initially, housing in a mental health cellblock. In some states, GBMI status is basically a requirement that the inmate get psychiatric clearance from a hospital before being imprisoned. When a crime is punished by probation, rather than imprisonment, a GBMI verdict can mean that mental health care is a condition of the probation. Then, if the probationer does not keep up with the required mental health care regime, she will have to go to prison.

HOW MENTAL HEALTH EVIDENCE AFFECTS CRIMINAL PUNISHMENT

When a verdict is reached in a criminal trial and the defendant is found to be guilty, we say that the "guilt phase" of the trial is over and the "sentencing phase" or "penalty phase" begins. The sentencing phase is the part of the trial in which the judge decides what the defendant's punishment will be. Criminal punishments are not completely arbitrary—the judge is limited by strict parameters called *sentencing guidelines* that establish a range of punishments to go with each crime. You may have heard about the punishment ranges on the news when reporters say, for example, "If convicted, he can get 5 to 10 years in prison." In felonies and cases involving multiple misdemeanors or a single misdemeanor that resulted in serious loss or damage, the sentencing phase involves a whole process that examines the particular defendant's circumstances in light of the sentencing guidelines.

If a defendant's mental illness was not necessarily the clear cause of the crime, her lawyer will not have claimed that she was not guilty by reason of insanity. If she was not found to be guilty but mentally ill or is not in a state that permits GBMI pleas, the judge will not have an obligation to incorporate mental health treatment into the punishment. Still, the judge has the discretion to include mental health treatment as part of the sentence and to reduce the severity of the punishment in light of how mental illness contributed to the defendant's criminal behavior and in light of how the sentence is likely to affect the defendant's mental health. The judge will be most inclined to do this if the defense lawyer presents facts about her client's mental health during the sentencing phase.

Specifically, the defense lawyer can submit a court document asking the judge to *take judicial notice* of the defendant's mental health. In this document, the lawyer will explain how the possible punishments are likely to provoke symptoms and to contradict the goals of criminal punishment. She will ask the judge to mitigate (lessen) the punishment in consideration of the mental health issue and she will recommend the most desirable punishment for her client. The prosecutor is also permitted to provide explanations and recommendations as the judge considers what sentence to impose.

Most of the critical input to the judge during the sentencing phase will come from a pre-sentence investigation. The judge orders this investigation, and a court-appointed officer carries it out. This officer is not a police officer. It can be someone whose full-time job is to conduct pre-sentence investigations or it may be someone else who works in the court system and handles pre-sentence investigations among other responsibilities.

The investigator will collect background information about the defendant and compile it into a pre-sentence report for the judge. The investigation will likely include interviews with family members and with mental health professionals who treat the defendant. It will probably involve an independent psychiatric examination, which the court will pay for. The content of the interviews and any examinations will be summarized and attached to the pre-sentence report.

After reading the lawyers' documents and the pre-sentence report, the judge will hold a sentencing hearing. At this hearing, the judge will identify all of the items that are on file for the hearing: the defendant's past criminal record, the pre-sentence report, the lawyers' documents, and possibly some other papers, such as a written statement from the victim and letters from people who know the defendant, depending on the circumstances. The judge will name the defendant's crimes and will talk about how the sentencing guidelines rank the severity of those crimes. He will note whether the state has a GBMI statute and whether the defense lawyer has raised a GBMI claim in the case. Lawyers generally submit a GBMI claim as a fallback when they present their claim that the defendant is not guilty by reason of insanity. It will say something like, "If you do not find my client to be not guilty by reason of insanity, and you believe that she is guilty, please consider her to be guilty but mentally ill."

The judge will give certain witnesses, including you, the victim, and the victim's loved ones, time to testify—unless you have already submitted your testimony in writing. Your testimony will be about your family member's good qualities. The victim and his family's testimony will be about how the crime has affected them. The judge will invite the prosecutor and defense lawyer to make any final oral comments advocating for a sentence that is at either the lighter or the harsher end of the sentencing guidelines. The judge may question the lawyers or the defendant at any point in the hearing. The hearing will come to an end when the judge imposes the sentence.

HOW TO Participate in Criminal Court Sentencing

Unless the defense lawyer thinks that you may make things worse for your family member, you can participate in the pre-sentence investigation and the sentencing hearing. Occasionally, a judge decides the sentence just on the basis of the pre-sentence report, or the lawyers negotiate a mutually acceptable sentence after reading the report. In these cases, the hearing is merely a 5-minute/no-witness session to formally declare the sentence.

If your relative lives out of town and never told you about the criminal charges or the trial and never told the defense lawyer about you, the sentencing phase may be your first chance to provide any help in the situation. Even then, you may only get that chance if the pre-sentence investigator discovers your relationship and makes contact with you.

Keep in mind that the pre-sentence investigator is not interested in your feelings; it will not help your convicted relative if you cry through the whole conversation or talk about yourself. The pre-sentence process is about finding the most appropriate punishment. If there is a chance that your relative can get lighter punishment or punishment that incorporates treatment for her mental illness, you can help that happen. You may know information that nobody else can convey.

Give the investigator facts about the kind of human being your family member is: Explain how he has been a good friend or a good citizen. Identify respectable groups that he has belonged to. Provide examples of ways that he is kind, helpful, or generous to other people. If you know that your relative has been working on self-improvement, talk about that and provide contact information to help the investigator connect with whoever helps in that self-improvement. Make sure the investigator knows if your loved one has made recent efforts to get an education or treatment. If your relative has a good boss who can attest to his responsibility, put the investigator in contact with that boss. And then call the boss yourself and give a heads-up to expect the investigator's call.

In the unlikely event that the investigator only asks you "yes or no" questions or mails you a short questionnaire that calls for only limited information, just push your information through any opening you get. If it is a "yes/no" conversation, add the word "and" to every reply. For example:

Q: Did your cousin Logan ever take illegal drugs?

A: No and because he is so diligent about his chores and other daily routines, he never would take drugs.

Q: If your sister Hannah does get a prison sentence, will she be allowed to live with you when she gets released?

A: Yes and I will be glad to have her because she is a quiet, gentle soul who will be extremely frightened if she lands in prison; she only got wound up in this crime because she was frightened and trying to defend herself.

If you get a written questionnaire that does not give you room to explain things, attach extra pages and number your compassionate, honest, and descriptive answers carefully so that the investigator can tell which answer goes with which question.

At a pre-sentence hearing, your information goals are to generate sympathy and demonstrate that your relative is not the awful person that the prosecutor makes her out to be. The defense lawyer will help you think about what information to use and how you should plan to get it across. When the defense lawyer contacts you about preparing for the sentencing hearing, be honest about your ability to testify. Let the lawyer know if you are too nervous to talk in public or if you have some reason to worry that you may just make your relative look worse. You do not have to testify. Maybe you can recommend another family member who can represent the family in the hearing.

RESOURCES FOR CRIMINAL COURT TRIALS AND MENTAL ILLNESS

1. The Social Security Administration publication *Transitioning From Incarceration* has facts about disability benefits during jail and prison and court-ordered inpatient treatment. It is available online at ssa.gov/reentry.

2. Thomas Grisso's book, *Evaluating Competencies: Forensic Assessments and Instruments* (2nd ed., 2003), is about forensic psychiatrists' and psychologists' roles in court. It supplies details about the various competence assessments and evaluations that are used with defendants who have mental illnesses (see especially Chapter 4, "Competence to Stand Trial," and Chapter 6, "Not Guilty by Reason of Insanity").

3. *Indiana v. Edwards*, 554 U.S. 164; 128 S. Ct. 2379; 171 L. Ed. 2d 345 (2008), is the case about the defendant who was originally unfit to stand trial and then, when he was fit for trial, wanted to represent himself in court. You can find this case for free online via scholar.google.com.

4. If your relative does not have a private lawyer and is relying on court-appointed counsel or the public defender's office, it is possible that nobody has told him who exactly will provide the representation. If this happens, contact the court clerk (find the clerk through the court's website) and ask for the lawyer's contact information. The clerk may not give you full contact information, but you can at least get the name and other clues from the call. If you know the lawyer's name, find out how to contact him or her via Findlaw's directory at criminal.findlaw.com or through the Martindale Hubbell directory at martindale.com.

5. The federal laws about defendants with mental illness and their competence for trial are in 42 U.S.C. §§ 4241 and 4242. Find the federal statutes regarding defendants who are not guilty by reason of insanity at 18 U.S.C. § 4243. Federal statutes are free online at law.cornell.edu/uscode and at uscode.house.gov.

6. The American Bar Association's *Criminal Justice Standards on Mental Health* are influential in all courts. Standard 7–4 is about competence to stand trial. Standards 7–6 and 7–7 are about the insanity defense—not guilty by reason of insanity. Standard 7–9 is about sentencing people with mental illness. They are available online at americanbar.org.

7. Just Cause Law Collective published a helpful article titled "Working with a Public Defender" that is available online at court.rchp.com, courtesy of RC Hill Publishing.

8. To find your state's statutes on competence to stand trial, on not guilty by reason of insanity, on guilty but mentally ill or guilty but insane, or on mitigating circumstances in sentencing, go to Justia (justia.com) or the Cornell Legal Information Institute (law.cornell.edu), select your state's name from the list, navigate to the state statutes, and then type the search phrase (for example, "not guilty by reason of insanity") in quotation marks to keep the words together in the same order. Alternatively, just browse in your state's criminal code.

9. In the federal government and in each state, sentencing guidelines set the range of punishment that can be imposed for a particular crime. When deciding where a defendant's punishment fits within a sentencing guideline's range of harshness, the courts consider facts like the amount of cruelty and pain inflicted on the victim, the defendant's criminal history, and the defendant's mental health. Find the applicable guidelines at the U.S. Sentencing Commission's website (ussc.gov) or at the National Center for State Courts' links to state sentencing guidelines (ncsc.org).

10. *Criminal Mental Health and Disability Law, Evidence and Testimony* (2009), a book by John Parry, is written for lawyers and has vast information about all stages of prosecutions against defendants who are mentally ill. Section 4.08 discusses research about courts that find mental health issues to be an aggravating factor that leads to a harsher sentence rather than a mitigating factor that leads to treatment as part of the sentence.

12

Mental Illness in Jails and Prisons

You may have read that state and federal prisons in the United States have large populations of inmates with mental illness. Now that your daughter Gina is incarcerated, you would like to think that the data have resulted in quality resources and services for the inmate population. To learn specifics, search on the term mental health *and peruse general information for families on the website of your state department of corrections or of the Federal Bureau of Prisons, depending on which system Gina is in. Then, using that information along with the news you get from Gina, you will know how to demand that she gets the mental health support that she is entitled to during her incarceration.*

SOURCES OF LAW

Prisoner rights arise from constitutional provisions, legislative statutes, and administrative regulations that have been enacted by federal and state governments. People who are incarcerated in federal prisons are protected by federal statutes and regulations. People who are incarcerated in state prisons are protected by state statutes and regulations. Inmates in both federal and state prisons are protected by the U.S. Constitution's due process clause, protection against cruel and unusual punishment, equal protection against discrimination, and rights to free speech, freedom of religion, and peaceable assembly. These legal provisions enable inmates with mental illness to communicate with supportive people on the outside and to get professional psychiatric treatment on the inside. Although the U.S. Constitution applies to situations in state prisons as well as federal prisons and entitles groups and individuals to sue their state prison system in federal court, the states have their own constitutions that mirror the provisions in the U.S. Constitution, which enable inmates and their families to sue a state correctional facility in their state's court system.

When Constitutional rights and federal statutes and regulations are not honored by federal correctional facilities, inmates can take legal action pursuant to two laws:

- The Federal Prison Litigation Reform Act requires prisoners to first file their complaint through the correctional department's full system of appeals, to pay the court fees up front, and to bring court cases only if the prison's actions resulted in physical injuries.

- Section 1983 of the Civil Rights Act authorizes individuals to bring lawsuits against government officials who violate the Constitution.

Without these legal provisions, federal inmates would have no recourse against their jailers.

State constitutions and statutes set forth the obligations of state-run correctional facilities and the rights of inmates at those facilities. State regulations and policy directives, written by each state's department of corrections, tell specifically how the statutes are to be carried out and authorize individual facilities to make rules. These laws, regulations, policy directives, and rules are about state prison operations as well as inmates' access to services and the quality and quantity of services available to them. The legal rights commonly significant for prisoners with mental illness are discussed below.

The Right to Punishment That Is Not Cruel or Harmful

"The touchstone is the health of the inmate. While the prison administration may punish, it must not do so in a manner that threatens the physical and mental health of prisoners." *Young v. Quinlan*, 960 F.2d 351, 364 (3d Cir. 1992).

Guards are allowed to use physical force with prisoners, but only to the extent that it is necessary to get them under control. The fact that an inmate may be traumatized or thrown into a psychotic episode by the use of physical force is not necessarily under consideration at that moment. Guards can opt not to come to the aid of an inmate, unless they know that the inmate is at substantial risk of serious physical harm. An inmate's anxiety, paranoia, or serious fear of abandonment do not figure into that equation. Prison staff can impose deprivations as a form of punishment, but not so severely that they deprive inmates of basic human needs like food, sanitation, and light. So, preventing an inmate from attending a class that he likes or taking away some of his stress-reducing recreational time would not count as cruel and unusual punishment.

All of these common-law understandings about cruel and unusual punishment are based on physical impact rather than mental effects. The only form of prison punishment that seems to be routinely considered in light of its mental impact is solitary confinement, and it has taken numerous court cases to finally reach even this consideration.

Prisoners with severe mental illness who are left in solitary confinement suffer extremely and unjustly. They mutilate themselves, kill themselves, or sink into fathomless despondency. These known effects of torment have come to prove that solitary confinement of seriously mentally ill inmates very often violates the Eighth Amendment prohibition against cruel and unusual punishment. Prisons and correctional systems all over the country are being urged to institute treatment pods, also called cell blocks or mental health pods, where inmates with serious mental illness can be confined in individual (not shared) cells but still have human contact and be assured of receiving medication and psychiatric visits. Activists pushing for these pods and other alternatives to solitary confinement want prison officials to realize that when a prisoner with serious mental illness behaves badly enough to warrant major intervention, something needs to be fixed in his psychiatric treatment.

Perhaps the cruelest and most unusual punishment is the kind that is imposed in retaliation for exhibiting mental illness. In 2012, the Department of Justice went after a Pennsylvania prison, in part, for putting mentally ill prisoners in full-body restraints after they had already calmed down or had harmed themselves beyond the point of being dangerous, for beating inmates after they were restrained, and for restraining inmates without involving mental health professionals. The trouble was over, but the inmates were put into full-body restraints anyway.

In 2014, mental health and disability advocates in Florida sued that state's department of corrections and its private mental health treatment provider for allowing staff to punish mentally ill inmates with long periods of time under scalding hot showers. This was known as "the shower treatment." The shower treatments were inflicted on inmates after they could not control their psychiatric symptoms.

There are many more examples, but the two from Pennsylvania and Florida are painful enough to illustrate the problem. These punishments, because they are used in response to manifestations of mental illness, are discriminatory. They violate the Americans with Disabilities Act (ADA) as well as the equal protection clause and due process clause of the U.S. Constitution and the comparable state laws.

The Right to Adequate Mental Health Care

Inmates are generally entitled to prison-provided mental health treatment when:

- The mental illness is serious.
- The symptoms of the mental illness can be substantially improved.
- The inmate is likely to suffer harm or worsening of the illness if mental health treatment is delayed or denied.
- The cost to the prison is not excessive.

These are the same conditions under which physical health care must be provided to prisoners. If physical health care is provided under these circumstances but mental health treatment is not, the prison is discriminating against its mentally ill inmates and, again, the ADA, due process, and equal protection are the legal bases for claiming discrimination.

Having been treated for psychiatric problems before getting arrested and then going through the mental health intake, assessments, and evaluations in jail, an inmate with mental illness usually arrives at prison with a file specifying a diagnosis and medications. Still, prison mental health teams conduct their own intake workups to verify each new inmate's existing mental health record and to match the inmate with available services. They may re-diagnose or re-medicate inmates. This is perfectly legal; in fact, it is often medically necessary because the prison does not necessarily have access to the same medications that the jail provided, or because the jail may have misdiagnosed the inmate, or because the inmate's condition has changed between the jail evaluation and the long-term prison confinement. What is not legal? Failing to provide mental health care at all, providing mental health care that is below the legal standard for quality, or failing to follow proper processes in delivering mental health care.

Federal court cases, interpreting the Eighth Amendment's "cruel and unusual" phrase, have concluded that prisons and other correctional facilities must provide *adequate* mental health care—not perfect or even great mental health care, just adequate. Prison mental health care is adequate when it is provided in a way that is not deliberately indifferent to an inmate's serious mental health needs.

Inmates can't choose their mental health providers; they have to work with whoever is assigned to them in prison. Sometimes the provider is a psychiatrist who makes monthly cell-side psychiatric check-ins—quick drop-in meetings at which the psychiatrist goes from cell to cell to see if any inmates need prescription adjustments. If the psychiatrist abruptly stops prescribing medication, or changes the dosage or type of an inmate's medication, or otherwise changes the inmate's treatment, it is hard to prove that the care was inadequate—harder than it would have been if the prison had provided no care. Prison administrations and courts usually bow to the providers' discretion. As long as providers provide treatment that is within the standard range and they document their reasons, the administration is likely to consider it adequate.

State prisons, and the state courts that have jurisdiction over them, follow this federal common-law requirement of adequacy as well as state-law standards for the quality of prison mental health care. The state standards vary across a vague spectrum of noncommittal promises: State correctional standards tend not to make descriptive concrete promises because state correctional authorities know that it may not be possible to live up to them in every single situation and because they have to avoid being sued for negligence if they are unable to fulfill a mandate that they have established.

For example:

- Maryland has an Office of Treatment Services that partners with private mental health agencies to work with inmates who are mentally ill. The office says that "clinicians work together with the private psychiatric services provider to ensure that the mental health needs of the offenders are met in the most clinically appropriate manner."
- In Texas, "The CMHCC [Correctional Mental Health Care Committee] strives to provide health care services of recognized high quality and deliver them uniformly, promptly and efficiently within the limits of appropriated resources."
- Illinois says, "Persons committed to the Department shall have access to mental health services as determined by a mental health professional."
- In Florida, "An inmate in a mental health treatment facility has the right to receive treatment that is suited to his or her needs and that is provided in a humane psychological environment. Such treatment shall be administered skillfully, safely, and humanely with respect for the inmate's dignity and personal integrity."

Although modern prisons offer a full continuum of mental health care and often contract with mental health companies that are supposed to be experts at managing mental health personnel and services, they do sometimes offer inadequate mental health care or mental health care that does not fulfill the state's standards. Courts have deemed prison mental health care to be inadequate or negligent when there were not enough mental health professionals available to treat the inmates, when inmates with mental impairments did not get appropriate follow-up treatment, when facilities did not have safe spaces for inmates experiencing bad episodes of mental illness, and when inmates were punished after exhibiting psychiatric symptoms rather than being given mental health treatment.

The Right to Refuse Medicine or Medical Treatment

Under the due process clause of the U.S. Constitution, prison inmates generally have the right to refuse medicine, but when the medicine is for a psychiatric problem and the inmate is a risk to himself or dangerous to others without it, correctional facilities can require the inmate to take the medicine. The mental health professions call this "treatment over objection."

Most states have treatment review committees in their prisons. The committees are authorized to review behavior and treatment files for prisoners refusing to take their psychiatric medicine and to order the medical staff to administer the medicine against the inmate's wishes. In the states that do not have these committees, prison officials either have to obtain a court order to force psychiatric medication on an inmate or they have to involuntarily commit the inmate to a mental hospital for treatment.

The Right to Communicate With People Outside of the Prison

Prisons and other correctional facilities can limit inmates' First Amendment freedoms of speech and assembly for "legitimate penological" reasons. Basically, this means that they will not allow prisoner communications that interfere with prison operations or safety or that create an unreasonable cost for the prison. These limits can prevent inmates from getting outside supportive contact exactly when they want it, but they do not usually prevent inmates from talking with, or writing to, anyone in particular—other than criminal associates, sometimes. When they have enough money to pay for it, inmates can usually find ways to use their outside communication rights to maintain some form of a therapeutic or at least emotionally supportive relationship.

Of all the realms of outside communications—mail, phone, and personal visits—the one that is allowed to be most restricted is outside visits. The Supreme Court ruled, years ago, that it was not cruel or unusual punishment to ban prison visits from children outside of the inmate's immediate family, to disallow former prisoners from coming back to visit friends who are still in the prison, or to declare that inmates who abused drugs in the prison could not have any visitors at all for two full years after the violation. Subsequent to that decision, courts have upheld just about every prison visitation limit except for some that dramatically prevent visitation altogether. Meanwhile, research consistently states that prison visitation results in better ability to cope with prison life and more successful returns to society after prison.

Courts have upheld prison mail rules on topics like quantity of postage, contents of letters and packages going into or out of prison, and inspections of prisoner mail. In all of the rules about prison mail, nothing prevents prisoners from corresponding with a supportive person unless that supportive person declines to participate in the correspondence. A prisoner who arranges to exchange mail with a therapist or other professional who has an obligation of confidentiality will probably have to sign a waiver of confidentiality for that professional since the only confidential mail that is uniformly honored in prisons is mail that comes from the defense lawyer or the judge.

Prisons also have strict rules about telephone access, similarly administered to prevent prisoners from participating in crimes, costing the prison money, or disrupting orderly functions. Most of the prison rules about telephones are about how and when inmates can have phone conversations with people on the outside. Although it is expensive, inmates or families can deposit phone call money in an account at the prison in order to pay the phone fee for regular, although brief, conversations with a therapist or other helping professional outside of the facility. Note that the professional will need to be paid for participating in each session.

Prisons routinely monitor inmates' phone conversations. Court cases about whether this violates Fourth Amendment search and seizure rights have concluded that it is legal to monitor prisoner calls because inmates do not have a "reasonable expectation of privacy" when they talk on the prison phone. Court cases about whether call monitoring violates fundamental privacy rights say that inmates waive their privacy rights when they pick up the phone and talk after seeing the "calls are monitored" sign that prisons always post at every phone.

Prisons do have ways of facilitating confidential calls between lawyers and inmates. Many of them also have ways of keeping track of approved outside phone contacts. It would seem easy to combine the two practices and to facilitate confidential phone conversations with outside mental health professionals, but that is not a widely reported practice. As with prison mail to and from inmates, therapists can satisfy their professional ethics rules by having an inmate sign a confidentiality waiver.

HOW PRISONS CAN USE INTERCEPTED COMMUNICATIONS BETWEEN INMATES AND PEOPLE ON THE OUTSIDE

Communications with friends, therapists, family members, and other supportive people are valuable to inmates, but they are not useful to monitors unless they affect the prison's efforts to maintain order inside the facility or to prevent crime outside of the facility. To illustrate how the prison monitors could react to common discussions between inmates and outsiders, here are some likely examples of conversation topics and possible prison responses:

- When an inmate expresses significant personal anger about a prison worker or another inmate, the mail or call may be considered a threat and may be used as proof that the inmate has to get stricter treatment or be moved to a different location.
- When an inmate confesses, in personal communications with someone on the outside, to bad behavior inside, the prison may use that information to punish the inmate.
- When an inmate conveys symptoms of major depression, particularly with suicidal thoughts, the prison may medicate or relocate the inmate.

Prison personnel cannot legally use the content of intercepted inmate communications for gossip or to torment inmates. Those are not "legitimate penological" behaviors.

PRISON GRIEVANCES AND INVESTIGATIONS

The way to start a claim against a prison is to use the facility's internal grievance procedure. Filing a grievance against a prison feels risky. Prison culture has a history of discouraging "snitches" from reporting bad treatment. Guards have been known to respond more slowly or not at all to the needs of prisoners who report problems in their units. But highly publicized cases and media attention to prison conditions in the past decade have brought positive changes to mental health treatment and other facets of prison management, proving to inmates that their grievances matter.

Prison grievance procedures are relatively easy for inmates to follow, often allowing complaints to be either oral or written and only requiring them to have basic facts, although they do have rigid deadlines. The staff end of the grievance procedure is strict, requiring much reporting and explaining. Prisons receive lots of inmate grievances about all kinds of things besides staff. Grievances can be about the food, the facility, the laundry, or anything else at the prison. Many prison grievances are resolved quickly and without drama. Perhaps a harassing cellmate is relocated or an abandoned routine is reinstated. But the grievance process for treatment of prisoners is slow. Both sides have to tell their stories and the investigations require numerous steps and much documentation. Prisons cannot risk losing employees simply because the inmates complain about them; not all of the complaints are true and not all of them demonstrate incorrect practices—as opposed to disliked practices.

The nondemanding standards for inmate grievances are probably meant to make the grievance process accessible. Unfortunately, the lack of requirements enables and practically causes inmates to file weak complaints. An effective inmate grievance should tell:

- Who did or did not do something
- When the event happened or should have happened
- What is problematic about what happened or did not happen
- How the inmate wants the problem to be resolved

To strengthen their grievances, inmates should reference applicable sections of the inmate handbook, the correctional staff manual (which is typically on file at the warden's office and may be requested through the prison library), and state correctional regulations.

Here is an example of a good grievance:

For the past eight days (from June 8 to June 16) the pill line has not had my Ativan which I am supposed to get every day for my anxiety. I just filled this prescription on May 28 and my refill card says I can't get a new prescription until July 28. I keep checking in case there's a mistake, but the pill worker named

Smith just says things like "You don't get any crazy pills today. The doctor does-n't like you anymore. You must be in some bad trouble." That's what he said today. Every day he says something like that to make me feel anxious when he knows that I'm not getting my anxiety medicine. This should not happen. I am following the exact pill line rules in part 5(b) of the Inmate Handbook. Also, the third line of DOC Employee Handbook says "We shall treat offenders with respect." Please get me my Ativan and make Smith stop talking to me like that.

If, after completing the prison's internal grievance process, an inmate does not have a resolution to the problem, she can appeal to the state correctional authority that supervises prisons. The correctional authority will begin by investigating the situation. It will either use its own investigative staff or it will engage the state's inspector general, depending on how the state's system is organized. The investigators will review staff logs, security videos, incident reports, and other documents associated with the prison and the problem. They will also interview staff and inmates. When they finish investigating the problem, the investigation office will issue a report detailing the investigative method, the prison's response to the investigation, and its findings. If the investigators find problems at the facility, the report will be followed by a list of corrective actions that the prison needs to take. Perhaps the prison needs to make operational improvements or to manage its staff differently. Once it has issued the list of corrective actions, the correctional authority ends its investigative role and begins to act in an oversight role to monitor the prison's implementation of the corrective actions.

If the correctional authority does not handle the matter satisfactorily, or if the prison does not make the correctional authority's recommended changes, or the problem continues to exist for any reason, families and inmates can file a report with the Special Litigation Section of the U.S. Department of Justice (DOJ). Under a law called the Civil Rights of Institutionalized Persons Act (CRIPA), this office has specific responsibility for enforcing the rights of inmates at local jails and state prisons. However, the DOJ will take action only in response to systemic problems. It is responsible for improving facilities, not for solving individual inmates' problems.

This means that reports to the DOJ have to demonstrate that the individual inmate's experience, such as that of your father, Brett, who has been diagnosed with bipolar disorder but has been denied a transfer out of the work detail that causes him to miss the psychiatrist's rounds, is merely one example of a bigger problem that exists in the facility. If your dad knows about other inmates suffering similar problems, he should put all of the stories into a report. Reports should group the inmates' stories under a clear collective problem statement like, for example:

- The Aardvark County Jail in New Hampshire is messing up inmate prescriptions.
- The Bison State Prison in Virginia is not giving prisoners access to the library.
- The Coyote Correctional Facility in California is not responding to inmate grievances.

When your father is making a report, after stating the problem and presenting examples, your father should explain how the inmates have attempted to resolve their problems using the prison grievance system and the investigative system in the state correctional authority. Then he should describe the response that the inmates have seen. At the end of the report, he should notify the DOJ that he is available to assist them as they begin their own investigation of the situation. By filing a strong and clear report depicting a systemic problem, an individual inmate has the best chance of catching the DOJ's attention. If the DOJ does follow up on the report, it will handle it using its usual civil complaint review and resolution process. (See Chapter 8 on police misconduct for explanation of this process.)

HOW TO Help a Prisoner Exercise Legal Rights

If you have an imprisoned relative who is suffering from injuries or worsened and apparently untreated psychiatric symptoms and is not able to seek help inside, you can intervene from the outside. You as a taxpayer/citizen/inmate family member/activist have power over the prison and correctional system because you represent the society in which they function. Imagine nesting dolls: The inmate is in the prison; the prison is in the correctional system; and the correctional system is in society. Society is you, your friends, your support group, the mental health service community, and your elected representatives. Your team is bigger than the correctional system. You do not have to stand by and watch bad things happen to inmates. Begin your intervention by looking through the prison's family handbook for any sort of invitation to communicate with the prison. You will almost certainly find a social work manager or some other family liaison available to hear your concerns and to get your relative the services that he needs.

If your relative, such as your cousin Beth, is able to self-advocate inside the facility and is preparing to either file a grievance or to participate in a post-grievance meeting, you can help with research. Research will be the core of any support that you give in the problem-resolution process. Despite your work schedule and other life demands, you probably have much easier access to the Internet than your cousin has. Concerned that inmates may connect with conspirators, commit Internet-based crimes, or antagonize their accusers and witnesses, prison libraries tend not to facilitate independent inmate access to the Internet. The librarian may look something up for an inmate but will not necessarily be thorough or imaginative in the search. You will probably have the time and interest to dig around in the websites of the correctional authority and the inspector general for reports and handbooks so that you and your cousin will know the best phrases to use in your communications. You will have the flexibility to try variations after an initial search does not yield enough results. You will have the freedom to Google for facts. You will be able to update or to elaborate on information that Beth finds in books at the prison library.

You can also help by keeping a back-up log of facts and incidents in the event that your relative is not keeping records or has records that get taken or destroyed. As your cousin tells you about different incidents and people, make a running list of the staff and inmates involved, the approximate date, and the facts. By doing this, you will be documenting patterns that may not otherwise be obvious.

Keep your eyes and ears open for any news about other people's complaints or investigations regarding that facility and, if there is anything happening, get in touch with those people to see if your relative's situation can be added to the action that these people already have underway. To find this sort of news, keep up with online communities that connect inmate families. PrisonTalk, Assisting Families of Inmates (AFOI), and Strong Prison Wives and Families all host opportunities for families to interact about facilities and inmate issues. The National Resource Center on Children and Families of the Incarcerated maintains an online directory of agencies and services that address family interests. Go through that directory to find local, state, and national entities that could do something about Beth's situation or a combination of problems that you and others have identified.

Spread the word. If you like to write, submit an article about your mentally ill and incarcerated loved one (with her permission) to the NAMI (National Alliance on Mental Illness) *You Are Not Alone* site, to your local NAMI news-letter, or to an inmate family support organization in your state (you can find them by typing the term *inmate family* and your state name into a search engine). Write a letter to the editor of your local newspaper. If you are not inclined to write something, offer the story to a local daytime talk show that broadcasts either on television or on the radio. The first goal in spreading the word is to connect with other families so that, together, you can deliver to the state authorities the fullest and most descriptive picture of what is going wrong at the prison. The second goal is to pressure the prison and the department of corrections or board of prisons to fix whatever is wrong.

In extreme situations, inmates have to file private lawsuits to pursue their individual interests in court. Begin this kind of lawsuit by contacting an advocacy organization, such as NAMI or the ACLU (American Civil Liberties Union), for any guidance or representation they may be willing to provide. These organizations will often be able to explain the relevant civil rights issues and refer the case to a local attorney. In rare and perfect circumstances, they will have their own legal team take the case to court, usually at no cost to the inmate or family. But when you approach them, do not expect to get anything more than some information. You will almost always have to hire your own civil rights lawyer in order to bring a lawsuit against a prison.

Tax Facts

- Money that inmates earn for work in the correctional facility is taxable, although it may not add up to a high enough amount to generate an income tax debt. Even the barter credits for commissary purchases count as taxable income. None of this prison income is eligible for the earned income credit. Inmates should identify prison income on their tax returns by writing the letters "PRI" on the dotted line in front of the tax form box where they enter their "wages, salaries, tips, etc." See Internal Revenue Service (IRS) Publication 596 and Brittany Benson's *Filing Taxes for an Inmate*, H&R Block Tax Institute (January 13, 2016).

- Damages or money awards that the government pays to people who were wrongfully incarcerated do not count as taxable income. More specifically, if somebody was convicted of a crime that he did not commit and then was pardoned or granted clemency or else the original case was either dismissed or a new court decision found him not guilty, the government may give him money as compensation for wrongfully convicting him. He does not owe income tax on that money. See the IRS web page titled "Wrongful Incarceration FAQs."
- If someone does not get around to filing a tax return in the year that the incarceration started, she can get a copy of old W2 forms from the IRS to find out how much income she had that year and she can also work out a payment plan to pay that back debt in small monthly amounts. It is sometimes possible to convince the IRS to reduce the tax bill. Alternatively, a family member can handle the tax return while the relative is incarcerated. See IRS Publication 4924 and IRS Publication 2848.

RESOURCES FOR THE RIGHTS OF PEOPLE WITH MENTAL ILLNESS IN JAILS AND PRISONS

1. An easy way to find operating rules and policy directives for your state prison system is to navigate through that system's website. To reach that website, use the Internet search pattern "[State] Department of Corrections" with your state's name instead of [State]. Keep the search phrase within quotation marks so that the words stay together in the same order. If your relative is in a city or county facility, just go to that facility's website to find the rules. Many of the rules are also published in a family handbook that is available on each prison or jail facility's website.
2. The Society for Prison Journalists maintains a portal to "Prison Access Laws." These are the laws that entitle outsiders to get information about things happening inside individual prisons and the correctional system. Families that encounter resistance when investigating their inmate's situation can refer to their state's access law. Find the portal at spj.org/prisonaccess.asp.
3. The National Conference of State Legislators manages a website called *State Sentencing and Corrections Legislation* where families can find their state's statutes about jails and prisons. See ncsl.org.
4. Find the state correctional system's regulations by searching for the term *corrections*, or *prisons*, or *law* in your state's administrative code. See the National Association of Secretaries of States' portal to state administrative codes at administrativerules.org. The state regulations establish basic standards, and individual facilities make rules to comply with the standards. The specific state standards for quality of prison mental health care that are quoted in this section of this book are from the following sources:
The Office of Treatment Services at the Maryland Department of Public Safety and Correctional Services (at dpscs.state.md.us).

The Texas Correctional Managed Health Care Committee (at tdcj.state.
tx.us).

Title 20 Illinois Admin. Code § 415.40 (at ilga.gov).

Title 47 Florida Statutes § 945.48 is online at leg.state.fl.us.

5. Columbia University publishes and updates a terrific *Jailhouse Lawyer's
Manual* that is free online at jlm.law.columbia.edu and that is available
for purchase in print. Many prison libraries have copies of the print
version. Chapters 23 and 29 of the manual explain federal requirements
for prison health care and prison mental health care and lead to lots of
cases about those subjects. Another great tool is the *Jailhouse Lawyer's
Handbook,* published by the National Lawyers Guild. The handbook is
easier to read than the manual and is free online at nlg.org.

6. The National Commission on Correctional Health (NCCH) *Care
Standards for Inmate Mental Health Care* are free online. The standards
must be met in order for prisons to be accredited by NCCH, but there is
no legal or professional requirement for them to have that accreditation
in order to operate, so the standards are merely optional. NCCH also
publishes a helpful glossary of prison health words. See ncchc.org.

7. See the Corrections and Mental Health blog operated by the National
Institute on Corrections, to read about issues from the institutional
perspective. (The blog is available at community.nicic.gov.)

8. The Association of State Correctional Administrators has a Behavioral
Health Committee that partners with federal agencies and mental
health service agencies to exchange ideas and develop initiatives about
best serving inmates with mental illness. Families wanting to suggest
improvements to a particular prison can find concrete examples on
the committee's Library page and its Projects page. Navigate to the
committee from asca.net.

9. The American Jail Association publishes articles about jail treatment
of offenders who are mentally ill. Some of its articles are heavy with
statistics, other present good examples, and others explain policy. Search
for the term *mental health* or *mentally* at americanjail.org.

10. The American Correctional Association also publishes numerous free
articles about mental health management in jails and prisons on its
website at aca.org.

11. The ACLU fights for inmates' rights and produces clear explanations of
how the Constitution justifies providing fair and humane treatment of
prisoners who are mentally ill. They also publish copies of all of their
court pleadings for free on their site. Look at their complaint in the case
of *Dockery v. Epps* for a good example of a multi-inmate lawsuit against
a correctional department for failing to enforce policies and improve
prison conditions. See aclu.org.

12. *The Treatment of Persons with Mental Illness in Prisons and Jails: A State
Survey* (published April 8, 2014) is a descriptive listing of each state
correctional system's mental health treatment protocols, emphasizing
how they handle mentally ill prisoners who refuse to take medication.
It is available online from the Treatment Advocacy Center at tacreports.
org.

13. The federal Prison Litigation Reform Act is in 42 U.S.C. § 1997e. The part of the Civil Rights Act that prisoners use when bringing constitutional claims is 42 U.S.C. § 1983. The Civil Rights of Institutionalized Persons Act is at 42 U.S.C. § 1997a. Find all of these in uscode.house.gov.

14. The Yale Law School has compiled and published for free online "Prison Visitation Policies: A Fifty State Survey." Check for the current version of your state's visitation rules using the citation listed for it in the survey, which is online at law.yale.edu.

15. The Bazelon Center for Mental Health Law publishes a booklet titled *For People with Serious Mental Illnesses: FINDING THE KEY to Successful Transition from Jail or Prison to the Community,* which is about re-establishing access to Social Security, SSI, and medical assistance benefits upon being released from prison. It is free online at bazelon.org.

16. The Society of Correctional Physicians has a valuable policy statement about segregating mentally ill inmates. It is titled *Restricted Housing of Mentally Ill Inmates* and is free online at societyofcorrectionalphysicians. org.

17. The Urban Institute's March 2015 report, *The Processing and Treatment of Mentally Ill Persons in the Criminal Justice System: A Scan of Practice and Background Analysis,* examines the ways that people with mental illness are treated medically, disciplinarily, and otherwise in jails and prisons. Acknowledging the barriers to better treatment, the report also depicts criminal justice practices that help to reduce incarceration and recidivism. See urban.org.

18. Prison grievance policies, including instructions for filing grievances, are available via the portal to prison grievance procedures at the University of Michigan School of Law (law.umich.edu).

19. The Association of Inspectors General maintains a directory of state prison oversight agencies at inspectorsgeneral.org.

20. Complaints about civil rights violations or policy infringements in federal prisons begin with the contact form provided by the Office of Inspector General at justice.gov/oig.

21. The Federal Bureau of Prisons has a publication in its "Clinical Practice Guidelines" series titled *Management of Major Depressive Disorder.* It is free online at www.bop.gov.

22. The American Library Association has a website called *Prison Libraries* that provides guidance, standards, and articles about the resources and services that inmates should be able to access in their prison library. Knowing about these professional expectations, prisoners can feel justified in expecting the library to help them access legal sources and correctional system policies. Find the site at ala.org.

23. To report systemic problems in local jails and state prisons, such as failure to improve after a pattern of misconduct has been reported to the state, write to the Special Litigation Section, U.S. Department of Justice Civil Rights Division, 950 Pennsylvania Avenue, NW Washington DC 20530. The office will also accept reports by telephone at (202) 514-6255 or toll-free at (877) 218-5228. Information about reporting prison

misconduct is on the doj.gov web page *Rights of Persons Confined to Jails and Prisons.*

24. *Fundamentals of Jail & Prison Administrative/Internal Investigations,* by D. P. Lyons (AuthorHouse, 2015), is available for less than $20 on Amazon. It instructs correctional facility administrators about all facets of investigating inmate grievances.

25. *Jail Standards and Inspection Programs: Resource and Implementation Guide* (National Institute of Corrections, 2007) is available as a free download from the National Institute of Corrections at nicic.gov. It has full instructions for developing and operating thorough standards and inspection practices that will uncover problems before inmates file grievances. It also tells how to properly follow up on grievances. Families and inmates can base their expectations on the standards set forth in this publication.

26. This chapter identifies three online networks for inmate families. Their web addresses are: PrisonTalk, prisontalk.com; Assisting Families of Inmates, afoi.org; and Strong Prison Wives and Families, strongprisonwives.com.

27. The National Resource Center on Children and Families of the Incarcerated, which maintains a directory of inmate family support services and publishes facts, reports, and coping ideas for inmate families, is online at nrccfi.camden.rutgers.edu.

28. Public Citizen's Health Research Group and The Treatment Advocacy Center published the research report *Individuals With Serious Mental Illnesses in County Jails: A Survey of Jail Staff's Perspectives* (http:// www.citizen.org/documents/2330.pdf). The report shows that jails have increasing populations of inmates who are seriously mentally ill and that approximately half of jails have made changes to their facilities or staffing to accommodate these inmates. The report also shows that fewer than a fourth of the jails provide post-release support as former inmates transition back to society and that people with mental illness tend to commit later crimes and return to jail at a higher rate than the general population.

29. The Center for Constitutional Rights has done some excellent fact finding about, and legal advocacy on, mass incarceration and solitary confinement. You can find their passionate arguments and fact sheets at ccrjustice.org.

Criminal Records and Reputations

Your Aunt Sylvia, whose mental health symptoms made it impossible for her to tolerate many work environments, spent years as a very successful homecare aid for senior citizens, until she was arrested for failing to pay a parking ticket that she hadn't even known about. She paid for the ticket and a traffic court processing fee immediately after being arrested, but she lost her job because her employer had a rule against having home visitors with traffic court records. Embarrassed and terrified by this experience, Aunt Sylvia has not dared to apply for any other jobs in the past few years. If you can help her get the record of the arrest and payment expunged, she will be able to return to the work she loved without having to explain what happened with the parking ticket.

EXPUNGING A CRIMINAL RECORD

There are occasions, involving the right kind of crime, a lack of criminal tendency, the passage of years, and an understanding judge, when you can get a criminal record expunged (meaning, wiped out). The criminal record can be an arrest record or a prosecution record. The record still exists in a hidden pocket of the criminal justice system's database, but it is not generally available. In most of the states that offer true expungement, the record is erased for almost all purposes—except for future police and prosecution purposes. Once a record has been expunged, the person accused and prosecuted never has to admit to the record's past existence, no matter who (outside of the criminal justice system) asks, be it a potential employer, a social service organization, a government agency, or anyone else. For all public intents and purposes, the record never existed.

Every state has its own laws about which kinds of crimes can be expunged and its own court rules about how to obtain the expungement. In general, expungements are only available for minor crimes and crimes for which the person was found to be not guilty. A felony or serious misdemeanor conviction typically requires a governor's pardon in order to be removed from someone's record.

Even minor crimes and not guilty verdicts, which are relatively small encounters with the criminal justice system, can compromise opportunities and leave someone feeling forever clouded by the whole bad situation. Consider, for example, your friend Ron, whose arrest and probation for harassment have made him ineligible for a particular group housing program that he wants to enter. Once he gets the record expunged, he will finally have a chance to live where he wants. Suppose your daughter Carrie was charged with public drunkenness and the charge was later withdrawn when she proved that she had not been drunk at all and was merely off balance because of her prescription medication. Getting that complete injustice off of her record will get her professional license back so that she can return to work as a preschool teacher. Maybe your co-worker Ayad remains so distressed about an old arrest that he can't even see a police officer in public without panicking. Having that record expunged could be a helpful step in supplementing his therapy.

People with mental illness do not have to explain or to demonstrate anything about their mental health in order to get a criminal record expunged. Whether the arrest was connected with mental health symptoms or the expungement is expected to alleviate mental health symptoms generally has no relevance unless the expungement happens to be part of an arrangement made by a mental health court. This is because the laws about expungement are rigid and function as checklists. If the record contains the type of crime that is identified in the expungement law, the person has not committed another crime since then, and the other legal criteria are satisfied, then it does not matter why the arrest happened in the first place or how the person's health might improve as a result of getting the record expunged.

Setting Aside a Criminal Record

A *set aside* (or vacated) record carries a note of excuse indicating that the conviction was set aside or vacated. This can mean that the conviction was minor and was cleared up with probation or it can mean that a conviction or guilty plea resulted from a mistake that has been corrected. Mistaken conviction records tend to result from having "ineffective assistance of counsel" (a lawyer who did not provide sufficient defense work) or from entering into a bad deal with the prosecutor. The bad deal would be one that the accused person should not have agreed to and took because of poor advice or misunderstanding. It is likely to have been a plea bargain in which he agreed to plead guilty to a lesser crime than he would have faced in a trial.

Maybe your son Phil, who was experiencing major depression, simply did not care what anybody said to him or told him to sign when he got in trouble for reckless driving. His defense lawyer did not take the time to get to know Phil and just wanted to end the case quickly. When the prosecutor offered to lower the charge to careless driving if Phil pled guilty, the defense lawyer was happy for the chance to be done with the case and told Phil to sign the plea. Phil never even had a chance to defend himself, although there could have been traffic-cam footage and witnesses available to prove that he was not guilty. Since he pled guilty to careless driving, he had to take a safe driving course, perform community service with the street crew that cleans up after car wrecks, and pay a hefty fine. If the lawyer hadn't taken advantage of Phil's depression and hadn't led him to take the plea, Phil would not have had to go through all of the punishment. In some states, this means that he has a legal basis for petitioning to have the conviction set aside. And, under particular circumstances, again depending on the state, if he is granted the set aside, he will not have to not admit to his arrest and conviction. In other places, if he succeeds with his set aside petition, he may still have to admit to the arrest and conviction, but he will have the right to explain that the situation was cleared up. Seizing the chance to give this explanation will take guts; employers and others will not necessarily ask for an explanation. They will merely ask questions like "Have you ever been convicted of a crime?" To make sure they know that his conviction was vacated or set aside, Phil will probably have to jam the phrase "set aside" into a small space on a form or say, "Yes, but it was set aside" in an interview just to have a chance to explain what happened.

In addition to having a less tainted record, people whose judgments are set aside can also get legal rights returned, if any were suspended along with their conviction. For example, Phil may have lost his driving privileges for three years with the careless driving conviction, but if he gets the conviction set aside after one year, he can get his driving privileges back at the same time.

Sealing or Suppressing a Criminal Record

Sealing and *suppression* are processes to hide an arrest or conviction record. They do not cancel the record the way an expungement does, nor do they excuse a record the way a set aside does. They merely put the record where the general public will not find it. And because sealing and suppression merely protect the record from gawkers, they do not protect against the "collateral consequences" of arrest or conviction. The collateral consequences can include the loss of civil rights, such as the right to vote or to serve on a jury, and the opportunity to obtain a professional license or driver's license or some types of state certification.

Despite being hidden from public access, a sealed or suppressed record still counts as a criminal record when a future criminal court looks back and counts past offenses to decide on a sentence. Suppose your friend Dade has narcissistic personality disorder and occasionally gets into trouble for fighting with people. Dade has already been arrested a couple of times in connection with fights. Both times, the court gave him probation and required him to complete anger-management classes. Dade now wants to seal those records because he plans to register with an online dating service and he doesn't want prospective girlfriends to find out about his criminal past. If the records are sealed, neither the dating service nor the girlfriends will know about them, but if Dade gets arrested for another fight, he is likely to face a much harsher criminal punishment than he has faced so far.

For some people with mental illness, the memories of an arrest and having to appear in court, no matter how the case turned out, can be a haunting disturbance for years afterward. Having to admit to the record makes the haunting even worse. If the record can be sealed, then at least the person will not have to think about it as much. Maybe your father, Nick, had a shoplifting conviction for which he served probation several years ago. It was only a one-time thing and he took his punishment, but he can't put it behind him because every time he applies for a new job he has to own up to it again. If he can get that record sealed, at least he won't have to show it on any more applications and risk having to explain it in interviews. Nick is not likely to get in trouble with the police ever again, so just having the record sealed will solve his problems with job applications and will help him to put it out of his mind.

HOW TO Expunge a Criminal Record

The process for expunging a record is typically very similar to the processes for sealing, suppressing, or setting aside a record. To keep this section from sounding garbled, it uses the term expunge, *but know that you can basically substitute the words* seal, suppress, *or* set aside *for that word as you read this HOW TO section. The processes differ in every trial court system, which means in every county or very large city, so the following material shows the standard pattern for taking this kind of action, rather than providing specific directions. Finally, beware of vocabulary. Having read the general distinctions among the processes, you will see that the words are not used the same way in every court system. For example:*

- *In Michigan courts, you would file an Application to* Set Aside *Conviction in order to get your case* expunged.
- *In Colorado, records of drug crimes and petty crimes committed by adults can be* sealed, *but not* expunged, *because that state permits expungements only for juvenile records.*
- *In New York, a court can* suppress *certain items that are used as evidence in a case, but it will* seal *the entire record of a case that was dismissed or that resulted in a not guilty verdict.*

The way to request expungement is to file a petition in the trial court where the original criminal charges were filed. The charges may have been dropped or the case may have been heard. The defendant may have been found guilty and served her sentence, or she may have been found not guilty. Either way, that court has jurisdiction over the expungement. The person named in the record (for example, your daughter Madison) typically has to file her own petition. Unless you are her guardian, this is not an action that you can take on behalf of your family member.

There is no time limit on seeking an expungement. It could be years or decades before Madison even needs the criminal record to be expunged. It is also possible that state law will change long after the criminal record was created. Perhaps the old law did not allow this type of record to be expunged, but the new law does.

The petition will require Madison to state a reason for the expungement. The reason has to show that she meets state law requirements. For example:

- The state law may say that expungement is available when someone successfully completed probation for a misdemeanor more than two years ago and has not had any police interactions in those two years. Where the expungement form asks for a reason, the petitioner who satisfies the legal conditions would write: *I successfully completed probation for [name of misdemeanor] on June 3, 2014, and I have committed no crimes and have not been arrested since then.*

Petitions have to be accompanied by various attachments. For example:

- States generally require petitioners to attach copies of their criminal records. This is annoying because the criminal court surely has access to the criminal records database. In fact, you typically have to obtain the record from that court's records office. You will likely have to pay a fee for getting the record.
- The petitioner may need to attach a new fingerprint card. This is aggravating, too: How could the fingerprints have changed? Your family member will have to find a time when the police department or sheriff's office can take the fingerprints, and then she will probably have to pay them for taking the prints and making the fingerprint card.
- The petitioner might also have to submit documents proving that she satisfied court-ordered activities, if those are not included with the copy of her criminal record. The documents may be certificates showing that she completed probation, a training course, or a rehabilitation program. They may be letters or attendance records from a community-service supervisor.

The petitioner will probably also need to submit her petition, including copies of the attachments, to the prosecutor's office in addition to the court. The court's instructions will explain how to address the copies if the judge and prosecutor who worked on the original case are no longer in office. It may not even matter whether those individuals are still around; your jurisdiction may have one designated judge and one designated prosecutor to handle all expungement petitions, no matter who worked on the cases initially. There is likely to be a filing fee for submitting the petition to the court. There may also be a "service" fee if the court requires your family member to have the sheriff or a constable deliver the petition to the prosecutor.

Once your family member's petition is received, it may be possible for the prosecutor to simply agree with it. If so, the prosecutor will sign the agreement notice on the petition or on a separate form and send it to the judge. The judge will then review the prosecutor's agreement, along with the rest of the petition packet, and decide whether to call a hearing. Most of the time, when the prosecutor has signed the agreement, the judge will order the expungement without holding a hearing.

Some jurisdictions require a hearing on every expungement petition even when the prosecutor has already agreed to the petition. This is likely to be a quick, low-stress hearing in which the judge simply needs to see and hear your family member explain in person why she deserves the expungement. She needs to come across as cooperative—which is a challenge after jumping through so many hoops and paying so many fees. The judge may ask some questions about how her life has been affected by the existence of the criminal record. These are fair questions; the answers demonstrate whether expungement is necessary. The judge will typically decide on the expungement right there while your family member is still in court.

Even though your local court or legal aid office will usually provide copies of the laws and forms that are needed for an expungement, many petitioners choose to hire lawyers for the claims. Legal aid offices handle expungement cases for clients living below the poverty level. Even non-impoverished petitioners who hire lawyers do not have to pay very much for this kind of representation. Since the process is so straightforward, the lawyer does not have to do much original work and will usually charge a relatively low fee. Look for a private criminal defense lawyer in a small practice. Shop around by looking at several local lawyers' websites. Call or email to ask about their prices as well as their success rates with expungement petitions.

If you notice an expungement schedule when you look at the court's website for instructions, you will know whether expungements are always held on a particular day of the week or month and where they are held. If your family member has the time, she may want to go and watch a few hours of expungement court. This way, she can get a feel for how the hearings operate in her area and she can see if she is inclined to hire any of the lawyers in those hearings.

FAMILY LIABILITY

It is impossible to miss the news reports about parents of people with a mental illness who are accused of crimes. The stories often have a subtext about how the parents are connected to the crime. The media know that people are curious about what kind of parents could have raised someone like this and why the parents failed to get help before their child did the bad thing. At least some people are looking for that sort of gossip. A lot of other people read the stories for validation. They know that the family had no way of preventing the incident. They know how many offices and groups and medications the families have tried. They know how hard it is to predict and to control an adult with mental illness because they have had the experience in their own families.

A major crime/big media combination is an extreme version of something that many families face on a much smaller scale. Most arrests are not widely covered. Nevertheless, families can find themselves having to explain things when one of their members has gotten into trouble with the police. Whether they are explaining to neighbors, the police, the media, or someone else, families who know their own potential liabilities and know the legal significance of particular facts will be able to give the best explanations.

Family liabilities can be criminal or civil. With criminal liability, family members are at risk of paying fines, being incarcerated, and/or losing their reputations. With civil liability, family members are at risk of having to pay money damages to victims. Both categories specify reasons that families can be guilty in connection with crimes committed by their relatives. Knowing the vocabulary and defenses associated with the reasons is the best way to prepare for questions and accusations.

Criminal Charges

CONSPIRACY
Conspiracy is a plan or agreement to commit a crime. Anyone who is involved with the plan can be guilty of conspiracy, even if he does not realize that the planned act was against the law and even if the criminal act never happened. People have a hard time defending themselves against conspiracy charges because criminal plans

are not usually put in writing and police have to rely on suspects' claims about who else was in on the plan. The best defenses against conspiracy charges prove that the accused conspirator did not have access to particular information and that he withdrew from the plan by communicating to the others involved that he would no longer be a part of it.

BEING AN ACCOMPLICE

An accomplice is someone who participates in carrying out the crime. In some circumstances, an accomplice may be called an "accessory." Accomplices provide weapons that criminals would not otherwise have. Accomplices distract victims so that other criminals can take advantage of them. Accomplices lead innocent victims to the place where the thief or attacker is waiting. Accomplices drive get-away cars. Accomplices supply money that is used to commit a crime. Accomplices may think that they are helping a relative with mental symptoms to calm down or that they have to assist that relative in a criminal endeavor to avoid being victimized themselves. Accomplices are punished as if they had committed the full crime.

The Model Penal Code, which is a compilation of legal standards that most states have incorporated into their own criminal codes, lists three defenses against accomplice liability:

- If someone was a victim of the offense that he is accused of participating in, he can use his victimization as a defense. Suppose, for example, that Aiden lets himself into his father's house, takes the car keys and the car without permission, and then intentionally runs somebody over with the car. The prosecutor might claim that by providing the car, the father is an accomplice. The father can defend himself by asserting that he was a victim of car theft, not a voluntary participant in vehicular homicide.
- If someone participates in a crime that inevitably requires two participants, he may be able to defend himself on the grounds that only one of the participants in that particular crime is able to be guilty. Suppose, for example, that distributing pornography is a crime. If Steve receives pornography from his brother who distributed it, Steve is not an accomplice because he was merely the necessary second half of the distribution.
- If someone ends her complicity before the crime, by either warning the police or undoing her part of the crime, she can defend herself by showing proof of her sabotage. Suppose Rebecca sets up a website with her cousin for the purpose of cheating people out of money. If Rebecca takes the site down and changes the account password before anybody tries to use it, she has a plausible defense against being an accomplice.

POSSESSION

Possession means people have control over various illegal objects, such as stolen goods, weapons, and particular drugs. To have "control over" the objects, the possessor can be the owner or renter of the place where the items are located, whether it is a home, vehicle, storage unit, safe deposit box, or other place that he is able to lock. To be found guilty, the possessor usually has to either know that it was illegal to possess the item or know that the item was within his possession, depending on how the state law is written. Here are some examples:

- People can be arrested for possessing illegal drugs simply because the drugs are in their house or car, whether or not they knew about them. But, in most states, they will be guilty of illegal drug possession only if they knew that they possessed the drugs. The Model Penal Code says in § 2.01(4) that knowing can even mean being aware that you have control over the item for a long enough time that you could have gotten rid of it. The federal crime of drug possession, which comes with a minimum penalty of one year in prison or a $1,000 fine, calls someone guilty only if they "knowingly or intentionally" possessed the controlled substance.
- It is also illegal to possess explosive devices. The Bureau of Alcohol, Tobacco, and Firearms regulates explosives and enforces a list of unlawful acts, which include "receiving" an explosive device from someone who has, at some point, been committed to a mental institution or who is simply not licensed to have explosives.

Clearly, the most helpful defense against a crime of possession is proving that you did not know you possessed the item. This is very hard to prove. Some defendants can demonstrate that the item was hidden from them or that they did not have the physical ability to discover that the item was in a place that they controlled.

DEALING, DISTRIBUTING, OR SUPPLYING
States have distinct statutes against illegal dealing, distributing, and supplying. These statutes make it easy to convict criminals' family members. For example:

Just outside of Pittsburgh, a few years ago, a mother was convicted for supplying guns to her son. This son had a history of involuntary mental health commitments. Knowing that his mother wanted to sell her guns, the son approached her one day, saying that he had a potential buyer. The mother removed the guns from safe storage and gave them to her son so that he could show them to the buyer. But he had deceived her. There was no buyer. He had a grudge and took the guns to a bar where he shot one person to death and wounded two others.

Nobody could be sure that the mother was in on the plan to shoot people at the bar, so even though she was charged with conspiracy, she was not found guilty of it. There was no question that she owned the guns and provided them to her son who, because of his mental health history, was not legally allowed to have them. She had to be found guilty of violating the Pennsylvania statute prohibiting any-one from supplying a weapon to a person with inpatient commitment history.

Even without knowing the state's full array of dealing/distributing/supplying offenses, families should expect that it is always a separate individual crime to pro-vide someone who is mentally ill with a gun, poison, drugs that were not prescribed for her, or a vehicle that she is not licensed to operate. Additionally, when families know that the unwell relative has a propensity to anger or impulsivity or that she is fixated on an injustice, they should expect to be scrutinized and possibly found liable if they have provided their loved one with items that are normally not dangerous but which did become implements of crime. Examples of these are locksmith tools, potentially harmful sports equipment, woodworking supplies, or small appliances. The main defense against charges of dealing, distributing, or supplying is to prove that the item was taken without permission from a secure location.

CIVIL COURT CASES: FINANCIAL LIABILITY FOR ANOTHER PERSON'S CRIME

Families are very rarely financially liable for crimes committed by their adult relatives. The people who might bring the civil cases would be survivors in a wrongful death case or injured parties in a personal injury case. They have to prove that the family members owed them a duty, usually a duty to protect them or a duty to warn them. In the unlikely event that the people can demonstrate a duty, they also have to prove that the family member breached that duty and that by breaching the duty he caused harm.

Suppose Warren threw a rock into the neighbor's window, breaking the guy's computer and damaging nearby artwork. In this case and similar cases, it is sometimes possible to respond effectively using common "damage control" techniques, such as apologizing on behalf of the relative who caused the harm and trying to show his side of the story without making anybody look foolish. For example, if Warren's wife June hurries over, offers to help pay for the breakage, and tells the neighbor how sorry she is, the neighbor may just offer to claim the incident as vandalism on his homeowner's insurance. If the neighbor doesn't make that offer, June could ask about the possibility of insurance coverage. Without giving too much information about what prompted Warren to throw the rock, June could ask the neighbor to put curtains or blinds over that window. If she gives too much information, including an explanation of Warren's delusions about the neighbor's computing, the neighbor is liable to ask why June didn't do anything to prevent Warren from being destructive, since she knew in advance that he was troubled by seeing the neighbor on the computer.

The family might hire experts to gather and explain information in support of the relative who committed the crime. The experts may include a forensic psychologist or psychiatrist, a private detective, or a forensic scientist. Together with the family, the experts can reveal the combination of factors that resulted in the bad event. This should always be done in consultation with a lawyer who understands the possible legal risks that the family needs to avoid. For example, June could get a consultation from a home security expert who would demonstrate that people who do not cover the windows of lit rooms at night are statistically more likely to be vandalized or burglarized. Then, if the neighbor starts talking about a lawsuit, June and her lawyer will already be thinking about using the expert's data in their response.

People can be quick to gang up on a person with mental illness, and they can be eager to exaggerate and exploit his condition. When families can show that their relative did not have control over mechanical issues, such as equipment failures, other people's actions, and additional facets of what happened, they counteract the swell of misunderstanding against their loved one. Standing by their unwell relative, they look like good, caring people who are doing the best they can.

Consider the case of Heath, a delivery driver who bumps into another vehicle when he's trying to avoid a pothole. Already managing chronic depression, Heath becomes despondent over the incident and having to go on mandatory administrative leave. When the other driver's lawyer learns that Heath is getting mental health treatment, he tells his client, and soon lots of people are suggesting that Heath intentionally caused the wreck and is a menace to society. Heath's family may worry that soon the groundswell will swallow them as well and that they will be blamed for not preventing Heath from driving. But Heath didn't do anything wrong and neither did his family. An accident happened. The family needs to put the word out that Heath feels worse about causing that accident than most people would. This, again, is a time when they may call upon an expert, in this case a mental health expert, to help them spread their message. If the story about Heath has gone mainstream, maybe someone from their support group can write a letter to the editor. Maybe they can hold a press conference, along with a psychologist and someone who has written about depression, at which they can inform the media about some of the ways that people with depression respond to upheaval. Perhaps they just want their expert to educate the other driver and that driver's lawyer, before things go too far.

Past Civil Court Cases About Family Liability

VOLPE V. GALLAGHER, 821 A.2D 699 (R.I. S. CT. 2003)

Volpe v. Gallagher is a well-known case in which a mother was sued after her adult son shot a neighbor. The *Volpe* court said that, "Because defendant knew about her son's mental illness but nevertheless, . . . allowed him to possess and to store guns and ammunition on her property, we are of the opinion that she had 'a duty to exercise reasonable care to so control the conduct of Gallagher as to prevent him from intentionally harming others or from so conducting himself as to create an unreasonable risk of bodily harm to them.'"

Neither the jury in the trial against Mrs. Gallagher nor the appellate judges believed her claims that she had not known that her son had guns in the house. The two of them had lived alone together for decades in the small home and the police had seen, right near the washing machine that this mother used in the basement, the son's shotgun behind the boiler and his shotgun box on top of the refrigerator. The courts that heard the case were also influenced by Mrs. Gallagher's claim that if she had known about her son's weapons, she would either have gotten rid of them herself or would have made him get rid of them. This claim showed that Mrs. Gallagher believed that she had control over her son and his possessions.

The courts reasoned that since the weapons, cartridges, and bullets were obvious to anyone in the house and the mother could control whether those dangerous items remained in the house where she was living with her son, who was paranoid and highly delusional, she had a legal duty to remove them so that her son could not use them to hurt anybody. The state supreme court even pointed out that she would probably not have been found liable if she had shown that her son had had control over her by being threatening or intimidating.

Most of the time, family members or other people who, like Mrs. Gallagher, are being sued for failing to prevent something bad from happening will defend themselves in court by saying that it was not their duty to rescue the person who was harmed. In other words, they invoke the "no duty to rescue" rule. Under this common-law rule, which has developed from many case decisions over the years, nobody has a legal duty to save another person from harm unless:

- A specific statute obligates them to do so.
- Someone attempts a rescue but then abandons it or does not do it right.
- Someone has caused the situation from which the other person has to be rescued.
- Someone has a special relationship with the person who caused the harm and could have influenced him or her to not take that harmful action.

In cases involving a perpetrator who is mentally ill and dependent on family members, people who have been harmed sometimes use the "special relationship" exception as a basis for suing the family.

A special relationship means that one person in the relationship has sufficient control over the other person to affect her decisions. Control does not have to be like hypnosis or even the strong disciplinary management that a parent has over a toddler. It can be the power that a boss has over employees, the strength of respect between siblings, or the general ability of a parent to convince an adult son or daughter not to do something.

WISE V. SUPERIOR COURT, 222 CAL. APP. 3D 1008 (1990)

Unlike the *Volpe* case above, *Wise v. Superior Court* is the first of three examples of court cases in which family members have not been found liable for the actions of relatives who were mentally ill. *Wise* is a case against a wife who ran away from home a week before her husband, who was depressed and aggressive, went up on the roof and launched a sniper attack "severely injuring a number of passing motorists." The court found that the wife did not have a duty to protect the passing motorists from a husband that she could not control. The injured people even argued that the wife should have had her husband committed when she felt so unsafe around him that she left home. Still, the court said that she had not been negligent because the harm was not foreseeable. The court contrasted this situation with the case of *Pamela L. v. Farmer*, 112 Cal. App. 3d 206 (1980), in which a wife was negligent for inviting neighbor girls to swim in her backyard pool when she was away at work and her husband, a known child molester, was at home and did molest the neighbor girls.

HAVEL V. CHAPEK, 2006 WL 3833871 (OHIO CT. APP.)

In *Havel v. Chapek*, a boyfriend with a history of self-mutilation and diagnoses of obsessive-compulsive disorder and depression killed his ex-girlfriend and then, after leaving the state, killed himself. The ex-girlfriend's family sued the boyfriend's family for failing to warn or protect their daughter. The court concluded that, since the boyfriend was being treated for his psychiatric problems and showed improvement by stopping his self-mutilation, he was an independent adult not under the control of his parents. The court also said that the boyfriend's parents could not have foreseen that he would be dangerous to the girlfriend because, until he killed her, he had only harmed himself.

PATTERSON V. FOLEY, 2009 WL 2357124 (CONN. SUPER. CT.)

Patterson v. Foley is a case about a young adult with anxiety disorder who was shouting profanities while riding his bike around the neighborhood and got mad at a neighbor who told him to go away. He got off of his bike and beat the neighbor so badly that the neighbor died a few months later. The neighbor's family sued the anxious man's family but lost because the attacker's mother did not have legal custody or guardianship of her unwell son. In that court, an adult's parent who was neither legal custodian nor guardian was not seen to have control or a special relationship.

HOW TO Interact With Police Investigators

If the police come to your home and ask to speak with you, you do not have to stop everything and have the conversation immediately. You can arrange to meet with them later. If you are willing and available to talk right then, you do not have to let the police into your house. You can step out into the yard with them, or bring them to your garage, or ask if you can take your car and follow them in their car to go and talk someplace else.

Why would not you let the police into your house? Your house may not be a very confidential space. If you have curious or talkative people around who might listen in on the conversation and then gossip about it, you may not want them to hear you talking with the police. Another reason that some people do not want the police in their house is that the police can gather a lot of information just by looking around the room. They are legally allowed to collect evidence that is "in plain view" without having a warrant to search. Even if there is not any evidence of a crime in the room, there may be clues that lead them to ask you questions that they may not otherwise have thought of. There may also be items in the room that provide them with a basis for obtaining a warrant to later search the house.

You have to be truthful and cooperative when the police seek your help in a criminal investigation. The police will probably find you before you even know that your relative has gotten into trouble. In that initial conversation, you will be shocked and will naturally want to receive information more than you will want to give information. Know that when you ask the police for information, you may inadvertently tell them something that will be used against your relative or against you.

Here are some examples:

- If the police say, "We're here about your son Howard" and you reply, "Oh no! What did he do?" you have just made Howard look guilty. This reaction also suggests that you may have known that he was planning something. If instead you say, "Oh no! What happened to him?" you will not give the police the impression that you expected any trouble from Howard.

- If the police say, "Your son Howard was in a bad car wreck this morning" and you ask, "Did he have his medicine with him?" the police will want to know what kind of medicine your son is supposed to take. You may have just given them the impression that there is something wrong with him. Once you reveal that the medicine was for a psychiatric condition, they will want more details about his mental health and may begin to make presumptions about his role in causing the wreck. Instead of giving the police this kind of clue as soon as they report that there was a crash, you can just be quiet and let them finish telling you what happened.

The police will ask you some precise questions to flesh out information that they have already gathered: *Does your son own a Batman costume? Did you give your daughter your credit card to use at the mall today? Has your husband ever been in a serious fist fight before? How often does your wife go to that bar?* They will also ask you open-ended questions hoping to get leads from your remarks: *Why was your daughter in that alley last night? How did your sister get the money to do this? What set him off?* If you do not know the answers to any of the questions, just say that. The police do not want you to guess; they are looking for facts. If you have any proof to back up your answers, tell the police about your proof. *My son was here playing cards with me until 10:00 last night, so were the next-door neighbors. Ask them; they will tell you that they were here with my son.*

WHY YOU SHOULD HIRE YOUR OWN LAWYER IF YOUR RELATIVE IS IN TROUBLE

There are several good reasons for hiring a lawyer to assist you with procedures and communications if a family member who has mental illness is accused of committing a crime. For one thing, a lawyer can help you to speak and write clearly and accurately in settings full of legal jargon and verbal traps. In the *Volpe v. Gallagher* case, a good lawyer would have made sure that Mrs. Gallagher did not claim that she could have gotten rid of her son's weapons. There was no way for Mrs. Gallagher to be sure that she would have been able to find and discard all of the son's guns and ammunition, but once she claimed that she could have done it, the prosecutor, judge, and jury could take her at her word and find her guilty.

A lawyer can also protect you from false accusations. All of your loved one's most irrational defenses and complaints about you, such as your boyfriend Zeke's assertions that you are poisoning him, could surface once he is under police scrutiny. The police are not therapists; they will not have long-term relationships with Zeke and they will not know which of his accusations are true. When they start to investigate his lies about your being behind the crime, you will want a good, smart lawyer to figuratively stand between you and the police and clear up the untrue claims before they evolve into criminal charges. When the police send investigators through your house looking for cyanide because Zeke told them that you used it to make him pass out so that you could use his computer to hack into other machines and steal information, your lawyer will (1) confirm that they have a warrant, (2) ensure that they only investigate within the limits of the warrant, and (3) tell you what to say or not to say.

Finally, you should have a lawyer just in case you did do something wrong. You may not have realized that you were breaking the law, but if you find out that you did, your role will quickly shift from merely supporting your loved one to also defending yourself.

Your lawyer will try to get your charge or charges reduced as much as possible and then will work to get you the lightest possible punishment. To reduce your charges, the lawyer will pick apart every element of any charge against you. If you are charged with conspiracy, for example, your lawyer can hound the prosecutor about how little you knew of your family member's intentions and demonstrate that you could not possibly have been in on the criminal plan when you did not even know that a plan was being hatched.

By arguing for the fewest and lowest charges, your lawyer is getting everything ready in case a charge does stick and the court has to punish you. Steering toward the least harsh punishment, the lawyer will emphasize how informative you have been and what your relative did to prevent you from even seeing, let alone avoid being gathered into, his criminal activity. Having studied your background and the array of punishments available in the jurisdiction, your lawyer will negotiate to keep you out of jail, perhaps getting you probation or community service.

RESOURCES FOR EXPUNGING A CRIMINAL RECORD

1. The Collateral Consequences Resource Center (CCRC) maintains a chart of state laws about expunging, sealing, suppressing, and setting aside criminal records. The laws in the chart are compiled and updated by the National Association of Criminal Defense Lawyers. See ccresourcecenter. org
2. The CCRC also publishes for free online an excellent collection of "State-Specific Guides to Restoration of Rights, Pardon, Sealing and Expungement," which include links to expungement forms or pleading samples for each jurisdiction. The documents typically differ within each county, so the CCRC links will take you to a statewide portal, if there is one, and the state portal will link you to the individual courts. If there is not a state portal, the CCRC will link to a few, but not all, of the courts in your state.
3. The National Association of Criminal Defense Lawyers, through its Restoration of Rights Project, shows whether and how each state and the federal government enable people with criminal records to restore their civil rights, resume their professional licensure, and get their record sealed or expunged. See www.nacdl.org/rightsrestoration.
4. Local legal aid offices frequently provide instructional packets telling exactly how to seek expungement in the local court. The packets list all of the steps to take, and they also have sample documents. If your local office does not provide such a packet, see if you can get one from a neighboring legal aid office in your state. Find legal aid offices via the federal Legal Services Corporation at lsc.gov.

5. The court where a conviction occurred will usually provide formal instructions for sealing, suppressing, setting aside, or expunging a record. The instructions will probably be less detailed than legal aid instructions, but they will certainly be authentic. Find the instructions by browsing in the court's website for terms like *forms* and *processes*. If they have a search box, type in the word *expunge*. You can usually get to the court's website by typing its name into a search engine.

6. The Electronic Privacy Information Center reports on data about state expungement practices. See epic.org/privacy/expungement.

RESOURCES FOR FAMILY LIABILITY

1. Justia has a free and authoritative criminal law glossary online at justia.com.

2. The National Center for State Courts offers a free assortment of authoritative articles about criminal procedure at ncsc.org.

3. *Common Steps in Criminal Investigation and Prosecution* is a plain English description of the criminal justice system from Lewis and Clark Law School (available at law.lclark.edu).

4. "The Interview: Do Police Interrogation Techniques Produce False Confessions?," an article by Douglas Starr, was published in the *New Yorker* (December 12, 2009). It is available for free online at newyorker.com.

5. The federal court system's introduction to criminal court is free online at uscourts.gov. It is titled *Understanding the Federal Courts: How Courts Work—Criminal Cases*.

6. Two American Civil Liberties Union (ACLU) guides to interacting with police are: *Know Your Rights When Encountering Law Enforcement* and *What to Do if You are Stopped by Police, Immigration Agents or the FBI*. Both of them are available at aclu.org.

7. Read about individual criminal charges at criminal.findlaw.com and in the legal encyclopedia at law.cornell.edu.

8. The National Association of Criminal Defense Lawyers has explanations of criminal court practices and defense legal issues on its website at nacdl.org.

9. The very interesting 2007 article by Dan Markel and Ethan J. Leib, "Criminal Justice and the Challenge of Family Ties" (*University of Illinois Law Review*, 1147), is tangential to the topic of family liability. Rather than focusing on family members who get blamed for a relative's crime, it focuses on all of the options that families have in regard to their relative's guilt: whether to turn him in or to help him flee, whether to testify against him in court, whether to harbor a fugitive, etc. The list of options extends through the entire criminal trial and incarceration. Search for the title of the article to find it for free online.

PART 3

Employment Law

14

Employee Reputations and Opportunities

You used to work with Diane and you have encouraged her to apply for a job where you work now. Diane was basically bullied out of her last job. She says that nobody liked her there. Out of work for six weeks now, she is already behind on credit card bills. This combination of social pressures at the last job and financial troubles at home makes her anxious about getting to know new co-workers and it also makes her worry about what might be in her record if her new employer does a background check.

LAWS THAT PROTECT EMPLOYEES WITH DISABILITIES

There are many state employment laws and two federal laws—the Americans with Disabilities Act (ADA) and the Rehabilitation Act—that were enacted to help people with disabilities, including psychiatric disabilities, to find and keep good jobs that match their talents and availability. But the symptoms of conditions that may at times interfere with work tasks can also prevent these individuals from asserting their legal rights. In fact, a person's own beliefs about himself may make him doubt that he can have a satisfying and stimulating job. For example, some people think that:

- If they have experienced serious mental illness and might experience it again, they probably cannot find a job.
- If they are collecting Supplemental Security Income (SSI), or Social Security Disability Insurance (SSDI), they are not permitted to get a job.
- If they experience an episode of serious mental illness, they will lose their job.

All of this is wrong. Employees with disabilities have legal rights from the time they apply for a job all the way through the end of the job. And much of the time, friends and family members can help enforce these rights when an employee is not able to. If they understand employment law, people with mental illness and their supporters can prevent a lot of work problems from getting worse.

The ADA means a job application process can be made feasible for somebody who otherwise would not even have a chance at the job. For example, what if, because of her psychiatric disability, your mother cannot participate in job interviews by telephone because she has to see people's faces when she is talking with them? She should be able to have her remote interviews online instead of over the phone so that she can look at the interviewers while she answers their questions. The ADA also ensures that work environments and job tasks can be adjusted to enable an employee to maintain a job while managing mental health symptoms.

If mental illness prevents someone from being able to sustain gainful employment, then Social Security regulations entitle her to financial assistance and medical insurance. The Social Security regulations also establish ways for employees with disabilities, including those who have a mental illness, to work part time while collecting disability benefits. When employees have to miss work because of their mental condition, they do not have to lose their jobs; in many situations, the Family and Medical Leave Act (FMLA) and the ADA entitle them to time off for treatment and recovery. Employees whose jobs cause severe mental upset, such as trauma brought on by a tormenting supervisor, can sometimes collect workers' compensation benefits to help them get through a recovery period. And workers who lose their jobs for reasons connected to their mental health can sometimes collect unemployment or disability benefits or file disability discrimination claims.

The one thing that makes employment law especially challenging is that any legal claims usually have to start at the workplace, rather than in a neutral court or regulatory agency. So suffering employees often have to make requests or accusations directly to the source of their misery face on:

- You discriminated against me.
- You caused me injury.
- I need a change to how things are going at work.
- I need to take time off.
- You made it impossible for me to do my job.

While employees may use different words or phrases, they do need to file grievances about mistreatment, requests for accommodation, and claims for insurance coverage directly with their employer. This can be a stressful process for anyone, and even more so for an employee who has, for example, clinical depression or an anxiety disorder. But there are ways that friends and families can help!

HOW TO Talk About Employment Law

When your loved one vents to you about a job search or an existing job, she is instinctively trying to protect her reputation. She relies on you to keep her secrets, to understand that she has to let off steam, and to give her good advice. If you are not a lawyer or paralegal and everything that you know about employment law comes from this book, and your loved one is already upset about an employment problem, you may feel intimidated about discussing possible legal remedies. You may think that you do not have sufficient legal knowledge to explain things to her, and you may worry that talking about legal action will agitate her. Here are some ideas for managing the conversation. These ideas are similar to the steps that a lawyer uses in a consultation with a prospective client.

1. *Acknowledge the injustice.* You probably do not know everything that went wrong when your family member applied for a job or had a bad experience at work. You only know what she has told you. She may recall certain events and conversations more vividly because they made her feel bad. She likely will not have full information about the employer's efforts on her behalf. Nevertheless, if she has expressed to you that an employer treated her unkindly or unfairly, then just out of loyalty you can acknowledge her feelings of injustice. This is what lawyers do when they meet consultation clients; they show appreciation for the client's version of events, while thinking to themselves about whether there is a basis for a lawsuit if everything that they are hearing is true. If it does not sound like the story requires legal action, the lawyer will not take the case. Similarly, you do not have to take up your family member's cause after you have enabled her to vent.

2. *Do not attempt to push your loved one to do something.* You know already that you cannot make another adult do something that she does not want to do. However, you can influence her thinking. When an adult in your family has a mental illness and is upset about something at work, your attempts to make her take a particular action will merely interfere with her thoughts. Maybe you think she should apologize to somebody. Maybe you believe that she should do whatever is necessary to get or keep the job. Maybe you think it is time to take legal action. All of these action plans come from your perception and personality, not from hers. Lawyers know that when people come to them for consultations, they are often just checking on their legal rights and will get scared if the lawyer jumps right in with a plan of attack. You, too, risk scaring or otherwise exciting your loved one at a point when her natural inclination may be to calm down once she gets the story off of her chest.

3. *Help her to gather information.* It is likely that your relative has some ambivalence about her employment situation; she is figuring out how to process it. She may need some information in order to decide what to do next. You may be able to help her figure out what kind of information she needs and think of where to find out what she needs to know. Depending on your own skills and your schedule, you could even offer to find the information for her.

   Suppose she wants to know if the boss can force her to work overtime. There are a few places to look for information about overtime: the employee handbook at work (if there is one); the federal Department of Labor's website about wages and hours; and the website for your state agency on labor. Perhaps she wonders how she can move to a different job within the same company. Her human resources office will have information about vacant jobs. She can contact them directly without telling her supervisor that she is even thinking about making a change. And depending on her situation, not doing overtime or getting a job transfer might be a reasonable accommodation. The Equal Employment Opportunity Commission (EEOC) website provides information on reasonable accommodation.

Maybe she thinks she is being harassed at work, but she isn't sure. She or you can reach out to a nearby women's rights organization or a disability rights organization to describe what has happened and ask if it sounds like harassment.

For any of these questions, she or you can also call your local bar association to ask if there are any free or reduced-rate services available in your community to provide legal advice and counsel to employees with disabilities.

Even if you do not immediately know where to get an answer, just telling your loved one that it sounds like she needs some information may help her to feel calmer and to know what to do with her energy, other than using so much of it to be upset. You can call a library reference desk later and find out where to look for answers. Lawyers do this, too; they identify an information need when they hear a prospective client's story. They will say out loud right there in the meeting, "Here's what we still need to know," or "I'll have to find out what the regulations say about this," or "I just don't know if your situation is like other cases around here." This last message can be deflating if the client was hoping for a fight, but that's okay; deflating is a form of calming, and if the situation does not sound illegal, the lawyer is modeling for the client that it is not wise to spend time and energy on it.

4. *Help her to formulate goals.* As you listen to your loved one's employment woes, consider the possibility that she is weighing legal options against some other interests, such as keeping her income. She may be angry and ready to quit her job at one moment and depressed about being considered a failure the next moment. Maybe she can't even get her foot in the door because there is something bad in her background check and she doesn't know whether to give up the job search altogether or keep pressing on. Let her work through these thoughts out loud, if she wants to do that. She will review the same thoughts with her therapist, caseworker, or job coach if she works with any of those professionals. In the meantime, this is when you may have an opportunity to verbalize what you have read about grievances, discrimination claims, getting time off through the FMLA or ADA, or other employment law protections that are covered in this book. Lawyers like to close their client consultations with options so that prospective clients have a convenient reason for pondering further before they decide whether to go forward with legal action. Similarly, you want to support your family member's efforts to make a decision about handling her employment difficulties.

EMPLOYMENT BACKGROUND CHECKS

These days, a lot of different jobs require new hires to undergo medical clearance or a criminal or financial background check before their hiring is complete. Employers seeking medical clearance are looking for confirmation that workers have the physical or psychological ability "to perform job-related functions." When assessing the health of new hires or existing employees whose duties are about to change, the employer has to obtain the relevant medical records from all of the workers in the same job category, not just selected individuals. And if one of those workers goes on leave for an illness or injury, he may have to undergo fitness-for-duty testing that includes medical exams again to confirm that he can still perform his job-related functions before he returns to work. Whenever employers collect medical records, they are required by the EEOC to file them separately from the rest of each employee's record and to maintain them as confidential documents.

Employers who check prospective employees' criminal records are usually trying to find out:

- Whether they can trust applicants with money,
- Whether applicants are safe drivers (if the job involves driving), and/or
- Whether applicants have a history of using drugs or committing violent crimes.

A criminal background check might look for arrests as well as convictions or it might just look for convictions, depending on the employer's information need. Since a lot of driving-related crimes are resolved with traffic citations, certain employers will require records of even those low-level offenses. When an employer seeks information about a prospective employee's trustworthiness with money, the background check may include the applicant's credit report in addition to his criminal record. One stray debt collection recorded in a credit report will probably not concern an employer, but a history of multiple nonpayments can suggest that the applicant does not handle money responsibly.

All of these common information needs are considered valid reasons for employers to collect employee background information. There can also be more formal reasons for background checks. In some instances, liability insurance requires employers to know about applicants' criminal backgrounds. In other instances, state laws mandate that particular professionals, such as teachers and elder-care providers, have no record of crimes committed against their client population. Whether background checks result from the employer's information need or from a state law requirement, they may only be used for legitimate hiring and employee-retention decisions. Employee privacy must be respected throughout the background check process.

Mental Health Commitments and Criminal Background Checks

Employment-based criminal background checks are not likely to include records of the police transporting someone to a mental health facility. Those police encounters are not arrests, and they are not part of a standard criminal record. In certain circumstances and jurisdictions, however, someone could be held in a mental health detention space operated by law enforcement. This kind of placement is more than simple transportation to a hospital and can appear in a criminal record.

An actual commitment to a mental hospital, as discussed in Chapter 5, is a medical determination usually made in the emergency department and is filed in civil court, not criminal court. Civil courts ordinarily do not make commitment records available to the public. However, according to federal law, they are supposed to submit them to the FBI's National Instant Criminal Background Check System (NICS).

The NICS is a limited-purpose database; it was created to control gun sales and is primarily used for background checks when people purchase firearms. Most employers cannot access it, although there are certain federal jobs that do require NICS background checks regarding mental health commitments. Typically, these are jobs for which a Transportation Workers Identification Card (TWIC) is necessary. Other jobs that need mental health background information prior to hiring will usually ask applicants to divulge their own commitment history.

Permission To Check Criminal Background

Most of the time, employers who need criminal background information only need it from their own state database of criminal records or from states where an applicant previously worked or resided. None of these checks will be done behind the applicant's back. State laws require employers to get permission from prospective employees before they can access criminal records. The release form on which the prospective employee gives this permission will list which records the employer is looking for. Employers cannot check these law enforcement databases themselves. They have to submit the prospective employee's permission slip along with a formal request to the law enforcement agency that has authority to search in the database. This, at least, is the formal and complete way of obtaining criminal records. On many local, county, and state court systems' websites, the public can navigate through judgment lists for free and at least find some facts about a particular defendant's involvement in criminal court. Employers tend not to bother with the free court records. The law enforcement databases provide more thorough information and the legal requirements for accessing them—especially getting permission from the job applicant—ensure open communication about how a record impacts the hiring decision.

Credit Reports in Background Checks

When employers use a credit reporting agency as a source for background information, they have to comply with the federal Fair Credit Reporting Act (FCA). Three communication tasks that the FCA requires of employers during the credit check process are:

- Get permission from the person whose credit report is being checked.
- Give that person a copy of the report before firing, reassigning, not hiring, or not promoting him.
- Inform the fired, reassigned, unhired, or unpromoted employee how the employer obtained the information that affected the decision and explain how to dispute and correct any information that may be wrong in the credit report.

Discrimination Arising From a Background Check

Once an employer has the information from the background check, they may not use it to discriminate on the basis of disability or any other EEOC protected class, such as race or religion. Here are two examples:

If the credit report shows that your father has unpaid bills owed to a psychiatric care provider, the employer cannot refuse to hire on the grounds that your dad has had psychiatric care. Employers are not even permitted to ask for extra information that might be connected with a prospective employee's credit report or criminal record. So an employer who sees that your father owes money to a psychiatric care provider cannot ask whether it was he or a different family member who required the care, what the care involved, or anything else beyond what was revealed in the credit check.

Suppose two job candidates have equal qualifications and committed equal crimes except that one candidate's criminal record includes the fact that she was temporarily not competent to stand trial and had to get mental health treatment. If the employer makes the hiring decision based on the disability information contained in the criminal record, the situation is probably worthy of an EEOC review. (See Chapter 15 on employment discrimination for information about filing an EEOC complaint.)

What Happens to the Private Background Record?

When a human resources office has no more use for private records, it can dispose of them. Criminal records disposal is generally covered by the federal regulation that requires confidential handling of criminal records at every stage of a background check. This regulation declares that employers have to ensure "integrity and security . . . to protect individual privacy." Credit reports have to be completely destroyed. The Federal Trade Commission (FTC) enforces a detailed "disposal rule" that requires employers to "burn, pulverize, or shred papers . . . so that the information cannot be reconstructed." The same rule requires employers to "destroy or erase electronic files.

The EEOC, which regulates all of the contents of employee files, not merely the records from a background check, is not as precise, however, in describing exactly how employers should ensure privacy when disposing of records; it simply declares when employers can dispose of employee records. The EEOC's emphasis is on preservation of evidence in case an employee sues the employer after leaving the job. If the employee files a discrimination claim, the EEOC requires the employer to keep everything that is in the personnel file until the case is completely over—including appeals. If an employee record simply contains the worker's initial application, his performance evaluations, and his resignation letter and he has never claimed discrimination, then his employer can dispose of his employment records one year after the last item was filed in the record. If an applicant is not hired by a particular employer, then the employer can discard the application after one year. There is one common exception to this one-year rule: Federal contractors have to keep employee records for three years instead of one.

When federal laws do not contain specific instructions for records disposal, such as the EEOC regulations and the federal regulations on criminal records, employers follow state data disposal laws that set forth requirements for disposing of private information that is contained in business records. These tend to require that records be destroyed, as opposed to simply being discarded, and they delineate requirements for managing technology systems and papers that are in transit for destruction.

Once the background check is over and the applicant is hired for her new job, she has a chance to develop her reputation. Suppose your cousin Maddie, who has major depression, is the person who has just been through this background check. No matter what happened at her past jobs or in her personal life, now that she has been hired for a new job, she can write a new chapter in the story of her life and take things in a different direction. Like many of us, she likes to have her personal identity associated with a job title and a workplace. In social situations, she will describe herself in connection with her employment. If she makes friends, does good work, and pleases the boss, any problems in her old record will become less significant over time. But if things go badly at work, the opposite can happen. A good employment record and clean background information can be marred by bad behavior.

POOR PERFORMANCE—INCLUDING BAD CONDUCT—AT WORK

We have all been around people who act badly when they feel bad. And we all know that severe mental health symptoms make people feel bad. So it stands to reason that an employee experiencing an episode of severe mental impairment may perform poorly on the job. Predictably, because the varieties of symptoms and job tasks are vast, the law does not provide a single prescription for managing employees whose disabilities cause them to perform poorly at work; sometimes they need to be disciplined and sometimes they need to be accommodated.

There is a series of questions that determines whether an employee is entitled to accommodation at work:

1. The first question is whether the employee has an impairment that interferes with at least one of her "major life activities."
2. The second question is whether she has a record of having the impairment or is regarded as having it.
3. And the third question is whether the employee is qualified to do the job either with accommodations or without them.

If the impairment interferes with a major life activity and the employee is qualified to do her essential work tasks, then she is supposed to get accommodation. If the answer to any of the questions is "no," then the employee is not considered disabled, is not entitled to accommodation, and can be disciplined. (See Chapter 15 for more details about workplace disability accommodation.)

The EEOC's regulations state that the following psychiatric conditions are, in virtually all cases, disabilities under the ADA because of how they affect the major life activity of brain function: major depressive disorder, bipolar disorder, post-traumatic stress disorder, obsessive-compulsive disorder, and schizophrenia. In addition to brain function, there are a number of additional recognized major life activities that are likely to be substantially limited for individuals with mental illnesses, including caring for oneself, eating, sleeping, reading, concentrating, thinking, communicating, interacting with others, and working. Some of these limitations, such as not being able to interact with others, may make someone unqualified for certain jobs. The facts of every case are different. In some jobs, such as your nephew Roy's customer service position at the building supply store, it is essential for employees to share, cooperate, and interact pleasantly with each other and with clients or customers. In those settings, social skills count as job qualifications.

Getting along with people is certainly not the only job qualification that can be compromised by a mental impairment; it is just more difficult to define than other job qualifications. For example, some people cannot focus on details when their mental health symptoms are bad. Others cannot sit at a desk all day, while still others cannot tolerate certain types of technology. To find out whether these are job qualifications, you or your family member who has a mental illness can check job descriptions contained in ads and performance evaluations for a particular position and the rules set forth by the employer in an employee handbook or other publication. These sources help to consistently categorize employee conduct.

Usually, the skills and tasks itemized in the job description and performance evaluation are considered essential functions of the job. If an employee cannot perform essential functions, even with reasonable accommodation, she is not qualified for the job. If particular conduct is merely listed in the employer's rules, but not in the job description or performance evaluation, the conduct may be a standard or an expectation but it may not be an essential function. The employee does have to comply with the rules, but he will not necessarily be considered unqualified if he fails to comply with them. Maybe your nephew Roy, the customer service agent, is in a manic phase that causes him to talk and move very quickly and to switch abruptly between things. His employer's rules require him to be patient with customers, but he is simply not able to respond patiently during this phase. It would make sense for him to request reasonable accommodations in this situation.

Examples of Bad Conduct by Employees

I once had a co-worker who would throw her office phone on the floor or against a wall whenever she got angry. She broke three phones beyond repair with this behavior. While her job did require her to talk on the phone, taking care of the phone was not among her job qualifications. If it had been a job qualification, and she had requested disability accommodation, the employer could have asserted that they owed her no accommodation because she did not know how to take care of phones and was therefore not qualified for the job. She did get in some minor disciplinary trouble for violating a provision

*in the employee handbook—not, however, a rule specifically about the phone.
It was a statement that employees should not damage workplace property.*

Here is an EEOC example:

*A loading dock employee whose work did not involve contact with customers or
co-workers was disciplined for wearing messy clothes and being "antisocial" for several weeks. The behaviors were symptoms of his mental health disability but were
also violations of the employer's dress code and courtesy policy. The EEOC says that
"rigid application" of the dress code and courtesy policy with regard to this particular
employee "would violate the ADA." In other words, the employer would be guilty of
discrimination if it disciplined this worker, whose conduct was symptomatic of his
mental impairment and did not involve his job qualifications.*

There are a couple of things to learn from the above examples:

1. Disciplining somebody who is simply exhibiting symptoms of a disability
   can be a form of discrimination.
2. An employee who is not necessarily disabled, like the telephone thrower,
   does not have to lose a job for demonstrating occasional minor symptoms.
   She can show that she is qualified to do her work, accept her discipline,
   take corrective action, and keep her job.

HOW TO Help Save a Job if an Employee Performs Poorly

Some employers can trick employees with disabilities out of their jobs by saying
that they are no longer qualified to do their work. For example, you may be able
to help your sister Ariana (who lives with ADHD) save her job by showing her
how to prove that her problematic performance (she impulsively printed an unnecessarily large quantity of expensive materials for the first program of the year
and now has no printing budget left for the remainder of the year's programs)
was merely inappropriate or unprofessional but not enough to get her fired. Urge
your sister to use her performance evaluation to her advantage. The good parts of
her evaluation will show how she is qualified for the job. The list of qualifications
itself will give her criteria to balance against the boss's complaints. If Ariana
does not have the energy or other wherewithal to obtain a medical statement and
request disability accommodation with the human resources office, then you
can do that legwork or find someone (a vocational counselor, another relative, a
disability lawyer, a social worker) to handle it.

Another way that you can sometimes save a job is to propose corrective action
as an alternative to either being fired or facing such harsh discipline that the employee would want to quit. Corrective action often includes redoing a ruined set
of tasks, having to be closely supervised for a set period, and writing apologies
to people. Participation in training sessions and therapy can also count as corrective action. Training sessions may be about teamwork, anger management,
communication skills, stress management, and other aspects of self-control.
In Ariana's case, the training would probably help her to develop more skill at
making plans. If she can show that the poor performance is a symptom of a
treatable mental health condition, an employee may be permitted to use sick

time or FMLA/ADA time to participate in training sessions. (Refer to Chapter 16 for guidance about making that request.) As long as you are in touch with the human resources department, you should ask if that office or any employee benefit programs at the workplace will pay for training or therapy.

Here are some ideas for communicating with your relative's employer:

1. Talk to your family member about how they want to handle the situation, and if they want you to help them communicate with the employer. It is important for someone—either the employee or someone speaking on behalf of the employee—to contact human resources before they make any decisions.

2. If your family member asks you to reach out to human resources on their behalf, all you need to say in this first conversation is something like:

My [spouse, son, daughter, sister . . .] has a disability and was involved in a bad situation at work yesterday. [He or she] works as a ___ in the __ department. I am just calling to let you know that while [he or she] is getting medical care related to yesterday's incident, I am available to help with any of your FMLA or ADA procedures for [him or her].

Any human resources professional—not the receptionist, but the actual professionals who are trained in human resources—will understand that you are putting them on notice as required by the two federal employment laws.

3. Do not admit to any wrongdoing by your relative and do not divulge private medical information. It is fine to convey that your relative is getting psychiatric care, but you should not say anything about the employee's psychiatric history or speculate about why the bad behavior happened at work. In the unlikely event that the human resource worker tries to get that kind of information from you, be ready to keep the conversation on track. You can say something along the lines of,

You seem to be asking me to guess what happened. I do not have that information. I am just calling to fulfill [name the employee]'s legal obligation to put you on notice for [his or her] FMLA and ADA rights.

4. If the human resources worker asks something like, "Has this ever happened before?" keep the attention on current events. Your goal is to save the job and any health insurance coverage that the employer provides. You could reply to the question in one of the following ways or in some other manner that is comfortable for you:

I really do not even know exactly what happened; is there a written report that you could send me? or *I am sorry, I do not have an answer to that question.* Or respond with the ever-uninformative *Why do you ask?*

WORKPLACE DISCIPLINE

It may be that the bad scene at work was not so big or so bad that an employee (such as your sister Ariana) needs time off under the FMLA or ADA, or even another accommodation under the ADA. Maybe Ariana is already getting accommodation, but the bad situation (her poor planning and impulsive squandering of the printing budget) happened, and now she is going to be disciplined. There are three legal concepts to know about employee discipline:

- Contract rights
- Due process
- Representation.

These are not likely to be actual formal, legal steps that someone would take, or legal rights that someone can enforce (except in a unionized workplace), but they are important concepts to understand because they provide bases for employees and employers to discuss the situation.

Contract rights are spelled out in documents, such as the employee handbook or staff policy manual, the workplace's list of rules, a formal union contract, and sometimes even lofty corporate policies on labor and human rights. The documents explain, among many other things, what is supposed to happen regarding salary, benefits, scheduling, and duties when an employee does something wrong.

Due process is about the way an employee gets disciplined. If there is a system for employee discipline, then every employee has a due process right to go through all of the steps in that system. If some employees have been treated differently from (better than or less harshly than) your sister, then she has a due process right to have the situation handled as the others were. Due process typically includes an opportunity for the employee to explain her perspective on what happened.

The concept of representation is simply the idea that, under the circumstances, a person who cannot express him- or herself should be able to have somebody else speak on his or her behalf. When an employee's disability interferes with her ability to represent herself, she can request representation as a reasonable accommodation in order to participate in the disciplinary conversations regarding her work performance. Combined with contract rights and due process, the opportunity for representation means that a family member, union representative, or caseworker would communicate with the employer about the poor performance and its effect on the employee's job.

Some offenses may lead to retraining, others to reprimands or write-ups, and some to demotion, while some will result in automatic firing. If there is a rule, policy, or contract about how particular types of offenses will be punished, employees need to know whether they are getting the treatment that is established.

Even without a policy in hand, an employee or her representative can ask whether the situation is being handled the way these things are always handled. Then, they can ask what comes next, in that policy, regarding the employee's ongoing employment or using the job as a reference for future employment.

If the workplace does not have a formal punishment scale and the employer arbitrarily made a decision in your relative's case, it may be possible to negotiate for mercy by offering to pay for property damage or to make any changes that the employer requests. A family member or caseworker could just say:

> *Ariana really likes this job and I want to help her build on the positive aspects of it. Is there anything that you want me to do to help ensure that there will not be a repeat of what happened?*

The interceding family member or the caseworker may be able to steer the conversation away from the employee's behavior and toward the needs of the workplace. For example:

> *I know that you need your staff to be here at 6:00 a.m., not three hours later like Ted has been lately, but putting him on bathroom-cleaning duty is not going to make him get to work any earlier. Can I work with you to come up with a punishment that is more likely to get him here and ready to work at 6:00?*

Poor performance like bad conduct at work is very often the result of stress—the temporary inability to reconcile pressures. *Temporary* is the important word here. Something is going wrong now, but it cannot always have been a problem. Maybe the job changed or maybe the employee is going through a change. Either one can change again, this time to rectify whatever brought about the bad conduct. But if neither the work situation nor the employee can change where they are heading, then an outside force—such as the ADA, FMLA, regular sick leave, and/or management training—can hopefully lead to a resolution.

In court cases about bad workplace conduct, it is easy to see how employees who are in the middle of mental crises and employers who lack understanding and are unwavering in their operations can get all tangled up. It is like viewing a weather map where a warm air mass and a cold air mass fly toward each other and swirl into a tornado when they collide. When it is over, others are left to clean up the destruction.

Court Cases About Poor Performance at Work

Baker v. City of New York, 1999 WL 33115 (E.D.N.Y.)
A social worker whose "unstable behavior was disruptive, threatening, and bizarre" was justifiably fired and was not a victim of discrimination because "no reasonable accommodation" would have enabled her to "perform the essential functions of her position."

Overton v. Reilly, 977 F.2d 1190 (7th Cir. 1992)
A chemist who lived with major depression and was tired during the day because of medicine that he took for his depression was authorized to proceed with a disability discrimination lawsuit against his employer after the employer fired him for occasionally taking catnaps and for poor communication with the public. His productivity was not compromised by the catnaps and communicating with the public

was not necessarily an essential function of his job. A trial court needed to decide whether he was entitled to accommodation.

CRANDALL V. PARALYZED VETERANS OF AMERICA, 146 F.3D 894 (D.C. CIR. 1998)

A rude and arrogant law librarian with bipolar disorder, who was verbally abusive to co-workers and almost got his library expelled from a trade organization, sued his employer for disability discrimination after being fired for his bad conduct. He lost the lawsuit largely because the employer had not even known that the librarian had bipolar disorder.

GAMBINI V. TOTAL RENAL CARE, 486 F.3D 1087 (9TH CIR. 2007)

An employee who had informed her employer about her bipolar disorder and was working to manage her symptoms was fired during her FMLA leave. She had taken the leave immediately after an angry outburst at work when she was blindsided by a sudden meeting at which her supervisor and a company administrator presented her with an "improvement plan." She sued her employer for firing her, and the jury upheld her firing, but the jury had not been informed that in the court's jurisdiction "conduct resulting from a disability is considered part of the disability, rather than a separate basis for termination." The appeals court decided that the case should be retried and that the next jury should be instructed on this point.

TAYLOR V. PHOENIXVILLE SCHOOL DISTRICT, 184 F.3D 296 (3D CIR. 1999)

A school principal's secretary was not accommodated when she returned to work after being hospitalized for bipolar disorder even though, during her hospitalization, her son had provided the school with medical documentation and other proof of his mother's bipolar disorder and her ongoing need for accommodation. In fact, when she returned to work, the school did the opposite of accommodating her. The principal began scrutinizing her and writing down every time she failed to deliver a message, had an interpersonal conflict, or even made an ordinary mistake. The initial trial court judge dismissed the case on the grounds that there was no question of law since the principal's lists proved that the secretary was not qualified and therefore was not eligible for disability rights. The appeals court held that a jury needed to hear the case. The appeals court further stated that, if the jury did find that the secretary was disabled, the school district would be obligated to interact with the secretary about possible accommodations and then implement reasonable accommodations for her.

CAMERON V. COMMUNITY AID FOR RETARDED CHILDREN,[1] 335 F.3D 60 (2D CIR. 2003)

The associate director of a thrift shop who had anxiety disorder got into a lot of trouble after a single angry exchange with a co-worker grew into a mess that attracted higher administrative attention. The associate director had been a highly

---

1 The agency later changed its name to Community Resources Staten Island and, in keeping with current terminology, states that it serves "people with intellectual and developmental disabilities."

praised and regularly promoted worker until this event. Ten days after it, she had to go on leave because of an anxiety attack. Meanwhile, the co-worker quit because she could no longer stand working for the associate director, although she did have to come to the building on a regular basis for her child's appointments at the service agency that was funded by the thrift shop.

When the associate director got back to work, she attempted to arrange a part-time schedule and requested that the job accommodate her anxiety by either refusing services to the former co-worker or giving her time off whenever the co-worker brought her child for services. Rather than satisfying these requests, the employer fired the associate director. The courts, at trial and on appeal, found that she was not qualified to be an associate director at this workplace for two reasons: (1) She would not admit that she was disabled by her anxiety, so it made no sense for her to claim disability discrimination, and (2) Having sufficient communications and relationship skills to manage people and control disputes was an essential qualification of the job. Seeking to avoid someone with whom she had argued was even more proof that she lacked that qualification.

PETRONE V. HAMPTON BAYS UNION SCHOOL DISTRICT, 03-CV-4539 (E.D.N.Y. JULY 10, 2013)

This case involved a new social studies teacher who suffered from a nervous condition. Medication kept him calm during his student teaching and the first few months of his professional job, but when he could no longer get to his VA psychiatrist (because the VA was open only during the hours when the teacher had to be at work), the teacher ran out of medicine and gradually became too nervous to be at the school at all. His union representative and the school district worked out a deal under which he was convinced to resign, so the lawsuit hinged on the fact that he had not been fired. Still, the appellate court summarized earlier cases about employees whose mental impairments made them unable to come to work. In summarizing them, this court showed that being present at work is often an essential qualification for the job.

COHEN V. AMERITECH, 15. A.D. CASES 363 (N.D. ILL. 2003)

Mr. Cohen was a telephone customer service representative whose job was to resolve and refer customer's problems and to inform customers about new and different products. He developed anxiety, for which he got counseling and prescription medicine, but he still could not tolerate two new company practices without suffering anxiety symptoms. The two company practices were (1) having monitors listen in on the customer service representatives' conversations with customers, and (2) requiring the customer service representatives to always recommend new products to callers, even when doing so was not related to the purpose of the call. Both of the practices were deemed to be essential functions of his job, since accommodating him by waiving those practices would mean that he did not have to do the full job. Because he could not handle these essential functions without unreasonable accommodation, he was not qualified to do the job.

If it bothers you that the employers won in so many of the case examples, do not be discouraged. The examples show the gaps that families can fill. Someone in the school teacher's family could have convinced him to take time off from work for routine psychiatric appointments so that he could continue with his medicine and keep his job. They could have helped him to request time off as an accommodation, which might have been necessary if he had not yet earned any sick time. The law librarian's family could have informed the employer, on his behalf, that he needed disability accommodations. That is exactly what the school secretary's son did. His proof of his mom's disability and her need for accommodation saved the day in her case. Finally, in the cases of the social worker, the associate director, and the telephone customer service representative, where the courts found that the employees were not qualified to do their jobs and therefore were not entitled to accommodation, the families could have helped their loved ones either to avoid going to court or to find more appropriate jobs after losing their cases.

Although the two subjects covered in this chapter show how the law applies to each individual employee's reputation, think about the general perception of mental illness, too. When your friend or family member tries to enter the workforce or move from one job to another, something about her association with mental illness may very well keep her from finding a good job match. Research by various experts and agencies conducted over time has consistently shown that employees living with mental illnesses have trouble finding and maintaining work that is appropriate to their intellectual abilities. The ADA can help workers with mental illness to overcome negative perceptions and have a fair chance at having employment that incorporates their interests and abilities; however, without the assistance of friends and relatives, it can be very daunting to face down discrimination.

RESOURCES FOR EMPLOYMENT BACKGROUND CHECKS

1. The Legal Action Center provides citations and summaries for every state's background check laws. See its *Roadblocks to Reentry* report for this information (available at lac.org).
2. The FTC establishes rules about employers using credit reports for employment background checks. In cooperation with the EEOC, it has produced an explanatory guide, *Background Checks: What Job Applicants and Employees Should Know*. See also the FTC guide titled *What Employment Background Screening Companies Need to Know about the Fair Credit Reporting Act*. These guides are free online at ftc.gov.
3. Employers usually contract with professional screening agencies to conduct background investigations. The National Association of Professional Background Screeners provides facts about background checks, a glossary of terms related to background checks, and frequently asked consumer questions at napbs.com.
4. The EEOC makes available free online guidelines, titled *Consideration of Arrest and Conviction Records in Employment Decisions Under Title VII of the Civil Rights Act of 1964*, at eeoc.gov.
5. State laws about data disposal, which mandate how employers are required to dispose of information obtained through background checks, are available through a portal at the National Conference of State Legislatures (at ncsl.org).

6. The Legal Action Center has developed an entire advocacy toolkit that includes model laws, action alerts, sample letters, and suggestions for steps that people can take to lobby their legislatures about writing better laws regarding background checks. See lac.org.

7. The National Employment Law Project (NELP) published a rousing report titled *Unlicensed and Untapped: Removing Barriers to State Occupational Licenses for People with Records.* Filled with data and examples of how people with criminal records are excluded from working in many fields, it calls on state licensing boards to change their rules. The report and NELP's entire campaign to advance "fair chance hiring" may inspire families dealing with the stigma of mental illness. See nelp.org.

8. The EEOC has helpful web pages, *Pre-Employment Inquiries and Arrest & Conviction* and *Background Checks: What Job Applicants and Employees Should Know*, on its website at eeoc.gov.

9. Nolo Press publishes summaries of state laws on use of arrests and convictions in employment in connection with its Employment Law Center at nolo.com.

10. The Bureau of Alcohol, Tobacco, and Firearms has a very informative website about the National Instant Criminal Background Check System (NICS) at atf.gov.

11. The federal regulations about "Criminal Justice Information Systems" are in 28 C.F.R. pt. 20. The regulations require that "criminal history record information wherever it appears is collected, stored, and disseminated in a manner to ensure the accuracy, completeness, currency, integrity, and security of such information and to protect individual privacy." The EEOC regulations permitting employers to dispose of employee and application records one year after employment ends or the application does not result in employment is at 29 C.F.R. § 1602.14. The EEOC regulation requiring employers to keep employee medical information in separate files from each employee's general employment record is 29 C.F.R. § 1630.14. These regulations are available for free online at ecfr. gov.

RESOURCES FOR POOR PERFORMANCE AT WORK

1. The EEOC's *Enforcement Guidance on Reasonable Accommodation and Undue Hardship* and *Enforcement Guidance on the ADA and Psychiatric Disabilities* are both available online at eeoc.gov. See also the EEOC fact sheet "The Americans With Disabilities Act: Applying Performance And Conduct Standards To Employees With Disabilities," which is also available at eeoc.gov.

2. The Society for Human Resources Management has a sample "Progressive Discipline Policy," which is a good example of how employers might deal with poor performance—depending on how many times the employee has done something wrong and how bad the wrongdoing is. You and your relative may want to have this kind of scale in mind if you try to discuss your relative's workplace punishment. The society also published a useful

article, "How to Accommodate Employees with Mental Illness," which could help you know what to ask the employer to do for your relative. See shrm.org.

3. The Partnership for Workplace Mental Health produces a newsletter, surveys, and other writings about the behavior and management of employees who have psychiatric conditions. These materials will be very helpful to you as you advocate for your relative and try to educate his or her employer about best handling or preventing poor performance. See workplacementalhealth.org.

4. *Road to Recovery: Employment and Mental Illness* is an extensive research study conducted by the National Alliance on Mental Illness (NAMI). The study reports that 60% of people who access mental health services have a desire to work but do not get employment support that would make it possible for them to manage jobs. The report also depicts model legislation that would mandate employment support. See nami. org.

5. Written testimony of Dr. Gary Bond, presented at the March 15, 2011, EEOC Meeting on Employment of People with Mental Disabilities, is a statement that provides a good summary of research studies referencing the discrepancies between actual talents and job quality for people with mental illness. It is available at eeoc.gov.

6. The Bazelon Center for Mental Health Law has policy documents, including reports, testimony, case briefs, and government papers, as well as employment data demonstrating that people with mental illness tend to be underemployed and unemployed. The Bazelon Center also has practical fact sheets about employment support services. All of the material is available at Bazelon.org.

15

Employment Discrimination

Your brother Jordan has had a mood disorder for all twenty years of his working life. It makes him unpredictable and occasionally unreliable. He is employed in a setting where the work is generally done in teams that consist of designers, fabricators, and merchandisers. He is a fabricator, but over time the boss has concluded that it is best to just have Jordan work alone in his own area, fulfilling work orders for overflow tasks. The boss thinks he is doing right by Jordan, but excluding him was really for the benefit of the other workers, not for Jordan, who feels more like an errand boy than a skilled tradesman. Working off to the side as he does, Jordan is not eligible for any of the industry awards that are available to his co-workers. And lacking the experience of working on teams, he has no basis for getting merit raises and no opportunity to develop skills and to advance in his job. Worst of all, the isolation depresses him. You and he would both like to know if he is a victim of employment discrimination, and, if he is, whether he can truly improve his work environment.

WHAT DOES JOB DISCRIMINATION LOOK LIKE?

Job discrimination can take various forms. It can be not hiring or not fairly compensating or not promoting somebody because of a disability, such as a mental illness. It can involve harassment, such as excluding or making fun of an employee, or it can be failing to adjust the work environment to make it feasible for an employee to do his work. It can include any treatment that causes the employee with a disability not to enjoy "equal benefits and privileges of employment" compared to co-workers in similar jobs at that workplace, even if the employee is still able to perform his or her job. When they are suffering any of these forms of discrimination, employees have the right to call for action by contacting their human resources office. If they feel harassed or unfairly treated, the appropriate first step is usually to file an internal complaint or grievance with human resources. If they feel compromised in their ability to get hired or to get their work done, the appropriate action is usually to request accommodation through human resources (if they are trying to get hired) or their supervisor (if they already work somewhere). For many people, including Jordan in the vignette above, the situation involves several of these problems. If an employee's internal efforts are not effective, the next step is usually to go to the Equal Employment Opportunity Commission (EEOC). Note: For some claims under the Americans with Disabilities Act (ADA), an employee may be required by an agency or court to arbitrate or mediate the issue with the employer first—before initiating legal action.

BULLYING, HARASSMENT, AND UNFAIR TREATMENT

The ADA prohibits unfair treatment by defining it as illegal discrimination. The ADA specifically forbids "limiting, segregating, or classifying a job applicant or employee in a way that adversely affects the opportunities or status of such applicant or employee" and "utilizing standards, criteria, or methods of administration . . . that have the effect of discrimination on the basis of disability." Bullying and harassment are not spelled out quite as clearly; they simply fit into the basic requirement that employers have to prevent and eliminate workplace behavior that interferes with disabled employees' "conditions and privileges" of employment.

Either to file an internal grievance with the employer or to make an ADA complaint about these behaviors, employees have to show examples of the behaviors. Documents that make good examples include:

- A log where the employee has kept track of discriminatory quotations and actions, along with dates and times when they happened and the names of people who were present; copies of negative performance evaluations; or employer communications that contradict positive work records.
- Copies of work products demonstrating the quality of the employee's performance.
- Copies of announcements in which the employer presents employee accomplishments and promotions, and similar materials.

A combination of documents will help to support the employee's own statements about being treated differently than his co-workers.

Unfairly treated employees who live with mental illness face a challenge when trying to show discriminatory treatment: the fear that they are setting themselves up for additional torment. In their grievance report or request for accommodation, they have to divulge embarrassing information, such as admissions about mistakes they made, revelations about their own weaknesses, private beliefs about co-workers, and attitudes about the administration. Furthermore, this information has to go to the employer who is both responsible for allowing the problems to exist and responsible for fixing the problems. To many people in this situation, the setup feels unjust and hopeless. However, by collecting and presenting documentary support, employees may feel more confident that they have justification for their claims. In addition, when the employer sees an employee bringing documentation to an internal grievance meeting, that employer knows that the employee is serious, validated, and preparing to take legal action.

CONFUSION AND MISUNDERSTANDINGS
ABOUT DISABILITY AND EMPLOYMENT

Sometimes employers think that they are being accommodating when an employee thinks that they are being discriminatory. This could happen, for example, when your son Jon's employer automatically exempts him from having to use the new technology, perhaps thinking that Jon will be less stressed that way. Meanwhile, Jon does not get an equal chance to do the work in the same way that everyone else does it. Employers should consult with employees about optional or adjusted participation, rather than excluding them automatically.

Another common confusion about job discrimination arises because, according to the Social Security Administration (SSA), being disabled means that someone has a medical condition that makes him unable to "maintain substantial gainful employment," but, according to the ADA, jobs are supposed to accommodate disabilities. So if a person is disabled, how does he have a job? At what point can the employer stop accommodating and suggest that the employee collect Social Security Disability Insurance (SSDI) or Supplemental Security Income (SSI) payments instead of going to work?

The answers to these questions come from this fact: There is not one standard legal definition of disability. Disability has a different meaning in the ADA than in the context of Social Security. In the ADA, the word *disability* means "(a) a physical or mental impairment that substantially limits one or more major life activities of such individual, and (b) a record of such an impairment, and (c) being regarded as having such an impairment." If an employee or job applicant satisfies this definition and is qualified to do the job, the employer must try to accommodate him, as long as the employer has at least fifteen employees and has been in operation for at least twenty weeks of the past year.

If one employer cannot accommodate an employee's disability, another may be able to. Alternatively, the employee may need to work in a different kind of job. Not being able to work in a particular job or field, or needing a reasonable accommodation, is different than not being able to maintain oneself by any kind of substantial gainful employment. (See Chapter 2 for a full explanation of how mental illness can qualify somebody for disability benefits from the SSA.)

THE ADA AND THE EEOC

The EEOC of the U.S. Department of Labor is the government agency tasked with enforcing the ADA. Chai Feldblum, Commissioner of the EEOC who speaks openly about her own anxiety disorder, has said that "the point of the ADA is to keep people with disabilities attached to the labor force." In other words, it is U.S. government policy that an employer who knows that an employee has a mental illness must try to find ways for that employee to accomplish his work tasks, rather than finding ways to get rid of that employee. The necessary accommodations may include changes in duties, revised routines, different methods of supervision, adaptive equipment (such as noise-cancelling headphones), office supplies that facilitate better task management, or modifications to the physical space.

Not believing that someone has a mental illness—but instead is lazy, spoiled, or fussy—is one of the main stigmas that people with mental illness face. For example, Julia's co-workers may think of her as lazy when she cannot get out of bed in the morning. They may see her as spoiled when she cannot control her mood. She seems fussy and uncooperative because she has compulsions. And maybe Julia comes across as manipulative when she requests accommodations. Whether or not her supervisor conveys these beliefs, Julia herself may have learned to expect them and may talk herself out of even requesting accommodations.

The ADA's basic requirements may help to counteract the stigma. Those requirements are (1) that the employee has to prove a legitimate need for reasonable accommodation, and (2) that the employer has to try to make the accommodation. Accommodations are reasonable when they do not create an "undue hardship" for the employer. Undue hardships are described as significant difficulties or expenses. If a proposed accommodation causes an undue hardship, the employer and the employee are expected to try to work out alternative accommodations that will be manageable for both of them. Accommodations may cost the employer some money and may obligate the employer to adjust other employees' schedules, routines, or workspaces, but those are not valid excuses for refusing to accommodate somebody.

ACCOMMODATIONS IN THE JOB APPLICATION PROCESS

Consider these examples:

- Maybe an employer's online application system requires more concentration and persistence than a particular applicant can muster up.
- Maybe the thought of being interviewed by a team, rather than being interviewed by a single person, causes an applicant so much anxiety that she declines to even go for the interview.
- Maybe the waiting room in the human resources department brings on a prospective employee's depression or panic attacks.

The process of getting hired for a job can be nerve-wracking for anyone, and job applicants with mental illness need to know that the ADA requires accommodations even in the application and hiring phases of employment. Employers have to adjust their practices when they learn that an applicant with disabilities will not otherwise have a fair chance at applying for and getting the job. Very often, applicants have to be self-advocates and state their needs up front. For example:

- When an online application is daunting, a paper application can be made available or the electronic version can be separately formatted in order to be saved on a desktop and completed in multiple sittings.

- When it is impossible for an applicant to face a team interview, the meeting can be divided into several separate, individual interviews.
- Applicants can bypass waiting rooms.

Rarely is there a part of the application, qualifying test, or interview process that cannot be altered.

You should understand, however, that employers—including the intake staff in the human resources office or the person at the front counter who happens to interact with an applicant—are not obligated to ask if a job applicant needs any accommodations while applying for the job. Unless an applicant has a very obvious medical condition, such as being visually impaired (i.e., blind), an employer would not even be expected to inquire about a need for assistance, equipment, extra time, or other adjustments to the application process. In fact, if an employer does ask an applicant if he needs accommodations based on something she perceives as symptoms of a mental illness and then for any reason does not hire him, the applicant might file an EEOC complaint on the basis that the employer's inquiry and the applicant's response about mental health doomed his chance to be hired.

So, with that looming legal threat, it makes sense that a potential employer would not question an individual about possible needs, although it is a good idea for employers to make general accommodation offers to all prospective employees. Large and sophisticated workplaces, especially those with professional human resources departments, sometimes have a phrase on their employment website or application that invites applicants to let them know if any accommodations are needed in order to apply for a job.

Some employers have a large-print line on the application that says "Please let us know if you need special arrangements in order to read or complete this form." Some have a standard question in the interview scheduling phone call that asks, "Is there anything about the interview conditions (which would be stated) that you need us to alter in order to accommodate you?" There may be other declarations of flexibility that welcome applicants with physical or mental medical needs to make arrangements in order to compete fully and fairly as job candidates.

When employers do offer disability accommodations to applicants, it is usually an earnest and nonjudgmental practice; it is not a trick or a sneaky way to weed out applicants who need a variance from the usual application process. Only the people who need to know about accommodations for the application, testing, or interview will know about them. If accommodations for the application process are related to duties that go with the job being applied for, such as needing to interview and eventually work in a private windowless space due to social phobia, then the supervisor has a legitimate need for that information and is entitled to it. Some jobs require new hires to undergo medical exams that may be for assessment of physical or mental health. This practice is legal under the ADA as long as the same medical exam is required for everyone who has been offered the same kind of job at that place. Depending on the industry and circumstances, there could also be government regulatory agencies that need to know about the accommodation. In such cases, the employer is permitted to disclose the information to the regulatory offices as confidential protected information.

HOW TO Request Job Accommodations

Someone, perhaps you if you have a family member with mental illness, has to notify a prospective employer when a job applicant or existing employee needs adjustments to the application process or the job. It is legal and professionally acceptable for a friend, relative, or job coach to provide this notification if the employee is not able to. Whether it is done in a conversation or in writing, the notification needs to contain the employee's name, the job title, and a clear, firm request. If the request makes the accommodation sound optional, it will make it seem that the applicant or employee does not really require accommodation. The human resources office may have its own system for receiving these requests. If there are no instructions in the employee handbook, call the person who handles scheduling or attendance and ask who to contact about disability accommodations.

The request for accommodation should name the medical condition and identify symptoms that are relevant to the application process or existing job. (The name of the medical condition is sufficient—the employee does not need to disclose the details of his or her symptoms or medical history. For example, the employee can state "bipolar disorder" without stating the date of onset, the medication regimen, or whether it is "rapid cycling.") Without this information, the employer does not know whether the employee has an actual disabling condition in need of accommodation or whether he or his support person is being unnecessarily demanding or uncooperative. The employer is allowed to ask certain questions about the medical condition and may ask for proof that the employee has the diagnosis.

Employers do not necessarily know how to accommodate every condition, so it is wise to suggest a possible and reasonable accommodation when making the request. In a job application situation, suggest ways that the hiring environment can avoid triggering an onset of symptoms. Here are several examples:

- *He cannot complete the application unless he is alone in a quiet room.*
- *She will need someone to read the questions to her and discuss them with her before she writes her responses.*
- *I cannot complete this application in one sitting because I need to re-read it and fine-tune my answers a few times before submitting it.*

In an existing employment situation, connect symptoms and modifications to each other. For example:

- *When I hear the person in the next cubicle arguing over the phone, I get very anxious; would it be possible for me to move to a different spot?*
- *I feel very stressed and dismayed by the constant inflow of tasks in our system. Is there a way that I can mark closure at certain points in the work routine? That would make me feel like I was accomplishing something and I would have an opportunity to release stress. What if I got up and walked around the room after every ten files? Would that be okay?*

If the employer asks questions about accommodating the disability, it may seem like a challenge or a criticism or some other affront to the employee or applicant. Since the employer is legally obligated to accommodate the disability, the employer's questions about the request for accommodation are legitimate as long as the questions are about the means of accommodation. When an employee requests accommodation but does not reply promptly to any employer inquiries, or if he doesn't cooperate with the employer's suggestions, he may give the impression that the accommodation request was not sincere.

It is possible and legally fine for an employer to come up with an accommodation that is different from the one suggested by the applicant or employee. (For example, an employee with seasonal affective disorder who requests a corner office with two windows can instead be provided with a light box.) The employer has to think about costs, timing, productivity, and fairness to other applicants and employees in addition to accommodating one employee. As long as the employer offers an accommodation that fixes the problem, it is probably a reasonable accommodation.

GETTING IDEAS FOR JOB ACCOMMODATIONS

The Job Accommodation Network (JAN) operated by the Department of Labor provides examples and consultations to help design feasible job accommodations when somebody is already in place at work or has just been hired for a new job. Employees and employers can browse in JAN's A–Z list of "Accommodation by Disability" to see suggestions for reasonable ways to accommodate employees who have depression, bipolar disorder, anxiety, and other mental health impairments. Additionally, employees and employers can chat online, over the phone, or by email with someone at JAN to brainstorm about accommodations.

At the local level, job coaches associated with disability service organizations and the state vocational rehabilitation office can help to create reasonable accommodations. These professionals usually become very well acquainted with their clients and can arrange job shadowing, equipment testing, and other experiments in the process of developing accommodations that best suit both the employee and the workplace. They are very good at educating employers and co-workers about an incoming employee's mental illness and, as part of arranging the accommodation, can provide the employer and co-workers with tips for interacting with him. For example, if your son Raj has an obsessive-compulsive disorder and cannot tolerate having people touch things that are on his desk, the job coach could advise his co-workers to always ask Raj to hand them papers, rather than reaching for the papers themselves.

Recommendations for accommodating mental illness and remedies from lawsuits about failure to accommodate mental illness may include staff training for co-workers who interact with the person who is mentally ill. The training is not meant to make a spectacle of anybody; it is intended to create an understanding work environment.

BRINGING IN THE EEOC

Employees do not have to go through the JAN or use a job coach to seek accommodations at work. They can have their own meeting with the boss or the human resources office in which they discuss their difficulties in accomplishing job tasks, hand over written proof of their mental illness and need for accommodation (perhaps a letter from their therapist), and suggest accommodations. This independent method can be especially challenging for people with certain types of mental illness, but it can also be effective. If it doesn't work, the employee can always turn to the EEOC for support.

It would be great if every employee with mental illness, independently or with professional support, could arrange calm and reasonable accommodations with an employer and if those arrangements could always preempt difficulties. Unfortunately, some employees encounter obstacles when they need to make changes in their jobs in order to continue working.

- If an employee already has job accommodations in place and her symptoms later require additional accommodations, she may be met with suspicion, if not resistance. For example, perhaps your neighbor Gerrie uses noise-cancelling headphones at her job and has a permanent pass on large group meetings to accommodate her social phobia, but now she hopes that she can also adjust her schedule to have her lunch hour at an off-peak time so that she won't have to eat with other people. Her boss may just say, "You already got what you asked for, and now you want more?" He may even turn her down, guessing that she is entitled to accommodations in her work but not in her lunch hour.
- Or, if she didn't formerly have accommodations but now needs them for the first time, Gerrie may get turned down on a technicality, such as she failed to tell her employer about the change in her health or she did not provide sufficient proof that her condition is disabling. Even if she does satisfy the technicalities—which are really the rules for demonstrating that she is entitled to accommodation—she may get turned down based on the substance of her request.
- What if Gerrie asks if she can work from home? Maybe the boss does not believe what Gerrie's documents say or maybe he simply does not see how he can give her the accommodation she is asking for. He may just hope that if he delays responding or does not agree to satisfy her accommodation request, she will quit the job.

Thanks to the EEOC, employers do not have the last word in discussions about employee accommodations. For whatever reason that attempts to arrange accommodations have failed, and at any stage of the arrangements, an employee can reach out to the EEOC for guidance, authoritative explanations, and, in some circumstances, even advocacy.

HOW TO File an Employment Discrimination Claim

When efforts to seek accommodations or resolve grievances with an employer are not successful, the next step is to file a complaint with the EEOC, where the complaint will be referred to as a "charge." Family members are legally permitted to file the charge if the unwell employee-relative wants them to. That authority (from which you can assist your loved one with mental illness) appears in the opening part of the U.S. Code section called *Power of Commission to Prevent Unlawful Employment Practices,* 42 U.S.C. § 2000e–5(b), which says, "Whenever a charge is filed by *or on behalf of* a person claiming to be aggrieved . . . ." This message is reinforced in an EEOC regulation at 29 C.F.R. § 1601.7, which says, "A charge that any person has engaged in or is engaging in an unlawful employment practice . . . may be made by or on behalf of any person claiming to be aggrieved."

If you live in a state that has its own Fair Employment Practices Agency (FEPA), the EEOC will send a copy of your charge to that office. The state agency can then opt to handle your claim. If it does, it will contact you with further instructions. See the Resources section at the end of this chapter for guidance on locating a state FEPA, should you need information about yours.

Being made to do something an employee hates to do is not discrimination, and neither is having to work with annoying people. The experienced workplace discrimination experts at the EEOC can tell the difference between a work situation that is just rotten and one that is actually discriminatory. To help workers know whether to even file a charge, they offer the EEOC Assessment System (https://egov.eeoc.gov/eas/), an online questionnaire that leads into the EEOC intake process and helps members of the public see if their circumstances have the characteristics of workplace discrimination.

The EEOC regulation about filing a charge on behalf of somebody else says that you do not need to identify yourself in the charge. You only need to provide the name, address, and phone number of the person you are filing for, such as your brother, Mike. The EEOC will then check with that person to see if he truly wants the charge to go forward. This is meant to be a protective step in reducing false claims. You would want to prepare your brother for that inquiry so that he does not get scared or suspicious when the EEOC reaches out to him and so that he is ready to interact with them. Note that, once the victim of discrimination has authorized the investigation, you cannot withdraw the EEOC charge. In fact, even the person you filed for can withdraw the charge only with EEOC approval.

When the employee authorizes the investigation to go ahead, he can also ask that the EEOC not reveal his identity to his employer. To the extent possible, the EEOC will try to honor that request. If you or a disability advocate filed the charge on behalf of Mike, for example, the EEOC can convey to the employer that someone has filed a complaint on behalf of an anonymous employee. Of course, as the EEOC progresses from the intake stage to a fuller inquiry, the employer will eventually need to know who the employee is.

EEOC Mediation

Since the investigative process takes a long time, typically about six months, the EEOC encourages employers and employees to mediate their disputes. Mediation is a facilitated conversation or set of conversations between the employer and the employee. It is a quick, calm, confidential, and cost-effective method of fixing discrimination problems at work. An employee who initially wanted to remain anonymous will have to reveal his identity in order to participate in mediation. Before even starting an investigation, the EEOC will notify the employee and the EEOC administrator at the workplace about the opportunity to mediate. If they both agree to mediate, the EEOC will postpone investigating the situation. And if mediation resolves the problem, the EEOC will not investigate the charge at all.

Here are some possible outcomes of mediation to have in mind as you prepare to help an employee go through the process:

- The employee may be given a leave of absence or a period of FMLA time.
- The supervisor or co-workers may be required to participate in training that will inform them about mental health conditions.
- The employer may make physical changes to the workplace.
- The employee may be moved to a different job in that workplace.
- The employee's job duties may be modified.
- The employee may do the same job at a different time of day with modified routines, or change to a part-time schedule (with part-time pay).
- The employee may either join a team so that he does not have to work alone or may leave a team so that he can work alone.
- The employee may have more frequent contact with the supervisor, with the goal of regularly interacting in a positive way. This contact can happen in person, by phone, or in writing and may have a built-in social component so that it does not feel oppressive or demeaning to the employee.
- Sometimes both sides come to the decision that it is best for the employee to leave the job, often with a severance.

HOW TO Assist With Employment Mediation

Let's continue with the example of your brother Mike—who lives with post-traumatic stress disorder (PTSD) from his time fighting in Iraq. Since the EEOC mediation is about Mike's charge of discrimination, it will have no purpose without his participation. As his well family member, you might recruit Mike's therapist or caseworker for some preparatory assistance to help ensure that Mike will show up and voice his position. This preparation should help your brother to see that the employer is not an enemy and that mediation is an opportunity to fix things at work.

The employee can have a representative at the mediation session. If you agree to be this representative, you can either speak on behalf of Mike or jointly with

Mike, but you should consider yourself to be only a team member, not a team leader. The employee is supposed to be the team leader.

The mediation will be conducted through your regional EEOC field office. These offices have staff mediators and also a panel of on-call mediators who are paid on a per-mediation basis and are not full-time employees of the EEOC. All of the mediators have completed professional mediation training that is either provided by or approved by the EEOC and they have mediated disputes in other settings prior to contracting with the EEOC. Field offices can operate their mediation systems differently, but you should expect that the office will appoint a mediator rather than letting you select one, and that it will have a general intake worker, who is not a mediator, coordinating details in advance of the mediation.

If you know of ways to help your brother participate in mediation, you may be able to convey those to the mediation intake worker in advance of the mediation, but there will also be an opportunity to do it when everyone is together in the mediation room establishing rules. EEOC mediators are required to provide reasonable accommodations, such as a quiet meeting space for Mike, who startles at loud, unexpected noises, so you have the option of presenting these thoughts as accommodation methods. If you handle this prior to mediation, tell the EEOC's field office if the methods have worked in past stressful communications with your brother. You may be able to provide written guidance from a therapist or caseworker who really knows your brother.

One thorough and succinct pattern for conveying these ideas, whether they are suggested rules or requests for accommodation, is to define the conditions under which Mike experiences a symptom, identify the symptom, and then suggest the accommodation for that symptom. To show respect to the mediator and the employer, you could phrase your suggestion as a question. Your relative may have multiple symptoms to accommodate. Present each of them separately and they will sound more reasonable.

Below are some examples of this pattern. Notice that they are phrased as if you are communicating with the EEOC field office in advance of the mediation. If you do not have that opportunity, review the pattern with your family member and, if he wants you to, help him plan requests that he can present when the mediator opens the session and calls for suggested rules.

When Carol is in highly stressful and formal settings, her other personalities come forward and communicate from a completely different perspective than she ordinarily has at work. If we could alleviate some of the intimidating aspects of the mediation setting, she will be more likely to participate from her usual personality. Would it be possible for Carol to come and visit the mediation room a few times in advance of the mediation and even have a few moments of casual conversation with a staff member each time—just about ordinary things, not about the job or this discrimination claim? I think that these visits will help her to feel calm and comfortable on the day of the mediation.

Greg's disability involves anger management. When he thinks that people are saying or writing anything about him, he gets loud and belligerent and distracted by his own anger. He does not become physically hostile. I expect that the mediator will take notes in the mediation session. Do you think we can use a projection system for the notes so that Greg can see them as they are being written? As another step to help Greg remain calm, can you make a point of personally inviting Greg to comment on things that are happening during the mediation?

You will know from the paperwork and conversations leading up to the mediation who will be there on behalf of the employer—probably the immediate supervisor and someone from the human resources office. Sometimes the employer will bring a lawyer. The mediator will invite all of the participants to suggest rules that everyone in the session will have to follow. Some rules that can help participants to communicate most effectively are: no loud voices, no name calling, and no cussing. This is also the point when employees can present preferences about how they like to be treated.

There are bound to be some surprises during a mediation session. You may discover that the workplace is not as bad as the employee has reported. You may even learn that the employer has already made multiple accommodations for your family member. You could find out that the workplace is undergoing some major administrative changes. If everything goes well, everyone together in the mediation room will contribute to a good idea for accommodating the employee—possibly an idea that neither side thought of before coming into mediation.

At times, however, the whole group environment of the mediation may become challenging, stifling, intimidating, or otherwise difficult for your family member. A very common mediation technique for handling these moments is called caucusing. A caucus is a separate, private conversation between one party and the mediator, during which that party (say, Mike) and his representative (say, you) express and work through something that is simply not coming out in the mediation session. For example:

- Maybe Mike feels like his employer is acting too paternalistic in the session.
- Maybe Mike is having a hard time following the conversation.
- Maybe he is trying to figure out how to say something.
- Maybe Mike just hates the whole direction that the mediation is going and wants to steer it another way.

As a family member who knows your relative better than the other people in the room, have your antenna up for times when your relative starts tuning out or otherwise conveying subtle discomfort that the other people in the room will not recognize. At those moments, you do not need to make personal comments to or about the employee. Just ask for a break, during which you and your loved one can, for example, go have a cold drink or a walk in the fresh air. Or ask for a caucus, so that the employee can get the mediator's private attention.

If you go into the separate caucus room and the employee refuses to say anything or else conveys disillusionment, use the caucus to find out what has brought about this sense of futility. Mike, for example, may say something like, "This is a waste of time; I don't even care what happens." In response to that, you and the mediator can talk with him about how to redirect the mediation or how to mark tangible progress as the conversation continues. Perhaps Mike could start keeping a list of good ideas or sensible statements that people are saying in the mediation. Know, also, that mediation does not have to be completed in a single session. It is common for mediation to take numerous sessions over weeks or months.

And if the employer and employee come to an agreement through mediation or at any other point in the EEOC process, it will be written into a legally binding settlement agreement. If either party does not uphold its promises, the other party may be able to sue them for breaching the settlement, although it is more likely that the settlement agreement will establish deadlines and conditions to help keep everyone on track with their promises. For example, the settlement agreement may say that the employer will provide Mike with a quiet workspace by the first of next month, and that if the employer does provide that quiet workspace, then by the end of the same month Mike will begin working with the Employee Assistance Program (EAP) at his job to devise a routine for managing his PTSD at work. The agreement may also require the parties to report back to the mediator after several months and to discuss their ongoing relationship.

It is possible for mediation to fail, in which case the mediator will generate a document reporting that the parties were unable to reach mutually acceptable terms. The parties and the EEOC will each get copies of that document, and the EEOC will then put the employee's discrimination charge into the investigation system. To assist your relative, keep track of the mediation report. If it turns out that he cannot be accommodated at work, it may be time to apply for short-term disability benefits (if available) or SSDI/SSI benefits. The mediation report, though it will not say anything specific about the employee's mental health, can help to support a disability claim. Combined with other materials about his current functionality, the mediation report can help demonstrate that your family member's mental health currently makes it impossible for him to maintain substantial gainful employment.

The EEOC Investigation

If mediation does not result in an agreement, the EEOC will look for proof of the claims set forth in the employee's discrimination charge. One EEOC investigator will be assigned to manage the case. That investigator will give the employer an opportunity to explain its perspective on what was happening at work when the employee felt discrimination. This explanation, the Respondent's Position Statement, will be provided to the employee upon request. The employee then has the option of responding to the employer's position. He may have proof, such as copies of break-room notices or other office documents, that the employer lied or exaggerated to look good in its Response Position Statement.

The investigator will get copies of all applicable personnel documents from the employer. These can include the employee's file and also the files on any co-workers or supervisors who were identified in the charge. This way, the EEOC can find out if the offending co-worker or boss has been in trouble before or is known to have any behavioral issues of the type that troubled this employee.

The investigator may visit the worksite to watch, to listen, and to ask questions in person. If your family member has identified witnesses to the discrimination, the investigator may arrange to talk with those people. Based on the information collected from the employer, it is possible that the investigator will seek additional information or clarifications from the employee. Still, no claimant should count on having this second opportunity to explain what happened. It is truly best to tell everything at the beginning.

The End of an EEOC Charge

Upon completing its investigation, the EEOC will conclude that (1) they have reasonable cause to believe that the employer discriminated against the employee, or (2) they do not have such cause. If the EEOC finds that it does not have cause to believe that the employer discriminated, this does not mean that the employer did not discriminate, it just means that the EEOC was not able to reach a conclusion in favor of the employee based on the evidence obtained during the investigation. If there is a "no cause" finding, the EEOC will dismiss the charge and notify the employee of his remaining right to file a private lawsuit. The no cause determination will not be admissible in such a lawsuit. The work involved in bringing the lawsuit would be similar to the work in a lawsuit about unlawful employment practices described in Chapter 17. If the EEOC finds cause to believe that the employer did discriminate, they will send a Letter of Determination to both parties, inviting them to participate in conciliation.

Conciliation differs from mediation because the EEOC investigator will play an informational role in the process and because the conversation will be about information gathered during the investigation. In other words, there is hard proof on the table, not merely one employee's impressions. The conduct of the conciliation meeting, which is likely to happen over the phone, will be respectful but relatively informal, much like the mediation. As with mediation, both the employer and the employee can suggest and discuss possible solutions in the conciliation meeting.

Conciliation is the last chance that an employer and employee have for reaching a peaceful resolution under the authority of the EEOC. They could have come to a settlement at any point before, during, or after mediation. Or they could put this charge to rest in conciliation. If none of the informal dispute resolutions has worked, the EEOC or the employee can sue the employer in court. Sometimes, employees opt to file their own discrimination lawsuits when the employer has rectified its discriminatory practices or workplace conditions to the EEOC's satisfaction but has not satisfied the individual employee's requirements.

WALKING AWAY

The EEOC's process for responding to workplace discrimination, like so many government processes, can be extremely challenging—even impossible—for some people who have mental illness. It seems so accessible, with its opportunities to communicate in person as well as in writing, its invitation to involve representatives and supporters, and its offer of accommodations, but it puts the employee under scrutiny and requires him to revisit bad experiences over and over again. In an initial burst of eagerness to seek justice, the employee may be tempted by the EEOC's Assessment System and even the intake process that is entirely focused on his perspective. But once the employer gets to respond and the parties are expected to interact with each other, the situation becomes less exciting. It may even make him feel more symptomatic. Dropping the charge and getting away from the employer may be a more positive experience for him than seeking to resolve the discrimination that he has been subjected to.

Tax Facts

- The damages awarded in discrimination lawsuits generally do count as taxable income. The full amount of the damage award has to be reported, but the costs of bringing a discrimination lawsuit are tax deductible. So the percentage that the attorney takes as a fee and any other litigation costs paid by the taxpayer can then be deducted later on the same tax return where the income is declared. See *IRS Lawsuits, Awards, and Settlements—Audit Techniques Guide,* Chapters 2 and 3, at the Internal Revenue Service (IRS) website (irs.gov).

- The cost of equipment and supplies that employees purchase at their own expense in order to be able to function at the workplace, such as noise-cancelling headphones, a light box, or an Alpha-Stim device, can be deducted as medical expenses on an employee's personal income tax return. See IRS Publication 502.

- Although employees generally obtain their own personal devices for job accommodation, the modifications to office spaces, computers, and other employer-owned equipment may have to be done at the employer's expense. Small businesses with fewer that thirty employees and less than one million dollars per year in annual profits can deduct the cost of "acquiring or modifying equipment or devices" for employees with disabilities. See IRS Form 8826.

- Several employer tax incentives are identified on the IRS website in *Tax Benefits for Businesses Who Have Employees with Disabilities.* Employees could inform the workplace about this document when they request accommodations. See https://www.irs.gov/businesses/small-businesses-self-employed/tax-benefits-for-businesses-who-have-employees-with-disabilities.

RESOURCES FOR EMPLOYMENT DISCRIMINATION

1. The ADA and the subsequent amendments and acts related to it were
   written and passed by Congress. The statutes from within the ADA
   about equal employment for individuals with disabilities are at 42
   U.S.C. §§ 12101–12213. The section defining disability is § 12102. The
   section defining all of the forms of discrimination is § 12112. The section
   authorizing family members to file EEOC charges on behalf of disabled
   employees is § 2000e-5(b). See uscode.house.gov.
2. The EEOC is an independent federal agency responsible for making
   and enforcing regulations that carry out the requirements of the ADA.
   Regulations about disability discrimination in employment settings
   are at 29 C.F.R. pt. 1630. The information about investigating disability
   discrimination complaints is in § 1640. See ecfr.gov or eeoc.gov.
3. The EEOC maintains fact sheets and guidance documents about
   disability discrimination at eeoc.gov. Two important guidance
   documents are *Enforcement Guidance: Reasonable Accommodation and
   Undue Hardship Under the Americans with Disabilities Act* (at https://
   www.eeoc.gov/policy/docs/accommodation.html) and *Enforcement
   Guidance on the Americans with Disabilities Act and Psychiatric
   Disabilities* (at https://www.eeoc.gov/policy/docs/psych.html).
   A useful fact sheet is *Employer-Provided Leave and the Americans with
   Disabilities Act* (at https://www.eeoc.gov/eeoc/publications/ada-leave.
   cfm). All of the statutes and regulations associated with the ADA plus
   case documents and technical assistance manuals are on a website
   managed by the Department of Justice at ada.gov.
4. The JAN has a very full and helpful compilation of accommodation ideas
   for workers with mental health impairments at askjan.org. Experts at JAN
   are available to consult on individual cases at no cost.
5. The quote from EEOC Commissioner Chai Feldblum about keeping
   people with disabilities attached to the workforce is from an American
   Bar Association training session called "The ADA and Mental
   Impairments in the Workplace," presented June 4, 2014. Ms. Feldblum's
   anxiety disorder is mentioned on her Twitter and Facebook pages and in
   numerous news articles about her.
6. Search in the EEOC's search box or any search engine for the EEOC
   guidance document on *psychiatric disabilities* using the italicized words
   as your search terms. Use the same method to search for the term *eeoc
   mediation* or navigate within the EEOC website for the page detailing its
   mediation system. See eeoc.gov.
7. See *How to File a Charge of Employment Discrimination* for instructions
   about beginning a claim with the EEOC. For information about the action
   following a disability discrimination charge, see the page titled *What You
   Can Expect After You File a Charge*. Both of these items are available on
   eeoc.gov.
8. To find a job coach who can help someone with a disability to find
   employment, arrange accommodations, and learn about self-advocacy,
   either contact the nearest United Way office (unitedway.org) or enter

your state name and the term *vocational rehabilitation* into a search
engine.

9. To find out whether your state has its own FEPA, either ask your local
EEOC field office or navigate from the EEOC's online map of field
offices to reach your state and local resources. Although you can begin
your claim with either the state FEPA or the EEOC, it is usually most
convenient to begin with the EEOC, since they will refer it to the state
FEPA if appropriate.

16

Taking Leave and Being Compensated

Your son Owen is hearing voices again and it has started to affect his job performance. The boss called Owen's job coach and the job coach called you. Working as a team, the three of you and Owen's therapist hope to convince Owen to get into intensive voluntary treatment. The job will be waiting when Owen is ready to come back. The boss just needs Owen's treatment provider to fill out some paperwork for the Family and Medical Leave Act (FMLA) to apply. You ask if Owen can get workers' compensation to pay for his treatment. The boss says no, but that the company's usual health insurance will probably cover it. He gives you the health insurance phone number so that you can find out details once you get Owen into the intensive treatment program.

FAMILY AND MEDICAL LEAVE

As touched on in Chapters 14 and 15, the FMLA is a federal law enacted for the purpose of saving people's jobs for them when they have to take some time off and devote their attention to a needy family member or to their own health. It is not necessarily paid medical leave, but it is a legally protected leave of absence. This means that the person taking the leave will remain an employee during the time off and will be welcome back at work to the same position or an equivalent position when the leave time ends. It is a legal guarantee of security for people with episodic mental illness who occasionally need a stretch of several weeks to get regulated, and it is a way for family members to be available for somebody who is experiencing severe mental illness. Importantly, during a FMLA leave, the employer is required to continue paying for health insurance to the same extent it does when the employee is not on leave.

Employees are entitled to FMLA leave when:

- They have worked for their current employer for at least twelve months.
- In those twelve months of employment, they have worked at least 1,250 hours, which is approximately 25 to 30 hours per week.
- The employer has at least 50 employees within a 75-mile radius of the employee (although state laws sometimes apply the FMLA or comparable state leave laws to smaller companies).

- The employee has a serious illness or has to care for a family member with a serious illness. Serious illness is defined in 29 C.F.R. § 825.113–115 as a condition that requires inpatient care or continuing treatment beyond the ordinary medical treatment that the employee routinely gets.

Examples of Situations When Employees May Take FMLA Time

Here are several examples showing when an employee could take leave in connection with mental illness:

- An employee with major schizophrenia has to be hospitalized for a few weeks and then requires several more weeks to get accustomed to new medicine and to participate in intensive outpatient treatment.
- An employee needs a course of electroconvulsive therapy treatments. The treatments need to be administered throughout approximately one month's time, under anesthesia. The doctor recommends that the patient then wait an additional two weeks before resuming the full schedule of normal activities.
- The wife of a man who has overwhelming anxiety needs time off from work in order to be almost constantly present with her husband and to help him manage the anxiety episode on an outpatient basis, since the initial days at the inpatient environment have made previous episodes even worse.

HOW TO Arrange for Leave From Work Under the FMLA

Let's look at the situation of your daughter-in-law Stephanie, who has the eating disorder anorexia nervosa and needs to take time off from her job in order to participate in a thirty-day intensive eating disorder clinic. Stephanie is not well enough right now to handle any communications, so you (as a supportive family member, worried about your daughter-in-law) will contact the human resources office directly. This contact should be made immediately when it becomes obvious that Stephanie needs time off that is beyond just taking standard sick time in the ordinary way at her workplace. Do not try to pressure your daughter-in-law to handle this communication herself; it just may not be possible for her to handle it at this point. Do not rely on a co-worker or supervisor to know what to do about FMLA time or to properly get the message to the right person in human resources. Make the contact yourself.

The law requires employers (typically the human resources office) to implement their FMLA leave process very soon after they learn that an employee has a serious illness requiring time off from work. Specifically, the regulation states, "When an employee requests FMLA leave, or when the employer acquires knowledge that an employee's leave may be for an FMLA-qualifying reason, the employer must notify the employee of the employee's eligibility to take FMLA leave within five business days, absent extenuating circumstances."

Since the law says that the employer's obligations begin when he or she "acquires knowledge," it is clear that the law allows family members to notify that employee's workplace when the employee needs to take FMLA time. The FMLA regulation states very clearly that "notice (to the employer) may be given by the employee's spokesperson."

To properly begin the FMLA process, you need to notify the human resources office, but unless your family member works for a large institution, you may not be able to find contact information for that office. In that case, it is fine to call your family member's manager, say that the employee needs FMLA time, and ask how you can contact the office that processes FMLA matters. You specifically want a phone number and an email address so that you can first call the human resources representative and then follow-up with an email to confirm the content of the phone conversation.

The subject line of your email should be something like "employee in need of FMLA time." The body of the message should then include the following information:

- The employee's name, job title (or general job description), and department.
- The fact that the employee is dealing with a serious illness and is under a doctor's care and/or in the hospital.
- A clear declaration that the employee is too sick to work and wishes to exercise her rights under the FMLA.

In your communications with the human resources office, you do not need to give details about the illness or predict how long it will last. The employer will get that sort of information (which may include the exact mental health diagnosis or symptoms) from the doctor or therapist who is treating your family member.

Scheduling Notes

The FMLA entitles employees to twelve "work weeks" off. Whether the employee's work week consists of twenty-five hours per calendar week or forty hours per week does not matter. If she only works two days of each week but in those two days she works at least twenty-five hours, do not worry that the law will count days instead of weeks. The employee will get twelve weeks according to the way twelve weeks would look on an ordinary calendar.

The FMLA only promises leave time, it does not guarantee that the leave will be paid. Employees may use any paid days off they have for income during their FMLA leave, including paid sick days, paid time off, or vacation days. The employer is allowed to require the employee to use up the paid days during the FMLA leave. Some employees will have access to short-term disability coverage through their employer or through a state program that replaces their income during FMLA leave.

Severe, debilitating episodes of mental illness cannot be planned. But people whose bad episodes tend to be foreshadowed by stress should know that it is fine to use their paid sick days when they just need a short time out for stress relief. Likewise, if someone has a cold or other ailment, she should use the paid sick leave to rest and recover. If, after that, she happens to need FMLA leave, she will still get up to the full twelve weeks off if she needs that much time to recover.

When To Tell the Employer That Someone Needs FMLA Leave

When an employee is able to predict a need for FMLA time, for example, when surgery is scheduled, he is supposed to give the employer thirty days' notice prior to taking the leave. Mental breakdowns do not come with thirty-day notices, however, and, as noted above, severe debilitating episodes of mental illness cannot be planned. Still, you or your family member may encounter an unknowledgeable manager or human resources worker who is stuck on the thirty-day requirement.

If that happens, tell that person to look at Title 29 C.F.R. § 825.303, which says that employees dealing with unplanned medical situations only have to notify the employer of a possible FMLA need within the standard amount of time that sickness is usually reported in that workplace. For example, if employees are required to call in sick by 10:00 a.m. in order to collect sick pay or have an excused absence, then somebody should try to notify the workplace by that time on the first day of the mental crisis.

Failure to exactly meet the employer's sick-notice rule on the first day probably will not cost the employee his job. The FMLA regulation explicitly allows for people dealing with emergencies to be late with their employer notification. But beware of the legal warning near the end of the regulation: "If an employee does not comply with the employer's usual notice and procedural requirements, and no unusual circumstances justify the failure to comply, FMLA-protected leave may be delayed or denied."

What Happens After You Have Put the Employer on Notice?

Employers are permitted to collect information legitimizing an employee's need for FMLA leave time. And, since an employer only has to grant FMLA leave for an episode of mental illness when that episode is a serious illness affecting the employee or the employee's relative, it makes sense that most employers require employees to submit FMLA medical certification demonstrating that the illness is serious.

Most of the time, employers ask that employees get the treating physician to complete a simple form attesting to the fact that the employee needs the time off in order to deal with the situation—either as a patient or as a family member who is helping a patient. That form will also call for the doctor to predict how long the patient will be unable to perform her ordinary work duties. The form may be a standard Department of Labor form or it can be one that is unique to the employer.

If your relative refuses to get mental health treatment, use the FMLA's promise of guaranteed employment at the end of the sick leave as an incentive to get her to seek medical treatment. Without a doctor's certification, the employer does not have to believe that the employee is seriously ill and in need of time off. Therefore, the employer does not have to grant leave under the FMLA. If the leave is not covered by the FMLA, there may not be a job waiting when the mental health episode is over.

Either you or your family member with mental illness should give the employer the form completed by the doctor and keep a copy of that completed form on file at home. It is critically important for your loved one to have a record proving that she fulfilled all of her legal obligations for FMLA. If someone at work loses or destroys paperwork, if management changes during an employee's leave time, or if a dishonest, vindictive boss fires an employee during FMLA leave or falsely claims that the employee walked off the job, you may need to prove that the employee is (or was) entitled to return to work with that employer at the end of the FMLA leave time.

What if the Employee Does Not Realize How Much Mental Illness Is Interfering With Work, but the Employer Sees It and Puts the Employee on FMLA Time?

Think about what it's like for a boss when an employee believes that spies have infiltrated the organization; or an employee is late, grouchy, and unproductive; or an employee is interfering with other people's workspaces. Obviously, the employee has some sort of mental disturbance. Clearly, the behavior is disrupting the workplace and possibly compromising sales and service. If the boss fires the employee, he risks being sued for discrimination and he loses his investment in the employee's training and experience. It makes sense that the boss would want the employee to go on leave and get better.

There is nothing in the FMLA that prevents an employer from putting a worker on medical leave when the employee does not ask for leave. Nevertheless, numerous employees have sued their employers for putting them on FMLA leave against their will. The federal courts have consistently said that when employers do that, it is not a violation of the FMLA. It may be disability discrimination—if the worker can prove everything required by the Americans with Disabilities Act (ADA)—but under the FMLA it is a perfectly legitimate action. It is also a situation that can help to prove disability to the Social Security Administration (SSA); just ask the employer to send the SSA all records relating to the FMLA leave, including behavioral documentation leading up to the leave.

As the coping person for an employee, for example your father, Stuart, you may bear the burden of the forced time off. Since your dad was in such a state that his boss pushed him onto medical leave, it is likely that his mental health treatment regime needs adjustment. It is also possible that he is not complying with his mental health treatment regime. A good course of treatment will likely get your father in shape to go back to work at the end of the twelve weeks, but even under these circumstances, there is no legal basis for forcing your dad to get mental health care.

What To Do if the Employer Does Not Cooperate With the FMLA Requirements?

If your loved one's employer refuses to follow the FMLA requirements, you should file a complaint with the local office of the Wages and Hours Division that is nearest to where the unwell employee lives and works. When you file a complaint on behalf of your relative, it is called a third-party complaint. You do not have to pay to file a complaint or to have the complaint investigated.

The Wages and Hours Division has a long list of facts that you should try to assemble in order to make the clearest possible complaint.

1. First, tell the facts about the employee. Provide the person's full name, address, and other contact information, as well as the person's current age and date of birth.
2. Next, provide your own name, your relationship to the employee who is mentally ill, and your own contact information.
3. In the third part of the complaint, give the facts about the employee's job. Identify the business or organization that employs or employed your family member. Provide the location where he works or worked and also tell if the human resources office is someplace else. For example, if your relative works in a grocery store, provide the address and phone number of that particular store, as well as contact information for the local corporate headquarters, if you can find all of that information. Give the employee's proper job title plus a list of his tasks. Tell how long the employee has worked there, the employee's salary, and the details about how and when salaries are paid. For example, you would write: *Sam is paid $12.50 per hour and he typically works 38 hours per week. He uses a time clock to stamp his time card when he starts and stops a shift. He gets paid every two weeks.*
4. Finally, explain what is wrong. In this last section, show that you and the employee fulfilled the rules of the FMLA: the employee had or has a serious illness, worked long enough for a big-enough employer, provided notice of the need for FMLA time, and gave the employer the medical provider's contact information so that the employer could verify that the employee had a serious illness and needed time off.

When the Wages and Hours Division investigates the complaint, they will base all of their questions and document requests on the details that you have provided.

RETURNING TO WORK AFTER FMLA LEAVE

While the FMLA is a straightforward law and most employees who need FMLA time to deal with mental health have a relatively simple experience when taking leave and returning from it, there are two cautions for employees and their families to keep in mind:

1. Returning to work can be particularly difficult for people who exhibited symptoms of mental illness at their jobs prior to going on leave. Workers may have to suffer indignities when they get back to work, such as going through fitness-for-duty testing or else having to provide apologies or explanations. They may feel that they are being watched and talked about by co-workers—and they will probably be right in feeling that way.
2. Although the FMLA promises that employees can return to work at the end of their leave, recent case law demonstrates that employees who committed offenses at work for which they could have been fired, even if the offense was a product of their mental illness, can be let go when they attempt to return to work after their FMLA leave.

Despite these issues, there are still good reasons for employees with mental illness to take FMLA leave rather than quitting their jobs or getting fired in connection with an onset of serious symptoms. For one thing, by remaining employed, they continue to be covered under their employer's health insurance plan. For another, despite the possibility of indignities or other discomfort, returning to the same job with familiar co-workers, tasks, and culture can still be less stressful than looking for a new job, going without income for an unknown period, and having to get acclimated to a new workplace. Finally, even if the job does have to end after the FMLA leave, either by firing or by the employee's choice, having a chance at returning to that job may help the employee in his recovery. Knowing that he achieved the goal of being able to go back, even if it didn't work out, ideally will propel him toward a positive search for a new job.

LEAVE OF ABSENCE UNDER THE ADA

Ordinarily, even when a worker with a disability is not eligible for FMLA leave, a state-mandated medical leave, workers' compensation, or a type of leave that the employer makes available (such as short-term disability), the ADA makes it possible for the worker to take leave as a disability accommodation. (*See* Chapter 15 for information about disability accommodations.) Under some circumstances, ADA accommodation leave is combined with one of the other leave options—for example, when somebody needs more leave time than the employer's short-term disability program provides. Like any disability accommodation, leave needs to be granted only when the situation fits the following ADA requirements:

- The employee has an impairment that interferes with at least one major life activity.
- The employee has a record of having, or is regarded as having, that impairment.
- The employee is qualified to perform the job either with or without accommodation.
- The accommodation does not create an undue burden for the employer.

As with FMLA leave, leave time that is arranged as an accommodation does not have to be a single big block of time. For example, an employee who needs to miss work once a week to see a therapist may be able to arrange for that weekly absence as a job accommodation. In some jobs, it is possible to simply schedule time off for those appointments without having to divulge a mental health diagnosis and arrange accommodation. In other jobs, a regularly scheduled absence, whether it is needed frequently or occasionally, could be disruptive to the workplace and will not be allowed unless the employee requests it as a disability accommodation.

The ADA forbids employers from punishing employees simply because they have been accommodated with leave time, so employees should not get demoted or fired, stuck with unfair work, or punished in other ways just because of having a leave time accommodation. Since the accommodation is only about being permitted to have the time off, there will still be other matters for employees to work out regarding their job responsibilities and their salaries when they take leave time as a job accommodation. Think about this in regard to your sister Bailey, who works as a computer network assistant and is accommodated with leave to participate in group mental health treatment sessions that occupy the entire afternoon every Monday. Bailey uses her paid sick time for her weekly leave, so she does not have to make up the hours in order to collect her full-time salary. However, because she gets a scheduling variation, the supervisor in her department requires her to stay behind and staff the help desk whenever the rest of the computer network staff go out to lunch together or attend entertaining morale-boosting events that their institution (not just the department) offers to all of its employees. Bailey would be justified in asking the disability expert in her human resources office whether this situation constitutes punishment for taking ADA leave. Since there may be other factors influencing the help desk schedule, it is best for Bailey to present her concern as a question and, at least initially, to raise it internally.

Here is another example: Suppose your son Vincent works as a billing manager in a local dentist's office that has only eight employees. The business is too small to come under the FMLA rules, so when Vincent has used up all of his sick days and needs to go into a short-term intensive treatment program for his psychiatric condition, it makes sense for him to request a leave of absence as a job accommodation. That way, he won't lose his job because of missing work while he is in the treatment program. He can't expect to be paid during his leave, since he has used up his paid sick time, but at least he can take the time he needs and will be able to go back to his job after he completes the treatment program.

When a Request for ADA Leave Is Denied

There are two common reasons for an ADA leave request to be denied:

1. Employers are not obligated to provide accommodations when doing so would cause them an undue hardship.
2. Employers are not obligated to grant leave as the accommodation when it is not medically justified.

To decide whether a particular leave accommodation would cause it an undue burden, an employer can consider how much time off the worker is requesting, how frequent and flexible that time off needs to be, whether a need for intermittent leave is predictable, how the person's leave may affect co-workers and their workloads, and how the leave will affect productivity or operations at the workplace.

What if your friend Andy, who works as a church secretary, experiences depression that, twice a year or so, makes it impossible for him to get out of bed for several days. Andy may not have any warning when one of the bad spells is about to start, but he knows that he has been having them since he was a teenager. Churches don't generally have large staffs of employees who can cover for each other, so Andy's boss may be concerned about how to manage communications and clerical duties when Andy suddenly has to miss part of a work week without any warning. With options like a temp agency and a voicemail message directing callers to another line for emergencies, along with the fact that most of Andy's work is not time sensitive, the boss should be able to come up with a back-up plan for the short, occasional staffing interruptions. In other words, Andy's absence seems not to create an undue hardship for the church and can probably be accommodated.

Now consider a work environment where Andy's attendance and institutional knowledge are more critical to productivity. Maybe instead of working as a church secretary, Andy manages a popular bike rental service near the train station. He opens the place early in the morning and staffs it alone. He knows all the quirks of the various bikes and is familiar with the regular customers' expectations. If he doesn't show up for work, nobody can rent a bike. A lot of commuters who rely on the bikes to get from the train to their jobs will be late because of not being able to get bikes. Since Andy cannot even make a phone call when he is debilitated this way, the manager who coordinates the city's bike concessions finds out about Andy's absence only when customers call to complain. The bike concession will lose business if customers cannot count on renting bikes there. In this example, Andy's need for unpredictable leave periods seems more likely to create an undue hardship for the employer, so the employer may not have to accommodate him by agreeing to allow him unplanned leave for random periods of time.

The second common concern regarding leave accommodations, medical documentation of the need for leave, is more concrete and less open to the employer's judgment. The employer (typically a human resources professional, not the employee's direct supervisor), with permission from the employee, will usually gather some facts from the employee's treatment provider. The facts are necessary to confirm that the employee does have the disabling medical condition that he claims to have and that he has to have leave time rather than another accommodation, such as flex-time or reassignment to a different job that is currently open and that the employee is qualified to do in the same workplace. When an employee is arranging ADA accommodation leave not in combination with FMLA leave, the employer is permitted to arrange a reasonable accommodation other than the one that the employee requests. If an employee requests leave time and the employer devises a different accommodation that effectively addresses the needs expressed by the employee, then the employee cannot sustain a claim that he is not being accommodated simply because he is not getting leave.

Suppose your friend Regan is a database developer for a chemical engineering company. Regan has PTSD that is triggered by loud noises, including banging and the sound of heavy machinery. When he learns that the company is going to dig up a section of the parking lot outside of his office and replace it with a garden, he is happy about the idea of the eventual garden, but he requests leave time for the days when workers will be using jackhammers and other loud equipment to remove the section of the parking lot. Regan's employer knows about the PTSD (it is already in Regan's personnel record) and does not require him to obtain a doctor's note before dealing with the accommodation request. But the employer does not think that Regan needs leave time during the parking lot demolition. Instead, the employer suggests that from now until the garden is installed, Regan's office and employee parking spot can be relocated far on the other side of the company's enormous campus, where he will not have to be exposed to loud noise. Since Regan can avoid the loud noise completely under this arrangement, it is a reasonable accommodation, even though it is not the accommodation (leave) that Regan originally requested.

Many people's work accommodations cannot be arranged as satisfactorily as Regan's are in this example. Mental illness has many varieties and affects people in different ways. If the person with mental illness that you know is in need of leave time as an accommodation and is not getting that or other accommodations that seem reasonable under the circumstances, see the section of Chapter 15 titled "Bringing in the EEOC."

HOW LEAVE TIME (FMLA OR ADA) AND WORKERS' COMPENSATION RELATE TO EACH OTHER

The words used in the title of the FMLA reveal what the law promises to employees—family and medical *leave*—and ADA accommodation *leave* gives time off, while workers' *compensation* (discussed in the next section of this chapter) involves money. FMLA promises leave no matter what caused the employee to be so mentally ill that he needed time off. The ADA promises leave if that is what is necessary to accommodate an employee. Workers' compensation pays money only if it was the job that caused the employee to suffer the particular episode of mental illness (if mental disorders are even eligible for workers' compensation in his state). Sometimes, these legal opportunities overlap: The job may cause a mental injury that entitles the employee to be paid workers' compensation until he recovers, and the job may require that the employee's recovery time be counted as FMLA leave. The U.S. Department of Labor has mandated that when state and federal laws about employee medical leave both apply to an employee at the same time, the employee is "entitled to the greater benefit or more generous rights provided under the different parts of each law." In other words, if the state workers' compensation law, the ADA, or another state law about leave for sick and injured employees would entitle that person to get more time off than he would under FMLA, then, even though his job may count the first twelve weeks off as FMLA time, the employee can remain on leave until he has used up the additional amount of time, beyond those first twelve weeks, that is permitted under the state law or arranged as an ADA accommodation.

WORKERS' COMPENSATION

As a chronic mental health condition becomes more troublesome over time, it is likely to affect the person's work performance or her responses to the work environment. Like a spilled glass of water that spreads out, wetting whatever it reaches in any direction, an episode of severe mental illness can invade the rational, well-disciplined parts of a good employee's mind. When events at work are the symbolic glass that spills, creating a creeping puddle of disturbance, such as when your son Isaac has a breakdown because everyone else in his data entry group was let go and he alone was left to enter more data in less time and still to be perfectly accurate, the employee may be able to collect workers' compensation benefits to pay medical expenses and replace at least some of his income for the amount of time that the episode prevents him from being able to work. Workers' compensation (also known as workers' comp) is a type of insurance that is paid for by employers and is mandated by relatively straightforward state laws. The laws distinguish between physical injuries caused by the job and mental injuries caused by the job. They discuss how the emotional distress or mental disorder has to be connected to the job, and they provide direction for how to prove that the emotional distress or mental disorder exists and affects the claimant's ability to work.

Note that, in many states, injuries to mental health can be compensated with workers' compensation coverage only when the worker has also suffered a work-related physical injury. In those states, the way that the physical and mental injury relate is very important. Much of the time, the mental health (or psychiatric) injury has to "arise out of" or be "caused by" the same event(s) that brought about the physical injury. The event or working condition that caused the mental health injury cannot be something common that happens in that line of work or a particular workplace. Most state laws require that something "abnormal" had to happen at work in order for the worker to be compensated for his mental health injury. Since psychiatric injuries may become evident only long after the physical injuries from an event at work, they can be described as "consequential" injuries and, with the support of expert medical opinions, later be added to an existing workers' compensation claim.

Historically, it has been difficult for rescue workers (police, firefighters, paramedics, and emergency medical technicians) to collect workers' compensation for traumatic stress because they are trained to manage their emotions during emergencies and disasters, and they have to know when taking rescue jobs that they will deal with stressful traumas. Yet, in Nebraska, there is a separate law specifically providing for compensation to first responders suffering mental trauma from "extraordinary and unusual" conditions on the job.

Initiating a Workers' Compensation Claim

Even the first step in a workers' comp claim—obtaining the injury report form—can be daunting for people suffering from severe mental symptoms. To get the form, commonly called a "First Report of Injury" (FROI), someone has to either telephone or go in person to the employee's manager or the company's main office and request it. This seemingly simple task can be very complicated and strenuous for someone whose job has brought on a bad mental episode. Many employees truly cannot do it and will miss the chance to collect their money if somebody else, such as a well and supportive relative, does not get the form for them. Requesting the claim form fills two purposes: it puts the employer on official notice of the injury and it provides the employee with the proper mechanism for getting the employer's workers' comp insurance to cover medical costs and pay the employee for having to miss work due to the injury.

The injury report form explains what the injury is, how it happened, and how it currently affects the employee's ability to work. Employers are legally obligated to direct injured employees to the form. The employer may provide the form directly or else provide a web link or contact information for their workers' comp insurance carrier. They may have a separate office that handles their workers' comp claims.

Some employees living with mental distress may feel nervous or anxious about dealing with strangers. They may be further bothered by having to sign something just to show that they received the form, which is a common requirement. Going through formalities can feel like a pointless run-around. If the ill employee has the impression that the employer is only acting in its own interest, he is right. The layers of formality and inconvenience exist just for the employer's benefit—to prove that the employer has fulfilled its legal duties. This is no comfort and does not feel promising to someone whose job has made him miserable. Meanwhile, the state can have such a short timeline for claiming workers' comp that a reluctant employee could lose his chance to get the benefits simply because he has not notified the proper office and obtained the form quickly enough.

Much is at risk here. At the very least, the employee's mental health injury may not be covered by workers' comp insurance. At the most, the employee could lose his job altogether. If the employee, for example your stepson Dennis, does not have a spouse or power of attorney authorized to conduct transactions on his behalf, someone in the family (perhaps you) should at least call his manager or the human resources office, say that Dennis has suffered an on-the-job mental health injury, and ask if you can begin the workers' comp claim process on his behalf.

The office may say that mental health injuries are not covered by workers' comp unless it happened along with an on-the-job serious physical injury. This is true in approximately twenty states. Faced with this response, you can say, "In that case, consider this to be notification that [name the person] needs Family and Medical Leave time effective immediately." (See the FMLA section in this chapter to read about that area of the law.)

If the office says that only the employee can initiate the workers' comp process, you can at least ask about the time limit and any other rules that the employee needs to know about. The employer will likely have a packet or the contact information for a different office that will provide the rules. Somewhere in the rules there may be a clause that begins with the phrase, "If it is impossible for the employee to . . . ." This is the cue that will either enable the family to start the claim, delay the claim, or proceed in a specified way. If the rules provide no entry point for the family, the employee truly cannot deal with the claim, and there is a time limit or other requirement that has to be met, it may be necessary for you or another relative to petition for temporary conservatorship (which may be called temporary guardianship where you live) in order to make the workers' comp claim for the employee. (See the conservatorship section in Chapter 21 of this book for information about doing that.)

It may also be helpful to contact a workers' compensation lawyer at this point. Most of the time, lawyers do not get involved with workers' comp cases until after the claim has been filed and acted upon. But when there is an impasse at the very beginning of the process, a lawyer may at least be able to buy time or file something with the workers' comp claims office to preserve the employee's opportunity to file the claim.

HOW TO Complete a Workers' Compensation Injury Report Form

When you or your family member gets the FROI form, expect that it will focus on physical injuries. Usually, the form will ask you to identify injured body parts and any equipment or conditions of the facility that caused the injury. If the form does not have a specific question about mental health, psychiatric harm, psychic injury, or something similar, then name the mental health problem where the form asks for facts about the injury. List all related physical conditions, such as hand tremors or the inability of the employee to sleep, in addition to the psychiatric condition.

The form will ask for physician contact information and the employee's permission to contact that doctor, although either the employer or state law may require employees (also referred to as claimants during this process) to be treated by an approved physician. The form may ask for the regular physician's contact information (note that this will be a psychiatrist when the claim is about a mental health injury) in order to confirm that the employee did not previously have the injury.

It is important to note that all workers' compensation claimants have to get medical treatment. The main point of workers' compensation is to enable injured employees to get treatment for workplace injuries without having to pay even a co-payment. An employee with a mental injury who refuses to pursue treatment cannot expect to collect workers' compensation.

Probably the most challenging questions on the form will be about how the injury happened. Psychiatric injuries usually need to have come on quickly and to be associated with something unusual or abnormal and major at work in order to be covered by workers' compensation. A gradual build-up of anxiety or depression, for example, would generally be covered by the employee's regular health insurance or the employer's short-term disability coverage, rather than workers' comp. Circumstances like bullying or undermining may fit better in a civil court claim for infliction of emotional distress as an unlawful employment practice than in a workers' comp claim.

To write a strong explanation of how the injury happened, present the facts in three phases. (Note that the examples below are written from the employee's point of view, but you don't need to do that if you are writing on his behalf.)

1. Identify the event that triggered the injuries. Examples include:
   - *When the customer attacked me . . .*
   - *When the other branch got robbed . . .*
   - *When my mentor got fired and I was suddenly demoted . . .*
   - *When something went wrong in accounting and we all got investigated and had to have lie detector tests . . .*
2. Explain in more detail how that event involved the employee. Examples include:
   - *I was thrown to the ground and beaten.*

- *I had to go through robbery reaction training.*
- *My income got cut significantly.*
- *I threw up and kept shaking and stammering all through the questioning.*
3. Highlight the event's lingering effects on the employee. Examples include:
- *I constantly see that attacker; I cannot sleep and am depressed and do not want to go anywhere.*
- *I just cannot focus on anything because I am so worried that every person who walks in might be a robber; I do not even want to look at people, let alone talk to them.*
- *When they fired my mentor and cut my salary, the ground fell out from under me; I totally lost my sense of security and started having panic attacks several times every day.*
- *Ever since the lie detector test, I have been in a state of major anxiety and paranoia; I am just waiting to get falsely accused and trapped in prison.*

Answer all of the questions on the injury report form. The claims administrator who reviews the form will not guess at the answers to parts left blank and may be able to deny the claim because of unanswered questions. One question that often stumps people is "Date of hire." You can at least fill in the month and year if you or your loved one do not recall the exact day. In response to a line that asks about a "substance or object" that caused the injury, you can identify an event.

Finally, you can feel very comfortable using the toll-free workers' compensation helpline or online chat service that is identified on the injury report form. State workers' compensation offices establish those service supports for the benefit of both claimants and claim offices: the more thoroughly and properly prepared the FROI is, the sooner and more correctly everything else can happen with the claim.

The Workers' Compensation Claims Administrator

Most of the time, the completed workers' comp injury report form should be submitted to a claims administrator at the workers' comp insurance company.[1] The injury report form and the instructions will explain how to submit the form to the administrator. The instructions will also indicate whether anything should be submitted along with the form—perhaps an incident report, contact information for witnesses, a hospital admission document, or other proof of facts in the claim.

The claims administrator (who may be called a claims adjuster, claims examiner, or something else that is similar to claims administrator) does not work for the company that employs the injured worker and has no obligation to save the

---

1 In states that allow self-insurance for workers' comp, some companies manage their own claims and payment system for workplace injuries. Since the programs are unique to the individual employers, they are not covered further in this book, although they are likely to be very similar to the descriptions here because they still have to comply with state law.

employer money. This professional is a neutral party responsible for assessing whether the claim satisfies the state's legal requirements.

The claims administrator is not supposed to analyze the claim in relation to previous cases or to make any presumptions about the work environment. Even if the injured claimant works in an insurance office, the workers' comp claims administrator, who also works in an insurance office, cannot presume to know anything about the office where the claimant's situation happened. Certainly, the administrator will not be in a position to understand the various symptoms and manifestations of mental illness. At this stage, the claims administrator is simply somebody who examines an injury report form against a basic checklist of the state's legal criteria for granting and denying compensation.

If the claim matches the criteria, the claims administrator will notify the employee about forthcoming payments and provide instructions for remaining in contact and planning a return to work. If the claims administrator does not have sufficient facts to conclude that the claim matches the legal criteria, which is likely because psychiatric claims often require more proof than the claim form allows, the claims administrator will send a denial notice. The denial will come with directions for pursuing the claim further.

Appealing a Workers' Compensation Denial

The safest way to proceed with a workers' compensation appeal is with legal representation. A workers' compensation lawyer will know whether the claim is worth appealing and, if it is, how to gather and present evidence. The lawyer will also be competent at disputing evidence that is presented against the employee. Evidence against the employee can include proof that the injury:

- was normal or foreseeable under the circumstances
- is not as serious as the employee claims it is
- did not occur at work
- does not prevent the employee from working.

The lawyer will help the employee to feel confident walking into a mediation session or hearing. If the case goes to mediation, the lawyer will know which mediator to select. If the case results in a hearing, the lawyer will already be familiar with the judge and will prepare the client for that particular judge's method for conducting hearings.

Workers' compensation lawyers often work in personal injury law firms. They are paid only if they win or settle the case and their payment will be a percentage of the employee's settlement or judgment. The percentage amount is set by state law, although judges can sometimes adjust the exact percentage within a range established by the law. Lawyers can also get reimbursed for their out-of-pocket expenses, such as the cost of having a medical expert examine and report on the claimant's condition, from the employee's settlement or judgment.

The workers' comp appeals process is an opportunity to present evidence that could not go with the original claim form. This evidence will usually include hospital records and input from various mental health professionals who have interacted with the employee about events at work and the resulting injury. An especially critical piece of evidence is a signed report from the worker's treating therapist and/or psychiatrist regarding the cause and disabling effects of the injuries. Additional helpful evidence will be copies of office emails between the employee, the boss, and others at work as well as witness testimony from people on the job who saw what happened. Either the employee or the insurer may call upon a vocational evaluator to assess the employee's aptitudes and abilities. Sometimes, family testimony is necessary in a workers' compensation appeal. The family can verify whether any events outside of work contributed to the employee's mental condition. The family can also describe the impact of the workplace problem on the employee's at-home mental functioning.

In some jurisdictions, parties to a workers' comp appeal are required to participate in mediation. These parties are the employee, the employer, and the insurer. The employee and the employer may both be accompanied by lawyers. The employee may also be accompanied by a supportive family member, if necessary. Mediation is meant to be an opportunity for claimants, not a roadblock. It invites more diverse and informal communication than a hearing does. Some employees, for example, need a chance to vent to their employer. They can do this in a mediation session. In a hearing, complaints about co-workers and the workplace and the way this claim has been handled would be considered irrelevant and the employee would have no opportunity to voice them.

Another benefit of workers' compensation mediation is that it reveals surveillance results that the insurer has gathered. If a "depressed" employee has been electronically recorded at dances or a "traumatized" employee has been working at another job, mediation will dispense with the case before everyone spends too much money and worry on it. Very often, the information can be obtained from social media. Of course, there are also times when the insurer's surveillance helps to support the employee's claim, such as when the surveillance video shows that an employee who claims to have been traumatized leaves his house only once during an entire week of surveillance and then it is in the company of a family member who appears to be urging him into the car for what turns out to be an appointment with the psychiatrist. If, however, any surveillance does not close the case and the mediation does not result in an agreement that is acceptable to both the insurer and the employee, then at least the employee will know what kind of opposition to expect at a hearing. He will have heard the employer's reasons for thinking that he did not become psychiatrically injured at work. Most of the time, there is no drama in mediation and it results in a swift and relatively low-stress conclusion for the employee. (See Chapter 15 for more on mediation.)

When there is not a mandatory mediation or if mediation fails to result in an agreement, the workers' compensation appeal process typically culminates in a hearing before a workers' compensation judge. Workers' compensation judges are employed by the state department of labor, not by the judiciary branch of government. In some states, they are called "hearing officers" or "commissioners" rather than "judges."[2] They are usually hired for this role after years of practice as attorneys in the workers' compensation field. Workers' comp hearings do not involve juries, but they can be open to the public, although the employee's lawyer can

---

2 Note: In Alabama, the civil court decides workers' comp cases, not a specialized judge in the labor department.

ask that the judge keep the hearing closed in consideration of sensitive psychiatric information that will be presented. Because they are operated by the state's labor department, the hearings tend to be conducted in ordinary state office buildings, rather than in a court house. Participants will have to go through security screening when they enter the building. Since workers' comp lawyers are in these buildings all the time, an employee with mental illness can easily arrange to meet his lawyer there in the weeks before his own hearing, just to get a feel for the place. On the day of the hearing, family members may come along to provide moral support or witness testimony, if the employee wants them there or if they are important to his case. The employee's lawyer will be there to present his claim and help him respond to anything that the judge or the employer's lawyer may ask. The facility will feel bureaucratic and the hearing room will be a simple space, but the hearing itself will be all about the worker.

The evidence in the workers' comp hearing will be sensitive. It has to contain mental health treatment records in order for an employee to prove a psychiatric injury. The insurer has a due process right to be fully informed about the injury in order to best assess whether it should be covered by workers' comp. Nevertheless, the employee's direct supervisor and co-workers do not need to see the records or necessarily to know about the mental health diagnosis or treatment, although they will likely have observed some symptoms at work. If a supervisor or other witnesses are involved in a workers' comp hearing, the employee's lawyer can try to make arrangements with the judge and the employer's attorney to allow the witnesses in the room only for their own testimony so that they will not be present to hear about any other evidence in the case. It is possible that their statements about seeing or hearing the injurious incident will be written and submitted in advance of the hearing so that they do not have to come in person.

Some of the evidence in the hearing may be graphic enough to revive or worsen the employee's mental health symptoms, such as when an employee was robbed and beaten by a customer or when a piece of large equipment dropped right next to the employee, causing him minor physical injuries and major traumatic stress. The employee does not have to stay in the room when that evidence is presented. His lawyer can make advance arrangements with the insurance lawyer and the judge to excuse the employee before the video of the robbery or photos of the dropped equipment or any other disturbing content is revealed. Since this is a hearing, the employee is supposed to be heard, so he will not be able to miss the entire event.

If the workers' comp hearing does not result in a favorable decision for the employee, there are still more opportunities for continuing the claim. The lawyer will usually review the judge's decision with the employee to talk about the judge's reasons for denying workers' comp benefits. If the lawyer is convinced that the judge mishandled the process or failed to honor the substance of any workers' comp laws, she can file a claim with the state's workers' compensation review board to review the facts and laws in the case. The review board is likely to uphold the hearing decision (i.e., agree with it) unless the judge or hearing officer was "arbitrary and capricious" by not following state norms in the case.

If the state does not have a workers' comp review board (at this point every state but Florida has one) or the workers' comp review board does not find fault with the hearing decision, the case can proceed to the state court system. The state court will be able to look at the employee's situation in a broader context than the workers' comp agency could. Rather than considering only the employee's injury in light of the workers' compensation laws, the state court can also analyze the workers' comp laws themselves. They may consider different meanings of a phrase in the law. They may compare the events at the workplace to similar non-workplace events that result in psychiatric injuries. They may consider whether the employee's experience demonstrates a legal flaw or omission that needs to be corrected.

Examples of Workers' Compensation Claims About Mental Health

ATASCADERO UNIFIED SCHOOL DISTRICT V. WCAB, 98 CAL. APP. 4TH 880 (CAL. APP. 2D DIST. 2002)
When an employee had an extramarital affair with a co-worker and everyone else at work was gossiping about it, the employee felt unable to continue performing effectively at that job and filed for workers' compensation. The legal question in this case was whether the problem arose from the job. Since the gossip really arose from the affair, rather than anything that happened at work, the court decided that this claimant was not entitled to workers' compensation.

ROMERO V. CITY OF SANTA FE, 134 P.3D 131 (N.M. CT. APP. 2006)
When a public swimming pool manager started having bad dreams and developed nausea, tremors, and photophobia (extreme sensitivity to light) from having to clean up dead pigeons and pigeon droppings at the pool, his state court was not able to award him workers' compensation benefits because in that state (New Mexico) psychological injuries are only compensable if they arise from a traumatic event, not from "gradual, progressive, stress-producing causes." In this job, dealing with the dead birds and thousands of pounds of droppings were just ordinary ongoing circumstances of the job.

STATE V. CEPHAS, 637 A.2D 20 (DEL. 1994)
In Delaware, a corrections officer whose workload tripled due to a staff shortage had to stay an extra sixteen hours each week just to get everything done. He became so stressed by the amount of work that he developed headaches, nausea, and hives and once passed out while driving home from work. The cumulative stress was found to be a mental injury resulting from work and the claimant was awarded workers' compensation. His case is often referenced in newer mental health workers' comp claims.

YOCOM V. PIERCE, 534 S.W.2D 796 (KY. 1976)
An old Kentucky case is also still relied upon in mental health–related workers' comp claims in that state. The case involved a middle-aged woman who color-coded garments in a clothing factory. She had worked at that job for thirty years and, when she made her claim, a doctor declared that she had "an anxiety neurosis that has gradually increased in severity over the past ten years. I think that the demands made by her work at the plant simply is a factor that tilted her over so that she was simply unable to cope with the requirements of her job." She won her case and was awarded worker's comp because the court clearly understood that

something dormant in this worker's mental makeup caused the working conditions to impact her so severely that she developed a nervous breakdown.

BABICH V. W.C.A.B., 922 A.2D 57 (PA. COMMW. CT. 2007)

In 2007, a Pennsylvania prison nurse with a history of mental illness filed a workers' compensation claim after being repeatedly tormented by inmates who threatened him, threw feces at him, and committed self-mutilation just to upset him when he made rounds to deliver their medicine. The appellate court found that he was not entitled to workers' compensation despite suffering depression and post-traumatic stress from the working conditions because employees working, as he was, in the criminally insane inmates' unit of a maximum security prison would be expected to experience the kinds of things he experienced at his job.

THE PSYCHOLOGICAL BENEFITS OF FMLA, ADA ACCOMMODATION LEAVE, AND WORKERS' COMPENSATION

Reading about the effort and potential opposition that your loved one may encounter when taking leave time or attempting to claim workers' comp benefits, you may think that he shouldn't bother with them. But these legal opportunities provide psychological benefits in addition to legal benefits. They empower employees to stick up for themselves and they provide security to people with mental illness who may not otherwise have the nerve to return to work after a bad episode. The return to work after leave is a chance for an employee to say, "I'm okay; you haven't seen the last of me. I refuse to be defined in this workplace by the episode that happened before I went on leave." And the communications about workers' compensation, even if the employees do not get compensated in the end, give them a legitimate stance to take against an employer whose actions or inactions caused them to suffer. Having asserted their legal rights, the employees can move forward not as victims or as people who couldn't handle their jobs, but as strong adults who not only got themselves through an episode of mental illness, but also proved to be brave and dignified.

Tax Facts

- Section 104(a)(1) of the Internal Revenue Code, regarding compensation for injuries or sickness, declares that "gross income does not include—amounts received under workmen's compensation acts as compensation for personal injuries or sickness." In other words, people who collect routine workers' comp benefits or workers' comp settlements ordinarily do not have to pay income tax on that money.
- Employees who are not paid for FMLA leave will not be charged income tax for their leave. If they do get sick pay for some of their FMLA days, then they will be charged income tax for just those days but not for any remaining unpaid days of FMLA leave. See IRS Publication 15A, *Employer's Supplemental Tax Guide.*

RESOURCES FOR FAMILY AND MEDICAL LEAVE

1. The Department of Labor (DOL) explains the FMLA online at dol.gov/ whd/fmla.
2. To file a complaint about an employer not following the FMLA, call or go to your nearest Wages and Hours office. Find a list of DOL offices and read full details about how the complaint will be investigated at dol.gov.
3. In the unlikely event that you are dealing with an employer that does not have a "medical certification" form for FMLA claims, get one from the DOL's collection of forms at webapps.dol.gov/libraryforms. You want form number WH380E if the sick person is the employee. Use form WH380F if you seek FMLA leave from your own job in order to assist the sick person. Note that the *WH* in the form numbers stands for Wages and Hours—the division of the DOL that makes and enforces FMLA regulations. The letter *E* stands for "employee" and the letter *F* is for "family."
4. *Sista v. CDC IXIS North America*, 445 F.3d 161 (2d Cir. 2006) and *Pearson v. Unification Theological Seminary*, 785 F. Supp. 2d. 141 (S.D.N.Y. 2011) are two examples of FMLA cases in which employees were fired when they attempted to return to work after their FMLA leave. In both of the cases, the employees had done things that were bad enough to get them fired prior to going on leave and in both cases the bad behavior was clearly the result of their mental illness.

RESOURCES FOR DISABILITY ACCOMMODATION LEAVE

1. The Code of Federal Regulations distinguishes between leave time as an accommodation under ADA and FMLA in the labor regulation at 29 C.F.R. § 825.702. This is free online at ecfr.gov.
2. The EEOC explains ADA disability accommodation leave in plain English, and provides many case examples, in an online page titled *Employer-Provided Leave and the Americans with Disabilities Act*. Type this title into a search engine or navigate to it through the EEOC's publications page. See eeoc.gov/eeoc/publications
3. The ADA Division of the EEOC's Office of Legal Counsel has issued *Enforcement Guidance: Reasonable Accommodation and Undue Hardship Under the Americans with Disabilities Act* to "clarif[y] the rights and responsibilities of employers and employees" that have to be reconciled when a worker who has any disability, including a psychiatric condition, needs accommodation. To reach the section that is specifically about leave time as an accommodation, hold the CTRL and F keys and then type the word *leave* in the search box that pops up. See eeoc.gov/policy/docs/ accommodation.html.
4. The Job Accommodation Network (JAN) at the DOL helps employers and employees to figure out the most reasonable accommodations in their situation. For clear explanations and examples of job accommodations, including leave time, and to reach the Ask JAN office for personal assistance, see askjan.org.

RESOURCES FOR WORKERS' COMPENSATION

1. The DOL links to state workers' compensation offices at dol.gov. You can also type your state name and the term *workers compensation* in a search engine to find your state office. The state workers' compensation agency website will include frequently asked questions as well as details about how claims are processed and can be appealed.

2. Find your state's specific rules, guidance, and other materials about its legal requirements via the National Association of Workers Compensation Judiciary at nawcj.org.

3. California's "DWC Glossary of Workers' Compensation Terms for Injured Workers" has a lot of phrases, words, and abbreviations that are used all over the country. Find it at dir.ca.gov.

4. Guide One Insurance also provides a thorough and free "Workers' Compensation Glossary of Terms" on its website, guideone.com.

5. The Workers' Compensation Institute is an industry association that writes about trends, cases, and evolving legal issues. Use the word *psychiatric* in their search box to read about questions and controversies regarding mental health claims around the country. See also its list of "payer acronyms" and its glossaries. All of this is available at wci360.com.

6. The National Council on Compensation Insurance (NCCI) "gathers data, analyzes industry trends, and prepares objective insurance rate and loss cost recommendations." Find assorted facts, training materials, and explanations about workers' comp on their website, ncci.com.

Responses to Employment Termination

After a year and a half on disability, Paul felt ready to work again. He thought that everything would be okay when he got hired to work on the city's street patching crew. City employees are set for life: There's always plenty of work and the fringe benefits are decent. The one thing he didn't really think about before starting this new job was the word crew. *Paul has to be a team player and get along with the guys and pretend to like all the dumb things they say. He just isn't like that. He has worked with a therapist on his social anxiety and his habit of pulling away from experiences that involve a lot of talking and cooperating, so he can handle some social contact, but yakking with these guys all day is just painful. After only a month, the crew has started to turn on him. They crowd up close to Paul in the truck and when they are outside working, they pester him with suggestions for finding a girlfriend. They take his tools just so he'll have to ask for them back, and then when he stammers or can't ask, they call him a little boy. No matter what Paul does, they gang up on him. He just can't take it anymore. He thinks that he may have to go back on disability. Witnessing all of this agony, you think he should sue the city's street department for causing this emotional distress.*

CLOSING A DOOR AND OPENING A DOOR

There is an old saying about opportunity—that when a door closes on one event in life, another door opens for the same person elsewhere. This is a good thought for families to keep in mind when a loved one with mental illness suffers a bad job loss. Jobs end badly when people are forced to leave them. For an employee who has a mental illness, two of the most legally significant causes of bad job loss are poor employment practices by the employer, in which case the former employee could sue the employer, and increased severity of the employee's psychiatric condition, in which case the former employee could apply for benefits, such as unemployment insurance, disability insurance, Social Security Disability Insurance (SSDI), or Supplemental Security Income (SSI).

A lawsuit alleging an unlawful employment practice, such as harassment that causes emotional distress, can itself be a traumatic event, although, like other assertions of rights, it can also be a healing triumph. Similarly, a period of disability can be restorative. If an employee with mental illness has been on disability for some time, but feels ready to return to work, the Social Security Administration (SSA) has several ways of supporting that transition. This chapter shows how an employee with mental illness can open new doors by bringing a lawsuit or returning to work after being on disability.

UNLAWFUL EMPLOYMENT PRACTICES OR OTHER TORTS CAUSING EMOTIONAL DISTRESS

No one should be tormented at work, and if this happens for an unlawful reason, employees can sue their employers for making them miserable! For example:

- Sexually harassing an employee causes emotional distress and is unlawful.
- Severe or pervasive harassment based on disability is also unlawful. Disability-based harassment can include such practices as targeting an individual based on their disability with bullying, unwanted touching, abusive teasing or joking, or knowingly "pushing buttons" to aggravate his or her susceptibilities. In some cases, the events could also constitute another claim, such as assault or intentional infliction of emotional distress.
- Demotion, termination, or refusal to promote based on disability is unlawful and can cause emotional distress.
- A denial of a reasonable accommodation is unlawful and can cause emotional distress.
- Depending on the facts, and the law in the particular state, a lawyer may also add torts to an employee's case, such as assault, battery, false imprisonment, or intentional infliction of emotional distress.

An employee may have various legitimate reasons to sue an employer for unlawful employment practices causing emotional distress, or for other torts, but the critical question is whether to do it. Families who know how these cases play out may be able to help with the decision and with managing the case.

Disability Discrimination and Workers' Compensation

Sometimes, the problems at work that result in emotional distress can count as employment discrimination, a tort under state law, and an on-the-job injury covered by workers' compensation. It is important that employees take steps to preserve their rights under each category.

- Unlawful discrimination—An employee who wishes to pursue a legal claim for disability discrimination (or another form of unlawful employment discrimination) causing emotional distress must begin by filing a charge or claim with the Equal Employment Opportunity Commission (EEOC) or a state Fair Employment Practices Agency (FEPA) within the statute of limitations (180 days in some states). If the employee works for the federal government, the statute of limitations is much shorter—the employee has 45 days to contact the agency counselor. (See Chapter 15 for more information about employment discrimination claims, including guidance about first raising the claim as an internal matter with the employer before making a legal claim with the EEOC.)

- Torts—Lawsuits alleging torts under state law, such as assault, battery, or intentional infliction of emotional distress, must comply with the state statute of limitations—usually one or two years from when the events happened.
- Workers' compensation—An employee who wishes to pursue benefits under workers' compensation must begin by filing a claim with his or her employer. Usually this must be done immediately. (See Chapter 16 for more information about workers' compensation.)

As you and the person who suffered emotional harm at work gather your thoughts before hiring an attorney who specializes in employment law, you might think about whether a single major event at work caused the harm to the employee or whether a series of events caused it. If it was one major event, then it may be a good case for workers' compensation, if your state even permits workers' comp claims for psychiatric injuries. When it was a series of events, then it may be a case of disability-based harassment or another type of unlawful employment practice or tort. The lawyer will have the expertise to decide which claims to raise, but you and your injured loved one will be able to communicate more productively with the lawyer if you have already considered some of these fundamental points.

Challenges in Bringing a Case Against a Former Employer

Finding a lawyer is the first challenge in bringing a case against a former employer. The second challenge is watching the evidence come together. Clients expect their lawyer to gather evidence, but seeing it all in one place can be horrible for clients, especially those living with mental illness. If, for example, the employee is your wife Iris, who has anxiety, the documents and witness testimony that her lawyer collects as evidence may remind her of how anxious she was previously and it may also cause her new anxieties. The third challenge is enduring the lawsuit process. For Iris, the chain of deadlines and appearances, and particularly her deposition, will likely provoke even more anxiety. There is also a fourth challenge, which is the internal personal work of moving beyond the emotionally distressing situation after not only living through it but also suing over it. This can be a crushing process for anyone, not just Iris or somebody else with mental illness. For some people, going through a lawsuit will batter a bad experience into a meaningless unrecognizable blob, the way a garbage truck dispenses with the trash we leave at the curb. Hearing the employer's crass explanations and repeating everything multiple times through trial preparation, the victims become numb to the story, lose interest in it, or simply stop allowing it to continue taking up space in their consciousness. Other victims are haunted by their emotional distress. Fighting a lawsuit against it solidifies the distress in their memories and guts, and no matter what comes of the lawsuit, the victims still feel bad. Perhaps at least reading about the first three challenges will help some employees and their families considering whether to bring an emotional distress lawsuit to predict whether such a lawsuit is worth the trouble for them.

CHALLENGE 1: FINDING A LAWYER

Lawyers who represent employees against their employers typically get paid on a contingency basis, which means that they make money on a case only if they win in court or settle out of court. Their payment is usually 30% to 40% of the amount that they get for their clients. They are constantly swamped by prospective clients who have suffered injustices and would not be able to pay out of pocket for legal representation. In other words, the lawyers get to choose which clients to take. They take the clients whose cases look winnable, because otherwise they will not get paid.

Two factors make a case winnable: a good client and a legitimate claim. A good client is one whose story is consistent and who cooperates by showing up at the right times, providing reliable facts, taking actions that the lawyer recommends, and remaining focused. Supportive family members can help with all of these items. A lawyer cannot be sure about these characteristics based on initial conversations, but he will usually ask some test questions to see if the prospective client tends to make excuses, alter facts, argue, or even just communicate badly. Whether the client has a legitimate claim is easier to figure out quickly.

A legitimate claim is one that satisfies the list of legal criteria. For example, disability-based harassment requires "severe or pervasive" conduct. Depending on the jurisdiction, the claim may also require that the victimized employee follow through with the employer's internal complaint process. If that is the claim being considered, the lawyer will listen to a prospective client's story with those requirements in mind. Take, for example, the situation of your niece, Becca, who has a panic disorder and works in a large regional real estate office. She is suing her employer for disability-based harassment because her co-workers made a joke out of her condition and played tricks on her to make her panic. Here are some of the questions that examine whether the behavior was sufficiently "severe or pervasive" to constitute unlawful harassment:

- *Did the co-workers know that they were doing something problematic and continue to do it anyway?* Everybody in the office knew about Becca's panic disorder. She was open about it when she was hired and arranged on her first day at work three years ago to have her desk in a spot where nobody could sneak up on her. Yet, one of the agents has gotten in the habit of yelling "Sold!" at the top of his lungs whenever a house sells, just to see if Becca will jump, another agent has learned to worry her by periodically moving and resorting the electronic files that Becca is responsible for, and the title searcher whispers "Don't mess up, Becca" at least once every week.
- *Did the co-workers have a legitimate business reason for their actions?* The realtors are supposed to notify Becca by email when they sell a house and they are supposed to attach their documents so that she, and only she, can properly place them in the electronic file database. There is no legitimate reason for any of them to yell "Sold!" or to interfere with the file system.
- *Did the co-workers consider the outcome of what they were doing?* The whole point of the annoyances was to try to make Becca panic.

Did the co-workers want to upset or cause trouble for the employee? The co-workers literally wanted to make Becca sweat. Because employer knowledge and responsibility is another criterion in a disability harassment case, the lawyer will want to be sure that the employer otherwise knew what was going on, and did nothing to prevent it.

- *Did Becca report the harassment to her supervisor? Did she let human resources know?* Yes, Becca told her supervisor and even wrote a complaint by email and cc'd HR. They took no steps.
- *Did the employer respond or take action upon learning that this was going on?* The employer told Becca to "loosen up" when she reported what the co-workers were doing.
- *Did the employer discipline the co-workers?* The employer was pleased with the good morale in the office and didn't want Becca's "jumpiness" to ruin the environment for everybody else.
- *Did the supervisor know what was going on?* The supervisor was present—and sometimes even laughed!

Unlawful disability-based harassment is severe or pervasive hostile conduct that is based on disability. The law does not define severe or pervasive conduct. Individual courts come to their own conclusions about it, based on the facts in each case. Here are questions that help to determine whether behavior is severe or pervasive:

- *Was it necessary or even justifiable in any way?* None of the actions by Becca's co-workers was needed in order for the business to function.
- *Was it in response to anything the victim did?* The co-workers who goaded Becca and the boss who made light of her panic disorder were responding to her workplace accommodation and her informing all of them that she had the disorder and could not predict when panic would strike.
- *Was there an element of shame in the behavior against the victim?* Becca is not ashamed of having a panic disorder, but the co-workers seemed to want her to feel ashamed. To them, it was funny when she became shaky, flushed, and sweaty.
- *How many times did the behavior happen?* It happened all the time, probably hundreds of times.
- *What was at risk for the victim?* Aside from the outward symptoms that made the co-workers laugh, Becca could feel her heart beating hard and fast, and she would get terrible chest pain and headaches during her panic attacks. Afterward, she would feel tired and embarrassed.
- *What made it different from anything else that happened in the workplace?* People joke around in this workplace, but these particular behaviors are mean-spirited, not funny.

The lawyer may not directly ask these questions; she may let Becca tell the story while she listens for the facts. She will consider Becca's situation in comparison with past cases that she has handled. Maybe Becca does not have an especially good claim for disability-based harassment, but she does have a strong claim for defamation or for privacy invasion or for refusal to provide a reasonable accommodation. Maybe it just sounds like routine bad stuff that does not warrant legal action.

Even if one lawyer thinks that a case has no merit, another lawyer may think it has lots of merit. Employees should seek consultations with law firms of different sizes and reputations in order to get a solid idea of whether their case is worth pursuing. If multiple lawyers decline to take the case and give reasons that show a lack of intent by the co-worker or a lack of severe or pervasive behavior, the case is probably not a winner.

Whether or not a lawyer eventually agrees to take the case, the victimized employee will have to go over the story repeatedly while shopping for a lawyer. The more he has to recall the bad treatment, the worse he will feel, and the more he and his family members will wonder whether to keep trying. Every time he has to tell what was done to him, his stomach may turn and his heart rate may quicken. It is a terrible story with at least one mean dominant character and a disappointing plot: The job did not turn out the way he had hoped it would. He feels rotten. He has either lost his livelihood or is on the verge of losing it. And surely he dreads the thought of looking for another job and starting over with an unknown group of new co-workers.

While the lawyer is assessing whether the case is winnable, the prospective client and supportive family member can assess the lawyer's humanity. Does this lawyer care what happened? Does she talk as if she wants to help? When she considers whether the co-worker's actions were "severe or pervasive," does she only consider the phrase as a legal standard or does she understand that the co-worker was really horrible?

CHALLENGE 2: GATHERING EVIDENCE

Once the lawyer is on board, it is time to build the case. This means gathering proof that meets the legal criteria that apply to the case. To use the example of disability harassment again, this would mean "severe or pervasive" hostile conduct that materially alters the terms and conditions of employment. The lawyer's part of the challenge is labor-intensive. She will send formal requests called interrogatories and requests for production of documents to the employer asking for copies of documents, such as records about the offending co-worker, facts about the workplace, and anything about the incidents and the victim. If the victim, such as your brother-in-law Tony, has symptoms of a mental illness, the lawyer will collect his mental health records to see if his therapist or psychiatrist has written about Tony's suffering harm from the events at work. The records will have to show serious mental harm, harm that has temporarily ruined Tony, and harm that is worthy of damages in a court case. The lawyer will probably depose people from the job, including the person accused. Depositions are personal interviews that are witnessed and transcribed by a court reporter.

As the lawyer pursues the information sources, she may learn some complicating things about her client. He could be exaggerating. He may have retaliated against co-workers. He could have caused the problem. He may be misinterpreting something. Events and behaviors that felt abusive to the employee may not have been what he thought they were. If the evidence does not support her client, the lawyer may recommend settlement rather than going forward with the case. If the evidence does support her client, she will have to divulge the opposition's claims to him. He has to know the case strategy and what they are up against, so he has to be confronted with the employer's version of things.

For a victimized employee, such as Tony, the challenge of gathering evidence is having to face this opposition. The process can be upsetting for anyone, especially for your brother-in-law with mental illness. Facing claims by the employer can make him feel as though he is stuck in the same old work problems, even though he now has a lawyer representing him. When Tony started the lawsuit, he was on the offense. But now that his employer is submitting its evidence, he is on the defense again, just like he was when things were bad at work and he finally became so miserable that he had to quit.

The employer's lawyer will also gather evidence. He will hire a mental health expert to at least review the plaintiff's records (Tony is the plaintiff in this legal action and the employer is the defendant) and possibly to meet with him. Again, Tony will have to relive his bad experience and tell a stranger about his private mental condition. As Tony's support person, you can at least be a sounding board after he gets out of the meeting. You probably will not be allowed in the room during the meeting because your presence may affect Tony's response to the mental health professional.

As the plaintiff, Tony will have to go through a deposition, answering questions for several hours in a closed room while a court reporter takes down every word. But there will be no feedback. A deposition is just lots of questions from the employer's lawyer, and when it ends, the person questioned walks away with nothing but a sore throat and questions of his own. Many months will have passed since the events at work. He may have gotten some facts wrong in the deposition, but the only way to know that is to think through the whole thing and try to remember what the lawyer asked and how he responded.

If it is okay with Tony and his lawyer, you can probably sit quietly in the room where he is being deposed. Tony's lawyer will have to clear this first with the employer's lawyer because the employer's lawyer will be in charge of the deposition. You will likely be made to sit out of the way where Tony will not be able to see your reactions, and if you make noise or otherwise disrupt the deposition, you will be told to leave. It costs a lot of time and money to conduct a deposition, paying the court reporter to be there and then later to produce a printed transcript of everything that was said in the room. Neither lawyer wants this valuable opportunity for gathering information to be ruined by an interfering family member who is not a party to the case. Nevertheless, having been there with Tony, you can help him to recall the strong and positive ways that he handled the questions and the intimidating environment in the deposition room. And if you are not allowed into the deposition, you can schedule an evening together with your loved one, hopefully with a good meal or at a comfortable place that he likes, and hear all about what he thought of the deposition.

CHALLENGE 3: PARTICIPATING IN THE LEGAL PROCESS
The legal process is a rigid collection of rules that are manipulated by opposing parties for the dual purposes of milking every benefit for themselves and thwarting every possible move from the other side. It is incredibly slow. Everything takes a long time, even the evidence gathering. While the lawyer sends requests for documents,

waits for the documents to come, and then reads through everything, the plaintiff has little to do with the case but wonder what is going on. The depositions will be scheduled far in advance, but they can still be delayed or rescheduled. The transcripts of the depositions will take a while to come; they have to be reviewed and revised before the lawyers can use them.

As each lawyer files pleadings with the court, the other lawyer will look for problems with them. The lawyers will file motions asking the court to exclude each other's evidence. They will petition for delays. They will each argue that the other has violated rules.

All of this fussing and stalling happens around the plaintiff, not with the plaintiff. He is not a part of the action. He is in limbo, waiting for a resolution. He may be ready to turn his attention elsewhere. At some point, depending on the jurisdiction, the court may order the parties to try to resolve the matter through mediation or negotiation. This detour away from the traditional court process involves selecting a neutral negotiator or mediator, working out schedules so that the employer, the employee, their lawyers, and the employee's supportive family member (should he want one there) can all attend as many mediation or arbitration sessions as it takes to either reach a resolution or to conclude that the case should go to trial.

If the parties reach a settlement in the alternative dispute resolution, at least the case will end, but the victimized employee will not have had his day in court. Mediation and arbitration have the benefit of being calm and peaceful ways to resolve disputes, but when all is said and done, some people are disappointed that they didn't get to experience courtroom drama. If the case does proceed to court, members of the public can show up to watch it—friends, enemies, and strangers. And the record of the trial will be available to people who go looking for it later. The mental health records likely will not become part of the public record, but references to the employee's mental health condition will be in other case documents since it is a central theme in the case.

HOW TO Reconcile an Emotionally Distressed Employee's Legal Options

- Help your relative (in this case, your mom Sandra, who can no longer effectively work as a teacher's aide in her local elementary school due to emotional distress inflicted by the lead teacher) decide whether she wants to go through a lawsuit. Clearly, bringing a lawsuit is itself emotionally distressing, but the suit does not have to happen right after the trauma at work. Your mom can file a claim with the EEOC (or the state FEPA) within the time limit, and see what happens with the EEOC investigation. When the EEOC dismisses a charge (perhaps because the employee and employer have resolved the problem) or completes its investigation, depending on the case, it provides the person who made the claim with a "Notice of Right to Sue," which entitles that employee to bring a lawsuit in court within ninety days.
- When she is ready, you can accompany your mom to consultations with lawyers or, if she goes alone, listen to what she says about the meetings and review any options that the lawyers discussed with her.

- You could suggest that, as your mom begins this series of events, she compile a timeline to remind herself about the order in which things happened at work. Maybe you can keep your own journal of names, dates, quotes, and recollections that could someday be useful in locating and questioning witnesses. Your journal may also help your mom later to decide whether she wants to revisit the trauma by going through a lawsuit.
- Make sure that your mom cooperates with the EEOC. Most people find it strategically wise to wait until the EEOC process has ended before dealing with the possibility of a lawsuit. First of all, the EEOC investigation will reveal evidence that may be good or bad for the employee. Second, the employee may be able to participate in the free EEOC mediation. The mediation process may satisfy the employee's financial and personal needs so that there is no reason to bring a separate court case.
- Help your mom access any available benefits. If she is looking for work but can't find a job, she can apply for unemployment insurance. If the emotional distress was so bad that your mom is not able to work at another job after leaving the one that upset her, help her to have an income and possibly health insurance while she works things out by putting her on track to collect disability, either from the benefits department at work, from state disability insurance (if she lives in a state that has this program), or from Social Security. An employee whose job trauma has made it impossible to work at any job can apply for SSDI or SSI benefits even though she is also taking other legal action. Keep an eye on the documents and statements presented to any benefits program. You want the statements made in connection with benefits to be consistent with the statements you might make in a lawsuit. (For more on Social Security benefits, refer to Chapter 2; for more on the EEOC, go to Chapter 15; and for more on workers' compensation, see Chapter 16.)

Tax Facts

- If an employee is awarded money damages in an out-of-court settlement or a court judgment, the damages for emotional distress will usually not count as taxable income unless they can be attributed to a "physical injury" or "physical sickness" as these terms are construed by courts and by the IRS. See IRS Publications 525 and 4345.
- Reimbursement for medical expenses is not usually taxable income. However, if the taxpayer previously took a deduction for paying some of the medical expenses out of pocket, then the damages that reimburse him for that payment do count as income on the current year's tax return. See IRS Publications 525 and 4345.
- An amount allocated for attorney fees is an "above the line" deduction when the case is brought under a civil rights statute, such as the ADA. In other words, money that the court awards a plaintiff to pay for his lawyer can be subtracted from that plaintiff's gross income when he is figuring out his adjusted gross income.

- Lost wages ("back pay") and punitive damages must be reported as taxable income on Form 1040, 1040A, or 1040 EZ. See IRS Publication 4345 and the *Lawsuits, Awards, and Settlements Audit Techniques Guide* at irs.gov.

RETURNING TO WORK AFTER SSDI OR SSI DISABILITY

Chapter 2 of this book focuses on the process of applying for SSDI and SSI, as well as what each is and how they differ. If your family member was successful in obtaining one of these disability supports and feels ready to try a job again, he will appreciate that the SSA has programs and policies that make it possible for recipients of either SSDI or SSI disability benefits to experiment with returning to work, to fully return to work, and then, if necessary, after leaving the disability program and being back at work for a few years, to later return to the disability program. The SSA knows well that many people with chronic mental illness can go through periods of years when it is not possible to work, followed by periods of years when it is possible to work. So disability support is available for all of the times when someone's mental illness makes it impossible to work—even if there are months or years of work in between those times.

Although the mental impairments are exactly the same in the SSI disability program and the SSDI disability program, there are differences between the return to work programs for people on SSI versus people on SSDI disability. Nevertheless, under both programs, people with disabilities are allowed to continue getting disability money while working part-time and while trying full-time work.

Whether someone is collecting disability benefits under SSI or SSDI, attempts at returning to work are good for the disability record for two reasons: They show that the person is not a malingerer (someone who fakes or exaggerates symptoms in order to collect disability benefits), which actually is a concern identified in the disability regulations, and they prove how the mental illness continues to affect the worker's ability to manage a job.

Working, SSI, and Medicaid

Beyond having money to live on, the biggest worry for a person with mental illness attempting to return to work after a period of SSI disability is whether her Medicaid (health insurance) coverage will continue. Most of the time, Medicaid will continue.

But when an SSI disability recipient earns money, her disability payments will be reduced. The reduction will not be a dollar-for-dollar exchange. There is no reduction at all for the first $85 that an SSI disability recipient earns. After that first $85, the cut in SSI benefits is only equal to half of the rest of the income. So if your relative feels happier or more secure or in any way better when she has a part-time job, do not get in the way; she will have more money in addition to the good feelings that come with working.

Here are examples of how the math works:

- *If you are on SSI disability and get paid $200 at a job, the SSA first counts that as $200 minus $85, which is just $115. Next, they say, "We're not going to cut your disability by $115; we're just going to cut it by half of that amount, which is $57.50." So you get to keep the full $200 of salary plus all but $57.50 of your usual disability money.*
- *If you are on SSI disability and have a job that pays $900 for one month, the SSA ignores the first $85 and says that you have earned $815. Then, they say that only half of that $815 will be cut from your disability payment. So they will take $407.50 out of your disability payment. You get to keep the $900 salary plus the remaining amount of the disability payment.*

Here is another way to think about this formula: A person collecting disability benefits under SSI can earn money from a job while also earning the disability benefits as long as the job income is no more than double the disability money plus $85.

Whether the person on SSI disability is just experimenting with a job or whether that person expects to keep the job for a long time, this formula is used to figure out how much money the person will continue to get in disability benefits.

When Someone on SSI Needs Training or Supplies in Order to Go Back to Work

Although SSI beneficiaries are not ordinarily supposed to have assets worth more than $2,000, the SSA does have a way for them to collect more than this amount in assets when they need to put aside money in order to go back to work. Beneficiaries can make a formal arrangement, called a Plan to Achieve Self Support, or PASS, with SSA to get the extra assets approved in advance.

Working with the state office of vocational rehabilitation, a job coach from a local mental health support organization, or any job placement service that cooperates with SSA, an SSI beneficiary—such as your friend Petra who has bipolar disorder—needs to make a job-related savings and spending plan. The plan might include getting educated for a completely new career or taking classes or license exams to update a past career. It might include buying tools or special clothing. Perhaps Petra would like to attend a one-year program to be trained as a pet groomer. She will need to put aside tuition money and funds with which to buy her own grooming tools. Petra will have to describe her plan and the items that she needs to buy on SSA Form 545-BK, which is available online or at the Social Security office.

Once the SSA receives the form, a local PASS expert will be assigned to review Petra's plan and to decide whether it is reasonable. Petra may have to meet with the PASS expert or talk with him over the phone. If the plan is approved, Petra will be permitted to have more than $2,000 in her bank account as she gathers the money to fulfill her PASS. Families and friends may contribute to that account or may buy some of Petra's supplies for her without compromising her SSI eligibility.

Notifying SSA That Someone on SSI Disability Is Working

No matter how informal or temporary the job is—even if it is just a couple of weekends wrapping packages at the mall in the month before Christmas—SSA has to be told about the job. If a disability beneficiary gets the kind of job that deducts Social Security and taxes from the paycheck and the SSA learns about the job from that instead of being told by the beneficiary, the disability benefits can be cancelled.

HOW TO Report That an SSI Beneficiary Is Employed

Either you or your family member with the disability must contact the nearest SSA office and provide the following information as soon as an SSI disability recipient takes a job:

- The date that the job starts.
- The duties, hours, and salary.
- Any impairment-related work expenses (IRWEs) that the employee has to pay that are due to the disability.

For example, an employee with depression may need to buy a light box for his workspace to help keep him from getting too depressed at work.

Here is another worthwhile IRWE to know about and report: The costs of having you or another person assist the person with mental illness to get ready for work, or to travel to work, or somehow to manage to perform the job. If this person, say your cousin Sam, has to pay you to do these things or if you have to give your time to help him instead of going to your own paid job, then the value of your help can be subtracted from the amount of job income the SSA will hold against Sam. (Read more about IRWE later in this chapter.)

- Pay stubs. These have to be mailed or delivered to the SSA office handling the employee's disability file by the 10th day of the month after getting the pay. Or the employee (or you) can call 1-800-772-1214 and report the earnings over the phone to the SSA. Just in case there is ever a claim that the employee did not report some income, keep the receipts that come from the SSA after you have reported the monthly job income to them.
- Also notify the SSA when the job ends—no matter why it ends—so that they know to resume paying the full disability amount.

At What Point After Returning to Work Does Someone on SSI Disability Lose the Disability Status?

There are three sources of information that the SSA uses to decide if an SSI disability recipient is still disabled:

- The SSA routinely reviews medical records to determine whether the disabling mental condition is still present.

- The SSA monitors the disabled worker's income record to see if that person is earning more than the "threshold" amount. The threshold amount is published every year at Title 20 Section 1574 and online at the SSA's Cost of Living Adjustments (COLA) web page.
- The SSA checks asset records to confirm that the person does not have more than a certain amount of assets and is not living in a government institution, such as prison.

If the disabling mental illness is controlled so well by medication, therapy, and other medical treatments that the SSI disability recipient can manage to work at substantial gainful activity, although she still needs Medicaid in order to continue her medical regime, the person will almost always continue to count as SSI disabled and to be eligible for the Medicaid benefits, even though she is employed full time.

For People Who Paid into Social Security and Collect SSDI

Unlike SSI recipients, someone on the SSDI program who experiments with returning to work and earns more than a certain amount of money per month is in a "trial work period" according to Social Security regulations. If she earns less than the threshold monthly amount for a trial work period, however, the work simply counts as a part-time job and does not interfere with the disability benefits at all. (See later in this chapter for more about part-time jobs.)

SSDI recipients can collect their disability payments plus their salary during a trial work period as long as they have been on disability for a full year. A trial work period is nine months of "substantial gainful employment" over the course of as many as five years. Some people work for nine months straight through. Others work for a couple of months and then take a break for a few months. Some people try working for a few weeks and then only try again after a year or so and, maybe, after a few sputtering attempts, manage to stay in the position for a span of several months.

HOW TO Report That an SSDI Beneficiary Is Employed

Either the SSDI beneficiary or a supportive loved one must report to the SSA every time the beneficiary starts or stops a trial work period. It is permissible to collect both the disability payment and the salary at the same time only if you or the beneficiary has arranged with the SSA for the beneficiary to be on a trial work period. (Warning: If work time is not reported as a trial work period, the person on disability can get into serious trouble. The SSA can report the situation to the federal prosecutor and then, in a trial, the federal court may deem the person to be guilty of fraudulent concealment of work activity.)

It is very easy to report that someone is starting or stopping a trial work period. Simply contact the nearest Social Security office by phone, in person, or in a letter and provide:

- The name of the person collecting disability benefits.
- The disabled person's social security number.

- The fact that this person is on disability and is starting or stopping a trial work period.
- The contact information for the place that has hired this person with disabilities.

When the SSA is notified about the trial work period, they will send a receipt to the person on disability. That receipt has to be kept with other important Social Security papers. If you are the one who keeps track of your family member's documents, keep an eye out for the receipts in case you are ever called on to prove that he truly did report that he was trying to work. If the person has multiple trial work periods, keep all of the receipts together in case you ever have to verify whether the nine months were all used up.

If the trial work period goes well and the employee feels able to continue working, the SSDI disability benefits will end, but the file will remain open for three years just in case the mental problems become so disruptive that the employee has to go back on disability. If the employee is able to work for more than three years before the next bad episode of psychiatric symptoms, he will have to reapply for disability benefits. As long as there are medical records and maybe even employment records showing that this is a bad episode of the same mental illness that previously disabled the person, the new disability claim will usually result in a faster decision than the original claim.

It is important to understand that someone with a mental illness cannot return to SSDI disability status just because he hates a job or gets fired from a job. To be deemed disabled again, the employee does have to experience the full listing of symptoms that the regulations identify for his mental illness.

Working Part-Time

A person collecting SSDI can work part-time without having that work count as a trial work period or a return to work. Remember that for the SSA, being disabled means not being able to maintain substantial gainful employment. Most of the time, part-time work is neither substantial nor gainful.

Substantial activity is assessed according to the kind of physical and mental effort that it takes and how that effort relates to somebody's particular mental and physical health. Gainful employment is defined by a dollar amount in the Social Security regulations. This amount is also on the SSA website under the topic "Substantial Gainful Activity."

Impairment-Related Work Expenses (IRWE)

People who collect disability benefits under either SSI or SSDI are likely to have out-of-pocket costs that make it possible for them to work. As already noted, the SSA calls the out-of-pocket costs IRWEs and subtracts them from the amount of earnings counted against the disabled earner. Reading about the IRWEs, you may wonder, "Aren't these accommodations and, if they are, shouldn't the job pay for them?" In fact, the job does not always have to pay for workplace accommodations; it just has to facilitate them and prevent interference with them.

Explanation of How Income Is "Counted Against" a Disability Recipient

As discussed above, in SSI disability cases, money earned at a job is counted to see how much of the SSI disability income the person gets to keep while also earning wages. When someone pays out of pocket for things that she needs in order to be able to go to work, the SSA acts like that amount of money was not earned:

- If someone earns $1,000 but has to pay $400 for IRWEs, the SSA says that the person has earned only $600.
- If someone earns $800 but has to pay $500 for IRWEs, the SSA says that the person has earned only $300.

Note that the IRWE costs have to be reasonable (in the standard price range for your community) and not reimbursed by insurance or the government. Some examples of costs that count as IRWEs are:

- A service animal
- An electrotherapy stimulation machine (for example, Alpha-Stim)
- Software to help the worker organize and remember tasks
- An environmental sound machine
- Noise-cancelling headphones
- Attendant care to help the employee to bathe, dress, cook, and otherwise get ready for work
- Out-of-pocket costs for medicine and counseling.

Tax Facts

- IRWEs can usually be deducted on an employee's personal income tax return as either medical expenses or unreimbursed employee business expenses, depending on the item and its use. See Tax Topic 502, *Medical and Dental Expenses,* and IRS Publication 529, *Miscellaneous Deductions* (regarding unreimbursed employee expenses). See also the chart of IRWE examples in the "Red Book" at ssa.gov/redbook.
- SSI benefits are not taxed. Wages and other income that an SSI disability recipient earns can be taxed and should be reported to the IRS on personal income tax returns.
- Depending on how much money you earn from part-time work, investment income, and other sources, up to 50% of your SSDI benefits can be taxed. Read Tax Topic 423, *Social Security and Equivalent Railroad Retirement Benefits,* for more details. See also *Benefits Planner: Income Taxes and Your Social Security Benefits* at ssa.gov.

RESOURCES FOR UNLAWFUL EMPLOYMENT PRACTICES

1. Read a sample fee agreement for a personal injury law firm on Findlaw. Its full title is *Sample Retainer and Contingency Agreement for an Injury Case.* See findlaw.com.
2. The Legal Aid Society—Employment Law Center has a straightforward fact sheet about intentional infliction of emotional distress. Find it online at las-elc.org.
3. Jessica Stender and Roberta Steele presented "Employment Torts," at the ABA Section of Labor and Employment Law at the 2009 Labor and Employment Law CLE Conference (November, 2009). This is a good essay about the array of personal injury claims, aside from inflictions of emotional distress, that employees can bring against employers: breach of privacy, defamation, interference with contract, negligent supervision, etc. The essay is available at americanbar.org.
4. James J. McDonald, Jr., presented "Assessing Emotional Distress Damages: Torture or Fair Play," at the ABA Section of Labor and Employment Law at the 2007 CLE Conference (November 9, 2007). It is a very detailed set of instructions for assessing the financial value of any given victim's experience with emotional distress. It can be found for free online at americanbar.org.
5. Leto Copeley and Narendra K. Ghosh presented "The Intersection of Workers' Compensation and Emotional Distress Employment Claims" to the American Bar Association (November 27, 2015). It is a very technical paper about legal strategies, and it is free online at americanbar.org.

RESOURCES FOR RETURNING TO WORK AFTER SSDI OR SSI DISABILITY

1. The SSA's Red Book is a thorough guide to all of the employment support that is available to people who are disabled. See ssa.gov/redbook.
2. Find the contact information for the nearby Social Security office online at socialsecurity.gov. Either you or the disability recipient must report job information to that nearby SSA office. Remember to keep copies of all documents exchanged between the disabled person and the SSA. You can also call 1-800-772-1213 to report that someone has started or ended a job.
3. You can read the full regulations about working after being declared SSI disabled at 20 C.F.R. §§ 416.260–269 at ecfr.gov.
4. The SSA's explanation about continuing Medicaid after an SSI disability employee returns to work is online at ssa.gov, on the page titled *Continued Medicaid Eligibility (Section 1619(B)).* The section number in the title is the section of the Social Security Act that provides for continuing Medicaid. The Congressional statute requiring the continued coverage is Title 42 of the United States Code § 1382(h). Navigate to the statute online from uscode.house.gov.
5. Read the full regulation about trial work periods for SSDI recipients in Title 20 § 404.1592 of the Code of Federal Regulations or online at ecfr.

gov. See also the Red Book chapter titled "Trial Work Period" at ssa.gov/redbook.

6. The quickest way to find the current year's disability earnings thresholds is go to the SSA's cost-of-living-adjustment page at ssa.gov/news/cola and look for this year's link to "tax, benefit, and earning amounts."

7. Substantial gainful employment is defined at Title 20 of the Code of Federal Regulations in § 404.1574.

PART 4

Consumer Law

18

Owing Money

Penny loves to shop. She says it comes naturally to her because she was named after money. When she's in a manic phase, she can stay up for days watching infomercials and buying things that catch her fancy. When you were at her place yesterday, she showed you a closet full of unopened boxes that have come in the past month's mail. She doesn't even know what's in them and she doesn't care anymore. She is a shampoo technician in a hair salon and does not have the money to pay for all of the orders. Overwhelmed by the quantity of boxes and the amount of her credit card bill, she is doing nothing about the situation. She is exhausted and says that she's so ugly and stupid she isn't even worth a penny. You can tell that she is becoming depressed and you hope that, if you can help her to return some of the purchases and get into a system for paying off her credit cards, she'll feel better.

INTRODUCTION TO MONEY AND MENTAL HEALTH

We do not always know which comes first, financial struggles or mental illness, but we do know that they are connected. There are plenty of data to prove the point, and most of us can understand this just from our own experiences. For example:

- We have worried about making ends meet.
- We have been depressed about having to make do with inferior items.
- We have felt embarrassed about not upholding our end of a deal.
- We have been on edge when we were between jobs or houses, not knowing if things would ever work out.

The temporary and mild versions of the struggles suffered by people who do not have psychiatric conditions are bad enough. The long-term, severe versions suffered by people who do have psychiatric conditions tend to make the financial issues even worse and compromise people's ability to manage adult life's fundamental transactions. Perhaps a mood disorder magnifies the impact of financial pressure or a thought disorder distorts the facts of the financial situation. Some people have disruptions in focus or memory, resulting either from a natural chemical imbalance or the medicine that is supposed to treat it, and these disorders prevent them from being able to cope with financial matters.

Families and trusted friends can help. In every area of consumer law, there are opportunities to assist, to represent, and, when things are especially bad, to take responsibility. Most of the help involves handling communications on behalf of the person who is unable to. Families can complete forms needed to make arrangements for their loved one or write letters to explain their relative's position on something, such as to offer a payment plan to the dentist's office when it is impossible to pay all at once or to notify the bank that there's an incorrect charge on the account. Family members can attend meetings about money issues on behalf of someone who, at least temporarily, is unable to communicate on her own behalf. For example, these might be meetings to arrange for the utility company's low-income assistance program or to orient a caseworker who does not realize the extent of the client's budgeting troubles. Families can often deal with consumer-support tasks in their spare time.

This is important assistance and, done right, it can preserve a person's dignity and independence. Imagine being the one who prevented your grandfather from being evicted or who helped your friend take a legal stand against someone who was cheating her. What if you could help somebody organize their bill payments and avoid going into debt? As a well family member or support person, you can reduce pressure on someone who is unable to sort out details. So many consumer issues complicate the lives of people with mental illness, and there are lots of ways for families to help!

DEBTOR-CREDITOR LAW

"Retail therapy" is not the kind of therapy that helps consumers with mental illness to manage their depression, mania, compulsions, guilt, or other serious mental symptoms. For many people, shopping will only worsen their symptoms. It leads to regret, disappointment, and the stress of either having to return merchandise or to pay for it over time with interest payments on top. Even when excessive spending is necessary, perhaps to replace something that is broken or to pay for an expensive service, consumers suffer the side effects.

The term *consumer* is defined as anyone accessing goods or services, and when a consumer does not have the mental energy to deal with the negative emotions and stressors that can come with paying for those things, he may not be able to handle the practical tasks of finding the receipt and sending or bringing something back or taking a part-time job that will generate money to pay debts. In fact, people with mood disorders are likely to be worse off if they add a part-time job to an already full schedule because disruptions to their regular sleep cycles usually compromise their mental well-being.

The legal category for spending and owing money is debtor-creditor law. Debtor-creditor law is about the allocation of rights and liabilities between consumers and creditors: consumers' rights not to be taken advantage of and creditors' rights to get paid for the goods and services that they provide.

Capacity To Enter Into Contracts

As a general rule, people with mental illness have the capacity to enter into contracts. When they buy something, such as a new bike, or arrange for services, such as getting a haircut, they enter into legally enforceable deals. They cannot claim that the deal is not valid and that they do not owe the money simply because they have a mental health diagnosis or were not thinking straight when they made the contract.

The default legal belief is that a person with mental impairment who experiences episodes of confusion, delusion, forgetfulness, or other cognitive issues was not experiencing those when she entered into the agreement. There are ways to negotiate out of contracts, but it is hardly ever legally sound to claim that one party's mental illness invalidates the deal. Only under very limited circumstances, when somebody with mental illness did not knowingly agree to the terms of the deal, could she have the contract declared invalid by a court.

The evidence that can occasionally void a contract on the basis of mental illness includes:

- Medical records showing that the person suffered from a pervasive mental impairment that compromised her ability to understand "the nature and consequences" of the contract.
- Affidavits and in-person witness testimony from people who interacted with the person on that day and at around that time.
- A resulting contract that is so absurd and disadvantageous (against the interests of the person who is mentally ill) that nobody in their right mind would have entered into it.
- Convincing proof that the party experiencing mental illness was under "undue influence."

Undue Influence

Undue influence is the legal phrase for what happens when someone takes over another person's free will. It begins when predators find adults who have mental illness and who are not comfortable managing their own money and property. The predators simply make an offer of help, and then, when a prospective victim accepts that help, they begin their exploitation.

The predators offer flattery and attention. For example, take the situation of your sister, Lucy, who has schizophrenia and lives in a group home. A predator, the handyman Gary, builds on Lucy's anecdotes about family members who ignore, betray, and minimize her—even if the stories are not true.[1] The predator may take advantage only one time or he may gradually convince the victim (your sister) to give him access to bank accounts, investments, and credit cards and then make himself a joint owner and beneficiary. Sometimes a predator—like Gary—gets his victims to buy him expensive gifts or to pay him an excessive salary for serving as a chauffeur, attendant, or other unnecessary staff. Sometimes predators are already on staff, either at the victim's home (such as with your sister, Lucy) or at an agency that serves the victim. Working for low salaries in staff positions, they become tempted by a victim's lack of attention to assets. Meanwhile, operating from their staff positions,

---

1 In some cases, a predator can even be a victim's own family member.

the predators can see and hear personal information that enables them to gain even more control over the victim.

Honest friends and family members like you can catch on to the undue influence when you see utilities being shut off, bills piling up, expensive items disappearing from the house, or accounts being unusually reduced, and when you hear the victim speaking in a dependent way. The victim may say things like:

> *I have to ask my housekeeper if I can make it to Cleveland for Thanksgiving this year.* (Why is the cleaning person making the travel decisions?)

> *My old rep payee was too stingy, so now my friend TJ from the gym is handling everything; he pays all the bills and gives me fifty dollars a week for spending money that the old rep never gave me.* (Presumably, TJ is pocketing the rest of the disability check and not paying bills.)

> *I had to get this new car; my neighbor said that I needed one, so he traded my old one in and he takes me where I need to go so I don't get lost driving the car by myself.* (Whose name is on this car's registration and who exactly paid for it?)

HOW TO Fix Undue Influence and Bad Contracts

Counteracting Undue Influence

If you suspect that someone is exerting undue influence over your family member, contact Adult Protective Services (APS) immediately. APS offices have legal authority to investigate claims of undue influence and to coordinate plans for removing the undue influence. They can get accounts frozen, locks replaced, live-ins evicted, and perpetrators arrested. In the unlikely event that APS is too slow or is not convinced about the victimization, you can get the same things done on your own. Know, however, that at every step people will ask you whether you have called APS yet.

If your relative gets services from any agency that employs professional social workers, speak to one of the social workers about the depletion and diversion of funds that you have witnessed. Professional social workers are mandatory reporters, legally obligated to notify police about vulnerable people who come under undue influence. If you have a suspicion that someone is victimizing your loved one but you lack concrete examples, consider hiring a private investigator to compile evidence of undue influence over your family member. Report any proof you have to the police (1) so that they can begin investigating the situation and (2) so that nobody can accuse you of failing to take action.

The tricky thing about involving these various professionals is that you want to stop the problem without tipping off the swindler. If the predator thinks that she is under suspicion, she may just disappear with the victim's money. This is why you contact a lawyer. Lawyers who specialize in elder abuse can help you to strategically plan a way to extricate your family member from the undue influence while preserving her assets and preparing to sue the swindler. Get a consultation with the lawyer as soon as you can after engaging APS.

Coping With Bad Contracts

If your family member is impressionable or impulsive or for any reason has entered into contracts that she cannot fulfill, you may be tempted to help extricate her from them. Unless you have conservatorship or power of attorney status authorizing you to negotiate contracts on behalf of your relative, or you have joint responsibility over the account used to pay a problematic deal, you will not have legal power to do anything about your relative's contracts. But if you feel compelled to speak or act on her behalf, and you are confident that she will not later turn against you for it, you can participate with her in whatever way works for the two of you. You could

- Conduct background research for her.
- Help her practice having mock conversations with promisees. (A *promisee* is someone who has been promised repayment, services, or cooperation in a contract.)
- Help her write some phrases or whole letters to send to promisees.
- Participate in conference calls or meetings that she has with promisees.

If your relative is very temperamental or tends to ignore obligations and instead to wish them away, she probably needs a financial conservator more than she needs the kind of help discussed here. (See Chapter 21 for more on conservatorship.) If your family member merely has a condition that makes it difficult for her to focus on details or if she is stressed by economic pressures, your assistance in the following transactions will likely give her valuable emotional and financial relief.

Renegotiating Contracts

Whether a contract is for services, an apartment, a purchase, or a subscription, the first step in getting out of it is to read its written terms. If your loved one with mental illness does not have a copy of the contract, request one from the other party. If the other party gives you a hard time when you ask for it or argues that he does not owe a copy to you or the consumer, point out that he claims to have entered into a deal with your family member and you need to see a signed agreement, with your relative's signature, that proves the claim.

If the deal was made online or via television, however, the contract will not be signed. It will simply be the seller's policies or rules, which may have come in the mail or which may be available only online from the company that your relative contracted with—not from the manufacturer.

See if the contract has a "liquidated damages" clause through which the consumer can make a payment and/or forfeit past payments and be done with the deal. That clause will usually include either the phrase "liquidated damages" or "early termination," and it will say how much one party to the contract has to compensate the other if it opts to end the contract before its promises have been fulfilled. The amount in the clause may be too much to pay, it may disproportionately benefit the seller or service provider, or it may apply only under limited circumstances. In those cases, it does not make sense for the consumer to offer to pay the liquidated damages amount, just for the sake of getting out of the contract. But if the requirements in the liquidated damages clause do look reasonable and feasible for your consumer, then he can save himself some stress by paying that money to buy his way out of the deal.

If your consumer is in an episode of severe psychiatric symptoms at the point when he needs to get out of a contract, somebody with durable power of attorney over his finances or conservator status can notify the other party to the contract that the deal needs to end early and that he or she, as durable power of attorney or conservator, has authority to settle the matter on behalf of the person who cannot participate. Suppose you have durable power of attorney over your brother's financial matters and, as his current severe psychiatric episode was developing, he entered into an agreement to replace all of the windows in his house, for $6,200. He really does not need all of his windows replaced and he would seriously deplete his savings if he went through with this plan. You look at the window contract and see that it has a liquidated damages clause indicating that if he pulls out of the deal before the windows are scheduled for delivery, he will lose the $800 deposit that he paid. Since the delivery has not been scheduled and that $800 has already been spent, you can notify the window company that, in keeping with the contract's liquidated damages clause, you, as power of attorney, are going to forfeit the deposit and cancel the order.

Now, it is certainly possible that the liquidated damages clause will be more complicated than this example is or that its terms are simply not possible for your consumer. In those situations, you may be able to negotiate a modified version of the liquidated damages clause. You probably don't want to attempt this negotiation alone, unless you are experienced at this kind of communication. This is definitely a good time to enlist the help of a lawyer, if your consumer can afford it or else is eligible for legal aid. If you can't get a lawyer and your consumer has a caseworker, or even a past caseworker, you can ask that person if she or her agency will help you negotiate out of the contract.

If negotiation isn't working or you don't want to even attempt it, and your loved one is breaching the contract by not paying money that she owes or not taking action that she is supposed to take, she (or you with authority to act on her behalf) can try an "accord and satisfaction" by writing a letter declaring that the disputed contract is over and that the enclosed payment serves as the final money owed under the contract. The enclosed payment should be a check for the amount that the consumer believes to be reasonable. She should use an ordinary bank check, not a cashier's check or travelers check and definitely not cash. On the memo line of the check and on the back of the check, she should put the phrase "final payment" or "accord and satisfaction." If the seller, creditor, or landlord cashes that check and does not refund it within a "reasonable time" (typically within 90 days), the common-law and state statutes say that he has accepted it as the final payment and cannot continue any further dispute about being paid under that contract.

If the contract is a sales contract, see if it has a clause about returning or exchanging merchandise. Online, at-home, and television purchases are covered by the Federal Trade Commission's Cooling-Off Rule and can be returned within three days without argument. Stores are not always required by law to allow returns or exchanges of nondefective goods, but if they do, their return or exchange clause will tell the circumstances under which the seller will take merchandise back. Stores make policies about returns and exchanges for two reasons: to maintain goodwill with customers and to protect themselves from dishonest people who attempt to get cash for goods that were not purchased from that store.

Even if a deadline has passed or a package has been opened, you can ask for permission to return undamaged goods and request at least a partial refund when you are able to prove that the goods did come from a particular merchant. If you cannot tell where a product came from, look through recent mail, browse through your relative's credit card accounts online, or wait for a forthcoming bill from either the seller or a credit card company. Once you know which credit card was used for the purchase, print the credit card record for proof of purchase that you can use in place of the missing receipt in order to return the merchandise.

As you read the initial contract, watch for the clause explaining what will happen if your relative breaches it. That clause may give clues about ending the deal or at least getting out of high payments. It may establish a timeline or series of events that you can help to interrupt. Think of an unpaid utility bill, for example. The utility may begin by charging a late fee when someone does not pay a bill, then proceed to contacting the customer who did not pay the bill or the late fee, and finally to discontinue the utility service. If someone can pay something on the customer's behalf or handle communications with the utility for the customer, then the service will not get turned off. If the clause says that failure to pay counts as a breach and that the seller or creditor will sue for nonpayment, look through the contract and the seller or service provider's policies (on its website) for a definition or explanation of what nonpayment means. Does it mean no payment at all? If so, perhaps your family member can make a partial payment or set up a revised payment plan to avoid being sued. If the breach clause says that collateral (property that is supposed to be given over if the person doesn't pay) will be seized if the debtor does not pay the amount owed, look for proof that the collateral was precisely identified and that your relative appeared to genuinely offer the particular collateral. Maybe it is okay to let the collateral go. If the breach clause says that disputes will be mediated, you could opt to wait until your family member is called to mediation and then help him to participate in the mediation.

Another tactic for ending (or "voiding") a contract is to file a claim with the Better Business Bureau (BBB). The BBB operates a full spectrum of dispute resolution services. Since the BBB is a neutral nonprofit organization and is not a part of the court system, its dispute resolutions are not based on contract law or consumer statutes or any other legal standards. They do not decide whether one party to the contract is wrong. They merely facilitate dispute resolutions to help contracting parties untangle their arrangements. Parties going into a conciliation, mediation, or arbitration through the BBB know that they are entering into communications that will get them out of the contract. Both parties will have to compromise. The BBB will coordinate the dispute resolution in a way that satisfies the parties' separate interests as much as possible.

If negotiation and mediation efforts fail, see what your state's consumer protection statute says about misleading customers. Consumer protection statutes prohibit service providers and sellers from tricking buyers about the quality or price of merchandise or services. Perhaps the business managed to talk your relative into the contract by exploiting the mental health symptoms that he demonstrated. For example, suppose your daughter was fixated on a previous bad experience when she entered into the contract; maybe a past gym membership had strict limits and so she entered into a new gym membership just knowing that she did not want to have all of those limits. Something about her particular psychiatric symptoms caused her to prioritize this issue so strongly that she did not realize how the membership person at the new gym was taking advantage of her by convincing her to purchase a disproportionately expensive long-term membership with extra features that were really beneficial only to couples, not individual members like her. Or maybe your son went to a particular car dealership because it advertised exactly the used car he wanted. When he got there, he learned that they didn't have that car or any other cars that were like it. The dealer, who could see that your son was socially awkward and extremely nervous (not necessarily realizing that he had a psychiatric condition), lured him into a false friendship and then convinced him to buy a much more expensive car and to grab it immediately without taking it for a substantial test drive or having his own mechanic look at it. Your son believed that his new best friend, the car dealer, would never have sold him a dud, so even though the engine whined and the car lurched, he never for a moment thought that there was anything wrong with it. Only when he took it to his mechanic after buying it did he learn that it needed serious, expensive repairs.

If your family member was somehow misled or manipulated by a seller or service provider, whether in person, online, over the phone, or via television, file a complaint with your state attorney general's office. The attorney general is responsible for enforcing consumer protection law and will investigate claims about deceptive sales practices. If the investigation reveals that the seller or service provider violated the law, the attorney general can make the business reform its practices. When a business has a routine practice of cheating people, the attorney general can shut it down and may sue to get money damages for deceived consumers.

Unpaid Bills

When a consumer gets behind on a series of bills and owes money to multiple creditors, the problem is no longer a simple matter of contract law. It belongs in the broader category of consumer law, which comes from federal statutes and regulations about leases, payment plans, credit cards, and debt collection. At the state level, consumers are also protected by laws about utility shut-offs, buying and selling cars, fees on "rent to own" purchases, and other long-term payment commitments.

When someone is behind on a payment or two with a couple of creditors, the usual way to handle the situation is to call or write directly to the creditors and work out a way to pay the back-due amount in small installments while paying the current amount in full. Occasionally, when the market is bad and creditors are desperate, they may renegotiate the entire deal to make all future payments more manageable for the debtor.

When a debtor owes a lot of money to several creditors and is not expected to come into additional funds very soon—for example, your son Wyatt, who has four active credit cards and a car loan—he needs professional advocacy and more formal help than you can provide as a layperson and not a lawyer. The debtor would probably benefit from the services of a credit counseling agency. The agency will negotiate with creditors for reduced payments over a longer pay-off time, for lower interest, and for removal of fees, and it will then arrange a debt-management plan for the debtor. Under a debt-management plan, your son would make a single monthly payment to the agency, and the agency would then divide that money among the creditors.

HOW TO Help Your Relative With Credit Counseling

For many people, credit counseling is a relatively easy and merciful way to get out of debt. But even the United States Congress has recognized the fact that mental symptoms can make it impossible for some people to participate in credit counseling. When it passed the Bankruptcy Abuse Prevention and Consumer Protection Act of 2005, requiring debtors to complete credit counseling before applying for bankruptcy, the legislature built in an exception saying that credit counseling is not required when "the debtor is impaired by reason of mental illness or mental deficiency so that he is incapable of realizing and making rational decisions with respect to his financial responsibilities."

Somewhere between the extremes of not being mentally healthy enough to participate in credit counseling and benefiting from credit counseling is the vast space where embarrassment and resentment prevail. For example:

For a person experiencing depression, embarrassment and resentment may be expressed by crying in the credit counseling session or by staying home and sleeping past the appointment time. The person may regret the happy expectations that got him into the debt.

To someone with compulsions or anxiety, the credit counseling office may be utterly intolerable: the furnishings, the bland receptionist, the germs, the desperate people sitting around, and the awful expectations about meeting with the credit counselor can all be tremendously stressful for someone already under pressure.

A debtor with anxiety or mania who has a thousand details to think about may worry that the credit counselor will not put any thought into his case at all.

For so many people, credit counseling is a harsh examination of what went wrong when they were hoping for something good, and it only comes to an end when they sign a pile of papers admitting that they have made a mess and are getting someone else to clean up after them.

If you are helping your relative with mental illness who is in debt, begin by honoring his legitimate feelings about having to work with a credit counselor. Then, help him to take charge and to understand that the credit counselor is his employee, hired to do work, not to be the boss. As the debtor, he is hiring the

credit counselor to identify which debts have to get paid the soonest, to identify which debts should not be paid, and to serve as an intermediary with the
creditors. These are valuable services requiring knowledge that most people do
not have. It is just like when someone does not know how to cut his own hair and
hires a barber to do it. Your relative borrowed money or enjoyed certain goods or
services and now has a legal obligation to pay for them. Hiring a credit counselor
is a major step in taking charge of the situation.

Here are four manageable tasks that you can do to help your loved one with
mental illness take responsibility and have a successful credit counseling experience that results in at least partially paying his creditors:

- Find a reputable credit counselor.
- Organize information.
- Facilitate communications.
- Suggest ideas.

Finding a Reputable Credit Counselor
To find a reputable credit counselor, go to the online list of credit counselors
approved by the bankruptcy courts or contact the federal Chapter 13 bankruptcy
trustee for your jurisdiction. The Chapter 13 bankruptcy trustee is employed
by the federal court system to coordinate all of the steps in the most common
form of personal bankruptcy. It is also a good idea to ask your public library if it
maintains a list of consumer resources that includes credit counseling services.
Credit counselors often give presentations at libraries, so reference desks typically have their contact information. Another way to find a reliable credit counselor is to go through the National Foundation for Credit Counseling (NFCC),
which is a professional organization with high membership standards that require credit counseling agencies to provide legitimate top-quality counseling, to
be accredited, to carry insurance, and to operate under strict ethical principles.

After critically reading each agency's website, check with the state attorney
general and the BBB to find out what kinds of complaints they have had about
the agencies and how frequently and recently they have been submitted. Ask
whether the agencies cooperated in the investigations and satisfactorily resolved
the complaints. Call the agencies directly and respectfully ask whether they can
match a consumer who has mental illness with an appropriate counselor. Maybe
you want someone who will be very protective, or someone who will give frequent assurances, or someone with particular demographic characteristics, such
as age, race, sexual orientation, or gender. Ask the agency how individualized
their services are and how they have accommodated past clients. You can even
see if it would be feasible to prepare a credit counselor, in advance, for interaction with your relative.

Family members can attend credit counseling sessions. The standards of
the Council on Accreditation specifically allow advocate participation. Since
financial issues are very personal, the agency will probably require the consumer to sign or say something before allowing you or another advocate into the
meetings. Once you are in the session, you can keep your eyes and ears open and

help to facilitate correct and complete communication between the consumer counselor and your relative.

Organizing Information
One way to ensure successful credit counseling is to provide the credit counselor with full and accurate information. No matter how uncomfortable the consumer feels at the session, he can get a useful conversation started just by handing over full and well-labeled folders containing papers that identify debts and assets.

Whether or not you participate in the credit counseling sessions, help your consumer to get the documents in order before the meeting. Make copies of everything and put the copies, not the originals, in a set of folders or separate paper-clipped bundles for the credit counselor. Make sure your consumer knows that the organized copies are for the credit counselor to keep on file for the consumer.

The packets should have titles like:

- Car and household bills
- Credit card bills
- Medical bills
- Court-ordered payments
- Personal loans
- Bank loans
- Collections agencies
- Recent pay stubs or government check stubs
- Bank account statements
- Investment or trust account statements
- Credit report

The credit counselor can order a credit report, but since consumers are entitled to get a free credit report every year, help your consumer to obtain and to print one for the session. If you have copies of credit card agreements, "terms and conditions," or other contracts for any of these items, put them into the folders.

Categorizing all of the asset and debt information this way will make it easy for the credit counselor to review payment options with the consumer. Different kinds of debts get negotiated in different ways. The credit counselor may, for example, make a pile of the separate folders representing secured credit purchases, such as a car or mobile home that can be repossessed. By organizing the information in advance, you will prevent confusion. Less confusion equals less frustration.

Facilitating Communications
The credit counselor needs to interact directly with the consumer, for example, your stepdaughter Sarah, who has a generalized anxiety disorder, so that together they can make a plan. The plan is more likely to succeed if Sarah takes a truly active part in making it. Some credit counselors expect consumers to complete worksheets and participate in other interactive processes during the session. Credit counselors need consumers to talk about their plans with comprehension and intent.

Without input and commitment from the consumer, the credit counselor cannot make a confident deal with the creditors. Creditors reduce their rates for credit counselors' clients only because they believe that the clients are genuinely planning to pay. The credit counseling service will lose its reputation and its ability to negotiate with creditors if clients do not fulfill their promises.

Consider practicing in advance of the first session. You might rehearse with the list of Frequently Asked Questions from the credit counselor's website. Show Sarah the kind of information that the credit counselor will need. This will help her feel less suspicious or defensive in the meeting. Point out that the credit counselor is not going to ask any questions that start with "Why." Credit counseling is not a forum for judging consumers. The session will be about "What," (as in, *What do you have?* and *What do you owe?*) and "How" (as in, *How often do you get paid?* and *How badly do you need to keep this item or service?* and *How can you be sure that you will pay that amount every month?*).

If the consumer tends to be very agreeable and always aims to please, there is a risk that she will not make a genuine plan with the credit counselor. She may feel happy in the meeting and may succeed at making friends with the credit counselor, but if she promises to pay more than she truly can every month, she will not improve her ability to get out of debt. An advocate like you may need to go along and play the "bad cop" just to be sure that the credit counselor gets accurate information and establishes a manageable plan. If no friend, caseworker, or relative is available, or if the consumer will not let anyone come, make a list of hard facts about her assets, ability to earn money, and typical spending practices. You can either mail the information directly to the credit counselor or give it to the consumer and say, "The credit counselor will like getting these facts and will make the best arrangements with you if he knows this stuff up front."

You may want to equip the consumer with some fallback phrases to use during the credit counseling session. For example, it will be very helpful for Sarah to know that it is okay to say things like: "Can you please explain that a different way?" or "I can't give up my car because public transportation is impossible for me," or "Will I have any money for recreation?"

Suggesting Ideas

You may know enough to predict how your consumer will act with the credit counselor and what it will take for her to follow through with the debt-management plan. The consumer and credit counselor, however, will not have this perspective: The consumer may not have accurate self-insight and the credit counselor will not have sufficient familiarity with the consumer to make predictions. Both of them can benefit from your ideas.

Because credit counseling sessions can get intense and certain psychiatric symptoms can come to the surface (such as a panic attack), you may have an idea about reducing the tension. What has worked in the past with the consumer? What does her therapist do in tense moments? If you know, then equip the consumer to deal with those moments or notify the credit counselor, in advance, of trigger words, beneficial diversions (such as deep breathing), the need for hands-on action, or other ideas that will enable the consumer to keep her head in the game.

If the consumer is going to get irritated by the waiting room (for example, the lights, the noise, or the décor), call her attention to that possibility ahead of time and plan ideas for self-soothing during the wait. She can pack a snack, bring a book or some music, write jokes or funny descriptions about the other people, work on crossword puzzles, or otherwise distance herself from the stressful delays and aggravations that could compromise her ability to stay and wait for the session.

Schedule a conversation for after the appointment so that the consumer can look forward to laughing at, venting about, and describing all of the day's annoyances. You could even provide conversation ideas in advance. For example, tell Sarah that, over dinner, you want to hear how the credit counseling office was like the Academy Awards: best dramatic role by a female performer, best sound effects, best costumes, and so on. You can even print her a score card or form where she can fill in the categories.

In anticipation of the credit counselor's guidance, make sure the consumer is ready to reduce her spending. She will probably have to give up some activities or ongoing expenses. For this part of the credit counseling experience, you might help her think of ideas for living without some of the treats she gives herself, like movies, fancy coffee drinks, and full-price magazines from the grocery store. If she enjoys any kind of creative pursuit, like making up songs, drawing cartoons, or writing stories, challenge her to use her creative mode to demonstrate the transition to life without whatever she is giving up. If she is more of the analytical type, give her a structure to work with: She might like a ledger book or a chart or phone app in which she can track how much she is saving. If she needs to figure out how to fill time with activities that won't cost money, you could inspire her to discover one new no-cost venue or event every week. She may even want to post online reviews or descriptions of her weekly discoveries. If she is concerned that her social life will be compromised when she cuts back on spending, guide her to think of alternative social settings. You can do this with questions, such as, "What if you invite the group over for a pot-luck instead of eating out?" and "How about starting a weekly card game instead of going to the mall every Saturday?" and "Have you thought about organizing walks and bike rides with some of the people that you'll miss when you stop going to the gym?"

By anticipating the various stressors that can come with credit counseling, and knowing your loved one's particular psychiatric makeup and ways of responding to stress, you can make her credit counseling experience much more tolerable and therefore successful than it otherwise would be, and, in doing so, you can help her avoid getting into legal trouble because of her debts.

Tax Facts

- Even when debtors cannot afford to pay their taxes, they need to submit tax returns (see 26 U.S.C. § 6011).
- Taxpayers can usually arrange to make installment payments to the IRS. The IRS's Taxpayer Advocate Service will help with the arrangements. See taxpayeradvocate.irs.gov.

- There are low-income taxpayer clinics all over the country that will advocate for taxpayers who have federal income tax troubles. See the Internal Revenue Service (IRS) Publication 4134.
- Using the IRS's online tool "Get Transcript," taxpayers can find out how much money they currently owe to the IRS.
- One way to reduce the likelihood of a future tax debt is to increase the amount of money that is withheld from paychecks. The IRS web page titled *Tax Withholding* has a good, thorough introduction to this topic. Use the IRS's online *Withholding Calculator* to figure out how to set the best withholding amount on your W-4, and then complete IRS Form W-4 to establish your withholding amount.
- Tax refunds cannot be garnished by private creditors. This means that private creditors (such as stores) cannot claim the money before the IRS refunds it to a taxpayer. Federal and state government entities are able to claim tax refunds before they are paid to the taxpayer. Once a tax refund comes into a taxpayer's possession, the private creditors can go after it. See online IRS Tax Tip 2012-59: *Tax Refunds May Be Applied to Offset Certain Debts* (March 27, 2012).

BANKRUPTCY

Bankruptcy and criminal law can feel equally terrible. Both areas of law involve irritating amounts of scrutiny, doubts about truthfulness, and being placed under government control for a long period of time. At least the criminal system (covered in Chapters 7 to 13 of this book) has built-in mental health assessments and treatment protocols. Bankruptcy court gives only the slightest nod to someone's mental wellness. Families can help the bankruptcy court to work with a debtor who is mentally ill and they can help that debtor to comply with bankruptcy court. Moreover, just by knowing how the bankruptcy process flows, families can moderate the pressures that bankruptcy's scrutiny, doubt, and lack of control can inflict on their loved one, who is already pressured with mental health symptoms. In many ways, but especially by providing information to both the debtor and the professionals as a bankruptcy progresses, families can be critical in helping someone who has a mental illness to participate effectively in bankruptcy's various tasks.

Comparing Credit Counseling Debt Management With Bankruptcy

Credit counseling debt management operates from the perspective that consumers are simply behind on their bills and that, with some organization and assistance, they can pay back the money they owe. It's a quiet and private way of getting back in control of personal finances. Both the debtor and the creditor benefit from credit counseling debt management: the debtor because his late fees and interest are reduced, and the creditor because he gets paid for his goods or services or is finally able to collect on a court judgment.

Bankruptcy operates from the perspective that the debtor needs to be bailed out. It is a court-based system that affects future opportunities. It costs more than credit counseling debt management, although some of the costs can get built into the regular debt-reduction payments that the consumer sends to the trustee.

The two advantages of bankruptcy are that the consumer usually does not have to pay back as many debts in bankruptcy as he would have to pay back through a debt-management plan (sometimes the debtor doesn't have to pay back any debts at all) and that bankruptcy is a form of court-ordered protection from creditors. If a debtor gets behind on payments under a debt-management plan, the creditors are allowed to reinstitute the fees and interest and go back to hounding the debtor for the money. If a debtor gets behind in a bankruptcy repayment plan, only the trustee deals with him and the creditors are not able to tack on any back-due fees that the court previously removed.

BANKRUPTCY BASICS

There are two different types of bankruptcy for individuals: Chapter 7 bankruptcy, in which debts are cancelled (discharged) and, although some valuables may need to be sold, most debtors are able to keep their assets, and Chapter 13 bankruptcy, which makes debtors pay their creditors back over a set period of time based on their ability to pay. The types of bankruptcy are named for the chapters where they appear in the bankruptcy code. The ability to pay back creditors is figured out by seeing how much money is left after subtracting the debtor's typical monthly household and business expenses from his typical monthly household income (which includes income earned by other adults in the family, not just the debtor). In both kinds of bankruptcy, the debtor is under very strict court supervision. The Chapter 7 bankruptcy process takes between four and five months. The Chapter 13 process takes between three and five years.

Some consumers, such as your wife's brother, Jaylyn, do not even have the option of going through Chapter 7 bankruptcy because they earn more than the median income in their state and have money left over after paying housing, transportation, and tax bills. A bankruptcy lawyer will handle the hard math and the many technicalities of a bankruptcy petition, but debtors (like Jaylyn) and people who help them cope with hard times (like you) should generally understand the process and its consequences.

HOW TO Assist With a Bankruptcy

Credit counseling (discussed earlier in this chapter) is a mandatory first step before filing for bankruptcy. However, people who are so incapacitated by their mental illness that they are not able to participate in financial decision-making with the credit counselor can be exempted from the credit counseling requirement in their bankruptcy.

If your consumer goes to a credit counseling session and is so unable to think clearly that he truly cannot follow what the credit counselor is saying, the credit counselor will probably advise him or her to apply for bankruptcy instead of paying the money back through credit counseling debt management. The counselor may even offer to provide written testimony about your family member's failed attempt at credit counseling. Even if the credit counselor does not suggest bankruptcy, you can encourage the consumer to look into it. If your family member is not good at keeping track of things, you may want to hold onto any paperwork that the credit counselor provides, including the credit counselor's business card, so that you can be sure that it gets to the bankruptcy lawyer, once one is hired. Helping to facilitate communications between the credit counselor and the bankruptcy lawyer is a useful step that you, as the well family member, can do.

Let's continue with the example of your brother-in-law, Jaylyn. If he has been through an unsuccessful attempt at credit counseling, you may need to motivate and focus him before he files for bankruptcy. Perhaps you can re-engage him by having him shop around for the right bankruptcy lawyer. A debtor can learn a lot about lawyers' personalities and people skills from their websites: Are they generous and clear at presenting information? Are there any videos where you can see how they talk and relate? Do they have either the casual or formal style that will appeal to your relative? If it won't insult Jaylyn, consider making him a chart where he can record answers to these questions. Bankruptcy lawyers will provide free consultations, so your relative can go alone or with you to select from among two or three lawyers before committing to one. Once hired, the bankruptcy lawyer will arrange to get paid out of the money that your loved one gives the bankruptcy court to divide among all of his creditors. In other words, your relative will not be expected to pay the bankruptcy lawyer up front.

Some lawyers consult by assessing an individual's debt situation and some by giving a generic summary of the bankruptcy process. The lawyer's office will tell you what to bring to the consultation. It is more efficient to have consultations with lawyers who will give a quick assessment of a particular debtor's actual circumstances. But if your family member is uncomfortable with new people or does not like to hand over personal information until he knows who he is dealing with, then the generic type of consultation will suit him better.

Once the debtor, such as Jaylyn, hires a lawyer, he will need to turn over copies of all of the papers you and he compiled for the credit counselor plus any new bills or records of additional funds. Jaylyn needs to inform the bankruptcy lawyer about every person and entity that he owes money to and any accounts or possessions he owns. Collecting and admitting to this financial information can trigger a debtor's anxiety, but once the lawyer has it, he will likely be able reduce that anxiety pretty quickly. Knowing about Jaylyn's assets and debts, the bankruptcy lawyer can tell Jaylyn which type of bankruptcy he will go through, whether the case will involve any special handling, and forecast almost exactly how his bankruptcy is going to play out. Many bankruptcies are very straightforward and follow a predictable series of steps. In fact, it is likely that a paralegal will complete much of the paperwork, so your relative should not think that he is getting inferior service if the paralegal, rather than the lawyer, interacts with him during the bankruptcy process.

As soon as the lawyer files the bankruptcy in court, creditors named in the case are legally forbidden to bother the bankrupt debtor any more. The legal phrase for this is "automatic stay." It is like the command a dog owner gives when he does not want his Doberman to lunge at someone: "Stay!" The bank-ruptcy court is telling the creditors not to lunge at the debtor anymore. When bankruptcy court issues an automatic stay, the creditors know that the debtor does not currently have the money to pay them in full. But if the debtor fails to list a creditor, even a friend or family member who has lent him money, that creditor will still be able to come after him.

The Bankruptcy Petition

The document filed with the bankruptcy court is called a petition. The petition includes the list of debts plus the plan for paying some of them and possibly cancelling others. The petition also lists the debtor's assets. The bankruptcy trustee is the court officer who will receive the petition. The trustee is authorized by the Bankruptcy Code to investigate the petition.

BANKRUPTCY AND PEOPLE WHO HOARD

People with hoarding tendencies tend to have trouble with asset disclosures (the list of assets in their bankruptcy petition) and trustee investigations. First of all, they have enormous quantities of assets to catalog. Second, they derive security from their possessions, and it can feel like a breach of security to tell an outsider what the possessions are. Third, itemizing possessions is the first step toward having to liquidate them for cash with which to pay debts. Of course, there are many people who would never even think of exchanging their possessions for money and so, when asked if they have assets, it honestly would not occur to them that the stuff that they have collected around their house counts as assets. In fact, most people's ordinary household items do not have to be sold, but some people do have valuable objects, such as antiques and collectibles, that do need to be sold in order to pay back creditors. People with hoarding tendencies may need therapeutic preparation before filing for bankruptcy so that they are not shocked by the inventory process or the possibility that the trustee will require them to sell some things.

In one of the well-known bankruptcy cases involving hoarding tendencies, a woman who not only hoarded certain things but also was unwilling to give up her best possessions, did not tell her bankruptcy lawyer that she had a collection of jewelry and artwork. Since the lawyer did not know about these possessions, he did not include them in the bankruptcy petition, which means they were not included in the list of items that could be used to pay off debts. In the very simplest part of the trustee's investigation—a basic check for past court records—the woman's di-vorce settlement showed that she had hundreds of thousands of dollars' worth of collectibles. The bankruptcy trustee and a U.S. marshal went to her house with a warrant, searched for and found the art and jewelry, and took it all away. Facing severe penalties, including a five-year prison term, the debtor finally agreed to a bankruptcy settlement in which her debts would not be discharged (cancelled) and the valuables would be sold to pay her creditors.

Another famous hoarding case came to light in bankruptcy court when married debtors listed cat care among their expenses. They reported, on their petition, that they had forty-five cats. Since they truly did own that many cats, the bankruptcy went through easily (except for a slight problem with their mortgage). In this case, nothing caused the trustee to think that the family was hiding assets, so it was not necessary to go and search the debtors' home looking for anything that could be sold.

Within three years, the people had over 200 cats, because kittens had been born to the existing cat collection. At that point, neighbors were complaining about the odor. Authorities (law enforcement and animal control) removed the animals, reporting evidence of hoarding throughout the house. Had the bankruptcy trustee thought about the possibility of breeding and categorized the original forty-five cats as an increasing expense, he or she could have arranged for the cats to be spayed or neutered and could have saved the couple from subsequent trauma.

Bankruptcy trustees are experts at spotting clues about possible assets. They can glean a full story just from stray facts in a bankruptcy petition. When the pieces of information in a petition do not add up, the trustee becomes skeptical about the debtor. Earnest debtors and good lawyers who file thorough petitions will have the most efficient bankruptcies.

Meeting of Creditors

Approximately one month after filing the petition, bankruptcy applicants have to be at a meeting of creditors. The name of the meeting makes it sound like a crowd of creditors will be there frowning at your loved one, but creditors hardly ever come in person because they already submitted their claims in writing and have nothing more to say. Ordinarily, this is a quick meeting with the trustee, and a supportive person (such as you) if the debtor wants one there, just to confirm that everything in the petition is true. The lawyer can shield a shy, anxious, delusional, or unnecessarily guilt-ridden client from coming across as unsure or untruthful. Someone should remind the lawyer, in advance, if the debtor has those tendencies.

If anything in the petition looks suspicious or incorrect, the trustee will inquire about it at the meeting. Having checked government records, tax filings, court cases, and bank records, the trustee may have discovered tips that may lead to further investigation. Lawyers try to prevent these surprise attacks by asking their clients many times before filing their petitions, "Are you sure you have told me everything?" The trustee can deny the petition for bankruptcy if there is reason to believe that the debtor is withholding information or trying to cheat.

MEETING OF CREDITORS AND PEOPLE WITH MENTAL ILLNESS
If your family member has severe anxiety or paranoia, she may be very uncomfortable with the scrutiny at this stage of the bankruptcy process and with the worry that she will be accused of cheating. As the well relative, you can recommend communication techniques and arrangements that will accommodate her needs. It is likely that you will have developed a relationship with the trustee's assistant by this time. The assistant will have communicated with you and your family member in connection with everything that you have submitted up to this point. This is the person for you or your lawyer to present your ideas to; he will be the one to set everything up for the meeting.

Some bankruptcy courts schedule all of their meetings of creditors, on any given day, to begin at the same time. Cases will be called for either the morning session or the afternoon session without any exact times, so everyone is in the same room together waiting for their meeting to be called up at the trustee's table in the front of the room. This means that, as each debtor has his or her meeting, the other debtors, creditors, and lawyers in the room can see and hear the whole meeting. If this is going to trigger psychiatric symptoms for your loved one, either you or he should ask his lawyer to arrange for him to go last in the session. Then, he may be able to leave the room and go someplace less stressful after signing in and, by the time it is his turn, all of the people connected with the other cases will be gone.

Perhaps the meeting of creditors will be more tolerable for your loved one if the trustee does not look directly at her and avoids using the word "you" as much as possible. A low-threat way to conduct the meeting would be to have three chairs next to each other, not too close to each other, facing a screen where the documents in the bankruptcy petition will be projected. The debtor can sit in the first chair, her lawyer in the protective middle chair, and the trustee in the third chair, farthest away from the debtor. You or other supportive people can remain in the room if your loved one wants you there.

As the trustee reviews each page of the petition, he can use neutral questions to check the content, such as:

- *Is this the full list of people who may be owed money?*
- *Should there be anything else on this list of debts?*
- *Are this bank account and this savings bond your only two sources of money, in addition to your monthly paychecks?*

These questions are less accusatory than:

- *Are you certain that you truthfully listed all of your creditors?*
- *Did you honestly list here all of the debts that you currently owe to other people?*
- *Have you failed to report any assets that we may need to use to pay your debts?*

If the trustee has uncovered court records or other blatant evidence of debts or assets that are not in the petition, he should not accuse the debtor of fraud. He can simply use a passive phrase, such as: *A basic public records search shows* … [whatever asset or debt was not in the petition]. The trustee can direct these remarks to the lawyer instead of to the debtor. And the lawyer can ask for an opportunity to modify the petition to include the newly discovered information.

Discharging Debts

Discharging debts means cancelling them. In Chapter 7 bankruptcy, unsecured debts are typically discharged. Unsecured debts are the bills that do not have collateral; credit card bills, utility bills, in-store credit charges, and back-due rent are the kinds of debts that tend to get discharged in Chapter 7 bankruptcy.

In Chapter 13 bankruptcy, debtors do have to pay off part of the debts. The amount of the payoff depends on the debtor's household earnings and expenses. Bankruptcy lawyers and the bankruptcy trustees have software to calculate the payback amounts. The software is used to make the plan, which is filed with the bankruptcy petition, for how much the debtor will pay each month during his bankruptcy. At the end of that time, the debts are discharged. In other words, the debtor has paid all that he is going to pay even though it is not the full amount that he originally owed.

Secured debts, such as loans for cars and expensive equipment, can also be discharged, but the creditors will still have liens on the items and can seize collateral or repossess them if the debtor stops making payments on them. Buyers know from their loan contracts when sellers have the right to repossess items or seize collateral.

The federal Bankruptcy Code and individual state laws identify the debts that can and cannot be discharged and list dozens of exceptions among them. There are several situations when discharge or nondischarge is specifically related to mental health: malicious or willful misconduct, spending when there is no money to spend, and owing money for higher education when it is impossible to fulfill career expectations.

MALICIOUS OR WILLFUL MISCONDUCT

Debts that result from malicious or willful misconduct cannot be discharged in bankruptcy. For example:

- If someone gets mad in a store and knocks over a display, he has to pay back the store owner; his malice caused the owner to lose money.
- If a driver purposely hits somebody else's car, she has to pay for the damage to the vehicle as well as for injuries suffered by occupants of the vehicle.
- Even when a criminal court has found someone to be "guilty but mentally ill," the bankruptcy courts will not cancel debts connected with malicious behavior that, according to the criminal court, happened only because of the defendant's mental illness.

Instinctively, we think that malice and willful misconduct are the result of intent, and we know that our family member who is mentally ill did not intend to cause damage and harm. He may act out when he is unwell, but the real person inside does not intend bad results. Unfortunately, bankruptcy law makes no exception for uncontrollable bad behavior.

SPENDING WHEN THERE IS NO MORE MONEY—INCLUDING PEOPLE ADDICTED TO GAMBLING

When a consumer knows that the credit cards are nearly maxed out and he does not have enough money to pay his existing bills, he cannot say, "Oh well, I'm going bankrupt anyway. I might as well buy a vacation and some other great things since they'll be cancelled in my bankruptcy." Those purchases will not be cancelled by bankruptcy!

Even if a debtor is not frivolous and realistically understands that he will not have another chance to purchase big and special items for several years after declaring bankruptcy, he should not run up more charges. If he does not have pocket money for groceries, transportation, and other routine costs, he should seek help from the county Department of Human Services and family members rather than putting more charges on his credit card. You, as that helping family member, could buy him a bus pass or fill up his car with gas. You could also take away his credit cards, if he will let you have them.

Some debtors who can tell that bankruptcy is looming think that they are being loyal or responsible if they dump the last of their money all on one particular creditor—probably the creditor who has hassled them the most. Others make generous gifts to loved ones and charities. The bankruptcy court will examine where that pre-bankruptcy money and those goods went and what the debtor intended. The bankruptcy trustee has the power to sue the recipients and get the assets back so that they can be included in the bankruptcy estate and be divided fairly among the creditors.

A debt that is built in anticipation of going bankrupt has to be paid back. It counts as nondischargeable debt because the debtor was trying to get away with not paying. In fact, the court can dismiss the entire bankruptcy petition, leaving the debtor with no bankruptcy relief at all, if he has intentionally spent beyond his ability to pay for things while planning to go bankrupt. People with gambling addiction encounter this law. They wishfully believe that they are just on the verge of winning a fortune. So they risk the last of everything just to keep playing. Then, when they lose and have to declare bankruptcy, the petition is either denied entirely or the bankruptcy is allowed to go through but the gambling debts are considered nondischargeable.

Some people with a gambling disorder have argued that their reason for continuing to gamble was that they were merely trying to earn money so that they could pay back their debts. Courts are not usually convinced by this claim unless the debtor has also taken some more practical steps toward earning money and has otherwise shown genuine intent to pay back debts.

In some bankruptcy cases, the trustee is impressed by a gambler's lack of intent. Here is the logic in these situations: Since bankruptcy will not cancel intentional charges made after a debtor knows that he will probably go bankrupt, some debtors have succeeded in getting their gambling debts cancelled by proving that they did not intend anything. Instead, their gambling disorder compelled them to keep gambling after they knew that they were out of money. One example of a court case on this topic involved a woman with a psychiatrically diagnosed addiction to gambling who went into bankruptcy because she was unable to pay the credit card bill from her last casino visit. The credit card company claimed that the casino debt should not be cancelled. The court decided against the credit card company and in favor of the debtor, stating that, since she had an addiction, she did not intend to cheat the credit card company—she was simply compelled by her mental illness to keep gambling. Therefore, she did not commit fraud and the debt could be discharged (cancelled).

Occasionally, gambling debts can be discharged, but when someone petitions for bankruptcy and then vaguely claims that while she used to have a lot of money she has now lost that money by gambling at a casino, the bankruptcy trustee has to be suspicious and wonder if the debtor is lying and trying to hide money. The trustee needs to see proof that the debtor truly does gamble, cannot control her gambling, and genuinely intended to repay her creditors. Casino records can show how often the debtor gambled. Therapy records can show that the debtor has a gambling disorder. Court records can also serve as proof of the gambling disorder. These are particularly likely to come from criminal court and family court because frequent gambling often leads to theft and divorce. But the proof of intent is harder to find because people with gambling disorder are not likely to keep careful ledgers of all their gambling losses and winnings. They do not want their families or the IRS to know the facts and they may not be able to face the facts themselves.

Bankruptcy courts are likely to believe that a debtor intended to pay back her debts if she made efforts to raise money for that purpose, perhaps by taking an additional part-time job in the evenings. When the debtor is someone who knew that she would be tempted to use the extra money for gambling, she needs to solidify the proof of her intent to pay back creditors by showing that she implemented a system for keeping the money away from herself. She may show bank records demonstrating that she signed every paycheck over to you or another family member as soon as she got it or that her checks were electronically deposited into an account that she could not access. Maybe instead of getting an additional job, she established a system for saving money in a way that prevented her from getting her hands on it. Again, this may involve you or another family member; the savings system may simply be that the two of you would get together for dinner every day, because she would otherwise go to the casino in the evening, and at dinner she would hand over any tips or other cash that she had accumulated during the day. She may even have given you power of attorney to manage her finances. These are the kinds of undertakings that will show the bankruptcy trustee that she was not merely putting money aside so that she could gamble, she truly was trying not to gamble so that she would have the money to pay her creditors.

HAVING NO EXPECTATION OF FULFILLING CAREER PLANS

Ordinarily, student loans cannot be discharged, but in some cases involving petitioners with severe mental impairments, the student loan debt can be discharged in bankruptcy. In these cases, it is evident that the student will show proof of how often and how tangibly her psychiatric symptoms disrupt her ability to function and prevent her from being able to use the expensive education she invested in.

Lots of young adults have mental health diagnoses. It is certainly not standard for graduates (or people who did not complete their degree plan) who experience mental illness to have their student loans discharged in bankruptcy. It can happen only when three criteria are met:

1. The former student has been unable to earn enough to pay for a minimal standard of living and also make payments toward the educational debt.
2. The former student's mental illness is severe and likely to continue for most of the bankruptcy term.
3. The former student has made a good-faith effort to repay the loans.

Debtor Education—Financial Management Class

Debtor education is a required part of every personal bankruptcy. It has to be completed online, over the phone, or in person within sixty days of the meeting of creditors or else the bankruptcy case will be closed and all of the creditors will be able to go after the debtor again. When the debtor completes the course, he will get a certificate that has to be filed with the bankruptcy court.

As with credit counseling, debtors can be exempted from this course when their mental condition prevents them from being able to understand or participate. The lawyer will have to file a motion with the bankruptcy court to get permission for the debtor to skip the course. To substantiate the claim that the debtor cannot handle the course, his lawyer will also have to attach medical records to the motion. Considering all of the work that has to be done for the debtor to get out of a two-hour course, it will probably be faster, simpler, and less expensive for the debtor to just sit with a friend or relative and get through either the online course or the phone course than to try to get out of it.

Concluding Bankruptcy

For Chapter 7 debtors, the bankruptcy process will end just a few months after the meeting of creditors and the financial management course. For Chapter 13 debtors, like your cousin Shawn who has an obsessive-compulsive disorder, there are a few more formalities. The creditors have to submit proof of how much they are owed. If their numbers do not match what Shawn initially told his lawyer and his lawyer put into the bankruptcy petition, both the trustee and Shawn's lawyer will need to see proof from the creditors. Maybe a creditor says that Shawn made only four payments on a debt and Shawn has cancelled checks proving that he made six payments. On the other hand, maybe Shawn thought that something, say his community center membership, was paid up through June and the community center has payment records proving that Shawn paid late for several months in a row leading up to June, but that the amount of the late payments met the member-ship fees only through April. The trustee can run the new numbers through her bankruptcy software to adjust Shawn's payback plan.

There is no need to get upset when a creditor's numbers do not match the debtor's numbers. It is bound to happen. A debtor will have a only finite amount of money to divide among all of the creditors, no matter what. If Shawn has continued to make his required payments during the first months of bankruptcy preparation and his creditors' claims prove to be legitimate, the repayment plan will be approved, and, in most cases, the payments will automatically go from Shawn's paycheck to the trustee's pay-out account for the remaining three or five years of the bankruptcy.

Bankruptcy and Disability Benefits

If someone petitions for bankruptcy during the long period of time when he is also applying for disability benefits, Social Security will have to cooperate with the bankruptcy trustee before releasing the person's lump sum of back-due disability benefits. Some or all of that money may have to go toward paying back creditors. In fact, many people who petition for bankruptcy after applying for disability have built up debt only because the disability approval process takes so many months. So the money in the lump sum of back pay would have gone to pay the same creditors on time, if the consumer had had it then. Even the attorney representing the consumer in the disability case can count as one of the creditors; however, in some cases, the attorney's fee for representing somebody in a disability case will be discharged in Chapter 7 bankruptcy. One more possibility that can arise in the relationship between bankruptcy proceedings and disability proceedings is that, when someone who is already collecting Social Security Disability Insurance (SSDI) petitions for bankruptcy, the Social Security Administration (SSA), which pays him monthly benefits, can also be one of the creditors entitled to get paid by the bankruptcy trustee. This would happen if the SSA mistakenly overpaid the person at some point and now needs to be repaid.

Bankruptcy and Conservators

Family members who serve as the conservator for a loved one with mental illness can petition for bankruptcy on behalf of their loved one. This means that the conservator would hire the bankruptcy lawyer and inform the lawyer of all of the ways that mental health symptoms have affected the ward's ability to work, his use of money, and his understanding of cause and effect. If you are the conservator, one of your inquiries to the bankruptcy lawyer should be whether bankruptcy makes sense under the circumstances. An experienced bankruptcy lawyer will be able to look through a debtor's credit report, account statements, and (if applicable) an SSA disability benefits letter and know whether it is worthwhile to petition for bankruptcy. If the lawyer concludes that bankruptcy will help to straighten out your loved one's financial tangles, you as conservator will stand in for the debtor throughout the bankruptcy process.

Final Thoughts About Bankruptcy

Reading about the steps in bankruptcy, you can see that it is not a flexible area of law. It is a rigid system of reporting facts and keeping deadlines. The rigidity may seem intimidating, but it is also what makes the bankruptcy process less stressful than a lot of other legal matters because it makes all of the legal interactions formulaic instead of personal.

In other words, although debtors have to reveal how much money they owe and who they owe it to, the bankruptcy system does not typically slow down to pass judgment on what happened. Bankruptcy courts only examine the debtor's motives in occasional circumstances, such as when the credit card company tried to convince the bankruptcy court that the credit card debt for gambling should not be discharged.

For most debtors, going through bankruptcy mainly requires short-term tasks that can be done in private, either alone or with the support of a family member or someone from the law firm. To be sure, the tasks—remembering details, making lists, and compiling bills and other records—can trigger psychiatric symptoms, but many people who are severely stressed and symptomatic because of their lack of funds and pressure from creditors can feel the benefits of undertaking these productive self-help tasks. They may especially like knowing that the federal court system's official definition of a bankruptcy debtor is "a person who has filed a petition for relief under the Bankruptcy Code." Relief: that is what bankruptcy is meant to provide, not an examination of the debtor, not an attack on the debtor, just relief from debts.

Tax Facts

- In Chapter 13 bankruptcies, tax debt is included in the repayment plan, so the IRS has to be listed among the creditors. See IRS, *Chapter 13 Bankruptcy— Voluntary Reorganization of Debt for Individuals (2016)* online at irs.gov.
- In Chapter 7 bankruptcies, income tax debts that existed for at least three years before the bankruptcy petition can often be discharged. This will only happen if the taxpayer filed tax returns (although she did not submit payment) for those years, the taxpayer did not commit fraud or evasion to avoid paying the taxes, and the IRS assessed the taxpayer's income and receipts more than 240 days before the bankruptcy petition. If the taxpayer already worked out a deal to pay the old IRS debts, the IRS will probably have assessed the taxpayer more recently than 240 days ago—when it received the most recent payment. In those cases, the 240-day rule can be adjusted to enable a current discharge.
- The bankruptcy trustee will obtain an employer identification number (EIN) to use on tax returns representing the bankruptcy. The individual taxpayer's social security number should not be used to represent the bankruptcy on tax returns.
- People in either Chapter 7 or Chapter 13 bankruptcy should continue to file individual tax returns during their bankruptcies. The obligation to report current taxable income continues to exist while the trustee deals with past debts.
- IRS Publication 908, *Bankruptcy Code Tax Compliance Requirements*, contains all of the details about bankruptcy and taxation.

RESOURCES ABOUT MONEY AND MENTAL HEALTH

1. An article by Amy Morin, "What Your Financial Health Says About Your Mental Health: Studies Show Your Debt Could Cost You More Than Just Interest," is available from *Psychology Today* online. It posted July 22, 2015, at psychologytoday.com.
2. Daniel C. Marson, J.D., Ph.D., Robert Savage, Ph.D., and Jacqueline Phillips, Ph.D., wrote "Financial Capacity in Persons with Schizophrenia

and Serious Mental Illness: Clinical and Research Ethics Aspects," which was published in 2006 in *Schizophrenia Bulletin, 32*(1), 81–91.

3. The 2013 article "Financial Victimization of Adults With Severe Mental Illness" (by Meredith Claycomb, M.A., Anne C. Black, Ph.D., Charles Wilber, M.Ed., Sophy Brocke, B.A., Christina M. Lazar, M.P.H., and Marc I. Rosen, M.D.) was published in *Psychiatric Services, 64*(9), 918–920.

RESOURCES FOR DEBTOR CREDITOR LAW

1. The National Consumer Law Center summarizes the Unfair and Deceptive Acts and Practices (UDAP) laws in all fifty states at nclc.org.
2. Find your state attorney general's office and its online consumer complaint form for reporting deceptive sales practices through the National Association of Attorneys General at naag.org.
3. The Federal Trade Commission publishes informative consumer support resources, including facts and instructions regarding its Cooling-Off Rule, a sample letter for correcting credit report errors, and articles about debt management, at consumer.ftc.gov.
4. The National Association of Consumer Advocates brings major lawsuits on behalf of consumers and has good instructions for dealing with debt collectors at consumeradvocates.org.
5. Federal consumer laws include: The Consumer Leasing Act 15 U.S.C. § 1667 (about all types of leases, not just cars); The Truth in Lending Act and Credit Card Accountability and Disclosures Act 15 U.S.C. §§ 1601–1666; and the Fair Credit Reporting Act 15 U.S.C. § 1681. Find them at uscode.house.gov.
6. Find the Bankruptcy Administrators' list of approved credit counseling agencies online at uscourts.gov. The list is not on the main page; the "resources" link and the "bankruptcy administrators" link will get you to it. Alternatively, call your local trustee's office and ask how to contact nearby credit counselors. The Department of Justice maintains a list of Chapter 13 trustees at justice.gov.
7. The National Federation for Credit Counseling sets standards for credit counselors and maintains a list of well-qualified members at nfcc.org.
8. Find your state's debt-management law by entering the phrase "debt management" in the search box on the website of the National Conference of State Legislatures at ncsl.org. Debt-management laws regulate the way debt-management services (also known as credit counseling services) conduct their business.
9. The American Bar Association's Commission on Law and Aging has a website about elder abuse that contains training materials, articles, explanations, and charts regarding several forms of debtor victimization, including undue influence. See americanbar.org.
10. The National Adult Protective Services Association publishes a lot of guidance about undue influence, as well as a compilation called "Financial Exploitation Case Studies." See napsa-now.org.

11. The Consumer Financial Protection Bureau (CFPB) publishes advice and facts informing banks about preventing, recognizing, reporting, and responding to financial abuse of senior citizens. The resources are voluntary best practices, not regulations. The CFPB encourages banks to use the information to train their staff. You can use the CFPB information if you are suspicious about your disabled relative's circumstances and as a source for phrases and explanations to use when approaching a bank about your relative's situation. See Consumerfinance. gov.

RESOURCES FOR BANKRUPTCY

1. The bankruptcy law that exempts people with mental illness from credit counseling when their symptoms prevent them from participating in their financial planning is at 11 U.S.C. § 109(h)(4). The bankruptcy law on willful and malicious misconduct is 11 U.S.C. § 523(a)(6). The bankruptcy law about not having to repay student loans is at 11 U.S.C. § 523(a)(8). The bankruptcy law about when debts will not be discharged is at 11 U.S.C. § 727. The law authorizing the trustee to investigate debtors' financial affairs is 11 U.S.C. § 704. All of these federal statutes are available at uscode. house.gov.
2. The Department of Justice publishes bankruptcy trustee manuals containing all of the rules trustees have to follow. Find them at justice. gov.
3. Find bankruptcy lawyers in your city by using the directory published by the National Association of Consumer Bankruptcy Attorneys at nacba. org.
4. Official bankruptcy forms are free online from the federal court system at uscourts.gov. Form B-423, "Certification About a Financial Management Course," certifies that the debtor's mental incapacity exempts him from financial management/debtor education. Some of the forms are applications to have fees waived or to pay fees in small installments.
5. One good case about discharging student loans for a bankruptcy petitioner with mental illness is *In re Larissa L. Johnston*, Bankruptcy No. 05-05136 (N.D. Iowa, Mar. 11, 2008). The case is available for free online at casetext.com. It references several similar bankruptcy cases.
6. The bankruptcy case about the people who hoarded cats is *In re Wheeler*, Case No. 05-30526 (Bankr. E.D. Tex.). The case about the woman who did not report her art and jewelry is *Youngman v. Bursztyn*, 366 B.R. 353 (Bankr. D. N.J. 2007). The case about the woman with gambling addiction and credit card debt from gambling is *In re Crutcher*, 215 B.R. 696 (W.D. Tenn. 1997).
7. Read the *Bankruptcy Basics* website available from the federal court system at uscourts.gov for clear and detailed facts about every action and document involved with every kind of bankruptcy. The site also has a glossary.

8. Two of the clearest sources on bankruptcy and disability are: Heather
   Frances, *How to File Bankruptcy While on SSI & Disability*, available from
   LegalZoom (http://info.legalzoom.com/file-bankruptcy-ssi-disability-
   25590.html), and *Bankruptcy Proceedings Overview*, from the SSA,
   Program Operations Manual System (POMS) § GN 02215.185, available at
   https://secure.ssa.gov/poms.nsf/lnx/0202215185.

19

Families and Finance

You and Gilly are practically sisters. You have been best friends since kinder-garten. All through school, she helped you with every art project. In fact, she grew up to be an artist and makes her living that way. Brilliant in numerous ways, she has a money avoidance disorder and cannot face her bank account statements or reconcile her income and payments. Sometimes she runs out of money and then can't pay for something that she needs. You and her family are glad to get her these things when she calls and says that she's out of money, but she seems to earn enough that this shouldn't happen. You are thinking about offering to handle Gilly's banking for her; you just want to know if there are any legal issues to be aware of if you to help Gilly with banking and some-times pay her bills out of your own money or give her things when she can't afford to buy them.

YOU, YOUR LOVED ONE, AND BANKING

There is a psychological explanation for why so many people with mental health problems have trouble managing money and bank accounts—it is known as poor executive functioning. Executive functioning is the ability to envision possible outcomes and adjust course to attain the best result. It is the basic, extremely small-scale, internal judgment version of avoiding a car wreck. When someone has poor executive functioning, he is generally not good at organizing or planning. He tends not to keep track of things. He cannot respond well to distractions or surprises. He is simply not wired to monitor account balances and numbers of debit card transactions and all of the other banking issues that can have bad consequences if not properly managed.

Bank customers with bipolar disorder may suffer more than anyone. On top of poor executive functioning, they have such great hopes when they overextend their accounts. To many of them, like your cousin Melissa, a wish and a plan can be pretty much the same thing, such as when she emptied her bank account to buy a popcorn machine and ingredients so that she could operate a popcorn concession stand at local festivals, not thinking of how strenuous it would be to spend every summer weekend acting cheerful and trying to convince strangers to buy bags of popcorn. Sometimes Melissa takes risks with money just because she is so hopeful. Then, when her hopes fall through and she is already disappointed, it seems like the bank hits her up with fines and sends scary and critical messages full of threats and accusations.

The banks may think these notices are straightforward statements of facts, and maybe they look that way to people who are not depressed, but they can seriously upset somebody with a depressive mood disorder like Melissa. Even worse is when banks play on customer loyalties. They encourage account holders to do something, maybe to use the debit card in stores or to use an ATM to make easy withdrawals, and then they punish customers who do that thing either too frequently or not enough. If it is difficult for your relative with mental illness to be a successful bank customer, you may want to serve as her power of attorney in connection with the bank account. (See Chapter 20 for details about financial powers of attorney.) You could also consider using the following banking tools to help her.

ABLE Savings Accounts

In addition to your loved one's standard bank account, you could establish an ABLE bank account in his name. ABLE stands for "achieving a better life experience." This is a new type of bank account that enables people with disabilities, including those with a mental illness, to have a slush fund for what the federal law calls "qualified disability expenses." Until ABLE bank accounts were authorized by Congress at the end of 2014, special-needs trusts were the only accounts where people in the SSI disability program could have money in excess of $2,000.

To open an ABLE bank account, your family member with mental illness (or someone authorized to handle banking on his behalf) needs to present certification (proof) of his disability and to show that the disability started before he was age twenty-six. (This age limit is likely to be changed soon.) People in the Supplemental Security Income (SSI) and Social Security Disability Insurance (SSDI) programs whose disabilities began prior to that age have the most convenient proof that they are eligible for ABLE accounts. They can simply bring a copy of their Social Security Administration (SSA) benefits letter. (You or the beneficiary can order a copy of the letter through the SSA website if he no longer has the letter that the SSA originally sent.) People who do not collect disability benefits from the SSA need to provide some sort of written communication from their doctor saying that they are disabled. The particular type of document and information needed differs across the states, but the bank will explain what the doctor should convey and whether to write a letter or to use a particular fill-in-the- blanks form.

Once the ABLE account is in place, it can receive up to the federal untaxable gift amount in total annual deposits. As of this writing, the gift tax law says that gifts of up to $15,000 from one individual will not be taxed. So, this year, your son Rod, who has an ABLE account, can have a total of $15,000 deposited into his account from all combined sources. Rod can put some of his own money into the account, you and other family members can put money into the account, and small windfalls, such as lottery winnings, can go into it. If a gift check arrives in November and $15,000 has already gone into the account this year, the recipient can either hang onto the check until January (when the new calendar year starts) or put it in a different account that is below the $2,000 SSI eligibility amount. The interest earned on the ABLE account will not be taxable interest. And, as with other bank accounts, withdrawals from the ABLE account will not be taxed as income.

Money in an ABLE account can be used by the person with the disability for the following list of expenses, which are named in the federal Achieving a Better Life Experience Act:

> education, housing, transportation, employment training and support, assistive technology and personal support services, health, prevention and wellness, financial management fees and administrative services, legal fees, expenses for oversight and monitoring, funeral and burial expenses, and other expenses, which are approved by the Secretary.

This is a good, flexible list that will make it much easier for families to assist someone with a disability to enjoy services, manage transactions, and avoid compromising SSI and Medicaid benefits. Note that the Secretary mentioned in the law is the Secretary of the Treasury, who can implement Internal Revenue Service (IRS) regulations approving additional expenses.

Online Banking

Just by logging in to your family member's online account with his user name and password, it is possible for you to handle his online banking without ever informing the bank that you are not the account owner. It is not advisable, but it is possible. There is also a way to be up front with the bank when you handle someone else's account: You and the account holder can arrange to make an existing account into a "convenience account" or an "agency account." These two account categories exist so that banks know when someone other than the account holder has the account owner's permission to handle deposits and withdrawals.

If your relative, like your son Rod in the above example, gives you access to his online banking service so that you can help manage his primary checking or savings account, the first thing to do is to arrange for all possible income to be directly deposited by payers. Direct deposits will ensure that you have funds to work with. Employers, the SSA, insurance companies, and courts (e.g., for support payments) are all equipped to make direct deposits. Arrange them so that Rod does not have to worry about keeping track of checks and dealing with deposit slips or even physically having to get to a bank or to use an ATM soon after receiving a check. (Rod may like using an ATM to get money, even if he is not good at keeping track of checks and depositing them in the ATM.)

Occasional checks, such as a refund from the IRS, may still arrive in the mail, but you can be ready for them and intercept them when they come. If you live far away, Rod will need to either deposit the checks himself or send them to you for deposit, but at least they will not contain the money that he depends on to make ends meet. Note that if you are just doing the banking informally, without having a convenience account or being named power of attorney, you will not want checks for Rod coming to your address—unless you are also willing to have collectors or legal opponents come to your door when they are after your relative.

Know exactly when predictable deposits are supposed to come into Rod's account and when routine payments have to go out. It is very easy to take a blank 30-day calendar page and write the expected financial events on it. The rent is due on the first day of the month. The SSI disability check will also come on the first of the month. The paycheck for his part-time job comes on the second and fourth Tuesdays, and so on. Considering when income will be deposited and when payments are due, you can plan the most sensible dates for automatic bill paying (which you and your family member will set up with the phone company and the credit card company and others on their websites, not on the bank's website). Mark those payment dates on the calendar page, too.

This is not a calendar that you should have to revise unless your relative experiences a significant change in circumstances, such as switching electric companies and getting on a new payment schedule. You definitely do not need to make a new page for every month or even every year. Just make one master calendar page and get into the habit of spot-checking the account online, maybe twice a month, to be sure that it has enough money to cover the automatic bill payments.

If you manage your relative's online banking and you are willing and able to occasionally supplement his bank account with your own money, simply make an online transfer. To do this, go online to your own bank account—no matter if it is in a different bank than your relative uses—and find the word "transfer" within the list of actions you can take. Transferring money into another person's bank account does not make you legally responsible for future payments to individual companies that get paid from his account.

HOW TO Avoid Trouble When Dealing With Your Relative's Banking

One serious legal concern when coping with banking—even if you have power of attorney—is that your relative with mental illness may accuse you of theft. If she tends to be suspicious, angry, or distrustful, consider whether she may claim that you are stealing from the account. Does she tend to blame people when she feels out of control? Just as bank robbery is still bank robbery when the bank leaves the vault open and does not have any guards posted, bank account theft is still theft even if the account owner has provided someone else with online access. This is different from joint ownership, which entitles each owner of the joint account to all of the money in the account. Your relative cannot legitimately claim that you are stealing from a joint account, but she can make a loud and ugly illegitimate claim. Organizing, monitoring, and occasionally subsidizing someone else's banking is a valuable package of services. It should not be a risky undertaking. If you think that your relative may become adversarial and make accusations when you are trying to help her avoid being overdrawn, just stay away from the bank account.

If you do take responsibility for sharing an account or for handling online banking associated with a relative's individual account—for example, you have agreed to help your mother, who has borderline personality disorder—prove that you are responsible by being a good communicator. Do not keep secrets from your mom. Be clear and complete. Show respect for her intelligence. These efforts will help your mother know what is happening in her bank account and prevent her from mistakenly thinking that you are stealing. Copies of your written communications will also serve as protective proof in your defense in case she ever does accuse you of wrongdoing.

You also want to open all possible communications that you can have with the bank. Having power of attorney or at least access to your mother's user name, password, and account number, you can register yourself for every notification service they have. If the bank has a "spending tracker" service that will let you know when the account is close to bottoming out, you definitely want to sign up for it so that you can deposit money and avoid overdraft fees. Banks can also alert you when direct deposits have come in and when there is a security concern with the account. If you have power of attorney and are permitted to communicate with the bank on your mother's behalf, keep either print or electronic copies of the communications between yourself and the bank and let your mom know about them.

Get into the habit of reporting regularly to your loved one about what is happening with her bank account. When you do this, remember that you are helping somebody who is either upset by banking or cannot concentrate on it, like your mom, who is unpredictable, but do it in writing so that you and she will both be able to put it into a file folder and refer back to it. It does not have to have a lot of words. Send the reports on a regular basis, either in connection with a monthly event or on a particular day of the month. If you time your reports to go with a monthly event, choose an expense rather than a deposit as the event. *Your rent of $800 was automatically paid on time today. On Tuesday, the bank sent your $250 monthly car payment.* If you notify your loved one only about money coming into the account, she may be tempted to spend too much.

Just convey essential facts and simple encouragement in the report.

- You could say things like: *We paid all of last month's bills on time and had $12 extra at the end of the month.*
- You can give banking tips in your report: *I see that you made twelve different debit card purchases. It is better if you click the "credit" link when you make those purchases. That will save us the $10 overuse fee and make it easier for you to return merchandise.*
- And when you mention anything from the bank alerts, do it without sounding critical or hostile: *The bank just sent me a note saying that a $50 debit at Target on Wednesday wiped out the last of the account. Don't use the debit card again until your salary gets deposited. I will let you know when that deposit shows up.*

Do you see how straightforward these notes are? They are much easier to handle than the standard bank statements that the bank will still continue sending to your mother, but that she may not read.

If ever you make a mistake with the account, fix it as soon as you discover it. Then, write a note to your relative that begins with an admission and explanation:

Mom, I made a mistake with your bank account, but I have fixed it. Having set up your rent payment to go out on the 29th of every month, I forgot to notice that February had only 28 days, so your March rent did not get paid on time. I didn't even know about this problem until your landlord sent the note about the late fee. I have already paid the late fee from my own money since this was my mistake. I personally handed that check and a rent check from your account to the landlord. (If you live out of town, you will send the checks to the landlord by return receipt mail.) I'm attaching here copies of both checks. From now on, your bank account will pay your rent on the 27th of each month.

In the unlikely event that you ever face a legal claim about misappropriating your family member's money, bring copies of these notes, reports, and bank statements to your lawyer. Do not give away your only copies. The more you can show, the more you can prove that you conducted yourself honestly.

Joint Accounts

A joint bank account is one that is owned equally by two people. It does not matter how much money each person has contributed to the account; they are each entitled to use all of the money in it. Each owner of the account is also equally responsible for any fees that the bank charges to the account. If one of the joint owners accesses the ATM machine too many times or writes a check for more money than is in the account and then does not pay the fees for breaking those bank rules, the other owner will have to pay them.

The fees can grow very rapidly. In addition to the fee for each bounced check or electronic payment, there is also an escalating fee for continuing to not have enough money in the account. This fee will get tacked on every single day until one of the account owners puts the necessary minimum amount of money into the account and pays all of the bank fees. The law does not set the fees, the banks do. The statutes about banking merely authorize the banks to set fees and to establish policies about when they will apply the fees. The amount and frequency of fees are set the way prices are set in most businesses: according to what the market will bear.

Another bank practice for joint owners to be cautious about is the way that banks count overdrafts. When account owners spend too much and then don't have enough money in their account to cover all of their checks and online payments, the bank will make the highest payments first. That way, the items that do not get paid are just small items. This seems like a helpful practice. The high expenses are likely to be rent, utility bills, and other necessities for living. The low expenses are likely to be minor debits at places like stores and gas stations. Here's the problem: The bank charges an overdraft fee for every single overdraft. By paying for one large check or debit instead of the handful of smaller checks or debits, the bank is entitling itself to collect fees for all of the separate small overdrafts. If it paid all of the small overdrafts instead of the single large overdraft, the customer would have only one overdraft fee.

The rules between banks and their customers are established by "terms and conditions," in other words, by contracts. These are one-sided contracts, not negotiable contracts. Applicants for bank accounts either accept the terms or they do not get the bank account. In the contracts, customers typically have no choice but to agree that if they violate bank rules, they may be frozen out of their accounts. When customers fail to pay fees, the bank can place negative claims about their "failure to pay" on their credit reports.

Before you decide to become jointly responsible with a family member who has a mental illness, remember that he will still be able to behave irresponsibly in connection with the joint account. He may get into fights or at least make a nuisance of himself at the bank. He may run up fees. He may make endless purchases, assuming that you will cover the costs.

HOW TO Respond To Your Relative's Questions About an Account

Every so often, your relative—this time, let's use your cousin Jose as the example—will ask you a question about an account that you manage for him. Maybe the question will come to you in a middle-of-the-night phone call. Maybe it will be in the form of an accusation. Maybe it will be delivered by somebody your relative is hiding behind. Maybe it will not make any sense. Even if it doesn't sound exactly like a question, but it is a statement expressing curiosity or worry about the bank account, a safe method for responding is to treat it as if it were a question. With that as your perspective in the conversation, you will help yourself to remain tolerant and in control of your own message.

And your message, at least to begin with, when you are blindsided by whatever your relative is conveying to you, should always begin with a respectful reply: "Tell me more." "I don't know about this problem, Jose; I'm glad you're telling me." Notice that these replies are not antagonistic. They invite your family member to explain what has upset him. The replies do not criticize or contradict your cousin. If you phrase your replies in the form of a question, you may come across as argumentative, so do not do that. In other words, if Jose asks you a question (although he doesn't necessarily phrase it as a question) and you question him in return, you may seem like you are ignoring the fact that he is curious or worried about the account that you are involved with.

Here are some examples of how a question from your family member may not be presented as a question:

- *I always used to be able to get my own money out of the ATM whenever I wanted to.* This is a way of asking "Why do you say that I can make only ten ATM withdrawals a month?"
- *You're blowing my savings!* This could be your loved one's way of asking "What happened to all of the money I thought I had?"
- *Stop telling me what to do with my own money.* This may be the way your loved one asks, "Will you please change the tone and content of your communications about my bank account?" If you have been saying things like "You can spend $50 on anything you want," you could instead say "Just making sure you know that you still have $50." In the second sentence, you don't sound as much like a parent giving permission to a child; you sound like an adult talking to another adult.

Once you get more facts, acknowledge the intelligence behind the question: "Oh, okay, you're reconciling the account and things are not adding up." "I see why you're calling now; it looks like there's been a mistake." You can be complimentary: "That's a good question." You could say, "That *is* odd" or "I agree with what you are saying." Above all, be open to the good possibility that you really have made an error that needs to be corrected. No matter what, you owe your relative a good explanation.

Once you know what is on his mind, promise to look into it and to fix it if it needs to be fixed. You can literally say, "I'm going to look into this." Or you could say, "Let me find out what's going on." Now, you may already know what is going on. You may be absolutely positive about exactly what has happened. But you need to dignify your cousin's concerns by taking the time to investigate before you respond. You may be wrong when you think that you know exactly what happened. Money worries are very stressful; investigate promptly and keep your loved one informed about what you are doing. Within a day, you should be ready to at least report that you have started investigating in some way. Take action that will enable you to make a statement like: "I scheduled an appointment for us to see the bank manager on Thursday." "I downloaded the bank's fee list and am going to circle some things on it and then mail it to you." "I pulled your account activity for the last four months and will go over it this weekend. Can we plan to talk on Tuesday?"

When you have the information he needs and are ready to answer, try to demonstrate information in a way that will hold his attention. You could use Monopoly money or a deck of cards, or have him draw or write as you talk. Or you could ask someone else whom he trusts, say a caseworker or someone from his peer-support group, to sit with the two of you and go over the most recent bank statement. The bank may even employ somebody who is available to review account information with customers.

If someone other than your unwell relative is questioning your management of the account, remember that you have no obligation, legal or otherwise, to discuss your relative's financial affairs with anyone else. Perhaps your relative is using the other person as a go-between because he or she is having difficulty trusting you. Maybe the other person is a con artist. It is possible that this is just some random do-gooder who does not know the facts. As long as you are dealing honestly with the bank and your relative, you can feel secure that you are fulfilling your legal obligations to him or her.

Nevertheless, you want to handle inquiries from outsiders with a balance of respect and suspicion. It is possible that someone who appears to doubt your bank account management may really need to be paid for something that your relative ordered. Not knowing whether they have any legitimate basis, require that all questions about your relative's bank account be submitted to you in writing. People will try to pry information from you by catching you by surprise. They will call you on the phone or make inquiries at stray moments. Especially when your loved one is entering into an episode of poor mental health, friends, cheats, or creditors may either attempt to take advantage of him or else try to rescue him from something that they are misinformed about.

Have a standard phrase ready for all of these people.

It could be: "My fiduciary relationship with [name] requires that I maintain written records of all communications. Please mail me your questions or comments and I will deal with them in that format."

Or you could say: "I am not at liberty to discuss [name's] private financial issues with you, but I will respectfully consider your concerns if you send them to me in writing."

People who have true claims in connection with your relative's bank account will be willing to put them in writing. If they are fakes, they might go away when you demand a written claim or they will submit something that you can keep on file in case it is ever necessary to prove that they attempted to defraud you and your relative. And, if they are just nosy, they will probably go away and stop bothering you.

Tax Facts

- ABLE savings accounts are generally tax exempt. However, if the person with the disability becomes temporarily not disabled, and some of the money in her ABLE account was earned income, the withdrawals of earned income that she makes during the not disabled period will be taxed. See IRS Publication 907.
- Holders of ABLE savings accounts will receive IRS Form 5498-QA from the bank every year. This form tells the IRS how much was deposited into the account in the past year and whether the deposits were actual contributions or interest income.
- Holders of ABLE savings accounts will also receive IRS Form 1099-QA from the bank every year. This form tells how much was withdrawn from the account and whether tax is owed on any of the withdrawals.
- Joint bank account holders are jointly liable for paying income tax on the interest that their account earns. One of the account holders can pay the tax on the full amount of interest or each account holder can pay half. If you intend to pay only half of the tax, report the full amount of the account's interest on Schedule B of your tax return and then write "nominee distribution" and your joint account holder's name on the very next line. In the column where you wrote the full interest amount, put a minus sign and half of that interest amount. When you come to line 2, which says "add the amounts on line 1," add whatever needs to be added regarding other your bank accounts, but for this joint account show only the half that you owe because you have already subtracted your relative's half of the joint account interest. See IRS Schedule B—General Instructions (search for *nominee*). The other owner of this joint account should also complete schedule B this way. To explain to the IRS why two separate taxpayers are each paying half of the tax on this interest, provide the joint account holder and the IRS with identical copies of Form 1099-INT on which you show that since the joint account holder owns half of the interest earned by the account, he owes half of the taxes on that interest. Finally, submit to the IRS Form 1096 which is a simple cover sheet for the 1099.
- To get a full explanation of taxes and bank account interest, see IRS Tax Topic 403, "Interest Received."

FAMILY FINANCIAL ASSISTANCE

Money problems can make anyone feel depressed, anxious, traumatized, or fu-rious. When financial shortfalls affect an already troubled person, their impact is magnified. Other family members, desperate to stop the snowball of trouble from rolling downhill and getting bigger, may find themselves handing over money with the hope that it will calm the person who is struggling with both financial troubles and psychiatric troubles. There are three common legal issues related to providing another adult with financial assistance:

- Creating gift tax liability
- Interfering with eligibility for government assistance
- The possibility of funding a crime.

Gift Tax Liability

In tax law, people who give (not those who receive) gifts valued at more than a certain amount are supposed to declare the gifts on a gift tax return and they may have to pay tax on part of the gifts' value. This tax is called "gift tax." The recipient does not have to pay income tax on the gift. Gifts worth less than a certain amount (which is set each year by the IRS), gifts to spouses, and gifts that directly pay tui-tion or medical costs for somebody else will not cost the donor a gift tax.

As of this writing, donors who make gifts of money or goods valued at over $15,000 to a single person in a single tax year are supposed to declare the gift on the IRS Gift Tax Return. This does not mean that the donor will have to pay tax, though. In fact, the tax code requires gift givers to pay the gift tax only after they have already given over $11,180,000 worth (to be exact) of gifts in their lifetimes. This sounds extreme, but there are people who give homes and collectibles, such as artwork, as gifts. Even if the donor has given gifts worth this much and now does have to pay gift tax, only the gift amount over $15,000 for an individual gift will be taxed. So if the gift is for $16,000 (or something worth that amount), the donor will only owe gift tax on $1,000. In most people's circumstances, it will not be necessary to pay tax on a gift made to an individual. Each individual taxpayer can give $15,000 in separate gifts to different people without reporting the gifts on a federal gift tax form and without being taxed on the gifts. Here are some examples involving people who have not gone over the $11 million amount.

- If ten different taxpayers each give $15,000 to the same person, say you, so that you receive a total of $150,000 in gifts one year, none of the donors will have to pay any gift tax and you will not have to pay income tax on that money. (You will have to pay income tax on interest or other earnings from the money, but not on the initial gifts.) Husbands and wives count as separate taxpayers for gift-giving purposes. So a couple can give $30,000 to each recipient without having to pay gift tax.
- And if one donor, say you again, gives $15,000 to ten different people, so you give a total of $150,000, you still will not have to pay the gift tax. The tax is just for individual or combined gifts from one giver to a single

recipient that total more than the amount allowed by the IRS. Search for the phrase "gift tax exclusion amount" on the IRS website to find the current year's tax-free limit.

Eligibility for Government Assistance

Government assistance programs are typically available only to people who earn less than a certain amount of money per year and who have less than a certain amount in assets (not counting their home and car). The actual dollar limits change periodically. Some programs prefer not to state a dollar amount for eligibility. Instead, they say that families and individuals living below the poverty limit are eligible for services. The poverty limit is set according to the census and can be found online through the Department of Health and Human Services.

The SSI disability program and Medicaid are two examples of federal assistance that limits eligibility according to assets as well as income. So, first they check to see if a claimant's income is below the poverty limit. If it is, then they check to be sure that the claimant has less than the allowed amount of assets. As of this writing, people can have a house, a vehicle, and up to $2,000 in other assets and still be eligible for SSI and Medicaid. Congress has periodically considered increasing the amount, but it has remained the same for decades.

SSI recipients can receive some cash gifts that will not affect their SSI eligibility. The cash gifts can be for no more than $60 each and they have to be "infrequent" or "irregular." "Infrequent" means that the gifts cannot come more than once every three months. "Irregular" means that they cannot come so regularly that the recipient would be able to plan on getting them.

If an SSI disability recipient is pursuing a "Plan for Achieving Self-Support" (PASS), contributions toward that plan will not count as assets that would compromise the recipient's SSI benefits. A PASS is aimed at the SSI recipient's getting a job. Healthy family members can give money or goods toward a disabled relative's collection of tools, clothing, accommodation devices, or other supplies that she will need in order to start a new job, but they should not be fooled every time a family member with mental illness claims to need job money. Some mental illnesses, such as antisocial personality disorder and narcissistic personality disorder, can include manipulative behavior. If the SSI recipient does not have a legitimate PASS in place, not only will the contributions likely be a waste of the donor's money, but also they may disqualify the relative with mental illness from continuing to get SSI benefits. Ask to see documentation of your loved one's PASS, or help him to interact with Social Security about creating one, before you give money for his work-related expenses.

For more information about gifts that do not count against SSI and Medicaid eligibility, see Chapter 20 of this book, in the section called "HOW TO Decide Whether To Buy a Tangible Gift or To Contribute to a Special Needs Trust". Just as the SSA has established dollar amounts and gift categories, other government agencies (including state and local governments) and organizations (including nonprofit service organizations) are legally allowed to set any eligibility limits that they choose, as long as they apply them consistently.

Funding a Crime

Knowledge and *intent* are the critical elements that can make gift givers guilty of crimes committed by recipients. Someone who gives a relative a weapon, or helps her to get a weapon, can expect to be charged as an accomplice to any crime committed with that weapon. Someone who pays for a relative to get a computer that she uses for online theft or other computer crimes probably will not get into any trouble with the police unless the giver knew that the recipient wanted the computer for an illegal purpose and he provided it anyway. (The computer giver could still be sued in civil court. Refer to the "Major Gifts" section later in this chapter.) Someone who gives the relative money with no awareness of how it will be used, especially if the person does not know that the recipient participates in any criminal activities, usually has very little criminal culpability.

HOW TO Cope if You Feel Conflicted About Giving Gifts

If for any reason you find yourself feeling conflicted about making small gifts to your loved one, keep in mind that sometimes there is legal support for giving gifts in ways that that benefit both givers and the recipients. Here is one example to consider: The tax laws entitle you to deduct charitable donations. If you can pay a local nonprofit organization to do something for your family member who has mental illness and you can claim part of that service cost as a charitable deduction, do it. You will be helping both your relative and the charity at the same time. Nonprofit organizations will provide you with a letter indicating how much of your contribution went toward costs and how much counts as a deductible donation. If they do not automatically send you the letter, ask for it.

Here are some common suggestions:

- Maybe your Aunt Mabel is not good at making meals. And maybe there is a local church that has food fundraisers—a seasonal ethnic soup sale or a monthly chicken dinner. If such a meal service exists, sign your aunt up for it and write off the permitted portion.
- Keep an eye out for organizations that provide rides, haul things away, or clean houses. Maybe Mabel could use that help, and you can get the tax write-off.
- Give the gift of membership. Membership in a nonprofit organization, such as a community center or museum, can entitle your relative to participate in activities and social engagements while you get a partial tax deduction for paying the membership fee. Not every membership has a deductible portion, so check on this before purchasing any membership for your relative.

Another way that the law supports gift giving is with the concept of exploiting contractual opportunities. This is not an explicit doctrine that would be spelled out in a textbook about contract law. It is simply the reality that you can take advantage of deals that may not have been designed to reward families for sharing with adults who have mental illness, but which have that effect. One example of this is the opportunity to use your grocery store loyalty card to purchase practical gift cards. That way, your family member gets the gift card and you get a discount on your own groceries. A side benefit of this kind of giving is that you can limit where your relative spends the funds. If you give her cash, she may not spend it wisely. If you give her a gift card to the shoe store, she has to use it for shoes. Other examples include volume discounts, "refer a friend" deals, buy one get one free offers, and similar opportunities to obtain goods and services for your relative in ways that make the items cheaper for at least one of you. As you discover great examples of these opportunities, put the word out to other families in your support circle.

Does your family member need a phone? Phone plans let you include your whole family in a group discount rate. Many family phone plan contracts will permit you to include someone who does not live with you. Read your terms and conditions to be sure that you can do this. Some plans do not try to limit the people whom you consider to be in your family, and others say that all family members have to be on your bill and making calls from within the same market area, but not that you all are required to live in the same house. If your loved one has a history of troubles relating to the Internet, consider providing him with a phone that does not include Internet access. If he already has a smart phone, you can later deactivate his Internet access from your service plan, should that become necessary. Providing even basic phone service is a very helpful thing to do for someone who lives with severe mental illness.

In fact, as another kind of gift, you can arrange to pay other kinds of routine bills for your relative.[1] You just need to be sure that you do it in a way that does not create a guarantor arrangement between yourself and the utility company, store, or other payee. If you become a guarantor, you will be responsible for the account. Companies have tricky ways of luring kindly, helpful relatives into becoming guarantors. They make it very easy to turn a single account into a joint account. They offer special "family pay" plans to help poor relatives. Not all of the family pay plans necessarily make you into a guarantor, but you want to be cautious about accepting liability for your relative's spending.

When companies cannot get you to become a guarantor, they are at least happy to have your contact information so that they can hassle you if the account holder ever gets behind on payments. You can avoid these traps by keeping your name and other contact details off any documents associated with the account. There are plenty of ways to pay someone's bill without identifying yourself on the account. One is old fashioned: Your relative can arrange for the bills to be mailed in print via the post office to her address and then she can pass them to you and you can pay them by check. At payment receipt centers, checks are removed and scanned by machines, so no human being is likely to record the fact that a name other than the account holder's name is on the check. Another method is to deposit money into her checking account for the exact amount of every month's bill (for example, the electric bill). This method can only work, however, if your relative is able to manage her spending and keep track of her

---

1 As discussed in Chapter 22 of this book, when you pay your relative's housing and food bills and he is on SSI, his SSI payments will be reduced. However, an SSI case example states that if you pay for non-housing and food items, such as a phone bill and cable bill, his SSI payments will not be reduced. See https://www.ssa.gov/ssi/text-living-ussi.htm.

bills. Each deposit is really just an allowance; you will have no control over the way it is spent. Arranging for automatic bill payments from that account can alleviate your family member's burdens, but it will result in bank penalties if she cannot keep sufficient funds in the account.

You can arrange to pay online, but to avoid confusion, the billing information should match the payment information. If your relative generally has good credit, online payments can be very convenient; you just take one of her existing credit cards or have her get a new credit card that will remain in your possession and use it exclusively to pay these bills. Of course you will then pay that credit card bill every month. If your relative has bad credit, you can buy a prepaid credit card in her name and use it to pay the bills online.

These contorted forms of gift giving would probably seem unwarranted in some circumstances. But various mental health symptoms, some arising from mood and some from unrealistic perceptions, play out as financial irresponsibility and leave people in need of help to obtain basic supplies and services. Families of people with severe chronic mental illness who find themselves giving gifts just to be sure that their family member has what she needs can take comfort from knowing how the law supports gift giving.

MAJOR GIFTS

Consumers who depend on federal disability benefits for their income are at risk of living without secure housing, reliable home appliances, certain educational opportunities, and their own vehicles unless they receive those things as gifts. Disability generally does not pay enough for people to buy these expensive items. In fact, there are also lots of full-time jobs that do not pay enough for workers to afford big purchases. And there are plenty of expensive things on the market that can make people's lives happier and more convenient.

When you think about why someone would give a very expensive item to someone else who has a history of serious mental illness, you intuitively realize that the giver has more than he needs, the recipient has less than he needs, and the giver feels either compassion or obligation toward the recipient. These three realizations will also come to mind when anything goes wrong after the gift is given. In the very rare event that something goes so wrong that the legal system becomes involved, both the giver and the recipient will instinctively want to use these realizations as legal defenses. They will say things like: *I didn't want it anymore. She needed it. I was only trying to help.* All of these are terrible excuses. They are good reasons for giving the gift, but they do not justify any legal problems.

When you honestly boil down these notions, you see that each is really about the fact that the recipient is mentally ill. Lawyers will start this boiling down as soon as they first meet with these people.

Q: *Why did you give him this car?*

A: *He couldn't afford to buy a car.*

Q: *Why couldn't he afford a car?*

A: *He can't work.*

Q: Why can't he work?

A: He's schizophrenic and has hallucinations.

Q: Oh, so you gave a car to someone who is known to have hallucinations? What did you think was going to happen when he had a hallucination on the highway?

Family gift givers should think responsibly, not merely compassionately, before giving something that the recipient may not be able to manage.

Unless you give your family member with mental illness something truly major, on the order of a house or car, or something dangerous like a sword or gun, you probably do not need to be afraid of lawyers coming after you for giving a gift. Household items, such as electronic devices, televisions, washer/dryers, and furniture, are not going to cause any legal trouble. A computer may lead to legal trouble— especially if the recipient uses it to hack into other computers, stalk, engage with criminals, lure children over the Internet, or commit other computer crimes. But unless there is a known legal risk associated with your relative's possession of a particular type of object, expect that gifts of household goods will be free of legal obligations for either the giver or the recipient.

Before you or anyone else gives a house, condominium, boat, motorcycle, car, or other really major gift to your family member with mental illness, remember that those gifts come with major legal responsibilities. The responsibilities are what the lawyers will actually be interested in if trouble arises, rather than the explanations about how badly the recipient needed it and how easy it was for the giver to buy it. Generally, the legal responsibilities fall into three categories:

- The laws associated with transferring that type of property.
- The legal obligations that the recipient will have once he takes ownership.
- The liability that the giver may have as a result of giving a gift to somebody who caused harm with it.

Legal Transfers (Taxes, Cheap Sales, Registrations)

Federal gift tax, mentioned earlier in this chapter, may be owed by the gift giver if the gift is worth more than the current minimum taxable amount—$15,000, as of this writing. Some gift givers disguise their gifts as cheap sales to avoid paying gift tax. They might sell their RV to a cousin for $5, for example. This is a legal sale. Sales prices are established by contracts between the seller and buyer, not by the legal system. But if the fair market value of the RV is more than $5, then the amount of the RV's value that is over $5 can be taxed as a gift. So, if the fair market value (the standard price where you live) of the RV is $16,000 and if you will be charged the gift tax for giving a gift worth more than $15,000, make the sale price $1,000. That way, you will not have to pay the gift tax because you will not have made a $5 sale and given a $15,995 gift. If your relative does not have $1,000 when you are ready to sell him the RV, you can arrange for him to pay you the $1,000 over time or you can allow him to work off the debt by doing chores for you.

When you present a gift in the form of a cheap sale, use contract formalities so that you are not later accused of giving a gift for which you failed to pay the gift tax.

Write a sales contract in which you specifically identify the item being sold, include the full names of the buyer and seller, tell how much is being paid for the item, give the date of the sale, and record any other promises or facts that are part of this sale. If the buyer cannot pay the full amount up front, one of the promises or facts will be his agreement to pay a certain amount of money per month for an acceptable number of months. Then, you and the buyer should both sign that document to show that you agree to the terms and you should both keep copies of the signed document and a photocopy of the payment—even if it is only a first installment check for $50. If your relative pays you cash, write him a receipt. It can be on any kind of paper and it can be handwritten or typed. A receipt is just a note saying that you received a named amount of money from a particular person for a specific purpose on a specific date.

For some gifts, such as jewelry and artwork, there are no legal obligations on the recipient of the gift. If the major gift is shares of stock, the recipient will have income tax liability on money that the stock earns, but probably no other legal concerns after receiving the gift.

Here is a useful fact about gifts of stock: When the recipient (let's say your daughter, Pearl) sells the stock, her profit (her "capital gain" in IRS language) is the difference between the price she gets for selling it and the price her gift giver (for example, your father) paid for it. So, if your dad paid $10 for the stock in 1974 and gave it to Pearl in 2012 and she now sells it for $10,000, she has to pay capital gains tax on her profit of $9,990.

If the gift is a vehicle, house, or condo, there are well-known legal formalities required in transferring the gift to a recipient. When the gift is a vehicle, the title has to be transferred to the new owner, the vehicle has to be formally registered with the state department of motor vehicles as belonging to the new owner, and the new owner will immediately have a legal obligation to insure the vehicle.

When the gift is a home, a title search and a deed transfer have to be conducted in order for the gift to be legally completed. The title search confirms that the home (whether it is a condominium, mobile home, free-standing house, etc.) truly belongs to the giver and is available for giving.

If a creditor has a lien against the home (such as a mortgage holder or home equity lender), the owner has to pay back the creditor before giving the house away. If the home is still deeded to a person who died (even if the death happened years ago) somebody (typically a realtor or real estate lawyer) will need to look at the will and transfer the house according to the will's instructions.

In the case where the homeowner has died, if the will says that the house is to be divided among all of the owner's children, then the home either has to be sold so that all of the children get equal shares of the home's value, or the kids have to all own it together, or some of the children can disclaim (give up) their shares of the house, or some of the kids can be bought out by the other kids. If the will says that the home is supposed to pass to just one person—for example, your sister Amanda, even if she has had nothing to do with the home—then Amanda has to be contacted and the home has to be transferred from the estate of the person who died to Amanda. It is then up to her to either keep the home, sell it, or give it as a gift to the relative with mental illness. These are some of the most common deed-related legal issues that we see when people give homes as gifts—whether or not there are family members with mental illness involved.

Legal Obligations That Come With Major Gifts

Think about these legal issues as they might apply to your sister: Homeowners have to comply with the fire code, health department regulations, property tax laws, building codes, and criminal laws. As covered in the family liability section of Chapter 13, a homeowner who takes in a drug dealer or mugger can be arrested as an accomplice after the fact. And a homeowner who lets a wanted criminal (someone who is already named in an arrest warrant) live in her house can be arrested for harboring a fugitive.

Homeowners also have a legal duty to protect people from being injured on their property, especially when they can predict that injuries will happen. So, for example, if kids coming home from school tend to run through a homeowner's front yard every day, and one day a child gets bad cuts because the homeowner did not sweep away the glass that broke at a party the night before, the homeowner is liable for the kid's injuries. This duty to protect against injuries is known as premises liability.

Owners of RVs have to park in legal spaces. The state motor vehicle code or the state landlord tenant laws usually direct where it is or is not legal to park an RV. If the RV is parked in an RV park, the RV owner is a tenant there, has to pay rent, and must follow all of the state's landlord tenant laws. Since an RV owner is both a tenant and an owner, he is liable for premises liability, helping or harboring criminals, and maintaining the dwelling. Meanwhile, he also has special legal rights, including the rights to utility access, grounds maintenance, privacy, hygiene facilities, and other items identified in the state's mobile home laws.

Condominium owners have similar combined obligations—some that are associated only with their unit and some that are associated with the shared spaces:

- Making too much noise can result in nuisance charges or citations for disturbing the peace.
- Putting out cigarettes on flammable surfaces may breach the condo contract and violate the fire code.
- Hoarding that attracts bugs and rodents can result in condemnation and a civil lawsuit for payment of cleaning and extermination fees.
- One person's excessive communications with, or demands on, the condo board may result in harassment charges.

Now, what if the homeowner has a serious mental illness?

- What kind of support does he need in order to keep the place habitable?
- What will it take to make sure that the property is safe for visitors?
- How can anyone prevent criminal associations with the property owner?
- Who could mediate the suspicions and misplaced loyalties that could ostracize this homeowner from his neighbors or cause him to house troublemakers?

These are the questions for families to think through when a member with mental illness receives a house, an RV, or a condominium as a gift. The questions should help you think of realistic ways to prevent legal problems for the homeowner—for example, your grandson Cedric, who has major depression.

Maybe someone in the family (perhaps you or your wife) can serve as a liaison between Cedric and the RV administration or condo association. Perhaps you can plan occasional family gatherings at Cedric's home so that several of you can eyeball the place every so often. At least consider going there yearly for a "we'll bring it" birthday party for Cedric. Is anyone in the family available to repair things? How will the yard be maintained? If the family is not available to cope with potential legal problems, then giving a house, an RV, or a condo to a relative with severe mental illness could just be a setup for failure and a trigger for unpleasant mental symptoms. (See the section of Chapter 20 titled "HOW TO Decide Whether To Buy a Tangible Gift or To Contribute To a Special Needs Trust.")

The Major Gift Giver's Possible Liability

If your friend Peter gives a car to his alcoholic brother or to another friend who is suicidal, knowing that the person has driven dangerously in the past, should Peter get in legal trouble for giving the car? Does it make a difference whether the car was lent or given as a gift? Many courts have discussed these questions. They use the phrase "negligent entrustment" to describe the gift or loan. This is a familiar concept from psychiatric malpractice and from the employment context, although it is usually called "vicarious liability" in those realms. (An extreme and tragic example is the depressed Lufthansa copilot who locked the other pilot out of the cabin and crashed the plane full of passengers into a mountain. Immediately, lawyers began planning vicarious liability lawsuits against the airline for allowing its depressed employee to fly the plane that day.)

Negligent entrustment is providing someone with a potentially dangerous item when you have reason to know that he will not use it safely. This definition certainly raises lots of questions:

- How dangerous is potentially dangerous?
- Isn't it possible that just about everything can be potentially dangerous?
- What sort of information counts as a reason to know anything about the person?
- Do you have to know how many traffic tickets he has had?
- Do you have to know his medical history?
- What exactly is the range of safe uses that you are supposed to be able to predict?

There are no solid answers to these questions. Each court asks these questions while deciding on the facts in a negligent entrustment case. Like all forms of negligence, negligent entrustment becomes a legal problem only if somebody suffers harm.

Sometimes, when the giver knew that the recipient was a dangerous driver, courts have found the person who gave the car to be guilty for the recipient's wreck.

In some of these cases, it was also important that the incompetent driver would not otherwise have had a car. He would not have been able to afford one, for example, had the giver not given it to him. But most of the time, courts hold only the driver to be liable, not the person who gave the driver the car as a gift. Making this decision, judges usually write that holding the gift giver liable would be like holding a car dealer liable. They can't hold car dealers liable every time somebody causes a car wreck.

When somebody lends a car to a dangerous driver who causes a wreck that injures people, the car lender is likely to be found guilty of negligent entrustment. What is the difference between lending the car and giving the car? Most courts believe that when somebody gives a car, he is relinquishing complete control of it. He does not know when the driver will use it or where it will be used, and he has no financial responsibility for the car. Courts that do hold the people who give cars responsible note that, if the giver had not relinquished control to the particular recipient, the injuries would never have occurred. Those are the contrasting views about giving cars as gifts. Courts commonly conclude that someone who lends a car does know the facts about its usage and does pay insurance and registration fees for it, so he does have control over its use.

Guns and cars are the two items most frequently seen in negligent entrustment cases because they are the most common dangerous objects that people provide to each other. The cases against those who give guns as gifts are not like the car examples; gun givers usually are held liable when the recipient uses the gun to hurt others.

There are specific laws that make it illegal to sell a gun to someone with a violent criminal past or a known mental illness. The laws exist to prevent dangerous people from having dangerous weapons. It makes sense that a person would be liable for giving a weapon to somebody who was not allowed to buy one. The gift giver made the danger possible.

In addition to negligent entrustment, which is the civil law problem with giving a dangerous gift, there can also be multiple criminal laws against giving somebody a gun, as discussed in Chapter 13 of this book. As with other civil harm, the punishment for negligent entrustment is payment of money damages.

Examples of Negligent Entrustment Cases

PACE V. DAVIS, 394 S.W.3D 859 (ARK. APP. 2012)
The father of a nineteen-year-old male who had been treated for anxiety and depression was not guilty of negligent entrustment for buying his unwell son a rifle, which the son used, just six months later, to shoot a romantic rival. Because the son had been a competent hunter since childhood and had not previously used a gun to injure any humans, the court found that the father had no reason to expect that his son would use the gun against a person. This conclusion is especially remarkable because the father admitted in court that his son had asked for the gun because he felt unsafe in his college apartment.

BROADWATER V. DORSEY, 688 A.2D 436 (MD. APP. 1997)

The parents of an adult son who had bipolar disorder and addiction disorder were not liable for a car accident that the son caused while driving a car that his parents had given to him eight months earlier. Although the parents knew about their son's psychiatric troubles and his bad driving record, and they continued to house and fund him, the court was convinced that they did not have control over his use of the car once they had signed it over to him.

KAHLENBERG V. GOLDSTEIN, 431 A.2D 76 (MD. APP. 1981)

A father who bought his adult son a car was liable for injuries to the passenger in that car when the son crashed it in a single-car accident just one week after his father bought it for him—before he had even registered it in his own name. The father definitely knew about his son's bad driving record, extremely unstable employment history, and generally irresponsible behavior. The court concluded that he had sufficient knowledge of his son's behavior to be able to predict that his son would not drive safely and that the son would not have had a car if not for the father's gift.

TALBOTT V. CSAKANY, 245 CAL. RPTR. 136 (CAL. CT. APP. 1988)

When a drunk driver killed someone with his car, the friends who had given him that car as a wedding gift, knowing that he was "an adult, licensed, albeit habitually drunk, driver," would have been liable if their gift had been the driver's only means of getting a car.

EDWARDS V. VALENTINE, 926 SO. 2D 315 (ALA. 2005)

The owner of a pickup truck was liable for injuries caused when his brother-in-law drove the truck into another car while he was under the influence of alcohol. The owner did not know that the driver was drunk that day or even that he had the truck, because he was at work when his brother-in-law took the keys. However, he knew that his brother-in-law had used the car before, could access the keys, was often drunk, and did not have a current license due to a DUI conviction.

If you feel confused after reading these case summaries, you are right to feel that way. There simply is no definite rule. Each court compares its current set of facts to earlier cases in that jurisdiction. Sometimes, the personal experiences of the judge and jury affect the case decision. Families just have to know that they can be found liable for harm that results from their gift giving and that they should think about the elements of negligent entrustment before they decide whether it is wise to give the gift.

Tax Facts

- Gift taxes are explained and demonstrated in IRS Publication 559.
- The tax form for reporting gift taxes is IRS Form 709.
- IRS Publication 550, *Sales and Trades of Investment Property*, explains capital gains that taxpayers owe when selling gifts of stock or investment funds.

RESOURCES FOR YOU, YOUR RELATIVE, AND BANKING

1. *American Banker* publishes a very technical "Banker's Glossary" of banking terms online at americanbanker.com. The U.S. Treasury publishes a plain English consumer-oriented banking glossary at helpwithmybank.gov.
2. The Consumer Financial Protection Bureau is a U.S. government entity that provides plain English information about many banking topics, including online banking, convenience accounts, and joint accounts (available at http://www.consumerfinance.gov/).
3. Access state laws about financial institutions and a general introduction to banking law via Cornell's Legal Information Institute at law.cornell.edu.
4. If you ever need to notify the government about a bank mistreating your relative, use the Treasury Department's complaint form at helpwithmybank.gov.
5. The National Down Syndrome Society pushed for the creation of the federal Achieving a Better Life Experience Act (the law establishing ABLE savings accounts), and the society has a thorough portal to state and federal laws about ABLE accounts. See ndss.org.
6. The ABLE National Resource Center has a very informative collection of webinars and case samples, and it links to state ABLE programs as well as articles about ABLE savings accounts at ablenrc.org.

RESOURCES FOR FAMILY FINANCIAL ASSISTANCE, INCLUDING MAJOR GIFTS

1. Federal poverty guidelines are published every year by the Department of Health and Human Services at hhs.gov.
2. Find the current year's SSI limits for cash gifts, income exclusions, and the amount of money that an SSI recipient can earn at the SSA's page about cost of living adjustments at ssa.gov. The list of possessions (and gifts) that do not count against SSI and Medicaid eligibility is also at ssa.gov under the heading "SSI Resources."
3. There is a portal to state laws about RV parks at mobilehome.net.
4. The American Bar Association has a glossary of real estate terms available online at americanbar.org. Navigate to the section on Real Property, Trust, and Estate Law to find the glossary.
5. E. Fuller Torrey's book, *Surviving Schizophrenia: A Family Manual*, includes a thoughtful section titled "Should People with Schizophrenia Drive Vehicles?" It has sensible facts about how that particular mental condition relates to the tasks involved in driving a car.

20

Trusts

Your mother established a special needs trust for your brother Raymond in 1999. She named your Uncle Seamus as the trustee. Now, Seamus is in poor health and has asked you to become the new trustee for Raymond's trust. You are willing to consider it, but you don't even know what this trust is supposed to do for Raymond.

HOW TRUSTS COME INTO EXISTENCE

A trust is created when someone establishes a bank account or investment account under its own identity as a trust account, rather than in the identity of the person whose money is in the account. In other words, the account will be named something like "The Irrevocable Special Needs Trust for Adam Green" or "The Adam Green Irrevocable Special Needs Trust." In these examples, Adam Green is the beneficiary of the trust—the person who will benefit from the money in the account. The trust is called a special needs trust because it satisfies the legal requirements that make it possible for someone collecting certain disability-related federal benefits to have this asset. The trust will be managed by a trustee who will control the way money in the trust is invested and spent. For many special needs trusts, the trustee is a nonprofit disability service organization that operates a pooled trust of its own and perhaps provides trustee services for other kinds of special needs trusts.

If you seek to establish a trust, you are not expected to know all of the mechanics and tactics necessary to set it up. You do need to know that there are two steps in establishing a trust: drafting the trust document and funding the trust.

Drafting the Trust Document

Drafting the trust document is technical work that involves tactical arrangements regarding the beneficiary's physical and emotional needs, other assets available to the beneficiary (including government benefits), the amount of money involved, the beneficiary's family, and tax laws. It has to be done by someone who knows the regulations and formalities, typically a trust attorney (also called an estate lawyer) and who can mesh the regulations with your family's particular circumstances. Here are some ideas for finding the right lawyer to draft a trust:

1. Use the "advanced search" feature in the Martindale Hubbell online legal directory to select the term *trusts* and limit the search to your city.
2. Ask people at NAMI meetings and other support groups about trust lawyers they recommend.
3. Visit the website of the Academy of Special Needs Planners and use its directory.
4. Contact the nearest pooled trust organization and, even if you decide not to get into the pooled trust, ask for leads to local trust lawyers.

Meet with several lawyers and hire the one who best satisfies your criteria for price, communication skills, empathy, patience, competence, and cooperation. You may not be comfortable conveying a lot of personal information in the initial consultation, but you should at least give the prospective trust drafters a sense of what you want them to do. Are you just looking for someone to draft the trust or are you looking for someone who will also serve as the trustee? Do you need a will or some other legal work in order to create the trust or do you really just need the trust? Specify if your relative is on Supplemental Security Income (SSI) so that the lawyers know whether it has to be a special needs trust (and, in that case, only engage a lawyer who has experience drafting special needs trusts). Ask the lawyers to describe their usual process for drafting a trust, and then listen for clues about how much they interact with each family and how well they hear and utilize any facts that you tell them.

Once you hire a lawyer, either the lawyer or a paralegal will communicate with you about the terms of the trust—how you want the trust to function. This will be a back-and-forth process involving several conversations. When the firm has gathered all of the necessary information from you, the lawyer will draft a trust for you to read. Consider this a first draft. You will probably already have previewed separate paragraphs before the full draft was written, but that does not mean that you can no longer edit or question anything. Seeing all of the terms together for the first time, you will almost certainly have some additional ideas or clarifications to include. You may even see that names are spelled wrong or that something was left out that you expected to have in the trust. Mark all of your comments and questions in colored ink on the draft and return it to the lawyer. You may have to go through the editing process two or three times.

Do not sign the trust until it satisfies you. When you are ready to sign it, the lawyer will host a signing ceremony, at which you go to the law firm and have your signature witnessed by the office notary, and then you receive an agreed-upon number of copies in official law firm packaging. If you are dealing with a budget firm that only does document drafting or if you are using a form instead of a lawyer, you can go to any notary to get your signature witnessed on the trust. Bring your passport, driver's license, or other government-issued photo identification with you to the notary's office. Do not sign the trust document until you are in the presence of the notary and the notary tells you to go ahead and sign your name. The notary will stamp, sign, and emboss the trust with their seal after you have signed it. Once that is done, your trust document is complete.

Funding the Trust

You can house the trust fund at any financial institution, such as a bank or an investment company, or, as noted previously, at a local nonprofit if there is one that provides trustee services. When you approach that entity, either in person or online, you will need to present two documents: the notarized trust document and an EIN Confirmation Notice from the IRS. (You will not have to provide these documents if you are entering into a nonprofit organization's pooled trust.) The EIN Confirmation Notice proves that you have created a unique tax identity for the trust. (See the Tax Facts box later in this chapter for more details.) Communicate to a trust officer at the bank, investment company, or nonprofit that you are opening an account for a trust. The trust officer will want to know whether the trust document names a trustee or whether you are asking the financial institution to serve as trustee. The trust officer will take the beneficiary's contact information and the trustee's facts and other details about the trust from the documents and will then have the trustee sign the application. If the institution is providing trustee services, the trust officer will talk you through some additional steps. If this is a third-party trust, either the grantor or the trustee should have an initial deposit ready for the account. The initial deposit can be a small check from a grantor or it can be an account transfer from an account that the grantor owns in the same bank or brokerage. If the private trust is going to be funded by a windfall that is coming to the beneficiary, perhaps a large lump sum of back-due benefits from Social Security, you may be able to establish the trust account before the money is available and without having to immediately deposit money into it. The financial institution should be able to provide the account number and other identifying information so that when the windfall payment becomes available it can be deposited into the waiting account.

Once the trust account is in place, the contributions that people make to it will look just like any other financial account contributions. Someone could write a check out to "The Adam Green Special Needs Trust" and mail it to the trustee, who will then indorse it as "Steve Smith, Trustee for the Adam Green Special Needs Trust account #12345." Someone else could do an account transfer or set up a series of direct deposits into the trust account. Another person may name the trust as beneficiary of a life insurance policy; then, when that person dies, the life insurance company will send the payment check to the trustee, who will deposit it into the trust account. Funding a trust is very straightforward business that will be familiar to anyone with a bank account.

TWO TYPES OF TRUSTS

Federal and state laws authorize a variety of types of trusts. This chapter covers two types: special needs trusts and spendthrift trusts. It also shows how special needs trusts can sometimes be classed as qualified disability trusts. These are the kinds of trusts that most are most commonly useful to people who live with mental illness and they can be combined. In other words, a special needs trust can include clauses that enable it to also serve as a spendthrift trust and/or a qualified disability trust.

SPECIAL NEEDS TRUSTS

Two categories of special needs trusts are authorized by federal law: payback trusts and pooled trusts. Court cases from throughout the country and decided over many years authorize another category—third-party special needs trusts, which are sometimes called "common-law trusts" or "supplemental needs trusts." These different categories of trusts have to comply with different rules, but they all share certain advantages for people who are disabled.

Who is disabled? The federal laws about special needs trusts define disability according to the standards set by the Social Security Administration (SSA). The beneficiary does not need to be collecting disability benefits from SSA in order to have a special needs trust, she is just supposed to have a condition that fits the SSA criteria. The SSA disability regulations recognize a wide array of psychiatric impairments. (See Chapter 2 to read about disability benefits from the SSA.) Suppose your son Ivan does not recognize that he has a mental illness and refuses to seek treatment, but you know that he cannot tolerate other people, experiences frequent delusions, and is not able to focus his thoughts. Since he will not accept psychiatric treatment and therefore does not have a medical record to prove his case in a disability claim, he has not applied for SSI disability benefits. Still, he has the symptoms that you and other witnesses can describe (if called upon) and that are included in the SSA criteria, so he fits the SSA definition of disabled.

The primary advantage of a special needs trust is that it enables the beneficiary to have a source of funding that does not compromise his eligibility for SSI, Medicaid, or other need-based government assistance. Even if the beneficiary does not need the government services but is disabled by his mental illness (perhaps periodically, in between periods when he is able to work) a special needs trust can be advantageous for him. It can:

- Protect his money from predators who may otherwise use undue influence to get access to his money
- Keep money aside for him when he would be tempted to waste it
- Enable him to be eligible for Medicaid during a time when he is collecting Social Security Disability Insurance (SSDI) and is not yet able to get Medicare
- Provide a place for loved ones to deposit funds that will be managed responsibly
- Pay for medical needs (including private health insurance, copayments, noncovered items, and more) as well as other kinds of resources and services that the beneficiary would not otherwise be able to obtain
- Prevent the beneficiary from having to "spend down" his assets if he loses his source of income and does require need-based government benefits in the future.

Special needs trusts also share some limits when the beneficiary is trying to stay eligible for SSI or Medicaid: The money in the trust account cannot be controlled by the beneficiary, even if he owned the money before it went into the trust; the trust money must be used for the sole benefit of the beneficiary; and the trust cannot be revoked (cancelled).

Categories of Special Needs Trusts

A special needs trust can be categorized as a payback trust (also called first party, or self-settled, or d(4)(a) for the law authorizing it) or third party, depending on how it is funded. If the money in the account comes from the beneficiary's own assets, such as her savings account, or assets that are slated to come to her from a windfall, such as an inheritance, a court case, lottery winnings, back pay from the SSA, or a large insurance payment, the trust is a payback trust. If the money in the special needs trust account comes from you or others wanting to set aside money for the person who is disabled, the trust is a third-party trust. Whether the trust is a payback trust or a third-party trust, it may be combined with other people's trusts in one big fund called a pooled trust.

PAYBACK TRUSTS

The phrase "payback trust" means that when the beneficiary dies, money in the trust will be used to pay the state back for Medicaid that the beneficiary received. If there is still money in the payback trust after the beneficiary's Medicaid debt has been paid back, the remaining money can go to loved ones or charities as instructed by the beneficiary when the trust document was written. The instructions for the use of his money after death have to be in the trust document instead of a will because once he puts the money into a special needs trust, he no longer has control over it; the trust controls it. If the beneficiary still had control over the money, it would make him ineligible for need-based government benefits.

Payback trusts are only for beneficiaries who are younger than age sixty-five when the trust is created and whose initial trust funds come from their own money, a windfall, or contributions by their parents, grandparents, or guardians. Money can be added to the trust at different times up until the beneficiary turns sixty-five. After that age, the only money that can come into the trust has to be from an annuity or a structured settlement. Friends and others can make gift contributions to the payback trust, once it has been established, but if the beneficiary dies before spending all of the money in the trust, the gifts will likely end up going to the state as part of the Medicaid payback. Here is an example: If your friend Scott has suicidal tendencies and a bunch of you have taken up a collection totaling, say, $8,000 to give Scott for his fortieth birthday, you will want to see about starting a third-party trust with that money, perhaps as part of a pooled trust, so that it will not go to the state if Scott does commit suicide.

To avoid unintentionally paying money to the state when they intended it for their loved one, many people make small periodic deposits into the special needs trust, rather than putting a large sum into the payback trust or going to the expense of establishing a separate third-party special needs trust. Some people do this simply out of necessity; they do not have a large sum of money. There are also times when people make periodic deposits into the payback trust because making the periodic payments elsewhere was making the person with mental illness ineligible for SSI and Medicaid. This is what happened with Diana, who has very painful arthritis in addition to her bipolar disorder. She can only get pain relief from a new medication that Medicaid does not cover and that costs hundreds of dollars a month. Diana's mother has been paying for private insurance in order for her to have that medicine. She has also been paying most of Diana's living expenses, but she would really like to retire from her job soon and stop having to pay so much for Diana. If she sets up a payback special needs trust and Diana gets on SSI, the SSI benefits will pay for Diana's living expenses and Diana's mom can periodically deposit money into the trust so that the trust can buy the private health insurance that enables Diana to get her expensive arthritis medicine.

Here is something important to know about payback trusts: States have ways of protecting their right to be paid back when the trusts pay for very expensive items. For example, if the payback trust purchases a home or vehicle for the beneficiary, the state may require the trust to place a mortgage on the house or a lien on the car to prevent the family from selling it and keeping the money when the beneficiary dies.

Third-Party Trusts

Families and friends create third-party special needs trusts when they want to set aside their own money in a long-term fund for an adult who has a mental illness. A third-party trust is a demonstration of loyalty. It shows that, at a time when the family (or friend) had extra money, they opted not to spend it on themselves and instead committed it to the future comfort of their loved one with mental illness. Maybe over the years, the family has already supported this person by paying for school, housing, and a couple of cars. And still they put additional assets aside into a trust just in case someday they no longer have extra cash, or they are not around and nobody else steps up to help, or their relative needs something and will not otherwise be able to have it. The trust can be created out of one initial deposit of assets or it can be created in a way that allows subsequent contributions from a defined group of people, such as the family, or from anyone at all who chooses to contribute to the trust.

The person who gives the initial money for a third-party trust and declares that it is to be held in trust for someone is usually called the grantor, although he may also be called the donor or the settlor. The grantor needs to establish the trust during his lifetime in order for it to be a third-party trust. If he merely states in his will that a special needs trust is to be established after his death for his daughter Gayle, who has schizoaffective disorder, Gayle will inherit the money before the trust exists. In other words, the money going into the trust will be Gayle's, not her father's, and then the trust will either have to be a payback trust or a share in a pooled trust.

The grantor does not have to put money into the trust during his lifetime; he merely needs to establish the trust by having the trust document drafted and setting up the account that will eventually receive the funds where the inheritance will be deposited later. Once the grantor puts money into the trust, management fees and taxes can be charged against the trust. Now, it is possible that the grantor will not have access to an institution that will allow him to establish a third-party special needs trust account without immediately putting money into it. In that case, he may be able to deposit a very small amount of money. Whether a deposit is needed and how small that deposit can be are questions to ask at any bank, investment house, or corporate trust establishment (such as a disability service organization that manages trusts) when deciding where to put the trust.

By establishing a third-party trust, the grantor can dictate how the money should be distributed after Gayle's death. For example, Gayle's father could name

Gayle as the primary beneficiary of the trust and Gayle's siblings or children as the secondary (or remainder) beneficiaries upon Gayle's death. The money left in the third-party trust after Gayle's death will then go directly to those people. It will not be used to reimburse the state for medical assistance, as it would in a payback trust, and it will not remain in the pool of money that comprises a pooled trust. If Gayle already has a payback trust, the grantor can instruct, in the document establishing this third-party trust, that the payback trust has to be tapped before this one. For example, if Gayle needs massage therapy that will not be covered by her medical assistance and there is enough money in her payback trust to pay for four massages in the coming month, then the third-party trust money will be available for this treatment only after Gayle has had her fourth massage. Grantors like this type of arrangement because it preserves more of the third-party trust money for other family members in the event that the person with the disability dies before using up the trust fund.

Just as the grantor can control what happens to third-party trust assets after the beneficiary's death, the grantor in this kind of trust also has significant control over how it is used for the beneficiary during her lifetime. When meeting with the lawyer who will draft his third-party trust document, a grantor may, for example, instruct that interest earned by the trust be used to pay for car insurance and other transportation-related expenses. There are two tactical reasons for putting this kind of instruction into the trust: (1) It gives the beneficiary financial assistance for transportation, but is not so limited that it will only pay for specific transportation costs, such as insurance, local rides, or a particular form of transportation, and (2) It sensibly prevents the interest from remaining in the trust where it would be subject to high income taxes. Another interesting effect of this trust instruction is that it does not explicitly prevent the trust from spending additional money on transportation, although it gives the impression that basically transportation payments from the trust should be limited to the interest amount. Some grantors and trust attorneys like this slight vagueness and others prefer to be more concrete.

Grantors who want to either reward or limit a beneficiary's particular behaviors can give instructions about spending the trust money in connection with those behaviors. For example, if Gayle's father knows and does not approve of the fact that Gayle would happily give her last penny to help stray animals, he can instruct the trust to never pay for any animal care. If he wants to encourage Gayle to keep her weight under control, he can instruct the trust to pay for her gym membership or personal exercise equipment. If, instead of establishing a third-party trust, Gayle's father merely contributed money to Gayle's payback trust, which was originally funded by her lump sum of Social Security back pay, he would probably not have the power to put instructions into the trust document.

POOLED TRUSTS

Pooled trusts are managed by 501(c)(3) nonprofit organizations and are especially efficient and desirable for families and beneficiaries who do not have vast amounts of money to put into the trust. First of all, the nonprofit organization operating the pooled trust will have its own master trust document with blank lines to fill in, so the family will not have to pay a lawyer to draft their trust document from scratch. Second, since the investments are managed centrally, each individual trust within the pool pays only a small part of the investment fees. Another benefit of joining into a pooled trust is having reliable and experienced investment management. The nonprofit organization will typically have a contractual arrangement with an investment firm that buys and sells investment shares on behalf of the many separate trust beneficiaries who are in the pool. The board of the nonprofit is responsible for negotiating the lowest possible fee with the investment firm, reviewing the firm's reports, and interacting with the firm about its decisions and operations. A nonprofit organization may also operate a payback special needs trust that will have the same experienced and reliable management.

The money for a pooled trust can come from the beneficiary or his parent, grandparent, guardian, or power of attorney agent, or by order of a court. When a beneficiary is joined into a pooled trust, his money will be invested along with everybody else's money in the trust. His percentage of that very large pool will be separately identified as his or her own trust.

If there is still money left in somebody's pooled trust when he dies, federal law requires that the leftover money go toward paying back Medicaid unless it is "retained by the trust." In other words, that leftover money can remain in the pool for other beneficiaries of the pooled trust instead of being used to pay back the state. State law and rules of the individual nonprofit managing a pooled special needs trust will dictate whether any part of funds remaining after a beneficiary's death will go toward payback.

HOW TO Manage an SSI Overpayment

When someone on SSI has control over more money than the maximum limit allowed by the SSA, which is $2,000 as of this writing, he will become ineligible for SSI until he gets below that amount again. This is a common challenge for SSI beneficiaries who have windfalls coming to them. Suppose we're talking about your sister Jennifer who developed suicidal tendencies after taking a particular medication and is now due to collect settlement money from a class action lawsuit against the drug manufacturer. Either you or Jennifer's trustee can try to shepherd the windfall payment so that it goes directly into her special needs trust. In other words, you would notify Jennifer's lawyer that the payment check should not be made in Jennifer's name; it should be made in the name of the payback trust or pooled trust that exists for Jennifer's benefit and it should be associated with the trust's tax identification number rather than Jennifer's Social Security number. If Jennifer does not already have a special needs trust when she joins into the lawsuit, she can establish one to receive her share of the lawsuit settlement.

The effort to have the money paid into a special needs trust is not an unusual request and most of the people collecting money in the lawsuit will likely ask for their payments to go into special needs trusts, but still the check may be made out to Jennifer. If this happens, Jennifer can endorse it to the name of her special needs trust. In other words, on the back of the check she would sign her name in cursive followed by the phrase "Pay to the order of the Jennifer [last name] Special Needs Trust."

The trust receiving the large amount of money can additionally be identified as a qualified disability trust, which means that the trust is qualified for a tax exemption as long as the beneficiary actually receives either SSI or SSDI disability benefits. If Jennifer does get those benefits and already has a special needs trust but the document that formed it lacks a qualified disability trust clause, you may want to establish a separate trust to receive the windfall in order to save on taxes. Many trust attorneys put a qualified disability trust clause into every special needs trust document just in case the beneficiary someday receives a windfall.

If the windfall has to go to the individual before it gets to the trust (and this may happen if the money is coming from an inheritance or if Jennifer was named as the beneficiary of a relative's insurance policy or investment account) then it will cause her to be ineligible for SSI in the month that the money was under her control—even if the money was only under her control for one day before it went into her trust. In this situation, Jennifer should not keep the disability check that comes that month. You or her representative payee, if she has one, should send it back to the SSA with a note indicating that some money passed through her bank account and on to her trust this month. Keep photocopies of the note, the check, and proof of the trust deposit in case the SSA ever mistakenly claims that Jennifer was overpaid that month. Social Security rules require beneficiaries to report within ten days if they have more than the allowed amount of money. Since it is going to make her ineligible for SSI that month anyway, it is fine to keep the money in the bank, within the same month, and use it to pay the bills that the SSI check would otherwise pay and to buy other items that Jennifer wants or needs. You just want to get it into the trust before Jennifer loses a second month of SSI benefits, and you definitely do not want it to interfere with her Medicaid eligibility.

If Jennifer does not return the SSI check for any months when she is ineligible for SSI, the SSA will discover the overpayment later, when it does a look back. A look back is when they look back over the past two to three years of a beneficiary's medical and financial records to confirm that she is still eligible for disability benefits. If Jennifer did have more than $2,000 (or the current allowed amount) in any months of the look-back period, the SSA will send Jennifer a letter called a "Notice of Overpayment." This letter will advise her that she can ask Social Security to waive the debt that she owes them, appeal their finding that she was overpaid, or do both of those things.

Jennifer will not be expected to pay all of the money back at once or to pay out of pocket. Social Security will collect the money that it overpaid by reducing Jennifer's payments by as much as 10% per month until the debt is paid back. But if you or she requests a waiver or appeal within thirty days, they won't reduce her payments until they reach a decision on the waiver or appeal. So if she ever says anything to you about Social Security threatening to cut her payments, ask her if she got a "notice of overpayment" and make sure that one of you submits the waiver or appeal request in time. If she wants you to help her interact with Social Security and you are willing to do it, then the forms you will need from the ssa.gov website are:

- Form 632—*Request for Waiver of Recovery or Change in Repayment Rate* (if you agree that your relative was overpaid, but hope that they will either waive the repayment or take smaller amounts over a longer period of time) and/or
- Form 561 *Request for Reconsideration* (if you disagree with the SSA and do not think that she was overpaid).

When you request a waiver or appeal, you and Jennifer can choose to submit only evidence or to submit evidence and have a conference with someone from Social Security. Whether she wants a conference or not, Jennifer can review the documents that caused the SSA to believe that she was overpaid. You and she can both look carefully at the documents to see if there are any mistakes (for example, if the record fails to recognize that Jennifer returned an SSI payment in a month when she received money from another source). If Jennifer's mental health symptoms make it hard for her to participate in a conference, she should not feel pressured to have the conference. All she really needs to do is explain her position, and she can do that in writing or she can designate someone else to do the writing. The written part involves filling in a Social Security form and attaching copies of proof. Jennifer may need to provide facts to the person completing the form. Whether or not she is the one who completes the form, she will have to sign the form herself.

If Jennifer does want to have the conference, you or someone else can participate with her. Jennifer can ask to have the conference in person, over the phone, or online. In the conference, an SSA representative will review the list of payments made to Jennifer and the records from her bank or other financial institution as well as any evidence that she has already submitted in writing. They will give Jennifer, and anyone participating with her, an opportunity to tell why she cannot or should not have to pay the money back. You can also bring proof to the conference. Even if you already sent copies by mail, bring to the conference copies of the letter and check that you sent back to SSA in the month that the windfall was temporarily in Jennifer's account and show the trust account statement with the date that the windfall was deposited there. If you have other reasons for asserting that Jennifer was not overpaid or should not have to pay money back, present them as well. Perhaps you have proof that Jennifer had less money than is shown in the Social Security record or that the extra money is not supposed to compromise her SSI eligibility (for example, if it was in an ABLE bank account or was part of a Plan to Achieve Self Support). After the conference, not during it, the SSA representative who participated in the conference will decide whether Jennifer did receive disability money that she was not supposed to get and whether she has to pay it back.

SPENDTHRIFT TRUSTS

Spendthrift trusts are good for adults who do not collect federal needs-based benefits but who sometimes run into trouble with debt collectors and other side effects of overspending. Most spendthrift trusts are third-party trusts, but a spendthrift clause can also be included in a pooled or payback special needs trust for someone who does collect SSI or Medicaid.

A "spendthrift" is someone who tends to waste a lot of money. Whether the spendthrift behavior is part of a manic disorder, or is simply due to a lack of education, or is due to anything else does not matter; nobody has to prove that the beneficiary truly is or is not a spendthrift. In fact, the beneficiary may be completely competent at managing money and the spendthrift trust designation will still be legitimate simply because the grantor believes that the beneficiary wastes money or may be chased by creditors. Designating a trust as a spendthrift trust is often just a cautious way to protect the trust from being drained too quickly. The person who designates it as a spendthrift trust will be either the grantor who provides money to establish the spendthrift trust or the drafter of a special needs trust that includes a spendthrift provision.

A spendthrift trust ensures that the beneficiary will have an ongoing stream of assistance but will not have the opportunity to squander the money—at least not all at once. If the spendthrift trust is a third-party trust with a grantor, the grantor can write into the trust instrument instructions telling the trustee about the wasteful spending she seeks to prevent as well as the range of acceptable spending. In the instructions, the grantor can make firm rules, and she can also convey some guidelines within which the trustee can make decisions.

The firm rules can include landmarks or conditions that the beneficiary has to reach in order to get payments from the trust. The landmarks can be as vague or as detailed as the grantor wants them to be. Here is a very simple landmark:

The trust will deposit into Laurie's bank account $100 per month.

Here is a more elaborate landmark example:

Within one month of the time that Denise completes her college education, the trust will purchase for her up to $1,000 worth of new clothing suitable for job interviewing and wearing to work.

The landmark can even indicate who will actually be paid the money. For example:

When Sachin provides documentary proof, in the form of pay stubs or an IRS W-2 statement, that he has completed one full year of employment in a single job subsequent to graduating from college, the trustee may use this trust to purchase a used car valued at not more than $10,000 for him. The trust payment for the car may be made only to the seller; the money cannot be provided directly to Sachin.

Of course, it is possible that the spendthrift beneficiary will immediately sell the car and use the proceeds for some foolish purpose. This example is merely written to show that a grantor can be as protective as she wants to be.

Another firm rule that a grantor may want to put into a spendthrift trust could be about sharing expenses. This kind of rule requires the beneficiary to raise a certain amount of money in order to get matching funds from the trust. It would say something like:

Funds from this trust may be used for any purchases, repairs, or other expenses connected with Marcus's home or vehicle. However, Marcus must demonstrate to the trustee that he has managed to set aside, from his own funds, half of the price for the service or purchase. If he has set aside sufficient money, the trust will pay for the second half of the service or purchase price.

Again, the trust can declare that it will make a payment on behalf of the beneficiary but not to the beneficiary:

The trust will pay its part of the service or purchase price directly to the vendor upon receiving the vendor's invoice for the actual total price.

Firm rules have to be written so that they will still have meaning as time passes. At one time, a grantor may have said, "Money from this trust may not be used to buy this beneficiary a camera." But now cameras are built into various other electronic devices. Is the trustee supposed to prevent the beneficiary from getting those devices from the trust? The lawyer writing the trust should know how to compose requirements that will stand the test of time.

One of the most common firm rules in a spendthrift trust is one requiring that payouts come only from the trust's interest or dividend earnings, but not from the principal. This may be written as a plain rule:

The maximum total amount that the beneficiary may use from this trust in any given year is the amount equal to the interest, dividends, and capital gains earned on the trust principal during the previous twelve months.

Alternatively, it can be the basis for monthly payments:

Interest and dividends earned by the trust investments will be disbursed to pay the beneficiary's service providers on the last business day of each month.

In addition to firm rules, remember that the instructions in spendthrift trusts will include guidelines. The guidelines should explain when and how the trustee can use her discretion. It is impossible to predict all of the circumstances that will leave the beneficiary in need of money, and it is unwise to make the trust so strict that it cannot help the beneficiary through hard times. The guidelines will give the trustee room to finance the unexpected needs and also to interpret the importance of various opportunities and to adjust with changing times and the beneficiary's mental health fluctuations.

Here are two examples of possible trust guidelines:

The trustee may allocate trust funds for any costs that she considers to be worthwhile investments in the beneficiary's career preparation.

The beneficiary may, from time to time, experience episodes of severe mental illness. During those periods, the trustee may allocate trust funds for nontraditional medical services that the beneficiary requests and that seem likely to provide at least temporary relief. Note that these services might involve nutrition, massage, recreation, acupuncture, or any other scientific or nonscientific means of supplementing standard medical mental health treatments.

One of the most important benefits of a spendthrift trust is that creditors are not permitted to grab the money out of it when they try to collect the debts they are owed. Once the trust makes a payout to the beneficiary, the creditors can try to get it from him, but they cannot get the money that is still in the trust fund. Knowing this, a trustee can make payouts around the beneficiary instead of making them to the beneficiary.

For example, suppose that your sister Babs ran up high credit card bills and now owes a lot of money. Meanwhile, she is in a terrible state of depression and cannot work. Since she is not working and has no job income, she is at risk of losing her apartment because she is not earning money that would pay the rent. If the trustee gives Babs the rent money, the credit card collectors can take it away from her. But if the trustee gives the rent money directly to the landlord, on behalf of your depressed sister, the collectors will not be able to take it because it will not have gone into the beneficiary's possession.

Here is a sample spendthrift trust clause demonstrating how these trusts prevent debt collectors from going after the money in the trust. This clause comes from Appendix 192 of *Revocable Trusts* (5th ed.) by George M. Turner.

The interests of the Beneficiaries in the principal and/or income of the Trust shall not be subject to the claim or claims of their creditors or others, shall not be subject to legal process, and may not be voluntarily or involuntarily alienated or encumbered before actual receipt by the Beneficiary.

A clause like this is likely to be the spendthrift component of a special needs trust that is either a payback trust or a pooled trust. This type of spendthrift clause can be included in any trust, even one that is not written for a beneficiary who wastes money. It is still called a spendthrift clause, no matter what kind of trust it is in, simply because it is designed to keep debt collectors away.

HOW TO Decide Whether To Buy a Tangible Gift or To Contribute To a Special Needs Trust

When someone with a disability collects SSI and/or Medicaid benefits, the following items will not count as assets when the government looks to see if the recipient has more than $2,000 worth of assets. Friends and family can give all of these items as gifts without compromising the person's disability benefits:

- A home and the land that it is on. This can be a stand-alone house, a townhome, a condominium, a mobile home, etc., as long as it is the SSI beneficiary's primary residence. (Refer to the "Major Gifts" section in Chapter 19 of this book to review the legal obligations that donors and recipients of large items like houses and cars can have.)
- If the home is on land that includes an area where edible crops are grown for the people who live in the house, the items necessary for growing the crops (garden supplies, seeds, composting equipment, etc.) will usually not count as assets. Likewise, the government will usually not count the supplies needed for raising animals that the family will eat or for keeping chickens to

get eggs. The animals, themselves, would also be uncounted assets. To confirm whether these gifts will count in your relative's situation, get a written confirmation about your plan for "property used for self-support" from your local Social Security office.

- Household gifts and personal effects. These include furnishings, appliances, electronics, tools, clothing, cosmetics, jewelry, and other items that people would ordinarily have in their home.
- A motor vehicle that the consumer actually uses. The person with the disability does not have to be the driver, just a user. Passengers count as users. The motor vehicle can be a car, truck, van, scooter, motorcycle, etc.
- A burial plot and burial expenses.
- Items that the consumer needs in order to prepare for becoming self-supporting or that he needs in order to continue working or operating a small business. Many people with disabilities do have occupations, even though they are not able to fully support themselves through their work. The types of gifts that people can give to help someone become self-supporting can include the price of getting a professional license or permit, tools, supplies, or uniforms. (Read about establishing a Plan to Achieve Self Support, called PASS, in Chapter 17.)

Financial donations to someone's special needs trust can pay for items that are not included on this list. Since the trust is meant to supplement the assets that are allowed by SSI and Medicaid, trustees have flexibility in deciding how to spend the trust money. (Read about trustees later in this chapter.)

Many people need things that are not in the SSI–Medicaid list of "not-counted" items. Recreation is not on the list, but we all know that recreation can be very helpful in managing mental health. Travel is not listed either, but almost everybody benefits from getting away sometimes. Cosmetic dentistry is another important expense that is not on the list and that can be paid for by a special needs trust. These are just a few examples. The government does not produce a list of legal and not legal purchases that trusts can make.

As explained in Chapter 19, families and friends who are deciding whether to give somebody a very large item, such as a home or a car, should consider whether the recipient will be able to maintain the item and handle the responsibilities that go with it. Sometimes, it makes sense to put the tangible gift into a special needs trust. The item (for example, a house), would then become the property of the trust so that the person with mental illness can live in it and rely on the trustee to manage it. It is possible to establish a separate trust just to pay for managing the house, but it is also possible for the house to become an asset within an existing special needs trust.

Putting a Home Into a Special Needs Trust
Rather than focusing on a house specifically, let's think about putting any type of home into the trust—a condominium, mobile home, townhouse, or detached house. How would the home get into the trust? Somebody can contribute money to the trust so that the trust can purchase the home; a beneficiary can transfer personal ownership of his existing home over to the trust; or a forthcoming

windfall (from a court case or inheritance, for example) can be directed to the trust with the condition that it be used for the purchase and maintenance of a home for the beneficiary.

Once the home is in the trust, the trustee will be responsible for paying for home improvements out of money that is in the trust. The trustee may also take responsibility for routine household expenses, such as utility bills, property taxes, insurance, and lawn mowing, if necessary. When the trust pays for routine household expenses, the beneficiary's SSI money will be reduced by as much as one third, because the SSA will consider the payments from the trust to be "in-kind support and maintenance." If the combined household bills are higher than the amount of the SSI reduction, then it makes sense for the trust to pay them.

If the home is not owned outright by the trust, but instead the trust makes mortgage payments on it, the mortgage payments will also count as in-kind support and maintenance that will reduce the beneficiary's SSI payments. In total, the SSI reduction for in-kind support and maintenance, whether it includes routine maintenance, mortgage payments, or both, will still be no more than one third of the SSI payment. Since the reduction in the SSI payment would be lower than the cost of almost any other kind of housing, even having a mortgaged home in a special needs trust is a good idea for many people—especially those who would have difficulty getting along with others in an apartment building or group home. (See Chapter 22 on housing for a fuller explanation of in-kind support and maintenance.) If the home is owned by the trust, it will have to be sold and used to pay back Medicaid when the trust's beneficiary dies.

For families with sufficient funds and in circumstances when a large-enough court settlement or other windfall is due, putting a home into a special needs trust ensures that the person with the mental illness will have decent housing and will not have to keep up with repairs. However, it does not make sense to put a house into a special needs trust if the trust does not have sufficient funds to keep the house in good shape and pay any related bills that are too high for the beneficiary to pay out of his disability benefits. If the house is falling apart and neither the beneficiary nor the trust can pay the bills, the trust will lose the house, and the beneficiary will lose the shelter and stability that he was supposed to enjoy.

Here is one last consideration about the idea of putting a home and maintenance money into a special needs trust: If the beneficiary is the type of person who does not like to be tied down to a single location, he will likely abandon the trust home (at least for occasional prolonged periods of time). The special needs trust document that puts the home under the trustee's control needs to give directions for handling the property when the beneficiary abandons it. The trustee can be authorized to sell it immediately and keep the proceeds in the special needs trust, or to sell it only after a certain amount of time passes, or to never sell it so that the beneficiary will always have a home available.

This has been a very long answer to the simple question of how someone should decide whether to give a gift directly to her relative with mental illness or put the gift into his trust. The summary answer is that it is good to give directly to your loved one any of the items in the SSI–Medicaid list of assets that are not counted, if he can manage the items and is not likely to abandon them or recklessly sell them. If your family member sells possessions, he may get enough money for them that he will lose his SSI or Medicaid eligibility. If your relative is already pretty well situated with all of the "not counted" items, then a donation to the trust is a good idea, because it can be used for so many additional kinds of purchases and services, and in the future it will serve as a financial cushion if your relative needs something.

THE TRUSTEE

Every trust has a trustee who manages the money in the trust and spends it on the beneficiary's behalf. The trustee may be an individual or a corporation, such as a disability service organization that provides trustee services. An individual trustee does not have to be a professional accountant or lawyer, but he or she does have to be someone who has the time, attention, and intellect to responsibly invest the money, make decisions about payments from the trust, and occasionally interact with government agencies, including the SSA, Medicaid, the Internal Revenue Service (IRS), and possibly the probate court. In consideration of these responsibilities, trustees are entitled to be paid out of the assets of the trust. Most state laws about trustee fees simply say that the fee is permitted to be "reasonable compensation." To get a sense of what counts as reasonable compensation in the local market, you may want to ask friends, colleagues, and support- group contacts about their trustee fees before you agree to hire an individual trustee. If you are considering a corporate trustee, contact a few different entities, maybe two banks and any nearby nonprofit trustees, to compare their rates and services.

Most of a trustee's work is making the day-to-day decisions about how, when, and why money can be removed from the trust. When a special needs trustee decides whether to pay for something using money from the trust, the law expects her to use good care and judgment. Law professor Robert B. Fleming (in an article titled "What Can a Special Needs Trust Pay For?") clarified that courts tend to uphold spending decisions made by a special needs trustee when:

- The expense is permitted within the terms of the trust.
- The payment is truly for something that the beneficiary will use or enjoy to his sole benefit.
- The purchase will not drain so much money from the trust that it will compromise the long-term potential of the trust.
- The expense goes along with a reason that the money came into the trust.
- The trustee has determined that there is no other reasonable way to pay for the item.

Trustees should make the decisions promptly and then arrange for the payment and logistics, if any logistics are needed. For example, if the beneficiary needs furniture, the trustee will need to order the new furniture, direct the seller to send an invoice or receipt to the trustee's address but to deliver the furniture to the beneficiary's address, schedule removal of the old furniture by a disposal service, and pay the disposal service.

The trustee's other major responsibility is to wisely invest the trust's assets so that they are in funds or accounts from which it is possible to remove money without penalty and the invested money will earn income (interest and dividends) for the beneficiary to use. A trustee who manages his cousin's $50,000 special needs trust and puts that whole amount into a Certificate of Deposit (CD) earning .15% interest is not fulfilling his responsibility. The interest rate is so low that it is useless and the bank will charge an early withdrawal penalty whenever he tries to remove money from the CD to buy something for the beneficiary, unless he happens to do it when it is time to renew (or not renew) the CD. In contrast, a responsible trustee is attentive to his beneficiary's typical needs and current circumstances and thoughtfully determines how to keep some of the money easily accessible, perhaps in a bank account, while the rest of the money earns a higher rate of return, perhaps in a mutual fund that is not as convenient or quick to access. This is not the only way to wisely invest trust assets; it is merely one example.

In carrying out the responsibilities related to spending and investing the trust assets, the trustee must always act in the best interests of the beneficiary. This means that he cannot be selfishly cause delays or unnecessary expenses for the sake of his own needs; all of his actions regarding the trust should be concerned with the beneficiary's needs. He has to be honest with the beneficiary and with anyone interacting with him as trustee. The interactions may be with the representative payee who directs the SSI checks, a power of attorney agent, a conservator, or someone representing an institution that provides resources or services to the beneficiary. Finally, the trustee is obligated to inform the beneficiary about the trust—making sure that the beneficiary knows when friends and relatives have deposited money for him, explaining how the investments are doing, giving him routine reminders about how the trust money has been spent in recent months or the past year, and providing other fundamental facts about the trust.

Because the role of trustee requires so much time, attention, and knowledge, and because so many special needs trusts have nonprofit organizations serving as their trustees, family members often leave trustee work to the professionals. Some find other ways to be involved with a loved one's special needs trust: They may just draft a detailed letter informing the trustee about the beneficiary's family context (including names), education, general medical history, preferences, aversions, calming influences, talents, and other characteristics and background facts that could be useful as the trustee decides on investments and payments over the years. Family members can serve as trust protectors, trust advisors, or co-trustees. In any of these roles, family members are likely to:

- Provide facts about the beneficiary to help the trustee make decisions
- Review and comment on the trustee's reports
- Take legal action to change fundamental aspects of the trust, such as moving the investments into a different financial institution or replacing the trustee.

These titles and responsibilities may be defined in the state's trusts code and can be written into the trust document or a note accompanying a pooled trust's master trust document. Family members should not feel pressured to involve themselves with a loved one's trustee. The whole purpose of engaging a trustee is to give that qualified person responsibility; if you do not trust his qualifications, you do not have to hire him, and if there is ever trouble with the trust, you can fight for the beneficiary's rights and needs even if you are not a protector, advisor, or co-trustee.

TROUBLES WITH TRUSTS

When you think about the fact that you must make up a name for your trust and arrange for it to have its own tax identification number, you will not be surprised to learn that in court cases and law books, a trust is a type of legal creature called "a fictitious entity" or "an artificial person." Like a real person, it has a function. For a beneficiary who has a mental illness, the trust's function is to hold funds when either the beneficiary's mental health or his SSI eligibility prevents him from having control over the money. The trust has relationships, too; the trustee and the beneficiary both interact with it. So, it has a recognizable identity, but you can always tell that it is fictitious or artificial because of one thing: it cannot make decisions. The grantor who creates it (unless it is funded by the beneficiary or a windfall and has no grantor) and the trustee who manages it make the trust's decisions. But real people are, after all, only human, and, given that people are not perfect, troubles can arise over the life of the trust.

The troubles will not be the fault of the artificial person, the trust itself, because without the power to make decisions, the trust cannot have done anything wrong. Troubles with trusts are caused by grantors who do not establish effective trusts in the first place and trustees who do not fulfill their duties. A good trustee can sometimes make up for vague or misguided instructions from a grantor. A bad trustee can get in the way of all the good that the trust is supposed to do. There are several known ways for a trustee to do a bad job. He could:

- Use money from the trust for his own benefit, such as when he pays himself a chauffeur's fee every time he gives the beneficiary a ride, even though the bus would be less expensive and more convenient for the beneficiary. This and similar behavior that benefits the trustee more than the beneficiary is called "self-dealing."
- Steal money from the trust.
- Invest the trust's contents irresponsibly.
- Lose track of where the beneficiary is and what he may need.
- Fail to pay for items that the beneficiary is supposed to get.
- Fail to notice an outside interference in the trust, such as cybertheft.
- Fail to file the trust's tax return.

When families and friends discover that any of these things have happened, they can rally around the trust, defending its purpose, either by mending the rift in its relationship with the trustee or else by rescuing the trust from the trustee.

Suppose the beneficiary of the trust is your niece Mim. Your brother was Mim's father, and he established the trust for her when he was dying. Mim has schizophrenia and was able to work full-time for only a couple of years in her early twenties. Since then, she has been on SSI. The trust is supposed to supply Mim with things that she needs and could not otherwise afford. Mim and her father enjoyed music together, and Mim continues to love music and finds it soothing, so it was important to her father and is still important to her well-being that the trust pay for Mim to attend concerts and to acquire any music recordings that she wants, as well as equipment that will play the recordings.

The current trustee is a local family service agency with a rigid new director. He has established a policy that special needs trust money may not be used for anything other than justifiable disability support items, no matter what the trust document says. He does not want the agency opening itself up to liability by mistakenly using trust funds for anything that could compromise beneficiaries' eligibility for SSI or Medicaid. In his view, concert tickets and recorded music are not disability support items. (Nobody knows how or why he came up with this phrase "disability support items.") Mim has not been able to attend concerts or download music since the policy was established. You, as a caring aunt, correctly believe that the trustee is doing a bad job by failing to provide items that Mim is supposed to get. You want to fix the situation so that Mim can get her music.

There are various ways for you to deal with the situation; you can take legal action on Mim's behalf,[1] but you may be able to handle this and other trustee problems with communication skills. Legal action is not always necessary to solve a legal problem.

If you do take legal action when a trustee proves to be, well, untrustworthy, it will typically be a petition in probate court seeking to have the trustee removed. The petition has to show how the trustee's action or inaction has compromised the purpose of the trust. The trustee can respond to the petition explaining why his action or inaction is valid. Then the court will hold a hearing to decide whether to remove the trustee. If the court does remove the trustee, it will then have to appoint another one. If the court does not remove the trustee, it might require the current one to change his practices and to submit routine reports to the judge for a period of time to be sure that he is performing responsibly. No matter how the hearing turns out, there is bound to be bad blood between you and the trustee and significant stress for the beneficiary. In many cases that involve bad trustee behavior other than stealing or unjustly benefiting from the beneficiary's money, it really is not necessary to remove the trustee.

Legal procedures, such as trustee removals, are established in part to put a neutral element between the people involved in a dispute. However, trusts already have

---

1 You may need to be appointed emergency guardian of the estate or emergency conservator in order to sue the trustee on behalf of your loved one. The Uniform Trust Code generally permits beneficiaries themselves to sue trusts, but since beneficiaries of special needs trusts are not permitted to require their trust to pay for something or to revoke or amend their trusts, they will not always be able to take their own legal action against their trustee. When a corporate or agency trustee is as blatantly wrong in its policies as the one in the example of Mim's music, the whole group of beneficiaries who rely on that trustee may be able to bring a lawsuit together on their own behalf.

a neutral element: the trust document itself—the artificial person. So, instead of using the court to authorize a change of trustee, a lawyer or qualified family member representing the beneficiary's rights under the trust may solve the problem by using the trust document to change the trustee's mind or behavior. Most trust documents contain specific words and phrases you can use in influencing the trustee, and there will also be clearly stated intentions that will influence him.

In the example of Mim's music, there is a clause in the trust document calling for the trust to pay for concerts and recordings. The agency director mistakenly believes that his policy (which is based on his fear of breaking the law) is right about what a special needs trust can pay for and that the trust document is wrong. If you can find in the language of the trust a way to go along with his policy, you may be able to solve the problem easily. Mim's father knew that music soothed his daughter, which is why he arranged for the trust to provide her with music. Soothing somebody who has a mental illness seems like an obvious way of satisfying a disability need. Perhaps the rift between the trustee and this particular trust can be fixed with proof that, for Mim, music is a disability need. If her mental health treatment provider can write a letter to the trustee identifying music as a disability need, then the trustee's policy will be satisfied and the trust will be able to pay for Mim's music again, which in turn will satisfy the music clause in the trust—all accomplished without having to go to court.

Another way of using the language of the trust document to influence the trustee's behavior is to use the trust document to explain things to the trustee. Sometimes the explanation will remind the trustee of the grantor's intent, such as: *Mim's father wanted her to be able to enjoy concerts and manage her own playlist; that's why he specified these items in the trust.* You could reinforce this explanation with a touch of guilt: *Can you really live with the fact that you are denying her exactly what her father wanted for her?* It is perfectly fine to make a trustee feel guilty when he has lost sight of what the trust is meant to do and the reminder is necessary to get him back on track. Why file a lawsuit when a guilt trip can solve the problem?

A third way to use the trust document's express statements (and the grantor's intent) is to compare them with examples from experts, such as disability organizations, legal publications, or lawyers. You could do this when you need to convince the trustee that his actions or inactions are wrong and to demonstrate acceptable actions. Regarding Mim's music, you could make this comparison: *You seem worried that the trust document is not legally permitted to authorize payment for concerts and recordings, but several law books and law firm websites show concerts and other entertainment as examples of legitimate expenditures for special needs trusts.* If it is not presented as a put down, the comparison will come across as support for the trustee, the proof that he needs in order to make the right move.

All of these methods of using the trust document are gentler and more efficient than using the probate court. They keep the discussion focused on the beneficiary's needs. And best of all, they enable the trust document, the artificial person that cannot make decisions, to have the last word.

Tax Facts

- The federal government and most states charge income tax on the money that trusts earn. Normally, trustees have to file an annual federal tax return, IRS Form 1041, to report interest, dividends, capital gains, and other income earned by the trust. Trusts pay high income taxes: They do not have to earn very much money before they owe taxes, and their tax rates are higher than the rates that individuals have to pay. Two of the common methods for avoiding very high taxes on a trust are: creating multiple small trusts (a different trust for each purpose or a different trust by each family member who seeks to help the person with mental illness) and making frequent payments out of the trust to, or on behalf of, the beneficiary so that earnings do not sit in the trust for long.

- Earnings that are paid out of the trust either to the beneficiary or on behalf of the beneficiary count as deductions on that year's Form 1041. The payments then count as income on the beneficiary's tax return. Since beneficiaries of special needs trusts always have low income, which is what makes them eligible for SSI, they are in a low tax bracket. Money from the special needs trust may be used to pay the beneficiary's income tax bill.

- There is a special tax exemption for "qualified disability trusts." The tax exemption, like the exemptions on personal income tax returns, is an opportunity to keep a certain amount of money from being counted as income on the trust's tax return. As of this writing, that amount is $4,050. So the first $4,050 of income that the trust earns in a year will not be taxed. The IRS sets the exemption rate each year and publishes it in the instructions for Form 1041 and on the form itself.

- The income tax exemption for qualified disability trusts is in 26 U.S.C. § 642(b)(2)(C)(ii). The Special Needs Alliance (specialneedsalliance.org) has a great, detailed explanation of qualified disability trusts that you can find by typing its title into a search engine: *What Is a 'Qualified Disability Trust' for Federal Income Tax Purposes?* The authors are Ron M. Landsman and Robert Fleming.

- Before you can put assets into the trust, you will need to get a taxpayer identification number for it. This is officially called an Employer Identification Number (EIN). It is the critical proof that the trust is a legitimate separate entity. To apply for your EIN, file IRS Form SS-4. There are a few tricky questions on the form because of all the different players involved in trusts. It asks for the name of the legal entity requesting the EIN; that is the name of the trust. It asks for information about a "responsible party." The trustee is the responsible party. It asks for a "TIN"; this is the grantor's Social Security number.

- The IRS will mail the trustee or the grantor (depending on who filed the SS-4) an EIN document after it has processed the SS-4 form. The EIN document is the official source of the trust's tax ID number and should be stored safely with all of the trust's official paperwork.

- Money from annuities and personal injury settlements does not count as taxable income when it is deposited into a special needs trust. However, the investment income earned on that money will be taxable along with the trust's other investment income. There are many more facts about federal tax issues involved with lump sum deposits in the following article, which is free online from the Special Needs Alliance: Shirley B. Whitenack, "Structuring a Personal Injury Settlement," *The Voice* (February, 2008). The URL to use is specialneedsalliance.org.
- There are dozens of specific tax facts that apply to the various types of trusts under particular circumstances. Please understand that the short list given here merely introduces a few points that are generally useful.

RESOURCES FOR TRUSTS

1. The Arc maintains a list of affiliates throughout the United States that provide trustee services on special needs trusts (the list is available at thearc.org). See also the Directory of Pooled Trusts compiled by the Academy of Special Needs Planners at specialneedsanswers.com.
2. The Special Needs Alliance publishes a free detailed manual called *Administering a Special Needs Trust: A Handbook for Trustees.* See specialneedsalliance.org.
3. The American College of Trust and Estate Counsel has links to professional tools that are used in trust creation and management as well as a directory where you can find local trust lawyers at actec.org.
4. The Martindale-Hubbell directory for finding lawyers is at martindale. com.
5. *Revocable Trusts*, by George M. Turner (5th ed., Danvers, MA, 2003) is a huge and detailed loose-leaf service that is updated regularly. This source is quoted in the section of this chapter about spendthrift trusts.
6. The SSA publishes its technical rules for special needs trusts in Section SI 01120.203 of the Program Operations Manual at secure.ssa.gov.
7. For many more details about pooled trusts, see *Pooled Trust Programs for People with Disabilities: A Guide for Families,* published by The Arc (2002). The guide is now available from Life's Plan, an organization in Illinois that coordinates care and trusts for adults with disabilities, at www. lifesplaninc.org/wp-content/uploads/2016/07/pooledtrustprogramsguide1. pdf.
8. There is much to learn about financial issues and special needs trusts. The Academy of Special Needs Planners is a professional association of financial experts, lawyers, and trust officers who have compiled a lot of this information on a website titled *Special Needs Answers.* See specialneedsanswers.com.
9. A very practical book to have on hand is *The Special Needs Planning Guide: How to Prepare for Every Stage of Your Child's Life*, by John W. Nadworny and Cynthia R. Haddad (Brookes Publishing, Baltimore, MD, 2007).

10. The SSI lists of assets that do not count against a disability recipient are on the SSI Resources page at ssa.gov.
11. Robert B. Fleming's article "What Can a Special Needs Trust Pay For?" is in the March 2008 issue of *The Voice*, a newsletter published by the Special Needs Alliance. It is available online at specialneedsalliance.org. The newsletter has many other informative articles about special needs trusts as well.
12. The federal law authorizing special needs trusts is 42 U.S.C. § 1396p. Find it online at http://www.uscode.house.gov. You will see that payback trusts and pooled trusts are explained in subparts of the statute. Spendthrift trusts are codified in § 502 of the Uniform Trust Code. The Uniform Trust Code is a model law that many states have adopted into their own laws. It can be found online at http://www.uniformlaws.org/shared/docs/trust_code/utc_final_rev2010.pdf. The law about qualified disability trusts is at 26 U.S.C. § 642(b)2(C).

21

Supportive Money Management

Your niece Fatima's impulse control disorder has put her at odds with just about everyone except for the charities; she can never say "no" to any charity that calls and asks for a donation. Meanwhile, the grocery store manager asked her not to come in again after the last time, when she accused a checkout clerk of not giving her the right discounts. Her condo board made a new rule limiting unit owners to speaking at no more than three meetings per year after Fatima disrupted so many meetings that no other unit owner could get a word in. She, in turn, kept getting fined and frustrated whenever she attempted to withhold her condo fee as a nonverbal way of protesting something the board was doing. Eventually, Fatima gave you power of attorney to handle her condo fees and other condo obligations. She was on the verge of walking away from her commitment to phone, cable, and Internet service until her therapist used supportive decision-making to help her think about priorities regarding those services. It seems that you, the therapist, and the other people who care about Fatima are forever having to "put out fires" that she starts in her various consumer interactions. Her financial behavior has become so irregular that you never know if she is going to continue getting the basic goods and services that she needs. You think it may be time for a conservator to start managing Fatima's financial responsibilities.

FINANCIAL POWER OF ATTORNEY

Financial power of attorney is the power to make financial arrangements and sign financial documents on behalf of another person. The person giving the power of attorney is called "the principal." The person taking the power of attorney is called "the agent." In other words, the person with serious mental illness is the principal and the person appointed to represent her is the agent. Sometimes the phrase "attorney in fact" is used instead of "power of attorney." Other powers of attorney exist to make health decisions. (Those powers are covered in Chapters 1 and 4 of this book.) It is possible for a beneficiary of Supplemental Security Income (SSI) or Social Security Disability Insurance (SSDI) payments to have a representative payee (Chapter 2) to handle disability payments in addition to someone with power of attorney for handling other financial matters.

Financial power of attorney status is granted in a contract between the principal and the agent; it is not something that happens in court. Most states have laws in place to protect principals from being tricked or not fully realizing how much power they are giving away. Here are some typical requirements in the laws:

- One or two witnesses also have to sign their names on the power of attorney contract. The witnesses should not be biased toward either the principal or the agent and should understand that they are witnessing an agreement that neither party is being forced or misled into signing. If a witness thinks that something is wrong, he can refuse to sign, which will make the whole deal fall through, at least until the parties find another witness.
- The contract has to be notarized. This means that the principal, the agent, and the witnesses all have to sign at the same time in the presence of a notary. The notary's seal is an attestation that the document was not forged because the signatories have shown credible proof of identification and have signed their names in the notary's presence.
- The contract should warn the principal and the agent that the legal system will uphold their agreement.
- The agreement has to include the date when it was signed and include the date or the circumstances when it will become effective. It can be effective immediately. It can be effective from the tenth of this month until the tenth of next month. It can be effective only during periods when the principal's psychiatrist declares him to be in specifically bad condition. It does not have to identify an end date, although it should have one if the principal expects to need the agent for only a limited period of time.

A principal who cannot, or who chooses not to, manage particular financial situations by herself should make this contract only with someone who is competent, honest, and willing to handle the responsibility. The agent with power of attorney is then empowered to take action on behalf of the principal in the way that the principal would. The agent does not get to override the principal's decisions, although he has to act in the principal's "best interests" and can avoid carrying out the principal's very bad decisions.

Note: As also mentioned in Chapter 1 of this book—which discusses the durable power of attorney for health care and related decisions—a power of attorney can be granted only by someone who has the mental well-being to make sound decisions. When someone is not able to make sound decisions, families, caseworkers, or other caring people can petition the probate court to appoint a guardian to make healthcare decisions or a conservator to make financial decisions for the person who cannot do it. Guardianship (covered in Chapter 3) and conservatorship (discussed later in this chapter) come with court authority and oversight that do not apply to power of attorney agreements. A person can revoke or ignore a power of attorney; he does not necessarily lose the right to act on his own accounts or contracts just because he has granted power of attorney to someone else. Guardianship and conservatorship, on the other hand, can be modified or ended only by a court order.

What Kind of Power Does a Financial Power of Attorney Grant?

Financial power of attorney can be granted for any range of financial dealings that the principal desires. The contract between the principal with mental illness, say your grandmother with clinical depression, and the agent, let's say you, can specify particular accounts, particular financial institutions, certain types of money management (stock trades, for example), full power to sign and make all of the principal's financial transactions, or even power to handle one single transaction.

To be sure that the state's legal requirements are satisfied and that the power of attorney document has all of the necessary details, your grandmother (the principal) and you (the agent) should meet together with a lawyer to plan the power of attorney and to arrange for the lawyer to put it in writing. Once the document is ready to be formalized, the lawyer will have a signing ceremony to satisfy the legal requirements about witnesses and notarization. Either state law or the agreement itself will establish a system for you to regularly report to your grandmother regarding how and when you use the power and to inform her about her current money situation.

Power of Attorney for Financial Decisions

Financial power of attorney can be a facet of an existing financial power of attorney through which the agent routinely manages particular financial matters or it can be in place for only those times when the principal is in a bad episode. When it is written to cover periods of severe mental illness, it gives an agent responsibility to act as power of attorney when the principal lacks legal capacity or does not have the attention, focus, rationality, desire, or other mental attributes necessary to know what the agent is doing. The principal does have to be sufficiently mentally engaged when he appoints the power of attorney. The idea behind the appointment is that the principal can anticipate times when he will experience such severe mental illness that he will not be able to handle accounts or transactions and he wants to be sure that his agent is committed to handling them for him.

If the power of attorney is meant to apply only when the principal is unwell, it may be officially termed "springing power of attorney" or "conditional power of attorney" and its message will be "My agent has power of attorney to manage my checking account only when I am in an episode of severe mental illness."

The power of attorney document will then explain how the agent, and others, will know that the principal is in an episode of severe mental illness. During the episode, the principal's durable power of attorney for medical decisions will also become active. (Read about that in Chapter 4, which covers psychiatric advance directives.)

There are various ways to demonstrate that a principal (your grandmother, for example) is ready for the power of attorney to be activated. The power of attorney document may say that the power will be activated when your grandmother cannot make or communicate decisions. That is not an especially clear indicator, but it can work, since the phrase represents a legal standard. In a better statement, the document will identify a particular assessment method, perhaps the Financial

Capacity Instrument, the Financial Competence Assessment Inventory, or parts of the Multidimensional Functional Assessment Questionnaire. All of these methods measure the ability to handle basic financial management. Unfortunately, they all require that the principal sit with a forensic psychology assessor and answer questions, which may not be possible during an episode of mental illness.

As an alternative, the power of attorney document (and a confidentiality release form) can say that your grandmother's therapist is authorized to notify you when your grandmother reaches the point of needing you to make her financial decisions. Of course, if grandma is so depressed that she has stopped going to therapy, this may also be impossible. The work-around for this possibility is to generically state that the power will become effective when a licensed therapist or physician verifies that the principal is not currently able to make financial decisions or handle financial transactions. That way, a doctor or therapist at the hospital or her general medical practitioner can provide the verification.

If the principal is so "out of it" that the agent believes it is time to step in, there is a good likelihood that the principal will either not realize that the power of attorney has become active or will not object to it. Her attention will be elsewhere and you will be able to handle legitimate transactions without having to explain the transfer of power. The document establishing the power of attorney will be sufficient authority for you to act on behalf of your grandmother. As long as you manage grandma's affairs responsibly, keep accurate, clear records for her to see once she sufficiently recovers, and only take actions that are permitted by the power of attorney, you should not run into any legal trouble.

What Do Power of Attorney Contracts Look Like?

Here is an example of a limited power of attorney: Suppose that a consumer (Steve) is burdened by debt and other pressures. He wants to sell his car but does not want to have to deal with selling his car. He can appoint someone (his brother Mike, in this example) as power of attorney just for the sale of the car. This appointment should be made in a detailed written agreement listing exactly which responsibilities the principal is relinquishing to the agent. The agreement must be clearly titled "Power of Attorney," it must be signed by Steve and Mike, and it must comply with all of the state's legal requirements. It would say something like:

> *Steve Jones appoints Mike Jones power of attorney to sell Steve's 2013 Volkswagen Jetta. Specifically, Mike is empowered to: investigate comparable cars (same make, model, vintage, and condition) on the market in order to establish a fair price for the car, advertise the car, accompany possible buyers on test drives of the car, negotiate the price of the car, transfer the title of the car, and utilize the services of the American Automobile Association to properly execute all of the car sale documents required under state law. Mike has no power of attorney over any of Steve's finances or property outside of this list of responsibilities that are specifically connected to selling this car. In exchange for serving in this capacity, Mike will be reimbursed (from the final sale income) for any out-of-pocket expenses that he incurs in connection with advertising, showing, or selling the*

car AND he will receive 10% (ten percent) of the final sale price in payment for his services. This power of attorney terminates upon successful sale of the car.

Here is a banking example: Suppose that someone with major depression has just been through a miserable divorce, a rotten debt-repayment period, or other bad financial situation. The person (let's call her Joan) still has a bank account, but she simply cannot face anything having to do with money, and she does not want to have to deal with her money at any point in the foreseeable future. She has asked her sister Victoria to take over her bank account, manage all of her payments, and just give her $20 a week for pocket money. The power of attorney between Joan and Victoria would probably have clauses like these:

This power of attorney is exclusively applicable to account #98765 at Porcine Bank in Anytown, USA, hereinafter known as "the bank account." The bank account belongs to Joan Ramos, principal. In accordance with state code section 12345, the agent [Victoria Ramos] is authorized to conduct the following transactions involving the bank account:

Writing and signing checks.

Writing and signing withdrawal slips.

Arranging and modifying automatic bill payments.

Endorsing and depositing any checks made out to the principal.

Conducting all types of online banking transactions.

Additionally, the agent is authorized to make administrative changes to the account, such as:

Implementing a new password or other security measures.

Ordering new checks.

Reconciling the account.

Interacting with the bank about any of its rules or practices involving the account.

The agent must pay from this account at least $20 in cash per week to the principal for any use that the principal desires. The amount may be renegotiated upward over time and it may be supplemented on any occasion upon the request of the principal as long as the account contains sufficient funds to fulfill the request. However, supplemental payouts will not be made to the principal when they will compromise her finances to the extent that she will not have enough money to pay for her necessities and current bills.

This power of attorney shall remain in effect until:

It is revoked by the principal.

The principal dies.

A court orders its revocation.

Financial institutions generally have their own forms on which account holders appoint powers of attorney. The forms are meant to ensure that the staff knows exactly where to look for particular information and that legal requirements are met. Account holders and agents should expect to complete the form at the financial institution in the presence of at least one employee. However, there is no rush. Anyone can pick up a blank form in advance so that the account holder and agent can discuss it and complete a first draft at home before filling in and signing the final form at the financial institution.

HOW TO Be a Good Agent

- Use the proper signature—Sign all documents with your own name "as power of attorney for" the principal. Literally, every check and other document should say "John Smith as power of attorney for Ann Jones" (although the names should be the principal's and yours as the agent). This is the correct way to show the authority under which you put your signature. When documents are signed this way, it is clear to anyone who sees the signature that you are an agent acting in the principal's interests and not in your own interests. In other words, it will not appear as if you are taking control of the principal's money for your own benefit.
- Never assume anything—Making assumptions about the scope of your power is a way to take on problems that you do not need to deal with. Making assumptions about your relative's motivation or planning is also risky. You may want to establish a routine set of questions that your principal has to answer before you will agree to act on anything for her. These can be questions like: *What are the prices of two comparable items and why do you want this one instead of the other? Is there anything significant about the timing of this transaction? Is anyone trying to pressure us into this?* Maybe you can simply convey that, since you never want to make any assumptions, she has to provide you with a justification every time she asks you to handle a transaction.
- Expect that you will get blamed for guessing incorrectly—If you ever have to guess whether it is right or wrong to pay for something, just expect that at some point the principal (for example, your stepbrother with bipolar disorder), will blame you for deciding either to pay or not to pay. Maybe he needed a new phone and somehow a salesperson convinced him to get a ridiculous long-term usage plan that included insurance and all kinds of extras with the elaborate phone that he picked. You thought it was extreme, but the monthly payments were manageable and so you signed the contract. Six months later, your stepbrother wants a different phone plan and says it is your fault that he is trapped in the long-term plan because you signed the agreement. That is just the way it is going to be: You will rarely be able to convince him that something else is more sensible, and then he will change his mind after you have followed his instructions and made a commitment on his behalf.
- Remember that the principal is not able to manage money responsibly— You, as the agent with power of attorney, have to serve as responsible eyes and ears for the principal. Make the principal provide you with proof and

background information when she tells you that she needs money for something big. Do not sign any payment agreements for her unless you are very comfortable with the terms and you are certain that there will be enough money to make the payments on time.

- Know and follow all of the guidelines granting you power of attorney—No matter how much you are pressured, look in your power of attorney document for confirmation that you are allowed to do whatever you are being asked to do—especially when you are asked to do something surprising. This should not take you a lot of time and it should not require major analysis. You should be able to handle it on the same day that the principal requests your assistance. If you are not convinced that the document gives you the power to take a particular action, such as getting a loan, selling something, or entering into a credit agreement, then do not take the action. Simply say, "I cannot agree to that; it is outside of my power." If the document requires you to take certain steps before you do something, such as collecting bids and checking references before hiring someone to do work on the principal's house, then inform the principal, in writing, that you are going to take those steps, and then keep proof as you go through the steps.

- Use the power of attorney document as your shield if ever you are accused of wrongdoing in your role as agent—The person most likely to accuse you of wrongdoing is the principal. She may file a court case accusing you of stealing or wasting her money. If she is so unable to deal with finances that a conservator is appointed to replace you, the conservator may bring a legal claim against you for mismanaging funds. It is also possible that other family members or a caseworker will file a petition in the probate court requiring you to provide a detailed record of all the transactions you have managed in your agent role. No matter who brings the legal claim or what legal rule it is based on, your first line of defense will be to show that you were acting within the power given to you in the power of attorney document. If you relied on an unclear part of the document, but you can show that you consulted with the principal or someone knowledgeable about that kind of spending, or that you shopped around, or that you did some other sort of research before taking action, your claim of satisfying the document will be more convincing.

Violating the Power of Attorney

The usual claim against people who do not fulfill contractual duties is a breach of contract claim. But when someone breaches his responsibilities under a power of attorney contract, he can also be liable for various civil and criminal offenses associated with misappropriating funds. The possible criminal charges against an agent who misuses the principal's money are violations of specific state statutes regarding agents, as well as theft and fraud. Theft, of course, is taking the other person's money. Fraud is intentionally misrepresenting important information in a way that causes somebody to suffer; in this relationship, the misrepresentation would cause the principal with mental illness to suffer. Fraud can be a criminal court claim, for which the agent may have to go to jail, as well as a civil court claim, for which the agent may have to pay money.

The major categories of civil court claims against agents accused of breaching their financial powers of attorney include conversion, negligence, and breach of contract:

- Conversion is turning someone else's money into your own money. An example of this would be an agent who uses the principal's bank account to purchase gift cards that could be used for the principal's needs but that are really used only for the agent's own purchases.
- Negligence is causing harm to the principal by failing to uphold duties that are established in the power of attorney document. If the agent is responsible for handling bank deposits, an example of being negligent would be losing and not depositing the principal's Internal Revenue Service (IRS) tax refund check and then not taking steps to get a replacement check. The agent's duties also include acting in good faith, demonstrating loyalty to the principal's needs, and avoiding conflicts of interest. An example of violating these duties would be when an agent uses his principal's money to support (buy things from) a business that the agent and his family operate. This is a conflict of interest and is contrary to the principal's needs if the principal really does not need the business's products and if the agent is working for both the business (as a seller) and the principal (as a buyer) at the same time.
- Breach of contract is failing to do the tasks that are identified in the power of attorney document, such as failing to file forms that are required by a government office—if the power of attorney document requires the agent to file the forms.

Agents are entitled to make honest mistakes, just like everyone else. The list of possible court claims shows how easily certain behaviors can make an error look like a rip-off. An agent who uses the principal's bank account or credit cards to give money to himself looks suspicious. An agent who uses the principal's money to hire members of his family (the agent's family) to "work" for the principal also looks suspicious. An agent who cannot answer questions or provide documents about the financial matters that he is supposed to manage justifiably appears suspicious. Avoid suspicion by using proper signatures, correcting your errors, doing only what you are authorized to do, and submitting thorough, regular reports to the principal, the court, or whomever else you are obligated to inform.

Tax Facts

- Taxpayers who want to appoint someone to handle their communications with the IRS have to file IRS Form 2848. This is the IRS's own specialized power of attorney form.
- There are circumstances when the IRS will accept "a non-IRS power of attorney." Instructions for this are included in IRS Publication 947, *Practice Before the IRS and Power of Attorney.*

SUPPORTED DECISION-MAKING

Many people have a "brain trust" or an "inner circle"—a handful of people whom they bounce ideas off. These relationships are often informal and imperfect. The person at the center—for example, your best friend Lisa, who has a binge eating disorder—may know that some folks in the circle (maybe her parents) will force unwanted advice on her. She can predict how her siblings will respond to her quandaries because she knows their standard perspectives. She may regret asking for opinions when it happens that any of these people try to take over, rather than just give the opinions that were asked for. She may worry that she is bothering you when she asks for input. To avoid these interpersonal burdens, Lisa can formalize her brain trust or inner circle with a supported decision-making agreement.

A supported decision-making agreement is a legal contract between someone who has difficulty making decisions and supporters who are willing to assist her with decisions. The assistance could involve brainstorming about possibilities, researching facts, prioritizing tasks and choices, or organizing ideas and information. Lisa has a brother with natural investigative skills, so she may ask him to handle the research end of her decisions. Since you are her best friend—and you are great at making lists and charts—you may be chosen to become the data organizer. Perhaps Lisa would rather organize her team according to categories of decisions, rather than according to skills. One supporter could consult on housing issues and another on shopping decisions, for example. It is also entirely possible that a decision maker like Lisa only needs one other person to support her in decision-making, rather than having a whole team.

Like many contracts, a supported decision-making agreement can be as flexible as the parties need it to be. The idea is to structure a system for the decision maker and her supporters to follow. Each supporter should have an independent contract with the decision maker. An individual supporter's promises in the agreement will be about the range of skills that he plans to supply, the topics he will deal with, his diligence, and his availability. He should promise to be as careful with the decision maker's circumstances as he would be with his own and to be prompt in dealing with decisions.

The decision maker's promises will be about her treatment of the supporter and her use of his services. For example, Lisa could promise that she will always give her supporter at least one full week to participate in each decision, as opposed to expecting immediate action. She could promise that she will not hold him financially liable for negative outcomes of decisions that he supports. Together, they will come to terms about what to do if the supporter is not available when she needs him. They will agree on a way to move forward when they cannot agree, perhaps deciding to involve a particular agency to help them through their discussion. They will formulate a termination clause so that they both know how and when to notify the other that they are ready to end the agreement.

There are free samples of supported decision-making agreements online, but the examples are extremely simple. Decision makers can recruit an organized professional, such as a caseworker, lawyer, or businesslike neighbor, to draft a personalized agreement that arranges for exactly the assistance they need while recognizing their autonomy and giving both parties a fallback plan if the other neglects a promise. The plan will likely be about repairing the situation, not about penalizing the person who breaks a promise. For example, there may be a phrase entitling Lisa to seek help from an alternate supporter if the designated supporter does not do the work within ten days. There may also be a phrase entitling the supporter to get out of participating in a decision if the decision maker nags him or does not provide complete background information about the pending decision.

The person who is drafting the agreement may recommend having several meetings with at least the decision maker in order to develop the agreement in layers. If the drafter is charging money to make the agreement (a lawyer is likely to charge) and it is too expensive to pay for that person's time at multiple meetings, decision makers and supporters can provide the drafter with a list of their desired terms at the first meeting and then ask if they can edit and comment on the first draft by email, rather than having to pay for another appointment in addition to the document fee. Having multiple meetings may also cause too many distractions and complications for someone who has trouble making decisions. Lawyers who write these agreements are specialists in elder law and disability law, and they should be flexible about arrangements. Decision makers and supporters can expect the lawyer to tailor the drafting and discussion process to their needs.

If the decision maker has a team of several supporters, she will probably be able to have the drafter establish one standard agreement that only needs to be slightly modified and separately printed for each supporter. When the document is completed, the decision maker and supporter(s) will sign their individual agreements. This final formality seals the bargain, making it binding and legitimate. Neither party will ever suffer serious punishment for breaching the contract because it rests entirely on trust and respect. Much of the trust and respect will have developed through the process of drafting the agreement and making it official.

What Do Supported Decision-Making Contracts Look Like?

Since the core purpose of a supported decision-making contract is to recognize that the person with mental illness is planning to make her own decision, the contract should begin by identifying her and stating her purpose. Here are two examples of the opening of a supported decision-making contract:

1. *I, Meredith Scott, am no longer happy working as an insurance office receptionist. I have the organizational and communications skills to work in a different environment and would like very much to work for a performing arts organization, possibly at the box office or behind the scenes. I am just not sure if it makes sense to change jobs right now and I don't know how to make this kind of change or what to say to my current boss.*
2. *This document is between Alan Wang, Ray Berty, and Kenny Wang. Alan seeks to make new plans for his daily transportation between the Fairweather Lodge where he lives, the Finer Points Auto Detailing shop where he works, and the Slide Hill Recreation Center where he hangs out.*

Next, the contract can introduce the people who will provide the decision maker with support.

1. *My friend Andrea, who is a librarian at the Pine Park Branch Library and my sister Gwen, who both have lots of job experience and are good at planning things, will help me to make this job transition. Andrea will help me find job ads and examples of letters that people write when they are changing jobs. Gwen will help me put together a resume and will practice job interview questions with me so that I will get to talk about this decision with her while I apply for jobs.*
2. *Ray is a caseworker at Winding Vine Behavioral Health. He has helped lots of clients to select from local transportation options and plan their commuting routines. Kenny is Ray's cousin and he operates a local ridesharing service. He has resources and industry contacts and believes that he can help Alan to avoid the crowds and waiting that bother him about public transportation at certain times of day.*

Now that the participants and their roles have been introduced, the contract should outline the plan. The plan may list the steps that the decision-making team will use, establish goals and deadlines, set a meeting schedule and general landmarks that the team hopes to achieve, or it may explain the team members' tasks.

1. *Andrea, Gwen, and I will meet at the library every Saturday afternoon at 2:00 for the next six weeks. After that, I will meet separately with Andrea and Gwen on a schedule that we will work out later. At the end of each library meeting, Andrea will give me at least one book to look through for the following week. She and Gwen will both give me practice tasks. I will bring the completed tasks to each meeting after that. By the end of the first six weeks, I hope to have a plan for when and how to change jobs and to have a system in place for responding to job ads. From then on, Andrea and Gwen will be on call to help me decide what to say in individual cover letters, interviews, and other job change communications.*
2. *Alan, Ray, and Kenny have already discussed Alan's transportation needs. Kenny is building a mobile app that will enable Alan to know whether a bus or train is nearby and how crowded it is. If the public transportation options are too crowded or not on schedule to reach him within ten minutes, the app will ask him if he wants to check with Kenny's ridesharing service. Kenny is prepared to provide Alan with a gift of four free rides per week in his ridesharing service. Between now and when Kenny's app is ready, Ray will take practice rides on public transportation with Alan and help him to arrange a work schedule that enables him to ride at off-peak times.*

The supported decision-making agreement should close with a statement about how the participants will finish their work together or else how they will manage an ongoing system of supported decision-making.

1. *Once I have completed my successful job transition, this contract will end.*
2. *When the app is functional and Alan is comfortable using it, Kenny will no longer be involved in Alan's transportation planning. Ray, in his capacity as Alan's caseworker, will continue to work with him on a weekly*

basis to coordinate his job schedule with rides, recreation, and curfew at Fairweather Lodge.

CONSERVATORSHIP

Conservatorship is court-ordered management of somebody else's money. Families seek conservatorship when a relative with mental illness has thwarted their more gentle efforts to help him manage. He has run up bills, emptied the joint account, ignored the power of attorney, failed to cooperate, and violated trust. Whether or not his misbehavior was intentional, it is time for somebody to take over.

Conservatorship is the financial version of guardianship. In some states, a conservator is called "guardian of the estate" and the guardian who manages health decisions is called "guardian of the person." When one person is responsible for both types of guardianship, he may be called the "plenary guardian." When separate people serve as guardian and conservator, they will need to jointly plan for situations in which their responsibilities overlap—for example, when the guardian is responsible for taking the person for medical tests and the conservator needs to arrange payment for the tests. (Refer to Chapter 3 of this book for more on guardianship.)

In order to get a conservator appointed for someone who has a mental illness, it is first necessary to convince the court that the person is no longer competent to manage his own finances—that he is "incompetent" or "incapacitated." This is a miserable, nightmare-inducing process. It requires the family to testify about foolish and embarrassing times when the unwell relative, let's say your father Jasper, has wasted money or missed bill payments—dumb things that anyone can do but that your dad has done so many times that his well-being is compromised. The family has to show a pattern of financial misbehavior that is not merely unorganized or even irresponsible but is so irrational that Jasper has to be characterized as incapacitated.

Petitioning To Have a Conservator Appointed

The process begins with a petition to the court, usually probate court. The petition may be called something else depending on where the person needing help lives; basically, it is a fill-in-the-blank form that is typically available on the local or state court system's website. You, the coping relative—tired of helplessly watching your unwell father's financial failures and avoidable complications—may be able to complete the form on your own, if you are generally comfortable doing that sort of thing. You will benefit from a lawyer's guidance as the process goes forward, and for the sake of efficiency, you may want to bring the completed form to your first meeting with the lawyer. You will want to hire a lawyer who specializes in elder law or disability law to submit the petition to court and to represent your assertions that your loved one is incapacitated and in need of a conservator in all of the court communications that follow your petition.

The first part of the form is fairly straightforward. It asks for facts: names, birthdates, and other facts. It will invite the petitioner (the person filling out the form) to nominate himself or someone else to serve as conservator. Eventually, the form will ask for descriptions of the unwell relative, examples of his financial ineptitude, and an explanation of his mental problems. Nobody can complete the form without feeling conflicted. The only way to succeed in the petition (and ultimately help to protect your dad's finances) is to make him look bad.

It costs a lot of money to bring an incapacity case—about $1,000 in many jurisdictions. That money has to be paid up front by the petitioner; it should not come out of money belonging to the person with mental illness. Petitioners who cannot afford the court costs can attempt to get them reduced or waived, but they should be aware that the high fees exist, in part, to prevent families from bringing false claims.

Once the petition is submitted, the court will seek proof of the claims that are stated in it. The judge will collect opinions from other family members, copies of financial records, and statements from mental health treatment providers. The judge may have a forensic psychologist analyze the person with mental illness for financial functionality and judgment. The judge will make sure that person who is unwell, known as the respondent in the case, is represented by a lawyer.

If the respondent does not have the wherewithal—financial, mental, or otherwise—to find a lawyer, the court will likely urge family members to help find a good lawyer for the person and may refer them to a legal aid office with expertise in conservator law. Some courts will be able to appoint a free lawyer to defend the respondent. As the court compiles information about the respondent's functional abilities and his family dynamics, this lawyer representing the person with mental illness will receive copies of everything. It is critical that the respondent have this advocate sticking up for him and watching out for his interests. The court will require the lawyer to keep the respondent informed and to report back to the court with any insights. Then, when the background research is finished, the court will schedule a conservatorship hearing.

The Hearing on Capacity and Conservatorship

On hearing day, the lawyers and parties all arrive dressed up and ready for their opportunity to be heard. In our ongoing example, you are the well family member (known as the petitioner in the hearing), and you come to the hearing in the spirit of helping your father, Jasper, but you probably also feel a sense of dread: You are an opponent here, accusing your poor, sick dad of reckless, embarrassing behavior, aiming to take away most of his decision-making power, publicly declaring that he cannot control himself, and knowing that if you succeed today, your reward will be permanent responsibility for depriving Jasper of financial independence.

The respondent (your father) will likely come to the hearing feeling defensive, disillusioned, dispirited, and demeaned. Or, he may be oblivious. He may even be cooperative. In his role as respondent, he is here to reply to the claims that you have made. He may want to say that his financial decisions have made sense or else that he is ready for someone else to handle the money hassles now. He is accustomed to critical accusations about the way he is. He almost certainly does not want to be a part of a spectacle in court. In fact, he may not even appear. If that happens, the judge will likely postpone the hearing and urge your dad's lawyer to make sure that your dad is present for his hearing next time. In some circumstances, the lawyer may be allowed to speak on your dad's behalf, although current courts are reluctant to remove a person's autonomy without actually seeing him. In the past, too many functional people were unjustly robbed of their independence when statutes and court practices permitted conservatorships without input from the person who was alleged to be incapacitated.

Having read through the whole descriptive petition and weighed the remarks submitted by the professionals and family members, the probate judge hearing a conservatorship claim listens for capacity as much as for incapacity. Conservatorship may not be necessary or it can apply to limited types of transactions or decisions. Perhaps the conservatorship can be temporary. On the other hand, maybe it is the only way to keep the person from becoming homeless. And, although the petitioner who brought the case may not want to believe it, the judge can agree to grant the petition for conservatorship but pick someone else to be the conservator.

The judges in these cases know what incapacity looks like and how it sounds. They see people with dementia, head injuries, and mental illness all the time. Having read the family's observations and the expert information, the hearing judge wants to know what the allegedly incapacitated person thinks about having a conservator. The judge also wants to hear this individual's opinion of the person that the petitioner has nominated to serve as conservator and whether he would prefer to have somebody else helping with his finances. Listening to the respondent's remarks, the judge will watch for signs of alertness and orientation.

The judge may ask questions that double-check the forensic psychologist's observations. One of the common legal questions for incapacity is whether the allegedly incapacitated person "can receive information effectively." Another legal standard, used together with that one, is whether he can "make and communicate decisions." Also, does he have the "ability to make reasonable decisions?" If he does not have that ability, he probably needs a conservator. The judge will have these questions in mind as she reads the petition file and observes the respondent at the hearing.

If the judge concludes that the respondent is incapacitated and in need of a conservator, she can decide whether the conservator will be responsible for all financial matters or for just certain categories of money management. She may also determine that the conservatorship should last for only a limited amount of time. Finally, the judge will name the conservator. If the petitioner does not want to be the conservator or if the judge has found him to be unqualified, she will identify someone else—usually a different family member, a friend, a nonprofit conservator service, or a local attorney.

The Conservator's Legal Obligations

Once the conservator (let's say that's you) is appointed by the court, it is as if the court has hired you for a job and the court is now your supervisor. You have to report regularly to the court, and you have to check with the court before making any major financial decisions for the incapacitated person (your father, who is now known as "the ward"). Your first report will be required soon after you are appointed. In that initial report, you will need to present an inventory of the ward's assets, your plan for managing the assets, and proof that you have notified all of the banks and other necessary entities about your conservatorship.

As a conservator, you can be paid, and although the court supervises you in this capacity, your very minimal hourly payment will come from the ward's assets, not from the court. In addition to the hourly wage (which many family members opt not to take), you are entitled to reimbursement for costs that you incur in satisfying your conservator duties. However, the court has to approve your fee and reimbursements.

Probate courts typically provide each new conservator with a detailed handbook that includes forms, deadlines, definitions, and rules. So there is nothing mysterious or tricky about the conservator's obligations to the court. Good conservators simply have to remain organized, be accurate, and follow the court's instructions.

The conservator's obligations to the ward are all about responsible money management. As your dad's conservator, you should always care about his money as much as you care about your own, and never mix his money with your own. Always avoid committing negligence or theft in connection with the ward's assets—those are the most common liabilities associated with conservatorship.

Responsible Conservatorship

Conservators can avoid mistakes and the suspicion of others by being well organized from the very start. The standard court reporting requirements will put any conservator on a good track by requiring him to compile a list of the ward's assets and debts and to replace the ward's name with conservatorship identification on accounts and contracts. Both of these steps sound simple, but they involve a lot of work. After they are done, the conservator just needs to use good judgment in all of his conservator transactions and decisions.

Most courts will require the conservator to post a conservatorship surety bond equal to the value of the ward's assets. Then, if the conservator wastes, loses, or steals any of the ward's assets, the bond will repay the ward. Conservators purchase the bond from a surety bond company. The court will probably provide the conservator with a list of local bond companies. The amount that the conservator pays for the bond will be a percentage of its face value. Each conservator's percentage will depend on his own assets and credit record as well as facts about the ward and the conservator's financial responsibilities on behalf of his ward. Some conservators may be able to pay as little as 1% of the face value of the bond. If the court finds that a conservator did waste, lose, or steal the ward's assets and orders the bond company to pay the ward, the bond company will then go after the conservator to collect the full amount that it had to pay the ward.

Compile a List of Assets and Debts

To compile the list of assets and debts, the conservator first has to find all of them. Even though this conservator may have served as power of attorney on a bank account or representative payee for Social Security benefits, he may not know about all of his ward's assets and financial obligations. Here are some sensible investigative steps that a conservator should take in order to compile a thorough list of assets and debts:

- The conservator will download the ward's credit report. That document should identify all of the ward's credit cards and bank loans. Not knowing which online sites have any of the ward's credit card information saved and not wanting the ward to continue being able to purchase online, the conservator will cancel (or at least freeze) the ward's credit cards.
- The conservator will take note of any automatic bill payments that are charged to the credit cards so that he does not miss payments or accidentally cancel service before arranging new payment methods. When he is dealing with high credit card debts, he should ask the companies to remove their fees from the account. They may not remove them entirely, but they may reduce them. If they insist on full fee payment, the conservator can go to a credit counseling service and have them negotiate on his behalf.
- In addition to credit card debts and bank loans, the credit report will identify any debts associated with court proceedings. These will include judgments filed by landlords who are owed back-due rent, child support arrearages, liens, bankruptcy, etc. The conservator needs to arrange payment plans to get the liens lifted as soon as possible, and he needs to find out about any bankruptcy obligations that he has to fulfill. If the bankruptcy happened in the last couple of years, he will look at the petition to see if his ward identified any financial accounts and then will check to see if the accounts still exist.
- Looking for assets, the conservator will check the unclaimed property databases in every state that the ward has lived in. These databases are maintained by each state treasurer's office. They exist because so many people lose track of, or do not know about, money that they are owed and because people forget to give forwarding addresses to banks, insurance companies, and government offices. At one time, the money in abandoned accounts would automatically become state government property after a certain number of years. Now, the states hold it for the rightful owners and list it in the unclaimed property databases. When people do not discover their own unclaimed assets before they die, their executors usually find them and distribute them to heirs. A good conservator will find his ward's money and use it to help him during his lifetime.
- The conservator will monitor the ward's mail, watching for any legitimate business communications that he needs to deal with. He may discover insurance policies that should be modified or cancelled. He may learn about unnecessary subscriptions and memberships that he can either cancel or avoid renewing. He will probably discover which dentist, doctors, and other professionals the ward visits. The conservator needs this information because he will now handle all of the business transactions with those offices. Monitoring the mail, he will also find out whether the ward has made any charitable commitments. The conservator has the power to cancel forthcoming payments on those donations.
- The conservator should kindly and respectfully interview the ward to gather clues about other possible assets. When the ward tells the conservator about his work history, the conservator may learn about jobs that ended badly. He can contact the employers' headquarters and find

out what happened to his ward's final paychecks; many shamed and angry employees simply walk away from the job, rather than going back to get the final paycheck at the end of the next pay period. If that happened with the ward, the conservator can have the payroll office issue new checks and send them to his attention. He may also discover that the ward should have applied for workers' compensation or unemployment benefits; it may not be too late to apply for them on his behalf. When the ward reminisces about his family, he may mention that somebody used to send him savings bonds or gave him stock shares as birthday gifts over the years. The conservator should be able to find those and either liquidate them or put them in the conservatorship account. Whether the ward tells the conservator about any of these financial gifts or not, the wise conservator will notify all of the relatives that he has been named conservator and ask that they let him know about any accounts or savings bonds that they have created for the family member who is the ward. As the conservator interacts with the ward, the ward may even tell him where he stashes cash. Hopefully, the conservator will not need to take away his ward's "comfort stash," but he should ensure that it is stored safely and he should keep a record of it in case the ward forgets about it or the conservator needs to move the ward out during a psychotic episode when he cannot think about the stash.

- The conservator will also need to inventory and secure the contents of the ward's home. Whether or not the ward has trust issues or tends to worry, it is usually best to involve him in the inventory process. Any of us would want to oversee the process if someone were going through all of our things, wouldn't we? Some of the ward's possessions will be legitimate treasures and, like most treasures, they will be buried and the conservator will have to dig for them. There may be a coin collection in a shoebox at the back of the closet in the middle stack of other boxes that merely contain junk. Inherited valuable jewelry may be rolled inside sock balls. If the conservator petitions for bankruptcy on behalf of the ward, these assets will need to be reported to the trustee. Even if the ward's debt situation is not extreme enough for bankruptcy, some of the treasures may need to be sold in order to pay his creditors.

- As the conservator looks through the ward's household for assets, he should be alert for clues about lifestyle issues to manage in the conservatorship: He may discover that the ward needs a handyman to come fix some things or that certain appliances need to be replaced. He may notice that the ward does not have curtains, or soap, or a vacuum cleaner, or other standard household items. It is appropriate for a conservator to obtain those items and services for a ward. If the ward has a separate person acting as his guardian, then the conservator and guardian together will decide which of them will take responsibility for assisting the ward with household and lifestyle matters.

The asset list that the conservator compiles has to include not only descriptive names of the assets, but also their monetary value and facts applicable to liquidating them in case some of them have to be sold. Here are a few examples:

The conservator discovers a $500 certificate of deposit (CD). On the list, he will write the name of the bank that issued the CD, the interest rate, and the date when it will become redeemable.

The conservator who finds that the ward has four televisions in an efficiency apartment will list each television according to brand and approximate age and the probable amount of money that it would sell for in a garage sale. Every price on the inventory list should be an educated estimate of its legitimate sales price, not its replacement value.

If the ward has tee shirts from lots of races that he has run, the conservator will just list those as "clothing" along with all the ward's other garments; he will not need to identify individual items unless they are valuable. Most of the items that the ward uses all the time, such as clothes, linens, and ordinary dishes, are still necessary to him; they do not have significant resale value and will not be liquidated.

If the ward has emotionally important collectibles or a secret money stash that the conservator truly could not deplete without compromising his ward's mental wellness, he will list it on the inventory but will avoid touching it unless he has no other choice and has arranged for emotional support to help the ward through the experience. When listing it on the inventory, he should think of it as something that he—as conservator—is supposed to protect.

All of the work that he does as conservator will be connected to the original list of the ward's assets and debts. He will make all of his decisions based on the knowledge that he gains from compiling it. He will file annual account reports to the court in which he refers back to the original list, noting where he has moved money, spent it, or added to it. In compiling it very carefully and thoroughly, he will earn the confidence of his ward and the court.

IDENTIFYING HIMSELF AS CONSERVATOR ON ALL DOCUMENTS

As the conservator discovers anyone engaged in business relations with his ward, he will introduce himself as the conservator who is now responsible for the ward's transactions with that entity. He will do this by sending a business letter and a copy of the court document appointing him as the ward's conservator.

In order to properly inform everyone whom he will do business with on behalf of his ward, the conservator will probably need to pay the court clerk for at least a dozen official stamped copies of the court's official conservatorship document. If he tries to use ordinary photocopies, recipients will send them back and refuse to recognize his conservatorship until they get an official stamped copy.

The conservator will notify the landlord, the utilities, banks, insurance companies, investment firms, a special needs trustee, and all of the ward's creditors that he will handle the bills from now on. He will tell them to send all communications to him. When the conservator first writes to the ward's bank, for example, his letter should summarize the attached court document and notify the bank that he is now taking responsibility for the ward's account. For example:

As you can see in the enclosed order by Judge Able Baker of the Anytown Probate Court, I have been named conservator for Jon Doe, as of May 1, 2016. In that capacity, I am writing to notify you that I will now manage Mr. Doe's account with you. The account is checking account number 12345. Please direct all future correspondence regarding the account to me at the address you see on this page.

The conservator will also use this letter to let the institution know if he plans to take any action on the account. For example, he may intend to rename the account, open a new account, transfer the account, or close the account. If he has not found an appropriate "name change" form on the institution's website, he will ask in the introductory letter whether there is a form to complete in order to have his conservatorship recognized on the account record.

He will either rename all of the ward's contracts and accounts to be in the name of the conservatorship or else establish new contracts or accounts in the name of the conservatorship. Depending on the circumstances, properly named conservator accounts identify the owner in these patterns: "Ann Smith, Conservator for Brian Smith" or "Estate of Brian Smith, a Disabled Person, by Ann Smith, Conservator." Although the contracts and accounts have both the conservator's name and the ward's name on them, only the ward's Social Security number should be affiliated with the assets and obligations. This is a critically important rule in keeping track of the ward's money. If the conservator puts any of the ward's assets under his own Social Security number, he may be guilty of criminal and civil offenses.

It is likely that the conservator will need to move some accounts around for convenience and higher earnings, since his ward was probably unable to focus on those kinds of concerns as he became less able to manage his finances. The conservator will arrange for paychecks to be directly deposited in the conservatorship bank account and for mail from the employer's benefits office to come to him. He needs to make sure that the doctors, therapist, dentist, and other healthcare providers understand whether he is just the conservator or whether he is also the guardian or healthcare power of attorney. (Refer to Chapter 3 of this book for information on guardianship and to Chapter 1 for more on healthcare power of attorney.)

By going to the trouble of renaming or establishing new contracts and accounts for the ward, the conservator becomes accustomed to his new and distinct identity in connection with the ward. As long as he keeps that identity and the ward's money apart from his own identity and money, he will not make the kinds of mistakes that look like theft.

Using Good Judgment

After compiling the assets and debts list and putting everything under his authority, the conservator's major legal responsibility is to use good judgment. Good judgment is the whole point of conservatorship. He was appointed to be the conservator because the court believed that his judgment should replace the ward's own judgment.

The conservator's judgment should be informed by the contracts he has taken over and the mail that he will now receive from the ward's accounts and service providers. He will read their policies, statements, and bills, and he will decide whether to keep doing business with them as their policies and prices either change or do not change. He will keep an eye out for better options in the marketplace. For example, the conservator may:

- Change the ward's fringe benefits at work, if it makes sense to do that.
- Negotiate for better rates wherever rates are negotiable.
- File a lawsuit to get the ward's money back if the ward has been ripped off.

- Buy the ward memberships and passes when they are cheaper than paying for individual visits to places that he frequents.
- Register the ward for any public benefits that he is eligible to receive.
- Find the ward better and more reasonably priced housing if the ward is living in a place that is too expensive. The conservator has this authority, and he may look for a place that is more convenient to shopping or public transportation; however, the court will likely need to approve a major transition like a move.

Remember that negligence exists when somebody breaches a duty and the breach causes harm. As long as a conservator uses ordinary reasonable skill and care when managing the ward's money, his judgment will satisfy the legal duty of conservatorship. Generally, this means paying the bills on time, planning and saving for unexpected costly events, and making decisions that are practical. Practical decisions help the ward to get the best bargains and to obtain the goods and services that he actually needs, rather than wasting money on silly things. All of this will come naturally if the conservator has the ward's best interests in mind whenever he takes action on behalf of the ward.

It is fine to use convenience as a factor in conservator decision-making. For example, a nearby bank may pay slightly lower interest than a more distant bank, but if it is quicker and easier for the conservator to get to the nearby bank and he frequently has to go to the bank in person, then he does not have to open the ward's account in the distant bank just to get the higher interest rate.

Notice that the legal expectations are only about money, not mental state. It is possible that a particular ward will have emotional associations with objects (like a ridiculously expensive car that he never should have bought) or places (like a business that terrifies or empowers him) that the conservator will need to honor when making his financial decisions. Honoring those associations does not mean giving in to them. If the car needs to be repossessed, the conservator has to make that happen as soon as possible, rather than continuing to waste money on it. Honor, in this context, means recognizing the importance of the association and providing emotional support for the transition. The conservator may enlist the ward's therapist to help with this. As explained in Chapter 1 about patient privacy, the therapist may not be authorized to share the ward's treatment information with the conservator, but she can hear about the conservator's intentions and help him to plan and carry out a healthy change in the ward's circumstances. If the conservator and therapist present consistent messages, the ward will get through the change with a minimum of stress or trauma.

The conservator's judgments will be monitored by the probate court when it reads his annual reports. Others who care about the ward, including you, will also watch the conservator and will notify the court if he begins to profit from the ward's assets. If he gets into a lazy and irresponsible pattern or makes a significant misjudgment, the court may replace him with a different conservator or draw on his bond to repay the ward's account. If he steals from the ward, the probate court can turn him over to the criminal justice system.

HOW TO Prevent and Handle Bad Conservatorship

The information that follows is for family members who are not petitioners or conservators, but who have an interest in their relative's financial well-being.

Family members who provide written statements and who testify at the conservatorship hearing are very influential. Find the time and information to participate as fully as possible in the process. If you hear that someone is going to petition for conservatorship over your relative, contact the petitioner and ask to be identified as a witness. If you do not know who filed the petition, but you have heard that one was filed, call the local probate court to say that you want to be a witness in the conservator petition regarding your relative. The person who answers the phone will either give you a docket number and tell you what to do or they will say, "We do not currently have a case involving that respondent," which will tell you that a petition has not yet been filed.

If there is a petition on file, follow the court clerk's instructions for getting your comments on record, either in writing or by testifying at the hearing. You may have first-hand knowledge of situations that other family members either did not see or do not understand. Whether you are in favor of the conservatorship or you are against it, you can give context to examples of your loved one's behavior that a caseworker or other professional may present. For example, your sister Kayla's caseworker may report to the court that Kayla once went into a fit when the gas company came to read her meter. You can complete that story by explaining any arrangements you have made to prevent such a situation from happening again. As evidence, you could show the meter-reading schedule that you obtained for your sister and copies of the official "We were here" cards that the meter reader has provided at each subsequent visit. You can help your loved one by conveying an accurate picture of her capacity for making financial decisions and fulfilling financial obligations. Doing this, you will help the judge either to decide on the most appropriate form of conservatorship or to decline a petition that is based on false or incomplete claims.

If a conservator is appointed, you can keep an eye on things, but realize that you do not have all the information that the conservator has. Understand that the conservator will make decisions and changes. To begin with, she will have to undo any bad arrangements that came to light through the hearing and her inventory process. She will probably have to reprioritize the ward's spending. She may have to cancel or reduce some costs in order to pay the ward's debts. You do not need to go running into court as soon as you see that the new conservator has discontinued the ward's phone plan or moved the ward to a different home. Just watch to be sure that the ward's legitimate needs are being met and that the conservator is not profiting from the ward's assets while the ward is being made to live in squalor.

If, however, you are close enough to the situation that you can see financial abuses, report them to the court. You can do this in one of two ways:

1. Either send a letter to the judge in which you detail problematic transactions and request that the judge inquire about them during the next accounting period.
2. File a petition to have the conservator removed.

If you file a petition, the court will hold a hearing to investigate the truthfulness of your claims and their significance to the ward's well-being. Your petition will be a public filing and you will be named as the acting party (petitioner) against the conservator. In other words, your name will be the first name on the case. This hearing will subject the conservator to serious scrutiny and the ward to stress. Granted, it is less stressful than having his money stolen. Just know that petitioning for removal of a conservator is a dramatic step that should be taken only when the conservator truly is bad for the ward.

In the hearing on a petition to remove a conservator, the court's options are to keep the conservator or to remove and replace the conservator. The petition to remove the conservator will identify another person or a local entity (typically a nonprofit agency) to replace the existing conservator. However, the court may put the conservator into a monitoring system and require her to obtain training in order to keep the conservatorship.

Note that the probate court dealing with conservator problems will not decide claims about theft, fraud, property destruction, emotional distress, negligence, or conversion of assets. Those claims belong in other courts. Contact the police to file theft and fraud charges; a criminal prosecutor will then bring the case to criminal court. The other items in the list are civil court claims that may be raised against bad conservators in order to get repayment for the person who is incapacitated. The civil claims generally fall into the category of personal injuries. Contact a lawyer who specializes in disability law, elder law, or personal injury law to bring claims in the civil trial court.

A POSITIVE END TO CONSERVATORSHIP

Remember that conservatorship is necessary only for someone who is incapacitated. Many people experience mental illness in varying episodes of severity and, if they are ever incapacitated, it is only likely to be for a temporary period. Their finances do not need to remain under the control of a conservator when their incapacity ends. They can petition the probate court to end the conservatorship.

This process will involve an investigation and hearing similar to those that the court conducted prior to establishing the conservatorship. As in the previous hearing, the ward will have a lawyer representing him, ideally the same lawyer. This time, if the evidence shows that the ward is now able to manage his financial responsibilities without the conservator, the court will declare him to be no longer incapacitated and will schedule a process for removing the conservator from the affairs of the person who is no longer his ward.

In the process, the ward will submit a letter and a copy of the court's Order to Restore Capacity (or a similarly named document) to all of the offices and institutions where the conservator has been representing him. The letter will state that the former ward seeks to remove the conservator's identity and authority from his record or account and that he will now assume responsibility for his own business with the office or institution. Some of the places may need the former conservator to complete a form that is unique to their way of doing business, and some may need both the former ward and the former conservator to jump through hoops.

None of this paperwork should be strenuous; institutions just want to keep their records straight. A former ward who runs into any difficulty in reclaiming control of his responsibilities should seek help from the lawyer who represented him in the hearing for restoration of capacity, not from the former conservator.

Tax Facts

- Conservators are required to file IRS Form 56, *Notice Concerning Fiduciary Relationship*, to notify the IRS when their conservatorship begins. They should file another Form 56 when the conservatorship ends. The only non-obvious answer on the form is the "identifying number." The ward's Social Security number should go on that line.
- Conservators are responsible for completing, signing, and submitting tax returns on behalf of their wards. This means that they can do the math themselves, use a reliable software product, or hire a tax service to deal with the tax return. The costs for software or a tax service can be paid from the ward's money.
- Conservators who are paid fees for their service have to pay income taxes on the fees.
- If conservators incur costs associated with caring for their wards, they can deduct the costs as long as they fit into ordinary deduction categories. Examples: If a conservator is in business to provide conservator services, some of the business expenses (such as mileage) will be deductible. See *Deducting Business Expenses* in the Small Business and Self-Employed section of the IRS website.

RESOURCES FOR FINANCIAL POWER OF ATTORNEY

1. The Uniform Law Commission created a model law, "The Uniform Power of Attorney Act," regarding financial powers of attorney. Twenty states have already incorporated it into their own state laws. Find the model law and a kit for lobbying your state legislature to adopt it at http://www. uniformlaws.org/.
2. There is a portal to "State Durable Power of Attorney Laws" at statelaws. findlaw.com.
3. The federal government's Consumer Financial Protection Bureau publishes a handbook titled *Managing Someone Else's Money: Help for Agents under Power of Attorney*. Find it online at consumerfinance.gov.
4. The American Bar Association Section on Real Property, Trusts and Estates has a fact sheet titled "Power of Attorney" at americanbar.org.
5. The Colorado Bar Association publishes a guide for agents, *So Now You Are an Agent under Financial Power of Attorney,* at cobar.org.
6. Many public libraries subscribe to electronic databases, such as Lawdepot, Gale Legal Forms, and U.S. Legal Forms, that provide fill-in-the-blank legal forms. You may want to use one of the free forms for a

single-purpose or short-term power of attorney arrangement. If you are not familiar with your public library, find it via publiclibraries.com.

RESOURCES FOR SUPPORTED DECISION-MAKING

1. The National Resource Center for Supported Decision-Making Project links to state laws and provides a free online collection of sample forms, webinars about supported decision-making, stories about supported decision-making, and instructional materials. This organization's website also has free articles about relevant policy issues, respecting autonomy, and providing good support to decision makers. See supporteddecisionmaking.org.
2. The Autistic Self-Advocacy Network has done significant research about supported decision-making in multiple countries, including the United States. Its publication, *The Right to Make Choices: International Laws and Decision-Making by People with Disabilities,* has an intimidating title, but it contains a very easy demonstration of how supportive decision-making agreements fit into the full spectrum of support services. See autisticadvocacy.org.
3. The National Gateway to Self-Determination develops training programs about self-advocacy and making plans. Families and consumers who are contemplating a decision-support agreement will find thoughtful relevant materials throughout the organization's website at ngsd.org.
4. Al Etmanski's book, *A Good Life* (Planned Lifetime Advocacy Institute, 2000), will be useful to consumers who want to read about building a support team (the inside circle or brain trust) for any purpose, who want to improve their planning skills, or who are thinking about the idea of supported decision-making. The book is available as a $20.00 (U.S.) ebook from the Canadian organization that published it. Families might like to implement some of the organization's service ideas in their own community. The website address is plan.ca.

RESOURCES FOR CONSERVATORSHIP

1. The American Bar Association's Commission on Law and Aging links to useful and current information about guardianship (conservatorship is also known as guardianship of the estate), including state laws, at americanbar.org.
2. The National Guardianship Association (NGA) offers educational training for conservators, sets standards for ethics and service, and provides very helpful information about issues that families face and resources that they may need. Note that NGA's site (guardianship.org) includes the entire Uniform Adult Guardianship and Protective Proceedings Jurisdiction Act plus related documents.
3. The National Center for State Courts maintains a good, practical *Guardianship/Conservatorship Resource Guide* at ncsc.org.

4. Someone who is accused of being incompetent or incapacitated and in need of conservatorship should be represented by a lawyer in the conservatorship hearing and related legal interactions. Many courts will appoint a free lawyer when the accused person cannot afford one. If the court does not provide a lawyer, the nearest affiliate of the National Disability Rights Network (ndrn.org) or the National Association of Elder Law Attorneys (naela.org) can help to find a qualified and affordable lawyer.

5. Some communities have Financial Abuse Specialist Teams (FAST) to investigate, prosecute, and otherwise deal with malicious conservators and others who take advantage of vulnerable people who have trouble managing money. See examples by using the phrase "financial abuse specialist team" in a search engine.

6. FindLaw manages a table of descriptive links to the courts that handle probate affairs, including conservatorship, in all of the states at estate.findlaw.com.

7. The Social Security Administration has a *Digest of State Guardianship Laws* that summarizes the legal standards for guardianship of the person and guardianship of the estate (conservatorship) throughout the country. U.S. Social Security Administration Program Operations Manual System (POMS) § GN 00502.300, *Digest of State Guardianship Laws,* is available at https://secure.ssa.gov/poms.nsf/lnx/0200502300.

22

Housing Law

Franklin doesn't like to stay in any one place for too long. He hears voices and sometimes the voices tell him it's time to get going. He was in a terrific group home for a couple of years, but when it started to feel stifling, he left and got a live-in job as a condominium handyman. He has had a number of live-in condo gigs since then. Franklin is well qualified for this work. He completed a plumbing apprenticeship right out of high school and later got an associate's degree in electrical technology. Also, Franklin hates to rent apartments. He did that only once and it fell through when the landlord evicted him for scaring the neighbors. He hadn't done anything to scare anybody, but the neighbors felt afraid of him when he seemed to be talking to himself, and so the landlord threw him out. Every so often, when he's in a bad way and can't work, either Franklin or a hospital caseworker will ask if anyone in the family can take him in for a while. You just got one of those calls and you'll probably give him a room, but the situation has made you curious about housing issues that affect people who live with mental illness.

INTRODUCTION TO THE LEGAL ISSUES

If it were not for the Fair Housing Act and U.S. Department of Housing and Urban Development (HUD) regulations on fair housing, people with mental illness would have a particularly hard time finding and keeping suitable housing. The fair housing laws protect against housing discrimination. In other words, the laws make it illegal for housing providers to refuse housing to people who have a mental illness, to treat residents with mental illness differently than other residents, or to make them leave their housing simply because they have a mental illness. Without fair housing laws, residents with mental illness would still be protected by basic contract rights, state and federal health department regulations, and state landlord–tenant statutes that would help them find and keep decent housing. The fair housing laws provide people with mental illness a legal basis for making changes to housing rules (referred to as accommodations) or modifications to physical spaces. The laws also provide a legal defense for some behaviors that may otherwise compromise the housing arrangement.

The Fair Housing Act requires that housing providers make reasonable accommodations or modifications for residents with disabilities when the residents cannot fully enjoy the property. Under this law and the HUD regulations that enforce it, residents with disabilities include people whose mental impairment "substantially limits one or more of such person's major life activities" and who have "a record of having" a mental illness. Because of these requirements, residents who seek accommodations or modifications have no choice but to disclose their disabling condition to their housing provider.

In addition to fair housing, HUD regulates affordable housing. People with mental illness who work in low-paying jobs or who collect Supplemental Security Income (SSI) may be eligible for HUD's affordable housing programs. Most of the affordable housing regulations affect housing providers, but, for residents, the regulations apply to moving dates and property conditions. People who get SSI disability benefits from the Social Security Administration (SSA) are themselves subject to regulations: they have to notify the SSA if they move to a different home. If they move in with family members, then their disability benefits will be reduced unless the family charges them for living expenses.

Housing-law problems that affect people with mental illness tend to be associated with shared properties, which include rentals, group homes, and homeowner associations. Therefore, the housing information that is covered in this chapter mainly focuses on shared housing, including when a family member with mental illness moves in with relatives.

Legal Rights, From Moving in to Moving out

Legal issues can arise at every phase of living in a place, beginning with the legal formalities of arranging to move somewhere, continuing with the rights and liabilities of living there, and ending with the obligations that go with leaving the household. Residents can exercise fair housing rights during each of the phases.

The search for housing and the moving-in phase depend on good contract negotiation. Mental illness can be a subject of the negotiation or it can cause the resident to be unable to negotiate or sign the housing contract. Some residents with mental illness have no special needs when they enter a new home, but they may later experience problems with the facility, the management, or the neighbors. For example, after living in his new place for a few months, Dereck realized that the housing provider misled him in the move-in negotiations. They said that the building had 24-hour security, which is critical for Dereck's sense of well-being, but it turns out that the exterior and interior boxes that appear to hold cameras do not really hold anything. And the lawn sign for the Iron Door Security Company is pointless, too; Iron Door went out of business years ago, and the housing provider never contracted with another security service. Dereck now feels genuinely endangered whenever he has to go in or out of the building. He wants to skip out on the lease and move immediately. When a housing provider tricks or confuses a resident like this, the state consumer protection statute may give the resident a reason to sue the housing provider and to get out of the lease early, or at least to defend himself against eviction, or, as in Dereck's case, the landlord's claim that by moving out early Dereck would be breaching the lease and would owe the landlord a full year's rent.

If a resident can no longer use and enjoy her place without accommodations or modifications, such as when Pippa developed frightening hallucinations and needed all of the interior doors (closets, bedroom, and bathroom) in her apartment to be removed, then the Fair Housing Act entitles her to get the changes made. And if, on the flip side, her disability causes her to trouble the management or neighbors, she can be evicted as a result of causing that trouble—although fair housing law can sometimes protect a resident with a disability from having to move. The landlord cannot arbitrarily evict her; he has to have good cause. If the time does come when a resident must move, the jostling upheaval that stresses just about everybody who has to move out of one place and into another can sometimes include legal consequences.

Housing Vocabulary

Here are key terms used in the area of housing and the law:

- *Person with a disability*—Someone who (1) has a physical or mental impairment that substantially limits one or more major life activities, (2) has a record of experiencing the impairment, and (3) is regarded as having such an impairment. These three criteria come from the Fair Housing Act 42 U.S.C. § 3602.
- *Major life activities*—Major life activities include, but are not limited to, caring for oneself, performing manual tasks, seeing, hearing, eating, sleeping, walking, standing, lifting, bending, speaking, breathing, learning, reading, concentrating, thinking, communicating, and working. These are defined in Americans with Disabilities Act (ADA) Amendments 42 U.S.C. § 12102(2)(A).
- *Accommodation*—Accommodation is an alteration in the ordinary rules, practices, and services in a housing community, whether it is a rental, a private place governed by a homeowners' association, a supportive housing program, or a public housing development. See 24 C.F.R. § 100.204.
- *Modification*—A modification is a change to the physical structure of the premises. Modifications may be necessary inside or outside and to the resident's individual unit or to areas that multiple residents share, such as hallways, laundry rooms, and gardens. See 24 C.F.R. § 100.201.
- *Necessary*—Modifications and accommodations are considered necessary if there is "an identifiable relationship" between the resident's professionally documented disability and the changes requested by the resident.
- *Reasonable*—Modifications and accommodations are reasonable if they make it possible for the resident to "have an equal opportunity to use and enjoy" the place and if they do not "impose an undue financial and administrative burden on the housing provider or . . . fundamentally alter the nature of the provider's operations." This quote and the necessity quote come from the HUD/DOJ Joint Statements listed in the Resources section of this chapter.
- *Resident*—In this chapter, the word *resident* is used for the person with the disability, who can be a renter, roommate, condominium owner, group home occupant, or otherwise named person living in a place where someone else controls the overall facility.

- *Housing provider*—In this chapter, a housing provider can mean anyone who represents the owner of a property that provides housing. It may be the landlord, someone on the condominium board, anyone who works in the rental manager's office, or a staff member at an independent living complex, for example.
- *Group home*—In this chapter, the term *group home* is used for housing that has staff on site, either part-time or full-time, to help the residents cooperate with each other and maintain personal and housekeeping routines in their own spaces. It may be called community residential treatment or community residential rehabilitation or a similar phrase that combines words representing home and services. Group homes operate on a broad spectrum. For example, some have shared cooking and dining facilities, some require residents to perform chores in the common areas, some include a shared vehicle, and some have arrangements with job providers. Caseworkers usually refer residents to group homes and can tell families about the various services and expectations at each facility.
- *Supportive housing*—In this chapter, this phrase means housing associated with support staff who are responsible for handling tasks that make it possible for an individual with mental illness to live there when his condition would otherwise prevent him from having permanent housing. The support staff do not necessarily live at, or work for, the place where the resident lives; they function as connecters between the resident and the facility. They typically arrange funding for housing and guide relationships with the housing provider, the utility companies, the neighbors, and others who have interactions with the resident. Most supportive housing programs are based in nonprofit organizations. The support services are optional and flexible. Some residents need support only to find housing. Others need support with just a single aspect of living in their housing: an example is Gail, who tends to isolate herself so much that she will not use the shared laundry room on her floor or go downstairs to the mailroom unless a program worker comes to get her once a week and accompanies her while she washes clothes and checks her mail in these locations in the building. Other residents need to have somebody on call but can handle most things by themselves. And some residents need routine assistance with cleaning, shopping, handling mail, and other tasks.
- *Public housing*—Public housing is housing that is operated and funded by the government, typically the city or county housing authority. It is expected to follow all of the federal, state, and local housing laws, everything from affordable and nondiscriminatory housing to health department standards and the criminal code, in order to keep people housed when they otherwise would not be.
- *Subsidized housing*—This phrase is often used to describe privately owned housing that receives funding from HUD to enable people with low incomes to live there. The subsidy is either project-based or tenant-based. For example, the Section 8 program has two forms of subsidies—the Section 8 project-based subsidy and the Section 8 voucher. The project-based subsidy is attached to the unit, while the voucher is portable,

permitting the recipient to move to a different apartment elsewhere in a jurisdiction.

FINDING AND ARRANGING HOUSING

Group homes and supportive housing services know if a prospective resident has mental health issues because residents in those housing arrangements have to prove that they have a mental illness in order to be eligible for the housing. Other housing providers generally do not need that information and are not likely to give any thought to a prospective resident's mental condition. In fact, when researchers planned to study discrimination against people with all kinds of disabilities who were shopping for standard apartments, they were challenged in figuring out how to test discrimination against prospective tenants with mental illness. In the end, they sent two actors pretending to be possible renters who both lacked rental history. One lacked history because of just getting out of college and one lacked history because of being in a mental health care facility.

The researchers were watching to see if the housing providers preferred the recent college student over the person who had been treated for mental illness. They also wanted to see if the housing providers tried to charge different prices based on the histories. Requiring a higher deposit or a higher rent from someone because of his mental illness would be discriminatory. The project, at this phase, "did not produce statistically representative measures of discrimination," so the researchers limited the next phase of their housing discrimination research to people who were deaf and people in wheelchairs.

Outside of this kind of scripted situation, in which the potential resident was instructed to convey that the previous home was a care facility, future residents' mental health issues will generally not be obvious to housing providers. Sure, a housing provider may notice if somebody is unwilling to touch anything or asks unusual questions about the place, but she is not likely to form a diagnosis or to conclude that the person should be charged extra or excluded from living there.

Housing providers' main concern when they meet a prospective resident is whether that person will be able to pay. For this reason, they may ask for proof of employment, permission to conduct a credit check, and/or a rental history. If the prospective resident does not have a rental history (for example, because of always living with family up to this point or living in a group home), he does not need to disclose why he has no recent rental history. He can simply state that he has not been renting. And if the housing provider tries to dig for more facts, the potential resident can say, "I really don't have a rental history. You can check my credit history; you will see that I have not been evicted and have managed my bills."

However, if a potential resident, perhaps your friend Max, does not have a good credit history, he may be able to give the housing provider a different form of assurance that he will be able to pay the rent. Beginning with the idea that the credit history is about the past and this housing contract is about the future, Max can show proof of his current income or a source of financial support. Perhaps he now receives disability benefits and can arrange for direct deposit of the monthly housing payment. Maybe his housing cost will be subsidized through a government program. It is possible that Max now has another person managing his money for him. There may be somebody willing to co-sign the lease. Having had a job for several months is good evidence of current financial stability. Bad credit history does not necessarily make it impossible to find new housing.

If someone knows at the outset that he needs the housing provider to adjust anything about the rules or the building because of his mental health, he should aim to get his requirements included in the housing contract, rather than surprising the housing provider later. Housing agreements, like all contracts, are supposed to be negotiated in good faith, which means that parties should be truthful and complete in their negotiations. A resident who signs the standard contract as if everything is fine and does not admit up front that he needs adjustments is not negotiating in good faith. Here are a few examples of proactive agreements:

> If Marco knows that his disability check will be deposited on the second Wednesday of every month and that he cannot pay his rent on the first of the month, he should not sign a lease requiring payment on the first of the month. He needs to arrange for his rent payments to be in the middle of the month.

> A resident can request that the housing contract be edited to accommodate glitches in disability payments or other agency funding. If the original line in the contract says, "A late fee of $50 will be added to all payments made more than one week after the due date," residents can ask whether following that line, the contract could say, "However, if the late payment results from a delayed government agency payment to, or on behalf of, the resident, the late fee will be waived."

> If Lena, a prospective condominium buyer, knows that she needs to put film over her windows and the homeowners' association (HOA) rules about window treatments may not allow the film, she can avoid getting herself into a conflict-filled housing situation by requesting a rule variance (in writing) in advance of purchasing the property.

Oral promises and assurances that are left out of written agreements usually do not get legal support. A housing provider or resident who truly intends to do something should put it in the written contract and expect that a court will uphold it as an obligation.

Doubts About Negotiating a Housing Contract

Some residents are reluctant to negotiate. Perhaps they want to avoid being in an uncomfortable interpersonal transaction, having to disclose information about their mental condition, or missing the chance to get the place because someone else grabs it while the negotiations are still going on. Knowing the legal aspects of these concerns can make them less worrisome.

Regarding the uncomfortable communications, residents should know that lawyers consider a written contract to be a "memorial" of an agreement after parties have worked out their terms. Most housing providers are accustomed to negotiating housing contract terms. They know that residents cannot always accept the standard terms and they welcome the chance to draft terms that satisfy their own needs as well as the resident's. Many housing providers are even knowledgeable about the fair housing laws. Whether or not they realize that an incoming resident will need accommodations or modifications, they know that if the adjustments are reasonable, they are legally obligated to accept them.

Residents can always appoint somebody to negotiate the housing agreement on their behalf. This can be a friend, family member, or caseworker; it does not have to be a lawyer. The safest way to make the appointment is in writing, either with a power of attorney document or by signing a form provided by the negotiator. In this document, the resident and the negotiator need to acknowledge that the negotiator is being appointed to represent the resident's specific requirements and preferences with the housing provider. The document should also note that the housing deal may fall through and that the resident will not get to hold the negotiator liable for a failed deal when she was merely representing the resident's interests.

An HOA may seem less comfortable with negotiations than other housing providers, but even the HOA industry association urges residents to clarify and negotiate before agreeing to HOA contracts. Residents in condominiums and community associations do own their own homes, but HOA contracts can include restrictions about how the yard or exterior of a resident's unit looks, about how many vehicles are parked outside, about behavior in the common areas, and much more. An HOA has the right to assess increasing fees if a resident breaks a rule and then does not correct the violation. Strict enforcement of HOA agreements is the only way that these associations can remain intact and function, so prospective residents have to be sure up front if they can live with the HOA rules.

Another important fact that residents need to know about negotiating for modifications or accommodations in any kind of housing is that they, the residents, will have to pay for them. This is stated explicitly in the Fair Housing Act. They also have to pay to have the changes undone when they move out, if the housing provider wants the place to be returned to its previous state. Explaining this to housing providers who are not familiar with the law can make housing contract negotiations much more comfortable.

Of course, modifications are more likely to involve costs than accommodations are, but some accommodations can come with a price. (Remember that modifications are changes to the physical space and accommodations are changes to rules or practices.) Here is an example of an accommodation with an associated cost:

Routine maintenance may be free to residents if the facility employs its own maintenance crew. But if Yves' mental wellness is affected by that crew and he needs to have a particular private contractor handle the occasional maintenance work needed in his apartment, he will be expected to pay out of pocket for his private maintenance worker—if he can prove to the housing provider (and possibly a HUD officer or judge) that this is a reasonable disability accommodation.

Residents ordinarily do not have to pay minor administrative costs that result from their accommodations; housing providers can absorb them. An example of a minor administrative cost could be the expense of having to drive to the bank and deposit a check from a resident who does not use the housing provider's electronic payment system.

Residents who need modifications or accommodations but are reluctant to reveal their mental health status before moving into a new home should know that they do not owe very much information to the housing provider. Fair housing laws do require residents to prove the disability and connect it to a particular modification or accommodation, but they do not require residents to be very descriptive of themselves. Certainly, residents do not have to convey anything about their treatment or any history of their mental condition when they request accommodations or modifications in housing. They only need to give bare facts. For example:

> Suppose your sister, Inez, is anxious or traumatized and will not answer the doorbell unless she knows who is on the other side. She wants to have a peephole installed in the door in order to be able to use and enjoy the apartment. She only needs to say that she is requesting a peephole as a disability accommodation because she has anxiety that prevents her from opening the door unless she recognizes the visitor or sees official identification. Her housing provider may require a verification letter from a care provider and may need to work out a system for confirming that staff will be admitted when necessary, but the provider should not need any additional details about the disability.

Residents who are concerned about missing a housing opportunity during slow negotiations can preempt that problem. They are right that the first person who arrives with the required money and signs the paperwork gets the place. If they are waiting for information before they can commit to the housing agreement, they may be able to literally buy time. Some housing providers will accept a pre-lease contract. In this agreement, a prospective resident pays money in exchange for the housing provider's promise not to let someone else have the place. The written deal will tell how long the promise is to last—how much time the resident is buying.

If the prospective resident is not waiting for information but is reluctant to agree to the place before his modifications are complete, then the negotiations will not get anywhere. Modifications are owed only to actual residents, not to possible residents. When the resident and housing provider write the lease clause about the modification, they can agree to a schedule for getting it accomplished. As soon as the modifications are justified and the clause is included in the contract, the deal is ready to go. The resident should sign and pay, and the housing provider should hand over the key.

POSSESSING A HOME

Once a resident moves in, he has to live within the terms of the housing agreement. No matter how ordinary the terms looked on paper, they may become very hard to live with. Various mental health symptoms can run afoul of the terms, but having a disability is not necessarily an excuse for violating the contract; very often it is merely a basis for requesting accommodations or modifications.

Housing Contract Terms

Here are some standard housing contract terms that may need adjustment for residents with mental illness:

- *Right of entry*—Housing providers may reserve the right to enter the unit at any time (typically in connection with maintaining the building or showing the unit to prospective residents) as long as they give the current resident a certain amount of notice. Residents can request accommodations as soon as they get that notice. They may need the housing provider to call thirty minutes in advance, or to come after noon, or to come only in the company of somebody the resident trusts. No matter what a resident requests, if he intends to package it as a disability accommodation, he will have to show how it relates to his mental health.
- *No pets*—Emotional support animals are a commonly permitted accommodation. However, the type of animal may be limited to accommodate other residents' fears, allergies, or other issues. Be aware that mental health providers are not always willing to attest in writing that having an animal will alleviate the client's mental symptoms. Without that documentation, many housing providers will not believe that the accommodation is necessary.
- *Tenant may not disturb neighbors' peace and quiet*—This term is just as likely to be used by residents with mental illness as it is against them. Housing providers rely on neighbors to be considerate of each other and to communicate directly with each other about noise. But it is hard for someone who does not feel well to confront a neighbor about loud music or arguments. And if the resident with mental illness is the one complained about, she may be shaken by the complaint. Realistically, the provider cannot require neighbors to tiptoe around and avoid disturbing someone else in the building; that sort of thing would not be a reasonable accommodation because it would interfere with the provider's fundamental operations. In extreme situations, a housing provider will evict a resident who chronically disturbs the neighbors. Residents have the option of suing neighbors for nuisance and intentional infliction of emotional distress, but the cases would be slow, expensive, and hard to prove. Most of the time, these problems are resolved by headphones or relocation, rather than the legal system.

Disposing of Trash and Waste

For people who hoard possessions, disposing of trash and waste is a difficult term to satisfy. Fortunately, there have been enough legal cases about hoarding tendencies that there is now a recognized accommodation to claim when housing providers attempt to evict residents due to the content of their households. Residents, through their disability lawyers, respond to the housing provider's eviction warning by requesting an opportunity to "cure" the lease violation. This request is filed in court as a response to the housing provider's notice.

Here is the accommodation: The housing provider must allow the resident to remain in place as long as he resolves the health, safety, and nuisance effects of having so much stuff in the unit. The health issues may involve infestations or germs from trash or waste. The safety issues may involve tripping hazards, fire hazards, and falling objects. The main nuisance is usually odor.

Because it is very traumatic for people with hoarding tendencies to discard and reorganize possessions, another accommodation that lawyers seek is sufficient time to make these massive household changes. The time will still be tight; the removal and reorganization process will not be gradual. Just as the lawyer obtains a psychologist or psychiatrist's affidavit establishing that the resident is disabled and in need of accommodation, she can ask the same professional (with the resident's permission) to provide the landlord and trial court with updates as the resident works through the housing upheaval. The evidence of progress demonstrates the resident's earnest desire to comply with the lease going forward and it can sometimes extend the removal and reorganization time.

As long as the resident discards enough content to remove health and safety concerns, pays cleaning and extermination fees, and demonstrates a plan to maintain the space in a safer and healthier way, he has a chance of succeeding in his eviction defense. He does not have to empty the place. He will probably have to get his place in compliance with local codes, such as the electrical, fire, plumbing, health department, and general building codes. There will be variations on this accommodation depending on the jurisdiction and the household. Sometimes, however, the court will not accept the accommodation and will proceed with the eviction.

HOW TO Request Housing Accommodations or Modifications

As a family member or support person for a resident with mental illness, you can approach the housing provider with a valid problem and a clear plan for resolving it. If you present only the problem, the housing provider will not necessarily know that you are asking for anything. If you present only the resolution plan without any justification for it, the housing provider may not believe that you need the modification or accommodation. The combination of the two messages (problem and suggested solution) is the strong opening move.

Either you or the resident can communicate the request over the phone, in person, or in writing, depending on the housing provider. If you communicate it orally, though, back it up with a written reminder within a day or two. By submitting the problem and plan in writing (print or email), you demonstrate that you seriously expect action. Be sure to sign, date, and keep a copy of your document in case you find yourself in a future legal situation in which you have to show a timeline or demonstrate that you requested an accommodation or modification for a disability.

Remember that you are submitting a request, not a demand. Phrase it as a question. For example: *As a modification for my son's disabling mood disorder, which is documented in the attached letter from Mountaintop Mental Health Services, would it be okay if we put up soundproofing material on the wall between his apartment and the one next to it so that he will not have to hear the neighbors yelling at each other?* Understand that the housing provider may have alternate ideas about how resolve to the problem. You, the housing provider, and the resident may have to go through a series of conversations with disability experts, contractors, and the resident's mental health provider in order to develop a mutually acceptable plan. Throughout your communications, be consistent in saying that the problem has to be fixed but also be considerate of the housing provider's legitimate interests as you seek changes to his property or practices.

As described in the hoarding example above, there are also times when the resident's need for accommodation only becomes obvious when he has violated the lease and is at risk of eviction. In those situations, either you or your loved one will need to ask the housing provider not to evict him and show proof that he can remedy whatever he has done to violate the housing agreement.

Again, whether the resident requests accommodation before experiencing a problem with the housing or after the problem has started, his request for accommodation will begin with presenting his accommodation need, which means revealing private mental health information. The resident may have to divulge vulnerabilities, explain things that upset him, and admit to not always having control over himself—all this just to keep living in a place.

If the resident is requesting accommodation in response to complaints from neighbors, the management, or an eviction threat, you or he will have to show that he has already taken steps toward changing his ways. Otherwise, the housing provider may not believe that he can comply with the lease. For some of this proof, you could show that the resident has purchased or been given certain supplies. You could present a new schedule and attest that he has already begun to follow it. You can get an affidavit showing that he has engaged peer support to deal with something so that he can avoid getting entangled with the neighbors.

You can have an occupational therapist or housing design expert provide a consultation and testimonial letter about helpful ways that the resident can function better in that particular place. You, the resident, and others in his support system may decide not to implement the functional changes until the housing provider accepts the plan and agrees to withdraw an eviction complaint from court, but at least the consultations will indicate readiness to fix the problems.

Paying for Housing

Article 1, Section 8, of the United States Constitution authorizes Congress to tax and spend for the general welfare. Ensuring that vulnerable members of society have housing is absolutely a way of providing for general welfare. When Congress allocates funds to HUD or the Department of Health and Human Services (DHHS) to institute housing and support programs for people with mental illness, the agencies are required to make regulations to frame the programs. In other words, housing and support programs are established by law, and people who satisfy the criteria to participate in the programs are entitled to them. Nobody should think that the word "entitlement" is negative and nobody should worry that there is something wrong with accepting a place in government-funded housing.

Even though housing funds are generated by HUD, which is a federal agency, they are managed by local, county, and state entities. HUD regulations primarily apply to those agencies and to housing developments, such as apartment complexes, public housing communities, and supportive group homes. The only ways that HUD regulations directly affect residents and their families are:

- By establishing criteria for living in HUD-funded housing
- By providing relocation assistance to residents of federally operated or funded housing that gets closed
- By operating the fair housing complaint process.

Residents are supposed to handle all of their government housing transactions with their local public housing agency, not with HUD directly.

The most well-known HUD program is The Housing Choice Voucher program, also known as Section 8. This program enables a limited number of people with sufficiently low incomes to select from any of the approved properties in their area and pay a fraction of the rent, with HUD paying the balance. (For a property to become approved, the landlord has to go through an administrative process that includes proving that the building meets certain "housing quality standards.") Some people with disabilities are able to get "certain developments" vouchers within the Section 8 program. These vouchers permit people with disabilities to live in certain Section 8 housing developments that are otherwise available only to senior citizens.

Aside from the Section 8 program, most of HUD's programs are basically ways of providing funds for states, counties, and cities to distribute. The Supportive Housing for Persons with Disabilities Program, known as Section 811, combines housing funds with access to supportive services. Other HUD programs prevent homelessness, or restore old properties, and so on. There are many HUD-funded programs that make accessible, supportive, and discounted rental units available to people who have disabilities and low incomes. Families can typically find these properties listed on their county's human services website and through the HUD Resource Locator.

Because they are legal entitlements, HUD-funded housing opportunities are wrapped in formalities. Consumers who cannot deal directly with their city or county housing authority can work with a caseworker to fill out the paperwork, possibly to participate in an interview, and to go look at multiple properties. Even after all of this work, they will typically have to sit on a very long waiting list, possibly for years, before eventually getting connected with housing. Along the way, there will be glimmers of hopefulness about getting a new start and periods of despair when it seems like a good housing solution is never going to work out.

HOW TO Help Someone Get HUD-Funded Housing

The best way to help a family member, for example your niece Luna, through waiting for HUD housing is to support her interaction with the process. Rules and regulations drive everything that HUD funds. If Luna is daunted by some of the tasks in the process, lend a hand or help her find someone else who can work through it with her.

Look for the facts that she needs to put on any forms that HUD or the housing authority requires. These will be standard facts about Luna's own life, such as previous addresses, income sources, and dates. You may need to order a copy of her credit report to get some of this information or else schedule a time when the two of you can go through the form together. Government forms can be very depressing and hard to focus on unless a kind and trusted friend or family member is next to you at the table talking through the questions with you. Once a form is complete, give Luna an envelope and postage, or computer access, or whatever is necessary to be sure she submits the form. Be sure to keep a copy of the form. If it is an online form and you do not have a printer, save it as a PDF or image before you send it and then email the saved version to yourself and to Luna.

When the housing authority calls or writes, help your family member respond promptly. Maybe Luna cannot summon the enthusiasm to deal with them herself, and you may not be thrilled about it either, because it may be yet another time when the housing authority has lost, changed, or forgotten something. But this communication could be really important. They may be calling to say that your loved one is approved for Section 8 housing—in other words she now has a voucher and can begin applying for properties in the Section 8 Housing Choice Voucher Program. Or perhaps they are calling to say that they received the last form, but it didn't have a signature at the bottom and they need your family member to come in and sign it this week in order to complete her file. The agency worker you are dealing with is merely trying to satisfy rules and regulations so that the rent subsidy or search for appropriate housing can begin.

Sometimes, if your family member has suffered through too many annoying complications with bureaucrats, it helps to turn the experiences into a sort of betting game. The two of you, and anybody else who wants to get in on the bet, can make a list of all of the possible hassles that may arise with the current bureaucratic communication. The list can also include positive items, such as "housing match." Each person can bet money that up to two items on the list are about to happen. Then, when the resident or, if she cannot do it, one of you on her support team responds to the housing authority's mail or phone call, she reports back to the others. You may want to continue the betting pool through several months of interactions with the housing authority, but it will only be fun if you make payouts after every call or letter.

Once your family member is approved for the housing program, switch to moving mode (unless it is a subsidy program that will reduce the rent payments where she already lives). Do not wait for an agency to find the actual housing unless you absolutely have to. Keep an eye on the HUD Resource Locator and local lists for places as they become available. Spot check every day and have all of your facts and documents handy so that your family member can pounce on new listings and get a signature from her case manager at the housing authority before anybody else does.

ENDING A HOUSING RELATIONSHIP

Early Termination

The same leases, group home agreements, and other housing contracts that record the price, rules, and expectations at a residence also contain "early termination" clauses explaining how residents can end the housing relationship early. At a place that specifically serves residents with mental illness, the early termination clause will likely respect residents' health-based reasons for needing to change plans. However, in other kinds of housing, the termination clause will usually say that the resident has to give the housing provider a certain amount of notice and pay a fee if he needs to end the contract early or does not intend to renew it.

The contract makes termination look clear and simple, but of course the circumstances of early termination complicate the situation; they blur the contract terms and cause a lot of stress. For example, early termination clauses typically require residents to pay a fee for getting out of the contract early. The fee may be a flat rate, a forfeit of the deposit, or the balance of the year's rent. When the early termination is the housing provider's fault, the resident usually does not have to pay the fee. If the property is noncompliant with state law—because of health or building code violations or a failure to pay property taxes—the housing provider is at fault and the resident does not have to pay the early termination fee. But when a housing provider is responsible for aggravating a resident's mental health symptoms, which makes it necessary for the resident to end the contract early (for example, when a housing provider employs a full-time maintenance worker who constantly plays loud music wherever he is working in the building and the music brings out one resident's delusional symptoms), the housing provider is not necessarily at fault; the (former) resident may have to sue the housing provider to get out of paying the fee. This makes no sense to people who understand the impact that mental illness can have, and that is why it is a good example of how standard housing contracts can lead to legal disputes involving a resident's mental health. The important thing to remember, when the housing conditions make it necessary for the resident to terminate early, is that almost every reason for early termination can also serve as a basis for fighting termination fees and trying to get the deposit returned. In other words, if the provider is not maintaining the place or the neighbors are causing trouble, the resident can assert that he needs to leave the place early because the housing provider's mismanagement is a breach of the lease contract.

Maybe a resident's Section 8 (housing choice) voucher has finally come through, making it possible for him to move to a different place, or perhaps his caseworker has found him a more supportive housing arrangement. It could be that his symptoms are worsening in the current environment and he has to move out in order to avoid going further downhill. All of these reasons are associated with being disabled. Since an accommodation is a change in the rules that is necessitated by somebody's disability, asking for the early termination fees to be waived can be a form of accommodation.

Here is another potential problem with early termination: What if a resident is in such a compromised mental state that he can hardly communicate at all and is currently being hospitalized? How can the resident be expected to notify a housing provider that he intends to move out? For that matter, how can he notify the housing provider that he is merely dealing with health issues and does not intend to move out? The housing provider, not knowing about the hospitalization, may believe that the resident has abandoned his home. This is not likely to happen if someone is just missing for a week or two, but if rent goes unpaid and mail piles up and a resident has disappeared without any explanation, a housing provider may think that the resident has taken off.

Of course, if the housing provider continues to get rent through government payments, a representative payee, or automatic deposits, she has no legal reason to concern herself with the resident's physical presence, and without further information she cannot presume that he has abandoned the place. Nevertheless, it is a good idea for someone who knows the resident to at least check in with the housing provider, say that the resident is away temporarily but will be back, and find out whether anything has to be done about the rent or the housing unit. This same caring friend or relative could also keep an eye on the mail and consider responding to any time-sensitive mailings—even if just to say that the intended recipient is dealing with a health issue and requires additional time to respond.

Here is a hassle to be aware of in regard to early termination fees: Housing providers can usually just deduct the money from residents' prepaid deposits. If the money is in the residents' hands, they can opt not to hand it over and then wait to see if the provider sues for it. But state landlord–tenant laws support the promises that people make in their housing agreements by telling how residents' deposits are allowed to be used. In almost all situations, the laws permit housing providers to tap into deposits when a resident owes them money or they have to repair damage caused by the resident who made the deposit. So when a resident seeks to have an early termination fee waived on the grounds that the housing provider's mismanagement is causing the early termination, or the fee waiver is a disability accommodation, he is generally asking the landlord to refund his housing deposit.

Eviction

When early termination is the housing provider's choice instead of the resident's, it is called an eviction. Most of the time, eviction begins with a warning, which is a notice to the resident that he has violated the lease and will be evicted if he does not take corrective action. Such actions can include paying back-due rent, keeping the windows closed when the heat is on, or stopping smoking in the hallway. Tenants are not necessarily owed a warning. The landlord may just send a "notice to vacate," a "notice to quit," or a "notice to cure" informing the tenant that, because of his lease violation, he has to vacate the premises (i.e., move out) by a certain date or else face legal action. That legal action is an eviction. If the resident lives in federally subsidized housing, the housing authority can evict a resident only for "good cause." Two standard examples of good cause are destruction of property and engaging in illegal activity on the property. As soon as a warning letter or one of the notices arrives, the resident or the family should bring in a caseworker to help figure out strategies and identify resources that can help the resident comply with the housing agreement. Again, this is something that sounds easier than it really is.

For the resident, maybe your good friend Sam who has a mood disorder, the notice or eviction warning may be only the most recent in a series of put-downs that he has been suffering. Whatever has been going wrong may have involved looks or comments from neighbors. There may have been criticism from multiple people more than once: Maybe the handyman griped at Sam for clogging the pipes too often or the lady next door told him not to hang around the entrance, even though his favorite seat is there. Sam may not even open the envelope with the eviction warning, and if he does open it, he may only feel worse. On top of everything else, he may be embarrassed to tell anybody that the housing is not working out. But if Sam remains silent, he may miss the chance to save his housing.

Eviction often comes with negative effects that are particularly troublesome for people with mental illness: a damaged reputation, a damaged credit report, a lack of money to deposit on a new place if the last security deposit went to pay for damage or a debt to the evicting landlord, and, almost always, stress and depression. To counteract stress and depression when eviction is looming, and to move the resident's focus away from the other possible bad results, families or advocates can review some neutral effects of eviction with a resident who has received either a warning or a court notice.

- If the housing has not been that good or the provider has been difficult, the resident may be perfectly happy to have an opportunity to get out of the lease early. In most evictions, the resident does not have to pay the full balance of the housing contract. As discussed earlier, when residents request early termination, they may have to pay the remainder of the contracted price, but in an eviction, the resident rarely owes any money beyond back-due rent and possibly the security deposit if he has damaged the property. Therefore, being evicted can save the resident some money while enabling him to move away from a bad situation.
- If the housing arrangement is not stable because the provider tends to make frequent eviction threats or taunts the resident about living at her mercy, and then the resident gets behind on rent or keeps getting in trouble just for being himself, he is better off taking the eviction rather than continuing to feed the housing provider's sense of power.
- Eviction is merely a legal transaction, just like negotiating the housing contract. A resident who gets evicted does not need to feel bad just because the arrangement is ending ahead of schedule.

Housing providers have to follow their state's procedures for evicting residents. Typically, the eviction procedures are in the landlord–tenant law, even if the housing arrangement is not strictly a standard apartment rental. If the housing provider is a disability support organization, it probably has its own more stringent rules to follow, in addition to the landlord–tenant law, before forcing somebody out of the residence.

The standard eviction process begins with a warning or notice, as noted above. If the resident does not make a payment toward back-due rent or take corrective action, the next step is a petition for eviction. The housing provider files the petition in court and the court issues an official notice to the resident. The notice may come in the mail or be posted on the resident's door. It will tell the resident to appear at a hearing about the eviction. The hearings are usually scheduled within just a few weeks.

The most common reason for eviction is nonpayment of rent, so the system seeks to resume the housing provider's opportunity to collect rent as soon as possible—by enabling him to get a new resident in the unit. As with all court appointments, either party can ask for the hearing to be postponed. (Sometimes this is called a continuance.) If a resident is experiencing a bad episode of mental illness and truly cannot represent his own position at the hearing, it only seems right that someone, perhaps you, ask the court to postpone the hearing until he can defend himself. A postponement form, or instructions for writing a petition, will be available either from the court clerk or on the court's website.

Technically, only lawyers and guardians or other appointees have authority to represent a party's interests in court, but since landlord–tenant hearings are relatively informal and health excuses are common, judges sometimes grant family requests for delays in these situations. It would be a good idea for someone close to the resident to include an explanatory note in the petition for postponement. The note could say something like,

> Please understand that my daughter [name of resident] has been unwell and is currently hospitalized. Her inability to pay the rent is connected with this period of poor health. Can you please postpone this hearing until she is well enough to be heard?

Understand that courts do not have to grant a postponement, no matter who requests it, and they can hold the hearing without the resident's being present. But an absent resident will almost certainly lose the eviction case, so there is a lot at stake here. If the attached note explains that the resident is receiving medical treatment for a disabling condition that led to the eviction proceeding, the judge may consider postponement to be a reasonable accommodation. If your loved one's condition satisfies the definition of disability that appears at the beginning of this chapter, then your note to the judge can include a line that informs the court about this. For example, it could say,

> Because my daughter's medical condition satisfies the Fair Housing Act's definition of a disability, please understand this request to postpone the eviction hearing is a request for disability accommodation.

If the eviction hearing goes forward, the resident's best defense will usually come from asking for an opportunity to cure his breach of the lease contract by changing his behavior (like the tenant with hoarding tendencies who was described earlier) or by working out a payment plan for paying back-due rent. The other defense that can sometimes save a housing arrangement would be one that is about fair housing principles—an assertion that the resident has not been reasonably accommodated. Sometimes, people with disabilities who are facing eviction will want to sue a housing provider for discrimination instead of merely using the discrimination claim as a defense against the attempted eviction. It is usually not necessary to take this extreme step. If the housing provider did discriminate against the resident, and the resident gets evicted, he or his supportive family member can still file a relatively low-stress fair housing complaint with HUD, even though the housing relationship has ended. (Read about reporting a discriminatory housing provider later in this chapter.)

HOW TO Testify at an Eviction Hearing

Eviction hearings move quickly. Judges handle dozens of them every day and can usually reach their decisions with just a few Yes/No questions. You, or more likely the resident—perhaps your brother Isaac who has PTSD—should be ready to answer the questions in a way that does not agree with the housing provider's claims. For example:

If the judge asks, "Did you pay the rent?" and the resident replies, "No, but . . ." the judge will cut him off. The provider claimed that the resident had not paid, and now the resident has admitted it. If instead, the resident says, "Yes, I paid the rent as long as I owed it—as long as the place was livable," then a real court argument has begun and both sides get to present their evidence.

In the standard format, the housing provider first presents her accusation that the resident breached the housing agreement. When she finishes her testimony, the resident (or her lawyer if she has one) can ask questions to see if the housing provider can back up her claim or to get her to admit to things that she did not say in her claim. Ordinarily, the judge will mark the end of the housing provider's testimony by inviting the resident to present his side of the case. The judge may do this by asking the resident if he has anything to say in his defense or the judge may ask the Yes/No questions at this point.

If your loved one is trying to represent himself without a lawyer and you are there with him, you may get the impression that the judge is about to dismiss the case or to announce a decision without giving your loved one a chance to state his position. This kind of thing tends to happen when the judge already has seen the housing provider in court a number of times and has gotten in the habit of believing her. If that is what is going on and your loved one needs support, go ahead and interrupt. You might say, "Excuse me Your Honor, may the defendant present his case now?" This may embarrass you, but it may also save the day for your loved one. If he has been hoping to express himself in court and it looks like the opportunity is about to pass him by, you have nothing to lose by reminding the judge that there are two sides to the case.

If your relative does not want you coming to court, you may be able to help him plan how he wants to communicate during the eviction hearing.

He should begin his defense with a strong statement that he did not breach the housing agreement. When questioning the housing provider, he may have shown some disagreement, but here he will try to lay it out clearly:

This is the housing provider's obligation. This is what I did. This is what the provider did. Now you can see that this problem resulted from the provider's failure, not mine.

The provider's obligations will be in the lease, in agency rules if the place is owned by a nonprofit, and in the law. At least some of the resident's complaints about the housing provider or the facility can probably be substantiated by the local building code or county health department regulations. You and your loved one can also look in the state's landlord–tenant law and consumer protection law. Refer to these laws and rules at every possible opportunity.

Here is a general example:

Suppose the lease or agency rules require the housing provider to provide laundry facilities. Several months ago, the dryer in your relative's building broke and the housing provider did not get it fixed or replaced. Instead, the housing provider hung a clothesline in the basement and told the residents to air-dry their clothes. All of the residents in the building have been angry about the lack of a dryer, but your relative cut the clothesline into small pieces and mailed the pieces to the housing provider with a note saying, "This is not a dryer!" The housing provider considers the rope cutting to be vandalism and is evicting your loved one on that basis. In the hearing, your relative will want to show that the housing provider is the one who violated the lease (and possibly an agency rule, if this is a group home, for example) by failing to uphold the common modern standard for a "laundry facility." Either he or you can search online for the phrase "laundry facility" to find a definition or examples proving that the phrase is understood to be about modern equipment, not a clothesline. He will also want to look at the vandalism clause in the housing contract to see if it uses a phrase like "damage to the building or fixtures" so that he can declare that a rope is neither a part of the building nor a fixture. Relying on rules and terms of the housing agreement like this can be a very effective way of turning the tables on a housing provider.

Here is a health department example:

Suppose the housing provider is evicting the resident for setting off smoke detectors every day, and suppose the resident knows that the smoke detector goes off because of shower steam, but she has to leave the bathroom door open during showers because of mold in the bathroom. Or maybe the smoke detector is set off when she uses the oven. The resident, or perhaps her supportive family member or close friend, can call the health department to inspect the place and see if the moldy bathroom, old oven, or other problems violate the health department code. If they do, the health department will issue citations and the resident will be able to use the inspection results to defend against her eviction. Her defense will be that the housing provider's health code violations caused her to set off the smoke detector.

Here is a consumer protection example:

Suppose the housing provider requires the resident to always be three months ahead with her rent payment. Then one day he notifies her that she has to move out of the place by the end of the current month. If the state consumer protection statute prohibits misleading consumers or causing a false sense of security, the resident can say that accepting her rent payments for months after the current one and demanding that she move this month is a violation of that part of the consumer protection law.

Here is an example of questioning the use of descriptive words:

Perhaps during the eviction hearing, the housing provider says the tenant did something "frequently." Ask the provider: How frequently? Where is the proof of that? Did she keep a calendar of the events? And did she say something to the resident every time she made a calendar note? Is she aware that she was harassing this resident by complaining to him about this issue all the time? If she only knows of a couple of incidents or did not keep records of them, then make her admit that she should not have characterized this is something that happened "frequently."

Maybe the landlord–tenant law or the housing provider's rules require the provider to give the resident a "reasonable amount of time" to find a new place before having to leave this one. What is reasonable? There is a lot of wiggle room with that word! Many factors contribute to how much time may be reasonable: the housing market, available funds, health symptoms, comparisons with how much time other people have needed, and so on. The resident's version of reasonable is at least as valid as the housing provider's version. And if the housing provider wants to argue about it, he has to go to the trouble of fighting the point in the eviction hearing.

If the resident did do something wrong, he may have had a valid reason for violating the lease. If disability is the reason, go through the whole fair housing analysis:

- *This resident has this disability_____.*
- *Because of the disability he_____.*
- *We have requested or now request that the housing provider accommodate this disability by_____.*
- *We submit this letter from the following professional who recommends this accommodation for this particular defendant.*
- *We believe that this is a reasonable accommodation because it will solve the problem for the housing provider and it will not interfere with his ordinary business practices.*

Here is a good strategy: If you listen carefully to the housing provider's testimony, you may hear her depicting the resident's disability. She may talk about moodiness or confusion or other symptoms. Use this as your opening to request accommodations. You can even say something like, "You yourself have noticed his mental health symptoms, yet instead of helping him, you seek to throw him out on the street." The idea here is to make sure the judge understands that, instead of accommodating his disability, the provider is evicting the resident because of it.

Possessions Left Behind

One of the typical results of either rushing or wandering out of housing is that residents do not take everything with them. Sometimes, they realize later that they are missing things. State landlord–tenant laws have provisions for these situations.

The provisions are the same no matter why the possessions were left behind—even if the resident went into the hospital and was unable to contact the housing provider.

If the housing agreement named an emergency contact or co-signer, the law may obligate the housing provider to contact that person and to report that the resident is gone but his possessions are not. The notice may look like a courtesy note, but it should be treated as legal notification that the resident has abandoned the dwelling and the possessions. This legal notice is required, in some states, before the provider can officially take the place back and rent it to somebody else.

Housing providers may not simply throw away their residents' belongings; they generally have to pack and store the stuff for a certain amount of time. If the resident tries to make contact and arrange to get his belongings, but the housing provider will not take his calls or will not agree to let him come for his things, the resident can petition (usually in the local small claims court—the same court that handles evictions) to get what belongs to him. This may be called a "petition for return of personal property," a "tenant's right of re-entry after lockout," or something similar to those phrases. The local legal aid office will likely have an online brochure about this process because the problem happens so often.

If at the end of the legally allotted time, usually a month or less, the resident has not made contact with the landlord and owes rent and otherwise seems to have walked out on the housing agreement, the law will characterize an absent resident's possessions as "abandoned." At that point, the housing provider is typically permitted to use the abandoned goods as repayment for back-due rent or to simply discard them if the resident does not owe any money. In many cases, housing providers will sell the items through an auction, rummage sale, or consignment store or else donate them to charity and get a tax deduction.

In situations when possessions are left behind after a dispute between a resident and his housing provider, whether or not there was an actual eviction hearing, the resident may never want to enter the premises again. This does not mean, however, that he loses the right to have his possessions; he should be able to get his things back. If the housing provider has a restraining order against the resident and the resident is not allowed to contact the provider or to return to the building, or if for any reason the resident is unable to remove his own possessions, the resident's friend or family member should be able to remove the his possessions from the premises without having to get a court order. You or another supportive person can simply call or write and ask when (not if) you can meet someone from management and collect your family member's possessions. If the housing provider gives you a hard time, then go to court—either to get an emergency conservatorship so that you have court authority to claim your loved one's possessions or, if your loved one can appear in court with you, to file for right of re-entry or return of possessions. (Conservatorship and the related topic of financial powers of attorney are covered in Chapter 21.) Even if you have the key and you believe that the possessions are still in the room or apartment that your family member occupied, you could run into trouble (or a changed lock) if you do not first make arrangements with the management.

If the housing provider gets rid of a resident's possessions before the law's time limit has passed or by preventing the resident and his support system from removing the belongings, the former resident can sue and get money to buy replacement items. In these circumstances, the likely legal claim against the housing provider would be the civil tort called "conversion."

HUD FAIR HOUSING CLAIMS

As part of its responsibility for enforcing the Fair Housing Act, HUD manages a complaint system for people who suffer housing discrimination. Fair housing complaints, which are initially called "claims" or "inquiries," can only be filed by "an aggrieved person," which means the resident who suffered discrimination. However, according to HUD's *Title VIII Complaint Intake, Investigation, and Conciliation Handbook* (fair housing handbook), there are circumstances when a family member can take action. "Any individual filing a complaint on behalf of an aggrieved person must present documentation that confirms that he or she has the authority to represent the interests of the aggrieved person. Examples of such documentation include a signed statement by the aggrieved person, or court orders appointing the individual as legal guardian, custodial parent, conservator or administrator on behalf of the aggrieved person."

If you do not have this kind of documentation and your relative is not comfortable filing a complaint, you can ask a disability support agency (for example, the nearest Obsessive Compulsive Foundation or the Depression and Bipolar Support Alliance) to make the claim. The handbook states that these entities have standing to bring housing discrimination claims. No matter who files the claim, the resident and the housing provider will both have to be identified and the resident will eventually have to participate in some aspects of the claim.

As an alternative to filing a housing discrimination complaint with HUD, you may be able to file one with a state or local Fair Housing Assistance Program (FHAP). Currently, thirty-eight states have a state FHAP, which means that they also have state laws against housing discrimination. The state law must be "substantially equivalent" to the Fair Housing Act in order for the FHAP to get HUD funding and be able to call itself a FHAP. Victims of housing discrimination may opt to file their complaints with the FHAP rather than with HUD and can expect that their complaints will be handled competently. Nevertheless, HUD invites all complaints to come in through its system. Sometimes, HUD will send a complaint that it has received over to the state or local FHAP. Victims who dislike or do not trust their state or local housing agency may indicate in their communications with HUD that they want their claim to stay with HUD and not be handled at the state or local level.

HOW TO Report a Discriminatory Housing Provider

As a relative of a resident with mental illness, you can help your loved one by filing a fair housing complaint with HUD. Either your loved one (through power of attorney) or a court (by appointing you as guardian or conservator) will need to authorize you to file the complaint. If the authorization is in place, begin by filing HUD Form 903, which you can find on HUD's website. Complaints are also accepted over the phone, in person, by email, or by postal mail. In the complaint, explain what has happened and why you think it is related to the resident's having a mental health condition or being disabled generally. You may have just one incident to report, but also indicate if you have gathered impressions, heard comments, or noticed other negative signals that are not exactly what you would call incidents. It is important for the complaint office to know whether you are dealing with a series of events and whether there is a discriminatory environment or just a single discriminatory person working for the housing provider. Even when you do not put the complaint in writing, the HUD worker who receives it in person or over the phone will write it down and require you to sign it before doing anything with it. If you do not sign and return the form within ten days, HUD will close your claim.

A HUD intake worker, also known as an equal opportunity specialist (EOS), will contact you within twenty days to ask additional questions. This conversation can feel suspicious or argumentative, but it is not meant to put anyone on the defense; it is merely for information gathering. The intake worker has to collect facts and enter them into a computer system.

The HUD complaint database is not connected to any other federal databases, and people who file housing discrimination claims do not need to worry that information from their fair housing complaint will be shared with other government agencies unless those agencies are involved in handling the complaint. An example of this is when HUD refers a complaint to a state or local FHAP. Another example is when HUD asks the Department of Justice (DOJ) to take action on a discriminatory housing complaint against a large-scale operator, such as the owner of multiple discriminatory housing complexes. Whether HUD pursues the case or not, it will keep a record about that provider in the event of future complaints. The complaint file will not be merged with other government records, and it will not be consulted in unrelated non-housing events involving the resident.

If the EOS is not able to match your situation with the fair housing process, she will refer you to the agency that does handle cases like yours so that you can file a claim with that agency. If the claim does look like a provable case of housing discrimination, however, the EOS will verify and supplement the information you have provided and then will send the completed complaint document via certified mail to you and to the housing provider.

Ordinarily, HUD will next pursue an investigation into the case. However, if the housing discrimination has put the resident at risk of serious harm or loss, such as homelessness, HUD can take emergency action before conducting its investigation. Suppose, for example, that the housing provider has started eviction proceedings, accusing a resident with mental illness of scaring the neighbors because he talks to himself. HUD can seek a restraining order to prevent the eviction from going forward. The eviction court does not have to grant the request for a restraining order, but HUD and FHAPs are known to arrange fair deals between residents and housing providers, so they are good at convincing eviction courts to let residents keep their homes through the fair housing resolution process.

HUD will use various research methods to investigate your fair housing complaint. Usually, HUD staff will gather documents (including those with facts about other residents served by this housing provider), ask questions of the housing provider, and visit the site in person. They will ask you and the housing provider to identify witnesses and then they will interview the witnesses. They may even conduct tests by having actors call or visit the housing provider to look and listen for discriminatory actions related to the issues in your complaint.

HUD Conciliation

Because so many housing discrimination problems can be resolved with an efficient exchange of information, HUD can convene a conciliation meeting at any point after the initial fair housing intake. Residents are usually permitted to include a support person in the conciliation, particularly if they need the support person to help them remember or communicate.

Conciliation involves a meeting. It is not adversarial like a trial. Participants usually sit around a table, although it is sometimes best if the resident and housing provider are in separate rooms and the conciliator travels between them, delivering messages. Or conciliation can take place over the phone—in a conference call. Whether in person or over the phone, the conciliator will take the lead in the meeting by stating rules for everyone to follow. In fact, the participants may have suggested some of the rules in advance. The rules do allow breaks, but they do not allow arguments.

The conciliator will make sure that the parties know that the meeting is confidential, that they both have the right to be represented by lawyers or other supportive people, and that they have the option of entering into binding arbitration to resolve some parts of their situation. After laying this foundation, the conciliator will summarize the current claim of housing discrimination and present some basic facts about housing discrimination. The parties will then get to comment on the summary.

The conciliator will often inform both the resident and the housing provider about some things that each of them communicated to HUD but not to each other. This is a helpful way of guiding the parties to understand each other. The conciliator may share examples of situations that were similar to what is happening with these participants, but mainly he will want them to suggest their own ideas for fixing their relationship. Residents and their support team should plan a list of desirable outcomes. Then, at the conciliation, they can state them with confidence. Desirable outcomes are not the same as final outcomes; residents will have to modify their expectations in the course of conciliation.

The primary goal of housing conciliation is to make plans for continuing the housing relationship without discrimination. If the housing relationship has already ended or definitely has to end, then the goals of housing conciliation will be to improve the housing provider's practices and to provide the former resident with an opportunity to describe the injustice that he suffered. Sometimes, depending on the resident's experiences and costs, conciliation can also result in money damages. Whether or not the relationship has come to an end, the housing provider may have to pay the resident for out-of-pocket expenses, such as the costs of photocopying documents, traveling to the conciliation, or meeting with a lawyer, which is not necessary for a HUD complaint or conciliation but does help some people to best explain their situations to HUD. If the housing relationship has ended, the housing provider may have to repay the former resident money that he lost by leaving the housing early and pay his moving expenses, and possible even extra costs associated with living in his new place. Sometimes HUD conciliators even order discriminatory housing providers to pay damages to their victim just for putting him through the trouble of having to bring the claim. When the money damages are owed to someone who collects SSI, the HUD conciliator can arrange for the payment to go straight into a special needs trust so that it will not compromise the recipient's SSI eligibility. (Read more about special needs trusts in Chapter 20.)

At the end of the conciliation meeting, the conciliator will draft a conciliation agreement. This document sets forth the housing provider's ongoing obligations to the resident and also to other residents with disabilities, current and future. The agreement may require the housing provider to supply routine reports to HUD as proof that he is fulfilling the conciliation agreement. Near the end, it will note that, if the housing provider fails to fulfill the terms of the agreement, HUD will submit the case to the DOJ for prosecution. Finally, the agreement will declare that the housing discrimination matter is now over and that the resident and housing provider are moving beyond it.

LIVING IN THE HOME OF FAMILY MEMBERS

Families are usually not legally obligated to house adult relatives with disabilities. In some states, however, filial responsibility laws do require that parents assist their indigent adult children and that adult children assist their indigent parents. These laws are written and interpreted differently in each of the states that have them, but none of the laws puts total outright financial responsibility on families and none specifically requires that families bring needy relatives into their own home.

The laws tend to identify particular types of expenses, such as medical and housing costs in need of supplementation, and to obligate only certain relatives— usually parents, spouses, and adult children, but not siblings, grandparents, or cousins. The laws do not relieve the federal, state, or local government of their obligations to poor people. They also do not require families to compromise their own well-being or to give the needy relative everything he wants. Filial responsibility laws simply identify circumstances when particular relatives who do have ample resources are required to provide some degree of help to their needy family members.

Whether or not a state has a filial responsibility law, many adults with mental illness spend periods living in relatives' homes simply due to the relatives' compassion and the practical reality that there are not enough supportive housing options available for all of the people who need them. When this happens, and the person with the disability receives SSI benefits, the SSI benefits will be reduced unless the person with the disability pays room and board expenses to the host relative. In other words, the Social Security Administration (SSA) considers free food and housing to be an asset. It is as if the government is saying, "If somebody gives you the gifts of food and shelter, then they are a form of income."

The SSA does not have a complicated formula for figuring out the value of the housing and food costs that families provide. Instead, they make a simple presumption: If the person with the disability lives in someone else's home and receives room and board without having to pay for it, then the SSI disability payment will be reduced by one third for every month that the residency lasts.

SSI beneficiaries will also have their disability income reduced if the parent or adult child with whom they live has an income. The SSA deems some of the host relative's income to be income belonging to the person with the disability. This same analysis applies to married couples; when someone with an income-earning spouse applies for SSI disability, part of the spouse's income is considered to be the SSI applicant's money. The SSI applicant or beneficiary is still considered disabled, and depending on his circumstances and state of residence, may be able to collect Medicaid. Note that when these family members, even spouses, live apart from each other, the income earner's money no longer counts against the SSI beneficiary.

Families who cannot afford to provide free food and housing or who simply do not want to give it away for free can charge their relative for living with them. In these situations, the SSI amount will not be reduced because the person with the disability will need the money to pay for living expenses. The SSA will not question the family's reason for charging room and board, it will just require proof of the arrangement. Suppose, for example, that your brother-in-law, Danny, is coming to live with you and your husband. The heads of the household (you and your husband) and the "tenant" (Danny) should all sign a document proving that the family does provide—and will continue to provide—Danny's food and housing and that Danny promises to pay his share of costs for the house and food. Danny's share truly should be an equal share of how much the home and food cost. In other words, the amount of his share is supposed to be figured out by adding the cost of your mortgage or rent, plus utilities, plus grocery costs, and then dividing that total by the number of people in the household. If your mortgage is $800 a month, your utilities are $200 a month, and your groceries are $500 a month, then your total monthly cost for housing and food is $1,500. If you, your husband, your two teenagers, and Danny all live together in the house, then that $1,500 has to be divided by 5 (since five people live there) in order to figure out how much Danny owes you every month. If you and your husband arrange for Danny to pay less than an even share, the SSA can say that he is not paying for room and board and they can then reduce his SSI payment by one third.

The SSA permits people to call and report changes in their circumstances, but sending the information in writing is more solid. Either the SSI recipient or the head of the household can send a copy of the agreement about living expenses, along with a cover letter, to the local Social Security office. The cover letter should include the name and Social Security number of the SSI beneficiary and it should say that the enclosed document is being submitted as proof that the beneficiary does pay for household expenses, despite living in a family member's home, and that he should not be deemed as receiving room and board as in-kind support.

Family Caregiver Agreements

A family caregiver agreement, sometimes called a personal care agreement, is a legal contract, written by a lawyer, in which a family member promises to provide a limited list of care services, usually along with room and board, to someone with a disability. In exchange for these services, the person with the disability may agree to pay money, take prescribed medicine, participate in therapy, and do chores for the family. If the person with the disability does not fulfill his end of the bargain, he can be made to leave the house. If the family does not provide a habitable space, decent meals, medication management, exercise equipment, or whatever other care services and resources they promised, the person with the disability will likely experience bad health symptoms and need to live someplace else where he can get better care.

These agreements are legally binding; the parties can sue each other if there is anything worth suing over. Lawyers, particularly those who practice elder law, are trained to write these agreements so that the parties can end the arrangement before things get bad enough to go to court. Lawyers do this by including guidelines for dealing with times when one of the contracting parties does not fulfill its part of the bargain, such as when a relative who has major depression, say your niece Jenny, moves into your house with her support cat Cleo and then does not clean up after Cleo.

When you discussed the family caregiver agreement with the lawyer, you said to him and to Jenny that Jenny has always liked to snuggle with cats and that she has a history of bad housekeeping. You told them both that while you were willing to provide a caring home for Jenny, you did not want to get stuck maintaining a litter box or cleaning Cleo's hair and dander from all over your house. The lawyer asked Jenny if she would agree to deal with the litter box, keep Cleo in defined areas, and dust and vacuum every Sunday. Jenny did agree to do all of that. "And what will happen if you miss a week?" asked the lawyer. Jenny said that she would do one of your chores (washing dishes) and make up for her missed cat cleaning. You weren't satisfied that this extra chore arrangement would keep Jenny on track, so the lawyer added some risk to Jenny's obligation. He told her, and wrote into the agreement, that if she failed to do her cat cleaning for three weeks in a row, you could take Cleo to the animal shelter.

Family caregiver agreements also include systems for avoiding foreseeable problems, such as the caregiver's occasional need to go out of town. Rather than scrambling to find a substitute caregiver right before they are about to travel, the family can put a plan for substitute caregiving into the agreement. To make this plan, the caregiver and the relative with mental illness can consult with the mental health treatment team or with other relatives about who can fill in when the caregiving relative goes away. The lawyer will want confirmation from the available substitutes and, with their input, will draft a routine for communicating and organizing in advance of a trip by the primary caregiver and providing coverage during the trip.

Families can discuss these issues when they meet with the lawyer to plan the document. In advance of meeting with the lawyer, families should think about the promises and requirements that they want to put into their agreement.

HOW TO Decide What To Put in a Family Caregiver Agreement

The first declaration in a family caregiver agreement should explain your household relationship. Explain why the adult relative lives in your home, in a way that is not a put-down. You may want phrase it formally like this:

This agreement establishes that A will provide the following care services to B for as long as B's disability prevents him from being able to care for himself or until either party elects to end this agreement.

However, you may prefer to have an agreement that sounds more like your usual way of talking:

We will let you live with us and we will do everything that this document says we will do, but only if you cooperate by doing what you promise to do in this document.

If the relative is living with you as a condition that keeps him from having to be institutionalized, you should reference the court order in your care agreement:

We are entering into this family caregiving arrangement pursuant to Judge Smith's order of September 15, [year] requiring that [name] either live with us or reside in [long-term care facility, jail, or other institution identified by the judge].

Include when the agreement becomes effective, whether on the date that it is signed or the first day of the next month, or some other specific day. Think about establishing either an end date or a "review and renew" date. This can be a general time period, such as in six months or a year, or it can be an actual date. For example:

We will review this agreement on June 1, [year] to decide whether to revise it, renew it, or end it.

To be clear, give the address of the residence and specifically list the spaces and furnishings that your relative will have access to. Say which bedroom he will have. Describe his kitchen privileges. Explain whether he has a private bathroom, access to a television, the yard, the bar, etc. It may be necessary to limit the rooms in which he may store his own possessions or alter the decor.

Specify that utilities are included. Since you will be living in a shared house, you really do not have the option of not providing utilities, but there are several reasons for stating that they are included:

- To show SSI the full range of in-kind support and maintenance you are providing
- To demonstrate to the Internal Revenue Service (IRS) that you are supporting this person as a dependent (if you are declaring him as a dependent)
- To be clear and accurate in your record-keeping
- To set the platform for rules about utility use.

Knowing your relative, you may need to require that showers not exceed a certain amount of time or that lights be turned off whenever he leaves a room. You may need to say that he is not permitted to adjust the thermostat or else that he can adjust the thermostat but cannot have a space heater in his room.

Set forth arrangements for cleanliness that both of you can honestly tolerate. Cleanliness issues include general housekeeping in the shared areas, care of your relative's private spaces, and washing laundry. If you house a relative who cannot tolerate germs and you keep such a dirty house that he is compelled to stay in his room all the time, then you cannot claim to provide him access to the whole house; your lack of housekeeping has made it impossible for him to use most of the house. On the flip side, you might house a relative who collects dirty abandoned objects or who never wants bed linens changed. Your family care agreement has to address the differences in housekeeping standards. Put rules and routines into the agreement so that you both know what to expect and what to ask of each other.

Between the facilities section and the services section of the agreement, you may want to address privacy and security. Your relative may need you to install additional security features in order for him to feel safe in your house. Alternatively, you may need to insist on standard operating procedures, such as:

Nobody leaves the house without ensuring that all doors and windows are locked.

or

Lit cigarettes are permitted only on the concrete back patio and must be disposed of in the sand bucket.

If your relative has a former spouse or enemy who presents a security risk, you all have to know about the person and agree not to let him or her in the house. As discussed in Chapter 13 of this book, in the section covering family liability, you may be criminally or civilly liable if you provide your relative with a dangerous weapon that he uses against somebody. There are ways to secure kitchen knives, shop tools, and guns. You and your relative can promise, in your family caregiver agreement, to take these security steps and then to follow them consistently.

Perhaps the most important service to establish is support for your relative's mental health treatment. He may need reminders about medication times, someone to practice skills with, motivation to attend appointments, and similar assistance. Maybe a treatment team has agreed to meet with him at home as long as you can ensure that he will be present when they come. Indicate that you will fulfill the tasks you know about and those that his therapist or team recommend later, and then include exactly what your relative has to do in exchange for the treatment support that you provide. He could, for example, agree to take the medicine as prescribed, participate fully in all forms of mental health treatment, cooperate with professional and family care providers, and not contradict efforts to help him be mentally healthy.

Similarly, you may need to promise that you will help your relative to satisfy court orders. For example:

- Your cousin Libby may need to participate in mandatory outpatient treatment.
- She may have a community service obligation to fulfill.
- She may need to meet with her probation officer.
- She may need to submit written reports.

Maybe Libby has a caseworker to help her handle these tasks. But if the caseworker is unreliable or if Libby will not cooperate, you may need to be the one who coordinates the compliance schedule, provides the rides, and generally makes sure that Libby does what the judge has ordered her to do. You have leverage because you are letting your cousin live in your house; formalize that power by putting it in the family caregiver agreement. Promise that you will support her efforts to satisfy court orders as long as she does her part.

Meals are another very important service to cover in the agreement. Indicate who will cook, how many meals per day will be provided, and whether everybody is expected to eat any of the meals together. Maybe you will buy the groceries and your cousin will do the cooking. If everyone has full access to the kitchen whenever they want it, set some guidelines about keeping track of grocery needs, making messes, and replacing broken objects. If anyone in the house has serious dietary limits, such as a peanut allergy, the agreement can require everyone to respect those limits. Explain how you will make sure that Libby has access to food when you need to be away for extended periods. Identify the food issues that everyone has to be flexible about.

You may also need to provide activities as part of your relative's care; being occupied and socially engaged are important to good health. You could facilitate socialization for Libby by setting her up with peer support, taking her to a clubhouse, or going along with her to activities. You may have to wake her for work every morning. You might provide her with a gym membership. Decide whether you will require Libby to do tasks in exchange for each thing you do for her. Here are some examples:

- If you do the laundry, Libby can be responsible for putting it in drawers.
- If you arrange activities, she has to bathe and groom herself and be ready on time.
- If you get her up in the morning, she has to feed the dog.

To offset any attempts by medical providers to bill you for your relative's care, consider including a declaration that you have no financial liability for any medical services that she receives. If you are paying for her health insurance (because she is not Medicaid eligible, because she is still in the waiting period for Medicare, or because you have to make sure that certain needs are covered), it does not mean that you are responsible for paying medical costs that are not covered by the insurance, even if you declare her as a dependent on your income tax return. Adult patients usually have to sign something at the doctor's office agreeing that they will pay for services that their insurance does not cover.

After you and your relative have written down all of the terms that seem necessary and possible to both of you, bring your list to a lawyer who specializes in either elder law or disability law. Elder law attorneys have the most experience with family caregiver agreements because senior citizens often pledge their own homes as payment for family care, arranging for the family to move in and care for them and then keep the house when they die. The lawyer will know how to make the agreement acceptable to the SSA and the state Medicaid office. He will also rephrase your terms to be sure that they are clear and enforceable, and he will build context around them. The context will provide for the "What if?" possibilities. For example:

- The lawyer will include a section on early termination, instructing everyone how to end the contract early.
- He will include the penalties that you and your relative agree to use against each other if you fail to keep your promises.
- He will help you devise a system for communicating about the household and the caregiver relationship, perhaps establishing when you have to give each other notice in order to do something differently.
- He will set forth instructions for modifying the agreement.
- He will help you plan a mutually acceptable way to manage during transitions and problems with service providers.

You will usually have a breathing period of at least several days between meeting to draft the agreement and going back to the lawyer's office to sign your names to the agreement. Ultimately, the lawyer will formalize the agreement by having you and your relative sign it in the presence of a notary. The lawyer will produce official copies of the agreement for Social Security, Medicaid, a judge (if this is court-ordered caregiving), and any other offices that need it as long as you inform the lawyer about those needs.

Tax Facts

- The costs that a taxpayer pays to modify his home for his disability are deductible medical expenses on his income tax return. If the person in need of disability accommodation lives in the home of a family member, the host who is the head of the household may claim this deduction only if he claims the person as a dependent. See IRS Publication 502, "Capital Expenses" section.
- The money that you spend to buy, train, and maintain a service animal is tax deductible as a medical expense, but note that the IRS clearly states that service animal deductions are only for people with physical disabilities. Expenses for emotional support animals are not deductible. See IRS Publication 502, "Guide Dogs and Other Service Animals" section.
- If a close relative (parent, sibling, step-sibling, adult child, in-law, aunt/uncle, niece/nephew, or former spouse) provides more than half of an adult relative's income, and that supported adult earns gross income (i.e., not counting government benefits, such as Social Security or income earned at a sheltered workshop) that is less than the current year's "exemption amount" (which is published in 26 U.S.C. § 151(d) and on irs.gov), then the supporting relative can claim the supported relative as a tax deduction. It is likely that someone who supplies room and board for another adult, whether or not it is in her own home, is providing more than fifty percent of that person's income.

- According to IRS Publication 503, families can get a tax credit for dependent care if they have earned income, claim as a dependent on their tax return a disabled adult who is not able to care for himself, and pay a care provider to help with the disabled adult relative. The criteria for not being able to care for oneself are "persons who cannot dress, clean, or feed themselves because of physical or mental problems" and "persons who must have constant attention to prevent them from injuring themselves or others." The IRS recognizes that the care provider may be needed for only part of the tax year (for example, during a temporary mental health crisis).
- A person who receives "nursing services" can deduct the cost of the services from his income taxes. The nursing services include dispensing medication and assisting with hygiene and may be built into a family caregiver agreement. Some group homes and supportive housing services may also be deductible as nursing services or possibly even "nursing homes" depending on the amount of care they provide. See IRS Publication 502, "Nursing Services" section, for more information.
- Taxpayers who work from home, even if the home is a rental, can deduct a space in their home that is used exclusively for work. They can also deduct the costs of heating, electricity (yes, every light bulb), and water that they use in their home work space as well as furnishings and office supplies that they purchase for their work. See IRS Publication 587, "Business Use of Your Home."
- State and local real estate taxes are deductible on federal income tax returns, but usually only for property owners, since they are the ones who are billed by the state and local government. Some states do allow renters to deduct their share of the landlord's real estate taxes from their state income tax returns when it is clear that the landlord is passing that expense on to the tenant. See IRS Publication 17, Chapter 22.
- Indiana and Minnesota permit renters to deduct parts of rent payments from their state income tax. See IC 6-3-2-6 *Information Bulletin #38: Income Tax* (Indiana Department of Revenue, May 2008) and Minnesota Department of Revenue Form M1PR, *Renter's Property Tax Refund.*
- IRS Publication 530 provides the tax information that all homeowners, disabled or not, need to know.
- Note that the "low-income housing tax credit" is a benefit to housing providers, not to residents. It allows owners of low-income housing to pay reduced taxes for building, buying, or rehabilitating housing facilities for low-income residents. See IRS Form 8609.

RESOURCES FOR HOUSING LAW

1. The Fair Housing Act and the Fair Housing Amendments Act are in 42 U.S.C. § 3601 through § 3619. Find them at uscode.house.gov.
2. Regulations that implement the fair housing statutes are in 24 C.F.R. § 100 through 125. Some specific sections to know about are 24 C.F.R. § 103(b) regarding fair housing complaints, 24 C.F.R. § 100.203 regarding

reasonable modifications, and 24 C.F.R. § 100.204 regarding reasonable accommodations. See also the definitions at 24 C.F.R. § 100.200 and the building accessibility standards that are listed at 24 C.F.R. § 100.201. These federal regulations are free online at ecfr.gov.

3. The *Joint Statement of the Department of Housing and Urban Development and the Department of Justice, Reasonable Accommodations Under the Fair Housing Act* (2004) and the very similarly titled *Joint Statement of the Department of Housing and Urban Development and the Department of Justice, Reasonable Modifications Under the Fair Housing Act* (2008) contain plain English summaries of the fair housing laws as well as good examples. Find them online by searching for their titles in quotation marks.

4. The housing discrimination research study that compared the way landlords treated a recent college student and a person coming from a mental health treatment facility is *Discrimination Against Persons With Disabilities: Barriers at Every Step* (by Margery Austin Turner et al., and published by the HUD Office of Policy and Development Research in 2005). It is available for free online at hud.gov.

5. If you are curious about other people's housing discrimination stories, read through the cases in HUD's online collection of documents on "Fair Housing Act Enforcement Activity." For each case, you can read a press release summarizing the situation, the full complaints that HUD filed in court, and the final resolutions.

6. HUD has a "Tenants Rights" portal that links to state landlord–tenant laws.

7. HUD's Fair Housing Equal Opportunities Library (FHEO Library) contains great technical guidance for housing providers. Families and residents can use the materials to phrase their communications with housing providers and to inform any inquiries or complaints that they are inclined to file against a housing provider.

8. *Tools for Tenants* is a guide to supportive housing. Written by the Substance Abuse and Mental Health Services Administration, it has short, clear explanations of tenants' rights and several checklists where people can identify their housing priorities, preferences, and needs. Find it at homeless.samhsa.gov.

9. The Community Associations Institute, which is the industry association for HOAs, provides good explanations, organizational guidance, and sample forms. See their publication "What You Should Know Before You Buy" at caionline.org.

10. The HUD Resource Locator at resources.hud.gov links consumers to programs, properties, and offices.

11. The *Multifamily Inventory of Units for the Elderly and Persons with Disabilities* is an online list of properties that are insured and subsidized with HUD funds. Find it by typing that title into a search engine. Each listing tells whether the housing is for the elderly or people with disabilities.

12. The National Housing Law Project publishes very helpful guidebooks, fact sheets, and other guidance on public housing. An especially

helpful resource is its packet of reasonable accommodations letters and pleadings, which contains "a variety of sample letters, pleadings, and documents that advocates have used to pursue reasonable accommodation requests." You will have to register for a free account at nhlp.org to see the letters and pleadings.

13. Search for the phrase "public housing agencies" on the HUD website. This will get you to a portal where you can find the proper name and full contact information for your nearest agency. Read through the housing agency's website to find out about local programs, people to contact, funds available, and property listings. Many people think that only caseworkers are allowed to locate properties, but individuals can do that for themselves once they know about the housing authority's website. Also look for the *Public Housing Guidebook* in the HUD search engine. This is the rule manual that public housing employees have to follow.

14. The *Housing Choice Voucher Program Handbook* is written in plain English and contains all of the HUD guidelines for Section 8 rentals. Chapter 5 of the handbook is "Eligibility and Denial of Assistance." Enter the chapter name and handbook title in a search engine to read this information for free online and to see how to best ensure that your relative satisfies the requirements to get in the program.

15. The article by Tom Cobb et al., "Advocacy Strategies to Fight Eviction in Cases of Compulsive Hoarding and Cluttering" (in *Clearinghouse Review Journal of Poverty Law & Policy*, Nov.–Dec. 2007, pp. 427–441), is practically an instruction manual for helping someone with a hoarding tendency to stay in a rental unit. It serves as a good example for using any kind of disability as a defense against eviction.

16. The Bazelon Center for Mental Health Law provides a free online manual titled *What Fair Housing Means for People with Disabilities* at bazelon. org.

17. The *Title VIII Complaint Intake, Investigation, and Conciliation Handbook* (8024.1) is the HUD staff manual for handling fair housing claims. This source has exact instructions for claims workers to follow. It specifically requires them to be helpful and courteous and to take the time to be sure that they and complainants understand each other. Because the handbook contains such full explanations of why and how the fair housing office does things, some residents or loved ones might like to read it before filing their own complaints. It is online at https:// portal.hud.gov/hudportal/documents/huddoc?id=80241c4FHEH.pdf.

18. Find links to state and local fair housing laws at http://lawatlas.org.

19. The DOJ Housing and Civil Enforcement Section (at justice.gov), enforces the Fair Housing Act and the Equal Credit Opportunity Act, typically by obtaining money damages for residents and forcing housing providers to change their conduct. Its website links to summaries and documents from recent cases.

20. The most efficient way to find out whether your state has a filial responsibility law is to contact your state's Area Agency on Aging, www. n4a.org, or the state office for AARP (American Association of Retired

Persons) at aarp.org. The laws are most commonly applied when aging
parents need assistance.

21. The Social Security information about reducing SSI payments when
families provide room and board is on the ssa.gov website under the
topic "living arrangements." For more detailed technical information
about this, see POMS Chapter 00835.001 titled "Introduction to Living
Arrangements and In-Kind Support and Maintenance," which you
can reach by entering that phrase and "poms" in a search engine. The
regulations on the topic are at 20 C.F.R. §§ 416.1121–1148.

22. Look in the *Social Security Handbook* for clear English lists of the
many rules about "deeming"—the times when a spouse's assets count
against someone with a disability who seeks SSI disability benefits. This
handbook is available at ssa.gov.

23. Facts and instructions about notifying the SSA of changes in housing
circumstances, whether cost, location, or anything else, are in a free
online publication, *What You Need to Know When You Get Supplemental
Security Income* (at ssa.gov).

24. The Family Caregiver Alliance provides many practical, compassionate,
and free resources for families who have adult disabled relatives living
with them. One page on their website, titled "How to Compensate a
Family Member for Providing Care," has very useful information about
family caregiver agreements. See caregiver.org.

25. The American Bar Association and state bar associations offer continuing
legal education courses about drafting family caregiver agreements. The
training materials from the courses are usually available at county law
libraries.

26. Legal aid offices in every major city and state provide landlords and
tenants with legal summaries, samples of court documents, and
handbooks. Even when a housing arrangement is not a traditional
landlord–tenant relationship, the materials will likely be instructive to
residents. If a resident satisfies low-income qualifications and the legal
aid office is not too busy, it may also provide a lawyer to represent the
resident. Search for your city or state name and the phrase "legal aid" to
find these free legal services and their online resources.

PART 5

Death and the Law

23

Missing Persons

When your ex abandoned you and moved across the country to be with someone "less rigid" years ago, you hoped you'd never have to see him again. Your son Brendan was fourteen at the time, big enough to go without you on commercial flights between your home and where your ex (Brendan's dad) moved. With your son's oppositional defiance, it wasn't always easy to get him packed and on the plane. It wasn't easy to get him to do anything. Now, he's grown up and has major depression and anxiety. Having flown between parents throughout his teenage years, Brendan is an experienced traveler who always seems to be moving from one miserable experience to the next. He'll stay with you for a few months until he remembers that you are the worst person in the world and then he'll disappear, wandering around the country in search of people he knows and sights that have been featured on the Weather Channel. You never know when or where he will pop up again. You've reached the point where you actually feel relief when your ex calls, because whenever he does, it is to tell you that Brendan has shown up at his place. The rest of the time, you worry. You don't know where he is, if he is okay, and whether you can do anything.

WHERE HAVE YOU GONE?

Lots of people opt to go "off the grid" for a time, just to take a break from dealing with everybody. This is generally legal, but if you disappear without letting someone else know, and you fit within the state's definition of a "vulnerable person," the police will likely investigate your absence as a possible crime. Families are terrified when this happens; they would much rather be in contact with their missing relative than with investigators. For example:

I know a woman who called everyone in her ratty twenty-year-old personal address book when her adult daughter (let's call her Candy) went missing. Candy had previously attempted suicide more than once and was now unhappy at her distant job. The mom thought that old friends might have heard from her daughter, and she was right. Candy was burrowed in a former boyfriend's summer home because it was off season and nobody was there to bother her.

Another woman told me that her son, let's call him Eugene, would slip away every three years or so. He would take buses around the country and live on the streets. After a month or two, a police department or social service agency would

*call her to come and get him. Then there was the time when he was gone for sev-
eral months and nobody called. Eugene had major depression, and his mother
started calling people she knew. Like the other mom, she contacted everyone
she could find who had ever known her son. She filed a missing person report.
Every time she heard on the news about the body of an unidentified man being
found, she called the police to ask if it might be her son. It never was. Then one
day somebody found Eugene deep in the woods, almost covered with leaves, and
dead from a self-inflicted gunshot wound. Forensic evidence confirmed the date
of the suicide note that was in his pocket; Eugene had died over two years earlier,
probably within days of leaving home.*

THE RIGHT TO DISAPPEAR

Most citizens of the United States are free to come and go as they please. Of
course, people who are confined by court order to a mental health facility, a correctional institution, or house arrest are not free to roam. Similarly, people who
have legal responsibilities, such as caring for a child or reporting to a probation
officer, cannot intentionally disappear without making arrangements to cover their
legal obligations. If those people abandon their legal responsibilities, they can be
arrested when they are found. Other than in these situations, people can go away
and stay away and not tell anyone where they are. This freedom is inherent in the
U.S. Constitution's Thirteenth Amendment promise that slavery "shall not exist" in
this country and the Fifth and Fourteenth Amendments' promise that neither the
federal government nor state governments may deprive any person of life or liberty.

Safety is the government's only reason for interfering with any free person's disappearance. Police have to investigate when they learn that somebody may have
been kidnapped, killed, or otherwise victimized. State-level missing person laws
further obligate police to investigate when vulnerable people disappear. In more
than half of the states, vulnerable people are identified as persons experiencing
symptoms of severe mental illness. The actual wording in state laws tend to be
"mental impairment," "mental disability," "high risk," or "mental condition that
subjects the person or others to danger." Of the thirty-seven states with alert systems for missing adults, twenty-eight call for the alert system to be implemented
when a missing person suffers from a mental or cognitive impairment.

Another way that police can intercept a missing person is to simply ask for identification. Police sometimes do this as part of a wellness check when they see somebody out in public who looks disoriented or unwell. Some police also try to get the
names of new folks in the homeless population, either to know who is around or
to connect the new person with appropriate local services. Twenty-four states have
"stop and identify" statutes specifically authorizing police to make people identify
themselves when the police suspect them of criminal activity. Even vague crimes,
such as loitering and blocking the sidewalk, are typically valid reasons for police
to ask for identification. Despite these legal authorizations for locating people who
have gone missing, people who do not want to be found can usually avoid attention.

Investigating the Missing

Police departments have internal protocols for investigating people who have gone missing. The protocols and state missing person laws permit people to report disappearances as soon as they are known. The traditional requirement for waiting a day or more before reporting a missing person is long out of style. The police may not take action immediately, but at least they no longer turn people away when they come to report a missing person before a certain amount of time has passed.

The police begin their intake reports by interviewing people close to the missing person. The interviews can be long, detailed, and unnerving. The police want to know about the missing person's relationships and physical characteristics, such as eye color, blood type, cosmetic implants, moles, and birthmarks. These questions—as well as inquiries about personal contacts, possessions, and interests—come from a printed list of standard questions that are meant to be thorough but often do not include characteristics that can be associated with certain psychiatric diagnoses. Examples include:

- The missing person has a tendency to bite nails, pick skin, pull out hair, or dress in a particular style.
- If he has a distinct way of walking or communicating, the police need to know.
- The person has multiple personalities with the following names and attributes.
- He has an alias or a character that he plays, and here are the things that he cannot resist or consistently avoids.

The more the police know about an individual's unique characteristics, the more easily they will be able to recognize him and get him home safely. Families should volunteer the information even if the police do not ask for it.

In addition to interviewing people who are very familiar with the missing person, the investigators will try to get DNA samples from the missing person's possessions, especially the hairbrush and toothbrush. They may also ask certain relatives to provide their own DNA samples. The police investigators will want to know about places where the missing person likes to go or places he has wanted to go. It will help if they know that the missing person, for example your younger brother Henry, who hasn't been seen for about a month, prefers to hang around with particular kinds of people (such as musicians) or engage in certain activities (like watching trains).

The police will put the information into their state or department database and will share it with other jurisdictions that are likely to encounter Henry. Once the report is in the state database, it will be forwarded to the National Missing and Unidentified Persons System (NamUS) database and to the National Crime Information Center (NCIC). The file will be coded as "high risk" if there is reason to believe that Henry is suicidal or in a severe state of mental disruption. Having completed their intake report, the police will ordinarily inspect Henry's home and the place where he was last seen. Knowing about Henry's mental health diagnosis, they will check to see if he is in an inpatient mental health facility. If he is not hospitalized, they will ask witnesses to provide any indications of Henry's plans and observations of his companions or departure. Predictably, the extent of their investigation will depend on department resources. Sometimes, in certain jurisdictions, the police may conduct their investigation and file their report in a single afternoon and then just wait for tips to arrive.

HOW TO Search for a Missing Person

Although there are situations when it is illegal to take personal action in connection with a police investigation, helping to locate a missing person is not one of them. The public information in the missing person database is meant to be shared. You can publish it in print and post it online without fear of being prosecuted.

Let's continue with the example of your brother Henry, who has borderline personality disorder. If you think that he could have changed his name, look for name change announcements in newspapers. Every U.S. jurisdiction requires that legal name changes be published in the newspaper. You can also organize a posse of searchers and hire a private investigator to help with the investigation. Know that your police department may want to register your volunteers—just to be sure that they know who is legitimately engaged in the search. Some police departments require volunteers to participate in search and rescue training. The training helps the volunteers to be safe and thorough in their hunting and canvassing. It also reduces the likelihood that they will accidentally ruin evidence.

Keep the police informed about your investigation. Tell your case investigator every time you begin a new facet of your search and every time you discover something about Henry. Feel free to ask your police case investigator for guidance and assistance; it is likely that she will offer advice every time you indicate that you want to expand the search. You can even ask her to come and speak at an event for your volunteers.

There are lots of expenses associated with searching for missing persons. It costs money to print flyers, tee shirts, and billboards; to equip searchers with flashlights and compasses; and to feed volunteers. You may need to buy two-way radios or a drone. When word gets out about your missing brother, people may come forward to offer money. You can accept the donations without knowing exactly how each financial gift will be spent on the search. However, if a donor limits the use of the money for a particular purpose, say for newspaper ads—especially if you requested it for that purpose—you should try to use the money that way or else get the donor's permission to use it for something else. It is not necessarily a contract violation to apply earmarked money to the general purpose of finding Henry, but you can avoid being sued for breach of contract by not promising a specific use in the first place or by fulfilling your promise if you do make one.

Any money that people contribute toward finding your missing brother should be kept in a bank account designated just for the search, and it should be used only for documented costs of looking for Henry. If there is any money left in the account after Henry is found and you donate it to a missing persons nonprofit, you can avoid the appearance of committing theft or fraud that could exist if you used the money for personal expenses. Since the money was donated only to help find your brother, not to make him well, even paying for medical care that he may need after he is found can be seen as making personal use of the donated money.

Some donors may ask for their money back once your relative is located. It is not illegal to refund donations, but it is also not required by law for two reasons:

1. Donations are considered irrevocable gifts—gifts that cannot be cancelled.
2. When the purpose of the donation ceases to exist before all of the money is used, you really cannot know exactly which donations were spent and which were not; all money is the same once it lands in the donation fund.

If your fundraising efforts will include raffles, bingo, or something like a carnival, check your state's "charitable gaming" law, and also find out whether your city has any restrictions on gambling. Sometimes nonprofit organizations will host games of chance as fundraisers when private groups do not have legal authority to collect donations that way. A church that has a weekly bingo game, for example, could donate one week's bingo income to the search for your missing loved one.

Unclaimed and Unidentified Dead Bodies

When somebody dies from suicide, a sudden and unusual medical event, homicide, or under mysterious circumstances, state law requires that the death be investigated. Every death involving someone who is alone and without identification is considered mysterious. To investigate these deaths, some jurisdictions have medical examiners, who are licensed physicians, and some jurisdictions have coroners, who are not necessarily physicians, although they do employ pathologists (doctors) to conduct autopsies. Autopsies are thorough examinations of the internal and external parts of the body. They are necessary only when the coroner or medical examiner cannot determine the cause of death more simply.

Every state has a statute describing how the coroner or medical examiner should attempt to identify bodies. Generally, the professionals are not obligated to look further than the government databases of criminals and missing persons. If they cannot figure out who the person is, they are supposed to submit all possible facts, photos, and dental information to the NamUS database of missing persons. The body will then be categorized as an unidentified dead body. If the coroner or medical examiner can identify the body but nobody in the family or community takes it for burial or other final disposition, the body will categorized as an unclaimed dead body.

The state laws about coroners and medical examiners are typically in the statutory code's "health and safety" category, and they also cover when and how to dispose of the unclaimed or unidentified remains. The coroner or medical examiner will have to hold the remains for a certain amount of time, usually at least a month.

After that, some states require burial or cremation at government expense. Other states allow the state's anatomical board to regulate disposal of the body, while others allow the body to be donated for medical research. A family who learns too late that their relative died and was either unclaimed or unidentified can obtain a copy of the autopsy report by following the instructions that the coroner or medical examiner provides online. If no autopsy was performed, the family can at least learn the cause and approximate date of their loved one's death by obtaining a copy of the death certificate from the state's vital records office.

CLOSING THE CASE

When a missing person is found either dead or alive, the police case file will be closed, although parts of it may be used as evidence in connection with related criminal charges. The related charges would apply if the missing person had been kidnapped, or if he was engaged in crime while he was missing, or if the missing person report was fraudulent to begin with. If the missing person died, the police will gather final facts from the coroner or medical examiner. To close the file, the police will generally write the results of their investigation, attach a closing code number, and save the information in their database. Then they will notify other agencies that helped with the case. Finally, they may have a practice of reporting "lessons learned" within their own professional development system.

When a missing person has not been found and the police have run out of clues to pursue, the case will be designated unsolved or it will be classified as a cold case. Police departments handle cold cases in different ways. The files may be moved to a different location, or they may get tagged as inactive. Some departments have special units that routinely review the files or implement new forensic tests on old evidence, and some continue to publicize the case so that members of the public can still submit clues. Every so often, someone from the police department may check with the family to ask if they have heard from their loved one.

Families who cannot tolerate the financial and emotional uncertainty of not knowing what happened to their loved one may petition the probate court to declare him dead. The actual petition may be titled something like "Petition for Presumption of Death." State laws and sometimes local court rules give precise instructions for filing the petition. Most of the time, the law treats the petition as part of an action to probate the missing person's estate.

The entire family does not have to petition together or even agree on the idea of having their loved one declared dead. Any one person can file the petition. Ordinarily, the petitioner is someone who needs to make a financial claim or to deal with a property matter that can only be handled in connection with probating the estate of the person who has been missing. The person may be a spouse who cannot get a home equity loan without proof that the other spouse has died or a spouse who wants to remarry. It could also be a sibling of the missing person who is the executor for their parent's estate, but who cannot make accurate distributions without a legal record declaring that the missing person is dead. Of course, it may also be necessary to file a petition for presumption of death when family members cannot otherwise collect the missing person's pension, investment accounts, or life insurance money. There are many valid reasons for filing the petition.

The petition is a simple form identifying the petitioner, the missing person, a few facts about the absence, and the reason for seeking the declaration. For many families with a missing loved one who is mentally ill, the most challenging question on the page is the one asking for "date of disappearance." Your guess may be weeks or months off from the actual date. The form will need to be accompanied by proof that the person has been missing for as many years as the state law requires— often five years, but sometimes as few as three—as well as proof that loved ones and others have been searching for him. The police report, the NamUS profile, and copies of any advertisements regarding the missing person will be convincing evidence to accompany the petition. The evidence should show that the search has been going on for as long as the person has been missing and that loved ones have tried multiple ways of hunting for any clues about what happened to him or where he may have gone. Having to repurpose the ad materials and revisit the whole search process for the Petition for Presumption of Death means looking at all of those hopeful words and efforts and admitting that now they are the opposite of hopeful; now they are being used to prove that the loved one is not coming back.

Tax Facts

- If you open a bank account for donations to help locate the missing person, you can obtain a federal tax identification number (EIN) for the account. This way, it will not appear that you are creating the account for personal benefit, and the interest earned on the account will not count in your personal income tax return. To obtain the EIN, complete Internal Revenue Service (IRS) Form SS-4. Use your own name as the legal name on the account and on the line that asks "reason for applying," check the box next to "banking purposes."

- If your relative owes income taxes and does not file a federal income tax return during the time that she is missing, the IRS will charge interest and nonfiling and nonpayment penalty fees. The mental health situation and other circumstances connected with her absence may be "reasonable cause" for the IRS to reduce or eliminate the fees. The IRS web page titled "Penalty Relief Due to Reasonable Cause" has instructions for making this claim in response to a fee notice. IRS Form 843, *Penalty Abatement,* must be filed with an explanation of your "reasonable cause," along with any proof you have to substantiate your cause.

- For personal guidance on handling your missing person tax quandary, you can request a private letter ruling from the IRS. The IRS instructions and a sample form for the request are at irs.gov on a page titled "How would I obtain a private letter ruling?"

- The IRS has a mail-forwarding process that you can use to get a message to a missing person. This will work only if the person has been in contact with the IRS since disappearing—for example, if the person has taken a job in a different city. Under this process, the IRS will forward a letter that serves a "humane purpose." The IRS defines humane purposes as those that have "urgent or compelling" messages that are not merely about finances. To access this service, you have to provide the IRS with a request that justifies your need for having the letter forwarded, the missing person's Social Security number, and a copy of the letter that you want the IRS to send to the missing person. Your letter to the missing person has to contain the following statement: "In accordance with current policy, the Internal Revenue Service has agreed to forward this letter because we do not have your current address. The Service has not disclosed your address or any other tax information and has no involvement in the matter aside from forwarding this letter." The IRS will not provide you with any information about the missing person and will not even confirm whether it found a new address for the person. Submit your request to IRS Disclosure Scanning Operation, Stop 93A, Chamblee, Georgia 30341. To read the full text of the procedure—Rev. Proc. 2012-35, see Internal Revenue Bulletin 2012-37, which is on the irs.gov website.

RESOURCES FOR MISSING PERSONS

1. An article by Tobias D. Wasser, M.D., and Patrick K. Fox, M.D., "For Whom the Bell Tolls: Silver Alerts Raise Concerns Regarding Individual Rights and Governmental Interests" (published in 2013 in the *Journal of the American Academy of Psychiatry and the Law*, Vol. 41, pp. 421–429), summarizes the state laws about adult missing person alerts.
2. The National Association of State Charity Officials links to the office in each state government that deals with charitable fundraisers—typically the Secretary of State or the Attorney General. It is a good idea to check with that office before collecting donations to use in the search for the missing person. See nasconet.org.
3. *Missing Persons: Volunteers Supporting Law Enforcement* is a free online guidebook from the Bureau of Justice Assistance, the International Association of Chiefs of Police, and Volunteers in Public Service. It has practical ideas and examples for police departments working with nonprofessionals to organize searches, staff phone banks, and spread the word about a missing person. See bja.gov.
4. The FBI's ViCAP (Violent Criminal Apprehension Program) resource collects and organizes information about missing persons who may be victims of violent crimes. Anybody can access it for free online. It contains two categories of records on missing persons: Records of persons whose names are known because they were reported missing and have not yet been found, and records of unidentified dead bodies. All of the entries contain basic physical descriptions of victims, including scars and tattoos. The entry for a person reported missing includes the missing person's name and photos provided by the family. The entries for unidentified bodies have images of clothing and possessions that were found with the bodies and, when possible, sketches of victims' faces. Find ViCAP at fbi. gov.
5. The FBI roster *Kidnappings and Missing Persons* tells the circumstances surrounding each person's disappearance in addition to providing photos and describing the person's physical characteristics. Find it at fbi.gov.

6. NamUS, the National Missing and Unidentified Persons System mentioned in this chapter, is made up of three databases: Missing Persons, Unidentified Persons, and Unclaimed Persons. The databases are free for the public to search online. The Missing Persons database has facts about people reported missing as well as information about people who have amnesia, dementia, delusions, head injuries, or other problems that prevent them from being able to identify themselves. Anybody, not just law enforcement agencies, can enter facts into the Missing Persons database. The Unidentified Persons database describes people who died but could not be identified by the coroners or medical examiners who entered their information into the system. The Unclaimed Persons database has information about deceased people whose identities are known, but whose families, friends, and faith communities did not claim their bodies. See namus.gov.

7. The University of North Texas Center for Human Identification Forensic Services Unit has numerous resources for families of missing persons. The center runs DNA tests on objects submitted by missing person investigators from all over the country. They also provide case intake forms and data entry guides for police departments to use. Families may want to browse through the sample documents to be sure that they have given all of the necessary information to investigators. Additionally, families are welcome to access the Center's series of free online courses about investigating missing and unidentified persons. The Center's portal to state missing persons clearinghouses will help families locate resources in particular states and regions. See untfsu.com.

8. *Police Chief Magazine* has two free online articles about police authority to demand identification. One is titled "Stop and Identify Laws," and the other is "Suspects Who Refuse to Identify Themselves." See policechiefmagazine.org.

9. The U.S. Supreme Court case approving police inquiries about people's identification is *Hiibel v. Sixth Judicial Court of Nevada Humboldt County*, 542 U.S. 177 (2004). Find it online by typing the first part of the case name into a search engine.

10. The Centers for Disease Control (CDC) has a free portal titled *Coroner/ Medical Examiner Laws, by State* where researchers can read and find laws about autopsies and the states' investigative systems. See cdc.gov.

11. See the *Medical Examiners' and Coroners' Handbook on Death Registration and Fetal Death Reporting* (free online at cdc.gov) for federal guidelines about the information that has to be collected and recorded in suspicious deaths.

12. To find a state's vital records office so that you can obtain a copy of a death certificate, either go through the cdc.gov page *Where to Write for Vital Records* or type the phrase "vital records" and the name of the state where the death occurred in a search engine.

13. The National Alliance on Mental Illness (NAMI) maintains a brief and clear online guide called *Finding a Missing Loved One* (available at nami. org).

24

Wrongful Death

Whitney and her family made careful arrangements for managing her eating disorder at college, but two months into school, when she was too busy and uncomfortable to deal with the dining hall, the arrangements started to fall apart. The RA was relieved when Whitney cancelled their dinners together. Somehow, she'd forgotten why Whitney even needed her as a dinner companion. She vaguely thought that Whitney was shy at first and had now found friends to eat with. The head of dietary services had lots of meals and students to keep track of; he had no idea that Whitney never asked for sack lunches or any of the other special services he'd offered her. The therapist at the campus counseling center met regularly with Whitney until mid-semester and then reached out to her when she stopped coming for appointments. Whitney agreed to a new therapy schedule but then never showed up for the appointments, and the therapist lost track of her. Meanwhile, Whitney was wasting away. Stressed by having to work so hard at everything on campus, she was depressed and not eating at all. Late one night, she had a massive heart attack in the dorm laundry room. The next morning, some students found her and called 911, but Whitney didn't survive. Her family can't get straight answers from anyone at the college. The family members don't know what went wrong after they made such careful arrangements, but clearly something went very wrong and they want to sue the college for Whitney's wrongful death.

WHAT IS WRONGFUL DEATH?

Wrongful death is a civil law claim that someone died because of action or inaction by particular people or entities. Its criminal version is homicide. Individuals bring civil cases, in which the punishment is primarily monetary damages, while the government brings criminal cases, in which the punishment can be incarceration and other losses of freedom. Whether or not the government arrests and prosecutes someone for causing a particular death, families can sue for wrongful death. Sometimes, the only way that a family can find out exactly what went wrong is to go through the discovery process in a wrongful death lawsuit. In the discovery process, the defendants accused of wrongful death are required to provide documents and to answer truthfully detailed questions about their actions and inactions leading up to the death. The questions asked in discovery are the same questions that will be asked in the courtroom. For this reason, many families are willing to settle their case out of court once they get explanations through the discovery process.

When wrongful death cases do go to trial, it is easier to win a civil wrongful death judgment than it is to get a criminal homicide conviction, because homicide has to be proven "beyond a reasonable doubt," whereas wrongful death only requires "a preponderance of the evidence," which usually means that just slightly more than 50% of the evidence proves that the defendant is liable. A famous demonstration of this was the combination of trials in which the football star O. J. Simpson was accused of killing his ex-wife and her boyfriend. He was found not guilty in the criminal trial because the jury still had some doubt about whether he had killed the couple. In the wrongful death trial, when the families of his ex-wife and her boyfriend sued him in civil court, he was found guilty because the jury was more than halfway convinced that he had caused the deaths.

Of all the sad and terrible stories about victimizing people with mental illness, wrongful death stories are some of the worst; they are all about ways that people could have helped, but did not. They ignored calls for help. They failed to show up. They did not pay attention. They did something wrong. Sometimes the details even show that people made mistakes because of the victim's behavior: He was strange in some way, and, because of that, they avoided him or did less than they otherwise would have.

Who Can Sue for Wrongful Death?

Most states have statutes that identify which people are entitled to receive damages from wrongful death claims; they are the only people who can bring wrongful death suits. Ordinarily, the executor, administrator, or personal representative of the estate is the one who hires the lawyer and in whose name the case is filed in court. Although the case is in the name of the executor, that executor relies on the statute to know which relatives, typically certain close family members, can get paid out of the proceeds of the case. A few state statutes specify that spouses or heirs may bring the case on their own without going through the executor. Since the wrongful death statute is about collecting assets in connection with someone who died, it is published in the probate section of the code.

HOW TO Begin a Wrongful Death Lawsuit

Personal injury lawyers—not estate lawyers—handle wrongful death claims. Note that personal injury lawyers get paid only if they collect money through a settlement or jury verdict. You want a lawyer who has won other wrongful death cases and will be tough against your opponent but kind to you. If the lawyer does not show compassion for your loss when she first hears the awful story from you, how will she show compassion in court? You may also want to know whether the lawyer is knowledgeable about mental illness. Contact your nearest National Alliance on Mental Illness (NAMI) chapter and other agencies that provide mental health advocacy or services to ask for names of lawyers. If an agency declines to give you names, look through its newsletter and websites for the names of board members or volunteers who have Esq. after their name. As you talk with each lawyer, you might float a few test questions to see how they explain some of your deceased relative's behaviors. You do not have to be sneaky about this; rather, you can say something like, "I want to be sure that I hire a lawyer who can explain mood disorders in a kind way. Can you tell me how you would prepare yourself to do that?" You can present it as a situational question, such as, "Knowing that my daughter did not perceive the world in the same way as most people do, how do you think you might argue against a claim from the other side that she caused her own death?" You might get a feel for the lawyer's knowledge and attitude by asking her to describe a past client who had a mental illness. For the best chance of getting a personal injury lawyer to represent you, bring a lot of facts to your first conversation, even if it is over the phone. As always, interview a few lawyers, confirm that they will not expect you to pay any money out of pocket, and compare their qualities before you decide which one to hire.

To prepare for these first conversations with lawyers, be ready to convey who, what, when, where, and as much as you can about how. When you explain who was involved, understand that the lawyer needs to know if it is an institution or individual with sufficient assets to make the lawsuit worthwhile. It sounds cold and cruel, but the primary remedy in a wrongful death lawsuit is money. True, there can be other punishments in addition to the money. Families often want the responsible people or institutions to be stripped of professional licenses, suffer damage to their reputations, and change their ways. These results can happen, but the actual legal remedy for wrongful death is monetary damages. It is important to understand that a law firm probably will not take a case unless it can be paid for the work, which means winning a settlement or judgment.

Describing what happened can be complicated. You will not have all of the details. Begin by itemizing the injuries that led to the death and by naming the official cause of death that appears on the death certificate. Then, tell as much as you know about the circumstances: whether equipment was involved, who was with your loved one during the incident that led to her death, whether she was okay prior to the incident, what kind of explanation you were given for her death, and anything else you know about what happened.

Your statement about when it happened will have two parts: (1) how long ago the death occurred and (2) how much time passed between whatever went wrong and when the person died. The state's statute of limitations determines how much time you have to file a wrongful death claim. You typically have two years after the injury that led to the death. So you do not have to rush, but the sooner you get a lawyer, the sooner the legal investigators can begin collecting physical evidence and talking with witnesses.

You tell where the death occurred so that the lawyer can figure out whether an insurance policy might pay for the lawsuit. Also, the location will give the lawyer ideas about evidence. It might be a place that has security cameras, for example, or that is obligated to produce incident reports when people get injured. If you know why your relative was in that place, provide the information to the lawyer as well.

When you get to explaining how the death occurred, you will be tempted to guess. Try to present as many facts as you can before you state any theories that you want the lawyer to consider. Was there a warning? Did people there previously show that they ignored, disliked, or disrespected your family member? Had she told you about faulty machinery, such as the unreliable elevator in her apartment building or the bad brakes on the group home's shared car? What kinds of medications was your relative taking at the time? Did anyone close to the situation share their impressions with you? If so, give the lawyer their contact information.

The heart of the lawyer's case will be about how the death came about. The firm will collect business records, medical evidence, police reports, and eyewitness testimony. They will make a timeline of events and diagram where everyone was and what they were doing. All of this information can be gathered over time, so you should not feel pressured to explain, in the first conversation, how exactly the person or institution caused your family member's death.

The strongest message that you have to convey when you first meet the lawyer is that you are truly suffering from the loss of somebody who should not have died the way she did. After all the years of sticking up for your loved one and facing down her opponents in all kinds of settings, this is your last chance to get back at someone who mistreated her. Never lose sight of that. Soon enough, those on the other side of the case will try to make your relative look bad; you want to be sure that you are hiring a lawyer who will not be swayed by those claims. When you tell the lawyer what your relative was like, watch and listen for a caring promise that this lawyer wants to get justice for your loved one.

Duty in Wrongful Death Claims

A legal claim for wrongful death is an accusation of negligence. This means that the survivors are suing a person or agency for neglecting their duty. To prove the case, they have to show that the particular duty really exists and that the defendant was responsible for fulfilling it. They also have to show that the defendant did not fulfill the duty (in other words, breached the duty) and that the breach resulted in your loved one's death. Here are some of the duties that are raised in wrongful death lawsuits:

DUTY TO PROTECT PATIENTS
Treatment facilities that know or should know about a patient's suicidal tendencies have a duty to keep the patient from hurting or killing himself. This typically means that the facility should keep the patient away from chemicals, sharp objects, ropes, and other potentially lethal objects, such as grab bars, towel rods, and drawer handles. Sometimes, patients have to be physically restrained. Hospitals also have to protect patients from being injured by other patients and from catching other patients' diseases.

DUTY TO PROTECT DETAINEES
Police departments and corrections agencies have a duty to protect people who are in their custody. If they put a detainee together with a dangerous person or fail

to protect a detainee from killing himself, they can be liable for wrongful death even though government immunity laws often prevent lawsuits against government workers. State courts differ on whether these entities can be liable only if they knew or should have known about the person's suicidality. (Read more about police and corrections liability in Chapter 12 of this book.)

DUTY TO FOLLOW PROFESSIONAL STANDARDS OF COMPETENCE

Police, medical providers, and other professionals whose malpractice results in somebody's death can be liable for wrongful death. It is easy to find stories of police departments that have been sued and paid settlements to families of people who were killed by officers who failed to recognize and correctly deal with suspects' manifestations of mental health problems. There are also many news stories and television shows about doctors prescribing the wrong types, quantities, or combinations of medicine and otherwise failing to follow professional standards for competence.

DUTIES TO MANUFACTURE SAFE PRODUCTS AND TO WARN CONSUMERS ABOUT SAFE PRODUCT USE

Foods, medications, small appliances, and many other consumer products are required to have instructions for safe use and warnings about the danger of unsafe use. If the warnings are not there or are inadequate, it is much easier to succeed in a wrongful death product liability lawsuit. Successful examples of such cases include those brought against manufacturers of prescription medications that drove people to suicide or psychosis, against automobile manufacturers whose cars had mechanical defects, and against manufacturers of food products who did not warn about allergens. Some professional football players' claims about head injuries leading to depression and suicide have been against helmet manufacturers. If a patient dies from an infection or other condition that happened as a result of initial negligence in production or labeling of a drug or equipment, the manufacturer can be liable as the "proximate cause" of death.

DUTY TO MAINTAIN SAFE PROPERTY

Businesses, hospitals, nonprofit organizations, and homeowners have to either fix dangerous conditions on the inside and outside of their property or else prevent people from entering the dangerous areas. Facilities may be liable for wrongful death when someone who is rightfully on the property is injured by another person on the property—especially when the facilities fail to have adequate security features. This is one of the reasons why so many places have security cameras and guards.

DUTY TO PREVENT SOMEONE FROM CAUSING HARM

This is a nebulous concept of duty, but lawyers devise versions of it in order to sue the families of people with mental illness. Although data show that most people who have a mental illness are not dangerous, there have been high-profile stories of mass shootings and other attacks caused by people with mental illness. Victims' families blame the killers' families for providing weapons, for not getting their relatives into hospitals, for not properly caring for their family members with mental illness, for not alerting society about these relatives, and for other omissions that families very often had no way of preventing. Sometimes, however, families could have prevented trouble—such as when they made drugs or weapons available or allowed their relative to use the car when he was obviously not in a safe condition to drive.

FAMILY INVOLVEMENT IN WRONGFUL DEATH CASES

Family members do not have to be present for most of the events in a wrongful death case. The executor who brings the case (who may or may not be a family member) will attend initial meetings with the lawyer and collect certain information for the firm. The information will likely include people's contact information plus documents from the decedent's home and computer. The executor might need to testify in the case, and she will get periodic updates from the lawyer. She will not, however, need to be present when the lawyer questions the opponents prior to the trial, and she will not need to be there when the staff in the law firm discuss the case among themselves.

The rest of the family, assuming that the executor is a member of the family, can just wait for the trial to start or the suit to be over, unless any of the lawyers want to question them. The pretrial phase, when the lawyers swap paperwork, gather expert opinions, and question each other's witnesses at depositions, will usually take several months. During that time, there probably will not be much to hear from the executor. Anyone who wants to follow the case can try two things in addition to keeping in touch with the executor: (1) see if the local court posts case documents on its website (there will not be many of them during the pretrial phase) and (2) offer to help the lawyer.

One of the most likely ways that a family member might help is by providing something similar to a victim impact statement that would be used in a criminal case. This can be done in a letter to the lawyer. It does not have to follow a specific format; it just needs to be a heartfelt declaration about how the person is affected by the death. The lawyer might not reply, but if she does, she might ask the relative to be interviewed privately in an office or even to testify in court. No matter what, the letter will help the lawyer to demonstrate how much harm was caused by the wrongful death. (Refer to Chapter 7 of this book for details about victim impact statements.)

DAMAGES IN A WRONGFUL DEATH CASE

Wrongful death survivors suffer in various ways and can collect damages for each form of suffering. If the family depended on the decedent's income, the court can pay them for the years of earnings that they will not get because of the wage-earner's death. Children suffer from the loss of guidance and companionship of a deceased parent and can get damages to compensate for the losses. If any relatives need treatment for mental distress following the wrongful death, they may be able to collect damages for their "mental anguish." Damages can also repay families for funeral costs and other expenses caused by their loved one's wrongful death. Sometimes, families can even collect damages on behalf of the person who died. In extreme cases, it is possible to get punitive damages, which exist solely to punish whoever caused the death.

When the lawyer representing the family asks personal questions about relationships, household finances, and mental health issues, it is usually for the purpose of figuring out how much money to seek in damages. Families can always ask, "Why are you asking me that?" if they are uncomfortable with a lawyer's questions.

Examples of Wrongful Death Cases

DEEDS, ROBERT CREIGH V. COMMW. OF VIRGINIA, VA 25TH JUDICIAL CIRCUIT, BATH COUNTY DOCKET #CL 15 000056-00 (FILED NOVEMBER 19, 2015)
This case is still pending, but due to its notoriety, the complaint is available online. A Virginia state senator sued a hospital, a mental health evaluator, and the state government for his son's wrongful death when his son shot himself after being discharged from the emergency department without getting necessary treatment. The son had a history of serious mental health issues. The mental health evaluator concluded that the son needed to be involuntarily committed but could not find a local facility for him and sent him home instead. The next morning, the son stabbed his father and killed himself. The legal complaint specifically asserted that the mental health evaluator at the hospital emergency department had a duty to find an inpatient facility with the space and competence to treat the son and that the region should have had a "web-based psychiatric bed registry." The complaint further asserted that the Department of Behavioral Health and Developmental Services had a duty to implement the Virginia Inspector General's recommendations for "emergency services to individuals in mental health crises."

DELANA V. CED D/B/A ODESSA GUN SALES, 486 S.W.3D 316 (MO. 2016)
The Brady Center to Prevent Gun Violence represented Mrs. Delana in the case, which is available on the Brady Center's website. In the case, a mother sued a gun store for selling her daughter a gun. The daughter used that gun to kill her father. The mother declared that, if the store had not sold her daughter the gun, her husband would still be alive. The daughter previously had been committed to a psychiatric facility and had been treated for paranoid schizophrenia; she should not have been able to purchase a gun because state law prohibited stores from selling a gun to people "adjudicated as being mentally defective." Since the gun store had a statutory duty not to sell the daughter a gun, but did sell her the gun that she used to kill her father, the mother asserted that the gun store was responsible for the wrongful death of her husband.

TATE V. CANONICA, 180 CAL. APP. 2D 898, 5 CAL. RPTR. 28 (CAL. CT. APP. 1960)
This is an early case (available free on Google Scholar) in which a family was able to sue for wrongful death when somebody caused their husband and father so much emotional distress that he killed himself. The family asserted that the defendant "intentionally made threats, statements and accusations against said deceased for the purpose of harassing, embarrassing, and humiliating him in the presence of friends, relatives and business associates." There have been many similar cases since this one.

SMITH V. UHS OF LAKESIDE, INC., 439 S.W.3D 303 (TENN. 2014)
This is a more recent emotional distress/wrongful death case (available online), in which a man who appeared to be depressed and delusional died from encephalopathy. The police had found him asleep in his car and, upon waking him, believed that he needed psychiatric help. They transported him to a psychiatric hospital, which misdiagnosed him as having psychiatric problems. This error enabled the encephalopathy to worsen and to cause permanent damage. Within months, the man was dead. In this case, the claim asserted that both the family and the patient suffered emotional distress because of the way the hospital handled the patient. (We do not know the final result of the suit, because the state's Supreme Court sent the case back to be retried and the result of that trial is not a published opinion.)

RD v. WH, 875 P.2D 26 (WYO. 1994)
In this case, a stepfather was sued for wrongful death and emotional distress. The stepfather had repeatedly sexually assaulted his stepdaughter when she was growing up. The sexual assaults caused her to suffer severe depression and to attempt suicide several times. She died from suicide using an overdose of a medication that the stepfather obtained for her, having days earlier failed in an attempt to shoot herself with a gun that the stepfather had provided.

AFTER THE WRONGFUL DEATH CASE

Wrongful death lawsuits can have an impact beyond whatever happens in court, even when they get settled out of court. They live on when legislatures, regulatory agencies, and institutions make new policies to prevent the same kind of death from happening again. Texas passed the Sandra Bland Act in memory of a woman who had depression and who was arrested after a minor police stop and an argument with the officer, and who then committed suicide in jail. The Bland family sued the county for wrongful death. Their out-of-court settlement in the case called for legislation in their daughter's name to implement specific improvements in jail booking and treatment for inmates who are mentally ill.

In Cincinnati, Ohio, a hospital that called police to intervene with a patient who was highly paranoid will now rely on its own expert practitioners instead of police to deal with psychiatric crises. This is because the police who encountered the patient with paranoia made him even more frightened and uncertain and then shot him with a Taser (an electronic control device, sometimes called a "stun gun"). The patient had a heart attack and died right after the tasing. His family called for the policy change and for the creation of a mental health advisory panel (which is also being implemented) when they sued the hospital for wrongful death.

Think about all of the pharmaceutical ads that now admit that their products "may cause suicidal thoughts or actions." Much of the pressure to establish those drug product warnings came from wrongful death lawsuits that unearthed little-known problems with the products, forced more thorough testing of them, and insisted that patients be alerted about the very dangerous side effects.

Not every wrongful death case results in immediate policy changes; sometimes it takes a collection of cases to reveal good ideas for improvements. However long it takes for policy changes come about, they supplement the legacies of people who die wrongful deaths. The stories of these people's lives do not end with the fact that they died; their lives mattered and should not have ended in the way and time that they did. The message underlying every wrongful death lawsuit and the policy changes that flow from it is, "Do not let this happen again."

Tax Facts

- Payments for physical suffering in a wrongful death judgment or out-of-court settlement do not count as taxable income. Payments for emotional distress or mental anguish in a wrongful death court case do count as income unless the problems originated from physical harm. Each recipient of money from the lawsuit will be taxed only on the amount he or she actually receives, not the total amount of the settlement before it was divided among people. See Internal Revenue Service (IRS) Publication 4345.
- If you previously filed a tax return deducting medical expenses because you paid out of pocket for medical treatment that you needed in connection with your loved one's wrongful death, then you are supposed to declare as income on your current tax return the part of your settlement or judgment that pays you back for the medical expenses. See IRS Publications 525 and 4345.
- Attorney fees in personal injury lawsuits (including wrongful death lawsuits) generally count as income to the plaintiff (the person who brought the lawsuit) when the lawyer was working on a contingency basis (getting paid only if she won or negotiated fees into the out-of-court settlement). Therefore, although the plaintiff does not get to keep the money, he does benefit from it, because his legal bill is being paid for him. This has been decided in cases interpreting 26 U.S.C.104(a)(2). See the IRS publication *Lawsuits, Awards, and Settlements Audit Techniques Guide* for details.

RESOURCES FOR WRONGFUL DEATH

1. To find your state's wrongful death law, enter your state name, the phrase "wrongful death," and the word *statute* into a search engine. It should look like this example: Montana "wrongful death" statute.
2. For a full, detailed presentation of the law about hospital liability for preventing suicidal patients from killing themselves, see Jonathan M. Purver, "Hospital's Failure to Protect Patient from Self-Inflicted Harm," *Proof of Facts*, 9, 2d, 223, Thomson Reuters—updated annually. This source includes checklists of proof to gather as well as sample questions to ask of various hospital employees. Find this publication at your county law library.
3. The National Institute of Corrections has articles and blog posts about detention facilities and liability at nicic.gov.

4. Facts and case stories about police liability for harm to detainees are available from the American Civil Liberties Union (aclu.org), FindLaw (findlaw.com), and the National Criminal Justice Reference Service (ncjrs.gov).

5. The Consumer Product Safety Commission (CPSC) accepts direct complaints about products that cause injuries. Reporting a dangerous product is an easy way for survivors to help prevent other families from suffering. The CPSC also maintains lists of dangerous products. If the product that led to your relative's death is on a CPSC list, there will likely be some lawsuits already pending against the manufacturer. See cpsc.gov.

6. The Brady Campaign to Prevent Gun Violence lobbies for gun safety legislation and participates in court cases about gun safety. Peruse their action-oriented materials at Bradycampaign.org.

7. A Texas lawyer named Skip Simpson maintains an online list of medications that have been associated with suicides and suicidal thoughts. See skipsimpson.com.

8. "Mental Illness and Violence," a *Harvard Mental Health Letter* (January, 2011; available from health.harvard.edu), is a clear but authoritative article that summarizes several research studies. It concludes that "violence by people with mental illness—like aggression in the general population—stems from multiple overlapping factors interacting in complex ways. These include family history, personal stressors (such as divorce or bereavement), and socioeconomic factors (such as poverty and homelessness)."

9. Lawyers publish lots of training materials in their professional journals. *The Brief*, published by the American Bar Association's Tort, Trial, and Insurance Practice Section, is a monthly publication full of practical guidance. For example, an article from *The Brief*, "Tragic, But is it a Wrongful Death? Tips for Defending a Suicide Case," tells lawyers how to protect clients in suicide wrongful death cases; in other words, the article shows the arguments that lawyers use against families that have lost somebody to suicide. Read it only if you can tolerate that perspective. Note that it includes a list of cases from all fifty states. The full citation is Matthew P. Smith, "Tragic, But is it a Wrongful Death? Tips for Defending a Suicide Case," *The Brief*, 44:3 60 (2015).

10. To find a lawyer who knows about mental health and wrongful death, look for lawyers who are on the boards of, or are associated with, your NAMI affiliate and your state or city's disability protection and advocacy agencies. To find these entities, start at www.nami.org and www.ndrn.org/en/ndrn-member-agencies.

Suicide Law

Alex, the only child of a single mother, was a year and a half into his first
professional job when his mom killed herself. He owned a car, had an apart-
ment, and knew how to handle a lot of things, but he didn't know what to
do after a suicide. The police talked him through the first steps of collecting
the possessions that were with his mother when she died and contacting a
funeral home. But then a lot of other questions and problems came flying at
him, mostly about money. The funeral home wanted to know how much his
mother's life insurance was worth so that they wouldn't charge more than that
for her funeral. His mother's landlords said he should sign the life insurance
policy over to them since they were owed the rest of the year's rent, according
to the lease. The owners of the hotel where she died wanted that life insur-
ance money, too. Alex didn't even know if his mother had any life insurance.
And he didn't want to talk to these greedy people. He only wanted to talk to
his mom.

HISTORY OF SUICIDE LAW

It used to be illegal to commit suicide. This meant that if someone intentionally
killed himself, the government got his assets. Of course, the person who died no
longer needed that land, house, money, or jewelry, but the family did. Essentially,
the law mandated that families had to suffer not only the loss of their loved one, but
also the loss of anything valuable that he possessed.

The practice of taking away the possessions of someone who killed himself was
first recorded in Ancient Rome, although at that time suicide was legally acceptable as long as it was the result of grief, disgrace, bodily suffering, or madness. In
medieval British common law, only insanity at the time of suicide would prevent
all of the person's assets from being taken by the king. No matter what might have
actually driven a relative to suicide, families would hurry forward with assertions
that he was out of his mind; it was the only way to save the family property. Under
the same medieval system, the family could at least keep the land (although not
the other assets) if the relative killed himself "from weariness of life or impatience
of pain."

Over time, the idea that "insane" people were unknowingly killing themselves
morphed into protectionism: People could be locked up so that they would not kill
themselves. The policy seemed helpful, but it really meant that people who were
suicidal lost all of their freedoms. With the growth of asylums from the mid-1800s

to the mid-1900s, the opportunity to confine became increasingly easy. Only in the 1950s did U.S. policy begin to formally shift toward confining people only if they were "likely" to injure themselves or others.

Now we have laws that automatically characterize people who are suicidal as dangerous, no matter what circumstances brought them to discuss or to attempt suicide. We continue to confine or restrain them even though they have not committed a criminal act. Nobody else in society, other than people who are known to have a mental illness or who have stated that they are thinking about suicide, can be confined simply on the basis that they might be dangerous. Even people who are planning to commit a dangerous crime cannot be arrested until they purposely take action toward committing the crime or attempt to commit the crime. And, as noted above, suicide is no longer a crime. The idea of dangerousness, which is cited in involuntary commitment and gun-control laws, is a form of blame. It is one of several random legal concepts that currently assign blame in connection with suicide and attempted suicide. Other such random legal concepts include defenses to certain insurance claims, malpractice assertions, and discrimination cases. The underlying messages in these legally valid defenses is, "She was the one who killed herself; it wasn't my fault." Perhaps someday suicide policy will be based on care instead of blame.

ATTEMPTED SUICIDE

Four prominent areas of law deal with attempted suicide: gun control, involuntary commitment, discrimination, and health insurance. All of them ignore known health facts about suicidality, and all are under review by legal scholars and mental health advocates. There is room for families to take action in each of these areas of law.

Gun Control

Gun-control laws are, to some extent, laws against attempted suicide. A legal scholar named Frederick Vars reported on the voluminous proof that many suicide attempts are impulsive and quickly regretted. Looking for a legally relevant way to respond to this reality, he pointed out that confining people on the grounds that they are dangerous is a misstatement: They were dangerous to themselves when they took too many pills or climbed out onto a window ledge, but now they probably are not. Now, they are more likely to be in survival mode: fighting to go on, grateful for another chance, and in need of control over their lives. He suggested that people should have the opportunity to put themselves on a list of consumers who are not able to purchase guns. If such a list were authorized by law and a government agency could facilitate easy registry, then people who battle periodic depression and suicidal thoughts could prevent themselves from taking one of the last steps toward fatality.

Involuntary Commitment

Vars is not the only scholar who sees the current involuntary commitment standard as an inappropriate anti-suicide law. Susan Stefan, a long-time expert in mental health law, explained that the legal standard for incompetence in most criminal situations, which is the inability to understand the nature and consequences of the act, is the opposite of how many people are when they attempt suicide: They decide on a method, they get rid of their possessions, they pick a location, they write a note. They look competent under criminal law analysis, yet we confine them as if they were incompetent. In fact, we confine them even before they attempt suicide if we discover that they are planning it. Stefan wrote that institutionalizing somebody after a suicide attempt is usually demeaning, not supportive, and not responsive to the negative beliefs that contributed to his suicidality. Her ideas about reforming official government responses to suicide attempts—demonstrating compassion, respect, and support—also serve as good models for families to follow.

Discrimination

Discrimination law looks at how students and employees are treated differently by their institutions after either attempting suicide or talking about suicide. This is not a frequent legal issue, but a discrimination claim does fit some of the responses that people get after attempting suicide. In the workplace, suicidality is rarely stated as the actual reason for being fired or assigned to a different job, although it may be the reason. When a New York employee who joked about committing suicide was immediately transferred to office duty and the person who replaced her was ordered to dig up proof of mistakes in her work, she got fired on the basis of the mistakes, but she had a legal remedy (discrimination) based on her suicidality. When a Tennessee employee requested a week off after a weekend suicide attempt and the personnel office fired her, claiming that she could not be trusted, the federal appellate court suspected that the firing was based on a stereotype of a suicidal person and sent the case back for a new trial.

Of course, the cases are not always in favor of the employee. Note that it is not discriminatory to fire somebody who is unqualified for his job. In Massachusetts, an employee who got fired after twice attempting suicide by overdose was found by the trial and appellate courts to be no longer qualified, since the job involved dispensing medicine. The Equal Employment Opportunity Commission (EEOC) investigates and remedies employment discrimination. Either families or employees can file the EEOC's online complaint form if someone is fired or otherwise discriminated against after attempting suicide. (See Chapter 15 of this book for more information about the EEOC and discrimination claims.)

Universities have different concerns than employers: They have to balance their obligations to protect students with their obligations to avoid discriminating against students. Several universities have been sued for their treatment of students who attempted suicide—evicting the students from their dorms and expelling them from classes. Meanwhile, other universities have been sued for negligence when they did not take action to prevent students from committing suicide. Although the law does not specifically advise universities about managing this balance, the professional literature of university administration shows that keeping students safe is a major priority and that universities are always increasing their efforts to avoid all forms of discrimination. Universities commonly have discrimination offices at the highest level of their administration, and families, especially parents, can call on that office to coordinate or reconsider the way a student who is suicidal is being handled.

Health Insurance

Ever since the Health Insurance Portability and Accountability Act (HIPAA) went into effect, group health insurance has had to pay for the costs of recovery from suicide attempts. Under the Affordable Care Act (ACA) and the Mental Health Parity Act, individual private health insurance plans now have to cover mental health treatment that is medically necessary. So instead of seeing the medical event as a suicide attempt, insurers are supposed to see it as medically necessary treatment for a mental health condition. Still, patients and families with private non-employer insurance plans may have to appeal initial insurance payment denials in order to get coverage. In many cases, families will have to demonstrate that their loved one with mental illness has a psychiatric diagnosis and suffered the injury because of symptoms associated with the diagnosis. It is similar to the way medieval families had to prove that property belonging to relatives who had committed suicide should not be taken by the king.

COMPLETED SUICIDE

The legal issues involving completed suicides are all basically financial. They involve wrongful death claims (which are covered in Chapter 24 of this book), government benefits, insurance claims, and use of the decedent's estate to pay expenses caused by the suicide.

Wrongful Death

Two possible criteria can make someone liable for another person's suicide: (1) either causing severe physical or emotional trauma that drives the person to suicide or (2) having a duty to protect the person from committing suicide.

Even when it is obvious that the defendant did cause trauma, it can be hard to prove that the trauma made the victim kill herself. A defendant can always show other influences and events that happened outside of his relationship with the victim. Among other things, he will point to the victim's mental health as the reason for her suicide. To contradict those defenses, families have to prove how the defendant's actions affected the victim. Their proof will include messages that the victim left behind and testimony from witnesses.

Most of the time, people do not have a duty to protect another person from killing herself. But, if somebody has a "special relationship" with someone who is at risk of suicide, then the duty may exist. The special relationship suggests that the person has influence or physical control over the one who is suicidal. Courts sometimes determine that a special relationship was in place when a defendant had custodial control (i.e., provided housing) over the person who committed suicide. Courts also conclude that there was a special relationship when the defendant had a known influence on the suicidal person and either used that influence to encourage the suicidality or else failed to use his influence when it could have reduced the suicidality. When a hospital patient, jail inmate, or college student living in a dormitory commits suicide, courts tend to find that the institution had a special relationship with the person who died.

Government Benefits

Ordinarily, spouses can collect Social Security survivors' benefits when their spouse dies. There are age limits for the benefits: The surviving spouse has to be over age sixty with no dependent children or under age sixty and caring for the decedent's children who are under age sixteen or disabled. There is also a limit relating to suicide. If the marriage has lasted for fewer than nine months, even if the couple was together for years before marrying, and the spouse died from suicide, the widow or widower will not be eligible for Social Security survivors' benefits.

Life Insurance

It is still legal for life insurance policies to exclude suicide, but most companies do cover it now as long as the policy was purchased a certain amount of time before the death, typically two years. The idea behind the old well-known exclusion was to prevent people who were suicidal from cheating the insurance company by buying life insurance when they knew that they were about to die. Under current plans, if a policyholder commits suicide before the two-year limit has passed, the insurance company will refund the premium—the amount that the policyholder paid for the insurance.

Accidental death and dismemberment insurance does not usually pay for deaths resulting from suicide, although court cases involving accidental suicides have sometimes been successful. One successful example was a case about someone who died from autoerotic asphyxiation. This person had intentionally cut off his breathing in order to attain sexual pleasure, but he had also set up a counterweight structure that was supposed to prevent him from going without air for too long. He even had a dinner date scheduled for that evening, which served as further proof that he did not intend to die. Since he did not intend for his temporary asphyxiation to kill him and he did intend to go out later in the day, the court found that his self-caused death was an accident and that the beneficiary of his accidental death and dismemberment insurance could collect under that policy.

HOW TO Collect Life Insurance After a Suicide

When someone purchases a life insurance policy, say your sister Leila, who had clinical depression and recently committed suicide during a particularly bad spell, she names beneficiaries who will get the money from the policy when she dies. Most people name two possible beneficiaries: a primary beneficiary, who is first in line and will collect the insurance money if he outlives the policyholder, and a secondary beneficiary (also called a contingent beneficiary), who is second in line and gets the money if the primary beneficiary dies before the policy-holder dies. Leila may choose to name her estate as her beneficiary, but this is generally considered unwise because it delays the payout and can result in state or federal taxes that the beneficiary has to pay. In this HOW TO box, the discussion assumes that you have been named a primary beneficiary.

Your first task is to find out if your sister had any life insurance coverage. If she was employed at the time of her death, contact the benefits office at her job and ask if they provided her with life insurance. Go through her household papers and her checkbook to look for anything that identifies a policy or a broker. Even if you see nothing indicating that she had a life insurance policy, submit an inquiry through the free online Life Insurance Policy Locator that is operated by the National Association of Insurance Commissioners (NAIC). To use this resource, you have to swear that you have already searched for a copy of your loved one's policy and you have to agree to cooperate with insurance companies that respond to your inquiry. The NAIC will pass your inquiry to life insurance companies that have agreed to participate in the policy-finding service. If any of the companies have policies with information matching facts that you have entered from your relative's death certificate (most likely her given name and city of residence), they will contact you directly. If the person who died had a common name, you may hear from multiple companies, only to eventually discover that the policies belong to other people.

The life insurance claim that you make after a suicide begins the same way as any other claim for a life insurance payment: On the insurance company's website, you click on the link that says something like "File a claim." The link will take you to a claim form and instructions for submitting it. You typically need to identify yourself and Leila and the policy number, indicate whether you want to get your payment in a lump sum or small amounts, and identify where the payment should be sent. Finally, you will probably have to print the form and sign it. Along with the form, you will have to submit a copy of Leila's death certificate and possibly a copy of her insurance policy. If your name has changed since Leila put you on the policy or you have other facts to update, attach a copy of a document that explains and depicts the change.

The "cause of death" (for example, poisoning, asphyxiation, drowning, or gunshot wound) and "manner of death" (accident, homicide, suicide, natural, unknown) on the death certificate will be very influential on your claim. If the death certificate has the word "suicide" on it, the insurance claim might get delayed or denied simply because somebody at the insurance agency did not properly read all of the dates or other information. If you do not get an acknowledgment within a few days of submitting your form or you do not get a decision within a month or so of submitting your form, get in touch with the customer service department to find out what is happening with your claim.

If your claim is delayed more than a month or is denied, contact an insurance lawyer to go over your documents and determine whether you should proceed with an appeal and possibly a lawsuit. Like personal injury cases, many insurance claims cases are billed on a contingency basis; the lawyer gets paid only after obtaining a settlement or judgment. Be aware, however, that an insurance lawyer might have to bill you regardless of outcome for a document review and consultation session.

If the claim is delayed, the lawyer will ask the insurance company what is holding up the process and will correct or complete any information that may have been lacking on your claim. Claimants' errors and omissions are often the cause of insurance processing delays. If this does not resolve the delay, the lawyer will likely involve the state insurance commission and make sure that the insurance company realizes that the family's costs and possible future lawsuit damages are growing higher as time passes. Note that you do not need to hire a lawyer to correct your claim errors or interact with the company and the insurance commission on your behalf, but having one to handle those tasks is a great convenience.

If the claim is denied, you really should involve a lawyer to study the situation and to determine whether there is a legal argument to make against the insurance company. The lawyer will carefully read over the insurance company's reasons for denying the claim. Maybe they contradict the insurance policy, violate the Constitution, or transgress either public policy or a statute. The lawyer might even conclude that the insurer acted in "bad faith," meaning that the company interpreted the policy so that they would not have to honor it. The lawyer might consider the possibility that the insurance company committed fraud—misrepresenting information with the intent to mislead somebody.

Occasionally, and not with great success, lawyers claim that insurers have caused emotional distress in their handling and denial of claims. Emotional distress claims only succeed when an insurer does something extreme and outrageous. What a sad cruelty it would be if an insurance company caused a family emotional distress after they had just lost a member to suicide.

The lawyer will also consider whether the broker or agent who sold the policy did something wrong. If the broker or agent misrepresented the policy when selling it to Leila, then you can file a claim against the broker or agent with the state licensing board. You might be able to sue the broker or agent if she did not use reasonable skill, care, and diligence in selling the policy. For example, the broker or agent can be liable for selling Leila the wrong kind of life insurance or for not informing her about possible risks, benefits, and limits associated with insurance options.[1] When it is appropriate, lawyers prefer to go after the insurance companies, rather than individual agents, because the companies have more money.

---

1 Ironically, insurance agents carry "errors and omissions" insurance to pay their costs in case they ever get sued for doing a bad job. But those are separate matters from disputes over a particular claim.

Families who have suffered a suicide loss may feel too drained to fight an insurance denial. They may believe that they are not entitled to collect anything. They may want to focus on more important issues than money. But the person who died had a reason for buying that insurance policy, probably to leave a legacy and to replace her income—exactly why the insurance companies encourage people to buy the policies.

Expenses Resulting From Suicide and Attempts

The legal system generally considers the person who causes damage to be responsible for fixing it—even if that person was committing suicide when the damage occurred. The family of that person did not cause the damage and does not have a legal obligation to pay for it, but the person who attempted or committed suicide is indebted as a result of the damage. In other words, people whose property suffers damage as a result of someone's suicide can usually count as creditors eligible to request payment from the estate of the person who died. A property owner's charge against the estate will reduce the family members' inheritance, but the relatives do not have a legal obligation to use their own funds to pay for damage that they did not cause. If the estate does not have sufficient funds to pay for the damage, then the property owner will either get no payment or partial payment.

If necessary, the property owners and others, including family members, who are affected by a suicide can usually draw on their own insurance policies to offset the expenses that arise after suicide. For example, someone who loses a loved one to suicide or who encounters a suicide scene might suffer from a sleep disorder, stomach upset, stress, and other medical conditions. His own health insurance will cover those conditions. Similarly, someone whose car was damaged in connection with somebody else's suicide will get compensated in the same way that he would be in a comparable situation that was not a suicide. In other words, if his car was hit by someone who intentionally sped down a street at high speed, intending to crash and die, then the dangerous (and suicidal) driver's auto insurance policy is supposed to pay for the damage. Somebody whose home or business was damaged during another person's suicide can make a claim on her own property insurance. Damage to homes and businesses is a common in suicide.

Depending on how and where a suicide occurred, cleaning up after it can be expensive. Body fluids alone can involve biohazard protocols: disinfection of the scene, replacement of carpets and textiles, and repainting or resealing stained surfaces. There may be bullet holes to fix. Broken objects may have to be replaced. If the suicide happened someplace other than a private home, the facility may need to implement new safety features and mount a public relations campaign to distract everyone from the story of the suicide.

The language of the property insurance contract will guide claimants in making the best declarations on their claim forms. If the contract says that it will cover crime-scene costs, decontamination, seepage, or other precise items, the claimant needs to specify those items on the claim form. This is a gruesome and upsetting task; owners of commercial buildings may be able to cope with it, but many families do not even want to know what has to be done to a place after suicide. There are damage-remediation and property-restoration companies that know well how to file these claims and will usually offer to file them for property owners.

When the remediation/restoration services offer to take responsibility for handling an insurance claim, the owner of the insurance policy may have to sign a written agreement assigning the claim rights to the remediation/restoration company. This is a legitimate practice that empowers the professionals to file strong claims. But it comes with risks: the insurance policy may prohibit policyholders from assigning their rights and the restoration/repair company might have a clause in the assignment contract entitling it to collect from the family whatever amount is unpaid by insurance. This is like requiring a blank check from the family. Families should have a plaintiff's insurance lawyer (a lawyer who represents claimants, as opposed to one who represents insurance companies) look at their insurance policy alongside the assignment contract to see if the assignment is feasible and to negotiate terms with the remediation/restoration company.

HOW TO Improve Suicide Law

To offset the towering pile of unpleasant legal tasks after a suicide—dealing with investigators, fending off bill collectors, managing insurance claims, and possibly bringing a wrongful death suit—you may want to involve yourself in advocacy to improve the way attempted suicide is managed and to develop kinder policies in support of families who deal with suicide. Here are ways to participate in positive advocacy:

- Support legislation that implements Frederick Vars' idea of "precommitment against suicide"—requiring your state government to create a registry where people can conveniently and voluntarily list themselves as not eligible to purchase a gun. The Vars proposition is listed in the Resources section at the end of this chapter. After you read it, send letters to your representatives in the state legislature. Summarize the parts of the idea that appeal to you, and ask them to introduce legislation putting it into action. If you know anyone who would be likely to register, say so in your letter, but do not give the person's name. You might also contact Frederick Vars to find out whether any states have already drafted legislation that you can share with your legislators.
- Testify at your relative's post-attempt commitment hearing if you have knowledge or experience allowing you to predict whether your loved one will recover more effectively at home than at the hospital. You may be one of the triggers that upset your relative and you may not be available to house your relative, but you can still fight for her dignity by informing the commitment judge about her particular personality and how she felt and handled things after past suicide attempts. These days, hospitals seem to be pretty swift in determining whether a patient is still dangerous to herself after an attempt. Your testimony can help to solidify that determination. (See Chapter 5 of this book for guidance on participating in commitment hearings.)

- Find ways to influence your state's commitment laws so that people who attempt suicide can get positive and comforting treatment instead of automatically being confined and restrained. Here are several ways to get started: Learn about treatment standards for attempted suicides in your region. You can get the information by participating in family education programs at local mental health treatment centers and by attending the annual conference of your National Alliance on Mental Illness (NAMI) chapter. NAMI is active in mental health policy reform, so your nearest chapter or affiliate may already be compiling ideas and information about improving services to people who have attempted suicide. Look for opportunities to serve on local and county government committees that deal with mental health issues. These entities frequently have nonpolitical citizen representatives on them. You might also discover that some of the mental health service agencies in your area welcome interested members of the public on their boards and committees.
- Once you have some connections and are informed about more situations than your own, work with like-minded people to explain how the law should change. Write a succinct statement in which you demonstrate problems with the current law and recommend improvements to it. Communicate this statement to the government entity that is responsible for changing the law; it might be the legislature or an executive branch agency, and it might be at the local, state, or federal level. Study the website of the government entity to see if they have a designated person or committee to deal with the issue. If there is no designee, then you and your team should at least reach out to your own representatives in the legislature or the director of the executive agency. Once you have made the government contact, you can confidently announce in a press release or your organization's newsletter that you are lobbying on the issue.

Tax Facts

- Generally, the payments that someone receives (the payout) from an accident or health insurance policy that is paid for by an employer will be taxable. Note that the amount the employee paid for premiums on the policy is subtracted from the payout when figuring out how much tax is owed on the payout. See Internal Revenue Service (IRS) Publication 525.
- The first $50,000 of group term life insurance (the standard kind of life insurance that employers provide) does not count as taxable income. The IRS has a formula for figuring the tax owed on higher amounts paid from group term life insurance accounts. See IRS Publication 525.
- Payouts from individual life insurance policies are ordinarily not taxable income. Interest earned on the policy can be taxed. See IRS Publication 525.
- If someone commits suicide within (usually) two years of entering into the insurance policy and the insurance company voids the policy by paying back the amount that the policyholder paid in, the paid-back money is merely a refund, not taxable income. See IRS Publication 525.

- Payments resulting from out-of-court settlements or court judgments for personal injuries, such as emotional distress, loss of companionship, and physical suffering, in a wrongful death case do not count as taxable income unless they resulted from physical injuries. If you previously filed a tax return deducting medical expenses because you paid out of pocket for medical treatment in connection with your loved one's wrongful death, then you are required to declare as income on your current tax return the part of your settlement or judgment that pays you back for those medical expenses. Each recipient of money from the lawsuit will be taxed only on the amount he or she actually receives, not the total amount of the settlement before it was divided among people. See IRS Publication 4345.
- Some "damage, destruction, or loss of property" resulting from a "sudden, unexpected, or unusual" event is deductible on a personal income tax return unless the taxpayer or the taxpayer's dependent or pet caused the event. The IRS requires taxpayers to prove that they have filed an insurance claim, if they have insurance, to offset the loss and reduce the amount of the deduction. Property damage from suicide will not be deductible in every situation. See IRS Publication 547.

RESOURCES FOR SUICIDE LAW

1. *Suicide: History of the Penal Laws Relating to it in Their Legal, Social, Moral and Religious Aspects in Ancient and Modern Times,* by R. S. Guernsey (Rev. ed., 1883), is a study that was originally presented to the New York Medico-Legal Society on September 23, 1875. It relates religious and national responses to suicide from ancient times until the late 19th century. Read it to learn about responsibility for self-murder (*felo de se*) and to see which cultures required distinct burial practices and property forfeitures after suicides. Sometimes, all of a person's assets had to be forfeited, sometimes just the land would pass to the government, sometimes only the money and valuables other than real estate would go to the government, and sometimes suicide was considered the honorable way to pay for a wrongdoing and would save the assets from forfeiture so that the family could have them.
2. Another interesting publication about the ancient history of suicide is H. C. White's article, "*Felo de Se*," published in 1898 in the *Western Reserve Law Journal 4,* 1.
3. A 13th century legal manuscript called *De Legibus et Consuetudinibus Angliae,* written by Henry Bracton, declared that when someone killed himself out of fear of punishment for committing a crime, he forfeited his assets to the government. "But if he has through phrensy or impatience of grief or by misadventure it shall be otherwise. . . . If he was insane when he did the act that caused his death, or if he did it by accident, he is to be held guiltless and forfeits nothing." This quote is part of a Bracton translation and analysis in William E. Mikell's article "Is Suicide Murder?," published in 1903 in the *Columbia Law Review, 3,* 6.

4. Federal Security Agency, Public Health Service Pub. No. 51, *A Draft Act Governing Hospitalization of the Mentally Ill* (1951), is the 20th century U.S. legal basis for recognizing mental patients' liberty interests. Intended to influence state mental health laws, it called for involuntary commitments to be used only if the patient was "likely" to be dangerous or else lacked insight or capacity to realize his need for care. A good article that contextualizes the draft act is Paul S. Appelbaum's "Commentary & Analysis: The Draft Act Governing Hospitalization of the Mentally Ill: Its Genesis and Its Legacy," published in *Psychiatric Services, 51,* 2 (2000).

5. In *Rational Suicide, Irrational Laws: Examining Current Approaches to Suicide and Law* (2016), Susan Stefan has written a fascinating and compassionate look at how law allows people experiencing suicidality to be misunderstood and mistreated. The author surveyed and interviewed hundreds of people who had contemplated suicide in order to devise her own ideas about how to improve legal policies.

6. Frederick E. Vars, in "Self-Defense Against Gun Suicide" (published in 2015 in *Boston College Law Review 56,* 1465) recommended creating a registry system for gun purchases that would enable people to deny themselves permission to purchase firearms. He likened the idea to Ulysses' asking to be tied to the mast of his ship so that he would not be lured by the Sirens when they sang.

7. *The Rights and Responsibilities of the Modern University: The Rise of the Facilitator University* (2nd ed., 2013), by Peter F. Lake, is an efficient book about university liability. Its section about suicide is clear and detailed. The book references facts and examples from its author's earlier article: Peter Lake & Nancy Tribbensee, "The Emerging Crisis of College Student Suicide: Law and Policy Responses to Serious Forms of Self-Inflicted Injury," which was published in 2002 in *Stetson Law Review, 32,* 125.

8. The Bazelon Center for Mental Health Law has online resource called "Campus Mental Health Issues," which includes copies of legal documents filed against universities that have evicted and expelled students who attempted suicide. See bazelon.org.

9. The court cases about employees who sued for disability discrimination after attempting suicide are: *Chandler v. Specialty Tires of America*, 283 F.3d 818 (6th Cir. 2002); *Peters v. Baldwin Union Free School District*, 320 F.3d 164 (2d Cir. 2003); *EEOC v. Amego Inc.*, 110 F.3d 135 (1st Cir. 1997).

10. The HIPAA rule requiring group health plans to cover suicide attempts is at 29 C.F.R. § 2590.702. Find it at ecfr.gov.

11. The part of the ACA that requires private health insurance plans to cover mental health care costs (which can include suicide attempts) is at 42 U.S.C. § 18031. This section of the code refers to the Mental Health Parity Act at 42 U.S.C. § 300gg-26. The laws are available at uscode.house.gov.

12. The American Foundation for Suicide Prevention offers online interactive tools to help people find the best-priced health insurance for their particular mental health treatment regime. See afsp.org.

13. The case in which accidental death and dismemberment insurance did
    have to pay beneficiaries when the victim accidentally killed himself by
    autoerotic asphyxiation is *Critchlow v. First UNUM Life Ins. Co. of Am.*
    378 F.3d 246 (2d Cir. 2004).
14. If you believe that an insurance company is unreasonably delaying a
    decision on your claim, handling the case in a sloppy manner (losing
    documents, not responding to communications, making mistakes),
    or behaving unethically, you may want to file a claim with your
    state insurance commission. The National Association of Insurance
    Commissioners (naic.org) maintains an online portal to the state
    offices, but you should also be able to find your commission by typing
    the phrase "insurance commission" and your state name in a search
    engine.
15. The Life Insurance Policy Locator is available from the National
    Association of Insurance Commissioners at https://eapps.naic.org/life-
    policy-locator/.

The Wills of People
with Mental Illness

The university law librarian found Joe's will in a library microfiche cabinet on the day after he died. Joe was homeless and for years had made frequent use of the law library and stored things in one particular microfiche drawer. Joe was guided by his own brand of fears and obsessions, and the law library was the only place where he felt safe around other people. He had written his will himself, carefully following the guidance in form books and a bar association manual in the library. The library director and another librarian had witnessed it and the notary from the financial aid office had certified all of the signatures. It was a perfectly legal will, and it stated that all of the investments Joe had inherited and never touched were to go to the Little Sisters of the Poor upon his death. He didn't want to give them the money during his lifetime; he wanted to have an estate. When the library director gave the will to Joe's brothers during a condolence call, they were shocked to learn what Joe had planned for his inheritance. They went to court and argued that Joe hadn't been competent to make a will, but the judge ruled against them and Joe got exactly the legacy he'd wanted.

AN INTRODUCTION TO WILLS

In a perfect world of estate administration (carrying out the last wishes of someone who died), a rational person has written a will following all of her state's formal requirements for language, signature, and witnesses. Suppose it is your will. You composed it thoughtfully and formalized it with the proper steps to clearly and correctly include instructions for disposing of all of your actual assets. The will identifies the people (for example, your spouse and children) and entities (maybe your college or favorite charity) that should inherit your assets, and it even has a "residuary clause" covering what should happen with assets that are not yet owned, conditions that are not upheld, and plans in the will that are no longer feasible at the time of your death. Finally, you (as the testator—the person making the will) have entrusted a conscientious executor to carry out your wishes.[1]

---

1 As an alternative to a will, you may have put all of your assets into a living trust, and named yourself as trustee and beneficiary, while also naming at least one heir as a successor trustee and successor beneficiary. With the living trust in place, you would know that when you died and could no longer serve as trustee, your successor trustee(s) would then take charge of the assets in your trust and benefit from them without having to go through probate court, as they would to collect your assets under a will.

But when a testator, let's say your father Edward, who has a delusional disorder, fails to follow formalities or to properly identify assets and heirs, either his estate will be complicated to manage or his will may be considered invalid. If the probate court determines that a will is invalid, then one of two things will happen: (1) either a will that your father wrote earlier will stand as the final will, or (2) if there is no previous valid will, your dad will be deemed by the court to have died intestate (without a will) and his estate assets will be distributed according to state law as if he had never written a will. It is certainly easy to imagine all of the ways that someone with a mental illness might not follow the perfect way of making a will.

THE SUBSTANCE OF THE WILL

Everyone has heard the classic opening line for wills: "I, John Doe, being of sound mind and body. . . ." There are a few different ways that you can prove that a testator with mental illness was not of sound mind when he wrote his will:

- You could show that the testator was delusional when writing the will and that the contents of the will were influenced by the delusion.
- You could show that the testator did not satisfy the common-law standards for being of sound mind.
- You could show that the testator wrote the will under the influence of someone who was tricking him or forcing him to make bequests that he otherwise would not have made.

The only people who are eligible to make these claims, in other words, the only people who can contest the will, are:

- Relatives who would reasonably expect an inheritance
- People who were named as beneficiaries in the same testator's earlier will or else the heirs of those people
- Creditors who are owed money by the testator
- People who have contractual promises from the testator that are somehow violated by the will
- Executors of either a former will or the current will.

There may be plenty of other people, including friends and caregivers, who believe that the will is not legitimate and does not convey the true wishes of the person who died, but unless those folks fit into the above list, they will not have legal standing to make a court case about the will's legitimacy.

Probate courts deal with the estates of just about everybody in society. They know a lot about people and they know that mental illness tends to be episodic, meaning that people who have a mental illness are not always experiencing symptoms of it. For this reason, there is a legal doctrine called "the presumption of lucidity" for people with dementia or a mood disorder, a personality disorder, a delusional disorder, or another mental health diagnosis. Under this doctrine, the court will presume that on the day someone with mental illness went to the lawyer's office to make out a will, that person was able to think rationally. The probate courts also rely on lawyers to draft wills only for people who are of sound mind during the will preparation discussions.

Bequests make up the majority of the will. Bequests are the gifts that the testator wants to have distributed upon her death. Bequests can be gifts of money or of possessions. Bequests can only be about assets that a testator actually owns when she writes her will, such as her home, her collections, her vehicle, and her money. Bequests have to identify the asset (for example, "my diamond ring"), or the source of the asset ("my safe deposit box"), or the quantity of the asset ("$500," or "all of my paintings," or "one third of everything I own"). To account for assets that the testator does not yet own, lawyers insert residuary clauses into wills. The residuary clause says that any other assets that the testator has not identified, or does not know about, or has not yet come to own will be distributed to a particular person or in a particular way. For example, this part of the will may say, "All possessions and assets that I acquire after writing this will are to be divided equally among my siblings."

Money that is in investment accounts and insurance policies is usually not included in wills because the owners of those accounts name beneficiaries in the account documents. Then, ownership of the account passes directly to the beneficiary when the original owner dies. The beneficiary has to claim ownership by providing proof of identification and the original owner's death certificate to the investment house or insurance company. When two people had a joint bank account together and one owner dies, the remaining owner becomes the sole owner of the bank account, so the money in the joint account also does not need to pass through a will. The money in a special needs trust does not pass to heirs through account identification or through a will because those trusts are not owned by the person with the disability. (See Chapter 20 of this book for more on special needs trusts.)

Case Examples: Being of "Sound Mind"

Here are modern examples of will contests in which courts decided whether wills were written while the testators were of sound mind.

MIAMI RESCUE MISSION V. ROBERTS, 943 SO. 2D 274 (FLA. 3D DCA 2006)

In this case, an elderly woman who was taking strong pain medicine developed depression and a mistaken belief that her caregiver, named Mrs. Roberts, did not take care of her and had allowed her dog to die. Although she had left a generous inheritance to Mrs. Roberts in a will written two years earlier, the elderly woman wrote a new will just three days after starting the pain medication. In the new will, she wrote that all of her assets were to be divided among four charities. On the fourth day of taking the medicine, and just one day after writing the new will, the testator died. Meanwhile, Mrs. Roberts had been visiting and assisting her every day for years and the dog was fine. When Mrs. Roberts petitioned the court to honor the old will and to declare the new will to be invalid, the court considered witness testimony from Mrs. Roberts and her daughter (who often visited the patient with her) as well as nurses and doctors who treated the testator before and during the time that she made the new will. The court also looked at medical records from the four days leading up to the testator's death. Since the witness testimonies and medical records consistently said that this testator underwent a personality change and had false beliefs about the dog and Mrs. Roberts in the last four days of her life, the court granted Mrs. Roberts' petition by throwing out the new will and upholding the old will.

In re Estate of Pilon, 9 A.D.3d 771, 780 N.Y.S.2d 810 (3d Dep't 2004)
Ephrem Pilon was a grandfather who left his estate to one grandson and declared in the will that he was leaving nothing to his other grandchildren "by reason of their total lack of concern for my well-being." The nonbeneficiary grandchildren asserted that their grandfather wrote the will while experiencing an insane delusion about a lack of attention from them, but the court had proof that the grandchildren "visited infrequently or not at all," which was enough to convince the panel of appellate judges that the grandfather's belief about their lack of regard for him was reasonable and not the result of delusion.

Newhouse v. Graczyk, 2007-Ohio-3302 (Ohio Ct. App. 9th Dist. Summit County 2007)
An adult granddaughter asserted that her grandfather was delusional when he wrote his will because he mistakenly believed that this granddaughter's mother had stolen from him. Witnesses testified that the daughter had taken tomatoes from the grandfather's garden and had taken back gifts that her family had given to the grandfather. Even the granddaughter who brought the claim admitted that her mother had taken tomatoes, although she said that it was because the grandfather was neglecting the garden. Evidence also showed that the grandfather had been neglecting to clean up after his dogs. Neither the trial judge nor the appellate judge was convinced that the grandfather was delusional. The appellate judge supported this conclusion by quoting several earlier cases that defined insane delusions. One of the earlier cases was *Kirby v. Kuhns*, 105 Ohio App. 294, 298 (Ohio Ct. App. 1957)] which explained that an insane delusion is "a belief in things that do not exist and that no rational mind would believe exist"

Accommodations During the Will-Drafting Process

A will can be created in a few standard meetings between the person wanting to create a will and her lawyer; it is just a matter of gathering a lot of facts and answering the lawyer's questions. However, making a will can be an upsetting process. For example:

- Consider how anxiety-provoking it can be for someone to reveal her financial secrets to a lawyer.
- Think about the ways that traumas and delusions can disrupt the long, involved process of itemizing assets, identifying relations, and going over dozens of tedious details.
- Realize that someone who avoids discomfort or scrutiny is at risk of not conveying her true intentions during the will-writing process.
- Understand how deeply depressing it is to think about dying.

Neither the laws about estates nor legal professional organizations have established a standard set of adaptations that enable someone to write a will when his or her mental health symptoms stand to interfere with the process. Because the area of estate law is very rigid, and a particular client may have rigid behaviors or rigid responses, the combination can make it very difficult to produce a complete and correct will.

If this is the situation for your family member with mental illness, a helpful step is to work with a psychiatric occupational therapist (OT). Whether it is you or your loved one who hires the OT, your loved one will need to agree to receive the OT's services. The OT, working together with the lawyer and your relative, can come up with ways to help your relative participate throughout the process. The OT will find ways to modify the legal tasks to enable your family member to participate in drafting a will. For example:

- If the lawyer's office is intimidating, the OT will recognize the problem and suggest that they meet at an off-peak time in a quiet corner of the cafeteria downstairs (so that people can't listen in) or in a confidential space where the testator goes regularly and feels secure.
- If the topic of bequests is too gloomy for your loved one, the OT may recommend that she hold something or do something with her hands to release tension (maybe even use a pen and paper to jot down her own thoughts), or else physically move around the room, while the lawyer drafts her bequests.
- The OT may even be able to train the lawyer and testator to work together. The lawyer may learn to separate the will-making process into small clusters of connected topics and tasks that will not distress or confuse this particular testator. The testator, in turn, may learn to avoid distraction and to focus on answering questions.

HOW TO Help Your Relative Plan His or Her Will

Most adults working with their lawyers can draft effective wills without any involvement from family members. In fact, family members who insert themselves into somebody's will-making process can create the impression of forcing the testator's decisions (the legal phrase for this is "undue influence"). The lawyer will insist that the family member stay out of the way so that he and the testator can finish their work. A will that results from undue influence is not a valid will.

Nevertheless, in some situations, there are ways that family members can help ensure that the testator presents herself as being "of sound mind." Remember that to truly have the mental capacity to make a legitimate will, it is not enough to be in a nondelusional state of mind. The formal common-law test of whether a testator has the mental capacity to make a will asks if she knows the answers to four questions:

1. Does she know the nature and extent of her property?

Of course, between the time that somebody writes a will and the time that she dies, her exact property is likely to change. This question about whether the testator knows the nature and extent of her property is meant to check on her rational awareness. If she genuinely and incorrectly believes that she owns a major landmark downtown, she may be suffering from a delusion or memory problem.

However, not every mistaken belief is proof of a delusion. If you are close to a person with mental illness who is planning to write a will, help her to compile a full and accurate list of her assets and, especially if she has paranoia or is given to negativity, make sure she knows that she has to tell the lawyer the truth about all of her assets. If possible, the testator should bring the lawyer photocopies of documents like deeds, insurance appraisals, or account statements. Using the documents, the lawyer can write the most accurate descriptions in the will and also advise the testator about when and how to name joint owners or direct beneficiaries who can obtain the assets without waiting for the will to be probated.

2. Can she identify the people who would be the "natural objects of her bounty"? This typically means that she can properly list who she is related to and how she is related to each person—even if she does not intend to leave anything to her relatives.

Notice that the testator is not expected to have completely accurate ideas about her relatives; she merely has to identify them. Wrong though her impressions may be, she does not have to leave anything to her children, spouse, or siblings. (Depending on state law, a spouse may be entitled to take a share of the estate even if the will attempts to disinherit him.) To help her prepare for the lawyer, and to prevent her will from being contested by someone claiming to have been left out only because the testator had a false belief, remind her that the will does not need to contain any information about her feelings about her relatives.

When a testator says what she thinks about a relative ("he is possessed by the devil," or "she is a thief"), she creates an opportunity for that relative to prove that the description is false. Then, the wrongly described relative can claim that the whole will is invalid on the basis of testator misperceptions. Instead of describing the relatives, the testator can merely say something to identify them and to show that she knows they would be "natural objects of her bounty" in the tradition of passing estates. Here is an example of how that could be done: "I have two children, Dick and Jane, who would automatically get my assets if I did not have a will, but I do have a will and in this will I choose instead to give my assets to the science museum." Sometimes testators leave small gifts to their natural heirs as proof that they recognize them and know that they expect to inherit something.

3. Does she understand the dispositions she is making?

A testator has to declare clearly and consistently that she wants her money, objects, or accounts to pass to named recipients. If you are helping someone whose mental illness prevents her from being able to make firm decisions or to understand consequences, you may want to recommend or even to facilitate a pre-will-making meeting between her and someone who has a history of helping her make plans. It can be a vocational worker, a mental health treatment provider, an occupational therapist, a probation officer, or a neighbor. Remind your loved one that she is merely calling on the planner to help her remember the steps or techniques that the two of them have previously used when making plans. They do not need to talk about the will, or assets, or death; they just need to practice reviewing the planning method. Or maybe you can provide the lawyer with a summary of the words and methods that best help the testator to be clear and organized.

4. Does she understand that she is making these dispositions of this property to these people in an "orderly plan" for the disposition of her property?

This line of inquiry is about the unemotional notion that the testator comprehends that she will die someday and that, by writing her will, she is deciding how all of her assets are to be handled when she dies. Depending on her mental health status, she may be distracted by parts of the inquiry. Someone has to deal with the distractions so that the lawyer can be confident that the testator truly means to execute the will.

This is one of the times when you may want to provide information to your relative's therapist, knowing that medical privacy laws will prevent the professional from telling you whether the information was used and how your family member responded to it. Specifically, you may want to let the therapist know that the will is being drafted. If your relative is depressed, fatalistic, or otherwise affected by the will-making process, the therapist will help her to cope with the emotionally difficult thoughts and tasks that she faces. The therapist may recommend some techniques to the lawyer and may also give you some advice about helping with the will process.

I Wish, I Want, I Hope

The expressions of desire—I wish, I want, I recommend, and I hope—have no legal power in a will. They may affect survivors' emotions and they may sway beneficiaries to take action, but they merely convey the testator's desires and cannot force anybody to do anything. In legal language, these are called precatory expressions.

Here is an example of how confusing the expressions can be: "It is my desire that all of my grandchildren either complete college or vocational education even if those expenses reduce by a million dollars the amount of money that my own children take under this will." Some courts may read this sentence to mean that the testator wants one million dollars of the estate to be set aside for the grandchildren's education. Others may believe that, since he did not name the grandchildren or tell how the money was to be divided among them, his desire to support their education is a nice idea but not a true bequest. Sometimes, when the expression sounds like "I rely on you" or "I am counting on you," a probate court will determine that the testator intended to create a trust. This is most likely to happen when the action he identifies is for the good of his family.

Wills are supposed to contain clear instructions, not sloppy expectations and wishful thinking. When a testator, such as your family member with mental illness who really wants to get his will in order, misunderstands this principle and tries to insert precatory expressions, he may run into a conflict with the lawyer. For example, suppose the testator is your uncle Clayton, who has a narcissistic personality disorder that is so disruptive that it causes him to be very easily offended and often angry when he interacts with people. Clayton has been banned from the deli in his neighborhood, and he once got into trouble with the police after an altercation with a parking lot attendant. He is known for storming out of businesses and events (including family gatherings) when he thinks he is not getting the respect he deserves. Clayton wants his will to say things his way, which is hopeful and includes lots of precatory statements, such as "I want my therapist, Herman Stikke, to buy some decent ties and get an eyelid tuck." He also wants his will to say, "It is my sincere desire that my longtime psychiatrist, Dr. Peter Olsen, get a much-needed vacation." Clayton's lawyer will be concerned that the precatory statements are not solid and could lead to fights, confusion, and wasting of the estate assets on a court case. When he says this, poor Clayton may feel that he is not being heard. He may have come to the meeting with the lawyer feeling proud and empowered to influence the future, and yet his lawyer can ruin that positive attitude in one moment, simply by dismissing it with the harsh and snooty word "precatory" and a swift declaration that Clayton's hopes will not accomplish anything.

You, as the person Clayton confides in and complains to, can explain the term *precatory expressions* to him in advance so that he won't be surprised when the lawyer wants to put Clayton's hopes and wishes into more concrete terms. You could talk with Clayton about phrasing his wishes as clear financial bequests, so that he will be ready for further discussions with the lawyer, or you could get his permission to go along for one of his meetings with the lawyer to be a teammate and to help him communicate without losing track of his message or emotions. If Clayton's hopes and wishes are about you, then you should not participate in the communications with his lawyer, but instead realize that this is a time when he should interact with his therapist, a psychiatric OT, or any trusted friend or family member who is good at handling formal communications, to work through the impasse with his lawyer.

Assuming that you or the other intermediary goes along to the lawyer's office, you may want to ask the lawyer to provide examples of other people's wills (with the names removed) where wishes were effectively translated into legal bequests. Another thing that you could do, right there in front of Clayton, is say to the lawyer, "I think we're having a translation issue here; am I right that you are not arguing with Clayton, and that you are just trying to translate what he said into the language of wills?"

Now, it is possible that Clayton's hopeful statements are not connected with money or gifts anyway and are simply messages that he wants to deliver. Maybe he just wants to say, "I hope that Dr. Stikke will always retain his good sense of humor and that one of these days he'll find a good wife." In that case, you or Clayton can ask the lawyer if it would be okay to write those wishes and hopes into a letter that can be sealed and kept with the will, to be opened only upon his death. Clayton doesn't really need a lawyer's permission to do that, but raising the question will be a good way of channeling away the expressions that should not be in the will and yet are interfering with the messages that do need to go in Clayton's will.

More than any other issue in estate law, the matter of precatory expressions demonstrates the spectrum of will-making. At one end of the spectrum is the promise of a legacy, the expectation of influencing the future, the hope that the beneficiaries will be well. At the other end of the spectrum are fear of death, disappointment that life will come to an end, and sadness about saying goodbye and missing all that is yet to happen in the lives of loved ones. We all experience emotions along this spectrum when we make our wills. And many people, not just people with mental illness, want to express hopeful messages in their wills. The issues with precatory expressions that are uniquely troublesome for people with mental illness are likely to be about perceptions: Maybe the only things that Clayton wants to express are hopes and wishes; he may not care about material goods. Maybe he feels criticized by the lawyer's particular way of saying that wishes do not belong in a will. Maybe he is unable to tolerate that his plan for the will conversation is disrupted by the lawyer's refusal to write his hopeful statements into the will exactly as he has composed them. These perceptions may make perfect sense to you because know Clayton; you can be the link connecting his wishes with his will when the lawyer does not understand him.

Conditional Bequests

Conditional bequests are a way to control people's lives from beyond the grave. They are inheritances that require beneficiaries to fulfill conditions (to do something) in order to collect their money. Conditions are established with words like *if*, *when*, and *as long as*. Classical examples of conditional bequests are statements like: "I leave to my nephew $20,000 for college education, but he may only have this money if the college he attends is Princeton," and "I hereby bequeath to my daughter our summer house at Chautauqua as long as she does not interfere with my plan for being cremated rather than buried."

Over the centuries, many people who did not want to comply with conditions have simply walked away from bequests without argument. Others have argued in probate court that they should not have to go along with the particular conditions that testators set. Examining these diverse conditions in thousands of probates through the years, American courts have consistently concluded that the conditions have to be "reasonable." If the condition is not reasonable, the beneficiary can receive the bequest without having to satisfy the condition.

Several categories of conditions have been recognized as unreasonable:

- Impossible conditions are unreasonable. When a testator calls for beneficiaries to go someplace or to do something that is not feasible under their circumstances, because of finances, physical capacity, time, opportunity, or other actual limits, it is fair to assert to the executor and, if necessary, to the probate court that it is impossible. So if your mother Celia, who was certain that she'd lived a previous life in Ireland, calls for you to move to Ireland, to buy a house there, and to keep her ashes on your mantle in order to collect your $10,000 bequest, a court will probably not force you to give up your entire life in the United States and move abroad to get that money from your mother's estate.

- Illegal conditions are unreasonable. When a testator tries to get a beneficiary to do something that is against the law in order to collect the inheritance, it is uniformly considered an unreasonable condition. Maybe your brother Buck wrote in his will that you can only collect your inheritance if you paint the sentence "Buck was here!" on the outside of the movie theater that fired him years earlier. Painting that message would be vandalism; you do not have to commit vandalism in order to collect your inheritance.

- Conditions that force the beneficiary to get divorced are often considered unreasonable, but if the testator had a protective reason for wanting the beneficiary to get divorced, even if it was to protect the money from being squandered by the beneficiary's spouse, these conditions are sometimes deemed to be reasonable. Your sister, who lived a frightening life filled with anxiety and paranoia, was also a kind and brilliant person. The one thing she most wanted to do, but could not do, was save you from the husband who, in her mind, constantly demeans you. Your parents were on to him, too, and for that reason they left their entire fortune to your sister. She wants you to have it upon her death, but only if you will finally pull yourself away from your husband. You do not have to leave him, but since the probate court may find your sister's condition to be valid, you stand to lose your inheritance if you stay with your husband.

- Conditions that require a beneficiary to remain unmarried are considered unreasonable because, as one writer phrases it, "marriage is central to the preservation of family structure and hence society." If your father seriously wants his money to stay in the family and not go to spouses, he would be better off putting it into trusts for you and your siblings.

- Conditions that require beneficiaries to never sell the property they inherit, or at least to keep it in the family, are considered unreasonable nowadays. Maybe your great-grandmother risked her life hauling her weaving loom to America from the old country. And maybe she, your grandmother, and your mother all helped their husbands and children through hard times by weaving on that loom. Without question, it is a magnificent loom. Yet you are legally permitted to sell it after you inherit it, even though your mother's will says, "I leave her great-grandmother's loom to my daughter as long as she agrees to keep it forever and pass it along to one of her own children when she dies."

Aside from these well-known examples of unreasonable will conditions, the conditional requirements that appear in a will generally have to be satisfied by the beneficiaries. Of course, testators do devise all kinds of annoying and inconvenient conditions that families do not expect. Perhaps in life they also involved family members in events that they would not have expected. Did you ever think you would have to pick your brother up from a mental hospital? Do you remember how reluctantly you went to that first family counseling session or support group meeting? Would you know how it felt to walk through a store with someone who was hearing voices if it weren't for your son's schizoaffective disorder? Carrying out conditions of a will that at first seem annoying can similarly bring you to understand and appreciate things that you otherwise would not value. Here is an example of how a legal but annoying condition in a will can play out: Maybe your cousin Miranda, who had depression and took comfort from living with several dogs, wrote in her will that you were to inherit her house as long as you allowed all of her surviving dogs to continue living in that house with you and you cared for the dogs in just the way that she would have if she were still alive. Whether or not you expect to enjoy living with the dogs, if you want the house, you will have to live with and care for the dogs that come with it—and over time you may well realize why the dogs meant so much to your cousin and why she wanted you to have them and her house.

When beneficiaries choose not to receive bequests because of conditions or when they fail to comply with conditions, one of two things will happen: (1) as the will directs, the bequest will go to somebody else, or (2) the state probate code will determine how the bequest is distributed to the testator's relatives. Depending on the size of the family, the probate code might entitle someone who does not fulfill a condition to the same inheritance anyway. After collecting and distributing all of the estate's assets, the executor has to swear to the probate court that he or she has fulfilled the terms of the will. For this reason, executors must do their best to see that reasonable conditions are satisfied and that unreasonable conditions are cancelled by the probate court.

FORMALIZING A WILL

The law of wills is old and stiff; like an elaborate antique gate, it is designed to protect the estate from invaders and marauders. Even after all of the terms have been carefully drafted, there are more formalities to observe when the will gets signed and witnessed. The testator must sign the will herself. She does not have to touch the lawyer's pen; she can bring her own. She does not have to sit down or smile at anybody. They can even arrange it so that she does not have to hang around and wait, but she does have to sign the will in her own handwriting and in the presence of other people—usually the lawyer plus two witnesses and a notary.

The witnesses can be people whom the testator knows and trusts. They do not have to be the lawyer's office staff (who usually witness clients' wills) and they do not have to know anything about the content of the will. In fact, the lawyer will not show them what is written in the will. He will inform them that they are present to witness the testator's signing of her will. Then, he will be sure that they watch her sign her name and that they sign their own names in the proper spaces on the will. After all of the signatures are completed, the secretary will scan or copy the will for the files and then package the original and a spare copy for the testator to take home. If your relative has symptoms that may later drive him to destroy the original will during a psychotic event or to lose the will amid hoarded piles or an unorganized lifestyle, offer to keep it in a safe place for him.

In cases where a lot of money is at stake and it is predictable that somebody will contest the will, some estate law experts recommend video or audio recording of the will-signing ceremony. As an added protection against claims that the testator was not of sound mind, the lawyer may review the four confirmation issues with the testator in the recording:

1. What is the nature and extent of your property?
2. Which of your relatives would naturally expect to be given assets in your will?
3. Can you tell me why we made this will?
4. Can you say what we are about to do to finish your will today?

If a testator does not want to be recorded, the lawyer will honor her wishes. A reluctant testator will look or sound troubled in the recording, and that appearance will only help whoever opposes the will to claim that the testator was forced to bequeath things the way she did.

WHEN A WILL IS MADE INFORMALLY

Certain that she can write or record a will in the style of her choosing, your sister Karyn, who has bipolar disorder, may handwrite her last wishes on paper at home, with nobody around. Maybe, to be sure that everyone gets her message, she will post an online video instead—possibly one with diatribes about all of the people who have ruined her life and reasons for choosing others to inherit her money and possessions. Maybe she will list her bequests in a blog or on social media. In situations like these, there are separate kinds of legal analysis for wills that do not follow proper formalities.

In thirty-five states, handwritten wills (also known as "holographic wills") are considered legitimate. They literally have to be handwritten, not typed, by the testator. Some states accept the handwritten parts of commercial will forms and some accept the entire forms, including the preprinted standard phrases. Handwritten wills and form wills have to be signed and dated and, in a few states, a witness has to have watched the testator write either the entire will or the last part where she signed her name on it. To some extent, handwriting a will may be the best method for some people to communicate their bequests; they can express their thoughts in the way that they ordinarily speak and write and they can explain what should happen without worrying that their message will be skewed by a grammatically uptight legal secretary. Such a will may seem to depict the testator's plans more honestly than any other document would be able to. On the other hand, certain assurances are lost when the will does not follow formalities. It will likely be easier for disappointed family members to claim that the testator, in this case, Karyn, was not of sound mind when she composed it. The informal will may distribute only some of her assets, and/or the writing may have been done impulsively or under undue influence.

You would think—in this modern age of communication technology and disability accommodations—that bequests recorded on personal electronic devices would be valid. They are not. Perhaps because troublemakers can edit the recordings or because they may be meant as jokes or get taken out of context, the law does not believe that they accurately convey testamentary intent—the testator's genuine goals. Spoken wills are acceptable in some states under very limited circumstances. The testator has to be in military service, in the throes of death, in imminent peril, only bequeathing a very small amount of money, or able to restate the bequest in writing at a later date. An acceptable spoken will has to be spoken in person to at least one witness who will swear to its accuracy.

The occurrence of eccentric millionaires leaving surprising bequests is so well known that it has become a stereotype. Yet, there are no legal practice guidelines for making estate plans with testators who experience serious mental illness. From one perspective this is good. It means that people with mental illness are treated equally and that the legal system truly does believe in the presumption of lucidity. From another perspective, it seems unfair because the will-making experience can be so stern and picky that some people will not even try to make formal wills. Then their money and possessions can end up in the hands of all the wrong people. But this is the current state of the law: formal wills are best, and handwritten wills are acceptable to some extent in most of the country.

HOW TO Contest a Will

Once a person with a will has died, the first thing that happens with the will is that the executor submits it to the local probate court in the county where the person resided. Upon filing the will, or soon thereafter, the executor is granted "letters testamentary" authorizing him to serve as the estate's personal representative in interactions with heirs, banks, creditors, debtors, and others who have business with the estate. Filing the will with the probate court puts it on public record; anyone can go and look at it. This is why celebrity wills are available online; researchers find the wills in the court files, copy them, and post them on the Internet. The will has to be on record with the probate court so that the estate can have its own identity. The estate needs an identity in order to be able to collect money that was owed to the person who died or that was in accounts under that person's name. The estate also needs an identity in order to distribute assets to beneficiaries. Most executors establish a checking account in the name of the estate and pay the testator's debts, bequests, and taxes out of that account.

Since the estate's identity is created in probate court, someone believing that a will is invalid has to make that claim in probate court (that is, they have to contest the will). Often, the probate court will have either a form for contesting a will or a rule with step-by-step instructions on how to notify the court that the will is not valid. The Resources section at the end of this chapter has instructions for finding the probate court's website, which may have copies of the form and instructions that you need or which will tell you where to call or visit for that specific local information. Here is a general outline of the process:

- The person contesting the will submits to the court a claim and proof that the will is invalid. This proof may be evidence about the testator's mental health, someone who tricked or cheated the testator, an attempt to commit fraud, a lack of formalities, incorrect statements, or the existence of other wills.

- The executor will receive a copy of the documents. Having been notified that somebody is contesting the will, the executor has to stop doing anything with the estate. Working with the lawyer who drafted the estate documents, the executor will then submit proof that this will is valid. This is when an audio or video version of the signing ceremony can be helpful.
- The probate judge will consider the evidence and decide whether to uphold the will. If the judge concludes that the will is invalid, but that a previous will is valid, then the earlier will can be executed. If the current will is invalid and there is no other valid will for a testator, the estate will be handled as an intestate estate.

WHEN SOMEBODY DIES WITHOUT A WILL

State probate codes have fallback methods for distributing assets when somebody dies without a will. Spouses, children, siblings, and parents of the decedent are assigned certain shares. But the court cannot believe every person who claims to be related to the decedent. A con artist or group of opportunists may claim to be entitled to inherit from the person. So probate courts have to hire somebody, usually a lawyer, to undertake a "due diligence" investigation to find out who the true heirs are.

In addition to reviewing the birth certificates, marriage licenses, and other evidence provided by legitimate family members, the investigator will look for additional relations, including children who are not necessarily known to the current spouse. Even the decedent may not have known about them. The investigator may discover relatives who are estranged from the decedent but still legally entitled to inherit from her. The investigator's fee and the costs of his investigation, which may include travel and public notices alerting creditors to the opportunity to claim debts, will be taken from the estate's assets.

The court will appoint a personal representative or administrator to manage the intestate estate. "Intestate" means that there is no will guiding the estate administration. The administrator will perform the same tasks that an executor does when there is a will: collecting assets, paying debts, distributing inheritances, and filing documents with the court. If someone in the family has come forward to handle this responsibility and the court is satisfied that he or she can handle the estate, then this person is likely to be appointed as administrator. Sometimes, courts have to choose from among several family members who volunteer. At other times, the court has to appoint a nonrelative, such as a local attorney, to administer the estate. Any estate administrator, whether a family member or not, is entitled to be paid for services. The state probate code establishes the payment rate. The payment comes from the assets of the estate and counts as one of the estate debts that has to be paid before the beneficiaries get their inheritances.

The three main problems with intestacies are that (1) the testator's money gets spent on the due diligence investigation, (2) the people who inherit may not be the people who would have been picked by the testator himself, and (3) the companies collecting automatic bill payments from the decedent's bank account may refuse to cancel the automatic payments under the belief that they only have to cooperate with executors, not administrators. There is also an especially sad dimension to intestacies: In order to be fair, the administrator usually has to sell the decedent's possessions and divide the proceeds among the heirs. Therefore, family members often are not able to have items that are meaningful to them. There are ways to work around this, however, particularly when only one relative wants to have a particular item. For example, Bruce was hoping to inherit his deceased brother's antique woodworking tools; an administrator can reduce Bruce's financial payout by the appraised value of the tools so that he can have the tools and the remaining dollar amount. Still, administrators are not obligated to extend this kindness. They do not have to deal with fights, personal requests, or other delays. They can sell or auction everything and distribute the money according to their own convenience as long as they do not cheat the heirs out of their rightful inheritance.

HOW TO Be an Executor or Estate Administrator

Once the questions have settled—whether there was a will, whether the will is valid, whether there are additional heirs—you can begin to manage the estate. The first part of this chapter has referred to "the executor" or "the administrator" as if it were not necessarily you. But very likely it is you—the same helper who has always been available, who went to the trouble of reading a book about mental illness and the law, and who has always watched out for your family member's legal interests.

You do not need to operate alone as an executor; many executors hire a lawyer to guide them through the process and to handle interactions with probate court (that is, to probate the will). Unless the will is contested, the court interactions will be with the office staff at the probate court. In many places, the lawyer will have a user account enabling her to upload probate documents straight from her office computer to the court's record-keeping system.

As with all of your other legal involvements, you will begin this one by gathering information. You will also want to order about twenty official copies of the death certificate, because you will need to enclose a copy with each of the various written actions that you take on behalf of the estate. In this situation, the information you need is about the decedent's assets and debts. Find it by looking through the mail, desks, files, and boxes. (If your loved one has a conservator, this information will already be compiled. See Chapter 21 for more information about compiling somebody's financial information.) As you find evidence of accounts, investments, old savings bonds, and other financial holdings, put it into a file called "Assets." If you find potentially valuable collectibles or jewelry, put pictures of them in the assets file. If you find cash around the house, gather it up and deposit it in the estate's bank account. As you find bills or other evidence of debts, put those in a file labeled "Debts."

As you discover ongoing expenses that are no longer necessary, such as the cable or magazine subscription bills, cancel them. Expect that as you collect assets from institutions or attempt to cancel services and subscriptions, you will need to provide a certified copy of the death certificate and a copy of the court order naming you as the administrator. Do not rush to shut off the utilities; they should not be turned off until you have removed your relative's possessions from his home. Wait until you know about any automatic payments before you cancel the decedent's credit cards or close his bank accounts; you need to cancel or pay off charges on those accounts to avoid incurring fees and hassles. You do not need to pay estate expenses just yet, even though some of the creditors will come rushing at you before you even know how much money you are dealing with. As long as you are in the information-gathering phase, your main responsibilities are to collect and to organize facts.

Having identified the existence of assets, your next task is to collect the assets and deposit them into the estate's bank account so that you can pay specific bequests and develop a pool of funds from which to pay the estate's debts. Most of the specific bequests will refer to objects, but in a wealthy estate, some will be about dollar amounts. If it becomes obvious at some point in the estate administration that the debts are minimal and manageable compared to the assets, state law may allow you to pay limited early distributions to the heirs.

To collect financial assets, such as the content of bank and investment accounts, notify the bank or investment service about the death of your family member and your status as executor or administrator. Recall that the estate will collect account assets only when the account, such as your sister's retirement fund at work or the stock that she owns, does not have a designated beneficiary. Most of the accounts will have a death notification form for you to complete. You will need to attach or later send a certified copy of the death certificate and a copy of your letters testamentary (the probate court document authorizing you to be the personal representative for this estate) or other court authorization to actually remove the assets from the account. If possible, arrange for electronic transfer of the assets to the estate account.

Nonfinancial assets that have not been bequeathed to anybody should be sold or donated in the name of the estate. You are responsible for getting the maximum value out of your family member's possessions. If you have reason to believe that any of his things are worth a lot of money, see whether he has insured them beyond standard household insurance. If the items are insured and have been recently appraised, use the appraised value as your opening sales price; you may not get that amount, but it is a reasonable place to start. If you find the insurance bill or receipt but not the appraisal, contact the insurance agent for a copy of the appraisal and referrals to dealers who can sell the item(s) for you.

Insurance is the not the only clue about which household items may be valuable. You may know that certain objects are very old, were created by experts, or were very expensive in the first place. You can find appraisers with expertise in jewelry, art, books, and everything else just by looking online, but you will not necessarily know whether they are legitimate. If a lawyer is helping you to administer the estate, contact the law firm and ask for appraiser recommendations. If you are not working with a lawyer, call the law firm that drafted the will and ask if they can refer you to reliable appraisers. You may also want to contact a good auction house in your area to ask whether they will sell or at least appraise certain estate items.

A lot of the stuff in the estate will be garbage. Throw it out. Some things will be potentially interesting or useful to other people, but not worth a lot of money. Try to sell those items online, at a consignment store, through a garage sale, or at a flea market. If any of it is still left over after the attempted sale, donate it to an agency that will provide you with a donation receipt. You may want to get the receipt made out in the name of the decedent so that you can deduct the donation on the decedent's final income tax return, if it makes more sense to itemize deductions on that return than it does to take the standard deduction. Or take the deduction on the estate's tax return.

The last category of responsibility for executors and administrators is distributing the estate assets. State probate codes typically list the order in which estate debts have to be paid. For an introduction to how the order will probably look, here is the debt payment priority list from Section 3-805 of the Uniform Probate Code.

- First, the funeral expenses have to be paid.
- Next, the estate administration expenses have to be paid. Estate administration includes the attorneys' fees, the executor's percentage, the cost of defending against a will contest, and the various expenses involved in cleaning, appraising, transporting, selling, and otherwise disposing of estate assets.
- Then, the estate has to pay the decedent's federal taxes. For most people, these are just income taxes.
- If there are any outstanding medical bills, including therapy bills, associated with your loved one's final illness, they should be paid after the taxes have been paid.
- After the medical bills, pay the state tax bills and other debts "with preference" under your state law. The probate court clerk will almost certainly be able to hand you a list of state debt payment priorities. Repayment of public assistance, such as Medicaid and Temporary Aid to Families, will probably be high on that list.
- Finally, pay any other outstanding bills.
- After paying off all of the debts, the executor can distribute the remaining money in the estate.

THE END

Then one day, after everything else has happened, you will file the final account document in probate court. This is the paper that identifies all of the assets you collected for the estate and tells how you distributed them. Technically, the estate lawyer will file the document because he is the one who has privileges to upload documents to the probate court. He may just ask you to email the document to his office, but try to go in person if you can, to watch the transaction go through. In fact, if the option exists, see if you can even go to the probate office and physically hand over the account document yourself.

This is when it is all over. People talk about burial or cremation as closure. Sometimes, learning the facts of a previously unexplained death is supposed to be closure. But, truly, concluding the estate administration is the end. The process of notifying people and going through all of your relative's possessions and counting his or her last pennies has brought you to closure. It is the last time you will do anything for this good person . . . and it is a legal matter.

Having stood beside your relative with mental illness against so many people who have cheated him or tried to push him away, you may have been closer to this fragile person than you are to anyone else in your life. It is possible that no one else you know has needed to deal with as many legal issues and been as vulnerable (and perhaps difficult) as this family member was. May your memories of your good and challenging times together always make you feel brave at exactly the right moments and may they help you relax and feel happy when less important things can otherwise trouble you.

Tax Facts

- The estate administrator is responsible for filing all federal, state, and local taxes for the decedent in accordance with the tax laws for the year of death. This will be Form 1040, 1040A, or 1040EZ at the federal level.
- The estate administrator is also responsible for filing an estate and trust tax return for any and all years that the estate or trust remains open and transacts business. This is Internal Revenue Service (IRS) Form 1041.
- Federal estate and gift taxes and state estate taxes are charged against the assets of the estate. The federal estate and gift taxes exemption is $11 million per individual for 2018, which means an individual can leave $11 million to heirs and his estate will not have to pay estate and gift tax on the distributions. Sixteen states have an estate tax; the exemptions and rates vary by state. See taxfoundation.org for more information.
- State inheritance taxes are charged against the gifts (money and possessions) that beneficiaries receive through an estate. To clarify: estate taxes are about giving, and inheritance taxes are about receiving. Only six states have inheritance taxes (Iowa, Kentucky, Maryland, Nebraska, New Jersey, and Pennsylvania). The rates and exemptions for state inheritance taxes are based on the relationship between the person who died and the heir. When a resident of one of the six states dies, the heirs will be taxed even if they live in other states that do not have inheritance taxes.
- The IRS has a very helpful guide for estate administrators: *Deceased Taxpayers—Understanding the General Duties as an Estate Administrator.* Find it at irs.gov.

RESOURCES FOR THE WILLS OF PEOPLE WITH MENTAL ILLNESS

1. The criteria for having the capacity to make a will are listed in *Restatement (Third) of Property* § 8.1 (2003). This same list is in the Wikipedia entry for "Testamentary capacity."
2. The American Bar Association has a free *Glossary of Estate Planning Terms* on its website at americanbar.org.

3. The American Bar Association also has a free book chapter online titled "Making a Will." It is easy to read, it includes suggestions for being precise, and it gives numerous examples. Find it at americanbar.org.

4. See the website of the National Association of Estate Planners and Councils for a free online video and a portal leading to local estate planners at naepc.org.

5. To read about making recordings of will-signing ceremonies and otherwise preparing for the possibility of a fight about whether somebody's will is valid, see Gerry Beyer's 2011 article, "Will Contests— Prediction and Prevention," in *Estate Planning & Community Property Law Journal, 4,* 1. This article is available for free online.

6. The book-length 2012 article by Joyce Moore, "Will Contests from Start to Finish," in *St. Mary's Law Journal, 44,* 97, unlike the previous article, tells how to fight a will, rather than how to make a will that prevents fights. Although the article emphasizes Texas law, it is a good guide for people in other states. The article is free online.

7. A chart identifying all of the state laws for will formalities (age of testator, required number of witnesses, and whether oral wills or handwritten wills are legal) is included in *National Survey of State Laws,* which is available in print and as a database in many law libraries. As an alternative, go to estate.findlaw.com, where you can link to state laws online and hunt for the formalities yourself.

8. One good article about conditions in wills is Jeffrey G. Sherman's "Posthumous Meddling: An Instrumentalist Theory of Testamentary Restraints on Conjugal and Religious Choices," which was published in the *University of Illinois Law Review* (1999). The statement about marriage being central to family structure comes from this article.

9. The American Occupational Therapy Association has several articles about how OTs help people with mental health diagnoses to actively participate in tasks at their highest level of independence. Find the articles by using the phrase "mental health" in the search box on the aota.org website.

10. Most probate courts provide instruction manuals and sample forms for executors of wills and administrators of intestacies. If you do not find this kind of publication on the court's website, ask about it in person. Someone in the office (not the judge) will know where to get the instructions. Note that not every state has a separate court for probate matters. The phrase "probate court" generally refers to whichever court deals with wills. Find links to these courts on the National Center for State Courts' page titled "Probate Courts: State Links" at ncsc.org.

ABLE bank account, 284–85
  expenses covered by, 285
  interest on, untaxed, 284
  resources on, 303
  tax considerations, 284, 291
ABLE National Resource Center, 303
Academy of Special Needs Planners,
    305, 325
  Directory of Pooled Trusts, 325
  Special Needs Answers, 325
Accessory, to crime, 167
Accidental death and dismemberment
    insurance, and self-caused death,
    412, 420
Accommodation
  definition of, 354
  disability, 37
    confusions and misunderstandings
      about, 199
    and court testimony, 89
    for crime victims, 86–87
    denial, 236
    for disability hearing, 27–28
    in EEOC mediation process, 207
    in housing (*see* Housing)
    in job application process, 202, 200–1
    in job interview, 200–1
    at work (*see* Workplace disability
      accommodation)
  during drafting of will, 424–25
  leave of absence under ADA as,
    220–23, 233
    denial of request for, 221–23

  psychological benefits of, 232
  and workers' compensation, 223
  necessary, definition of, 354
  reasonable. *See also* Housing,
    accommodations/reasonable
    accommodations
    definition of, 354
    EEOC information on, 181, 195
    workplace (*see also* Workplace disability
      accommodation)
      ADA and, 199–200
Accomplice
  definition of, 167
  liability for being, 167, 294
Achieving a Better Life Experience Act,
    285, 303
Addiction treatment
  programs approved for court-ordered
    services, 120
  records from, in intake for mental
    health court, 124
Administrative law judge (ALJ)
  disability hearing, 23–24, 28–29, 31–32
  manual for, 37
  mistakes by, 32
Adult Protective Services (APS), 44, 47
  and counteracting undue influence, 258
Advanced Self Advocacy Plan, The
    (ASAP), 55
Advocacy groups
  locating, 110
  support for victims of police
    misconduct, 99, 103

Advocacy Handbook, 112
Affirmative defense, 136
Affordable Care Act, and coverage of
      recovery from suicide attempt,
      411, 419
Agent
   in durable power of attorney for mental
      health decision-making, 53
   in financial power of attorney
      and accusations of wrongdoing, 333
      and adherence to power of attorney
         document, 333
      avoidance of making
         assumptions, 332
      and blame by principal, 332
      breach of contract, 334
      civil court claim against, 334
      conduct and responsibilities
         of, 332–33
      conflict of interest, 334
      criminal charges against, 333–34
      definition of, 327
      duties of, 334
      guide for, 349
      misconduct by, 333–34
      mistakes of, 334
      and principal's best interests, 328
      signature of, 332
   in psychiatric advance directive,
      54, 48, 53
Alabama, workers' comp cases in, 229–30
American Bar Association
   Commission on Law and Aging,
      280, 350
   *Criminal Justice Standards on Mental
      Health,* 145
   Glossary of Estate Planning Terms, 438
   glossary of real estate terms, 303
   "Making a Will," 439
   portal to state and local bar
      associations, 132
   portal to state guardianship laws,
      46, 350
   power of attorney fact sheet, 349
   *A Practitioner's Guide to Hospital
      Liability,* 81
   Standards on Treatment of
      Prisoners, 112

Standing Committee on Legal
      Aid and Indigent Defendants
      (SCLAID), 121
American Civil Liberties Union (ACLU).
      See also Advocacy groups
   advocacy for fair and humane treatment
      of prisoners, 158
   civil rights lawyer referral list, 111
   guides to interacting with police, 175
   information on police liability for harm
      to detainees, 407
   on reforming police practices, 110
American College of Trust and Estate
      Counsel
   directory of trust lawyers, 325
   tools for trust creation and
      management, 325
American Correctional Association,
      articles on mental health
      management in jails/prisons, 158
American Counseling Association, ethics
      information from, 13
American Foundation for Suicide
      Prevention, 419
American Hospital Association (AHA)
   behavioral health resources, 66
   Hospitals in Pursuit of Excellence, 66
American Jail Association, articles
      on treatment of mentally ill
      offenders, 158
American Library Association, *Prison
      Libraries* (website), 159
American Medical Association (AMA)
   Code of Ethics, 13
   link to psychiatrist licensure
      boards, 80
American Nurses Association,
      Professional Standards, 13
American Occupational Therapy
      Association, 439
American Probation and Parole
      Association, resources from, 120
American Psychiatric Association
   Code of Ethics, 13
   Policy Finder, 80
   Principles of Medical Ethics with
      Annotations Especially Applicable
      to Psychiatry, 13

American Psychiatric Nurses Association,
resources on restraint and
seclusion, 56
Americans with Disabilities Act
(ADA), 110
case documents and technical
assistance manuals, 212
definition of, 212
definition of disability, 199
definition of major life activities, 354
EEOC information on, 195
employee's rights under,
communicating with human
resources about, 189
and employment
discrimination, 197–98
leave of absence as disability
accommodation under,
220–23, 233
denial of request for, 221–23
psychological benefits of, 232
and workers' compensation, 223
and police misconduct, 100
prisoners' rights under, 149
and protection of employees with
disabilities, 179–80
section on filing EEOC charges on
behalf of someone else, 212
section on forms of discrimination, 212
sections on equal employment for
individuals with disabilities, 212
statutes and regulations associated
with, accessing, 212
and workplace accommodations,
199–200
Americans with Disabilities Act
(ADA) Compliance Division,
and police misconduct, 100,
102, 110
Animal(s). See Emotional support
animals; Service animal(s)
Appelbaum, Paul S., "Commentary &
Analysis: The Draft Act Governing
Hospitalization of the Mentally
Ill," 419
Application for Disability Insurance
Benefits, 19
Appraiser(s), for estate items, 436

Arc, The
list of trustee services, 325
Pooled Trust Programs for People with
Disabilities, 325
Arrest, 104. See also House arrest;
Inmate(s)
collateral consequences of, 163
resources on, 111–12
Arrestee(s), mental health screening of,
107–8, 111
Arrest records, in employment decisions,
194, 195
Assault, statute of limitations for, 237
Assessment. See also Evaluation
jail-based, records from, in intake for
mental health court, 124
mental health, for inmates, 108, 111
Asset(s)
in bankruptcy petition, 271
and eligibility for government
assistance, 293, 303
of estate, 435
distribution of, 437
free food and shelter as, SSA
and, 376–77
identified in will, 426, 423
listing, for credit counselor, 265
not counted against disability
recipient, 316–17
SSI list of, 326
spouse's, and SSI disability benefits, 386
ward's
conservator's list of, 341–44
liquidation of, 343–44
resale value of, 343–44
Social Security number and, 345
Assisting Families of Inmates, 160
Association for State and Provincial
Psychology Boards, 80
Association of Inspectors General,
directory of prison oversight
agencies, 159
Association of Social Work Boards, 80
Association of State Correctional
Administrators, Behavioral Health
Committee, 158
Atascadero Unified School District v.
WCAB, 231

Attorney fees
    awards for, in court case, tax
        considerations, 80, 243, 406
    discharged in bankruptcy case, 277–78
    in personal injury lawsuit, tax
        considerations, 406
    in wrongful death case, tax
        considerations, 406
Attorney general, state
    and consumer protection, 262
    office, locating, 280
    online consumer complaint form, 280
Attorney in fact, 327
Autistic Self-Advocacy Network, *The Right
    to Make Choices,* 350
Automatic stay, for creditors, in
    bankruptcy process, 270
Autopsy(ies), 393–94
    state laws about, 397

Babich v. W.C.A.B., 232
Background check(s)
    credit report in, 183, 184, 194
    criminal
        permission for, 184
        of prospective employee, 183
    discrimination arising from, 185
    for employment, 182–86
    FTC guide to, 194
    for mental health commitment, 183–84
    records of, disposal of, 185–86
    resources for, 194–95
    state laws on, information on, 194
Baker v. City of New York, 191
Bank(s)
    communication with, 287
    notification of conservatorship, 344
    notification services, 287, 287
    spending tracker service, 287
Bank account
    conservatorship and, 345
    convenience, 285, 303
    for donation to help locate missing
        person, 395
    fees, 288
    gift deposits into, 295
    interest earned, tax considerations, 291
    joint, 286, 288–89, 291, 303, 423
    mistakes with, reporting to relative, 287

online transfer to/from, 286
outsider's questions about, responding
    to, 290
relative's questions about, responding
    to, 300
terms and conditions (contract)
    for, 288–89
transfer to estate, 436
for trust, 306
Banking. *See also* ABLE bank account
    agency account for, 285
    direct deposits for, 285
    glossary for, 302
    legal considerations, 286
    mental health and, 283–84
    online, 285–86, 303
    overdrafts in, 288
    power of attorney for, 331
    reporting on, to relative, 286
    resources on, 302–3
Banking law, resource on, 303
Bankruptcy, 268–79
    advantages of, 269
    assisting with, 263
    and back due SSI benefits, 16–17
    Chapter 7, 269, 273, 277
        tax debt and, 279
    Chapter 13, 269, 274, 277
        tax debt in, 279
        trustees, DOJ list of, 280
    concluding, 277
    conservator and, 278, 342, 343
    credit counseling debt management
        and, comparison of, 268–69
    and debtor education, 277
    and disability, 277–78, 282
    and filing tax returns, 279
    glossary for, 281
    lawyer for, 269, 272, 273, 278, 281
    money spent in anticipation of, 274–75
    and people who hoard, 271–72, 281
    as relief from debts, 278–79
    resources on, 281–82
    tax considerations, 279
    tax returns representing, EIN for, 279
Bankruptcy Abuse Prevention and
    Consumer Protection Act, 263
Bankruptcy Basics (website), 281
Bankruptcy case(s)

cat hoarders', 271–72, 281
  on discharging student loans, 281
  of gambling addict and credit card debt
    from gambling, 281
  of woman who did not report art and
    jewelry, 271, 281
Bankruptcy forms, from federal court
    system, 281
Bankruptcy law(s), resource on, 281
Bankruptcy petition, 271, 272
Bankruptcy trustee(s), 271, 272–73
  Chapter 13, 264
  investigation of debtors' financial
    affairs, bankruptcy law on, 281
  manuals for, from DOJ, 281
Bar association. *See also* American Bar
    Association
  locating, 36
  and locating criminal defense
    lawyer, 132
Battery, 58
  statute of limitations for, 237
Bazelon Center for Mental Health Law
  advocacy for patients' civil liberties, 65
  "Campus Mental Health Issues," 419
  chart of state statutory codes, 65
  fill-in psychiatric advance directive
    template, 55
  information on underemployment and
    unemployment in people with
    mental illness, 196
  publication on transition from jail/
    prison to community, 159
  reports on mental health courts, 130
  *What Fair Housing Means for People
    with Disabilities,* 385
Beneficiary(ies)
  of disability benefits, 16
  of insurance policy, 423
  of investment accounts, 423
  of life insurance, 413
  of trust, 304, 309–10
Benson, Brittany, *Filing Taxes for an
    Inmate,* 156
Bequest(s), 423
  conditional, 429–31
  management of, 436
Best interests, patient's, decision making
    in, 53–54

Better Business Bureau (BBB), dispute
    resolution services, 261
Beyer, Gerry, "Will Contests—Prediction
    and Prevention," 439
Bill payment
  automatic, 295, 285–86
  calendar for, 285–86
  conservator's management of, 342
  as gift to relative, 295
  online, 109
  for SSI disability recipient, and SSI
    benefit amount, 295
Bipolar disorder
  as disability, under EEOC
    regulations, 187
  and money management, 283–84
Blandford, Alex M., and Fred Osher,
    *Guidelines for the Successful
    Transition of People with
    Behavioral Health Disorders from
    Jail and Prison,* 120
Body(ies), unclaimed/unidentified, 393
  NamUS databases on, 397
  ViCAP records on, 396
Boruchowitz, Robert C., Malia N. Brink,
    and Maureen Dimino, *Minor
    Crimes, Massive Waste,* 120
Bracton, Henry, *De Legibus et
    Consuetudinibus Angliae,* 418
Brady Campaign to Prevent Gun
    Violence, 407
Brady Center to Prevent Gun
    Violence, 404
Brief Jail Mental Health Screen, 111
Broadwater v. Dorsey, 302
Building accessibility standards, 383
Bullying, 226
  workplace, 198
Bureau of Alcohol, Tobacco, and Firearms,
    website about NICS, 195
Bureau of Justice Assistance (BJA)
  Justice and Mental Health
    Collaboration program, 97
  Mental Health Courts (manual), 129
  technical support for police
    departments, 97
Burial plot/burial expenses, not
    counted in disability benefit
    eligibility, 317

California
  "DWC Glossary of Workers'
    Compensation Terms for Injured
    Workers," 234
  parents' attempts to intercept their son's
    crime spree in, 93, 97
Californians for Safety and Justice,
    *Victims of Crime Act and the Need
    for Advocacy,* 96
*Cameron v. Community Aid for Retarded
    Children,* 192–93
Capacity/incapacity
  conservatorship and, 338
    hearing on, 26, 39–40, 339–40
  legal standards for, 340
Capital gains, 298, 302
Car. *See* Vehicle
Cash, ward's, conservator's management
    of, 342, 344
Caucusing, in mediation, 208
Cause, in negligence claim, 76, 78
Center for Constitutional Rights
  civil rights lawyer referral list, 111
  research and advocacy
    on mass incarceration, 160
    on solitary confinement, 160
Center for Elders and the Courts
  Guardianship Basics, 47
  information about guardianship
    courts, 47
  information about legal issues
    and quality of service in
    guardianship, 47
Center for Ethical Practice, 13
Center for Guardianship Certification,
    The (CGC)
  credentialing process, 43, 46
  online training and certification by, 46
Centers for Disease Control (CDC)
  *Coroner/Medical Examiner Laws, by
    State,* 397
  Where to Write for Vital Records, 397
Centers for Medicare and Medicaid
    Services
  filing a grievance with, 81
  summary of federal regulations
    governing psychiatric hospitals, 66
Chandler v. Specialty Tires of America, 419
Charitable gaming/fundraisers, 393, 396

Child abuse, reporting requirements, 6
Citizen's Commission on Human
    Rights, 56
Civil commitment. *See* Involuntary
    commitment
Civil commitment hearing office, 59
Civil court cases, 79, 398–99
  against conservator, 348
Civil rights
  restoration of, 174
  violations of, in federal prisons,
    complaints about, 159
Civil Rights Act
  and prisoners' rights, 159
  Section 1983, 148
Civil rights lawyers, 103
  locating, 111
  referral lists for, 111
Civil Rights of Institutionalized Persons
    Act (CRIPA), 154, 159
Claimant
  definition, 15
  for disability benefits, 15
Client consent. *See* Consent
Closed-circuit television, for crime
    victim's testimony, 89
Closed period of disability, 25–26
Cobb, Tom, et al., "Advocacy Strategies
    to Fight Eviction in Cases of
    Compulsive Hoarding and
    Cluttering," 385
Code of Federal Regulations
  confidentiality of substance abuse
    patient records, 121
  definition of substantial gainful
    employment, 251
  HIPAA privacy rules, 121
  on leave time as accommodation under
    ADA and FMLA, 233
  listing of impairments qualifying for
    disability, 37
  on restraining hospital patients, 56
Cohen v. Ameritech, 193
Collateral consequences
  of arrest or conviction, 163
  breach of contract and, 261
  definition of, 261
Collateral Consequences Resource
    Center (CCRC)

chart of state laws on expunging
    criminal records, 174
collection of state-specific guides to
    restoration of rights, pardon,
    sealing, and expungement, 174
Colorado, process for expunging criminal
    record, 164
Colorado Bar Association, guide for
    agents, 349
Columbia University, *Jailhouse Lawyer's
    Manual,* 158
Common-law trust(s), 307
Communication
    about banking, with relative, 286
    about financial matters, 255–56
    with bank, 287
    with credit counselor, 265
    with employer, after employee's poor
        performance, 132
    with mental health professionals, 3–4
    prisoners', with people outside
        prison, 151–53
    monitoring/interception of, 152–53
Community Associations Institute, "What
    You Should Know Before You
    Buy," 384
Community service, 116
    compliance with, 117
Competence, 134
    assessment, for defendant with mental
        illness, 145
    of criminal defendant, 133–34, 145
    resources on, 56, 145
    to stand trial, 133–34, 145
    state statutes on, 145
Complainant, definition of, 71
Complaint(s)
    about professional ethics, 72–73
    about professional misconduct, 69–70
    about professional or institution, 71
    content of, 70
    definition of, 69–70
    direct, 71
    filing, institutional systems for, 70
    remedy/resolution in, 70
Conciliation
    for employment discrimination
        case, 210
    for fair housing complaint, 375–76

Condominium. *See also* Home
    legal obligations with, 299
Confidentiality
    attorney–client, 75
    ethics rules about, 7
    and prisoners' mail, 151–52
    and prisoners' phone calls, 152
    state laws about, 11–12
Confidentiality of Substance Abuse
    Patient Records, 121, 124
Consent
    for disclosure of mental health
        information, 5, 7, 10
    in legal context, 111
    state laws and, 11–12
Conservator. *See also* Conservatorship
    appointment of, petition for,
        27, 338–39
    and bankruptcy, 278
    business expenses of, as deductible, 349
    civil court claims against, 348
    collaboration with guardian, 41, 42–43,
        338, 343
    collaboration with therapist, 346
    criminal charges against, 348
    decision-making by
        convenience and, 346
        and honoring ward's emotional
            associations, 346
    definition, 47
    handbook for, 341
    identification as such, to everyone doing
        business with ward, 344–45
    legal obligations of, 340–41
    list of ward's assets and debts compiled
        by, 341–44
    misconduct by, 346
        reporting of, to court, 117
    naming of, by judge, 340
    need for, 259
    payment of, 341
        tax considerations, 349
    possible actions undertaken by,
        347, 345–46
    removal of, petition for, 117
    reports to court, 340–41, 344, 346
    surety bond posted by, 341
    use of good judgment by, 345–46
    ward of, 340–41

Conservatorship, 38, 39, 328, 338. *See also* Conservator–48
  bad, prevention and management of, 26
  and banking, 344–45
  capacity/incapacity and, 338, 348
    hearing on, 26, 39–40, 339–40
  and contracts, 345
  court costs for, 339
  emergency, to reclaim resident's belongings from former housing, 372
  end of, petition for, 348
  legal duty of, 346
  legal standards for, 351
  positive end to, 348
  resources for, 350–51
  responsibilities of, 341–46
  tax considerations, 349
  temporary, 340
Conservatorship document, official copies of, 344
Conservatorship hearing, 26, 39–40, 339–40
Conspiracy, 166–67
Constitution, state, prisoners' rights in, 147, 148
Constitution, U.S. *See also specific amendment*
  Annotated, 111
  prisoners' rights in, 147
  text of, 111
Consultative examination(s), in disability application process, 21–22, 37
Consumer(s)
  definition of, 256
  rights of, 256
Consumer Financial Protection Bureau (CFPB)
  information on banking, 303
  Managing Someone Else's Money: Help for Agents Under Power of Attorney, 349
  resource on financial abuse of elderly, 281
Consumer law(s)
  federal, 280
  and unpaid bills, 262
Consumer Leasing Act, 280

Consumer Product Safety Commission (CPSC), and dangerous products, 407
Consumer protection statute(s), 261
Consumer support, family assistance with, 255–56
Contempt (of court), 9
Contract(s), 52
  accord and satisfaction, 260
  bad, coping with, 75
  bank account, 288–89
  breach of, 261
  capacity to enter into, 256–57
  conservatorship and, 345
  copies of, obtaining, 259
  early termination clause, 259
  HOA, 358
  housing (*see* Housing contract)
  liquidated damages clause, 259
  mental illness and, 256–57
  renegotiation of, 259
  sales, 297–98
    Cooling-Off Rule and, 260
    returns and exchanges under, 260
  supported decision-making, 335–37
    decision maker described in, 336
    ongoing, 337
    opening of, 336
    plan outline in, 337
    supporters described in, 336–37
    termination statements, 337
  voiding, 261
Contract dispute(s)
  mediation of, 261
  resolution of, 261
Contract rights, and employee discipline, 190
Conversion
  by agent with financial power of attorney, 334
  definition of, 334
  legal action against professionals for, 78
  of resident's belongings from former housing, 372–73
  as theft, 79
Copeley, Leto, and Narendra K. Ghosh, "The Intersection of Workers'

Compensation and Emotional
Distress Employment Claims," 250
Cornell Legal Information Institute,
111, 145
information on banking laws, 303
Coroner. *See* Medical examiner
Corrections agency(ies), and wrongful
death, 401–2
Council of State Governments
*A Guide to the Role of Crime Victims in
Mental Health Court,* 129
Justice Center
Advocacy Handbook, 112
Consensus Report on mental health
care in jails, 111
online curriculum for setting up a
Mental health court, 129
Counselor(s), mental health, legal resource
for, 80
Court
civil (*see* Civil court cases)
criminal (*see* Criminal court)
mental health (*see* Mental health court)
probate (*see* Probate courts)
Court appearance, compliance with, 117
Court order(s)
compliance with, 117–20
and disclosure of private
information, 7, 8–9
Covered entities, access to private medical
information, 10–11
*Crandall v. Paralyzed Veterans of
America,* 192
Credit card(s)
for bill payment, 109
conservator's management of, 342
fees, conservator's management
of, 342
Credit Card Accountability and
Disclosures Act, 280
Credit card debt
and bankruptcy, 274–75
from gambling, and bankruptcy,
275, 281
Credit card record, as proof of
purchase, 261
Credit counseling, 263
advantages of, 268–69

advocate participation in, 255, 266
exemption from, 263
mental illness and, 263, 281
facilitating, ideas for, 93
failed attempt at, 269
organizing information for, 265
Credit counseling agency(ies)
approved by Bankruptcy
Administrators, list of, 280
conservator's use of, 342
reputable, locating, 264
services provided by, 263
Credit counseling services, regulation
of, 280
Credit counselor(s)
communication with, 265
list of, 280
reputable, finding, 264
services provided by, 263
standards for, 280
Credit history, and finding
housing, 356–57
Creditor(s)
automatic stay, in bankruptcy
process, 270
bankruptcy applicants' meeting
with, 272–73
mental illness and, 272–73
rights of, 256
Credit report(s), 265
in background check, 183, 184, 194
in background record, disposal of, 185
correction, sample letter, 280
ward's, conservator's use of, 342
Crime(s). *See also* Minor crime(s)
committed by relative, family liability
for, 166–68
components for proof of, 136–37
confession to, 105
funding of, by gifts, 294
intent and, 136–37
by mental health professionals, 79
mental illness and, 136
against people with mental illness,
prevalence of, 96
prosecution of, standards for, 96
Crime spree, California parents' attempts
to intercept, 93, 97

Crime victim(s), 85. *See also* Victim
     impact statement; Victimizationof
     people with mental illness;
     Victims' rights–90
  as accusers, 86
  advocate for (*see* Victim rights
     advocate)
  bearing witness by, 88–89
  compensation rights of, 96
  mental health court and, 127–28, 129
  personal information disclosure by, 86
  resources for, 96
  re-victimization of, 99
  right to be heard, 88–89
  right to notification, 88, 96
  right to restitution, 88
  support services for, 87–88
  testimony by, 89, 96
Criminal activity, of relative, options for
     family in regard to, 175
Criminal charges, information about/
     explanation of, 175
Criminal conviction
  collateral consequences of, 163
  mistaken, setting aside, 162–63
Criminal court
  affirmative defense in, 136
  defendants with mental illness
     and, 131–32
     resources on, 144–46
  expert witnesses in, 138
  federal, explanation of, 175
  multiple defenses in, 136
  practices, explanation of, 175
  resources on, 144–46
  sentencing phase, mental health
     evidence and, 142–44
Criminal court cases, 79, 398–99
Criminalization of mental illness
  prevention of, 90
  resource on, 111
Criminal justice information systems,
     federal regulations about, 195
*Criminal Justice Interventions for
     Offenders with Mental illness,* 129
Criminal justice system
  Advocacy Handbook for, 112
  description of, 175
  resources on, 96, 97

Criminal law, 85–86
  glossary for, 175
Criminal procedure, 104
  state's rules for, link to, 111
Criminal punishment, mental health
     evidence and, 142–44
Criminal record
  in background record, disposal of, 185
  check
     permission for, from job
        applicant, 184
     of prospective employee, 183
  copies of, 165
  in employment decisions, 194, 195
  expunging, 64, 161–49
     process for, 164
     resources for, 174–75
  sealing of, 163, 175
     resources for, 174
  set aside (vacated), 162–48, 175
     resources for, 174
  suppression of, 163, 175
     resources for, 174
Crisis intervention team (CIT), 59, 85, 90–95
  advocating for, 95
  and criminal charges/arrest of troubled
     person, 92
  de-escalation of crisis, actions
     for, 91–92
  emergency calls to, 92–93
  evaluation of troubled person, 91
  funding for, 97
  getting to know, 93–94
  locating, 97
  non-emergency request for, 93
  program objectives for, 90, 97
  and referrals, 91
  resources for, 97
  starting a program for, 95, 97
*Critchlow v. First UNUM Life Ins. Co. of
     Am.,* 420
Cruel and unusual punishment, 148–49

Damage award(s)
  for emotional distress, 250
     tax considerations, 79, 243
  for employment discrimination, tax
     considerations, 211
  for housing discrimination, 375–76

for wrongful conviction, tax
considerations, 157
in wrongful death case, 403–4
tax considerations, 406
Damage control techniques, 169
Danger/dangerousness. *See also*
Imminent danger
and involuntary commitment, 57, 60
legal concept of, 409
from relative, advice for family
members about, 66
Dangerous products
reporting, 407
and wrongful death, 407
Data disposal, state laws about, 194
Dealing, liability for, 168
Death. *See also* Suicide;
Wrongful death
investigation of, legal requirements
for, 393
petition for presumption of, 394–95
suspicious/mysterious, 393
information required to be collected
and recorded about, 397
Death certificate, copies of
for executor's use, 435
obtaining, 397
Debt(s)
in bankruptcy petition, 271
discharging (cancelling), in
bankruptcy, 273–74
of estate, 435, 436, 437
listing, for credit counselor, 265
nondischargeable, bankruptcy law on,
275, 281
payback amounts, in Chapter 13
bankruptcy, 274, 277
related to court proceedings,
conservator's management of, 342
secured, 274
tax refunds and, 268
unsecured, 273
ward's, conservator's list of, 341–44
from willful and malicious
misconduct, bankruptcy law on,
274, 281
Debt collectors, dealing with, resource
on, 280
Debt management

by credit counseling, and bankruptcy,
comparison of, 268–69
state laws on, obtaining, 280
Debt-management plan, 263
Debtor(s)
in bankruptcy, definition of, 279
financial affairs of, investigation by
trustee, bankruptcy law on, 281
mental incapacity of, 281
tax returns of, 267
unpaid bills of, 262–63
victimization of, resource on, 280
Debtor-creditor law, 256
resources about, 280–81
Debtor education, in bankruptcy, 277
Decision-making
by conservator
convenience and, 346
and honoring ward's emotional
associations, 346
guardian's power for, 42
mental health, durable power of
attorney for, 48–49, 52–55
in patient's best interests, 53–54
resource on, 56
supported (*see* Supported
decision-making)
*Deeds, Robert Creigh v. Commw. of
Virginia,* 404
Deeming, 386
Defamation, 78–79
Defendant
competence determination for, 133–34,
135–36, 145
insanity when committing crime,
proving, 138
with mental illness
federal statutes regarding, 145
prosecution of, resource on, 146
mental symptoms of, ebb
and flow, 139
not competent to stand trial, 133–34
management of, by court, 134–35
participation in own defense, 133
*Delana v. CED d/b/a Odessa Gun
Sales,* 404
Delaware, mental health-related workers'
comp claims in, 231
Delusion(s), insane, 424

Department of Justice
  ADA Compliance Division (*see*
      Americans with Disabilities Act
      (ADA) Compliance Division)
  bankruptcy trustee manuals, 281
  Civil Rights Division
      and police misconduct, 100, 102, 110
      and prison misconduct, 159
  descriptions of laws on police
      misconduct, 110
  Disability Rights Section, and police
      misconduct, 100, 102, 110
  findings letters, 110
      on police misconduct, 110
  Housing and Civil Enforcement
      Section, 385
  list of Chapter 13 trustees, 280
  Office for Victims of Crime, 96
  Office of Inspector General, contact
      form, 159
  and police misconduct, 100–2, 110
  *Rights of Persons Confined to Jails and
      Prisons* (website), 159
  *Smart on Crime: Reforming America's
      Criminal Justice System,* 121
  Special Litigation Section, and inmates'
      rights, 154
  Victim Assistance Training
      (VAT), 87, 96
Department of Labor. *See also* Wages and
      Hours Division
  explanation of FMLA, 233
  link to state workers' compensation
      offices, 234
  medical certification forms for FMLA
      claims (Form WH380E or
      WH380F), 233
Direct deposits, 285
Directory of Pooled Trusts, 325
Disability, 235
  accommodations, 37
      confusions and misunderstandings
          about, 199
      and court testimony, 89
      for crime victims, 86–87
      denial, 236
      for disability hearing, 27–28
      in EEOC mediation process, 207
      in job application process, 202, 200–1

  in job interview, 200–1
  undue hardship caused by, 200, 221–22
  at work (*see* Workplace disability
      accommodation)
age of onset, and ABLE account
      eligibility, 284
and bankruptcy, 277–78, 282
certification, and ABLE account
      eligibility, 284
closed period of, 25–26
confusions and misunderstandings
      about, 199
definition of, 199, 307
and eligibility for programs, 18
employee with (*see* Employment
      discrimination)
and employment support, 250
episodic, 26
equipment and supplies needed for
      workplace functioning, as medical
      expense, 211
evidence of, 218 (*see also* Functional
      limitations)
how to help with, 26
harassment about, 236
impairments qualifying for, 37
mental symptoms and, 20, 22
onset date, 16–17
  for new claim, 35
people with
  Fair Housing Act criteria for, 354
  protection and advocacy (P&A)
      agencies for, 65
physical symptoms and, 20
psychiatric conditions qualifying as,
      with EEOC, 187
and return to work, 235–36
and special needs trust, 307
symptoms of, disciplining employee for,
      as discrimination, 188
threshold earnings amount with, for
      SSA, 247, 251
unlawful employer practices based on,
      236, 250
Disability accommodation leave. *See*
      Americans with Disabilities Act
Disability application, 15, 19–21
  administrative law judge hearing
      on, 23–24

consultative examinations for, 21–22, 37
costs, reducing, 20
information sources for, 20
losing (claim denial), 32–34
medical records for, 20
new, after claim denial, 32, 34–35
reconsideration, 22
rejection, 22–23
representative for, 23–24
resource for, 37
results, 22
Disability benefit(s), 243. *See also* Social
    Security Disability Insurance
    (SSDI); Supplemental Security
    Income (SSI)
application for (*see* Disability
    application)
cash, 16–17
claims, 15
closed period of, 25–26
court-ordered inpatient care and, 144
eligibility for, 15
income and, 249
during jail and prison, 131–32, 144
lump sum payments
    and bankruptcy, 277–78
    tax considerations, 36
reapplying for, after three years of
    employment and new onset of
    disability, 248
representative payee for, 35, 37, 327
resources for, 36–37
resumption after release from
    confinement, 132
tax considerations, 36, 249
types of, 16
Disability denial, 32–34
appealing, 32
Disability discrimination, and workers'
    compensation, 236–37
Disability hearing
ALJ's questions in, 31
arriving for, 28–29
check-in for, 29
claimant's demeanor and, 23, 29
debriefing after, 29
disability accommodations for, 27–28
hearing room for, 31
people present at, 31

preparation for, how to help with, 26, 30
process during, 31–32
representative for, 23–24
    fees/payment for, 23–24
representative's questions in, 31
as video conference, 28
vocational expert in, 31–32
Disability lawyer, 23
fee paid to, as tax-deductible
    expense, 36
locating, 36, 46
Disability Rights Network, 36
directory of protection and advocacy
    (P&A) agencies, 65
Disability support agency, and fair
    housing complaints, 373
Discrimination. *See also* Disability
    discrimination; Employment
    discrimination; Housing
    discrimination
arising from background check, 185
forms of, ADA section on, 212
against inmates, 149
suicidality and, 410, 419
Distributing, liability for, 168
Diversion, for mental health care, of jail
    inmate, 109, 112
Dockery v. Epps, 158
Documentation, in intake for mental
    health court, 123–25
Drug possession, 167–68
Drug product warnings, 405
d(4)(a) trust. *See* Trust(s), special needs
Due process, 147, 149
and employee discipline, 190
Durable power of attorney
for health care, 49, 329
for health care and related decisions, 10
    creation of, 10
for mental health decision-making,
    48–49, 52–55
    agent with, 52–55
    state laws on, portal to, 349
Duty(ies)
breach of, 68, 69, 76, 77
    action-based, 77
    inaction-based, 77
to follow professional standards of
    competence, 402

Duty(ies) (*cont.*)
  for institutions, 69
  in liability for another person's crime,
      169, 171
  to maintain safe property, 402
  to manufacture safe products, 402
  in mental health treatment, 76
  and negligence claim, 76
  to prevent someone from causing
      harm, 402–3
  to protect, 8, 14
  to protect detainees, 401–2, 406, 407
  to protect patients, 401
  to use reasonable skill and care,
      professionals', 68
  to warn, 8, 14
  to warn consumers about safe product
      use, 402
  in wrongful death claims, 401–2

Edwards v. Valentine, 302
EEOC v. Amego Inc., 419
Eighth Amendment, 107, 148, 150
Electronic Privacy Information Center,
    data on state expungement
    practices, 175
Emergency department, mental health
    workup in, 63
Emotional distress
  financial value of, 250
  intentional infliction of, 236
    fact sheet about, 250
    legal action against professionals
        for, 78
    statute of limitations for, 237
  with life insurance claim denial, 414
  payments for, as taxable income, 79, 243
  unlawful employment practices and,
      236, 250
  and wrongful death, 404, 405
Emotional support animals
  and housing contract, 360
  tax considerations, 382
Employee(s)
  bad conduct by, 186–88
  with disabilities, laws that
      protect, 179–80
  with mental illness, negative
      perceptions of, 193–94

poor performance by, 186–88
  corrective action for, 188
  court cases about, 191–93
  resources on, 195–96
  saving a job after, 34
Employee business expense,
    unreimbursed, IRWEs as, 249
Employee discipline, 190–91
Employee records, disposal of, 185–86, 195
Employer(s)
  communication with, after employee's
      poor performance, 132
  former, lawsuit against, 235
    alternative dispute resolution in, 242
    challenges in, 237–42
    distress caused by, 237–38
    evidence in, 237–38, 240–41
    good client in, 238, 240–41
    lawyer for, 237–40
    legal process for, 237–38, 241–42
    legitimate claim in, 238
    mediation for, 242, 243
    negotiation in, 242
    options for, helping to
        reconcile, 242–43
    winnable case in, 238
  torts causing emotional distress, 236
  unlawful practices, 235–42, 250
Employer identification number (EIN)
  for bank account for donations, 395
  for tax returns representing
      bankruptcy, 279
  for trust, 306, 324
Employment. *See also* Substantial gainful
    employment
  background checks for, 182–86
  disability and, confusions and
      misunderstandings about, 199
  discrepancies between actual talents
      and job quality in, 196
  medical clearance for, 182–83
Employment application, disposal of,
    185–86, 195
Employment discrimination
  claim (charge)
    on behalf of somebody else, filing,
        205, 205, 212
    filing, 205, 212
    how to file, 205

investigation of, 209–10
"no cause" finding for, 210
Respondent's Position
Statement, 209–10
walking away from, 211
damages awarded for, tax
considerations, 211
definition of, 197–98
FMLA time and, 218
grievances about, 197–98
mediation for, 206, 212
outcomes/resolutions of, 206
regulations about, 212
reporting, 197–98
resources for, 212–13
settlement agreement, 209
statute of limitations for, 236
suicidality and, 410, 419
and workers' compensation, 236–37
Employment law, 179–80
managing conversations about, 75
Employment record, disposal of, 185–86
Employment support, 196
Employment termination. *See also*
Job, loss
disability and, 235
unlawful employment practices and,
235–42, 250
Equal Credit Opportunity Act,
enforcement of, 385
Equal Employment Opportunity
Commission (EEOC)
Assessment System, 205
Background Checks (web page), 195
and discrimination claim after suicide
attempt, 410
*Employer-Provided Leave and the
Americans with Disabilities Act,*
212, 233
employment discrimination case, 185,
197–98, 236, 242, 243
conciliation for, 210
end of, 210
filing a charge in, 205, 212
and filing charge on behalf of
somebody else, 205, 205, 212
investigation of, 209–10, 212
Letter of Determination for, 210
mediation of, 206, 212, 242, 243

"no cause" finding for, 210
"Notice of Right to Sue" in, 242
resources for, 212–13
walking away from, 211
*Enforcement Guidance: Reasonable
Accommodation and Undue
Hardship Under the Americans
with Disabilities Act,* 212, 233
*Enforcement Guidance on Reasonable
Accommodation,* 195
*Enforcement Guidance on the
ADA and Psychiatric Disabilities,*
195, 212
explanation of ADA disability
accommodation leave, 233
guidance document on psychiatric
disabilities, 212
guidelines on consideration of arrest
and conviction records in
employment decisions, 194
*How to File a Charge of Employment
Discrimination,* 212
information on reasonable
accommodation, 181, 195
Job Accommodation Network
(*see* Job Accommodation
Network (JAN))
policy on disposal of employee records,
185–86, 195
*Pre-Employment Inquiries and Arrest &
Conviction* (web page), 195
psychiatric conditions considered
disabilities by, 186
*What You Can Expect After You File a
Charge,* 212
and workplace accommodations,
199–200, 204
Equal opportunity specialist (EOS), in
HUD, 374, 374
Esq. (Esquire), 132
Essential functions, for job, 187
Estate
administration of, concluding, 437–38
assets of, 435
final account, filing in probate
court, 437–38
identity for, 433
intestate, 434
tax considerations, 438

Estate administrator
  guide for, 438
  for intestate estate, 434
  payment of, 434
  resources for, 439
  responsibilities and tasks of, 435, 438
  and wrongful death lawsuit, 399
Estate lawyer. *See* Trust attorney(ies)
Estate planners, 439
Estate taxes, 438
Ethics. *See also* Professional ethics
  books with information on, 13
  resource on, 55
Ethics codes, 72
Etmanski, Al, *A Good Life,* 350
Evaluation. *See also* Assessment
  of inmate, by professional, 108
  jail-based, records from, in intake for
    mental health court, 124
  of troubled person, by crisis
    intervention team, 91
Eviction, 353–54, 366–68
  corrective action to avoid, 366, 367
  defenses against, 369, 368–69
  FHAP action in, 374
  for good cause, 366
  hoarding tendencies and, 360–61, 385
  HUD action in, 374
  negative effects of, 367
  neutral effects of, 367
  notice, 366, 367
  procedures for, 367–68
  for violation of housing agreement,
    steps to remedy, 362
  warning of, 366, 367
Eviction hearing, 367
  postponement of, 368
  testifying at, 369
Executive functioning
  definition of, 283
  poor, consequences of, 283
Executor
  and contested will, 433
  and filing will in probate court, 433
  resources for, 439
  responsibilities and tasks of, 435
  and wrongful death lawsuit, 399, 403
Experts, battle of, in criminal trials, 138
Explosive devices, possession of, 168

Expungement
  of criminal records, 64, 161–49
    process for, 164
    resources for, 174–75
  definition of, 63
  of involuntary commitment record,
    63–64, 66
Extra Help program (SSA), 18, 37

Facility(ies)
  safety, and wrongful death, 402
  security of, 402
Fair Credit Reporting Act (FCA), 184,
    194, 280
Fair Employment Practices Agency
    (FEPA), 205, 213
  employment discrimination case, 236
Fair Housing Act, 352, 353–54, 358
  criteria for "person with a
    disability," 354
  enforcement of, 385
  text of, 383
Fair Housing Amendments Act, text
    of, 383
Fair Housing Assistance
    Program (FHAP)
  and eviction prevention/resolution, 374
  fair housing complaints with, 374, 373
Fair housing complaint, 368–69, 373
  filing, procedure for, 373
  HUD conciliation and, 375–76
  HUD staff manual for handling, 385
  investigation of, 374
  regulations governing, 383
Fair Housing Equal Opportunity Library,
    from HUD, 384
Fair housing law(s)
  examples, 384
  plain English summaries of, 384
  regulations that implement, 383
  state and local, links to, 385
Fair market value, and gift tax, 297
False imprisonment, 78–79
Families Against Mandatory Minimums
    (FAMM), 121
Family and medical leave (FMLA
    time), 214–15
  arranging for, 133, 225
  duration of (number of weeks of), 216

eligibility criteria, 214–15
employee need for
    employer's knowledge of, 215
    notice to employer about, 215, 217, 225
    sick-notice rule and, 217
employer noncooperation with
    complaint about, 219, 233
    third-party complaint about, 219
employer's placement of employee
    on, 218
examples of, 215
job loss after, 220, 233
legal aspects of, 214
paid, 216
    tax considerations, 232
predictable need for, notice to employer
    about, 217
process for, 217–18
psychological benefits of, 232
reason for
    employer's knowledge of, 215
    medical certification of, 217–18, 233
resources for, 233
return to work after, 217–18, 219–20
unpaid, 216
    tax considerations, 232
and workers' compensation, 223
Family and Medical Leave Act (FMLA),
    214. See also Family and medical
    leave (FMLA time)–15
communicating with human resources
    about, 189, 225
online explanation of, 233
and protection of employees with
    disabilities, 180
Family Caregive Alliance, 386
Family caregiver agreement, 378
arrangements and conditions specified
    in, 379
communication provision in, 382
early termination clause in, 382
effective date, 379
end date, 379
facilities section of, 379
formalizing, 382
and medical costs, 381
modifications of, instructions for, 382
nursing services in, 383
official copies of, 382

penalty provisions in, 382
privacy and security arrangements
    in, 380
reason for, declaration of, 379
resources on, 386
review and renew date, 379
and service provider problems or
    transitions, 382
services section of, 380, 380
signing, 382
and substitute caregiving, 378
Family liability, for crimes committed by
    relative, 166–68, 402–3
civil, 166, 169–72
criminal, 166–68
resources on, 175
FBI. See also ViCAP (Violent Criminal
    Apprehension Program)
and police misconduct, 100, 102, 110
roster of kidnappings and missing
    persons, 396
Federal Bureau of Prisons, Management of
    Major Depressive Disorder, 159
Federal Trade Commission (FTC)
consumer support resources from, 280
Cooling-Off Rule, 260, 280
on debt management, 280
rules on background checks, 194
sample letter for credit report
    correction, 280
Feldblum, Chai, 199–200, 212
Felo de se, 418
Fifth Amendment, 105–6, 390
Filial responsibility laws, 376
your state's, locating, 385
Financial Abuse Specialist Teams
    (FAST), 351
Financial assistance, from family, legal
    considerations, 292
Financial capacity, serious mental iIllness
    and, 279
Financial institutions, state laws
    about, 303
Financial liability, for another person's
    crime, 169–72
Financial management. See also
    Conservatorship
ability to handle, assessment
    of, 329–30

Financial management class, in
  bankruptcy, 277
Financial power of attorney, 284, 327–31
  activation of, 329–30
  for banking, 331
  contract for, 327–28
    dates in, 328
    effective date, 328
    legal considerations, 328, 329
    notarization of, 328
    witnesses to, 328
  document for, 329
  laws related to, 327–28
  limited, 330
  model law for, 349
  power granted by, 329
  and principal's episodes of mental
    illness, 329
  and reports to principal, 329
  resources for, 349
  for sale of car, 330
  violation of, by agent, 333–34
Financial victimization. *See also* Undue
    influence
  of persons with serious mental
    illness, 280
  resources on, 280, 281
FindLaw
  information on police liability for harm
    to detainees, 407
  links to probate courts, 351
  portal to states' durable power of
    attorney laws, 349
  *Sample Retainer and Contingency
    Agreement for an Injury Case,* 250
FindLaw directory, 145
Find Legal Aid directory, 36
Fines, for criminal activity, 117, 121
Fingerprint card, 165
First Amendment rights, 58
  prisoners and, 151
First-party trust. *See* Trust(s),
    special needs
First Report of Injury (FROI), 224–25
  how to complete, 226
Fischer, Mary Alice, *The Ethics of
    Conditional Confidentiality,* 13
Fleming, Robert B., "What Can a Special
    Needs trust Pay For?," 319, 326

Florida
  and mental health care in prisons, 150
  Title 47 Florida Statutes § 945.48, 158
Forensic interviewer(s), 86
Forensic psychologist/psychiatrist, and
    competence determination,
    133–34, 145
Fourteenth Amendment, 390
Fourth Amendment, 104–5
  prisoners' phone calls and, 152
Frances, Heather, *How to File Bankruptcy
    While on SSI & Disability,* 282
Fraud, 78–79
  by agent with financial power of
    attorney, 333
  by conservator, 348
Functional limitations, 16
  evidence of, 23, 24–25
    faked, as evidence against
      disability, 25
    how to help with, 26

Gains Center for Behavioral Health and
    Justice, 111
Gambini v. Total Renal Care, 192
Gambling addiction, and bankruptcy,
    275–76, 281
Gambling laws, and fundraising, 393
Gift(s)
  cash, and SSI eligibility, 293, 303
  as charitable deductions, 294
  cheap sale as, 297
  conflicting feelings about, coping
    with, 294
  financial, conservator's management
    of, 342
  home as, 298
  legal considerations with, 294, 296–97
  major, 296
    giver's possible liability with, 300–1
    legal considerations with, 297
    legal obligations with, 299–300
  memberships as, 294
  to person with mental illness, family's
    role in, 299–300
  of stock, 298
  tangible
    as contribution to trust, 27
    decision-making about, 316

untaxed, 284
vehicle as, 298
Gift cards, 188
Gift tax, 297, 438
  definition of, 292
  exceptions to, 292
  exclusion amount, 292
  liability for, 292
  resources on, 302
Government assistance. *See also* Disability
      benefit(s); Medicaid; Social
      Security Disability Insurance
      (SSDI); Supplemental Security
      Income (SSI)
  eligibility for, 293, 303
Grisso, Thomas
  *Assessing Competence to Consent to
      Treatment,* 56
  Evaluating Competencies, 111, 145
Group home
  definition of, 355
  and tax-deductible nursing services, 383
Guarantor(s), 295
Guardian(s)
  collaboration with conservator, 41, 42–
      43, 338, 343
  court appointment of, 38
  decision-making power of, 42
  definition, 47
  individuals as, 38
  institutions as, 38
  and lawsuits on behalf of incapacitated
      individuals, 74
  locating, 46
  and mental hospital admission, 41
  need for, 38–39
  online training for, 46
  plenary, 42–43, 338
  problems with, 41, 44
  professional, business expenses of, 45
  and psychotropic medications, 40
  record keeping (files maintained by), 42
  reports to court, 41
  spouse as, and income tax filing, 45
  standards of practice for, 46
  training and support programs for,
      locating, 43
  ward of, 40
Guardian(ship) of the estate, 39, 338, 350

legal standards for, 351
Guardian(ship) of the person, 38, 338
  legal standards for, 351
Guardianship, 328
  arrangement, terms of,
      establishing, 40–41
  competent versus incompetent, 41–42
  cross-border issues in, 47
  incapacity and, 38, 39
  modification/restoration, 43–45
  process for, 39–41
  resources for, 46–47, 350
  state laws on, resources for, 46
  tax considerations, 45
  termination, 43–45
  terminology, glossary for, 46
  training and support programs,
      locating, 43
Guardianship court hearing, 38, 39–41
  defendant's lawyer in, 40–41
Guardianship investigation, 39
Guardianship petition, 39
Guernsey, R. S., *Suicide,* 418
*Guidebook for Social Work Disciplinary
      Actions,* 80
Guide One Insurance, glossary for
      workers' compensation, 234
Guilty but insane, state statutes on, 145
Guilty but mentally ill (GBMI), 131,
      141–42, 143
  state statutes on, 145
Gun(s), negligent entrustment of, 301
Gun-control laws, and suicide prevention,
      409, 416, 419
Gun law, 66
Gun sales
  legal regulation of, 301
  NICS information for, 14, 184
  and wrongful death, 404

HALLEX, 37
Harassment, 236
  disability-based, 236, 237
    severe or pervasive conduct in, 238–40
  at work, 182
  workplace, 198
Harm
  in negligence claim, 76, 77–78
  protection against, police and, 98

Havel v. Chapek, 171–72
Health and Human Services,
    Department of
    guidance on health information
        privacy, 14
    HIPAA complaint form and process,
        12, 12, 14
    Office of Civil Rights, 12, 12
    portal to health regulations, 66
    poverty guidelines from, 303
Health care payers, access to private
    medical information, 10–11
Health care proxy, 38, 49
Health Information and the Law, 13
Health information privacy, 3. *See also*
    Privacy–14
Health insurance
    and coverage of recovery from suicide
        attempt, 411
    locating, 419
Health Insurance Portability and
    Accountability Act (HIPAA),
    3–4, 124
    complaint, about privacy violations,
        12, 12, 14
    and coverage of recovery from suicide
        attempt, 411, 419
    and "covered entities" with access to
        medical information, 10–11
    definitions, 14
    and family access to medical
        information, 5–6, 7
    HHS guidance on health information
        privacy under, 14
    privacy rules, 14, 121
    and psychotherapy notes, 6, 14
    state laws and, 11, 14
Hearing(s), 58. *See also* Disability hearing;
    Eviction hearing; Involuntary
    commitmenthearings about–59
    conservatorship, 26, 39–40, 339–40
    judicial review, mental health court, 128
    versus trials, 58–59
    in workers' compensation case, 229–30
Hearsay rule, 60
HHS. *See* Health and Human Services,
    Department of
Hiibel v. Sixth Judicial Court of Nevada,
    Humboldt County, 397

HIPAA. *See* Health Insurance Portability
    and Accountability Act (HIPAA)
Hoarding
    and bankruptcy, 271–72, 281
    and housing, 360–61, 385
    and trash/waste disposal, 360–61
Home
    abandonment of, by special needs trust
        beneficiary, 318
    business use of, tax considerations, 383
    as gift, 27, 298, 316
    group (*see* Group home)
    legal obligations with, 299
    as property of trust, 27
    purchased by payback trust, 309
Home improvements, trustee
    responsibility for, 318
Home inventory, ward's, conservator's
    management of, 343
Homelessness, prevention of, 33
Homeowners' association (HOA),
    contract, 358
Homicide, 398–99
Hospital, mental/psychiatric
    accreditation, 66
    content of services in, 62
    liability issues, resources on, 81
    quality of services in, 62
    quality standards for, 66
    regulations governing, 62, 66
    standards for, 62
Hospital care, complaints about, 62
Hospitalization. *See also* Involuntary
    commitment
    draft act governing, 419
    Medicare coverage for, 18
Hospital liability, for preventing suicidal
    patients from killing themselves,
    401, 406
Hospitals in Pursuit of Excellence
    (HPOE), 66
House. *See* Home
House arrest, 115–16
Household expenses, paid by trust, 318
Household gifts, not counted in disability
    benefit eligibility, 317
Household items, in estate, 436
Household management, conservator
    and, 343

Housing. *See also* Home; Section 8
    housing
    accommodations/reasonable
        accommodations, 352, 353–54
        definition of, 354
        guidance on, 384
        for hoarding tendencies, 360–61, 385
        HUD/DOJ joint statement on, 384
        payment for, 358
        regulations governing, 383
        request for, information included
            in, 359
        requesting, process for, 18
    affordable, 353
    family members' provision of, 376–77
    finding, 356, 385
    government-funded, 362
    HUD-funded, 363, 363
    legal rights related to, 353
    low-income, tax considerations, 383
    moving into/moving out of, 353
    paying for, 362–63
    physical modifications of, 352, 353–54
        definition of, 354
        HUD/DOJ joint statement on, 384
        payment for, 358
        regulations governing, 383
        request for, information included
            in, 359
        requesting, process for, 18
        schedule for, 359
    possessions left behind in, 371–72
    public (*see* Public housing)
    resident's absence from, 365–66, 371–72
    shared, problems with, 353
    subsidized (*see* Subsidized housing)
    supportive (*see* Supportive housing)
    tax considerations, 382–83
Housing and Urban Development,
    Department of, 352–53
    conservator's management of, 346
    equal opportunity specialist (EOS) in,
        374, 374
    and eviction prevention/resolution, 374
    "Fair Housing Act Enforcement
        Activity" (online resource), 384
    fair housing claims, 373, 373
    Fair Housing Equal Opportunity
        Library, 384
Form 903, 373
Housing Choice Voucher Program
    (Section 8), 364, 355, 363, 385
*Housing Choice Voucher Program
    Handbook,* 385
housing funds and regulations, 362–63
housing programs, disability status
    and, 18
programs, 363, 363
properties insured and subsidized by,
    list of, 384
Public Housing Guidebook, 385
Resource Locator, 165, 363, 384
Supportive Housing for Persons with
    Disabilities Program (Section
    811), 363
"Tenants Rights" portal, 384
*Title VIII Complaint Intake,
    Investigation, and Conciliation
    Handbook,* 373, 385
Housing contract
    adjustments for residents with mental
        illness, 359–58
    and deposits, 366
    and disturbances of peace and quiet, 360
    early termination of, 365. *See also*
        Eviction–66
        fee for, 365, 366
        provider mismanagement and,
            365, 366
    living up to, 359
    negotiating, 357–59
    negotiator for, 358
    no-pets rule, and emotional support
        animals, 360
    pre-lease, 359
    termination clause in, 365–66
    terms used in, and adjustments
        for residents with mental
        illness, 359–58
Housing discrimination, 368–69
    cases, HUD online resource on, 384
    claims, with HUD, 373
    HUD conciliation and, 375–76
    HUD online resource on ("Fair
        Housing Act Enforcement
        Activity"), 384
    protection against, 352
    research on, 356, 384

Housing law, 352–53
    resources for, 383–86
    terminology, 354–55
Housing programs, disability status
        and, 18
Housing provider
    definition of, 355
    discriminatory, reporting, 373
    low-income housing tax credit, 383
    and negotiation of housing
        contract, 357–58
    and resident's absence, 365–66
    right of entry, 360
    technical guidance for, from HUD, 384
    testimony, in eviction hearing, 369
HUD. *See* Housing and Urban
        Development, Department of
Human resources, communication
        with, after employee's poor
        performance, 132

Identification, police authority to request,
        390, 397
Illinois
    and mental health care in prisons, 150
    Title 20 Illinois Admin. Code §
        415.40, 158
Imminent danger, 7–8
    CIT responses to, 91
    definition, 7
    protecting potential victims
        against, 8, 14
    warning about, 8, 14
Impairment-related work expenses
        (IRWEs), 248–49
    tax considerations, 249
Incapacity. *See also* Capacity/incapacity
    and guardianship, 38, 39
    temporary, periods of, 48
        agent in, 54
        state laws on, 49
Income
    and eligibility for government
        assistance, 293, 303
    threshold, for SSA, 247, 251
Income tax(es). *See also* Tax
        considerations
    on conservator's fees, 349
    debt and, 267–68

and disability benefits, 249
on gift of stock, 298
and gifts, 292
guardians and, 45
and inmates' income, 156
on insurance payout, 417
missing persons and, 395
SSI recipient and, 249
on trust's earnings, 324
Indiana
    rules on client consent, 11
    state income tax deduction for
        rent, 383
Indiana v. Edwards, 135–36, 145
Ineffective assistance of counsel, 162
Information, patients' right to, 58
Infraction(s), 113. *See also* Minor crime(s)
    court cases, 114–15
Inheritance tax, 438
In-kind support and maintenance, 318
Inmate(s). *See also* Prisoner(s)
    communications by, prisons'
        monitoring of, 152–53
    deprivations as punishment for, 148
    discrimination against, 149
    diversion for mental health care,
        109, 112
    evaluation by professional, 108
    families of
        online networks for, 160
        support services for, 160
    grievances against correctional
        facilities, 153–56, 159, 160
    income tax filing by/for, 157
    laws and, 147–48
    mail rights, 151–52
    mental health assessment for, 108, 111
    mental health of, supporting, 109
    with mental illness, 107–9
        Advocacy Handbook for, 112
        numbers of, 160
        post-release support for, 160
        punishment of, 148–49
        recidivism among, 160
        resource on, 111
        segregated housing of, 159
        shower treatment, 149
        treatment pods for, 148
        Urban Institute report on, 159

monitoring, 96
participation in mental health care, 109
physical force used against, 148
post-release transition to
    community, 159
restraints used on, 149
right to adequate mental health
    care, 149–50
right to communicate with people
    outside prison, 151–53
right to punishment that is not cruel or
    harmful, 148–49
right to refuse medicine or medical
    treatment, 151
taxable income of, 156
telephone access by, 152
treatment for, 108, 405
visitation rights, 151, 159
Inpatient care
    court-ordered, 134–35
        disability benefits and, 144
    for detainee not guilty by reason of
        insanity, 139
    Medicare coverage for, 18
In re Crutcher, 281
In re Estate of Pilon, 424
In re Larissa L. Johnston, 281
In re Wheeler, 281
Insanity defense, 136–41
    ABA standards on, 145
Insurance. See also Accidental death and
        dismemberment insurance; Health
        insurance; Life insurance
    medical, government-funded, 17–18
    payout, tax considerations, 417
    unemployment, 243
Insurance companies, access to private
        medical information, 10–11
Insurance policy(ies), beneficiaries
        of, 423
Intent, insanity defense and, 136–37
Intentional torts, 69
    criminal equivalents of, 79
    definition of, 78
    legal action against professionals for, 78
    types of, 78
Internal Revenue Service (IRS)
    Bulletin 2012-37, 395
    on capital expenses, 382

Chapter 13 Bankruptcy, 279
    as creditor in Chapter 13
        bankruptcy, 279
Deceased Taxpayers—Understanding
        the General Duties as an Estate
        Administrator, 438
Deducting Business Expenses, 349
Disclosure Scanning Operation, 395
Form 56 (Notice Concerning Fiduciary
        Relationship), 45, 349
Form 709 (for gift tax), 302
Form 843 (Penalty Abatement), 395
Form 1041, 324, 438
Form 1096, 291
Form 2848, 334
Form 8609, 383
Form 8826, 211
Form 1099-QA, 291
Form 5498-QA, 291
Form 109r-INT, 291
Form SS-4, 324, 395
Form SSA-1099, 36
Form W-4, 268
Gift Tax Return, 292
installment payment arrangements, 267
IRS Lawsuits, Awards, and
        Settlements—Audit Techniques
        Guide, 211
Lawsuits, Awards, and Settlements
        Audit Techniques Guide, 406
mail-forwarding process through, 395
online "Get Transcript" tool, 268
"Penalty Relief Due to Reasonable
        Cause," 395
power of attorney for dealing with, 334
private letter ruling from, 395
Publication 15A (Employer's
        Supplemental Tax Guide), 232
Publication 17, 45, 383
Publication 502, 45, 211, 382
    "Capital Expenses," 382
    "Guide Dogs and Other Service
        Animals," 382
    "Nursing Services," 383
Publication 503, 383
Publication 525, 243, 406, 417
Publication 529 (Miscellaneous
        Deductions), 249
Publication 530, 383

Internal Revenue Service (*cont.*)
  Publication 535, 45
  Publication 547, 418
  Publication 550 (*Sales and Trades of Investment Property*), 302
  Publication 559 (on gift tax), 302
  Publication 587 (*Business Use of Your Home*), 383
  Publication 596, 156
  Publication 907, 291
  Publication 908 (*Bankruptcy Code Tax Compliance Requirements*),C18.P121
  Publication 915, 36
  Publication 947 (*Practice Before the IRS and Power of Attorney*), 334
  Publication 2848, 157
  Publication 4134, 267
  Publication 4345, 80, 243, 406, 418
  Publication 4924, 157
  Schedule B–General Instructions, 291
  Tax Benefits for Businesses Who Have Employees with Disabilities, 211
  Taxpayer Advocate Service, 267
  Tax Tip 2012-59, *Tax Refunds May Be Applied to Offset Certain Debts*, 268
  Tax Topic 403 ("Interest Received"), 291
  Tax Topic 423 (*Social Security and Equivalent Railroad Retirement Benefits*), 249
  Tax Topic 502 (*Medical and Dental Expenses*), 249
  Tax Withholding (web page), 268
  Withholding Calculator, 268
  "Wrongful Incarceration FAQs," 157
International Society for Ethical Psychology and Psychiatry, materials on ethics, 55
Interview(s), forensic, 86
Investment accounts
  beneficiaries of, 423
  transfer to estate, 436
Involuntary commitment
  of criminal defendant, 134–35
  criteria for, 57
  of detainee not guilty by reason of insanity, 140
  draft act governing, 419

  emergency, 59
  hearings about, 58–59
    after suicide attempt, 416
    parties to, 59
    witnesses in, 59–61
  hearings office, 59
  illegal, 64
  improvement, work toward, 65
  of inmate from jail, 109
  inpatient, 57
  legal considerations with, 57–58, 419
  length of time of, 61
  outpatient, 57
  procedural rules for, 58–59
  processes for, 58–59
  resources for, 65–66
  by staff, 59
  state laws and, 57–58, 59, 64, 65
  suicidality and, 410, 416, 417
  terms of, 61
Iowa, inheritance tax in, 438
Israel, Andrew B., *Using the Law*, 80

Jail(s) and prison(s). *See also* Inmate(s)
  access laws, 157
  grievances and investigations of, 153–56, 159, 160
  mental health assessment of inmates in, 108, 111
  mental health care in, 107, 149–50, 405
    adequacy of, 150
    criteria for, 111
    inadequate, 150–51
    inmate participation in, 109
    negligent, 150–51
    providers, 150
    resources on, 111–12
    standards for, 111
    state standards for, 150
  mental health screening of arrestees, 107–8, 111
  and mentally ill persons, 107–9
  professional's mental health evaluation of inmates in, 108
  release from, and transition to community, 159
  resources on, 111–12
  rules and policies, accessing, 157
  visits to prisoners in, 151, 159

Jailhouse Lawyer's Handbook, 158
Jailhouse Lawyer's Manual, 158
Job
 essential functions for, 187
 loss (*see also* Employment
  termination)
  after FMLA leave time, 220, 233
 saving, after poor performance by
  employee, 34
Job Accommodation Network (JAN), 37,
  203, 212
 Ask JAN office, 233
 personal assistance from, 233
Job application process, disability
  accommodations in, 200–1
 requesting, 202
Job coaches
 and creation of job
  accommodations, 203
 locating, 212
Job discrimination. *See* Employment
  discrimination
Job interview(s), disability
  accommodations in, 200–1
Joint bank account, 286, 288–89, 303, 423
 interest on, tax considerations, 291
Joint Commission
 accreditation standards, 66
 filing a complaint with, 81
*Journal of the American Academy of
  Psychiatry and the Law,* 56
Just Cause Law Collective, on working
  with a public defender, 145
Justia, 145
 criminal law glossary, 175
 lawyer finder, 36

Kahlenberg v. Goldstein, 302
Kansas, rules on client consent, 11
Kentucky
 inheritance tax in, 438
 mental health-related workers' comp
  claims in, 231–32
Kirby v. Kuhns, 424

Lake, Peter F.
 and Nancy Tribbensee, "The Emerging
  Crisis of College Student
  Suicide," 419

*The Rights and Responsibilities of the
  Modern University,* 419
Lambda Legal, civil rights lawyer referral
  list, 111
Landlord-tenant laws
 resource on, 386
 state, online link to, 384
Lawsuit(s), 74
 on behalf of incapacitated
  individuals, 74
 class action, 74
 employment discrimination, 210
  tax considerations, 211
 against former employer, 235
  challenges in, 237–42
 police misconduct, 102–3
 professional misconduct, 74–75
 settlements or court judgments in, tax
  considerations, 418
 wrongful death, 398–99
Lawyer(s). *See also* Attorney fees;
   Disability lawyer; Public defenders;
   Trust attorney(ies)
 bankruptcy, 269, 272, 273, 278
  directory of, 281
 on boards of mental health
  organizations, 132
 civil rights, 103
  locating, 111
 for conservatorship hearing and related
  legal matters, 338, 339, 348, 351
 contingency fees, 75
 for contract renegotiation, 260
 criminal defense, 136
  locating, 132–33, 145
 defendant's, in guardianship court
  hearing, 40–41
 defense
  for minor crimes, 114–15
  and referrals to mental health
   court, 123
 for drafting will, 425, 424–25, 428
 for expungement of criminal
  record, 165
 for family caregiver agreement,
  381, 378
 free consultations, 75
 for guardianship modification/
  restoration hearing, 43–44

Lawyer(s) (*cont.*)
in hearing for restoration of
capacity, 348
hiring your own, if relative is in
trouble, 173–74
for intentional tort cases, 78–79
for involuntary commitment
hearing, 59, 60
in lawsuit against former
employer, 237–40
for life insurance claim, 414
locating, 325, 351
in mental health court, 132
personal injury, 75
sample fee agreement for, 250
for wrongful death lawsuit, 75
for police misconduct case, 102–3
for probating will, 54
prosecuting, protection of crime
victims, 86
for respondent in conservatorship
case, 339
specializing in elder abuse, and undue
influence, 258
for supported decision-making
agreement, 335–36
workers' comp, 225–26, 228, 229–30
for wrongful death case, locating, 407
Least restrictive alternative, 58
Leave of absence. *See also* Family and
medical leave (FMLA time)
under the ADA, 220–23
need for, medical documentation of,
217–18, 221, 222
options for, 220
and workers' compensation, 223
Legal Action Center
advocacy toolkit for background check
laws, 194
information on state background check
laws, 194
Legal aid
for expungement of criminal
record, 165
finding, 36, 174
free legal services, 386
instructions on seeking expungement of
criminal record, 174
resources on housing law, 386

Legal aid office, locating, 36, 174
Legal Aid Society, Employment
Law Center, fact sheet about
intentional infliction of emotional
distress, 250
Legal forms, sources of, 349
Legal Services Corporation, 174
Find Legal Aid directory, 36
Letter of Determination, for EEOC,
for employment discrimination
case, 210
Letters testamentary, 433
Lewis and Clark Law School, *Common
Steps in Criminal Investigations
and Prosecution,* 175
License verification, psychologist, online
resource for, 80
Licensure, professional, 68
Licensure boards
disciplinary decisions of, 73
making a complaint to, 72–73
professional ethics and, 72–73
psychiatrist, 80
psychologist, online resource for, 80
Liens, conservator's management of, 342
Life insurance
payout, tax considerations, 417
premium refund
after suicide of policyholder, 412
tax considerations, 417
primary beneficiary of, 413
secondary (contingent) beneficiary of, 413
suicide and, 413, 412, 420
Life Insurance Policy Locator, 413, 420
Life's Plan, 325
Lifestyle, conservator and, 343
Living wills, 49
Lyons, D. P., *Fundamentals of Jail &
Prison Administrative/Internal
investigations,* 160

Mail
forwarding, by IRS, 395
ward's, conservator's management
of, 342
Maine, rules on client consent, 11
Major depressive disorder
as disability, under EEOC
regulations, 187

in prison inmate, management
    guidelines for, 159
Major life activities
    definition of, 354
    limits to, and disability, 354
Malingerer, definition of, 244
Malpractice
    definition of, 68
    lawsuits, issues involved in, 74–75
    in mental health professions, 68–70
    not responding to family input about
        client's suicidality as, 74–75, 80
Manufacturer, as proximate cause of
    (wrongful) death, 402
Markel, Dan, and Ethan J. Leib, "Criminal
    Justice and the Challenge of
    Family Ties," 175
Marriage, as central to family structure,
    430, 439
Marson, Daniel C., Robert Savage, and
    Jacqueline Phillips, "Financial
    Capacity in Persons with
    Schizophrenia and Serious Mental
    Illness," 279
Martindale Hubbell Directory, 36, 111, 145
    and locating criminal defense
        lawyer, 132
    and locating trust attorney, 305, 325
Maryland
    inheritance tax in, 438
    Office of Treatment Services, 150
Maryland Department of Public Safety
    and Correctional Services, Office
    of Treatment Services, 157
Massachusetts, employment
    discrimination and suicidality case
    in, 410
McDonald, James J., Jr., "Assessing
    Emotional Distress Damages," 250
Mediation
    caucusing in, 208
    of contract disputes, 261
    definition of, 206
    of employment discrimination problem,
        206, 212, 242, 243
        failure of, 209
        report, 209
        settlement agreement in, 209
    of workers' compensation case, 228, 229

Medicaid, 17–18
    and asset limits, 316, 293
    and confinement for criminal
        case, 131
    eligibility, special needs trust and, 307
    information on, 36
    payback trust and, 308
    and return to work, 244–45
    and SSI, 17–18, 244–45, 247
    for SSI recipient who is employed,
        247, 250
Medical assistance benefits, re-
    establishing, after release from
    prison, 159
Medical examiner, 393
    state laws about, portal for, 397
Medical exams, for new hires, 201
Medical expenses
    for disability equipment and supplies
        needed in workplace, 211
    family caregiver agreement and, 381
    home modifications as, 382
    IRWEs as, 249
    for personal injury, tax
        considerations, 80
    reimbursement for, tax
        considerations, 243
    for service animals, 382
    special needs trust and, 307
    with wrongful death of loved one, tax
        considerations, 406
Medical insurance,
    government-funded, 17–18
Medical planning documents, 49
Medical privacy, 3. See also Privacy–14
    exceptions to, 5–6
    reasons for, 3
Medical providers, and wrongful
    death, 402
Medical records
    collected by employer, confidentiality
        and storage of, 182–83, 195
    for disability application, 20
    and mental health court referrals, 125
    privacy, and mental health court
        referrals, 124
Medicare, 17–18
    and confinement for criminal case, 131
    information on, 36

Medicare (*cont.*)
  mental health treatments and services
      covered by, 36
  Part A, 18
  Part B, 18
Medicare Advantage Plan, 18
*Medicare and Your Mental Health
    Benefits,* 36
Medicare Prescription Drug Plan, 18
Medication(s)
  associated with suicide and suicidal
      thoughts, list of, 407
  information on, resource for, 56
  for inmates, 107, 149–50
  warnings about, 405
Mental anguish, payments for, as taxable
    income, 79
Mental Health America (MHA)
  advocacy for mental health
      courts, 129
  information on psychiatric advance
      directives, 55
  work on mental health resources, 65
Mental health commitment, background
    check for, 183–84
Mental health court
  case management, 126–27
  charges dropped or lowered by, 127
  crime victims' interests and,
      127–28, 129
  definition of, 122
  intake process for, 123–25
    victim participation in, 128
  judicial review hearings, 128
  lawyers who practice in, 132
  manual on, 129
  participants (defendants) in, 125
  partners with, 122
  portal to, 129
  proceedings in, 125
    manual for, 129
  purpose of, 122
  referral of cases to, 123
  resources on, 129–30
  sanctions, 126
  setting up, curriculum for, 129
  staff teams in, 122
  supporting, 128
  and treatment plan, 125–26

*Mental Health Declaration of Human
    Rights, The,* 56
Mental Health Parity Act, and coverage
    of recovery from suicide attempt,
    411, 419
Mental health power of attorney. *See*
    Durable power of attorney, for
    health care and related decisions
Mental health record, in intake for mental
    health court, 123
Mental health service agency, employment
    with, 34
Mental illness
  faked, and mental health court, 124
  and violence, research on, 407
Mentally Ill Offender Treatment and
    Crime Reduction Act, 97
Miami Rescue Mission v. Roberts, 423–24
Michigan, process for expunging criminal
    record, 164
Mikell, William E., "Is Suicide
    Murder?," 418
Minnesota
  Family Involvement Law, 13
  mechanism for expunging involuntary
      commitment record, 66
  rules on client consent and
      privacy, 12, 13
  state income tax deduction for rent, 383
Minor crime(s). *See also* Infraction(s);
    Misdemeanor(s)
  alternatives to incarceration for, 121
  court cases, 114–15
  defenses for, 114, 115
  definition of, 113
  examples, 113
  police response to, 113
  probation for, 117
  punishments for, 115–17
    community service as, 116
    compliance with, 115
    training and treatment as, 116
  resources on, 120–21
  successful outcomes with, 120
Miranda v. Arizona, 105
Miranda warning, 105–6
Misdemeanor(s), 113. *See also* Minor crime(s)
  court cases, 114–15
  lawyers' workloads from, 120

Missing persons, 389
    alerts, state laws about, 396
    closing of case file on, 394–95
    as cold case, 394
    FBI roster of, 396
    high risk, 391–92
    and income taxes, 395
    interception of, by police, 390
    investigation, 391
    legal considerations, 390
    NamUS databases on, 397
    reporting, 391
    resources for, 396–97
    searching for, 138, 396
        and collaboration with police, 392
        money/donations for, 392, 395, 396
    state clearinghouses for, 397
    ViCAP records on, 396
    vulnerable people as, 389, 390
Missouri CIT Council, program objectives
        for CITs, 97
Mistreatment, 68–70
Mobile home. See Home
Mobile mental health crisis team, 91
Model Penal Code, defenses against
        accomplice liability, 167
Modification. See also Housing, physical
        modifications of
    definition of, 354
    necessary, definition of, 354
    reasonable, definition of, 354
Money
    and mental health, 255–56
        resources about, 279–80
    your relative's, accusation of
        misappropriation, 36
Money management. See also
        Conservatorship
    mental health and, 283–84
    representative payee and, 35, 37
    supportive, 327 (see also
        Conservatorship)–51
Montana, rules on client consent and
        privacy, 11, 13
Moore, Joyce, "Will Contests from Start to
        Finish," 439
Morin, Amy, "What Your Financial
        Health Says About Your Mental
        health," 279

Mortgaged home, in special needs
        trust, 318
Multifamily Inventory of Units for
        the Elderly and Persons with
        Disabilities, 384

NAACP, civil rights lawyer referral
        list, 111
Nadworny, John W., and Cynthia R.
        Haddad, The Special Needs
        Planning Guide, 325
Nagourney, Adam, article on parents'
        attempts to intercept their son's
        crime spree, 97
Name change, 206
National Adult Protective Services
        Association, 47
    "Financial Exploitation Case
        Studies," 280
    guidance about undue influence, 280
National Alliance on Mental
        Illness (NAMI)
    Finding a Missing Loved One, 397
    lawyers associated with, 407
    and mental health policy reform, 417
    Road to Recovery: Employment and
        Mental Illness, 196
    toolkit for starting a CIT, 97
National Association for Court
        Management, Adult Guardianship
        Guide, 47
National Association for Psychiatric
        Hospital Systems, quality
        standards and accreditation
        provision, 66
National Association for Victim
        Assistance, 96
National Association of Attorneys
        General, 280
National Association of Consumer
        Advocates
    activities of, 280
    instructions for dealing with debt
        collectors, 280
National Association of Consumer
        Bankruptcy Attorneys, directory
        of, 281
National Association of Crime Victim
        Compensation Boards, 96

National Association of Criminal Defense
    Lawyers
  explanation of criminal court practices
    and defense legal issues, 175
  Restoration of Rights Project, 174
National Association of Elder Law
    Attorneys, 351
National Association of Estate Planners
    and Councils, 439
National Association of Insurance
    Commissioners (NAIC)
  Life Insurance Policy Locator, 413, 420
  portal to state insurance
    commissions, 420
National Association of Professional
    Background Screeners, 194
National Association of Secretaries
    of States, portal to state
    administrative codes, 157
National Association of Social Workers,
    Code of Ethics, 13
National Association of State Charity
    Officials, 396
National Association of State Mental
    Health Program Directors
  Criminal Justice Primer for State Mental
    Health Program Directors, 97
  portal to government authorities in
    states and territories, 56
National Association of Workers
    Compensation Judiciary, 234
National Center for State Courts, 97
  articles on criminal procedure, 175
  data on criminal fines, 121
  Fines, Costs, and Fees Resource
    Guide, 121
  Guardianship/Conservatorship Resource
    Guide, 350
  links to mental health courts, 132
  links to state sentencing
    guidelines, 145
National College of Probate
    Judges, information about
    guardianship, 47
National Commission on Correctional
    Health (NCCH)
  Care Standards for Inmate Mental
    Health Care, 158
  glossary of prison health words, 158

2014 Standards for Health Services in
    Jails, 107
  Standards for Mental Health Services in
    Correctional Facilities, 111
National Commission on Domestic
    Violence, self-protection advice
    from, 66
National Conference of State Legislators
  debt-management laws available
    from, 280
  information on data disposal laws, 194
  information on duty to warn and duty
    to protect, 14
  State Sentencing and Corrections
    Legislation, 157
National Consumer Law Center, summary
    of Unfair and Deceptive Acts and
    Practices (UDAP) laws, 280
National Council of La Raza, civil rights
    lawyer referral list, 111
National Council on Compensation
    Insurance (NCCI), workers' comp
    info from, 234
National Council on Disability, 66
National Crime Information Center
    (NCIC), missing persons reports
    collected by, 391–92
National Crime Victim Law Institute, 96
National Criminal Justice Reference
    Service, information on
    police liability for harm to
    detainees, 407
National Disability Rights Network, 351
  links to advocacy groups, 110
  member agencies, lawyers associated
    with, 407
National District Attorneys Association,
    National prosecution
    Standards, 96
National Employment Law Project (NELP)
  campaign for "fair chance hiring," 195
  report on criminal records and
    employment, 195
National Foundation for Credit
    Counseling (NFCC), 264
  list of members, 280
  standards for credit counselors, 280
National Gateway to
    Self-Determination, 350

National Governors Association, *HIPAA, Corrections, Law Enforcement, and the Courts,* 121
National Guardianship Association (NGA)
 Model Code of Ethics for Guardians, 46
 resources available from, 350
 Standards of Practice for Guardians, 42, 46
 training programs and materials from, 43
National Guardianship Network (NGN), 46
 Decision Making without Guardianship, 46
 information on Working Interdisciplinary Networks of Guardianship Stakeholders (WINGS), 46
National Guardianship Summit, Third, 42, 46
National Housing Law Project, 384
National Instant Criminal Background Check System (NICS), 14, 183–84, 195
National Institute of Corrections
 Corrections and Mental health blog, 158
 information on detention facilities and liability, 406
 Jail Standards and Inspection Programs, 160
 resources on inmate mental health services, 112
National Institute of Mental Health (NIMH), medication information from, 56
National Lawyers Guild
 civil rights lawyer referral list, 111
 Jailhouse Lawyer's Handbook, 158
National Library of Medicine, guide to medications and supplements, 56
National Mental Health Consumers' Self-Help Clearinghouse, information on psychiatric advance directives, 56
National Missing and Unidentified Persons System (NamUS), 391–92, 393

databases in, 397
National Organization for Social Security Claims Representatives (NOSSCR), information on disability claims, 37
National Register of Health Services Psychologists, 80
National Resource Center for Supported Decision-Making, 46, 350
National Resource Center on Children and Families of the Incarcerated, 160
National Resource Center on Psychiatric Advance Directives, information from, 55
National Survey of State Laws, 439
Nebraska
 inheritance tax in, 438
 workers' compensation to first responders in, 224
Necessary [term], definition of, 354
Negligence, 68
 by agent with financial power of attorney, 334
 in conservatorship, 341
 definition of, 68
 institutional, 69
 in wrongful death, 401
Negligence claim
 elements of, 76
 statute of limitations for, 74
Negligent entrustment, 300
 examples of, 301–2
Newhouse v. Graczyk, 424
New Jersey
 inheritance tax in, 438
 mechanism for expunging involuntary commitment record, 66
New Mexico
 mental health-related workers' comp claims in, 231
 rules on client consent and privacy, 11, 13
New York, process for expunging criminal record, 164
NICS. *See* National Instant Criminal Background Check System (NICS)
Nolo Press, Employment Law Center, 195

Nonprofit organization(s), and pooled
    trust operation, 310–11
Not competent to stand trial, 133–34
    management of, by court, 134–35
Not guilty by reason of insanity,
        131, 136–41
    challenges to proving, 138–39
    in federal cases, 139
    federal statutes regarding, 145
    goal of claiming, 137
    legal significance of, 139–40
    in state cases, 139, 140
    state statutes on, 145
Notification, crime victims' right to, 88, 96
Nursing services, as tax-deductible
        expense, 383

Obsessive-compulsive disorder,
        as disability, under EEOC
        regulations, 187
Occupational therapist (OT), 439
    psychiatric, and drafting will, 424–25
Ohio, rules on client consent and
        privacy, 11, 13
Oklahoma, rules on client consent, 11
Overdrafts, bank account, 288
Overton v. Reilly, 191–92

Pace v. Davis, 301
Pamela L. v. Farmer, 171
Parry, John
    Civil Mental Disability Law, Evidence
        and Testimony, 13
    Criminal Mental Health and Disability
        Law, Evidence and Testimony,
        13, 146
Parry, John Weston, Mental Disability,
        Violence, Future Dangerousness, 66
Partnership for Workplace Mental
        Health, 195
Part-time work, SSID beneficiary and, 248
Patterson v. Foley, 172
Payback trust. See Trust(s), special needs
Paycheck(s), ward's, conservator's
        management of, 342, 345
Payers, access to private medical
        information, 10–11
Pearson v. Unification Theological
        Seminary, 233

Peer specialists, 34
Pennsylvania
    inheritance tax in, 438
    mechanism for expunging involuntary
        commitment record, 66
    mental health-related workers' comp
        claims in, 232
Periods of temporary incapacity, 48
    agent in, 54
    state laws on, 49
Personal care agreement. See Family
        caregiver agreement
Personal injury
    by conservator, 348
    payments for
        resource on, 325
        as taxable income, 79–80
        and trusts, 325
Personal injury lawyer(s), 75
    sample fee agreement for, 250
    for wrongful death lawsuit, 75
Personal representative of estate, and
        wrongful death lawsuit, 399
Peters v. Baldwin Union Free School
        District, 419
Petition for diversion, 109
Petition for Presumption of Death, 394–95
Petrone v. Hampton Bays Union School
        District, 193
Phone plans, 295
Planned Lifetime Advocacy Institute, 350
Plan to Achieve Self Support (PASS), 245
    contributions to, 293
Plenary guardian, 42–43
Police. See also Crisis intervention
        team (CIT)
    encounters with, 85
    family cooperation with, 8
    family members' reluctance to
        call, 94–95
    interaction with, resources on, 175
    interrogation techniques, New Yorker
        article on, 175
    liability for harm to detainees, 407
    and management of psychiatric
        crises, 405
    negative encounters with, 98 (see also
        Police misconduct)–103
    and qualified immunity, 102

violence against person with mental
illness, 98
and wrongful death, 401–2
Police investigators, interaction with, 172
resources on, 175
Police misconduct, 98–103
civil complaints, 102
criminal complaints, 100, 102, 110
definition of, 98
DOF findings letters on, 110
federal complaint about, 100–2, 110
federal statutes about, 110
local complaint, filing, 99
patterns and practices of, 100
resources on, 110–11
types of, 98–99
Pooled trust. See Trust(s), pooled
Possession
definition of, 167–68
liability for, 167–68
Posttraumatic stress disorder, as disability,
under EEOC regulations, 187
Poverty limit
and eligibility for government
assistance, 293, 303
federal guidelines on, 303
Power of attorney. See also Durable power
of attorney
conditional, 329
financial (see Financial power of
attorney)
for health care, 38, 345
for IRS matters, 334
limited, 330
springing, 329
Precatory expressions, 427–29
Prejudice, against people with mental
illness, 66
Premises liability, 299
Prescription management
for jail inmates, 107
negligent, as drug dealing, 79
Presence of mind, insanity defense
and, 137
Pre-sentence investigation, 142–43
Presumption of lucidity, 422
Principal, definition of, 327
Prison(s). See Jail(s) and prison(s)
Prisoner(s). See also Inmate(s)

rights of, 147–48
DOJ information on, 159
resources for, 157–60
Prison library(ies), resource on, 159
Prison Litigation Reform Act, 147, 159
Prison oversight agencies, 159
PrisonTalk, 160
Privacy
books with information on, 13
HIPAA rules about, 14, 121
of medical information, 3–14
legal exceptions to, 124
and mental health court referrals, 124
prisoners' phone calls and, 152
of psychotherapy notes, 6
resources for, 13–14
right to, 58
state laws about, 11–12, 13, 14
violation of, 12
HIPAA complaint about, 12, 12, 14
Privilege, therapist–client or
doctor–patient, 9
Probate courts, 422
contesting will in, 433
filing of will in, 433
resources for executors and estate
administrators, 439
Probation
as alternative to incarceration, 117, 120
and guilty but mentally ill status, 142
compliance with, 117–20
for minor crime, 117
post-incarceration transition to, 120
Problem(s), communication of, to mental
health practitioner, 3–4
Product liability, and wrongful death, 402
Professional ethics
codes of, 13
complaints about, 72–73
and patient privacy, 7
Professional misconduct, 68, 69
client/family response to, 69–70
complaints about, 69–70
criminal equivalents of, 79
as criminal offense, 69
lawsuits, 74–75
legal considerations with, 68–69
penalties for, 69
resources on, 80–81

Professionals, and wrongful death, 402
Program Operations Manual System
    (POMS), 37
    Bankruptcy Proceedings Overview, 282
    "Introduction to Living Arrangements
        and In-Kind Support and
        Maintenance," 386
Promisee(s)
    and contract negotiations, 259
    definition of, 259
Property damage, tax deduction for, 418
Property insurance, and remediation/
        restoration after suicide, 415–16
Property tax. *See* Real estate tax
Property used for self-support, as
        uncounted asset, 316, 317
Protection and advocacy (P&A)
        agency(ies), 65
Protection from abuse order, 60
Psychiatric advance directives (PADs)
    agent designated by, 48
        and periods of temporary
            incapacity, 54
    as communication, not contract, 52
    contents of, 48
    forms for, 49–50, 51
    hospital noncompliance with, 52
    legal considerations with, 52
    misuse, speaking up about, 52
    modification/replacement of, 52
    need to follow, determination of, 49
    reasons for, 48–49
    resources for, 55–56
    state laws on, 49
    state practice information on, 55
    treatment preferences in, 48–51
        agent and, 53
    writing, inquiry techniques for, 49–51
Psychiatric crises, management. *See also*
        Crisis intervention team (CIT)
    by expert practitioners, 405
    by police, 405
Psychiatrist(s)
    code of ethics, 13
    licensure boards, 80
    in prison mental health care, 150
    standards of practice, 80
Psychologist(s)
    code of ethics, 13

    legal obligations of, 80
    license verification, 80
    licensure boards for, 80
    practice standards for, 80
Psychotherapy notes, HIPAA rule
        for, 6, 14
Public Citizen's Health Research Group,
        report on mental illness in
        inmates, 160
Public defenders, 114–15, 121, 133
    and referrals to mental health
        court, 123
    working with, resource on, 145
Public housing
    definition of, 355
    finding, 385
    resource on, 384
Public housing agency(ies), locating, 385
Public Housing Guidebook, 385
Public library(ies), 349
Punitive damages, as taxable income, 80
Purver, Jonathan M., "Hospital's Failure to
        Protect Patient from Self-Inflicted
        Harm," 406

Qualified disability trust, 311, 306
    federal law authorizing, 326
    resource on, 324
    tax exemption for, 324
Qualified immunity, 102
Question(s), leading, in drafting
        preference statements, 51

RD v. WH, 405
Real estate tax, as tax deduction, 383
Real estate terminology, glossary of, 303
Reasonable [term], definition of, 354
Receipt(s)
    definition of, 297–98
    for payment, 297–98
Rehabilitation Act, and protection of
        employees with disabilities, 179
Rehabilitation Act of 1973, and police
        misconduct, 100
Remediation/restoration services, after
        suicide, and insurance claims, 415–16
Rent, as state income tax deduction, 383
Representation, and employee
        discipline, 190

Representative payee
  for disability benefits, 35, 37, 327
  training and guidance for, 37
Reputation, 186
Rescue workers, mental injuries to,
    workers' compensation for, 224
Resident, definition of, 354
Respondent's Position Statement, in
    EEOC investigation of job
    discrimination, 209–10
Restitution, crime victims' right to, 88
Restoration of capacity, 43
Restraint
  resources on, 56
  used on inmates, 149
Retail therapy, 256
Return to work
  after SSDI or SSI disability, 244–46
    loss of disability status with, 246–47
    resources for, 250–51
  and fitness-for-duty testing, 182–83
  Medicaid and, 244–45, 247, 250
  training and supplies for, SSI and, 245
Rights of mental patients, 58, 65
Right to disappear, 390
Right to remain silent, waiver, 106
  intelligently made, 106
  knowingly made, 106
  voluntary, 106
Romero v. City of Santa Fe, 231
RV
  cheap sale of, as gift, 297
  legal obligations with, 299
RV parks, state laws about, 303
Salvation Army, 33
Sanctions, mental health court, 126
Schizophrenia
  as disability, under EEOC
    regulations, 187
  and driving, 303
Search and seizure, 104–5
  consent to, 104
    unknowing, by person with mental
    illness, 104–5
Seclusion, resources on, 56
Section 8 housing, 364, 355, 363, 385
Self-advocacy, resources for, 350
Self-incrimination, Fifth Amendment
  protections against, 105–6

Self-murder. See *Felo de se*
Self-settled trust. *See* Trust(s),
    special needs
Sentencing
  mitigating circumstances in, state
    statutes on, 145
  of people with mental illness, 145
Sentencing guidelines, 142, 145
Serious illness
  definition of, 215
  and family and medical leave, 215
  medical certification of, 217–18, 233
Service animal(s), expenses for, tax
    considerations, 382
Sexual assault, 79
Sexual harassment, 236
Shapiro, David L., and Steven R. Smith,
    Malpractice in Psychology, 80
Sherman, Jeffrey G., "Posthumous
    Meddling," 439
Shower treatment, 149
Sick days, paid, use of, 216
Simpson, O. J., 399
Simpson, Skip, 407
Sista v. CDC IXIS North America, 233
Sixth Amendment, 140
Slate, Risdon N., Jacqueline K. Buffington-
    Vollum, and W. Wesley Johnson,
    *The Criminalization of Mental
    Illness,* 111
Smith, Mathew P., "Tragic, But is it a
    Wrongful Death?," 407
Smith v. UHS of Lakeside, Inc., 405
Social Security Act, Section 1619(B), 250
Social Security Administration (SSA)
  Appeals Council, 32
  and asset limits, 245, 247
  Bankruptcy Proceedings Overview, 282
  benefits letter, 284
  *Benefits Planner: Income Taxes and
    Your Social Security Benefits,* 249
  and changes in housing
    circumstances, 386
  Complaint Adjudication Office, 27–28
  and confinement for criminal
    case, 131–32
  Continued Medicaid Eligibility, 250
  Cost of Living Adjustments (COLA)
    web page, 247, 251, 303

Social Security Administration (*cont.*)
  as creditor in bankruptcy case, 277–78
  definition of disability, 199, 307
  Digest of State Guardianship Laws, 351
  disability programs, 15–16
  Extra Help program, 18, 37
  and free food and shelter as
      assets, 376–77
  guidelines for consultative
      examinations, 37
  list of assets not counted against
      disability recipient, 326
  Notice of Overpayment from, 312
  notification, about SSI recipient who is
      working, 246, 250
  Office of Disability Adjudication and
      Review (ODAR), 23
  offices, contact information for, 250
  Program Operations Manual System
      (POMS), 37, 282, 386
  proving disability to, 218
  questions about disability
      application, 19
  Red Book, 250
      "Trial Work Period" (chapter), 250
  and representative payee, 35, 37
  *Request for Waiver of Recovery or
      Change in Repayment Rate* (Form
      632), 312
  and return to work, 244–46
  "SSI Resources," 303
  on substantial gainful activity, 248
  support for return to work, 235–36
  technical rules for special needs
      trusts, 325
  threshold income amount determined
      by, 247, 251
  Transitioning From Incarceration, 144
  *What You Need to Know When You Get
      Supplemental Security Income,* 386
  work incentives program, 26
Social Security Administration (SSA) forms
  545-BK, 245
  Application for Disability Insurance
      Benefits, 19
  Authorization to Disclose Information
      to the Social Security
      Administration (Form 827), 20
  Program Discrimination Complaint
      Form (Form 437), 27–28, 37
  Request for Hearing by Administrative
      Law Judge, 23
  Request for Reconsideration (Form
      561), 312
Social Security benefits
  and employment, 180
  information on, 36
  re-establishing, after release from
      prison, 159
Social Security claims representative, 23
Social Security Disability Insurance
      (SSDI), 16, 243. *See also* Disability
      benefit(s)
  amount of benefits, 16, 36
  back due benefits, 17
      tax considerations, 36
  and bankruptcy, 277–78
  beneficiary
      employment, how to report, 247
      trial work period for, 247, 250
  benefits letter, 284
  and employment, 179
  example of, 17
  and Medicaid, 307
  and Medicare, 17–18
  onset date for, 17
  and part-time work, 248
  reapplying for, after three years of
      employment and new onset of
      disability, 248
  resources for, 36–37
  and return to work, 244 (*see also* Return
      to work)–46
  tax considerations, 36, 249
Social Security Handbook, 386
  disability chapter, 36
Social Security survivors' benefits, suicide
      and, 412
Social work
  license verification, 80
  regulatory boards, 80
Society for Correctional physicians,
      *Restricted Housing of Mentally Ill
      Inmates,* 159
Society for Human Resources
      Management

"How to Accommodate Employees with
    Mental Illness," 195
sample discipline policy for poor
    performance, 195
Society for Prison Journalists, portal to
    prison access laws, 157
Solitary confinement, 148, 160
Sound mind, of testator, 425, 426,
    422–21, 432
case examples, 423–24
Special Needs Alliance (SNA)
    *Administering a Special Needs Trust: A
        Handbook for Trustees,* 325
    Find an Attorney page, 46
    information on guardianship, 46
    The Voice (newsletter), 326
    *What Is a 'Qualified Disability Trust' for
        Federal Income Tax Purposes?,* 324
Special needs trust. *See* Trust(s),
    special needs
Special relationship
    and liability for another person's
        crime, 171
    and liability for another person's
        suicide, 411–12
Spendthrift, definition of, 313–14
Spendthrift trust. *See* Trust(s), spendthrift
SSA. *See* Social Security
    Administration (SSA)
SSDI. *See* Social Security Disability
    Insurance (SSDI)
SSI. *See* Supplemental Security
    Income (SSI)
Staff training, in job accommodations, 203
Starr, Douglas, article on police
    interrogation techniques, 175
State(s)
    constitution, link to, 111
    correctional system mental health
        treatment protocols, list of, 158
    correctional system regulations,
        accessing, 157–58
    department od corrections rules and
        policies, accessing, 157
    professional boards, 72
    rules for criminal procedure, link to, 111
    statutes about jails and prisons,
        accessing, 157

State laws
    about patient privacy and disclosure of
        information, 11–12, 13, 14
    ethics codes and, 7
    and family access to medical
        information, 7, 11–12, 13
State mental health code, accessing, 65
State v. Cephas, 231
Statute of limitations, 74
    and wrongful death claims, 400
Stefan, Susan, 410
    Rational Suicide, Irrational Laws, 419
Stender, Jessica, and Roberta Steele,
    "Employment Torts," 250
Stigma(s), mental illness and, 200
Stock, gifts of, 298
Stress, and bad conduct at work, 191
Strong prison Wives and Families, 160
Student loans, bankruptcy and, 276, 281
Subpoena
    definition, 9
    motion to quash, 9
    and testimony about private
        information, 9
Subsidized housing. *See also* Section 8
    housing
    definition of, 355
    project-based, 355
    Section 8 project-based subsidy
        and, 355
    Section 8 voucher and, 355
    tenant-based, 355
Substitute decision maker, in durable
    power of attorney for mental
    health decision-making, 53
Substance Abuse and Mental Health
    Services Administration
    (SAMHSA), 120
    portal to mental health courts, 121
Substantial gainful employment, 15
    definition of
        in CFR, 251
        SSA, 248
    disability and, 199
    part-time work and, 248
    for SSDI beneficiary in trial work
        period, 247
Substituted judgment, 53–54

Suicidality
    family input about, psychiatrists'
        liability for not responding to,
        74–75, 80
    laws dealing with, 409–11
    and wrongful death, 401–2
Suicide. *See also* Wrongful death
    accidental, 412, 420
    attempted
        expenses resulting from, 415–16
        laws dealing with, 409–11
        recovery from, health insurance
            coverage of, 411
        treatment for, 417
    and blame, 409
    completed, legal considerations, 411
    expenses resulting from, 415–16
    lawsuits related to, 74–75, 80
    and life insurance, 413, 412, 420
    remediation/restoration services after,
        and insurance claims, 415–16
    risk of, screening arrestees for, 107
    and Social Security survivors'
        benefits, 412
    treatment facility's duty to protect
        patients against, 401, 406
    as wrongful death, 411
Suicide law
    history of, 408–9, 418
    improving, advocacy for, 416
    resources for, 418–20
Supplemental needs trust(s), 307
Supplemental Security Income (SSI), 16,
        243. *See also* Disability benefit(s)
    and asset limits, 245, 316, 245, 284, 293
    back due benefits, 16–17
        tax considerations, 36
    benefit amount, 16, 36
        bill payment and, 295
    benefits letter, 284
    and changes in housing
        circumstances, 386
    eligibility
        cash gifts and, 293, 303
        special needs trust and, 307
        windfalls and, 245
    and employment, 179
    and free food and shelter as assets,
        376–77, 386

    and host relative's income, 377
    and housing, 353
    in-kind support and maintenance and,
        318, 386
    list of assets not counted against
        disability recipient, 326
    living arrangements and, 386
    and living expenses, 377
    Medicaid and, 17–18, 244–45, 247, 250
    onset date for, 16–17
    overpayment, management of, 245
    and paid room and board with
        family, 377
    recipient who is working, notifying SSA
        about, 246, 250
    recipient who returned to work, loss of
        disability status, 246–47
    re-establishing, after release from
        prison, 159
    resources for, 36–37
    and return to work, 244 (*see also* Return
        to work)–46
    spouse's assets and, 386
    and spouse's income, 377
    tax considerations, 36, 249
    and training and supplies for return to
        work, 245
Supplying, liability for, 168
Supported decision-making, 335–37
    resources for, 350
Supportive housing
    definition of, 355
    guide to, 384
    and tax-deductible nursing services, 383
Support services, 33
Support team, resource for, 350

Talbott v. Csakany, 302
Tate v. Canonica, 404
Tax considerations. *See also* Income
    tax(es)
    ABLE bank account and, 284, 291
    awards for attorney fees in court case
        and, 80, 243, 406
    bankruptcy and, 279
    capital gains and, 298
    conservatorship and, 349
    with court settlements, 79–80, 211, 418
    with damage award

for emotional distress, 79, 243
for employment discrimination, 211
for wrongful conviction, 157
in wrongful death case, 406
with disability benefits, 36, 249
lump sum payments, 36
with emotional support animals, 382
estate, 438
with family and medical leave (FMLA
time), 232
for guardians, 45
housing-related, 382–83
impairment-related work expenses
(IRWEs) and, 249
insurance payout and, 417
joint bank account interest and, 291
life insurance payout and, 417
life insurance premium refund and, 417
with medical expense
reimbursement, 243
for personal injury, 80
with wrongful death of loved
one, 406
with out-of-court settlements,
79–80, 243
payment of conservator and, 349
service animal expenses and, 382
with Social Security Disability
Insurance (SSDI), 36, 249
with Supplemental Security Income
(SSI), 36, 249
with support or care of adult relative,
382, 383
with workplace disability
accommodations, 211
Tax credit, for dependent care, 383
Tax refunds, 268
Tax return(s)
of debtor, 267
filing, during bankruptcy, 279
of trust, 324
*Taylor v. Phoenixville School
District,* 192
Tennessee, rules on client consent, 11
Testamentary capacity, 438
Texas
Correctional Mental Health Care
Committee (CMHCC), 150
Sandra Bland Act, 405

Texas Correctional Managed Health Care
Committee, 158
Theft
by agent with financial power of
attorney, 333
by conservator, 348, 346
in conservatorship, 341
Therapeutic Justice in the
Mainstream, 65
Third-party trust. *See* Trust(s), third-party
Thirteenth Amendment, 390
Threats. *See* Imminent danger
Ticket(s), compliance with, 117
Tools for Tenants, 384
Torrey, E. Fuller, *Surviving Schizophrenia:
A Family Manual,* 303
Tort(s). *See also* Intentional torts
causing emotional distress in
employee, 236
definition of, 78
employment-related, 250
statute of limitations for, 237
Townhouse. *See* Home
Training, court-ordered, 116
compliance with, 117
Transportation Workers Identification
Card (TWIC), background check
for, 184
Treasury Department
banking glossary published by, 302
complaint form for bank
misconduct, 303
Treatment
court-ordered, 116
compliance with, 117
right to accept or not to accept, 58
Treatment Advocacy Center
chart of state statutory codes, 65
data on prevalence of crimes against
people with mental illness, 96
and elimination of barriers to
treatment, 65
Mental Health Diversion Practices, 129
report on mental illness in inmates, 160
research on mental health courts, 129
*The Treatment of Persons with Mental
Illness in Prisons and Jails,* 158
work of, 129
work with families, 65

Treatment facility(ies), and wrongful
      death, 401
Treatment plan, mental health court
      and, 125–26
Trial work period, for SSDI recipient,
      247, 250
Trust(s)
   as artificial person, 321
   bank account for, 306
   beneficiary of, 304
   contributions to, 306
   creation of, 304–5
   d(4)(a), 308
   earnings of, tax considerations, 324
   EIN Confirmation Notice for, 306
   as fictitious entity, 321
   function of, 321
   funding, 306
   investment income, tax
      considerations, 325
   living, 421
   pooled, 304, 305, 306, 308, 310–11
      directory of, 325
      federal law authorizing, 326
      and funds remaining after
         beneficiary's death, 311
      resource for, 325
      spendthrift clause in, 313, 316
   qualified disability (see Qualified
      disability trust)
   resources for, 325–26
   special needs, 284, 304, 306, 423 (see
      also Trustee(s))
      advantages of, 307
      annuity money deposited in, 325
      assets of, investment of, 320
      common-law, 307
      contribution to, decision-making
         about, 316
      disability and, 307
      family members' involvement
         with, 320–21
      federal law authorizing, 326
      first-party, 308
      lawsuit settlement and, 245
      lump sum deposits in, 325
      payback, 307, 308–10, 326
      personal injury settlement money
         in, 325

   purchases by, 317, 319, 326
   putting home into, 27
   resource for, 325
   self-settled, 308
   spendthrift clause in, 313, 316
   SSA rules for, 325
   supplemental needs, 307
   third-party (see Trust(s), third-party)
spendthrift, 306, 313–16
   federal law authorizing, 326
   guidelines in, 315
   instructions for (firm rules
      in), 314–15
   landmarks/conditions for beneficiary
      to receive payments, 314
   and protection against creditors/debt
      collectors, 316
tax identity for, 306
taxpayer identification number (EIN)
   for, 324
tax return of, 324
terms of, 305
third-party, 307, 308, 309–10
   funding of, 309
   grantor of, 309–10
   instructions for, 310, 314
   primary beneficiary of, 309–10
   secondary (remainder) beneficiaries
      of, 309–10
   troubles with, 321–23
   windfall-funded, 306, 308
Trust attorney(ies)
   directory of, 325
   locating, 304–5, 325
Trust document(s)
   drafting of, 304–5
   signing, 305
   used to influence trustee, 322–23
Trustee(s)
   bad actions of, 321
   corporate, 319
   individual, 319
   legal action against, 322
   payment of, 319
   removal of, 322
   responsibilities of, 319–20
   self-dealing by, 321
   services that serve as, resource for, 325
   of special-needs trust, 304, 306, 319–21

handbook for, 325
spending decisions by, 319
Truth in Lending Act, 280
Turner, George M., *Revocable Trusts,*
316, 325
Turner, Margery Austin, et al.,
*Discrimination Against Persons
With Disabilities: Barriers at Every
Step,* 384

Unclaimed property
conservator's search for, 342
databases of, 342
Underemployment, of people with mental
illness, 196
Undermining, 226
Undue hardship, disability
accommodations causing,
200, 221–22
Undue influence, 257–58
counteracting, 258
definition of, 257
and drafting a will, 425
mandatory reporting of, 258
resources on, 280
Unemployment, of people with mental
illness, 196
Unemployment benefits, ward's,
conservator's management
of, 342
Unemployment insurance, 243
Unfair and Deceptive Acts and Practices
(UDAP) laws, summary of, 280
Unfit to stand trial process, 124
Uniform Adult Guardianship and
Protective Procedures Act
(UAGPPA), 47
Uniform Adult Guardianship and
Protective Proceedings
Jurisdiction Act, 350
Uniform Power of Attorney Act, 349
Uniform Probate Code, Section 3-805, 437
Uniform Trust Code, 326
Union Gospel Rescue Mission, 33
United States Code
Deprivation of Rights under Color of
Law, 110
Police Misconduct Provision, 110
statutes about police misconduct, 110

United Way, 212
lists of disability services, 18
University(ies), and suicidal students,
410–11, 419
University of Memphis, resources on
CITs, 97
University of Michigan School of Law,
portal to prison grievance
procedures, 159
University of North Texas Center for
Human Identification Forensic
Services Unit, 397
Unpaid bills, 262–63
Urban Institute, *The Processing and
Treatment of Mentally Ill Persons in
the Criminal Justice System,* 159
U.S. Sentencing Commission, sentencing
guidelines, 145

Vars, Frederick, 409, 416
"Self-Defense Against Gun Suicide," 419
Vehicle. *See also* RV
as gift, 298
negligent entrustment of, 300–1, 302
not counted in disability benefit
eligibility, 317
purchased by payback trust, 309
ViCAP (Violent Criminal Apprehension
Program), 396
Vicarious liability, 300
Victim Assistance Training (VAT), 87, 96
Victim impact statement, 89–90, 96
mental health court and, 128
and wrongful death lawsuit, 403
Victimization, of people with mental
illness. *See also* Crime victim(s)
prevalence of, 96
resources on, 96
Victim rights advocate/advocacy, 87
resources on, 96
states' offices of, 96
Victims' rights, 85–86, 87
resources on, 96
Victim Support Services, 87–88, 96
VINE, 96
Violence
mental illness and, research on, 407
by or against person with mental
illness, 98

Vital records, state office of, 397
Vocational expert, in disability
        hearing, 31–32
Vocational rehabilitation, 34, 37
Volpe v. Gallagher, 170–71, 173
Voluntary commitment, 61
Volunteer(s), community service and, 116
Vulnerable people
    definition of, 389, 390
    as missing persons, 389, 390

Wages, lost, awards for, in court case, as
        taxable income, 80
Wages and Hours Division, and complaint
        about employer not cooperating
        with FMLA requirements, 219, 233
Ward, of guardian, 40
Warrant(s), for police search, 104
Wasser, Tobias D., and Patrick k. Fox, "For
        Whom the Bell Tolls," 396
Welfare check, 93
Wellness check, 93
*What You Should Know Before You apply
    for Social Security Disability
    Benefits,* 36
Wheeler, Anne Marie (Nancy), and Burt
        Bertram, *The Counselor and the
        Law,* 80
White, H. C., *"Felo de Se,"* 418
Whitenack, Shirley B., "Structuring a
        Personal Injury Settlement," 325
Will(s), 421–22
    bequests in, 436, 423
        conditional, 429–31
    capacity to make, criteria for, 438
    contesting, 426, 433, 422, 439
    contests, prediction and prevention, 439
    drafting of
        accommodations during, 424–25
        therapist's assistance with, 427
    executor for, 421
    filing, with probate court, 433
    formalities, state laws on, 439
    formalizing, 431–32
    handwritten (holographic), 432–33
    helping a relative to plan, 425
    invalid, 433, 422
    made informally, 432–33
    precatory expressions in, 427–29

recorded on electronic devices, 432–33
residuary clause in, 421, 423
resources for, 438–39
signing, 431–32, 439
spoken, 432–33
substance of, 422–23
tax considerations, 438
witnesses to, 431
Willful and malicious misconduct,
        bankruptcy law on, 274, 281
Winick, Bruce J., *Civil Commitment,* 65
Wisconsin, rules on client consent, 11
Wise v. Superior Court, 171
Work, poor performance at. *See*
        Employee(s), poor performance by
Workers' compensation, 223–32
    claim for
        family and, 225
        initiating, 224–25
        lawyer for, 225–26, 228, 229–30
        temporary conservatorship for, 225
        time limits on, 225, 237
    claims administrator for, 227–28
    and consequential injuries, 224
    denial, 228
        appeals process for, 228–30
    disability discrimination and, 236–37
    and emotional distress employment
        claims, 250
    glossary for, 234
    hearing of case for, 229–30
    injury report form for
        contents of, 225
        how to complete, 226
        obtaining, 224–25
        submission to claims
            administrator, 227–28
    laws applicable to, 223–24
    leave time and, 223
    mediation of case for, 228, 229
    mental health claims
        examples, 231
        resource on, 234
    and mental injuries, 226, 223–24, 225
        to rescue workers, 224
    payer acronyms, 234
    and physical injuries, 226, 223–24, 225
    psychological benefits of, 232
    resources for, 234

service supports for, 227
state court and, 230–31
state offices, link to, 234
state review board and, 230
state-specific information on, 234
tax considerations, 232
ward's, conservator's management
    of, 342
Workers' Compensation Institute, 234
Workers' compensation judge, 229–30
Work incentives program, SSA's, 26
Working Interdisciplinary Networks
    of Guardianship Stakeholders
    (WINGS), 46
Workplace disability accommodation,
    186, 199–200, 222–23
  EEOC and, 204
  employers' expenses for, tax
      considerations, 211
  ideas for, sources of, 203, 212
  JAN consultation about, 212
  leave time as, 220–23
  reasonable, 202, 203, 181, 195, 200
  requesting, 202, 181, 195, 197–98
  tax considerations with, 211
  and undue hardship, 200, 221–22
Workplace discipline, 190–91
  sample policy for, 195
World Health Organization (WHO),
    materials on mental health
    patient's rights, 55

Wrongful conviction/incarceration,
    damages/money awards for, 157
Wrongful death, 398–99, 411
  definition of, 398–99
  duty and, 401–2
  lawsuit, 398–99
    how to begin, 75
  legal remedy for, 400
  resources for, 406–7
  settlement or court judgment for, tax
      considerations, 418
  state statutes on, locating, 406
  who can sue for, 399
Wrongful death case(s)
  attorney fees in, tax considerations, 406
  damages in, 403–4
    tax considerations, 406
  examples of, 404
  family involvement in, 403
  lawyer for, locating, 407
  resources for, 406–7
  social/legal/policy effects of, 405–6
  suicide, information for lawyers
      about, 407

Yale Law School, "Prison Visitation
    Policies," 159
Yocom v. Pierce, 231
Young, Marlene A., *Victim Assistance,* 96
Youngman v. Bursztyn, 281
Young v. Quinlan, 148

CPSIA information can be obtained
at www.ICGtesting.com
Printed in the USA
BVHW072237260619
552064BV00004B/11/P